# EFFECTIVELY EDUCATING STUDENTS

## WITH

# HEARING IMPAIRMENTS

# EFFECTIVELY EDUCATING STUDENTS WITH HEARING IMPAIRMENTS

## BARBARA LUETKE-STAHLMAN AND JOHN LUCKNER

*Northern Illinois University*

Longman

**Effectively Educating Students with Hearing Impairments**

Copyright © 1991 by Longman
All rights reserved.
No part of this publication may be reproduced,
stored in a retrieval system, or transmitted
in any form or by any means, electronic, mechanical,
photocopying, recording, or otherwise,
without the prior permission of the publisher.

**Longman, 10 Bank Street, White Plains, N.Y. 10606**

Associated companies:
Longman Group Ltd., London
Longman Cheshire Pty., Melbourne
Longman Paul Pty., Auckland
Copp Clark Pitman, Toronto

Executive editor: Naomi Silverman
Development editor: Elsa van Bergen
Production editor: Dee Amir Josephson
Text design adaptation: Dee Amir Josephson
Cover design: Susan J. Moore
Production supervisor: Joanne Jay

**Library of Congress Cataloging-in-Publication Data**

Luetke-Stahlman, B.
    Effectively educating students with hearing impairments / Barbara
Luetke-Stahlman and John Luckner.
        p.    cm.
    Includes bibliographical references.
    ISBN 0-8013-0317-6
    1. Children,  Deaf—Education—United States.  2. Hearing impaired
children—Education—United States.  I. Luckner, John.  II. Title.
HV2440.L84   1990
371.91′2—dc20
                                                    90-5648
                                                    CIP

5 6 7 8 9 10-CRW-99989796

**This book is dedicated to**

Laurent Clerc,
a bilingual, Deaf man
who could sign French and English
and who was the first person to serve
as chief executive officer of a school for the deaf.

He said:

Education is the care which is
taken to cultivate the minds of youths,
to elevate their hearts and to give them
the knowledge of the sciences and of what
is necessary to teach them to conduct
themselves well in the world.

# Contents

# Foreword

In the field of education of the deaf, there have been, over the past 200 years, three generic areas of disagreement, controversy, and conflict. In simple terms, these might be presented as three questions: (1) How should deaf children be taught? (2) What should deaf children be taught? (3) Where should deaf children be taught? The first question, of course, relates to the "methods" controversy, which is most commonly referred to in terms of oral versus manual modes of instruction but which also includes differences in opinion among supporters of manual communication. In the United States, these differences revolve around the extent to which communication should involve combined or simultaneous oral-manual communication and the relative roles of English-based signing systems and American Sign Language (ASL), which is distinct from English.

The second question deals with decisions about curriculum. Deaf children obviously have special needs and require unique services in areas such as English instruction, use of residual hearing, and exposure to sign communication (for the large majority who do not have deaf parents), among others. At the same time, they must have access to the general school curriculum in reading and writing, mathematics, science, social studies, art, and physical education. Given limitations on the school day and the attention span of children, educators of the deaf must make difficult curriculum decisions as they balance the needs of the children whom they serve.

The third basic question deals with school placement and is concerned with issues of separate placement, "mainstreaming," and socialization of the deaf child. Passage of Public Law 94-142, the Education of All Handicapped Children Act of 1975, with subsequent amendments, has concentrated attention on such concepts as least restrictive environment, free appropriate public education, and individual educational planning.

*Effectively Educating Children with Hearing Impairments* addresses all three questions and concentrates quite impressively on the second one: What are the curricular needs of deaf children and how do we go about meeting them? The authors advocate the coordinated use of speech and sign and rely heavily on the Cummins Model of Communication Proficiency to develop a process for integrating academic instruction and the development of communicative fluency. Designed for teachers of the deaf and for students who are in training to become teachers of the deaf, the text is an excellent source for several of the methods courses offered in teacher training programs. These include methods of teaching school subjects, speech, and English. Practical and effective procedures and materials are provided for planning, data collection, and assessment in the various chapters.

Education of the deaf is a very special profession that includes large numbers of special practitioners, both hearing and deaf. With this text, the authors have made a significant contribution to the field.

Donald F. Moores

# Preface

We have written a book cooperatively that we believe shares a personal statement and provides a practical text as well. Several common threads are woven throughout the text. We support a bilingual, bicultural goal in the education of hearing-impaired students, lessons based on assessment and structured to meet specific goals and objectives. We contend that it is important to be knowledgeable about effective instructional techniques, students' first language, and teacher instructional input based on that "first language." We advocate that teachers provide input that consistently corresponds with speech and that communication goals be integrated into academic lessons. The Cummins bilingual model of language proficiency has been presented as a method of assessment and intervention. Finally, we argue for language intervention motivated by genuine communication.

We have sought to provide a readable text that links research to practice for the undergraduate or graduate student training to be a teacher of hearing-impaired students. Graduate students in speech pathology, audiology, counseling, or a similarly related course will find this a valuable resource, also. We perceive the text as one to be used in one or two methods courses, after a basic course in deaf

education has been acquired. For us, this is the book we wish we had when we were studying to be teachers of the deaf. Also, it is the book that we wish we had as professors last semester. It is the book we sincerely hope will assist teachers in training and teachers in the field to teach effectively the heterogeneous hearing-impaired population that currently receive educational services in various settings.

The book provides a foundation for assessment and intervention. Communication is defined and intervention is exemplified in key areas (e.g., reading, writing, math, and science). Chapters that can be helpful to all teachers include those on effective instruction, self-esteem, behavior management, deaf culture, and working with others. We regret that it was beyond the scope of the book to discuss students with multiple-handicaps in addition to deafness.

We would like to thank the hearing-impaired students that we have worked with through the years. It is because of them that we have maintained our love for this field and worked so hard to improve the quality of services that each student receives. Our experiences as teachers of the deaf have colored every page of this book.

We believe that the field of education of

hearing-impaired students is an exciting one; it always has been, and will continue to be. Like most fields, it is not static, and for this reason we must reexamine continually what is happening and how it is affecting those with whom we are concerned. Today's teachers of hearing-impaired students face very difficult tasks. They need to develop competencies and expertise in many and varied areas. Not only do they need to acquire theoretical and practical knowledge in a wide range of subjects, but they also need to abstract, synthesize, and apply such knowledge to meet the individual needs of students. At times, these tasks will seem insurmountable. However, we sincerely believe that the challenges are worth the effort and that the rewards are lifelong.

Our thanks to the Department of Educational Psychology, Counseling, and Special Education at Northern Illinois University (especially Marvin Powell and Deb Holderness) for supporting this project. Our thanks to Naomi Silverman who guided us through the publishing process. We used the helpful feedback of C. Tane Akamatsu (Michigan State University), Jean F. Andrews (Lamar University), David F. Conway (University of Nebraska at Omaha), Jerry B. Crittenden (University of South Florida), Bruce F. Godsave (State University of New York at Geneseo) and Jeri F. Traub (San Jose State University) who reviewed the initial drafts of the chapters.

On a personal note, Barbara would like to thank her children, Breeze, Hannah, and Mary Pattie, and her colleagues, Mary Pat Moeller, Don Moores, her brothers and sisters, and the River Road Gang for their support and love in the year this text was written. She dedicates this book to her husband, Kent D. Luetke-Stahlman, and to her parents: Elizabeth W. Luetke, William V. Luetke, and Rita C. Meinert. John would like to thank his wife, Sue, for being such a wonderful partner and his dad, Bill, for his continual support. He dedicates this book to his mom, Marion, who set the standard for caring and striving that has made a project like this possible.

# PART ONE

## Preparing for Instruction

# CHAPTER 1

# Communication and Cognitive Development

## OVERVIEW

In this chapter, basic concepts and themes are presented that are critical for the application of material presented throughout this text. First, the components of language are defined and described in an operational manner. Likewise, other key components of communication (i.e., speech articulation, speechreading, and audition) are defined briefly. This practical format will allow for assessment and intervention tools, strategies, and materials to be provided in a cohesive and useful way in subsequent chapters.

Several distinctions are made in this chapter that should help you clarify how particular terms are used throughout the text: *Speech* is defined in contrast to *language; language acquisition* is contrasted to language learning. Terminology inherent to the field of bilingual education is defined, discussed, and applied to linguistic situations involving hearing-impaired children. These distinctions allow for information regarding "first language" assessment to be provided.

The link between language, cognition, and play is explained in this chapter as well. This information is presented in a very operational way so that you can conduct assessment (and write goals and objectives) for your students. The Cummins model of bilingual language proficiency, utilized throughout the text, also is explained, with examples given to illustrate the application of the concepts to situations involving hearing-impaired children. The chapter concludes with 15 thoughtful features of the optimal language learning environment.

---

### CHAPTER TOPICS

The Components of Language
Language Acquisition Compared to Language Learning
Bilingual/Bimodal Language Possibilities Defined
The Link Between Language and Cognition
Setting Cognitive Goals
The Cummins Model of Language Proficiency
Optimizing The Language Acquisition/Learning Environment

---

# THE COMPONENTS OF LANGUAGE

One of the major goals in educating children with impaired hearing is to facilitate their ability to communicate effectively with others. Our efforts as educators should result in competent young adults who are able to make purchases, access services, socialize, and feel comfortable within the bilingual/bicultural communities in which they live. To this end, it seems logical that educators define *communication* globally to include the components of language, speech articulation and audition, and speechreading. Each of the terms is introduced in this chapter and explored further in later chapters.

## Language Defined

Language is the medium that allows people to transmit thoughts to other human beings, to identify their innermost feelings, to aid in solving personal problems, and to explore the world beyond their sight and current time frame. In addition, language has been considered by many to be the singularly most important tool for obtaining knowledge and skills in our society. Modern evidence has shown that *language* must be defined and understood as a dynamic interaction between the *cognitive, linguistic*, and *communicative domains* (Clark & Stewart, 1986).

Bloom and Lahey (1978) have defined *language* as the intersection of *use, content,* and *form*. We believe that all hearing-impaired children should be assessed in these three areas with regard to spoken and signed or cued (if utilized) English; assessment of these same components for American Sign Language (ASL) might be appropriate also. (It may be also that educators working with hearing-impaired students from homes in which two oral languages are spoken would be interested in discerning the language skills of bilingual students who are exposed to Spanish, Vietnamese, Portuguese, Cambo-

dian, or other oral languages; however, information presented in this chapter is stated with regard to English, and it is assumed that readers can make adaptations to other language situations as necessary.)

*Language use* or *pragmatics* deals with the conditions under which linguistic symbols function as communicative acts. *Language acquisition* strategies in nonhandicapped infants occur with the actual and active participation of the language learners (Mahoney & Weller, 1980). So too, *language intervention* should be designed to increase the learners' use of language (e.g., to make a request, to describe something, to start, maintain, or end a conversation). Central to the approach of this book is the belief that every intervention strategy that is used with hearing-impaired children should be communicative in nature and should use language in authentic contexts. The most important variables for the interaction of language are the provision of opportunities for conversations and the exploitation of real-life experiences (Clarke & Stewart, 1986). To impart language to the hearing-impaired student, you must interact with the student as a language user and arrange the classroom environment in a manner that fosters interaction among your students. (Guidelines for managing the learning environment are offered at the end of this chapter and in Appendix A.)

*Language content* is defined as the meaning or *semantics* conveyed in an *utterance*. A student might mime running, sign RUN, or say "run" and be encoding the content of "action" in each case. In analyzing how language is used and meanings expressed, educators focus on the contents that students combine (e.g., running = action + time) and the complexity of those contents (based on developmental information). Your goals in this area might involve students' use of agent-object (e.g., *mommy sock*), object-object (*shoe sock*), and other relationships, the use of single or combined specific contents, or the use of complex semantics, such as causality (e.g., . . . *because*. . . .), mood (e.g., *I should make*. . . .), or antithesis (e.g., . . . *but*. . . .).

*Language form* is defined as the *grammar* and *syntax* of a language; how words combine to form sentences and the rules that govern the formation of sentences. To assess and set goals, you decide if behaviors such as using a sentence, using a sentence of a particular length, using subject-verb agreement, choosing the appropriate pronoun, or including a relative clause construction, and so on, are demonstrated by your students. This is the area of language for which there are the most commercial tests and materials available—and the area in which most teachers of the deaf feel comfortable in setting goals and preparing consequent lessons. We believe that you need to focus on the form of English primarily after a student has demonstrated both comprehension of the reason for the form and knowledge as to how the form is used. For this reason, we have arranged the chapters that provide a detailed examination of assessment and intervention techniques in the order of use, content, and form (Chapters 5, 6, and 7) to highlight this sequence.

## Speech, Language, and Listening Skills

Speech and language are separate components of communication; they are often confused. You will probably teach some students who are capable of receptively or expressively knowing language but are not able to articulate speech in a manner that is comprehensible (meaningful) to anyone trying to communicate with them. Other examples might include a child with paralyzed vocal chords who expresses herself in an age-appropriate manner by using a computer keyboard and screen or a mute deaf adult who writes intelligible notes, letters, and position papers. A Hispanic child might speak Spanish fluently and not be able to read or write it, yet write age-appropiate English for a wide range of purposes. When researchers and educators outside the field of deafness theorize, for example, that students must process phonetic (oral) coding abilities to be proficient readers (e.g., Carroll, 1986), it is apparent that they are confusing speech with language abilities and have not considered hearing-impaired students whose speech is unintelligible and unheard by them but whose language skills enable them to read at grade level (Luetke-Stahlman, 1988d).

Speech can *encode* a language, but success with speech skills does not guarantee success with language. An elementary-age hearing-impaired child who can produce almost perfect phonemes may not be able to make a polite request, combine complex meanings in an utterance, or communicate beyond a three-word level. Yet another deaf student might have unintelligible speech but demonstrate the English skills necessary to pass a college entrance exam. Our goal as educators should logically be to facilitate the development of bilingual/bicultural adults who have the skills to access both hearing *and* deaf cultures. These students will then be prepared to decide as adults with which group of people they will choose to socialize and work. Therefore, as educators, we strive for students to develop both their oral and manual skills to the best of their abilities.

Many educators believe that most hearing-impaired students can be taught to improve their ability to vocalize, incorporate features of *prosody*, pronounce sounds, words, or phrases and use rhythm, stress, and intonation appropriately so that they are intelligible to listeners. *Speech articulation* and *speechreading* are reciprocal abilities. What this means is that an individual's speechreading ability can aid the oral communication process if the student is able to obtain meaning from another's speech movements. In general, this ability is dependent on the language knowledge of the student. The point being emphasized is that an individual's development in the areas of speech and speechreading are highly dependent on the strength of the language base that has been achieved. More specific information on strategies for assessment and intervention in the area of speech are offered in Chapter 8.

Assessment and intervention of auditory or listening abilities allow students to develop their hearing potential. The procedures used to assess and train audition can be adapted easily for speechreading work. Because successful auditory intervention involves developmentally appropriate speech, language, play, cognitive, and speechreading knowledge, it is referred to also as *communication training*. It emphasizes integrated intervention—a concept that we promote throughout this text. Auditory training and speech reading are the focus of Chapter 9.

As educators, we would like to be able to determine a student's ability in each of these communication areas shortly after the hearing impairment is verified. The youngest children are at the *critical age* for improvement to occur. During this period, communication skills can be acquired more easily than when the child is older. However, we need to possess the skills to assess these abilities for each child and to determine the extent to which intervention is appropriate. Research with hearing-impaired students has indicated that they progress in each of the developmental areas in the same sequence but at a slower rate than hearing children (Kretschmer & Kretschmer, 1978; Moores, 1987; Quigley & Paul, 1984; Wilbur, 1979). We believe that all students deserve the right to demonstrate empirically whether or not they can make progress in each communication area.

## LANGUAGE ACQUISITION COMPARED TO LANGUAGE LEARNING

Some researchers and educators make a distinction between the terms *language acquisition* and language learning, and therefore, we

have used these terms carefully throughout this text. We use the term *language acquisition*, a natural process of development, to clarify the period of *first language* development. We have had to expand this concept to include the bimodal and/or bilingual nature of "first language acquisition" that may occur with hearing-impaired children (see next section). This is because, in actuality, many hearing-impaired children acquire more than one first language. Oral bilingual research on language acquisition at the one-word stage has supported the notion of "bilingualism as a first language." (Swain, 1972). This means that the child first acquires one linguistic system with different entries from two or more languages (or systems) and later sorts out the languages into two distinct systems. This theory has been supported by preliminary research when sign is acquired in addition to speech (Prinz & Prinz, 1981; Schlesinger & Meadow, 1972). Hearing bilingual children (those who speak two oral languages) begin to separate the two languages between the second and third years. It is about this same period in development that such bilingual and bimodal children become "language specific" and begin to use one language or system with a particular person. Schlesinger and Meadow (1972) documented that two hearing children living with their deaf grandmother constantly signed to their grandmother and spoke to their hearing parents. This behavior is called *code-switching*. Prinz and Prinz (1981) and Luetke-Stahlman (1983) also found that bimodal children begin to code-switch at about 2 years of age. Children who are exposed to a proficient language model during this time and an environment conducive to language acquisition (as delineated at the end of this chapter) progress through predictable developmental milestones of use, content, and form in at least one language or system of communication.

We use the term *language learning* to refer to that learning which occurs after the initial first time period (typically birth to 5 years) of language acquisition; that is, language can be acquired before about age 5 and must be taught to a child after that time period. The language learned then is either a first language (because the child was not given the opportunity to acquire a first language before this time) or a second language (learned after a first one has been acquired). For example, a child might acquire ASL from his parents and learn English during the preschool years from siblings, neighbors, and television.

## BILINGUAL/BIMODAL LANGUAGE POSSIBILITIES DEFINED

We are using the term *bilingualism* to refer to the use of two different languages (e.g., Swedish Sign Language and American Sign Language, or ASL and manual English) and *bimodalism* to refer to two modalities of communication (e.g., an oral, manual, or written mode of language). The word *system* is used to distinguish between a natural language and a created mode of expressing a language (e.g., Signed English, Seeing Essential English, Signing Exact English, etc.) If a person has use of two modes of communication, he or she has bimodal language ability. Although bilingualism can generally be described as the use of two different languages, researchers involved with the study of different languages and dialects disagree as to the extent and measurement of linguistic proficiency required to be so labeled. We have chosen to use the term to mean any degree of ability, as long as the user has some knowledge of two languages.

Two other descriptive terms commonly used in the field of bilingual education are *balanced* and *dominant bilingualism*. Depending on sociolinguistic factors, such as the type of assessment instrument used and the investigator's language background and status, a person tends to use either equal (balanced) or unequal amounts of the two languages (so,

one of the person's language uses is more dominant than the other).

Lindholm (1980) further delineated two types of childhood bilingual language acquisition processes: *simultaneous* and *successive*. In *simultaneous acquisition*, the child is exposed to two languages from birth (e.g., the mother speaks one language and the father, another). Preschool children who acquire a second language are usually considered to be simultaneous bilinguals, even if they are exposed to the second language after the first one, because research has indicated that the process of language acquisition in these children does not differ from true simultaneous acquisition, even though the two languages are acquired at slightly different times (Ervin-Tripp, 1974).

An alternative process, *successive acquisition*, is defined by Lindholm (1980) as a student's acquisition of one language from birth and a second language later in life (e.g., upon entry into school). Since many hearing-impaired students learn a second language (e.g., Signed English, SEE-2) at school, they seemingly could be labeled successive bilinguals. However, many hearing-impaired children enrolled in preschool programs may qualify as simultaneous bilinguals if the Lindholm rationale is applied because of the age at which they acquire a sign language or system. It is unknown at this time whether later literacy obtainment is enhanced by simultaneous or successive language processing.

### Types of Input Used with Hearing-Impaired Students

As we have noted, there are several methods or modes of communicating that have been used historically with hearing-impaired children. Before we discuss how we might assess which of these is most beneficial to a particular student, it might be useful to review those that are most popular.

A number of different languages are used with hearing-impaired students in the

United States. English is both spoken and/or signed to 99 percent of these students; American Sign Language (ASL) is used with 1 percent (Woodward, Allen, & Schildroth, 1985). In addition, there may be other languages used with hearing-impaired students. For example, at the Rhode Island School for the Deaf, Spanish, Vietnamese, and Portuguese are spoken to deaf children and paired with a sign system. No doubt, other bilingual program options have evolved in communities where there are large numbers of non-English speakers.

The results of a survey by Woodward, Allen, and Schildroth (1985) indicate that 33 percent of the hearing-impaired students in the country are taught in only English. These students attend public, private, and residential schools in all parts of the country.

About 1 percent of hearing-impaired children are exposed to Cued Speech, a method of cueing a listener as to what English phonemes are being spoken. It is a receptive system, invented by a hearing man, Dr. Orin Cornett. The system involves four vowel positions in the mouth and neck area and eight hand shapes. A listener decodes the cue by attending to the cued hand shape and position as well as by speechreading. It may be that the student is exposed to oral English or a SEE system for academic instruction (and uses one of these two methods for expressive language) and that only the speech therapist and family members cue to the child. In other programs, Cued Speech is used as an input by the classroom teacher. While there is little research available to determine the effectiveness of the Cued Speech method, many isolated families throughout the United States have found success with it. Usually Cued Speech users are from white, upper-middle-class families.

Of the remaining 67 percent of the hearing-impaired students who are exposed to sign in the United States, most are in programs in which sign is used in conjunction with speech. This type of invented communication input is referred to as a sign system throughout this text (Wilbur, 1978) and differs from American Sign Language (which evolved naturally and was not invented artificially) with regard to grammar and many lexical items. A number of sign systems were invented in the late 1960s and early 1970s.

Seeing Essential English or SEE-1 (Anthony, 1971) is a system that attempts to complement speech and is not signed in the concepts of American Sign Language. It serves both an educational and a social need, with a goal of "giving comprehension of correct, colloquial English" (Anthony, 1971). It was invented by a hearing-impaired man, David Anthony, and is used in isolated areas of Colorado, Iowa, and Texas. The system utilizes word divisions, prefixes, and suffixes and is presented in English words. Multiple meanings are signed literally. Examples of SEE-1 include:

1. has
   HAVE + S
2. invariably
   IN + VARY + ABLY + Y
3. motorcycle
   MOT + R + CYC + LE
4. butterfly
   BUTTER + FLY
5. boys
   BOY + S
6. running
   RUN + ING
7. I ran the machine
   I RAN + PAST TENSE the machine
8. yesterday
   YESTER + DAY

SEE-1 is very similar to SEE-2 but differs in several important ways: (1) SEE-1 reference books are not available commercially, and homemade versions are difficult to obtain; (2) Anthony continues to modify the system, so that changes are made more frequently than with the other systems of communicating with hearing-impaired students; and (3) SEE-1 has a sign for almost every syllable of a word (so that *butterfly* would be made with two signs and *motorcycle*, with four signs).

Signing Exact English or SEE-2 was invented by Gerilee Gustason, a deaf woman, and her colleagues (Gustason, Pfetzing, & Zawolkow, 1973). Users of SEE-2, like those of SEE-1, always voice when they sign (which is called simultaneous communication) and sign to represent almost exactly what they are saying. Signs in SEE-2 correspond with the morphemes (or smallest units of meaning) of English. For example, *butterfly* and *motorcycle* are represented with only one sign, because, if the words were broken down into smaller units, those units would not mean anything in relation to the whole word (*butter* has nothing to do with *butterfly*). Gustason and her colleagues based the system on the "two-out-of-three rule": If a word had two of three components (spelled or sounded the same, or meant the same thing), it was signed with the same sign. Therefore, in SEE-2 the word *run* is signed as *run*, whether it means *to run*, *to have a runny nose*, or *to run a machine*, and so on. Many public and private school programs use a version of SEE-2, and almost all teachers have copies of the Gustason, Pfetzing, Zawolkow book. Almost pure versions of the system can be found in Sedalia, Missouri, Omaha, Nebraska, and parts of California. Some examples that differ from SEE-1 are ·as follows:

3.  motorcycle
    MOTORCYCLE (single sign)
4.  butterfly
    BUTTERFLY
8.  yesterday
    YESTERDAY

(*Has, invariably, boys, running,* and *I ran the machine* would be signed as they are above).

Signed English (SE) is an invented system that is very similar to Manual English (ME). It was developed by Harry Born-

stein and Karen Saulnier, both hearing educators. The system is spoken as it is used and basically follows English grammatical structure. Some signs are borrowed from American Sign Language, and others are similar to those used in the SEE systems. The rules for using Signed English are not detailed, so users have more freedom than with the SEE systems in deciding how they will sign figurative English (e.g., *my nose is runny*, *you are neat as a pin*), use sign markers (e.g., *figured out, electricity, unworkable*), and sign novel words (e.g., *toddler, gallop, range, cattle*). Luetke-Stahlman (1988d) found that teachers often use a Signed/Manual English *register* that resembles "foreigner talk" (Cokely, 1983). Features include: short sentences; paraphrases of lexical items and certain constructions; reduction of *inflections*; lack of function words; avoidance of slang in favor of more standard forms; use of full forms instead of contractions; repetition of words; and slow, exaggerated enunciation (Ferguson, 1959). The following samples of Signed English are from teachers' videotaped spontaneous language (underlined words were signed as well as spoken). Many words are signed and meanings of spoken utterances are changed for the deaf student.

OK—any other word?
Yea, I would not like to go there, too.
You do not want to walk through that
    water, *right*?
You don't scream out . . .
My favorite car is, I think, Ms. S's
    white car.
OK—go ahead.
Come on, bunny.

Students who have been exposed to Signed/Manual English (SE/ME) for school instruction have lower test scores on English language and reading tests than do students who have been exposed to oral English, the SEE systems, and ASL (Luetke-Stahlman, 1988a). However, several districts are meeting currently to decide how they can modify the Signed English system in order to make it more comprehensible to students. Many teachers in public, private, and residential schools use Signed and Manual English, and the Bornstein, Saulnier, and Hamilton (1980) book is used as a fundamental teaching resource throughout the United States.

Pidgin Sign English, or PSE, is not an invented system but, like natural pidgins, is a contact language and the result of something that occurs when two groups of people need or desire to communicate. For example, deaf people who typically would use ASL try to string their signs in English-like word order, may fingerspell function words (*to, the, a*), and may sign more slowly and use simpler grammar when they use PSE with hearing friends. Hearing people, who would typically speak English, might try to sign what they are saying, use one sign to represent several words, use gesture and mime to support the meaning of their speech, and communicate in slower, more simplified grammar when they communicate with deaf friends. PSE is a social language that has been adapted for more formal purposes. It does not adhere to English grammar and may not encode the meaning of the speech that may accompany it. Students exposed to PSE for instruction purposes have not done as well on tests of English language and reading as have students exposed to oral English, ASL, and the SEE systems (Luetke-Stahlman, 1988a).

The Rochester Method is familiar to many teachers of the deaf, although no school program actually uses it any longer. The method of fingerspelling each spoken word began as the policy of Mr. Zenas Westervelt,

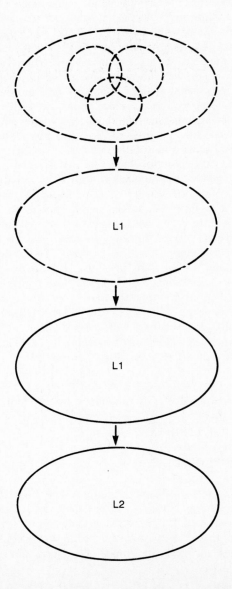

**EXHIBIT 1.1.** Assessing which language and/or system (L/S) operates as the first language for a hearing-impaired student so that the literacy curriculum in the second language (i.e., English) can be most successfully learned. Dotted lines indicate a weak language base; solid lines indicate a strong language base. L2 indicates a second language (e.g. English). The intersecting circles within the top circle represent various combinations of developing languages or systems (e.g., oral English, home sign, ASL, etc.).

the first (hearing) superintendent at the Rochester School for the Deaf. He required that signs be eliminated and that fingerspelling be used exclusively at the school (Williams, 1984). The Rochester Method was thought to be a way in which hearing-impaired students at the school could gain familiarity with the English language. Speech was combined with the 26 letters of the manual alphabet, and the proficient teacher attempted to spell every letter of every word at approximately 100 words per minute (Moores, 1988). In research compiled by D.F. Moores (1987), the result of two studies by Steven Quigley were that students using the Rochester Method were superior to students exposed to "oral-only" input on tests of fingerspelling, reading, and written English. (The reader should note that, given the time in which this research was conducted, it is unlikely that all "oral-only" students were appropriately placed.)

These languages or systems must be made available to students based on their needs, as determined by assessment and as documented in the Individualized Education Program (IEP). Yet, because this may not be feasible financially, some students who need an ASL, oral English, Cued Speech, or SEE program are assigned to an available placement. As a result, students rely on the integrity and skill level of their teachers to supply them with the language or system that is most beneficial for learning new, unknown information.

Signed and Manual English and PSE are forms of input that do not correspond closely to spoken English (Luetke-Stahlman, 1988d). This input has been found to be of two types:

1. *Fossilized input.* The content and form do not represent proficient use, and the learning of form has ceased. The term implies that the forms used are frozen and will not improve without specific content and form intervention. For example, figurative English and multiple meanings are not signed literally by most users (Luetke-Stahlman, in progress).

2. *Developmental input.* Errors are made while developing system competency. These errors could indicate progress in learning to sign (Cordor, 1967; Lange, 1977) and may not be fossilized.

## "First-Language" Assessment

Given all the available languages and systems for use with hearing-impaired students, it is important for you to know which one is most beneficial to each of your students. Because 92 percent of all hearing-impaired children are raised in homes with hearing parents (Schein & Delk, 1974), profoundly deaf children's first language may not be identical to that of their parents; that is, since most of these students cannot hear spoken English to a sufficient degree such that it can be acquired as an age-appropriate first language, spoken English does not develop as their "first" or "native" language. Instead, the composition of this manner of communication may include gesture, home sign, formal sign, cues used as signs, and/or oral words. Most of these children do not have a proficient language base in either English or American Sign Language at the time that they enter an educational program.

We believe that there may be numerous languages and/or systems comprising the first language of hearing-impaired students (see Exhibit 1.1) and that the dominant first language (or system) should be identified empirically. The importance of identifying the first language (which may, in actuality, be a system) is of critical importance, because this then should be the language or the system used by parents and teachers to teach literacy skills of the dominant culture (e.g., reading and writing in English). Once assessed, this input (language or system) should be used for instruction to teach new, unknown information to these students (e.g., English communication and academic skills). We predict that numerous methods for such first-language or system assessment will be developed in the coming years. At present we are familiar with only two such procedures (e.g. DEIP and single subject design); they are outlined below.

***Diagnostic Early Intervention Project.*** The Diagnostic Early Intervention Project (DEIP) is housed at Boys Town National Research Hospital in Omaha, Nebraska. DEIP is a research-based, clinical process that involves hearing-impaired infants, toddlers, and preschoolers. The procedure is designed to document data-based techniques so that an objective placement into either a local oral or Signing Exact English school program can be made.

Students are enrolled in the project for six months and attend assessment sessions on a regular basis with a parent. Assessment includes direct diagnostic teaching, using a variety of inputs (e.g., speech, sign, cues, etc.), parent interviews, and team discussion. Both formal and informal data are collected via a variety of tools. The result is an educational audiogram (see Exhibit 1.2), in which areas of interest are summarized as being of no concern, mild-moderate concern, or significant concern with regard to intervention. Summary case reports from Moeller et al. (1987) of hearing-impaired students enrolled in DEIP appear in Exhibit 1.3.

After having completed assessment and placement of an initial group of students, DEIP project members (Moeller et al., 1987) stated that (1) placement should not be based on audiological information alone; (2) testing across the developmental areas was necessary; (3) an educational audiogram proved to be a useful format in graphically portraying complex factors and assisting the team decision-making process; and (4) long-term objective monitoring and program revision based on data from the student was required.

***Single-Subject Design.*** The purpose of single-subject design is to allow a student who is at least 3 years of age to demonstrate empirically which of several languages and

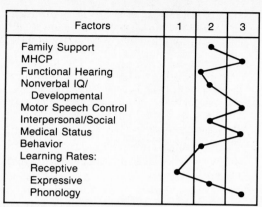

**EXHIBIT 1.2.** Educational audiogram. Level of concern rated independently by DEIP team members according to preestablished guidelines. A "1" means "of no concern" and suggests that the behavior or factor assessed is within normal limits or within expectations for routine clinical care. (For example, a rating "of no concern" would be indicated for a child whose parents are appropriately involved or who is requiring only routine health care.) A "2" means "of mild-moderate concern" and would be indicated if the family had difficulty participating and complying with the program. A "3" means "of significant concern" and would be indicated if the family was having difficulty being minimally involved or if the child had several medial problems interfering with educational needs. MHCP means that there exists multiple handicapping conditions.

SOURCE: M. P. Moeller, M. J. Osberger and J. Morford in J. G. Alpiner and P. A. McCarthy (eds.) *Rehabilitative Audiology: Children and Adults.* Baltimore: Williams and Wilkins, 1987.

systems are the most beneficial in learning new and unknown information and therefore function as a first language. It is not predicted that hearing-impaired students would be homogenous in this regard. In fact, empirical assessment to determine the first language (or system) would result logically in groupings of students based on language or system type and age appropriateness for at least some school subjects.

Case 1

*Background and Presenting Problem*: The child was followed from age 3 until age 10. He had a moderate to severe sensorineural hearing loss in the right ear (a). The suspected cause was rubella. The child, who also had asthma, was followed closely because of a delay in oral language development.

*Clinical Findings.* Diagnostic teaching and monitoring revealed (b) oral formulation problems, significant visual and auditory memory problems (learning disabilities), significant word retrieval deficits, and an inability to process multisensory input (e.g., simultaneous communication did not facilitate learning). This child could not efficiently process information from simultaneous forms of communication.

*Disposition.* Recommendations included continued placement in an oral education program with intensified language intervention and a resource consultant for his learning disabilities.

*Key.* R indicates aided right ear; L indicates left ear. X indicates unaided left ear; 0 indicates unaided right ear.

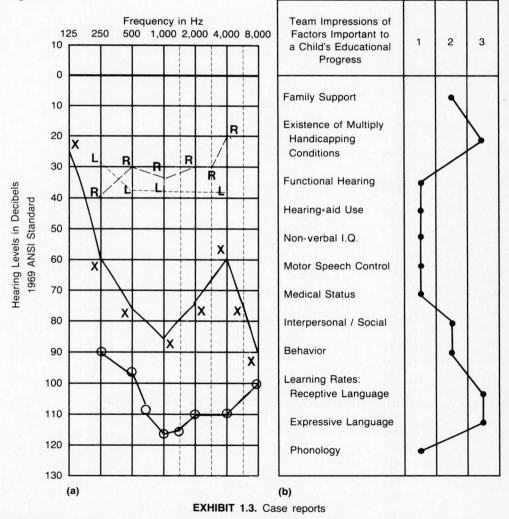

(a)  (b)

**EXHIBIT 1.3.** Case reports

SOURCE: M. P. Moeller, M. J. Osberger and J. Morford in J. G. Alpiner and P. A. McCarthy (eds.) *Rehabilitative Audiology: Children and Adults*. Baltimore: Williams and Wilkins, 1987.

**EXHIBIT 1.3.** (cont'd)

Case 2

*Background and Presenting Problem.* This Waardenburg's syndrome child had a severe to profound hearing loss (c) that was identified in early infancy. She was also followed and treated for chronic otitis media. At 8 months of age, she was enrolled in an intensive auditory-oral intervention program.

*Clinical Findings.* Six years of longitudinal evaluation revealed (d) excellent use of residual hearing, superior nonverbal intellectual abilities, nearly normal receptive and expressive language growth intensively involving parents, and impaired but improving speech.

*Disposition.* When this child was an infant, several clinicians predicted that she was not a good candidate for oral education based on the severity of her hearing loss. Her progress, however, justified the approach taken. By 6 years of age, she was mainstreamed in a regular kindergarten class with resource help. Continued auditory-oral programming was recommended.

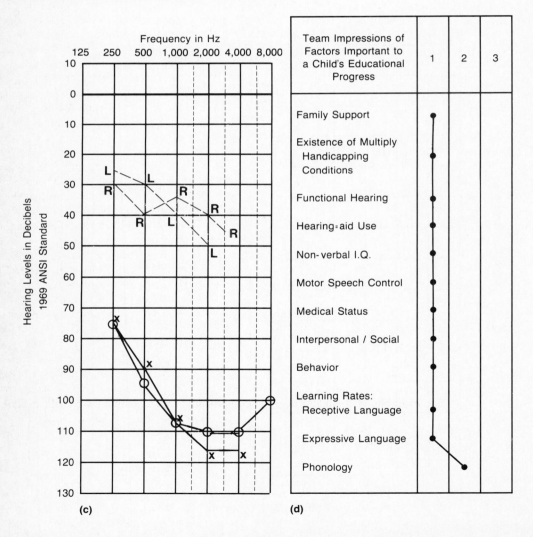

(c)                    (d)

The first step in designing a single-subject study is to choose stimuli that are challenging but possible for the student to learn and that can be drawn or written. If the student can read, then it is best to use written stimuli. Examples include single nouns or verbs, phrases, or short sentences. Stimuli must all be of the same type and must be depicted in a similar fashion. Since the assessment should include a variety of language or system possibilities, the tester will need 4 to 10 stimuli for each language or system to be tested.

The single-subject design used by Luetke-Stahlman (1982, 1987) was a receptive task. Students were asked via each language or system to point to each stimuli in the baseline condition (i.e., the part of the assessment process before teaching occurred). Those items that the students could identify correctly were eliminated from the stimuli set and replaced with items that the students could not identify. At least two baseline trials were administered, and data were graphed (see the baseline phase illustrated in Exhibit 1.4).

When the teaching phase of the assessment begins, the teacher asks the student in the language or system assigned to that group of stimuli to find the stimuli. The teacher needs no special training to learn this phase of the design, but he or she must know all the languages or systems to be used with the student. If the student identifies the item correctly, reinforcement is given in that same language or system. If the student identifies the item incorrectly, teaching of the item is provided in the language or system assigned to that group. (For example, if a student does not point to car when asked in oral English to do so—"Show me a car"—then the teacher would say, without signing or cueing, "Look, here is the car. Can you say *car*? Good.".) The teaching phase continues until the student has learned to locate all stimuli items assigned to a particular group of items. Results are graphed and visual inspection is used to discern which input is functioning as the student's dominant first language. Some results from past assessments are presented in Exhibit 1.4.

The control in a single-subject design is a condition in which some items are baselined and rebaselined periodically but are never taught. These items are presented to the student about every third trial. Credence is given to the student's ability to learn new material from various input (because the student can comprehend one or more of them effectively) if the student does not learn to identify this group of control stimuli. The results of a single-subject design provide insight with regard to first-language ability only for the student being assessed. Luetke-Stahlman has used the procedure to identify first language, spelling, and vocabulary methods for individual hearing-impaired students (aged 3 to 7 years) and for discerning the value of computer use for particular hearing-impaired students (1982, 1987).

Once significant adults have identified the language or system that is functioning as a dominant first language for the student, it is expected that the student would be exposed to that input during literacy instruction. Luetke-Stahlman (1982, 1987) assessed 11 deaf students, using single-subject design methodology, and found that a mismatch occurred between the first language demonstrated empirically by the student and the input used by the classroom teacher for seven (64 percent) of the children. We predict that literary and academic abilities of such students might improve if teachers supplied a matched input for instruction. Practitioners in hearing bilingual education have explored possibilities for accomplishing this outcome. We will describe several of their most workable models in the following discussion.

## The Immersion Model

The immersion or single-medium model (Ramirez, 1980) denotes that a student is immersed in one language for the entire school day. The school staff uses the dominant input

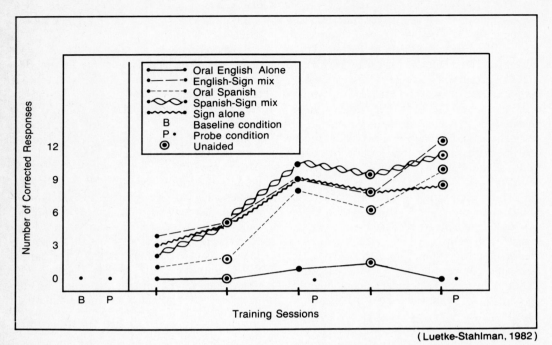

( Luetke-Stahlman, 1982 )

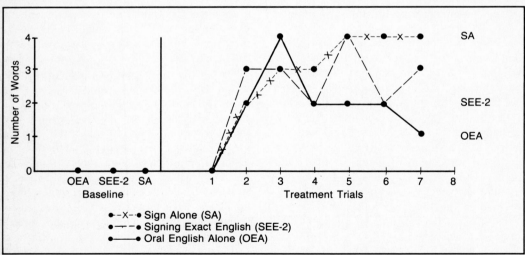

Subject 1. SA words: dreaming, digging, dancing, driving; SEE = 2 words: shopping, shouting, standing, stealing; OEA words: waving, winking, weaving, waiting (Downs, 1982 in Luetke-Stahlman, 1987).

**EXHIBIT 1.4.** Some examples of single-subject linguistic assessment

source: B. Luetke-Stahlman, "Applying bilingual models in classrooms for the hearing impaired." *American Annals of the Deaf*, *128* (7) (1983), 21–29.

(that used by the majority of speakers in the community) at all times, and students are discouraged from speaking in their home (minority) language. Some hearing bilingual educators feel that the immersion model is ineffective for students who do not have an age-appropriate first-language base. For example, Cummins (1979) reported,

> For the *minority language child*, instruction mainly through the native language has been shown to be just as, or more effective, in promoting dominant language proficiency as instruction (solely) through the dominant language [immersion]. (p. 202)

The immersion model closely resembles the oral approach historically used to teach English to hearing-impaired students. Many students who use sign language as their native language because their parents are deaf, as well as those students who have learned sign language from peers or Deaf adults, find their language base unassessed, unused, and ignored at school. In the past, students may have been insulted or punished for signing in an oral school program.

After a decade of use of sign systems, a new adaptation of the immersion model has evolved in the field of deaf education. Some cities, and whole states, provide only one input of instruction for hearing-impaired students at school. Hearing-impaired students are immersed in a form of simultaneous communication that may not match their first language and may not be advantageous for literacy obtainment. These students deserve the opportunity to demonstrate empirically their dominant language and have it matched (used) by their teachers for instruction.

## Partial Bilingualism

Partial bilingualism uses two languages for literacy instruction and the teaching of subject matter. For example, mathematics and science might be taught in the dominant school language (e.g, English), and the first language (e.g., Spanish) might be used for social studies and literature. Ramirez (1980) discussed several other forms of partial bilingualism—the preview-review approach, the concurrent model, and the alternate language program—in which two oral languages are interchanged to various degrees throughout the day.

Teachers of hearing-impaired students could use similar models by choosing from several languages or systems, depending on assessed student needs, and by systematically alternating them throughout the school day. Exhibit 1.5 provides some examples for consideration. Such models may represent a necessary compromise to true bilingual programming with hearing-impaired students, because relatively few reading materials, especially beyond the preschool level, are available in ASL or sign print. Yet, in other situations, a student who has been assessed to use SEE-1 most effectively would be exposed to both this first language and the dominant school system (e.g., Signed English or SEE-2).

## Transition

Another bilingual model that teachers could use in deaf education is the transition model. In this model, the hearing-impaired student in the early grades would be instructed in the language or system demonstrated to be the first language and in later grades, in another language or system. In hearing bilingual programs, the school language is introduced typically in the second or third grade. This model allows an age-appropriate, strong first-language base to be established in one language or system before English literacy skills are taught and expected to be learned. A variation of the transition model is a maintenance program. In a maintenance program, the native language or system is never completely absent from the academic program. An example would be a native ASL signer who has been transitioned to SEE-2 and studies ASL culture and history as a high school senior.

When ASL is demonstrated to be the

**EXHIBIT 1.5.** Some examples of bilingual instruction models

| Model | General Comments | Disadvantages for Hearing-impaired Students | Advantages for Hearing-impaired Students |
|---|---|---|---|
| *Half-day of Two L/S* The student is instructed in one language or system (L/S) in the morning and the other L/S in the afternoon. For example, ASL in the morning and SEE-2 in the afternoon. | *Other Combinations* *Morning*  *Afternoon* SEE-2     Rochester<br><br>                Oral SEE-2     English<br><br>ASL         See-2 | Language mixing beyond that normally demonstrated by young bilinguals (e.g., at less than 3 years of age) possibly occurs, and the language base acquisition of the child may suffer. (Luetke-Stahlman, 1982)<br><br>The curriculum would need to be considered—which subject would be taught in which L/S, or would subject matter be duplicated in the different L/S? | Teachers could rotate from the morning to afternoon so fewer ethnic Deaf adults would be necessary. |
| *Bilingual Teacher* The teacher says/signs an utterance in one L/S and then repeats it in the other L/S (e.g., first ASL, then SEE-2, or first ASL, then Rochester.) | A second version of this model would have an ethnic Deaf adult and a hearing teacher team-teach, each providing a separate and distinct L/S. | Same as above. | Same as above. |

most beneficial manner of communication for a student, the student must be exposed to fluent users of the native language. Providing instruction in ASL means that *ethnic Deaf adults* must be hired as teachers and assistant teachers. Just as a dedicated bilingual-bicultural staff is an essential part of any bilingual program with hearing students, a ethnic signing staff would be a necessary component of a school program for hearing-impaired students using ASL. Concomitantly, a proficient sign system staff would be neces-

sary in programs using a sign system.

The bilingual models presented in this chapter would most likely need to be altered should these models be adopted in programs for hearing-impaired students. However, the purity of the models is not the issue. Beginning to use them—changing the exposure of students to incomplete forms of languages and systems (e.g., Signed English, poorly signed SEE-1, SEE-2, etc.) that are employed currently in classrooms for hearing-impaired students—is the goal.

## THE LINK BETWEEN LANGUAGE AND COGNITION

The method used to assess the first language of each hearing-impaired student proposed by Luetke-Stahlman (1982) includes characteristics that are found also in the model of bilingual language proficiency proposed by Jim Cummins (1984). Before we explain this model, we wish to review some of the necessary principles of cognitive development.

### Early Cognition

Most parents delight in and often record the beginning vocabularies of their children. Examples of typical first utterances are available for study from all types of language acquirers (Collins-Ahlgren, 1975; Greenfield & Smith, 1976; Maez, 1984; McIntire, 1974; Prinz & Prinz, 1981; Schlesinger & Meadow, 1972; Wilbur & Jones, 1974). Have you ever known a baby whose first word was because or now or but? Can you deduce why it might be that such a phenomena would never occur? It is because there are strong parallels between cognition and language development (Bates, 1976a; Westby, 1980). This fact has encouraged us as authors to promote the Cummins model of bilingual language proficiency, thereby defining language proficiency by reference to both cognition (or the ability to think and reason) and content (or the nonlinguistic support that can be used in communicative and/or instructional situations).

Piaget believed that the ability to comprehend and reason develops through a process of assimilation (which he called *construction*) and organization that begins at birth and continues throughout life (Piaget & Inhelder, 1969). The Piagetian stage of the sensorimotor period (birth to 2 years) is useful to educators who work with infants and toddlers or to those who assess older children with developmental delays. When specific cognitive skills representative of this period are listed and defined, as they are in Exhibit

1.6, adults can act on clues from children and facilitate cognitive abilities. For example, if you were a teacher of a 20-month old child, you could hypothesize that your student can evoke internal representations of absent objects. While playing with the student, you would observe that she is able to put together independently a simple puzzle and string beads and that she no longer requires a model to imitate. You could facilitate development by encouraging application of skills to new situations.

Certain cognitive prerequisites appear to be necessary (but not sufficient) for communication skills to emerge. For this reason, it seems useful for educators working with infants, toddlers, and preschoolers to have access to charts of cognition, communication, and play behaviors grouped by age levels so that a skill in one area can be used to guide the appearance of skills in another area. In Exhibit 1.6, such a compilation based on spoken monolingual language development is provided. (Additional information provided on the chart will be explained in detail in later chapters.) For example, the exhibit indicates that at 8–12 months a child might vocalize in recognition of familiar persons. Let us imagine that you are working with a child who does just that. Information from Exhibit 1.6 would support your suggestion to significant adults that they now pair proper names (in voice and/or sign) with the vocalization, since a child at that age might also be capable of saying da-da or ma-ma, and so on. Your strategy of using developmental data helps ensure optimal growth across several developmental areas.

### Social-Emotional Growth, Play, and Language Acquisition

Parents' inability to communicate effectively with their hearing-impaired children about things or events that are not present affects their social and emotional development (Schlesinger & Meadow, 1972). Moeller and

**EXHIBIT 1.6.** A compilation of developmental skills based on hearing, monolingual langauge development

| Age in Months | Cognition | Play | Use | Content | Form | Speech or Auditory Training |
|---|---|---|---|---|---|---|
| 0–1 month | No discernible separation in development from object. | | Vocalizes occasionally. | | | Is startled by stimuli. |
| 1–4 months | Very little, if any, search for a vanished object—"out of sight, out of mind." Shifts from attending to contours and movement to preference for complex and moderately worded objects. | Repeats actions that accidently produce interesting results. | Smiles, coos in response to voice and adult smiling. Emits distinguishable cries for anger, pain, hunger, etc. | Attends and responds to voice affect (anger, playfulness). | Babbles repetitive syllable series (e.g., da-da-da). Often repeats a gestural or vocal response if someone has immediately mimicked the production. Reductions are limited and are only gross approximations of the model. | |
| 4–8 months | Continues manual search for object *if* grasping interrupted by removal of object. Looks at point where a moving object should reappear. Searches for partially hidden object. Behaves as if object no longer existed when it | Bangs objects together; shakes shakeable objects (e.g., rattle, bell). Performs some *differentiated* actions with objects (e.g., crumbling paper, sliding toys, tearing, stretching, rubbing, mouthing). Visually inspects an object while | Exhibits facial and vocal surprise when a hidden toy is uncovered. Responds by being called by name. | | | Vocalizes to source of voice sounds and noise makers. |

| 8–12 months | drops out of sight. Reacts with only mild surprise if retrieved object differs from the one hidden. Demonstrates new actions on objects (related to object properties). | tactually exploring it. Continues to attend to and repeat actions that produce interesting results. Requests continuation of a play activity by touching adult's hand, smiling, or performing some motor element of the activity. Takes turn in familiar action games with caretaker. Performs joint action "rituals" with caretaker (turn-taking routines). | Shouts to attract attention, listens, then shouts again. Responds to requests (e.g., waves "bye, bye") Expresses anger and distress when a toy is taken away. Looks at care | Appreciation of causality outside self demonstrated by pushing adult's hand to continue an interesting sensory effect; anticipating the occurrence of events from signs (e.g., crying when | Says da-da-da or ma-ma and three or more other words. Responds "No, No" to inhibitory words. | Vocalizes familiar sounds on hearing novel ones. Imitates sounds if in vocal repertoire. Imitates nonspeech sounds (cough, tongue click, lip smacking). |
|---|---|---|---|---|---|---|

(continued)

**EXHIBIT 1.6.** (Continued)

| Age in Months | Cognition | Play | Use | Content | Form | Speech or Auditory Training |
|---|---|---|---|---|---|---|
|  |  | Repeats a behavior when others laugh at it. Uses imitation to continue interesting events and to learn new behaviors. Only imitates vocalizations and actions that are similar to those in repertoire. Intentionally drops and throws objects. Uses objects in a socially relevant manner (e.g., puts necklace around neck, pretends to drink from cup, hugs doll, sniffs flowers.) | giver, as if to acknowledge receipt, when receiving an object. Vocalizes in recognition of familiar persons. Responds by giving objects to requests. | father gets his coat out). Shakes head for "no." |  |  |
| 12–18 months | Varies actions on objects to experiment with different effects (e.g., explores gravity). Notices relationships. Not successful at | Changes actions on objects to produce variations. Links objects in functional relationships (e.g., puts cup on saucer and | Responds to requests to locate familiar people and to get objects (e.g., toys) from predictable locations by pointing. | Use two words to express the semantic relations of existence negation recurrence attribution possession | Says from five to ten words (usually nouns referring to animals, food, or toys). Begins to name absent objects and events. | Imitates novel sound sequences. |

| 18–24 months | | | | | |
|---|---|---|---|---|---|
| retrieving object if hiding is not visible because cannot yet think where it might be. (Therefore searches where last seen and not where last found.) Experiments with means to an end to see what will happen and to learn about properties. | pretends to drink). Shows, offers objects to others to look at. Can place 6–9 cubes in a cup and then remove them (seeing model) Pulls out and replaces one peg in pegboard. Puts pellets and removes them from bottle. Places round shape in three-shape form board. Imitation used in a trial-and-error fashion to discover the properties of objects. | location agent–agent action–object agent–object<br><br>Makes requests by handing toy to adults, turning doorknob to request going outside, handing book for story, etc. Uses pointing to direct adult attention. Indicates wants by gesturing and vocalizing. | Has ability to evoke internal representations of absent objects and events evident in mental problem solving. Immediately looks for cause of his or her actions. Systematically searches as many as three hiding places for a missing item.<br><br>Imitation no longer requires that the model be present. The child is now capable of mental representation and long-term memory for what was modeled. Also capable of imitating complex new acts and objects as well | Requests desired objects. Vocalizes immediately following the utterance of another (but vocalizations are not necessrily contingent or related to the prior utterances.)<br><br>Responds to simple two-step directions Uses two-word utterances to code relational meanings (e.g., more cookie—recurence). | Uses words to make wants and desires known. Names objects in the presence of others. Produces successive single-word utterances, coding different aspects of the same event (e.g., mommy . . . juice). Produces approxi-<br><br>At least 25 percent of the speech of hearing children is intelligible. |

(continued)

EXHIBIT 1.6. (Continued)

| Age in Months | Cognition | Play | Use | Content | Form | Speech or Auditory Training |
|---|---|---|---|---|---|---|
| | Matches on the basis of color. | as persons. Demonstrates an understanding of the functions and social meanings of a large number of objects (e.g., holds telephone to ear and vocalizes, tries to put socks and shoes on, lines truck and trailer as if truck were pulling trailer). Attention attracted by things that move and can be acted upon. Actions with objects reflect the unique functional properties of the objects. | | | mately 50 words. Says "What's that?" to elicit object names. | |
| 2–3 years | Indicates object missing from a small array of familiar objects. Solves match-to-sample problems (with shapes, objects, pictures, colors). Groups objects by | Enjoys simple pictures and stories. Performs more realistic and expanded action scenes (4–5 appropriately chained actions). Uses newly | Answers questions dealing with familiar objects and events. Uses more and different words to encode the same semantic relations. Initiates spontane- | Recognizes and names colors. Vocalizes about the actions of others. | Produces simple noun phrases (modifier and noun). Produces simple verb phrases with main action verb (no inflections). Produces ex- | At least 60 percent of the speech of hearing children is intelligible. Engages in vocal play. |

single dimen-sions (color, shape, size).
Applies previous experiences to solve new problems.
Demonstrates the ability to remember absent objects and events.
Vocalizes about objects and events that are not immediately present.
Compares differences (2–7 years).
Constructs series of objects of different lengths but only attends to one end (2–7 years).

acquired behaviors in varied settings.
Engages in prolonged domestic make-believe play.

ous vocal interactions.
Adds information to the prior utterances ot communication partner.
Answers simple questions appropriately.
Asks increasing numbers of questions (particularly about location and identity).
Uses increasing numbers of utterances that serve the interpersonal function: calling attention to self or objects and events in the environment; regulating the behavior of others; obtaining desired objects or services; participating in social interaction rituals (e.g., *Hi; Bye*); commenting about objects and ongoing events; engaging in vocal play.

panded noun phrase [demonstrative and modifier (or article) and noun].
Marks present progressive (*ing*); uses *s* for plurality; uses the preposition *in*.
Indicates negation with *no* or *not* (*mommy no*).

(continued)

**EXHIBIT 1.6.** (Continued)

| Age in Months | Cognition | Play | Use | Content | Form | Speech or Auditory Training |
|---|---|---|---|---|---|---|
| 3–4 years | Compares differences. | Places as many as 10 shapes in place. Remembers daily routine sequences. | Responds to *whose, who, why* and *how many* questions; refers with increased frequency to the activity of others. Refers with increased frequency to objects and events removed in time. Changes tone of voice and sentence structure to adapt to listener's level of understanding. Uses some alternative forms to take context differences into account (e.g., speaker/hearer pronoun distinctions, definite/indefinite articles, and ellipsis based on shared information). | Knows shapes, sizes, positions, and colors. Knows number symbols 1–10. Knows time (e.g., day/night) and seasons. | Produces expanded noun phrase (demonstrative + article and adjective + noun) Uses *to be* as copula but not as auxiliary. Uses preposition *on*. Uses possessives. Uses "wh" to introduce questions. Uses *can't* and *don't* to mark negatives. Uses prepositional phrases. Begins to use past tense. | At least 85 percent of the speech of hearing children is intelligible. At least 95 percent of the speech of hearing children is intelligible. |

| 7–11 years | Seriates systematically; constructs two-dimensional arrays. | Elaborates and expands the prior utterances of another. |
| 12+ years | Seriates abstract and hypothetical arrays. | |

Luetke-Stahlman (in press) have suggested that the inability to refer to linguistically complex meanings in play may handicap the social, emotional, and linguistic development of young, hearing-impaired children. For these reasons, guidelines for social-emotional development appear in Appendix A (e.g., toileting, behavior, etc.).

Play is a natural and important activity for all children. Maria Montessori said that play is children's work. Students can clarify, practice, and master many fundamental physical, social, intellectual, and linguistic skills through repeated play experiences. Play should be identified as an important opportunity for development by significant adults working with hearing-impaired children.

Play behaviors parallel growth in other developmental areas (as can be seen in Exhibit 1.6) and are vehicles through which cognition and language can be facilitated (Westby, 1980). For example, children who

engage in symbolic or representational play evidence advances in general emotional growth, are persistent at tasks, distinguish reality from fantasy, cooperate well with others, and have the ability to tolerate delays, show empathy, and provide leadership. Further, children who engage in symbolic play perform significantly higher on prereading tasks than peers who do not engage in symbolic play.

## Play Assessment

Play should be assessed just as other important areas of growth for children are assessed. For example, *Westby* (1980) has designed an assessment tool that assists in goal setting and that provides insights into intervention strategies in this important developmental area. Her 10-stage checklist is reprinted as Exhibit 1.7.

**EXHIBIT 1.7.** Symbolic play scale Checklist (Westby, 1980)

| Play | Language |
|---|---|
| *Stage I—9 to 12 months* | |
| —— Awareness that objects exist when not seen; finds toy hidden under scarf | —— No true language: may have performative words (words that are associated with actions or the total situation) |
| —— Means-end behavior—crawls or walks to get what he wants; pulls string toys | Exhibits following communicative functions: |
| —— Does not mouth or bang all toys—some used appropriately | —— Request (instrumental) |
|  | —— Command (regulatory) |
| *Stage II—13 to 17 months* | |
| —— Purposeful exploration of toys: discovers operation of toys through trial and error; uses variety of motoric schemas | —— Context-dependent single words, for example, child may use the word "car" when riding in a car, but not when he sees a car; words tend to come and go in child's vocabulary |
| —— Hands toy to adult if unable to operate | Exhibits following communicative functions: |
|  | —— Request     —— Protesting |
|  | —— Command     —— Label |
|  | —— Interactional     —— Response |
|  | —— Personal     —— Greeting |
| *Stage III—17 to 19 months* | |
| —— Autosymbolic play, for example, child pretends to go to sleep or pretends to drink from cup or eat from spoon | Beginning of true verbal communication. Words have following functional and semantic relations: |
| —— Uses most common objects and toys appropriately | —— Recurrence     —— Agent |
|  | —— Existence     —— Object |
|  | —— Nonexistence     —— Action or state |

**EXHIBIT 1.7.** (Continued)

| Play | Language |
|---|---|
| ─── Tool-use (uses stick to reach toy) | ─── Rejection   ─── Location |
| ─── Finds toys invisibly hidden (when placed in box and box emptied under scarf) | ─── Denial   ─── Object or person associated with object or location |

*Stage IV—19 to 22 months*

Symbolic play extends beyond the child's self:

─── Plays with dolls; brushes doll's hair, feeds doll a bottle, or covers doll with blanket

─── Child performs pretend activities on more than one person or object: for example, feeds self, a doll, mother, and another child.

─── Combines two toys in pretend play, for example, puts spoon in pan or pours from pot into cup

─── Refers to objects and persons not present

Beginning of word combinations with following semantic relations

─── Agent-action   ─── Action-locative
─── Action-object   ─── Object-locative
─── Agent-object   ─── Possessive
─── Attributive
─── Dative

*Stage V—24 months*

─── Represents daily experiences: plays house—is the mommy, daddy, or baby; objects used are realistic and close to life size

─── Events short and isolated; no true sequences: some self-limiting sequences—puts food in pan, stirs, and eats

─── Block play consists of stacking and knocking down

─── Sand and water play consist of filing, pouring, and dumping

─── Uses earlier pragmatic functions and semantic relations in phrases and short sentences

The following morphological markers appear:

─── Present progressive (ing) on verbs
─── Plurals
─── Possessives

*Stage VI—2½ years*

Represents events less frequently experienced or observed, particularly impressive or traumatic events

─── Doctor-nurse-sick child

─── Teacher-shopping

Events still short and isolated. Realistic props still required. Roles shift quickly.

Responds appropriately to the following "Wh" questions in context:

─── What
─── Who
─── Whose
─── Where
─── What . . . do
─── Asks "Wh" questions—generally puts "Wh" at beginning of sentence
─── Responses to why questions inappropriate except for well-known routines, such as, "Why is the doctor here?" . . . "Baby sick."
─── Asks why, but often inappropriate and does not attend to answer

*Stage VII—3 years*

─── Continues pretend activities of Stages V and VI, but now the play has a sequence. Events are not isolated, for example, child mixes cake, bakes it, serves it, washes the dishes; or doctor checks patient; calls ambulance, takes patient to hospital and operates. Sequence evolves . . . not planned.

─── Compensatory toy . . . reenactment of experienced events with new outcomes

─── Associative play

─── Uses past tense, such as, "I ate the cake . . . I walked."

─── Uses future aspect (particularly "gonna") forms, such as, "I'm gonna wash dishes."

*(continued)*

**EXHIBIT 1.7.** (Continued)

| Play | Language |
|---|---|
| *Stages VIII—3 to 3½* | Descriptive vocabulary expands as child becomes more aware of perceptual attributes. Uses terms for the following concepts (not always correctly): |
| ——— Carries out play activities of previous stages with a doll house and Fisher-Price toys (barn, garage, airport, village). | ——— shapes |
| ——— Uses blocks and sandbox for imaginative play. Blocks used primarily as enclosures (fences and houses) for animals and dolls | ——— sizes |
| ——— Play not totally stimulus bound. Child uses one object to represent another. | ——— colors |
| ——— Uses doll or puppet as participant in play | ——— texture |
| | ——— spatial relationships |
| | ——— Gives dialogue to puppets and dolls |
| | ——— Metalinguistic language use, such as, "He said . . ." |
| | ——— Uses indirect requests, such as, "Mommy lets me have cookies for breakfast." |
| | ——— Changes speech depending on listener |
| *Stage IX—3½ to 4 years* | Verbalizes intentions and possible future events: |
| ——— Begins to problem solve events not experienced. Plans ahead. Hypothesizes "what would happen if . . ." | ——— Uses modals (can, may, might, will, would, could) |
| ——— Uses dolls and puppets to act out scenes | ——— Uses conjunctions (and, but, if, so, because) *Note*: Full competence for these modals and conjunctions does not develop until 10–12 years of age |
| ——— Builds three-dimensional structures with blocks which are attempts at reproducing specific structures child has seen. | ——— Begins to respond appropriately to why and how questions that require reasoning about perception |
| *Stage X—5 years* | |
| ——— Plans a sequence of pretend events. Organizes what he needs—both objects and other children. | ——— Uses relational terms (then, when, first, next, last, while, before, after) *Note*: Full competence does not develop until 10–12 years of age |
| ——— Coordinates more than one event occurring at a time | |
| ——— Highly imaginative. Sets the scene without realistic props. | |
| ——— Full cooperative play | |

SOURCE: C. Westby, "Assessment of cognition and language." *Language, Speech, and Hearing in the Schools, 11*, 154–188. Reprinted by permission of the American Speech-Language-Hearing Association and the author.

## Linguistic Maps of Cognitive Development

As children mature they need to have the concepts that they are constructing paired with the language labels and phrases conveying those concepts. Typically, children make many mistakes as they try new forms of language to convey their ideas. In the following

examples, a child did not have the cognition required to express an idea as an adult would have expressed it.

*4 years 1 month*

**HANNIE:**  Will I be old when you die?

**MOM:**  Could be. You never know. I could die tomorrow or when I'm older than

Grandma. Jane wasn't old when she died.

**HANNIE:**   Was she new?

*4 years 6 months* (new vocabulary acquisition)

**HANNIE:**   Oh, I'm getting this all nervous. (trying to glue a little paper house)

*4 years 6 months*

**HANNIE:**   (talking about scotch tape and masking tape) You can't have my tape, Mama. You (already) have about three pairs of it—a big kind and a little kind.

*5 years 3 months*

**HANNIE:**   Is it night on the other side now? (said in the morning and apparently talking about the earth but not using the word)

**MOM:**   What are you talking about? Oh, the earth? Yes.

**HANNIE:**   Do they have Christmas, too?

When language such as this is used by hearing-impaired children, the adult can model the adult language required to express the idea for the child. It is important that children are provided with the language on which to map their *cognition,* so that a "cognitive-linguistic gap" does not develop in which their *nonverbal* thinking ability tests higher than their language (in voice or sign) ability (Moeller & McConkey, 1983).

## SETTING COGNITIVE GOALS

After assessing the cognitive abilities of your students, you will need to be able to list and define cognitive skills and to set appropriate goals in this area. (Assessment is covered in Chapter 2; the writing of goals and objectives is covered in Chapter 3.) Examples of cognitive skills that you may want to consider when you are working with hearing-impaired children are listed in Exhibit 1.8. They have been adapted from the Weikert preschool curriculum.

**EXHIBIT 1.8.** Examples of cognition skills for which educators need to write goals.

### Key Experiences in Active Learning

Exploring actively with all the senses
Discovering relationships through direct experience
Manipulating, transforming, and combining materials
Choosing materials, activities, and purposes
Acquiring skills with tools and equipment
Using the large muscles
Taking care of one's own needs

### Key Experiences in Using Language

Talking with others about personally meaningful experiences
Describing objects, events, and relationships
Expressing feelings in words
Having one's own language written down by an adult and read back
Having fun with language: rhyming, making up stories, listening to poems and stories

### Key Experiences in Representation

Recognizing objects by sound, touch, taste, and smell
Imitating actions
Relating pictures, photographs, and models to real places and things
Role playing, pretending
Making models out of clay, blocks, and so forth
Drawing and painting

*(continued)*

**EXHIBIT 1.8.** (Continued)

## Key Experiences in Developing Logical Reasoning

### Classification

Investigating and/or labeling the attributes of things
Noticing and describing how things are the same and how they are different
Sorting and matching
Using and describing something in several different ways
Distinguishing between "some" and "all."
Holding more than one attribute in mind at a time (*Example*: Can you find something that is read and made of wood?)
Describing what characteristics something does not possess or what class it does not belong to

### Seriation

Comparing: which one is bigger (smaller), heavier (lighter), rougher (smoother), louder (softer), harder (softer), longer (shorter), taller (shorter), wider (narrower), sharper, darker, and so on
Arranging several things in order along some dimension and describing the relationship (the longest one, the shortest one, etc.)

### Number Concepts

Comparing number and amount: more/less, same amount; more/fewer, same number
Comparing the number of items in two sets by matching them up in one-to-one correspondence (*Example*: Are there as many crackers as there are children?)
Enumerating (counting) objects, as well as counting by rote

## Key Experiences in Understanding Time and Space

### Spatial Relations

Fitting things together and taking them apart
Rearranging a set of objects or one object in space (folding, twisting, stretching, stacking, typing) and observing the spatial transformations
Observing things and places from different spatial viewpoints
Experiencing and describing the positions of things in relation to each other (e.g., in the middle, on the side of, on, off, on top of, over, above)
Experiencing and describing the direction of movement of things and people (to, from, into, out of, toward, away from)
Experiencing and describing relative distances among things and locations (close, near, far, next to, apart, together)
Experiencing and representing one's own body: how it is structured, what various body parts can do
Learning to locate things in the classroom, school, and neighborhood
Interpreting representations of spatial relations in drawings and pictures
Distinguishing and describing shapes

### Time

Planning and completing what one has planned
Describing and representing past events
Anticipating future events verbally and by making appropriate preparations
Starting and stopping an action on signal
Noticing, describing, and representing the order of events
Experiencing and describing different rates of movement
Using conventional time units when talking about past and future events (morning, yesterday, hour, etc.)
Comparing time periods (short, long; new, old; young, old; a little while, a long time)
Observing that clocks and calendars are used to mark the passage of time
Observing seasonal changes

Adapted from High/Scope Foundation, 800 N. River Street, Ypsilanti, MI 48198.

Bloom's hierarchy (Bloom & Krathwohl, 1977) of cognition skills has been used by educators from many fields to assess and intervene with older learners; it appears in Exhibit 1.9 (Chamot, 1982). Educators have used this taxonomy to set goals and to develop questions that increase and decrease the level of difficulty. The levels, in increasing order of difficulty, include knowledge, comprehension, application, analysis, synthesis, and evaluation of information (reading from the bottom up in the exhibit). Taxonomies help to set goals, based on the needs of each hearing-impaired student. For example, a goal involving analysis might require that the student utilize factual information in formal speech to persuade classmates to purchase a product. A goal involving knowledge of the same material might require that the student list desirable attributes of two familiar products.

**EXHIBIT 1.9.** Language and cognition organized in a hierarchical manner (Chamot, 1982)

| Cognitive Domain Taxonomy | Linguistic Process | Internal Language Skills | External Language Skills |
|---|---|---|---|
| | | Use of information acquired through reading and listening in decontextualized situations. | Formal, academic speaking and writing. |
| Evaluation | Judging | Evaluation of accuracy and value. Applicability of ideas. | Expression of judgments. Use of rhetorical conventions. |
| Synthesis | Generalizing | Find relationships. Make inferences. Draw conclusions | Explanation of relationships, inferences, and conclusions. |
| Analysis | Informing | Acquisition of factual information. | Application of factual information acquired to formal information. |
| Application | Communicating | Understanding meaning of what is listened to in informal situations. Emergence of silent reading for basic comprehension. | Communication of meaning, feelings, and intentions in social and highly contextualized situations. Emergence of expository and creative writing. |
| Comprehension | Recombining | Recognition of and response to new combinations of known words and phrases in listening and oral reading. | Code switching and first-language transfer. Writing from guidelines and recombination dictation. |
| Knowledge | Recalling | Discrimination of and response to sounds, words, and unanalyzed chunks in listening/seeing. Identification of labels, letters, phrases in reading. | Production of single words and formulas; imitation of models. Handwriting, spelling, writing of known elements from dictation. |

SOURCE: A. U. Chamot, "Second language learning." *Forum 8*, 5. National Clearinghouse for Bilingual Education, 1980. Reprinted by permission of the author.

## THE CUMMINS MODEL OF LANGUAGE PROFICIENCY

The older the hearing-impaired student is, the more intertwined language and cognition skills become. Cummins (1984) recognized this phenomenon and proposed a model to define language proficiency that included both the dimensions of cognition and context. Because the model is based on hearing bilingual research, it has proven to be useful for discussing assessment or for task analyzing any area of communication or academic skills to teach bilingual and/or bimodal hearing-impaired learners (Luetke-Stahlman, 1987).

## Adapting Hearing Bilingual Proficiency Assessment

When a hearing child from a hearing bilingual home enters school, the child placed in a classroom in which monolingual or bilingual instruction is used. In the case of a Mexican American student, for example, the placement would be based on the child's age, language proficiency in English or Spanish, and parent preference. Tests of language proficiency would be administered to such a student and, generally, an English-dominant student would be placed in an English-only classroom, and a bilingual and minority-language-dominant child could be placed in a classroom in which both Spanish and English were used for instruction. The goal of education in both English-only and transitional classroom placement is to facilitate the students' development of cognitive and academic skills.

The goal of educators of hearing-impaired students parallels that of educators of hearing bilingual students: The students should obtain English literacy skills that will lead to full participation in the majority culture. When a young, hearing-impaired child enters school, a classroom placement is not made typically based on the results of language assessment, however. Language proficiency in oral English might be assessed and used either to place a child with intelligible speech in an oral-only English classroom or to suggest to the parents of an older, non-orally proficient child that signed instruction appears necessary, since the child is significantly below grade level. Rarely is the student's ability to use oral-only, simultaneous communication (cues, sign, gesture, etc.), fingerspelled-only communication, or ASL communication assessed, as we have recommended in this chapter. Traditionally, placement is made on the basis of the child's age and the parental or educational system's pref-

erence in terms of use or nonuse of signs in the instructional school program. Signing children are exposed typically to the system or to the mixture of languages and systems that are used by the teacher. Educational programming organized on the basis of language or particular system dominance rarely exists.

The degree of dominant language proficiency (e.g., English or ASL) of a student should be considered when the student's classroom placement (e.g., English-only or bilingual classes) is being determined and is advocated if the Cummins (1984) language proficiency model is adapted to situations that face us as educators in the field of deafness. Cummins noted that some Hispanic children (with normal hearing) were able to use English to survive on the playground but not to explain a reading story to a classroom teacher. He suggested that this seemingly contradictory behavior could be understood by analyzing both the cognitive-linguistic and contextual demands of tasks involved. His model of overall language proficiency is represented by two intersecting continua (see Exhibit 1.10). The familiar language of the playground would be characterized by quadrant A; the demands of the classroom, by quadrant D.

In the Cummins model, the horizontal continuum of context moves from embedded (content available) to reduced (little or no) context. Examples of a speechreading task sequenced on this context continuum would include a live speaker (providing a lot of content), a videotaped speaker, colored photographs of lip and tongue positions, black- and white-line drawings of lip and tongue positions, and printed speech sounds. Other types of contextual cues would involve the familiarity of the topic and how much has been said about it already. Stimuli on the right side of the continuum have less context with which the student can deduce meaning than those on the left side of the continuum, that is, the student must discern meaning from linguistic information alone when skills are listed on the far right side of the context continuum.

**EXHIBIT 1.10.** The Cummins model of language proficiency

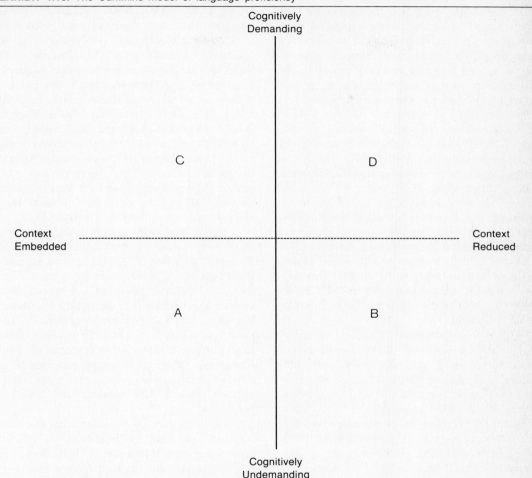

On the vertical continuum of cognitive-linguistic skill, tasks are organized that require low to high cognitive-linguistic involvement. Cognitive examples have been added to the model by Chamot (1982) and are presented in Exhibit 1.9. Linguistic examples moving up the continuum include a clozed set of phrases or sentences of known words, a familiar rhyme or story, an open set of isolated words, isolated phonemes, or a story with new or difficult vocabulary. Cognitive examples could entail knowledge (at the bottom of the continuum) and judging (at the top of it).

Cummins stressed that tasks characterized as being both cognitively demanding and of little or no context are those typical of the classroom and would be charted in the upper-right-hand quadrant of the model (quadrant D in Exhibit 1.10). A task in this quadrant might require that a hearing-impaired student read a story from a basal reader or give a formal speech without visual aids, and that requiring comprehension and synthesis of newly acquired, difficult vocabulary and/or complex grammatical structures.

According to the Cummins' model of linguistic proficiency (1984), it is not performance with cognitively undemanding, context embedded tasks (quadrant A), but with cognitively demanding, context reduced tasks (quadrant D) in a student's first language that can be used to predict performance in learning a second language and that should be the basis for classroom placement; that is, despite obvious differences between the first and second languages in terms of *surface features* e.g., phonology and syntax), there is a common, underlying *use* and *content* proficiency that determines an individual's ability on cognitive/academic tasks in both the first and second languages. For example, an adult might be able to say "girl" and easily remember the sign for *girl* (made with an A-hand to represent the strap of a bonnet on a cheek), because an underlying knowledge of the characteristics of an old-fashioned bonnet exist and do not need to be taught. This ability may not exist for a toddler (who is not able to associate the characteristic of a bonnet with the sign).

It is important that this underlying ability for cognitive-academic tasks be developed and serve as a language base on which second-language cognitive-academic skills can be developed. For example, if a student has been successfully assessed via ASL on a number of receptive (e.g, pointing, showing) and expressive (e.g., saying, signing) tasks, characterized by the cognitively demanding, context reduced constraints of the model, the prediction would be that there would be a similar successful performance in those same tasks via Signing Exact English (or another language or system), provided that the student is given sufficient exposure to learn the second language or system and could comprehend it. There is some evidence (reviewed by Moores, 1987) that this has been demonstrated in several studies in which ASL users out-performed oral subjects on academic and communicative measures.

The feasibility of using first-language quadrant D behaviors to predict a second language (i.e., English) in hearing-impaired populations was evidenced also by a study conducted at the National Technical Institute for the Deaf (NTID). This study used a questionnaire based on variables that Woodward (1973) found correlated to proficiency in adult users of ASL (Hatfield, Caccamise, & Siple, 1978). The questionnaire was administered to NTID college students in conjunction with a receptive comprehension test of ASL and a similar test of Manually Coded English (MCE). Results supported the validity of Cummin's model: Students who scored highest on the questionnaire also scored highest on the MCE test. Their performances supported the hypothesis that high first-language quadrant D behaaviors can predict high second-language quadrant D behaviors.

Luetke-Stahlman (1989) found the predictability feature of the Cummins model to be useful with hearing-impaired students with regard to speechreading ability. One of her students, Sherry Swanson, assessed two college-age women in their ability to answer the same set of questions. Her work is discussed in Chapter 9. Ling (1976) also found relationships that were in agreement with Cummins' model of language proficiency: a positive relationship between language competence, speech intelligibility, and auditory perception.

Unfortunately, the assessment of first-language quadrant D behaviors to predict second-language quadrant D behaviors has been ignored traditionally in policy decisions regarding school placement for both hearing bilingual and hearing-impaired students. Instead, school placement has been based on "natural communication" (quadrant A) tasks, if it is assessed at all. If first-language quadrant D behaviors should be assessed to predict second-language quadrant D behaviors, then a further assumtion in the assessment of language proficiency of hearing-impaired students is that their "first language" may not be English or only English (e.g., several languages or systems may function as a "first language"). This assumption is not without empirical support (Luetke-Stahlman, 1982).

In summary, the Cummins (1979, 1984)

model for assessing language proficiency breaks such proficiency into four components, based on context and cognition constraints. Further, first-language or system quadrant D behaviors should be assessed to predict second-language or system quadrant D abilities. If the goal of language proficiency assessment is English literacy development, it seems necessary to suppose that, since English is probably not the first language of all hearing-impaired students, an age-appropriate, complete quadrant D language base needs to be developed on which to build English literacy skills. If a hearing-impaired student is allowed to demonstrate which language or system is the most beneficial in acquiring cognitive-academic skills, then classroom placements should be based on these findings. For example, sign dominant children should be provided with sign dominant ethnic instruction, system dominant children should be provided with an accurate, consistently signed English language model, and cueing or oral dominant children should be provided with an accurate, proficient cued or oral model for instruction.

The feasibility of the Cummins model in assessing language proficiency of hearing-impaired students is that a multimodal assessment can be planned rather than a monolingual or a bilingual one. Further, academic goals can be organized systematically by using the four quadrants of the models. Examples of such uses are provided throughout this text.

## OPTIMIZING THE LANGUAGE ACQUISITION LEARNING ENVIRONMENT

When educating hearing-impaired students, teachers must give attention to the language acquisition environment, to the acquisition process itself, and, in particular, to the language input and activities that are necessary to compensate for the sensory deprivation of their students (Blackwell, et al., 1978). The features listed and described in the following paragraphs as those needed to provide optimal input for acquisition of a language are not presented in an order that signifies that any one feature is more important than another. Rather, these factors have been found to be necessary if a language is to be acquired.

1. *Optimal input is comprehensible.* Steve Krashen (1982) wrote an entire book about this principle. For some students who are exposed to oral English, Cued Speech, American Sign Language, SEE-1, or SEE-2, it may be that one or more of these codes are too complex for the student to comprehend. As we have discussed in this chapter, we believe that every hearing-impaired student has the right to demonstrate empirically which of all possible *languages* and/or *systems* are most beneficial in learning new and unknown, challenging information. By definition, the assessed language(s) and/or system(s) would be those that are comprehensible to the student in academic situations and are referred to in this text as the student's "first language."

2. *Optimal input must be complete.* The student must hear or see a complete language model, or *acquisition* cannot occur. Krashen's research can be applied by educators in the field of deaf education to mean that students with impaired hearing must be able to hear or see a complete representation of spoken English if they are to express the form of that code. ASL users need to see competent native users of ASL if they are to be taught academics via that language. Even when significant adults are conversing in simple, short sentences and are using oral English or a sign system, they should use grammatically correct language. Certainly users of oral-only, Cued Speech, SEE-1, and SEE-2 advocate this philosophy as they strive to determine which students can succeed with these methods of communication.

Several researchers have reported that it is not possible to voice and sign simultaneously to an accurate degree (Kluwin, 1981; Marmor & Petitto, 1979; Strong & Charleston, 1988). However, work by Luetke-Stahlman (1988d) has revealed that 25 teachers using SEE-1 or SEE-2 could sign the content and form of English in a manner that corresponded closely with spoken English. She found also that 12 teachers using SEE-2 signed 92 percent of what they said. The majority of teachers in the sample (which exceeded 50 videotaped transcripts) could sign over 70 percent of the meaning conveyed by their speech. A four-year study by Luetke-Stahlman (in press), involving over 175 hearing-impaired students representing seven different languages or systems, revealed that students exposed to a language or to an invented system that corresponds closely to a spoken language, scored significantly higher on reading and English language tests than did students exposed to Signed/Manual English and the input that teachers labeled as Pidgin Sign English (PSE). Significant adults using one of these methods of simultaneous communication need to supply input as completely as possible. (See Exhibit 1.11 for information regarding the adaptation of Signed/Manual English to a more complete system.) Users of Signed/Manual English or PSE are encouraged to use fingerspelling, to borrow affixes from SEE-2, to sign figurative English in a literal manner, to use ASL features (e.g., modification, placement, sightline, reduplication, directionality, etc.), and to employ mime to make their input more complete and their meaning more salient.

3. *Optimal input must be at a level that is slightly above that of the student.* Krashen labeled this concept "input + 1," and we have adapted the concept to mean that significant adults must target their input with respect to the cognitive and linguistic abilities of those whom they are teaching. Krashen uses an analogy of an English speaker who is trying to comprehend Spanish spoken on a radio program. Those of us who have a beginner's ability to speak Spanish and who have listened to a Spanish radio broadcast know how frustrating (and incomprehensible)

it can be to try to attend to input that is just too complex and that lacks a visible context from which we can deduce clues. Moeller and Luetke-Stahlman (in press) found that parents might sign to their deaf children using input that is below that of the child (i.e., input − 1).

We believe that educators must assess the use, content, and form of the student language that they are *facilitating* and aim their input at a development level slightly above the assessed *phase* in each area. Significant adults can make input optimal if they know the level of "parentese" or "teacherese" that they should be using. (Tools to ascertain these levels are described in Chapters 5, 6, and 7.)

4. *Optimal input provides context to those who need it before comprehension is expected in context-reduced situations.* Earlier in this chapter, the Cummins model of language proficiency was explained and exemplified. This model has been used to task analyze many areas of communication for students with impaired hearing. The model provides for a systematic manner in which context can be faded when it is no longer required. For example, a teacher might use diagrams rather than photographs to reduce context, talk about unfamiliar (but not present) items rather than familiar (but not present) items, or to discuss events that happened in the distant past rather than the immediate past.

5. *Optimal input must be modeled by at least one proficient user of the language.* This person must have a command of the target language, must be physically and psychologically available to the student for communication, and must both initiate conversations with the student and reply sensibly and grammatically to most of the student's utterances (Bonvillian, Nelson, & Charrow, 1976). Adults must expand the student's utterances within a relevant context (McCormick & Schiefelbush, 1984), and they must ask questions that check comprehension

and insure that their input is at an appropriate level (Krashen, 1982; McCormick & Schiefelbush, 1984).

6. *Optimal input is learned in situations in which the* "affective filter" *is low* (Krashen, 1982). The *affective filter* is a screen of emotion that can block language acquisition or learning if it keeps the user from being too self-conscious or too embarrassed to take risks during communicative exchanges. All of us have experienced situations in which someone has criticized something we said or the way we formed a cue or a sign. Immediately we lose our motivation to continue, because we focus on the form of what we are saying or signing, or because we are inhibited in our motivation to communicate. It is logical that interrupting a student's message so that speech or grammar can be imitated correctly would create anxiety, lower any motivation to risk using the target content or form, and damage self-esteem and self-concept. Fillmore-Wong (1978) found that low anxiety, high motivation, strong self-esteem and self-confidence all positively influenced second-language acquisition. Unfortunately, the teacher's typical reaction to a student's mistakes is to correct the student's errors. Instead, the teacher must try to remember that errors can be viewed as signals of language growth. All hearing children make mistakes as they acquire language, but their parents focus on the meanings that they are trying to convey rather than on correcting their form.

As a teacher, your job is to reinforce the emerging behaviors that deserve attention and praise. Try to find something positive to say to each student about his or her performance during an activity and keep the situations challenging but fun!

7. *Optimal input occurs in situations in which adults possess a positive attitude towards the various cultures represented by their students.* Language proficiency involves both linguistic and cultural dimensions (Cummins, 1984). Cazden, Vera, and Hymes (1972) found that exceptionally high rates of academic achievement and success were the result of cultural congruence in the classroom. We should strive to accept the bilingual/bicultural heritage of our hearing-impaired children and be sensitive to their need for identity and role models. (See Chapter 14 for specific ideas on implementation.)

8. *Optimal input uses a consistent lexicon and grammar.* A data set of teachers using Signed/Manual English and PSE, currently being analyzed, has demonstrated the severity of the need for teachers to sign words and figurative English as do the other teachers in their programs. In this study, teachers sign identical words in more than one way, regardless of the language or the system that they indicated they were using. Little consistency in the signing of figurative English or the use of ASL features has been found among teachers representing the same programs. Teachers using simultaneous communication need to meet regularly and discuss the standardizing of signed words, affixes, and figurative English. Invented signs need to be recorded such that all users have access to them.

9. *Students will attend to input when they have an interest in the topic, material, or activity* (Loban, 1978; McCormick & Schiefelbush, 1984). Optimal input is whole, interesting, relevant, and genuine (Goodman, 1986). Experimental evidence suggests that students pay little or no attention to the meaning of utterances after the first few repetitions in a pattern drill, and the same result is most likely true for dialogues and grammatical exercises that are memorized by rote (Krashen, 1982).

10. *Optimal input must be supplied in sufficient quantity.* Krashen (1982) suggested supplying 40–50 minutes of input (of the type provided in this section) to students each day until the student is an intermediate user of the target language. Unfortunately, we do not have enough data to know how much input is necessary to reach each phase of lin-

**EXHIBIT 1.11.** Adapting Signed English to correspond more closely with spoken English

1. The Bornstein, Saulnier, and Hamilton text (1983), *The Comprehensive Signed English Dictionary*, is used as a standard.

2. Words are signed in the same order as they are spoken in an English utterance. If you say, "Move back and take your hands off Tom's back," you would sign MOVE BACK AND TAKE YOUR HAND + S OFF TOM + 'S BACK. (The convention of capital letters is used to show signed words.)

3. The 14 Bornstein markers are used consistently; that is, *climbed* is signed CLIMB + D, stuck and went are signed STICK + PAST TENSE MARKER, GO + PAST TENSE MARKER. To sign *gone*, use the GO + N MARKER. This is not always the way these words are illustrated in the text. For example, Bornstein and colleagues provide an ASL sign for *stuck*, but for consistency we advocate signing STICK + PAST TENSE MARKER. They do not use suffix markers consistently for MENTALLY RETARDED and EMOTIONALLY DISTURBED; we advocate that you do so.

4. The SEE-2 affix markers are used for all words requiring them. For example, *unzip* is signed UN + ZIP (and not signed NOT + ZIP), and *undress* is signed UN + DRESS. These two words appear as different signs in the Bornstein text, but the use of affixes can help us consistently and completely encode English. Affixes are used regularly when you are talking to young children (e.g., "Can I unbutton your dress?") and appear often in children's literature. For example, the Disney version of *Cinderella* contains the sentences, "To Cinderella's *amazement*, the pumpkin changed into a carriage. The whole *kingdom* was wondering."

5. SEE-2 (Gustason, Pfetzing, & Zawolkow, 1973) signs will be used only when Signed English signs are too similar to distinguish between them (e.g., DRESS + CLOTHES) or do not exist (e.g., AVOID, ITEM). If a sign cannot be found in either book, fingerspelling is used (see 6).

6. When deaf adults fingerspell words, the words are less than seven letters long (Akamatsu, 1983). Novel words that are seven letters or less could be fingerspelled. Signs could be invented for longer words and recorded in a systematic manner.

7. Signed English (SE) signs that encode two or more words (e.g., FIGURE OUT, STICK IN, GET OUT, HAVE TO) are signed as separate words (e.g., STICK + IN, GET + OUT, etc.).

8. English is signed literally. For example, in Walt Disney's *Cinderella*, several sentences would be signed like this:

| On the | stroke | of | midnight, | the | spell | will | be | broken |
|--------|--------|-----|-----------|-----|-------|------|------|--------|
ON THE S-T-R-O-K-E OF MIDNIGHT, THE SPELL WILL BE BREAK + N

| When | the | prince | saw | the | charming | Cinderella, | he | fell | in | love | instantly |
|------|-----|--------|-----|-----|----------|-------------|-----|------|-----|------|-----------|
WHEN THE PRINCE SAW THE CHARM + ING CINDERELLA HE FALL + PT IN LOVE INSTANT + LY

a. Signed like fingerspell
b. CHARM from SEE-2
c. Signed FALL + past tense of IN LOVE even though this is a figurative use of the word fall.

9. Signs are be used as they are spoken or written in English and not based on the iconicity of the sign. For example, the word or sign *animal* is used to convey utterances such as,

You animal.
You brought out the animal in her.
That's a huge animal.

40

*Boy* would be signed to encode utterances such as,

Oh boy!

That's a boy!

The boy is running.

The old boys' club is in operation.

This decision is based on two things:

Research that has shown that children do not depend on (or even realize) iconicity of signs (reviewed in Paul & Quigley, 1988)

Research by Luetke-Stahlman (1988a) that has shown significantly higher reading and English language abilities of severely and profoundly (unaided) deaf children exposed to SEE-2 and SEE-1 (in that order and when compared to groups of oral English, SE/ME, PSE, and ASL users)

## Needs

For those programs that prefer to use a "conceptual" approach to signing, two things should be considered by adult signers:

1. Are all adults signing a conceptually different sign for all the different meanings of a particular word? For example, we have found over 15 different meanings for expressions that include *heart*. Would your group be signing these expressions 15 different ways?

2. Will there be consistency among all signers so that the students have comprehensible models?

Parents and teachers who seek to use SE/ME in a manner that is linked to literacy will need to

1. Meet regularly to discuss signs

2. Establish a systematic method of recording SEE-2 and invented signs

3. Look up signs consistently

4. Use videotaped language sampling techniques to record and analyze their own bimodal input

**41**

guistic development. However, we believe that each student should receive instruction in the language or system that has been demonstrated to be most beneficial for that student for at least part of the school day.

Quantity of input also is supplied when adults are repetitive. One researcher found that children are prone to attempt those constructions that significant adults use most frequently. Therefore, significant adults need to repeat multiple sets of the use, content, or form of targeted behaviors.

11. *Optimal input is positioned so that the new information is at the front or the end of the utterance.* Young children seem to have a bias towards processing sounds, hand configurations, or constructions that are either in the initial or final position (Furrow, Nelson, & Benedict, 1979; Newport, Gleitman, & Gleitman, 1977; Slobin, 1970). For example, a hearing child, Hannah, called herself "Nah" and her dog Primo, "Mo" as a toddler. Another practical example of this principle is found with one of our recommended question prompts (see Chapter 10). This prompt usually brings the question form to the front of the request so that it is more salient. Depending on what you are trying to teach, you can move the important information to a key position in the sentence (e.g., when you are focusing on color, say "The chair is *red*," not "The red chair").

12. *Optimal input occurs when users have a positive attitude about language acquisition.* Significant adults have to believe in their children's abilities and eventual progress (Nelson, 1973), and students have to be positively motivated. Students who are encouraged are likely to do a better job at any task (Johnson & Johnson, 1984).

13. *Optimal input is cognitively salient.* For the use, content, and form of a language to be acquired by a student, the match between an action, object, or process must be labeled for the child such that it is noticed (Carroll, 1986). The teacher has to take advantage of teachable moments that occur and provide language labels for students during these moments.

14. *Optimal input involves feedback.* Feedback such as acknowledgment (e.g., "uh huh") and head nods signal an approving environment in which the student is free to take risks (Furrow, Nelson, & Benedict, 1979; Johnson & Johnson, 1984; Newport, 1977). Also, when parents correct children, language acquisition is affected in a positive way if an explanation follows the correction (e.g., "That is not a car; it's a truck. See, it has a place to put things.")

15. *Optimal input is obtained via a conversational approach.* Successful conversation with a user of the desired language may be the best language lesson of all, as long as the significant adult succeeds in fulfilling the other conditions for optimal input as they are listed here. A conversational approach would entail that adults take more time simply to talk or sign to hearing-impaired students and capitalize on topics and content that are motivating to the students. For example, calendar time could be replaced by problem-solving or planning time during which students have an opportunity to express something that they truly wish to make others understand or to convince someone of something (Loban, 1973). During planning time, hearing-impaired preschoolers could explain in which learning center they would like to play, with whom, and what they are going to do there. Older students in a contained classroom could begin the day by providing a rationale for the order in which they would like to move through their lessons, explain what they plan to do at recess, or discuss why they would like to work at a particular learning center when they finish their work.

## SUMMARY

The material presented in this chapter lays a groundwork of principles for concepts that will be discussed in future chapters. *Com-*

*munication* is defined as including the components of language (use, content, and form), speech articulation and speechreading, and audition.

Also included in this chapter is information pertaining to the development of cognition and its relationship to bilingual and bimodal language proficiency and assessment (i.e., the Cummins model). Fifteen factors that are believed to be necessary to facilitate optimal language acquisition are listed and described. These important features will be exemplified throughout the text.

## ACTIVITIES

1. Draw a diagram that illustrates how the following words are related to each other: *use, content, form, communication, language, speech, speechreading, speech articulation,* and *cognition.* Write a paragraph that describes your diagram.
2. Draw the two intersecting continua of the Cummins model. Pick any area of communication (that is not already diagrammed in the text) and list five skills in each of the four quadrants.
3. Administer portions of the Denver, Uzgarius, and Hunt scales, Bayley scales, Wechsler Preschooler Primary scales, or McCarthy scales to a hearing or hearing-impaired child who is from 1 to 7 years of age.
4. Conduct a Piagetian task with several hearing and/or hearing-impaired children. Discuss the individual differences in the children.
5. Plan play activities for three different ages of young children, using Exhibit 1.6. Write out a description and purpose for these activities, which then could be given to parents.
6. Find pictures of 30 different toys and organize them by age appropriateness. Find toys that are appropriate for infants, toddlers, preschoolers, and kindergartners.
7. Assess a learning environment according to the factors that we have discussed as being necessary if language is to be acquired. Evaluate your findings with regard to two other topics that were discussed in this chapter.

# CHAPTER 2

# Assessing Students' Needs

## OVERVIEW

In Chapter 1, we discussed how a hearing impairment has a profound effect on the communication and cognitive development of a hearing-impaired student. In Chapter 2, we begin to look at ways in which you can plan educational programs to meet the needs of your students so that you can help them overcome the impact of their hearing loss. Fundamental to the development of educational plans is the process of gathering information about your students so that you can determine what their individual strengths and areas of need are. This process is traditionally referred to as *assessment* or *evaluation*.

In order for a hearing-impaired student to receive special education or related services, that student must go through several stages of assessment. While terms that are used to describe the various steps in the assessment process will vary from school system to school system, we are using the term *assessment* to describe the systematic process of collecting information from a wide variety of sources in order to make decisions regarding the student's placement and instructional program (Davis, 1983).

Any discussion of assessing hearing-impaired students must be prefaced with an understanding that there are legislative considerations that guide the assessment process. In the last three decades, the federal government has moved from demonstrating little involvement in special education to become a major partner in state and local programs for hearing-impaired students. As an educator in the 1990s, you have inherited a major responsibility. After well over a century of lawsuits and state and federal legislation, it is now the right of all special-needs students, regardless of the type or degree of their handicapping condition, to be treated fairly and equally with respect to education. It is our job as educators to see to it that these students receive an education that is suitable to their needs.

An understanding and appreciation of the current legislation and social climate will help you to analyze existing programs and public policies as they affect hearing-impaired students. This chapter begins by reviewing two important federal laws that lay the foundation for the assessment and intervention procedures that we will then examine in detail. As a teacher, acting as an advocate for your hearing-impaired students and their families, you need to understand and execute the provisions of these laws.

```
┌─────────────────────────────────────────────────────────┐
│                     CHAPTER TOPICS                       │
│                                                          │
│   The Legislative Foundation                             │
│   Forms of Assessment                                    │
│   Using Assessment for Intervention                      │
│   Modifying Assessment Techniques                        │
│   Overview of Assessment                                 │
└─────────────────────────────────────────────────────────┘
```

## THE LEGISLATIVE FOUNDATION

### Public Law 94-142

Legislation at both the state and the federal level has had a major impact on the education and treatment of hearing-impaired children. In November 1975, Congress passed Public Law 94-142 (Education for all Handicapped Children Act). The implications of this law are extensive and have had a direct impact on classroom activities, changing drastically the roles and responsibilities of parents and school personnel. Enacted in 1978, PL 94-142 was the result of a discovery that only about 50 percent of handicapped school-age children in the public schools were receiving the special education services that they needed and that 1 million children were being excluded from the public school system (Cartwright, Cartwright, & Ward, 1985). The federal government mandated that state and local agencies were responsible for correcting these conditions. PL 94-142 was implemented to help the states handle the costs of providing educational programs for special-needs students.

PL 94-142 requires that all handicapped children and youth be provided with appropriate educational services from 3 to 21 years of age. According to Kirk and Gallagher (1986), the law has several major components that have shaped special education over the past decade. They include the following.

1. *Zero Reject*. All children must be provided with a free and appropriate public education, regardless of their handicapping condition.

2. *Nondiscriminatory evaluation*. Each student must be fairly and accurately evaluated. The tests must be appropriate to the child's cultural and linguistic background. Tests should be provided and administered in the child's native language or typical mode of communication. The tests should be selected and administered so as to best ensure that, when a test is administered to a hearing-impaired child, the test results accurately reflect the child's aptitude and achievement levels.

3. *Individualized Education Program*. An individualized education program (IEP) must be developed, implemented, and evaluated for each student who is receiving special education services. The components of the IEP are specified in the law and outlined in detail in a later section of this chapter.

4. *Least-restrictive environment*. As much as possible, handicapped children should be educated with nonhandicapped children. School systems should provide a continuum of services that facilitates student movement from one type of service to another as the need arises.

5. *Due process.* Due process is a set of procedures that ensure fairness and accountability. These procedures include the parents' right to be consulted about their child's educational program prior to its implementation, to obtain an individual evaluation from a qualified examiner outside the school system, and to call a hearing when they do not agree with the school's plan for their child. The role and responsibility of a teacher during a due process hearing is presented in Exhibit 2.1.

6. *Parental participation.* Parents of a hearing-impaired child have access to their child's educational records and the right to participate in the development of the educational plan for their child.

**Formulating an Individualized Education Program.**    The educational and related services that must be provided by law to a hearing-impaired student emerge from the assessment of the student's present performance level. As we have mentioned earlier, the federal government requires certain components in an individualized education program (IEP) for each hearing-impaired student who needs special education and related services. The

IEP is a planning document that is the starting point for the development and coordination of a student's special education curricula. Currently, there is no one standardized IEP form. While many IEP plans may include additional information, each IEP must include at least the following components.

1. *A statement of the student's current level of performance.* According to the IEP interpretation guidelines published in the Federal Register (1981), current performance levels should include an accurate description of the effects of the handicap on the student's academic performance (language, reading, math, etc.) and nonacademic performance (self-help, psychomotor, social skills, vocational, etc.). The information should be presented in objective and measurable terms. There should be either test protocols, academic work samples, or other data to support the analysis of the student's skills. Additionally, the information must be relatively recent (no more than one or two months old) in order to be considered current.

2. *A statement of the annual goal, which describes what will be accomplished by the end of the year.* Annual goals are usually stated in terms that are broad enough to reflect expected behavior changes, yet specific enough to suggest component short-term objectives. The annual goals should be based on

**EXHIBIT 2.1.** Guidelines for preparing for due process hearings (Scandary, 1981)

Teachers need to be prepared to:

1. State their professional credentials, certifications, training, and experience relative to their position, title, and current status in the educational system of the student in question

2. State the extent and nature of their contact with the child

3. Make statements about the unique needs of the student

4. Discuss the kinds of evaluative tools and methods used in arriving at their conclusions concerning the student's academic and behavioral abilities.

5. Discuss the validity and reliability of the evaluative materials used

6. Explain terms and terminology specific to education and/or the particular professional field of expertise that they represent

7. Sit down and work with the parents after the hearing is over

8. Seek a consultation or intervention when they feel that parental dissatisfaction is being expressed

SOURCE: J. Scandary, "What every teacher should know about due process hearings. *Teaching Exceptional Children 13,* 92–98. Reston VA: The Council for Exceptional Children, 1981.

the data presented in the current level of performance section. They should reflect established priorities that are based on entry behaviors, realistic expectations of performance changes anticipated over the school year, and an assessment of the amount of time and type of instruction necessary for achieving the goal. Examples of appropriate annual goals are:

> Mary will be able to subtract numbers without regrouping.
> Steve will use his auditory training system daily.
> Kenny will achieve a 2.0 reading level by May.

3. *A statement of the short-term instructional objectives in measurable steps.* Once annual goals have been developed, the teacher must write more specific short-term objectives. Short-term instructional objectives describe in behavioral terms what the student needs to learn and how to measure when that learning has occurred. The instructional objectives define how each annual goal is reached and are, therefore, more detailed. Essentially, the objectives break the goals down into concrete, teachable components. They should be logically sequenced and built from the student's current abilities to the annual goal. In some cases, there may be only one instructional objective for each annual goal, but usually there are several. Instructional objectives tend to follow a four-part sequence. Specific information for developing short term instructional objectives is provided in Chapter 3. Examples of instructional objectives are:

> Greg will solve addition problems of one-digit plus two-digit numbers with carrying, with 90 percent accuracy.
> Chris will identify the characteristics of evergreen trees with 90 percent accuracy.
> Given 10 locations, identified only by

their latitude and longitude, Leona will locate their corresponding positions on a map with 80 percent accuracy.

4. *A statement of the specific educational services or materials needed by the child.* The designation of programs and services to be provided to the student may be the most critical aspect of the IEP (Schloss & Sedlak, 1986). Special education services generally include information about the educational setting in which the student will be placed to achieve the annual goals.

For example, Sherry, a 9-year-old hearing-impaired student, receives most of her educational program in a fourth-grade class with her hearing peers. Sherry has a full-time educational interpreter. In addition, she works with a teacher of the deaf for one hour a week on language. The services that are provided by the educational interpreter and the teacher of the deaf need to be listed on Sherry's IEP.

In addition to the actual special education services that will be provided, the IEP must also indicate *related services*. Related services are special programs—developmental, corrective, and supportive—that the student may need outside of the special or regular education program. These might include speech therapy, physical or occupational therapy, transportation, and counseling services. Specific materials or equipment that a student needs should also be included (e.g., a hearing aid, an auditory trainer, or large-print books).

Placement options that currently are available to hearing-impaired students are displayed in Exhibit 2.2. The use of a circle to show the continuum of services, as suggested by the Commission on Education of the Deaf (1988), helps us to see that one program is not necessarily better than another and that the individual student's needs should be matched with the program that can best provide the appropriate services. Generally speaking, hearing-impaired students can be

**EXHIBIT 2.2.** Placement options available to hearing-impaired students.

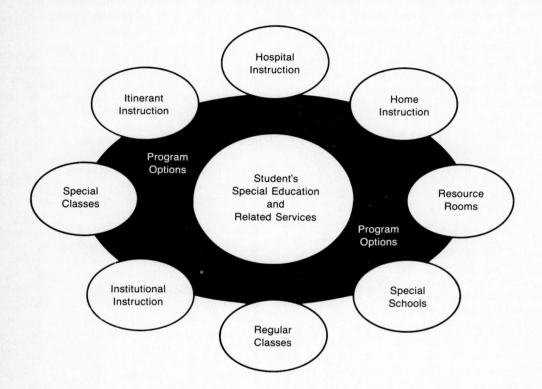

placed in educational environments that range from full-time special education services in special schools, such as residential and day schools for the deaf, to more integrated settings in which they can attend academic and/or nonacademic instruction with their hearing peers. For a more thorough breakdown of educational options, see Paul and Quigley (1990).

5. *An explanation of how much time the student will participate in a regular education program.* The IEP must indicate academic and social areas where the student is able to benefit from interacting with hearing peers. These can range from being mainstreamed into formal academic subjects to informal set-

tings, such as the lunchroom, school assemblies, and the playground. For example, the IEP may include regular class for third-grade math, five times a week for 40 minutes per day, and physical education with a regular fourth-grade class, two times per week.

6. *Procedures for measuring objectives.* The law requires appropriate objective criteria and evaluation procedures, as well as schedules for determining whether the goals are being achieved. At least once a year, an objective assessment of the student's progress must be made. This process facilitates the determination of new goals and objectives, the revision of current objectives, and the selection of effective teaching strategies.

The IEP should list the specific assessment instruments—the means of testing—or data collection procedures that will be used. Instruments and procedures must be valid and reliable. Vague or subjective measurement procedures should be avoided. Data that is collected on a regular basis and used to modify the instructional program should be pulled together prior to the annual review. The type of data that is taken will depend on the objective. Examples of data that may be included in the annual review are: (1) achievement test scores, (2) skills checklists, (3) criterion-referenced tests results, (4) attendance data, (5) data from direct observations, and (6) data from permanent products of the student's work.

7. *The date that services will begin and the length of time that services will be provided.* This aspect of the IEP specifies the date on which IEP services are to be initiated, as well as the anticipated period of time that the IEP is to be in effect (e.g., beginning 9/15/90, 3 times per week for 20 minutes each meeting, for a total of 60 minutes per week). The IEP must be reviewed on an annual basis in order that the appropriateness of educational placement and services can be reconsidered. If the student's progress indicates that a change needs to be made, the change must occur. For example, Gary, who has been placed in a regular third-grade class for all academic subjects, is falling behind in the areas of reading, science, and language. At the annual review, it was decided that Gary would benefit from an educational environment that was designed to provide more intensive work in those academic areas. It was also decided that Gary needed auditory training. Therefore, it was decided that Gary would receive services from a deaf educator in the areas of language, reading, science, and auditory training and would continue placement in the third-grade class for all other academic and nonacademic subjects.

According to Westling and Koorland (1988), ways in which the usefulness of the IEP can be increased include the following:

1. Write IEPs that are based on objective data.
2. Keep IEPs readily available and look at them on a regular basis.
3. Prepare individual lessons based on the IEP.
4. Communicate with other teachers and therapists about students' goals and objectives, and encourage their cooperation.
5. Work toward achieving the goals specified on the IEP.

## The Education of the Handicapped Act Amendments Law

Another important law for hearing-impaired children and their families is the Education of the Handicapped Act Amendments Law, Public Law 99-467. The federal government passed PL 99-457 in September 1986, after gathering evidence concerning the effectiveness of *early intervention* with handicapped children. Over a period of approximately 20 years, educators and legislators had become aware that delays in development and family stress could decrease if support and services to children and their families were made available. For example, by providing parents with counseling services when their child was diagnosed as having a hearing loss, the opportunity for family members to express their feelings and concerns helped them to learn to accept their hearing-impaired child and to provide a nurturing environment for their child's development. Further, early intervention—as early as needs became apparent—could prevent costly public services later in life, because children and family members were more able to contribute to their communities (Smith, 1987). Educators and behavioral scientists now view even very young infants as capable of participating in complex interactions with *significant others* (parents, siblings, neighbors, etc.). They have found that heightened social competence leads to accelerated cognitive development (Gilkerson, Hilliard, Schrag, & Shonkoff, 1987).

Public Law 99-457 includes provisions for students of all ages, but the major focus of the law relates to handicapped children between the ages of birth and 6 years. All states were mandated to serve these children by 1990–1991. Children can be served by the law without being given a categorical label (e.g., learning disabled, blind, emotionally disturbed), and parent instruction is supported through government funding. Variations in the length of the school day, type of service model (e.g., home-based, center-based), and mainstreaming opportunities are encouraged by the law.

Monies are granted to states based both on the number of handicapped preschoolers served and the number predicted to be served. States that refuse to serve special-needs children lose all federally disseminated preschool grant funds, PL 94-142 dollars generated by preschoolers, and all grants and contracts related to preschool special education funded under the Education of the Handicapped Act discretionary programs. To implement the law, states need to establish standards to evaluate appropriate placement options, and personnel standards need to delineate competencies across many disciplines.

*Handicapped Infant and Toddler Program.* Public Law 99-457 also established a voluntary Handicapped Infant and Toddler Program. The purpose of this landmark early intervention program is to provide financial assistance for states (1) to develop and implement a statewide, comprehensive, coordinated, multidisciplinary, interagency program of services; (2) to facilitate the coordination of resources from federal, state, local, and private sources; and (3) to enhance states' capacity to provide quality early intervention services (Ballard, Ramirez, & Zantal-Wiener, 1987). Children from birth to 3 years of age are eligible if they evidence a handicapping condition or are "at risk" medically or environmentally for substantial developmental delays if early intervention is not provided.

Families of children who meet these criteria are eligible also for services.

## Individualized Family Service Plans (IFSP)

Public Law 99-457 promotes a coordinated and multiagency approach to implementing new early childhood initiatives. Lawmakers acknowledged during the formation of the provisions that a wide variety of service providers should be involved in the provision of cost-effective services.

A multidisciplinary assessment, an evaluation conducted by professionals from diverse disciplines, such as, a classroom teacher of the hearing-impaired, a speech-language pathologist, an audiologist, a psychologist, a social worker, and other appropriate personnel, and a written IFSP are required for each eligible child receiving early intervention services. The services provided may include special education, speech, language and audiological services, occupational and/or physical therapy, psychological services, parent and family training and counseling services, medical and health services, and so forth, which are necessary to enable the child to benefit from other early intervention components. These services are provided at no cost to the family.

## Perspective on the Legislation

We are part of a new era in education in this country. No longer is the exclusion of children with special needs from educational programs either justifiable or legal. No longer is our principal concern whether or not we should provide full educational opportunities to students who are hearing-impaired; our concern now is how best to do this. The laws tell us that we now must plan, in advance of placement, how, where, what, and how fast students will learn. It tells us that the students have the right to be made aware of their performance and to be protected so that a fair judgement of their abilities can be made. It tells us that all hearing-impaired students must receive an individually planned program of instruction and that the program must be reviewed and evaluated at least annually. As a teacher, you will have the responsibility to understand and to carry out on a daily basis the intent of the laws that affect your students.

## FORMS OF ASSESSMENT

The focal point of Public Law 94-142 is the Individualized Education Program or the IEP. As we have seen, the IEP is intended to establish a highly individualized structure for learning that is based on objective evaluation procedures. It is through assessment that educators can gather the information needed to make decisions about possible educational alternatives and interventions. This process of assessment is aimed at discerning individual characteristics that are important for establishing an instructional program to meet a student's educational needs. Assessment involves more than just administering tests and calculating scores. It should be approached in a systematic manner as an interactive process, whereby on occasion you go beyond the standard test procedure in order to gain additional information about the student's abilities (Sattler, 1982). The objective of such adaptation is not to increase the student's score, but rather to discover what support or cues are needed to get the student to respond correctly to the items failed. It is recommended that this type of interaction not be initiated until the administration of standard tests has been completed. Examples of alterations to standardized tests that can be used to gain more information include providing extra clues to the student, giving explicit feedback on performance, or having the student explain his or her approaches to problem solving (Sattler, 1982). In sum, assessment is best viewed as a method of inquiry that results in obtaining information about the strengths, weaknesses, and expectations of a particular student.

## Purposes of Assessment

The primary purpose of assessment is to apply pertinent information about a specific student as you make decisions about appropriate placement and effective methods of instruction. There are four purposes of assessment:

1. *Placement*. To aid in deciding what the appropriate educational environment for the student should be.
2. *Program planning*. To assist in determining the skills and knowledge that the student has and has not mastered. The results enable the *multidisciplinary team* to design an educational program that meets the needs of the individual student.
3. *Student evaluation*. To monitor a student's achievement and progress.
4. *Program evaluation*. To measure the effectiveness of a specific method or set of materials in a program.

## Assessment Methods

*Norm-referenced Tests.* Norm-reference tests are commercially prepared instruments that have been standardized by being administered to groups of students. The primary purpose of norm-referenced tests, which are also called *formal tests* or *standardized tests*, is to help educators compare one student with others of the same age or grade level. They are most frequently used with hearing-impaired students in order to help document placement decisions. Norm-referenced tests can sample a broad range of skills. They are best used to measure long-term objectives or as screening tools to identify areas in need of a more precise and thorough evaluation. Norm-referenced tests are accompanied by manuals that provide essential information for the appropriate use of the test. Generally included in the manual is a description of the various parts of the test and directions for how to administer to assure that the test will be given, scored, and evaluated in a standardized manner.

Typically, correct student responses are totaled and referred to as a *raw score*. This score is then converted by using a normative table into derived scores, such as grade and age equivalents or a percentile rank. These scores permit a measure of student behavior that is interpretable to professionals and parents across geographic areas and disciplines of study. For example, if a hearing-impaired student were administered the Stanford Achievement Test, Special Edition for Hearing-Impaired Students, the student's scores on each of the sections of the test could be compared with those of other hearing-impaired students as well as hearing students across the country. Another value of norm-referenced tests is that they are an annual evaluation in which the current score can be compared with the scores from the previous year to monitor efficacy of the student's IEP.

Several major problems limit the usefulness of norm-referenced tests. Many norm-referenced tests are not appropriate because they have not been normed on hearing-impaired students (Moeller, in press; Salvia & Ysseldyke, 1988). Similarly, norm-referenced tests have been shown to discriminate against minority students (Anastasi, 1976). Another limitation of norm-referenced tests stems from the amount of time that it generally takes to administer and score the test or test battery. M.P. Moeller (1988) stated in regard to assessing language that norm-referenced tests rarely provide a comprehensive sampling of students' functional language skills, because students are tested outside of relevant communicative contexts, and that norm-referenced tests, by nature, have too few items sampling each language behavior to be of prescriptive value.

Some of the most common norm-referenced tests that are used with hearing-impaired students include the Hiskey-Nebraska Test of Learning (Hiskey, 1966), the Wechsler Intelligence Scale for Children-Revised (Wechsler, 1974), the Metropolitan Achievement Test (Prescott et al., 1984), and the Stanford Achievement Test-Hearing Impaired (Madden et al., 1972). Specific tests that can be used for each academic area are discussed in the appropriate chapters that follow.

*Criterion-referenced Tests.* Criterion-referenced tests differ from norm-referenced tests in that they do not produce scores for comparative purposes; rather, they describe what a student knows and can do, and they determine the student's own mastery level (Taylor, 1984). Criterion-referenced tests, which also are called *domain-referenced* and *objective-referenced assessment* (Bigge, 1988), can be either commercially or teacher made. This type of assessment is made up of a specified set of skills of activities, called *criterion behaviors*. They provide answers to specific questions about a student, such as:

Can Joey write his name?
Can Kathy button her sweater?
Can Jane divide two-digit numbers by two-digit numbers using regrouping?

Items on criterion-referenced tests are often associated directly with specific instructional objectives and thus assist in the writing of IEPs and in evaluating student progress. Skills assessed by criterion-referenced tests are stated in behavioral or performance terms and are associated with a specific instructional area so that little inference is made when evaluating the test results. For example, if you wanted students to use basic addition facts from memory, a test could be used in which the student was expected to do 20 addition problems, with sums to 20, within two minutes with at least 90 percent accuracy. If the student was successful, then you could conclude that the student had reached mastery on this particular skill. If the student was not successful, then more practice or a different intervention approach would need to be undertaken. As each new objective is introduced into the curriculum through daily instruction, a criterion-referenced test can be administered to evaluate student progress and the effectiveness of the teacher's instruction. The tests can uncover learning difficulties by examining the data to identify patterns of errors that need to be remediated. In sum, the primary value of criterion-referenced tests is in their ability to help the teacher identify the particular skills or knowledge that a student has acquired or is lacking and to provide a relatively continuous assessment of the skills related to a specific curriculum.

Some of the most common criterion-referenced tests that are used with hearing-impaired students include the Brigance Diagnostic Inventories (Brigance, 1980), the Metropolitan Achievement Tests (Instructional Batteries) (Prescott et al., 1984), and the Key Math Diagnostic Arithmetic Test (Connolly, Nachtman, & Prichett, 1976). Specific criterion-referenced tests that can be used for each academic area are discussed in the appropriate chapter.

*Curriculum-based Assessment.* Curriculum-based assessment (CBA) is a set of standardized procedures that educators can use to obtain measures of student achievement. The term refers to the approach that uses direct observation and recording of a student's performance in the school's curriculum as a basis for gathering information to make instructional decisions (Deno, 1987). Fuchs (1987) reported that curriculum-based assessment involves four basic steps:

1. *Identify long-range student goals.* The curriculum level, at which the student should be proficient within the next three to nine months, the student's current level of functioning on the material, and the level of proficiency that the student should achieve are established.

2. *Create a pool of test items.* Test items are written based on the content of the long range goal.

3. *Measure pupil performance.* Pupil performance is measured on a sample of goal level material at least twice a week.

4. *Evaluate the database.* The student's performance is reviewed and a determination is made as to whether the instructional program requires modification so that pupil performance can be improved.

Here is an example. Suppose you are working with Katie, an 8-year-old profoundly deaf child, and you want to get an idea of her math computation skills. Specifically, you want to determine if she is accurate on basic math facts. You will select stimulus materials from the curriculum that sample a broad range of computation skills. You will give Katie the paper, some scrap paper and a pencil, and have her complete the worksheet. You will establish a criteria for acceptable performance. Then you will score her paper and compare it to the established criteria. If she meets the criteria, then she can move on to more complex computations, or you can begin to focus your instruction on improving her rate or application. If she does not meet the criteria, then you can go back over the paper and examine the types of errors that she is making and adjust your instructional plans accordingly.

CBA can be used to measure a student's performance in any academic subject. It can follow a sequenced curriculum, such as in the areas of reading, math, and spelling, or it can look at areas that tend to be more teacher developed, such as writing or study skills.

*Informal Assessment Procedures.* A variety of nonstandardized assessment procedures can provide information about what and how to teach. *Informal assessment procedures* may consist of teacher-made tests, rating devices, checklists, and observation. They are used as a means of initially and periodically assessing student performance and skills. Informal assessment procedures may be used by themselves or as a way of supplementing the information obtained from norm-referenced or criterion-referenced tests. By giving an informal test, you can determine what specific skills a student already knows and what skills a student has not yet mastered relative to the specific subject. Teacher-made tests may be constructed from instructional materials, so that the items closely parallel the curriculum that is being used. A precise educational analysis can be accomplished by repeatedly administering informal tests over time to assess student growth. In addition, direct observation is a valuable assessment skill for teachers. Checklists, rating scales, interviews, and student records are all forms of informal assessment that can be useful tools to assist you in gathering information about student performance. It is important to note that an essential element in informal assessment, regardless of the method being used, is maintaining accurate records.

## USING ASSESSMENT FOR INTERVENTION

Assessment for intervention aids in individualizing instruction to meet a student's identified educational needs. As we have previously mentioned, one of the major provisions of PL 94-142 is the requirement that an IEP be formulated for each student who receives special education services. The IEP serves two primary purposes. First, it is a written plan that prescribes specific educational objectives and placement for an individual student. Second, it serves as a management tool for the entire assessment and teaching process.

### The Process

The stages of the IEP planning sequence are displayed in Exhibit 2.3. They include: referral, the multidisciplinary evaluation, the staffing, implementation of the teaching plan, and monitoring of student progress. The following is a brief explanation of each stage.

*Referral.* The initial referral of a student who has a suspected hearing problem for special education services can come through several sources (e.g., as a result of school-wide screening, a parent or teacher's concern, or a doctor's examination). School personnel must notify the parents and acquire written permission for an evaluation once the referral has been made. The type of assessment data needed and who will be responsible for gathering this information should be decided at this time.

*Multidisciplinary evaluation.* A team of specialists, who represent various disciplines, gather information about the student by assessing the impact of the hearing impairment on the student's speech and language skills, academic performance, and behavior. The purposes of the evaluation are to determine the student's present level of functioning, to identify specific needs, and to consider services for meeting those needs.

*Staffing.* After the multidisciplinary information is gathered, the parents are contacted so that a conference can be arranged to discuss the evaluation results and the ensuing decisions and recommendations regarding the student's educational program. The staffing committee must include a special education administrator, the student's teacher, and a member of the evaluation team. The parents or school district may request that other individuals or agencies that they feel are suitable be present. If it is determined that the student cannot receive reasonable benefits from regular education without assistance, the student's needs must be identified, and annual goals and characteristics of services to meet those

**EXHIBIT 2.3.** The IEP process.

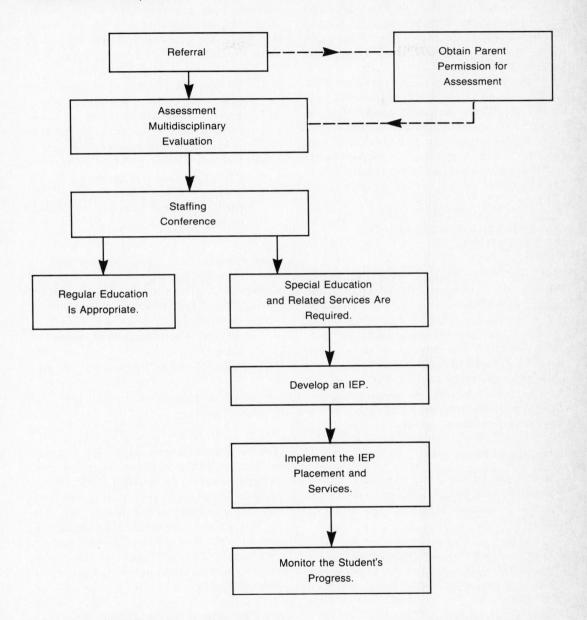

goals must be jointly established. This process then culminates in the development of the IEP. Educators should encourage parents to participate actively in the development of the goals and objectives included in their child's IEP. They must be at least aware of its content and indicate their approval by signing the IEP.

*Implementation of the teaching plan.*

The student is placed in the educational setting that has been agreed upon by the team and receives instruction designed to help him or her reach the goals and objectives delineated in the IEP.

*Monitoring of the student's progress.* The student's IEP must be reviewed and reevaluated at least annually. Plans to show how the evaluation will be accomplished, who will conduct it, and the assessment instruments and criteria to be used must be included.

## MODIFYING ASSESSMENT TECHNIQUES

The most direct approach for assessment of students who are hearing impaired is to use tests designed for hearing students. However, to do so, teachers may need to make certain modifications in either the stimulus demands or the response requirements—how the questions are presented and how answers are given. According to Bigge (1988), there are five types of changes, or accommodations, that alter the measurement techniques but do not interfere with the standard content.

### Accommodations

Changes can be made in (1) sensory modality; (2) written format; (3) time constraints; (4) test conditions, and (5) performance method.

*Sensory Modality.* Hearing-impaired students may need a change in the stimulus presentation. An appropriate change involves administering the test in American Sign Language (ASL), Signed English, SEE-2, Cued Speech, oral English only, or any other mode used by the student.

*Written Format.* Students may have problems if they are distracted by too much material on a page, or they may have difficulty keeping their place while working on the page. Possible modifications in the written formats of the assessment tools suggested by Bigge include:

1. Reduce the number of questions per page.
2. Enlarge the print.
3. Provide more space between problems or columns on a page of problems.
4. Use graph paper for math problems.
5. Put all the material necessary for answering the test question on the same page rather than requiring the student to turn pages.

*Time Constraints.* Some students may be able to do the assessment activities as presented but may need more time. Changes in the time constraints of assessment include:

1. Administer tests in more than one session.
2. Allow a longer time period for each test.
3. Present more breaks within each testing session.

When standardized tests are used it is essential that the teacher include information about the time extension in the final report. It is a valuable practice to mark on the page what was completed during the regular test time and then to allow the student to continue. By comparing the two pieces of information, the teacher may gain additional information on how the student would perform under regular time constraints.

*Test Conditions.* When students have problems taking standardized tests in large groups with standardized instructions that dictate how the teacher and student interact, specific accommodations can be made. Changes in test conditions include:

1. Administer the test individually or to a small group.
2. Present the directions to the students in their primary mode of communication.
3. Repeat directions or reexplain them until the students indicate understanding.
4. Give extra examples along with the instructions.

***Performance method.*** If students are unable to use conventional methods, such as giving a spoken response or using a paper and pencil, they may need to be able to modify their responses. Such modifications can include the use of signing their answer or making use of a multiple-choice pointing response.

## Assessment of "Difficult" Students

From time to time you will encounter students who are not cooperative during the assessment process; we will refer to them as "difficult" students. Some practical suggestions might be useful when you are working with students that are resistant to testing. First, it is important that you spend some time prior to the testing communicating with the students, and possibly with their parents. When the students see you interacting with someone that they trust, you may seem less threatening to them (Urey & Biasini, 1989). Also, try to adopt a nonthreatening posture. By squatting down to the students' level, you may be able to eliminate some of their feelings of intimidation. In addition, you may want to offer students your hand and escort them to the testing area. Show them where to sit and take your seat across from them. Whenever possible, begin with several practice items or material that is relatively easy for the students to perform.

If students are negative or nonresponsive during the testing process, it is important for you to communicate to them that, in the end, the test will be completed. A statement such as, "We can continue or we can wait until you are ready to work," lets them know that there is work to be done (Urey & Biasini, 1989). If you need to wait for students to decide to cooperate, it is best to have them remain seated. Generally, the waiting period will not be very long. If students are attempting to "wait you out," you may want to do something else during the testing session. While you are engaged in this productive activity, be certain that the task that you want the students to do remains in front of them. Eventually, they will want to regain your attention and will begin to work on the task. An alternative strategy is to take a short break and spend some more time trying to build a more positive rapport (Sattler, 1988). Focusing attention on their interests, family, and friends also may help the situation.

For students who are very active and highly distractible, you will want to keep the pace of the testing session in accordance with their disposition. It is important to plan some activities for students during downtimes and between subtests. You may want to have materials such as crayons and paper, dolls, or toy cars on hand for them to use (Urey & Biasini, 1989). If students are not attending, it may be appropriate simply to reach across the table and gently touch their arms or hands. If students begin to give you responses that are nonsensical, you will want to communicate to them that this is not acceptable behavior and that you want them to stop playing around. You can say something like, "You are being very silly right now. Let's try again." If this is not successful, you may have to consider presenting a contingency for more appropriate behavior, such as, "Answer these next four questions, and then we will take a little break."

Being mentally and cognitively prepared to work with students who are less than happy to comply with the assessment process is part of good teaching. By being one step ahead of them and by developing a good rapport with students, you can circumvent many of the common problems that teachers encounter.

## OVERVIEW OF ASSESSMENT

An essential component of effective teaching is knowing what questions to ask, performing the appropriate assessment to gain information, and linking assessment results to specific educational goals and objectives. Assessment is a multifaceted and dynamic data collection process through which educators seek to identify students' strengths and weaknesses, thereby providing a basis for decisions that will enhance their educational opportunities. Numerous commercially available assessment devices are available. However, many teachers soon learn that precise, direct instruction often requires developing specific assessments for their own class or for one particular student. (Examples of these are provided in the chapters concerning communication, reading, and writing.)

Once educational programs have been implemented, pupil progress and program success should be evaluated systematically. This ongoing process determines whether the hearing-impaired student is receiving appropriate services or whether specific changes need to be made. Ongoing assessment procedures are designed to provide frequent measurement of performance over time, allowing a comprehensive evaluation of specific skills and components of the instructional program. Frequent collection of student performance data results in the making of more accurate and appropriate educational decisions. By collecting data in this manner, instructional problems may be precisely identified so that modifications in the school program may then be made. For more in-depth information, the reader is encouraged to refer to more comprehensive sources such as Salvia and Ysseldyke (1988), Sullivan and Vernon (1979), and Zieziula (1983).

## SUMMARY

Assessment is the cornerstone of good teaching. Only through the process of determining a student's strengths and areas of need, can we plan and then implement an appropriate educational program. We began the chapter by reviewing legislation—specifically PL 94-142 and PL 99-457—and by looking at how these two laws shape and delineate how you work with hearing-impaired children.

The different reasons for undertaking assessment were discussed. It is suggested that you undertake the assessment procedure by functioning somewhat like a private investigator who tries to gather as much information as possible from various sources in order to put together the best possible educational program that you can for each student that you work with. In doing so, you must know what assessment tool to use for what purpose. Understanding the differences between norm-referenced tests, which compare one student to other students of the same age or grade level, and criterion-referenced tests, which compare a student to a level of mastery, is essential. Curriculum-based assessment and informal assessment procedures such as teacher-made tests, observation, rating scales, and checklists are additional tools that can be used to gather data.

We also presented ways in which you can modify the assessment process to get results that accurately reflect a student's ability. Knowing when and how to make these modifications can help turn a potentially time-wasting experience into a more positive fact-finding venture. Finally, we discussed ways in which you can assess the student who is resistant to testing of any sort. Hopefully, you will never need to refer back to this section of the text, and all of the students that you teach will be anxious and excited to work with you in any capacity. However, if that is not the case, you want to be prepared to make the testing situation a positive one for you and the student. Developing a positive rapport, being firm about what you want completed, and being organized are examples of some behaviors that you can incorporate to help overcome any resistance.

## ACTIVITIES

1. Write a scenario about a student who is given or denied one of the provisions guaranteed by PL 94-142. Share your work with your classmates and have them identify the component you have targeted.

2. Collect examples of IEP formats as a class. Compare the various forms and identify the information that is required and that which is additional.

3. Practice writing annual goals and objectives that are written in an appropriate form.

4. Review one hearing-impaired student's school file to determine the assessments that have been conducted. Note how these procedures were linked to IEP objectives and program intervention.

5. Review one norm-referenced and one criterion-referenced test.

6. Invite a professional involved in the assessment of hearing-impaired students to discuss modifying assessment techniques with your class.

# CHAPTER 3

# From Planning to Data Collection

## An Overview of the Teaching Process

### OVERVIEW

There are a series of important events that lead to the development of each hearing-impaired student's IEP. First, as described in Chapter 2, the multidisciplinary team assesses the student and shares the information that they have gathered in order to determine the appropriate learning tasks for the student. Crucial to instructional planning is the writing of goals and objectives based on the information gained from the assessment process. These goals and objectives should be written in a manner that facilitates accountability. This chapter picks up where Chapter 2 left off, by describing how to take assessment results and develop educational goals that are student oriented, clearly written, and observable. It then proceeds to task analysis: the procedure of taking an objective and breaking it down into incremental teaching steps. A brief overview of curriculum selection is presented prior to focusing on developing units and writing lesson plans. Classroom strategies are touched upon and are further developed in Part Two. Finally, several practical methods for collecting student data are provided for monitoring student performance and conducting program evaluation.

---

### CHAPTER TOPICS

The Process of Instructional Planning
Curriculum as a Guideline
Units as Steps Towards Long-Term Goals
The Spiral Curriculum
Writing Lesson Plans
Data Collection

# THE PROCESS OF INSTRUCTIONAL PLANNING

One of the primary tasks of a teacher is to make planning decisions, which range from such seemingly simple matters as organizing the arrangement of the classroom to more complex problems such as determining what it is that the students need to learn. There are five basic types of planning in which teachers regularly engage: yearly planning, long-term planning, unit planning, weekly planning, and daily planning. Each is important for effective instruction.

The rapid pace of events that occurs in most classrooms provides the underlying reason why planning plays such an essential role. Huberman (1983) pointed out that, in the average classroom, teachers engage in about 200 interchanges per hour. There is no data available that specifically focuses on teachers of the deaf, but we can both remember lots of occasions when we had reached the 200-interchanges-per-hour mark in the first 30 minutes of the day.! Therefore, in order to increase the success of your students, you need to set aside time to plan a systematic instructional program to address each student's individual needs. This does *not* imply that each student must be taught in a one-to-one instructional format. It does mean that the student should receive daily instruction that is tailored to his or her educational needs. We need to match the student, the task, the input, and the instructional interventions to ensure optimal student development.

Exhibit 3.1 provides a six-step model for planning instruction and making decisions about the appropriateness of the instruction. Making data-based decisions is an essential condition for providing quality instruction. This is a consistent theme throughout this text and is exemplified in the model. The six steps include: assess, determine instructional goals, sequence teaching steps, plan instruction, implement the teaching plan, and evaluate.

## Step 1: Assess

Successful instruction begins with the selection of appropriate learning tasks. Data provided by the multidisciplinary team during the primary assessment should provide sufficient information for selecting initial instructional goals and instructional strategies that are most likely to be effective for each individual student. New information will be gained as you work with your students and continue to evaluate their progress through the use of formal and informal assessment techniques. This dynamic, ongoing process is called *formative data collection*: evaluation that occurs as skills are being developed. Teachers who accept the responsibility of formative data collection will reap the benefit of a systematic plan that brings organization and continuity to their teaching.

## Step 2: Determine Instructional Goals

If you are going to make a significant difference in the lives of your students, you must know what you want your students to accomplish. When teachers have clearly defined behavioral objectives, better instruction occurs, more efficient learning results, and better evaluation occurs (TenBrink, 1986). These objectives provide guidelines for instructional program development by furnishing a detailed written overview of where the student should be going and by supplying directives for the measurement and evaluation process. According to Ryan, Johnson, and Lynch (1977), the reasons for writing objectives are: (1) to guide curriculum development and sequence instruction; (2) to provide a basis for evaluation of student progress; (3) to provide the teacher with criteria to determine when an educational target has been reached and when to begin instruction on new behaviors; (4) to provide parents and administrators with information regarding achievement expectancies; and (5) to meet legislative requirements.

The two major characteristics of behaviorally stated objectives involve (1) emphasiz-

**EXHIBIT 3.1.** Elements of instructional planning

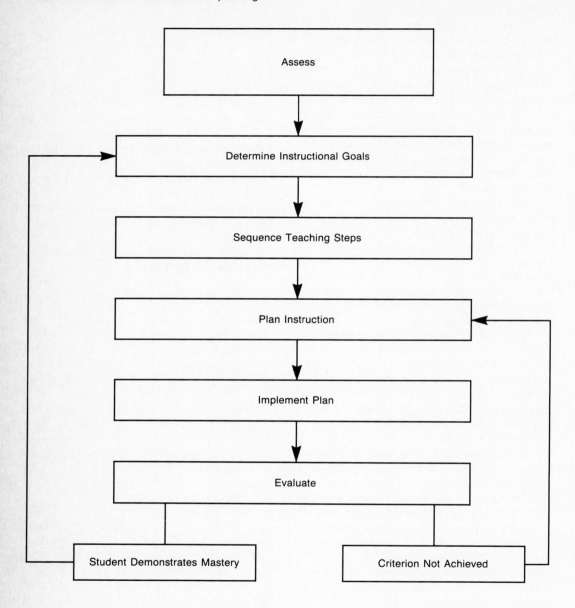

ing student rather than teacher behavior and (2) specifying precisely what the student is expected to be able to do following instruction (Meyen, 1981). A behavioral objective should contain four components (Van Etten, Arkell, & Van Etten, 1980):

1. *The student for whom the objective is intended.* Objectives should specify exactly for whom the objectives are written.

2. *A statement of the precise, observable behavior that the student is expected to display.* An understanding of what is meant by

the term *behavior* is important if you are going to write objectives in behavioral terms. The learning of a computational skill, the understanding of a concept, the development of an attitude, and the reduction of a disruptive behavior are all examples of changes in behavior. However, much of what is taught in school involves the acquisition of knowledge that may not necessarily be reflected in the student's overt behavior. For example, we cannot observe thinking or the process of learning. Therefore, we can set up learning opportunities that require students to perform selected tasks. As they perform these tasks, their behaviors demonstrate what they do or do not understand. It is not possible for us to observe the thinking process of a student as the student strives to solve a multiplication problem, but we can examine the solution that the student arrives at and decide whether it is correct or not. If it is not correct, we can then attempt to break down the steps that have been undertaken in order to analyze where an error in understanding may have occurred.

Identifying the behavior that you want the student to accomplish is not difficult. Think about what you want the student to be able to do. Then, think of how you will be able to recognize when the student has accomplished the objective.

One of the primary keys of this entire procedure is choosing an explicit verb that connotates an observable behavior. Here are two lists. One gives vague, unobservable verbs or phrases that should be avoided; the other gives terms that are more appropriate.

| Unobservable Terms | Observable Terms |
|---|---|
| To know | To identify (name, say, label, cue, sign) |
| To understand | |
| To master | To explain |
| To be aware | To write |
| To appreciate | To demonstrate |
| To realize | To list in sequence |
| To enjoy | To discriminate |
| To learn that | To compute |

To believe
To recognize
To discover

To recall
To predict
To locate
To analyze
To present
To draw
To list
To underline

3. *The conditions under which the student is expected to display the behavior*. It is important for behavioral objectives to specify the conditions under which the student's behavior will be demonstrated. Words and phrases such as the following help to structure and to individualize instructional programs:

*Given* 10 flash cards with sight words and the instruction "Read these words," . . .

*Using* a map of the solar system, David will label each planet in its proper position from the sun . . .

*Following* the reading of a passage on an appropriate reading level, . . .

*Without the aid of* manipulative objects, Sue will complete a worksheet of 20 single-digit subtraction problems . . .

*Provided* with a series of questions on one study technique, . . .

*When asked* to identify the main characters of a story, . . .

4. *Criteria for successful performance of the behavior*. When you are determining objectives, you must consider also the level of performance that indicates acceptable attainment of the objective. Students are expected to meet these standards before they can proceed to the next objective in the instructional sequence. By assuming that a student has mastered a concept or a skill when, in fact, the student has not, you may set the stage for future problems and frustration for both the student and yourself. In order to be certain that mastery of a task has occurred, standards must be established by which the student's

knowledge of the skill can be evaluated. The following are some ways in which you can state criteria for successful mastery:

With 90 percent accuracy
Eight out of ten times
Without assistance and within two minutes
For five minutes

An example of a behavioral objective that specifies for whom the objective is written, and includes, an observable behavior, the condition, and the criteria, would be the following:

When given a worksheet composed of 10 two-digit plus two-digit addition problems, the student will compute the sums with 80 percent accuracy in five minutes.

*A Key to Behavioral Objectives.*   One way in which you can remember the four parts of an instructional objective is by using the acronym ABCD:

*A*udience: Who is to accomplish the task?
*B*ehavior: What is the task to be accomplished?
*C*ondition: What are the circumstances for performing the task?
*D*egree: At what level of proficiency is the task to be accomplished?

For more specific information on preparing instructional objectives, you may want to review the text by Mager (1984).

## Step 3: Sequence Teaching Steps

All annual goals, such as master basic computation facts at the first grade level, and most short-term goals, such as be able independently to clean a hearing aid, must be broken down into smaller instructional steps in order for students to experience mastery.

Breaking down a body of tasks into subtasks is referred to as *task analysis* or *skills sequencing*. The process of task analysis involves the specification of important subtasks that are essential to the completion of a task or the attainment of a skill. Task analysis consists of dividing learning tasks into parts to identify the skills that are used in performing those tasks. The perspective that learning is cumulative and that skills build upon one another is basic to task analysis. Instruction gradually proceeds through the hierarchy of steps until the student has learned to perform each step. By the time the student completes the sequence, the goal has been learned (see Exhibit 3.2). These component objectives and task sequences are the foundation of the daily lesson plan.

Objectives that are too complex most likely will result in frustration and failure on the part of the student. Objectives that are too simple may produce boredom and disinterest on the part of a student. For example, in mathematics, teachers typically do not teach division until the component skills of subtraction and multiplication have been mastered. Task analysis involves isolating, describing, and sequencing the necessary subskills,

**EXHIBIT 3.2.** Task analysis

Given a calculator and a math problem that involves addition of two-digit numbers and the procedure of carrying, the student will complete the proper sequence of steps to compute the correct answer with 100 percent accuracy.

Task Sequence

1. Turn on the calculator.
2. Clear calculator by pressing *C*
3. Press key for numeral in tens place (4).
4. Press key for numeral in units place (5).
5. Press "+"
6. Press key for numeral in tens place (3).
7. Press key for numeral in units place (8).
8. Press "="
9. Write or state numeral on display.

which, when mastered, will enable the student to perform the long-range behavior or annual objective. Frank (1973) outlines four steps in task analysis:

1. Clearly state the long-term goal.
2. Identify the subskills of the terminal behavior and sequence them from simple to complex.
3. Informally assess to see which subskills the student already can perform.
4. Start teaching in sequential order, beginning with the easiest subskill that the student has not yet mastered.

Academic and communication tasks can be broken down by using two methods. These methods are *reverse analysis* and *forward analysis*.

*Reverse Analysis.* Specific skills may be identified by working in reverse from the annual goal to the short-term goal by asking the question, "What skill must be taught prior to the long-term goal in order for the student to be successful?" For example, an annual goal for a student may be subtracting two-digit numbers by using the procedure of borrowing. In order for the student to reach that goal, there are several prerequisites that must be mastered. The student should be able to subtract a one-digit number from a two-digit number with borrowing. Preceding that skill, the student should be able to subtract a two-digit number from a two-digit number without borrowing, and before that, be able to subtract a one-digit number from a two-digit number without borrowing. Skills should be listed in receding order until the identification of subskills reaches the current level of performance of the student, in this case, addition and subtraction of two one-digit numbers.

*Forward Analysis.* Another method of systematic identification of specific teaching steps is to begin with the student's current level of performance and proceed forward, identifying each subsequent skill until the annual goal has been reached. For example, a student currently may be able to identify the numbers 1–12. The annual goal may be to tell time by five-minute intervals. In order to accomplish this, the task that the student must master first is to discriminate the small and large hands on the clock and then identify the function of the small and large hands. The subsequent skills may be to identify an hour, to identify "before" and "after" an hour, to identify "half-past" the hour, and so on.

Scope-and-sequence lists provide a general breakdown of objectives that are arranged in a hierarchical order. They can be a valuable resource and great time saver. Commercial programs and criterion-referenced tests are good sources of scope-and-sequence skills lists. An additional source of scope-and-sequence material can be found in Mercer and Mercer (1985).

## Step 4: Plan Instruction

Once you have determined the instructional needs of the student by assessing *what* to teach and by breaking your material down into sequential steps, the very important process of determining *how* to teach begins. Although task analysis facilitates instruction, it is not part of the actual instructional process. Task analysis provides a blueprint for instruction by furnishing you with a layout of skills sequence through which the student should proceed to achieve the long-term goal. How the component skills should be taught is a decision that must be made separately for each student. The key to this step is analyzing how each individual student learns best. This information can be gleaned through both the formal and informal assessment procedures that were described in Chapter 2. In addition, ongoing interaction with the student will provide you with more information on which to base your decisions. Coordination of this information with the approaches presented in this book lead to the selection of materials, methods, and procedures to be used during instruction.

## Step 5: Implement Plan

Specific techniques that should be attended to during this step include establishing a positive learning environment, being organized, maintaining student attention, anticipating potential problems, and providing clear instructions.

## Step 6: Evaluate

Teachers must know if their students are making adequate progress towards specified instructional objectives so that they can modify instructional procedures. You have many choices in selecting evaluation activities: commercial tests, criterion-referenced skill inventories and checklists, and teacher-made instruments. Assessment should be frequent and should be the basis for making instructional decisions. As indicated in Exhibit 3.1, following evaluation you would go back to the planning stage. If the student is making adequate progress, then it is time for you to begin work on the next objective. If the student is not making appropriate progress, you have four options: (1) repeat the same instruction, (2) modify the instructional procedures, (3) introduce a new teaching strategy, or (4) change to an easier task. Deciding which of these choices to implement is really situational. Take time to reflect on the student, the materials, and the quality of teaching. Try to sort out the factors that are interfering with the teaching/learning process and then decide what can be done to change it. Making the time to examine the problem usually provides the stimulus for correcting it. When that is not the case, make use of the resources around you. Talk to your supervisor or other teachers. They have a wealth of experience and a fresh look at the problem that they can share with you.

# CURRICULUM AS A GUIDELINE

## What Is a Curriculum?

Developing students' current and future capabilities in a variety of situations at home, in school, and in the community is a primary goal of education. The educational system's *curriculum* specifies the content of the academic subjects, such as science and social studies, and nonacademic subjects such as art and physical education, as well as their scope and sequence that should be followed to help students reach their potential.

The curriculum results from the influences of the "normal" sequential development of skills, the nature of publishers' textbooks and materials, university teacher education programs, and the expectations of educators, parents, and the community (Gloeckler & Simpson, 1988). The curriculum is the central organizing tool of an educational program. Teachers are expected to follow the guides in preparing and implementing their instructional programs so that the outcome of their educational intervention in the classroom is consistent with the shared goals of the curriculum.

In general, the curriculum for most hearing-impaired students is focused on implementing the goals and objectives stated in each student's IEP. It is through the assessment process and use of materials such as curriculum guides that teachers are able to choose appropriate goals for each individual student. A problem in the field of education of hearing-impaired students is that, outside the areas of speech language and auditory training, very little has been done in the way of developing special curricula for students (Moores, 1987). Therefore, a major challenge that you face is to choose the goals and objectives that will have the most positive impact on the development of your students. When determining the courses of study and sequence of presentation, educational programs and teachers have several options for choosing curricula for their hearing-impaired students. The following options have been adapted from Bigge (1988):

1. Use a curriculum and objectives that have been specifically developed for hearing-impaired students.
2. Use the regular education curriculum and try to meet the same standards and expectations that apply to regular students but allow for special and/or related services and methods.
3. Use the regular education curriculum and accompanying objectives but reduce the level of complexity.
4. Use a lower grade-level curriculum.
5. Use curriculum objectives that have been developed for other special-needs students.

There are many factors that will interact to help you make the decision concerning what you will teach your students. Some of the primary variables that will influence this decision are the type of program you work for, the educational philosophy of the program, the curriculum that has been used in the past, and the financial resources that currently are available for you to spend on curriculum materials. Being aware of the different resources that you can use with your students is an important time-saving measure.

## Preschool Curricula

A curriculum should reflect the developmental abilities of the students for which it is intended. A curriculum for preschoolers typically includes the areas of cognition or thinking skills, play, language, self-help, and motor skill. As students mature, play is replaced by art, music, and physical education, and cognition expands to include work with academic subject matter. Because the majority of hearing-impaired students do not possess age-appropriate communication abilities, the curriculum to which they are exposed should include the aspects of language, speech, and listening skills described in Chapters 5–9. An example of a curriculum developed specifically for hearing-impaired preschooler is the Kendall Demonstration Elementary School, Preschool Curriculum Guide (KDES faculty and staff, 1989).

Of the several choices of curriculum orientation that might be available to hearing-impaired preschoolers (e.g. Montessori, behavioral, developmental, academic focus, etc.), a cognitive-linguistic approach has been recommended by Moeller and McConkey (1983). Trends in preschool education should be away from a focus on academics (Murley, 1988). A cognitive-linguistic curriculum is designed to develop students' capabilities in making connections between events and objects and to allow them to construct mental representations of themselves and their environments. This type of curriculum focuses on key experiences with language and on emergent cognition (e.g., classification, seriation, number, space, and temporal relations).

*Components of a Cognitive-Linguistic Curriculum.* Developed as a result of 15 years of work in education by Weikart and his associates, the curriculum that we will outline has adaptations suggested for hearing-impaired preschoolers. The open framework requires a thinking, creative teacher who can relate the actions and language of young children to underlying developmental principles (Ispa & Matz, 1978). Students and teachers work together mutually to initiate daily activities. This approach involves four basic components:

1. Teachers are encouraged to facilitate the development of cognitive skills by broadening and strengthening them; the skills are not taught directly (Ispa & Matz, 1978). Chil-

dren are aided in using language, in being actively involved in activities, and in practicing thinking skills.

2. The room is arranged with the message that children can make decisions about what they are going to do and how they are going to do it. Yet, it imparts a sense of order. The room is divided into several distinct areas: a block area, an art area, a housekeeping area, a quiet area, a workbench area, and a sand and water area. There are real tools, real kitchen equipment, and so on. Storage cabinets, sinks, and shelves are at the child's level. Similar items are stored together, and the locations of these items are outlined and labeled.

3. A consistent daily routine allows students to predict events and to understand time concepts and the sequencing of activities. A beneficial routine might include planning time, work time, cleaning-up time, recall and snack time, activity time, and circle time (Ispa & Matz, 1978). A capsule description of each element in this daily routine appears in Exhibit 3.3. The activities listed explain the shift between independence and structure and help to foster social competence in the children. We believe this atmosphere provides hearing-impaired students with opportunities to practice independence and build self-esteem and to obtain the language and cognition skills needed for future academic success.

4. Paramount to the Wiekart curriculum is the notion that the preschool teacher and student need to plan. Murley (1988) has suggested several planning strategies that appear in Exhibit 3.4 to help children plan in creative ways. Planning allows hearing-impaired children to use language within a predictable

---

**EXHIBIT 3.3.** Daily routine (Ispa & Matz, 1978)

The central purpose of a consistent daily routine is to give both adults and children a focus that allows them to use their creative energies on the task at hand without worrying about what comes next. Children feel more *secure and more in control* of their actions when they can predict the order of events. In addition, the routine helps children to develop an understanding of time in terms of a sequence of events that they participate in each day. A capsule description of each element in the daily routine follows:

*Planning time.* The children decide what they are going to do during work time and indicate their plans to an adult, who helps the children think through and elaborate their ideas. The adult also records the plans, helps during work and recall times, and also helps the children get to the proposed work area.

*Work time.* With the support and assistance of adults and peers, children actively pursue the ideas, activities, and projects that they decided on at planning time. Teachers move about the room, conversing with children, asking them questions about what they are doing, and helping them follow through on the plans that they made. Children who complete their initial plans make and work on another set of plans.

*Clean-up time.* Children sort, order, and put away materials that they have used during work time. They store unfinished projects.

*Recall, snack, and small-group time.* The same small group of children meet together each day with an adult to snack, recall work time activities, and work with materials in an activity usually planned by the adult to provide one of the key experiences. A small-group time activity might involve each child making a batch of playdoh and observing changes that occur, for example, or each child building with boxes and blocks and talking about spatial relations.

*Activity time.* Children and adults are involved in large motor play and conversation about what they are doing either outside, if possible, or indoors when it rains.

*Circle time.* All children and adults meet together as a large group to sing and make up action songs, play musical instruments, move to music, play games, and sometimes briefly review an upcoming social event.

SOURCE: J. Ispa and R. Matz, "Integrating handicapped preschool children within a cognitively oriented program." In M. J,. Guralnick (ed.), *Early Intervention and the Integration of Handicapped and Non-handicapped Children.* Austin, TX: PRO-ED Inc. Reprinted by permission.

context. In addition, the planning strategies that you use with the students can be combined with the planning strategies utilized by you (see Exhibit 3.5). For example, a student might place a symbol in a square on a planning board for the activity that they plan to do first. Students can be given the opportunity to arrange several symbols sequentially on a planning board to indicate what they plan to do first, second, and so on. Use of pictures, planning boards, and symbols provides hearing-impaired children with context to support expressive linguistic attempts (e.g., "First I will go to toys, then I'll go here"— pointing to picture).

As a teacher of hearing-impaired preschoolers, you can use several strategies to help the students describe their plans. An ex-

ample appears in Exhibit 3.6 and illustrates how both language and cognition are facilitated through planning. Moeller and Mc-Conkey (1983) found it useful to use contextual cues or to repeat familiar discourse during planning time so that preschoolers could use the familiar routine to support emerging language content and form.

During work time and recall periods, you serve as an observer and facilitator. Use the language intervention strategies explained in Chapters 5–9 to promote needed skills. You might ask the children what they did during work time, how they could get more snacks, or to mutually solve a particular problem.

Because of the emphasis on language and cognition, the Weikart curriculum has

---

**EXHIBIT 3.4.** Verbal planning strategies (Murley, 1988)

---

1. Sing a planning song. When the song stops, one child will share his or her work plans.

   (sung to the tune of London Bridge)
   "Tell us where you'll work today,
   work today, work today.
   Tell us where you'll work today
   My friend _____."

2. Provide red, blue, and yellow sunglasses (or make paper glasses). Instruct children to choose a pair of glasses. Look through the glasses to a work area and share what they will do in the area.

3. Provide each child with a written numeral on a card to correspond with the number of children in the group. Verbally share plans in numerical order.

4. Instruct children to select an object that they would like to work with that day. Bring the object back to the planning table and share what each child will do with their objects.

5. Have all the children sit in a circle on the floor. Roll a ball to a child. The child will share his or her work plans and then roll the ball to another child.

6. Instruct children to think of two areas to work in. Use temporal terms when asking questions about their work plans (e.g., "What will you do first? What will you do last?").

7. Place hula hoops on the floor to represent each work area. Place an object from each area inside the hoops. Children are to stand inside the hoop that corresponds with the work area of their choice and share their plans. When everyone is finished sharing, count the number of children standing inside each hoop. Ask, "Which area will have the most children working in it today? Which area will have the least?"

8. Instruct children to sit in a circle on the floor. Have the children close their eyes and place a block (behind, next to, or in front of a child). The selected child will tell the location of the block and share his or her work plans. Repeat this with each child.

9. Provide two telephones. Call each child on the phone and ask where he or she will work.

---

SOURCE: J. Murley, *Application of the High Scope curriculum in special education early childhood classrooms.* Paper presented at the Illinois Division for Early Childhood, Springfield, IL, March 1988. Reprinted by permission of the author.

**EXHIBIT 3.5.** Planning time strategies (Murley, 1988)

1. Hang a symbol in an area where a child wants to work.
2. Make area symbol cards. Have the children pick the area that they want to work in.
3. Ask the children to hang their names and symbols on an area planning board.
4. Ask each child to bring one object that they will work with to the table. Trace around the object and label or take dictation if it is appropriate.
5. Select one object from an area and imitate an action with the object. Have classmates guess the child's plan from the action.
6. Use the same activity as above, but exclude the object and role play only.
7. Have the children write their names and symbols on a paper located in a work area. Papers should be collected and names read during recall time. Papers may be different shapes, depending upon the key experience or theme (e.g., pumpkins at Halloween, shapes for spatial relations).
8. Make area planning forms. Have the children fill in the name of the area they will work in.
9. On blank planning forms, ask the children to draw a picture of what they will do or what materials they will use.
10. Select one familiar object to represent each area (e.g., paintbrush, block, bowl). Place the objects in a "feely" box. Have the children feel for the object that represents their work area.
11. Cut pictures that represent materials in interest areas out of catalogs and magazines. Let the children choose pictures of one thing that they will use and tell how they will use it.
12. Have the children pretend to take a photograph of an area that they will work in. Come back to the planning table and draw a picture or trace an object to represent the photograph.

SOURCE: J. Murley, *Application of the High Scope curriculum in special education early childhood classrooms*. Paper presented at the Illinois Division for Early Childhood, Springfield, IL, March 1988. Reprinted by permission of the author.

been used successfully with hearing-impaired children. The approach includes features of whole learning, genuine learning, problem solving, low affective-filter, effective questioning, effective teaching, context-embedded learning, and the importance of play. These features are summarized in Exhibit 3.7.

## Elementary Curricula

Teachers working with hearing-impaired students always have had to design curricula as well as teach. This is difficult, because it requires that the teachers (1) have a command of the scope and sequence of each develop-

**EXHIBIT 3.6.** Teacher's questions help the child describe the plan (Moeller & McConkey, 1984)

| | |
|---|---|
| CHILD: | "First I will play in building area." (The temporal concepts like *first* and *second* arose naturally out of repeated encounters with choosing and following a plan using the planning board.) |
| TEACHER: | "Oh, and what will you do there?" |
| CHILD: | "Build a fire station." |
| TEACHER: | "A fire station? Neat. What will you use?" |
| CHILD: | "Those tinker toys and the costumes and three towels for beds." |
| TEACHER: | "Oh, beds. You will have a few firemen. Good idea. Who will you play with?" |
| CHILD: | "Matthew" (Matthew shakes his head "no" and says he is going to play at the water table.) |
| TEACHER: | "What will you do now? Matthew doesn't want to play." |
| CHILD: | "Ask somebody else." |
| TEACHER: | "Good, have fun." |

SOURCE: M. P. Moeller, M. J. Osberger and J. Morford in J. G. Alpiner and P. A. McCarthy (eds.) *Rehabilitative Audiology: Children and Adults*. Baltimore: Williams and Wilkins, 1987.

**EXHIBIT 3.7.** Summary of concepts underlying a cognitively based intervention program (Moeller & McConkey, 1984)

| Strategy | Description |
| --- | --- |
| Method of presentation lends organization to the child's learning. | Child is encouraged to see whole relationships and to organize content in contrast to learning isolated facts or vocabulary. |
| Emphasis on *active* learning. | Child has opportunities to initiate and carry out own learning rather than having knowledge transmitted to him or her didactically. Child becomes involved physically and mentally in the discovery of relationships. Comparison and contrasts are used to clarify relationships. |
| Provision of opportunities for child to actively solve verbal (sign, cued, or spoken) problems in flexible ways. | Child is exposed to daily problems and alternate solutions. Emphasis is placed on learning that the child can devise many solutions to various problems. |
| Encouragement of divergent thinking. | Technique instills attitude that no solution is "wrong"; child has opportunity to explore divergent solutions. |
| Use of inquiry learning strategies. | Teacher uses thought-provoking and divergent questions to encourage discovery of relationships (e.g., thought-provoking question during clean-up time: "Jeremy, can you help me pick up all the blocks that are long and round?" Divergent question during clean up time: "These blocks won't all fit in the wagon. How are we going to put them away?"). |
| Emphasis on highlighting key conceptual relationships. | Teacher continually relates content to broad, main concepts rather than bombarding children with isolated details. Emphasis is placed on the process of learning concepts. |
| Use of a daily routine that encourages decision making, predicting, and reasoning. | Teaching strategies organized throughout the day to lead children to think in increasingly abstract ways. |
| Associative learning. | Concepts not presented in isolation but related to familiar, established knowledge or key concepts. |
| Key experiences are provided to support the children's development of logical thinking. | Following areas form a basis of curricular content: representation of experiences and ideas; classification; seriation; numeric concepts; problem solving; summarizing |
| Provision of goal-directed play experiences and sociodramatic play routines. | Teacher guides children in their ability to represent through play, progressing from concrete to abstract levels. |

SOURCE: M. P. Moeller, M. J. Osberger and J. Morford in J. G. Alpiner and P. A. McCarthy (eds.) *Rehabilitative Audiology: Children and Adults*. Baltimore: Williams and Wilkins, 1987.

mental or instructional area; (2) organize the material so that the basic components can be followed and improved the next year; and (3) have evaluation schemes for the content, materials, and procedures utilized. This is an overwhelming task, and it is no wonder that these teachers acknowledge that skills are missed or unit themes readdressed in sequential years. Therefore, it is important for you to find out what the curriculum is in the program that you are using. If there is no curriculum, then it is best for you to acquire one on your own. Curriculum resources that have been developed and used with hearing-impaired students for specific areas of study are presented throughout the text. Additional resources can be found in Bunch (1987) and Kirby (1980).

## UNITS AS STEPS TOWARDS LONG-TERM GOALS

Just as curricula provide a general overview, *units* provide a framework for the achievement of smaller steps that will eventually lead to the attainment of the long-term goals that are delineated in each student's IEP. Each individual unit should focus on a central theme and make use of a variety of resources, student interests, and experiences (Sanders, 1988). For instance, your self-contained class of third-grade hearing-impaired students might be about to begin a unit of study on the topic of "safety." Some of the subunits that you may want to include are (1) important people in safety; (2) safety in the classroom; (3) safety in the car or on a bus; (4) safety in the home; (5) fire safety; (6) bicycle safety; (7) water safety, and (8) safety signs. Some of the resources that you may want to use include *Dinosaurs Beware: A Guide to Safety* (Brown, 1982) and *The Dangers of Strangers* (Vogl, 1983). You may want to use filmstrips. Deaf adults could be invited to discuss their use of safety precautions. Resource people that you may want to invite to class are a police officer, a fire fighter, and an emergency medical technician. Some field trips that you may want to take are visiting a recently burned home, riding in an ambulance, or visiting the police station.

Units represent a method of organizing the content, objectives, materials, and evaluation techniques for a teacher or group of teachers as a preparation for teaching subject matter. According to Meyen (1981), the use of teaching units can be justified for four specific reasons: (1) to teach information; (2) to integrate skills; (3) to motivate students; and (4) to facilitate transfer.

In many cases, it is not necessary for you to develop your own resource units or to revise available units. Some educational systems have prepared resource units for each grade level or for a block of grade levels. The resource units are sometimes bound into courses of study or accompany the curriculum guides. Curriculum materials centers at many universities keep a collection of commercial or published units, as well as teacher-made or unpublished resource units (Ogletree, Gebauer, & Ujlaki, 1980). The ready-made resource unit or school curriculum guide can save you considerable time. In most cases, some revision is necessary, which may come about as you update subject matter, content, materials, and resources and revise the objectives and activities to meet the specific needs of your students. For example, if one of your colleagues developed a unit on transportation a few years earlier, some of the information may still be valuable. However, the library may have received some new books and/or films on this topic. The pictures may need to be updated to reflect more contemporary modes of travel. The bus, train, and airline schedules should reflect current use. The list of resources, such as guest speakers will be different, contingent upon any contacts that you have or the occupations of the parents of the students in your class. Another consideration is that the activities and worksheets that were previously developed may not necessarily be appropriate for your students. The information may need to be broken down further, or the language level of the materials may need to be made more challenging to fit your students' current level of functioning.

When you are constructing the instructional unit, the process can be divided into two areas: *preliminary steps* and *lesson plans*. The preliminary steps are designed to facilitate the writing of lesson plans, which become the body of the unit and represent the teaching strategies from which you teach (Meyen, 1981).

## Developing a Teaching Unit

According to Sanders (1988), when you are planning a unit there are some specific points that you should take in consideration:

1. Units should be structured in terms of central themes or problems.
2. Units should be developed based on the interests, needs, and problems that the students will confront as they grow and mature.
3. Units should be appropriate to the developmental as well as age level of the students.
4. Units should have clearly stated outcomes or objectives that function as steps or guides to completing the units.
5. Units should be structured in such a way as to enable all students to participate and to share in their successful completion.
6. Units should offer several opportunities to use and reinforce previously learned skills and concepts.
7. Units should have a variety of activities that are significantly related to the subject matter.
8. Units should include effective evaluative strategies to determine how effectively the material was learned by your students.

Meyen (1981) presents a six-step approach for developing a teaching unit:

*Step 1: Rationale.*  Focus on the overall purpose of the unit and its relationship to the students' instructional program. State the rationale in a broad descriptive manner and include information that reflects the reason for teaching the unit. The rationale should also indicate expected outcomes from teaching that unit.

*Step 2: Subunits.*  Determine the scope of the unit. Identify possible related themes on which lessons can be grouped within the context of the unit topic. Listing all the possible subunits facilitates the organization of learning experiences and activities pertaining to the unit. From this point, the subunits can be organized into a logical sequence.

*Step 3: General Goals.*  State the goals in general terms. This provides the foundation for the development of instructional objectives and the potential sequence in which the unit will be taught.

*Step 4: Core Activities.*  List possible teaching activities through which the content and skills can be taught more effectively than if a textbook approach were being used to teach mathematics, reading, language, health, social skills, and so on. After randomly listing the activities, it is important that you organize them by core areas (i.e., which activities will enhance a math lesson, a science lesson, etc.).

*Step 5: Resources.*  If all the books, instructional materials, audiovisual media, community resources (both persons and places), and sources of obtaining additional information and materials have been thoroughly investigated, and the feasibility of appropriate and adequate materials has been established, the success of the unit is enhanced.

*Step 6: Vocabulary.*  Compile a basic list of words and expressions that are relevant to the unit. This should be done by trying to identify the words and phrases that can best be taught in conjunction with the unit topic. Make sure you are able to sign all needed vocabulary if you are working with bilingual or bimodal students. Additions to your list should occur as the unit is taught.

The length and detail of the unit depends on the content of the subject matter and the grade level of the students. If the unit is well developed, you will have a resource of ideas regarding the content and scope of the unit from which to draw upon as you write your lessons. Following the planning stage of the unit comes the organizational component. Each subunit should be broken down into two or three lessons. Behavioral objectives need to be developed, and methods and activities for meeting those objectives need to be prepared. Materials need to be either acquired or made. Resource people need to be contacted, and field trips need to be scheduled. When all these pieces have been put together, you can plan weekly lessons.

## THE SPIRAL CURRICULUM

Another perspective on curriculum and unit planning is presented by Blackwell, Engen, Fischgrund, and Zarcadoolas (1978). They suggest the implementation of a *spiral curriculum* that allows for a sequential approach towards building on existing knowledge and understanding. The concepts that are presented one year are added to and become more intricate each additional year. The ultimate goal of the curriculum is to involve students in the process of categorizing and making inferences about a growing body of knowledge.

Implementation is composed of three processes, referred to as (1) the acquisition of information, (2) the transformation of information, and (3) the evaluation of information. Exhibit 3.8 illustrates each of these.

During the acquisition stage, attention should be given to guiding students through the three levels of representation that are suggested by Bruner et al. (1966). The levels are (1) the enactive processes, which involve representation by action and experimentation; (2) the iconic representation, which involves perceptual imagery, such as pictures and diagrams; and (3) the symbolic representation, which involves mainly language. Blackwell et al. (1978) recommend that you progress through this sequence when you are introducing new material. The second process, the transformation of information, requires that students go beyond the recognition and comprehension of facts. This stage focuses on generalizing the material that has been learned to other instances. The final process is the evaluation of information. This step seeks to help students integrate new information and offset the natural tendency to overgeneralize and develop stereotypes.

The themes that Blackwell et al. suggest for courses of study, and how these topics are interwoven, can be found in Exhibit 3.9.

## WRITING LESSON PLANS

Teachers write lesson plans in many different ways. One thing that almost all lesson plans have in common is a list of steps or procedures that the lessons will follow. According to Morine-Dershimer and Pfeifer (1986), lesson plans serve three basic functions. First, the act of writing down the purpose and the

---

**EXHIBIT 3.8.** Objectives addressing the processes of the spiral curriculum

1. *Acquisition of information.* Following two units of instruction on families from different countries, students will identify four similarities and four differences between the family structure of country X and country Y.
2. *Transformation of information.* Having successfully identified the similarities and differences in the family structure of country X and country Y, students will give four reasons why the family structure of country Z (new information) is more like that of the family structure in country X or country Y.
3. *Evaluation of information.* Given a description of a family structure that is different from those of country X, Y, or Z, students will provide an argument as to why the new description does not fit each of countries X, Y, or Z.

**EXHIBIT 3.9.** Curriculum outline and units of study

| Level | Thematic Outline |
|---|---|
| Preschool I<br>*3–5 years* | A.  The child in the family and at school |
| Preschool II<br>*5–6 years* | B.  The family in society |
| Lower School I<br>*6–7 years* | A.  The child and family in other societies<br>B.  Personal awareness (physical, psychological, emotional) |
| Lower School II<br>*7–8 years* | A.  The environment in which people live<br>B.  Family roles |
| Lower School III<br>*8–9 years* | A.  The history of peoples and societies<br>B.  Social roles |
| Lower School IV<br>*9–10 years* | A.  Racial origins and cultural expression<br>B.  The movement of peoples and cultures |
| Middle School I<br>*10–11 years* | Cultural interaction: changes that occur when cultures interact with each other |
| Middle School II<br>*11–12 years* | The human condition: people need to respond to situations and events |
| Middle School III<br>*12–13 years* | The riddle of the past: the various ways that we learn about people in other times |
| Middle School IV<br>*13–14 years* | Being human: some factors that make people distinctively human |

planned procedures for a lesson can help clarify them in your mind. Second, the written plan can serve as a record of your ideas and classroom activities. You can refer back to them during the lesson to remind you of the next step. The same notes can be used later to remind you of what was done and how effective it actually was. Third, a lesson can be used as a guide for classroom observers. It allows an observer to focus on the main points of the lesson.

## Format of Lesson Plans

Most teachers' plans are informal and are comprised of some combination of general statements, phrases, or a brief outline of what will happen during the lesson. While this may be sufficient for the experienced teacher, beginning teachers may need more structure to help guide them. Westling and Koorland (1988) suggest that a format of a lesson plan answer the questions what, when, where, how, and why.

*What.*    The goal or objective of the lesson is the starting point. As discussed earlier, it should describe student behavior, it should be observable, and it should be measurable.

*When.*    The lesson plan should indicate at what time of the day the lesson is going to take place and what the estimated time for the lesson will be.

*Where.*    The lesson plan should indicate the part of the room where the lesson will take place. Will it be a small-group lesson, large-group lesson, or a tutorial? Will the students work at their desks individually at some point during the lesson or will they be working together on a cooperative project?

*How.*    How the objective of the lesson is going to be taught is a critical part of the lesson plan. This is the opportunity for you to choose the materials, procedures, questioning strategies, and behavioral control methods that you expect to use.

*Why.* It is a valuable practice to be certain consistently that what you are teaching is coordinated with the goals that you have delineated on the IEPs. The lesson plan allows you to structure a learning situation so that you can work on multiple objectives for each student during the same lesson.

Lesson plans can be written in many other forms, but usually they should list the steps that the lesson will follow. You will find that the notes on the sequence of the lesson serve as a useful reminder before, during, and after the lesson. A fairly common format for writing lesson plans is (1) state the objective of the lesson, (2) list the instructional materials that will be used, (3) indicate the steps that will be followed during the les-

son, and (4) identify how the students' progress will be assessed. Exhibit 3.10 is an example of a basic lesson plan. Note that it includes a spot for any questions that you may want to ask or for specific comments that you may want to make.

Another example of a format for a lesson plan appears in Exhibit 3.11. The format provides an opportunity for you to link the long-term goal with the daily objective. While the long-term goal can be stated in general terms, the objective should be written using behavioral terminology. The three components of the procedural section insure that the lesson is related to the objective, that demonstration and extended practice are planned, and that question prompts are con-

**EXHIBIT 3.10.** Sample lesson plan

Name: _____    Date: _____

Subject of the Lesson: _____

Time Estimate: _____    Grade Level: _____

I.  Behavioral Objectives:


II.  Preparation:
  A.  Purpose of the Lesson:


  B.  Materials:


III.  Procedure:                              Questions, Comments, and Directions:
  A.  Introduction:


  B.  Body of the Lesson/Development Guided Practice:


  C.  Closure/Concluding Activity:


IV.  Evaluation:

**EXHIBIT 3.11.** NIU/Deaf education lesson plan format and sample content

Teacher: Michelle Gavin                                                                 Student: Marlin
Instructional Area: Sight Words
Date: 11/15/89

   I.   Long-term Goal: Increase expressive sight vocabulary.
  II.   Behavioral Objective: Given the words TWO, HE, CAN, and NO, Marlin will be able to tell the
        teacher the presented word when asked, 9 out of 10 times.
 III.   Lesson Presentation:

   A.   Introduction:                                          Teacher Behavior:
        Explain to Marlin what will occur today. He will       Sit next to Marlin at the round table.
        be given four words to learn; we will practice
        them in sentences; we will add them to our             Child Behavior:
        concentration game. Be sure to say that we             Be attentive and ask questions as necessary.
        will only play the game if Marlin participates.
        Ask if there are any questions.

   B.   Demonstration:                                         Teacher Behavior:
        Show him each new word (i.e., *two, he, can,*           Show the cards. Ask what letters are in the
        *no*) separately on a flash card. Then, tell him,      word. Fingerspell with him. Have him write the
        "This is the word        ". Say the word and          words and give assistance if needed.
        then have Marlin say the word. Have him
        repeat. Next, ask him, "What letters are in this       Child Behavior:
        word?" Repeat his answer and then fingerspell         Repeat the words when asked. Say the letter.
        the word. Next, ask him to write the word five         Fingerspell with teacher. Write words.
        times on a note card, the chalkboard, on
        paper, etc., making it large, then small. If he
        gets it wrong, have him trace it, then slowly
        fade out the letters. Example: *two, tw_, t__,*
        *t__, ___, ___.*

   C.   Question Prompts:
        Exaggerated interrogative: *Which* letters are in
        this word.
        Visualization: use of one space per letter in
        word. Example: He __ __.

   D.   Extended Practice:                                     Teacher Behavior:
        The child will read sentences with the new             Give sentences. Pick certain words to make
        vocabulary words, invent sentences with flash          up a sentence. Give him a premade card with
        cards, and use context to find which word fits         sentence and two words from which to
        in a blank. We will play a game of concentra-          choose.
        tion with the new words.
                                                               Child Behavior:
                                                               Read sentences. Make sentences. He figures
                                                               out through context which word is correct.

  IV.   Lesson Adaptations:

   A.   Lower Level:                                           A lower level of this task would be to
                                                               introduce only two words and have Marlin
                                                               trace the words, as with a faded procedure. In
                                                               this procedure, he would be given the word,
                                                               then he would be asked to trace it. Each
                                                               consecutive time he traced it though, the
                                                               letters would be fading. Example: *will, wil_,*
                                                               *wi__, wi__.*

                                                                                          (*continued*)

**EXHIBIT 3.11.** (Continued)

    B.  Higher Level:                                 A higher level of this task would be to simply give Marlin more words each time. Also, he could make up and write out his own sentences with the new word. The sentences that Marlin makes from the flash cards that I choose could be longer and more complicated.

    C.  Cognitive Level: Knowledge

  V.  Materials: Teacher-made sight-word cards.

  VI.  Evaluation Method:

    A.  Description of Method: I will record sight words identified correctly as we play *Concentration*. There will be from three to five opportunities to read the word during the game.

    B.  Criterion: Marlin will say the words with 90 percent accuracy.

    C.  Recording Method: I will write on a chart how many words Marlin can read. Also, I will note which words (if any) Marlin cannot read.

| | | | | | | | | | | | | | | | | | | | | | | |
|---|---|---|---|---|---|---|---|---|---|---|---|---|---|---|---|---|---|---|---|---|---|---|
| | | | | | | | | | | | | | | | | | | | | | | |
| | | | | | | | | | | | | | | | | | | | | | | |

  VII.  Communication Objectives:

    A.  Auditory Training: Marlin will listen for each word as he stands at the board. He will write each word he hears with 80 percent accuracy.

| | | | | | | | | | | | | | | | | | | |
|---|---|---|---|---|---|---|---|---|---|---|---|---|---|---|---|---|---|---|
| | | | | | | | | | | | | | | | | | | |

    B.  Speechreading: Marlin will speechread each word and write it to indicate comprehension with 80 percent accuracy.

| | | | | | | | | | | | | | | | | | | |
|---|---|---|---|---|---|---|---|---|---|---|---|---|---|---|---|---|---|---|
| | | | | | | | | | | | | | | | | | | |

    C.  Speech Articulation: Marlin will say one sound for each word with 80 percent accuracy.

| | | | | | | | | | | | | | | | | | | |
|---|---|---|---|---|---|---|---|---|---|---|---|---|---|---|---|---|---|---|
| | | | | | | | | | | | | | | | | | | |

  VIII.  Behavioral Management Techniques:

    A.  Target Behavior: The target behavior is to have Marlin participate without whining or complaining about the task.

    B.  Consequences: If Marlin complains about the task and refuses to do what he is asked, then we will not play the game at the end of the lesson.

    C.  Schedule: This will be the condition for each sight word introduced.

  IX.  Evaluation and Comments:
I think that Marlin acted appropriately in both staying on task and behaving. The guided practice went very well. I think this was because I had sufficient number of items to practice and also because the lesson was structured loosely. He enjoyed it and did not want to stop when I told him our time was up. No changes are necessary.

sidered (see Chapter 10). Often when student teachers and beginning teachers write out these steps, they are able to incorporate them more easily into their actual lesson. Lesson adaptation allows a teacher to be ready for problems—whether the lesson is too difficult or easily grasped. Task analysis on the Cummins model of language proficiency (see Chapter 1) insures that you will be prepared to individualize according to the needs of your students. The materials section should include all needed resources. Within the evaluation section, the evaluation method (related back to the objective for the lesson) and how the data will be charted are described. Finally, the evaluation and comments section is completed after the lesson, and comments as to how to improve the procedure or materials are listed.

One final suggestion about planning is worthy of mention. It is important not to let the instructional planning process become too routine. Students learn more and like school better when they are taught by teachers who vary their instructional procedures from time to time (Morine-Dershimer & Pfeifer, 1986). Therefore, as you plan your lessons, you might find it helpful to ask yourself some of the following questions:

> What skills will students practice in this lesson?
> How much practice will each individual student actually get?
> What alternative instructional methods can be used?
> What are some ways in which individual differences can be provided for in the lesson?
> What alternative instructional materials can be used?

## DATA COLLECTION

Teachers must constantly strive to provide learning and specific activities for skill devel-

opment at the level required by the student, to modify instructional approaches, and to monitor the student's progress. Formative data collection procedures should be designed and utilized as an integral part of the teaching process. Formative data collection— evaluation *while* skills are being built—and record keeping allow teachers to monitor both the student's performance and their own management skills. An analysis of the records enables teachers to make necessary midcourse program corrections and to be responsive to each individual's unique needs. For example, without some form of systematic record keeping, it is very difficult for teachers to remember just how well a given student was doing with specific vocabulary tasks at the end of the day or which methods, or rewards seemed to be related to improvement. In addition, without a usable basic data system, it is most difficult to determine when program changes should be made and the nature of any changes that are needed. When teachers use data-based programming to monitor and adjust instruction in special education classes, their students learn faster: They achieve scores 26–37 percentile points higher than standard special education classes (Fuchs & Fuchs, 1986).

Many teachers are reluctant to collect data because they believe that they cannot measure student progress and teach simultaneously or that evaluation is a complicated and time-consuming process. The outcome of this is that, all too often, student progress is only casually or subjectively assessed. Teachers may complain that there is not enough time to collect all the different types of data that are required. However, King, Wesson, and Deno (1982) note that trained teachers require only two minutes to prepare for, administer, score, and graph student performance. Additional approaches that may be used in an effort to offset time concerns include enlisting the help of volunteers, parents, aides, or the students themselves. As you incorporate data collection procedures into the teaching process, you should gather information that focuses on answering two basic questions: (1) "How are my students doing?"; (2) "Are the instructional programs working with each student?" (Lund, Schnaps, & Bijou, 1983)

## Types of Data

Regardless of the type of data that are collected, you must be able to compare a student's present performance with past performance. Deciding which records to keep depends on several factors, including the nature of the task to be recorded, the time needed for recording data, and how the information collected is to be used (Evans, Evans, & Mercer, 1986).

The data that are collected commonly are of three types: (1) raw data, (2) proportional data, or (3) frequency data. One type of data might be more appropriate than another, depending on the skill or the behavior that is being measured.

*Raw data* reports the number of correct and/or incorrect responses that a student makes or the number of specific behaviors that a student displays. Raw data would be suitable for objectives such as these:

> Edison will use his voice to get someone's attention.
>
> Sharlene will use the pronoun *he* when communicating with significant others.

Some examples of the charting of raw data appear in Exhibit 3.12.

*Proportional data* may be reported in two ways: as percentages and as ratios. Percentages are computed by dividing the number of correct responses by the number of opportunities. For example, 8 correct responses out of 10 opportunities would equal 80 percent. One limitation of percentage reports is that it does not provide information about the quantity or amount of work completed. Ratio reports are similar to percentage reports, except that the number of opportunities are always noted. Ratio reports give the ratio of correct responses to the number of

opportunities, such as 8/10 or 8 out of 10. When you are using proportional data, it is a good practice to try to keep the number of opportunities constant from session to session. For example, if you are working on sight word vocabulary, it is best to work consistently on 20 words per day, rather than work on 10 on Monday and 15 on Tuesday. Proportional data are most useful for objectives in which a margin of error exists during repeated performances (Lowenbraun, Appelman, & Callahan, 1980). Proportional data would be suitable for objectives such as the following:

> Victor will multiply one-digit by one-digit numbers with 90 percent accuracy.
>
> Pedro will identify the capitals of the 50 states with 80 percent accuracy.

When accuracy rather than speed is the primary aim, such as when a student is acquiring a skill, a proportional score is an appropriate method of collecting data.

*Frequency* or *rate data* refer to the number of responses in a given unit of time. It is usually expressed in terms of behavior for each period of time (e.g., 20 one-digit math problems in one minute). Frequency data should be the measure of choice when speed is concerned. Frequency data allow you to discriminate between the students who have acquired skills with 100 percent accuracy but are slow and students who have acquired skills with 100 percent accuracy but are fluent. This type of measurement is more sensitive than proportional data because both accuracy and frequency (speed) are specified. Frequency data would be most appropriate for objectives such as the following:

> Rhonda will compute two-digit plus two-digit numbers without regrouping at a correct rate of 30 problems per minute.
>
> Melissa will spell vocabulary words at a

**EXHIBIT 3.12.** Example of the charting of raw data (Johnson & Paulson, 1976)

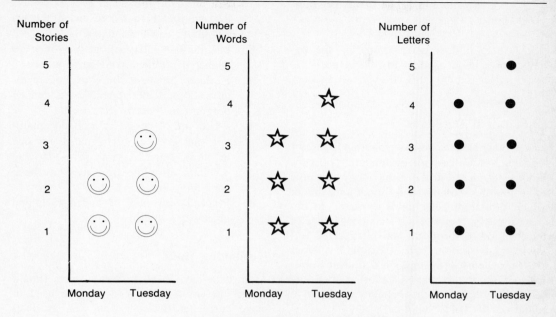

"Warm Fuzzy" stickers as tokens of progress

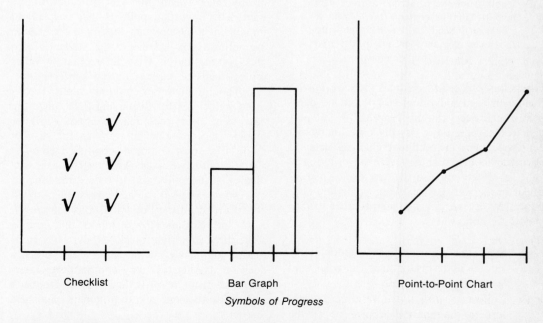

| Checklist | Bar Graph | Point-to-Point Chart |

*Symbols of Progress*

SOURCE: F. Johnson and C. Paulson, *Individualizing the Language Classroom*. Cambridge, MA: Jacaranda Press, 1978.

correct rate of 15 words per minute with no more than two errors per minute.

A helpful data grid, comparing the behavior of a target student to that of peers, is displayed in Exhibit 3.13 (Bursuck & Lessen, 1987).

## Data Based Decisions

The lesson plan serves as your blueprint for teaching, as well as for evaluation. The condition statement of the behavioral objective indicates the stimuli and conditions under which the target behavior is expected to occur. Similarly, the criterion statement indicates the level of performance that is expected following intervention. For example, if your short-term goal is to improve a student's ability to discern the main idea of a story, the following might be the behavioral objective found on his IEP:

> Given five stories to read, varying in length from one paragraph to three paragraphs and in content (*the condition statement*), Sandy will select and write the main idea in four out of the five stories (*the criterion statement*).

Using this objective, you can then work with Sandy on each individual story until he demonstrates mastery at the criterion of 80 percent for several days. If this criterion is not achieved, then instructional changes need to be made to help Sandy reach the criterion.

To effectively use data to make instructional decisions, the following procedure suggested by Evans, Evans, and Mercer (1986) should be followed:

1. State the short-term instructional objective in terms of specific goals and level of performance.
2. Collect *baseline data*. Baseline data refers to the natural occurrence of the behavior before intervention occurs. It serves a purpose similar to a pretest in that the data provide a level of behavior against which the results of an intervention can be compared.
3. Institute an intervention. Continue to collect data and record performance.
4. Evaluate progress. Introduce other interventions if the student has not made progress in three to five days.
5. When the objective is attained, maintain that level of performance for one to three days. Assess on a variable schedule after the objective has been achieved.
6. Proceed with more advanced goals and objectives. Return to step 1.

## Displaying Data

After data have been collected, you should record the information so it can be used to make curricular decisions, as well as decisions about the most appropriate teaching strategies. You can use a teacher's grade book or any other system that you feel comfortable with. The important point is that you should implement a system that is simple for you to use, allows you to review the student's progress often, and is easy to explain to other professionals or parents during conferences.

Though there are no universally recognized guidelines for displaying data (once the data have been recorded), simple charts or graphs may provide a very useful display mode. The most common graphing method is a graph with two axes. The vertical axis (ordinate) is generally used to record the amount of responses; units of time (sessions, days) are recorded on the horizontal axis (abscissa). Kerr and Nelson (1983) report that graphs serve three important purposes: (1) They summarize data in a manner that leads to daily decision making; (2) they communicate intervention effects; and (3) they provide feedback and reinforcement to the student and the teacher.

When changes in a student's program are

**EXHIBIT 3.13.** Data grid for Work Habits Perception Check (Bursuck & Lessen, 1987). Behaviors at Specific Points in Time

Use this sheet to record behaviors that occur at specific points in time during the day. Examples of these kinds of behaviors are: begins work on time, organizes self for work, follows directions, behaves appropriately during transitions, etc. Score + if the student is appropriately engaged in the behavior. Score − if the student is not. For behaviors such as work completion or work accuracy, space may be used to record %s (% of accuracy, % completion).

Student _____  Teacher _____

Grade _____  Dates _____

Behavior(s) _____

_____

| | Setting/Subject _____ _____ Time _____ | Setting/Subject _____ _____ Time _____ | Setting/Subject _____ _____ Time _____ | Setting/Subject _____ _____ Time _____ | Overall % of Behavior Across Settings/Subjects |
|---|---|---|---|---|---|
| **D A Y 1** | Target _____ Peer 1 _____ Peer 2 _____ Peer 3 _____ Peer 4 _____ Peer 5 _____ | Target _____ Peer 1 _____ Peer 2 _____ Peer 3 _____ Peer 4 _____ Peer 5 _____ | Target _____ Peer 1 _____ Peer 2 _____ Peer 3 _____ Peer 4 _____ Peer 5 _____ | Target _____ Peer 1 _____ Peer 2 _____ Peer 3 _____ Peer 4 _____ Peer 5 _____ | Target _____ Peers _____ |
| **D A Y 2** | Target _____ Peer 1 _____ Peer 2 _____ Peer 3 _____ Peer 4 _____ Peer 5 _____ | Target _____ Peer 1 _____ Peer 2 _____ Peer 3 _____ Peer 4 _____ Peer 5 _____ | Target _____ Peer 1 _____ Peer 2 _____ Peer 3 _____ Peer 4 _____ Peer 5 _____ | Target _____ Peer 1 _____ Peer 2 _____ Peer 3 _____ Peer 4 _____ Peer 5 _____ | Target _____ Peers _____ |
| **D A Y 3** | Target _____ Peer 1 _____ Peer 2 _____ Peer 3 _____ Peer 4 _____ Peer 5 _____ | Target _____ Peer 1 _____ Peer 2 _____ Peer 3 _____ Peer 4 _____ Peer 5 _____ | Target _____ Peer 1 _____ Peer 2 _____ Peer 3 _____ Peer 4 _____ Peer 5 _____ | Target _____ Peer 1 _____ Peer 2 _____ Peer 3 _____ Peer 4 _____ Peer 5 _____ | Target _____ Peers _____ |

**Overall % of Behavior Within Settings/Subjects, Across Days**

| Target _____ Peers _____ | Target _____ Peers _____ | Target _____ Peers _____ | Target _____ Peers _____ | Target _____ Peers _____ |
|---|---|---|---|---|

SOURCE: W. D. Bursuck and E. I. Lessen, "Curriculum-based assessment: Benefits to handicapped and non-handicapped learners and their teachers." *Learning Disability Focus, 3* (1), 1987.

made, phase lines are inserted. Changes may consist of an alteration in the classroom environment, a change in the presentation of the task, the reinforcement, or the curriculum. Phase lines are vertical lines that are drawn between day lines or sessions from the top of the $y$ axis to the $x$ axis, and they indicate a change in instructional conditions or teaching techniques. Other important points to remember when you are charting conventions are: (1) Use a pencil so that errors can be easily corrected; (2) connect data points by drawing a straight line from one plotted day to the next; and (3) do not connect data points over weekends, holidays, and absences or across phase lines (Evans, Evans, & Mercer, 1986). Exhibit 3.14 is an example of a graph that has been used to chart a student's progress.

A simple data sheet is another option that can be utilized for record keeping. It should include the student's name, the objective, the criterion, a code that indicates the student's responses (for example, " + " means correct, " − " means correct but hesitant, "0" means incorrect), criterion, date, and a space for comments. This data sheet can be explained to students, who can be shown how to monitor and record their own progress. Lund, Schnaps, and Bijou (1982) suggest that a large chart with a student's name, followed by rows of blank boxes, be drawn on construction paper and covered with clear plastic so that it can be wiped off and reused. Students can record their own accomplishments by drawing stars, happy faces, or some favorite character, or by pasting stars or stickers each time they respond correctly or reach a criterion.

Student performance should be measured frequently until mastery or proficiency of the skill has occurred. Formative evaluation measures should be taken at regular intervals, so that progress can be measured continually. Although daily measurement and charting is the ideal procedure, research has indicated that satisfactory educational decisions can be made on the basis of data that have been collected three times per week (Ysseldyke et al., 1983).

## Perspective on Planning and Data Collection

All teachers plan. Effective teachers approach planning systematically by making data-based decisions. Selecting and devising goals and objectives is an important part of planning. The problem that faces teachers on a daily basis is determining the extent to which students have attained the objectives set out for the lesson. When you are engaging in lesson planning on a daily basis, your evaluation can be formal and informal, depending on the lesson and time restrictions. An important consideration for you to make when you are evaluating a student's progress is whether the technique employed needs to provide data directly related to the objective that is being evaluated. The important point here is that evaluation, like instruction, must be planned.

In an age when accountability is so important, keeping records is a simple method for demonstrating and communicating program effectiveness. Kerr and Nelson (1983) suggest that to "be an effective teacher (i.e., to ensure that your students are progressing as rapidly as their capacities and present educational technology allow, you need a system for monitoring their progress on a frequent and regular basis" (p. 29). The process of data collection means that teachers must act as researchers in their own classrooms by systematically evaluating the effects of instructional decisions on the basis of measurable changes in student performance. The best measure of good teaching is not what the teacher does but what the student does. Frequent measurement of student progress reduces the time and effort used in nonproductive instructional methods, identifies student areas of difficulty, and cuts down on student frustration. Haring, Liberty, and White (1980) found that teachers who employed a formative data collection procedure

**EXHIBIT 3.14.** Example of a graph used to chart progress (Evans, Evans, & Mercer, 1986)

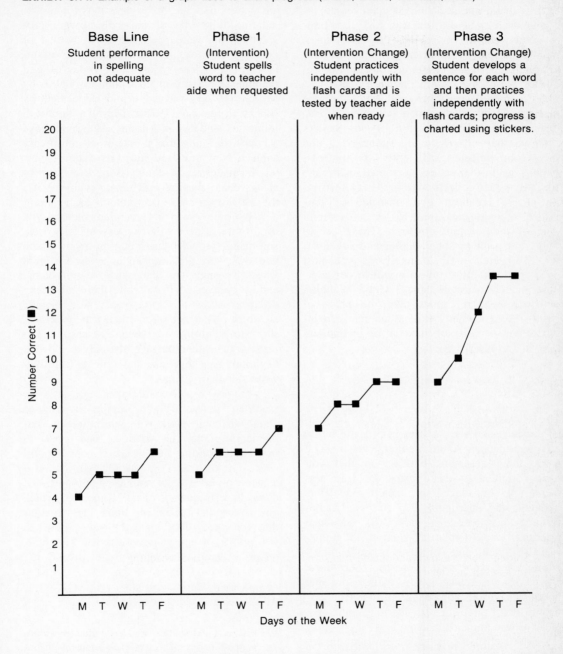

| Base Line | Phase 1 | Phase 2 | Phase 3 |
|---|---|---|---|
| Student performance in spelling not adequate | (Intervention) Student spells word to teacher aide when requested | (Intervention Change) Student practices independently with flash cards and is tested by teacher aide when ready | (Intervention Change) Student develops a sentence for each word and then practices independently with flash cards; progress is charted using stickers. |

Number Correct (■)

Days of the Week

made almost twice as many instructional decisions that increased student achievement as did teachers who did not use this procedure.

For data to be useful, the information must be displayed in an easy-to-read fashion. Graphing and using charts are common methods of presenting data. Because a visual display is provided, graphs and charts enable teachers easily to document changes in student performance over time. Also, student progress may be effectively summarized and then communicated efficiently to students, parents, and other school personnel. Although formative data collection at first may seem to be an added burden, good instructional programs include measurement as an integral part of the teaching process. These procedures are a matter of planning and organization. To be successful, plans of this type must be carried out systematically with a considerable degree of consistency. Good planning and organization cannot take the place of good overall teaching skills, but they can increase the benefits of such skills in application in the classroom.

## SUMMARY

This chapter focused on your need to be both an architect and a researcher in order to be an effective teacher. As an architect, you will be using the assessment information that you have compiled to make plans for your students. We introduced a six-step model for planning and instruction: (1) Assess, (2) determine instructional goals, (3) sequence teaching steps, (4) plan instruction, (5) implement the plan, and (6) evaluate student progress. The importance of writing behavioral objectives was made. It was pointed out that good behavioral objectives are student oriented, descriptive of the learning outcome, clearly written, and observable.

This chapter included information on curriculum, which provides the basis for the content that you will be teaching your students. The use of a cognitive-linguistic curriculum with preschool students was advocated, and specific suggestions for implementing this type of curriculum were provided. Units were presented as a method of planning and teaching that lead to the attainment of long-term goals. Two types of unit planning were presented—one advocated by Meyen (1981), and a second advocated by Blackwell et al. (1978). Meyen's approach immerses students in a topic. They undertake a course of study that is integrated into every subject. New units are added as students master the material. In comparison, Blackwell et al. advocate a spiral curriculum with specific themes woven into and built on each year.

No matter which curriculum method you use, you will need to write lesson plans. Lesson plans provide the blueprint from which you will work. We looked at a few different ways in which you can write lesson plans, and we suggested that, while there are many different forms of lesson plans, most include an objective, a list of instructional materials, steps to be followed when teaching, and a method of evaluation. We also advocated that beginning teachers take the time to carefully write out their plans.

Finally, we discussed your role as a researcher: constantly developing hypotheses about what will work with your students, implementing the intervention, and—just as important—taking data to see if your hypotheses were correct. The data that you can collect are of three types: raw data, proportional data, and frequency data. Choosing which one to use is contingent upon the behavior that you want to evaluate. However, the data will not be of any value unless you review it, record it, and, when appropriate, display it.

## ACTIVITIES

1. Pick a social studies or science chapter from a popular series. Discuss each element of instructional planning (outlined in Exhibit 3.1) with regard to the chapter you have located. Write any goals and objectives in the correct

format. Sequence the necessary teaching steps, employing the principles of task analysis.

2. Design a unit and include Meyen's six steps in your plan.

3. Using the Blackwell et al. (1978) spiraling curriculum approach, develop a set of goals for an elementary school class of hearing-impaired students. Then, plan a series of goals for the following year that would extend the students' knowledge and thinking abilities.

4. Write two lesson plans, experimenting with different formats.

5. Take data while you observe a teacher working with a hearing-impaired student. Chart the data related to different objectives in several ways.

# CHAPTER 4

# Working with Others

## OVERVIEW

The manner in which we provide educational services to hearing-impaired students has changed in the last decade as a result of federal and state mandates. Teachers of hearing-impaired students who work in *mainstreamed settings* are changing their roles from those in which they provide educational intervention solely to hearing-impaired students to those that include the provision of continuous support, from a *consultation* perspective, to parents, regular class teachers, speech-language pathologists, paraprofessionals, and administrators as they endeavor to mainstream hearing-impaired students (Luckner, Rude, & Sileo, 1989). Classroom teachers, *specialty teachers,* and other professionals have become involved with setting specific goals and objectives for individual hearing-impaired students and with helping the students attain those goals. Consequently, professionals providing services to hearing-impaired students must communicate effectively and coordinate programs jointly to a greater degree than ever before.

Because of these changes, teaching hearing-impaired students now involves more multidisciplinary, adult-to-adult interaction. These changes are best viewed in a manner that conceptualizes the teacher of hearing-impaired students as the "program manager" of the instructional team (Boomer, 1980). As such, it will be your responsibility to help define the program goals and to manage the resources to reach those goals. In doing so, you will have to coordinate your actions and the actions of others in a very organized and professional manner. In an effort to assist in that process, a discussion of your role with regard to the various significant adults who may be involved and tips for successful interaction with these adults are provided in this chapter.

# CHAPTER TOPICS

Multidisciplinary Team
Paraprofessionals
The Speech and Language Pathologist
The Interpreter
The Regular Education Teacher
The School Psychologist
The School Nurse
The Counselor
The Social Worker
Supervisors, Special Education Directors, Principals
Volunteers
Tutors
Parents
Working Parents
Single Parenthood
Low-Income Families
Rural Parents
Substitute Teachers

## MULTIDISCIPLINARY TEAM

Working as a member of a team has become an integral part of the educational process, both in the delivery of services and in the assessment process through which the services are prescribed (Day, 1985). As a teacher of the deaf, you will spend a great deal of your time at various types of meetings. Many of these meetings will be team meetings in which you will get together with other professionals and/or parents to discuss students' needs. As we have discussed in Chapter 2, federal and state legislation requires team meetings for the purpose of gathering information from individuals with different areas of expertise when decisions regarding assessment, placement, and program planning for hearing-impaired students need to be made. These teams are called by many different names, such as *pupil evaluation team, interdisciplinary team,* or *child study team*, de-

pending on the school system that you work for. However, the roles and responsibilities of the members of the team usually are very similar. For the purposes of continuity, we will refer to the team as the *multidisciplinary team.*

How the multidisciplinary team makes decisions will vary from group to group. Yet, there are some things that you will want to consider and do in order to have a positive influence on the success of team meetings. First, you will want to develop a level of comfort, whereby you can be an active, contributing member. Yoshida, Fenton, Maxwell, and Kaufman (1978) report that individuals on a team express satisfaction with the process in direct relationship to their level of participation or self-perceived influence on the decisions being made. Two specific behaviors you should avoid are trying to be a person who has all the answers or a person who agrees with everything and defers to other team members. Neither of these approaches contribute to the overall effectiveness of the multidisciplinary team.

Team meetings can be very effective and valuable, or they can function in a manner that is less than positive. All too often, the meetings lack focus on the specific issues to be addressed, the time to reach closure on issues is longer than expected, and equal participation by team members fails to occur (Day, 1985). There are certain things that you can do to help make the time that you spend with the team efficient. Initially, you may think that some of the recommendations may not be appropriate for you, since you will not be the individual directing the meeting. However, many teams have found that having the teacher chair the meeting helps to keep the meeting focused on educationally relevant issues and increases the teacher's feeling of participation and influence (Day, 1985). Therefore, while you are trying to use your time wisely and are advocating for the students that you work with, you may want to make suggestions to the group as to how it may be able to function in an efficient manner. The following suggestions, which have been adapted from Davis (1983), are valuable.

1.  Establish the roles and responsibilities of all team members.
2.  Identify what the purpose of the meetings is, for example, whether the team will be establishing a student's eligibility for special education or deciding placement.
3.  A written agenda should be developed and distributed prior to the meeting.
4.  Meetings should begin and end at scheduled times.
5.  Minutes of the meeting should be taken, so that decisions that are made can be clearly recorded at a later time.
6.  The process of how decisions will be made should be discussed prior to the

meeting. Will voting be done by majority or by consensus?
7.  Conversations during the meetings should focus on the student being discussed. Irrelevant conversations and report writing should be done at some other time.
8.  Long-range schedules for future meetings should be established. This precaution attempts to ensure that members attend and are prepared for future meetings.

Currently, being a member of a multidisciplinary team is an important part of being a teacher of the Deaf. Developing a personal style that permits you to contribute and help other team members actively participate in meetings is an essential skill.

## PARAPROFESSIONALS

Among the resources that are being used increasingly to assist teachers in providing quality services to hearing-impaired students are paraprofessionals or teacher aides (Boomer, 1980). Paraprofessionals are employed typically in contained classrooms or resource rooms. These workers may be parents or adults who enjoy contact with children and are not certified as teachers. Many distinct advantages are provided when paraprofessionals are used appropriately. These include (1) increased opportunities for giving students individualized attention, (2) a contribution of strengths and talents to the classroom not possessed by the teacher, (3) emotional support for the teacher, (4) a liaison between the teacher and other programs, and (5) partial relief from time-consuming noninstructional tasks (White, 1984).

In order that you can start the school year off smoothly, you should arrange a meeting with the paraprofessional before school begins. At this meeting, you will want to show the paraprofessional around the building and your classroom or work site and introduce him or her to various school personnel. The importance of regular attendance, daily starting and finishing times, and dress codes also should be explained. In addition, procedures for fire drills and expected duties on the playground, in the lunchroom, and at other junctures in the day should be discussed. When classes begin, you will want to go with the paraprofessional to the playground, to the lunchroom, and other places that your students will be traveling to during school hours. In this way, you can be a role model for handling various situations. As the paraprofessional gains experience and confidence, many responsibilities can be assigned to him or her. You should provide the paraprofessional with copies of your daily schedule, task analysis procedures, and the IEPs of the students. The paraprofessional should be allowed opportunities to observe new methods and materials and should be expected to become skilled in their use. You should explain the use of parallel talk, self-talk, and informative talk (see Chapter 5) and expect the paraprofessional to use these strategies daily. The importance of *confidentiality* should be discussed, and you should act as a role model in this regard. In addition, a long-range goal for you to work towards is to have the paraprofessional be able to explain the philosophy and daily routines of your program.

You and the paraprofessional should meet on a weekly basis to review the previous week's activities and to plan for the coming week (Boomer, 1980). By planning together, the paraprofessional can feel a greater investment in the program and, as a result, take more initiative in helping students to reach specific goals. Also, you should take the time during these weekly meetings to provide feedback on the paraprofessional's job performance. Statements—positive or negative—should be related to specific job skills. When you give negative feedback, it is best that you include information that gives the paraprofes-

sional an alternative way of doing things. Similarly, there are moments when you will need to spend time and listen to some of the paraprofessional's concerns. It is best to view the paraprofessional's role as a dynamic and constantly expanding one (White, 1984). A quality relationship between you and the paraprofessional will be based on your ability to provide direct supervision while at the same time being secure enough to accept honest feedback from this individual (Moore, 1974).

## THE SPEECH AND LANGUAGE PATHOLOGIST

You will need to communicate effectively with the speech and language pathologist. Exactly what your role will be in providing these services to the appropriate students must be negotiated between the two of you. Dilka (1984) suggested that the speech and language pathologist be responsible for assessment and intervention of articulation and language goals and that this professional might conduct workshops, counseling, and guidance for school personnel, parents, and students. We advocate that teachers of hearing-impaired students be highly involved in the assessment and intervention of speech and language goals and objectives for each of their students. It is essential that the monitoring and practice of these goals be integrated into various activities within contained and mainstreamed situations. Yet, you may need the resources, methods, and specific materials that the speech and language pathologist can provide. If a student is being seen at a clinic outside the school setting for speech, language, and/or auditory training, it can be the role of the speech and language pathologist to communicate with the professionals at that facility and coordinate services. Data on progress can be charted by the speech and language pathologist and shared regularly with the teacher, parents, regular education teachers, and other professionals who are working with the student.

## THE INTERPRETER

The purpose of the interpreter is to extend communication between individuals who may not share a common communication mode. Dilka (1984) defined an *interpreter* as one who listens to spoken English and communicates it via American Sign Language (ASL) and a *transliterator* as one who listens to spoken English and communicates it in a form of manually coded English (or cues). We will use the term interpreter much more generally throughout this chapter, and we define an interpreter in educational settings as one who does either of these functions. Since ASL is not used typically in educational settings (Woodward, Allen, & Schildroth, 1985), it is most likely that these professionals will be using some form of oral English, Cued Speech, SEE-1 or SEE-2, Signed or Manual English, or Pidgin Sign English to link adults and children who do not sign proficiently to hearing-impaired students. The interpreter's responsibility is to convey spoken messages within listening range through the use of the input used by the hearing-impaired student. The interpreter conveys the message among the individuals but does not enter the dialogue as a contributing member of the communication. The interpreter has become an important member of the educational team for hearing-impaired students in elementary, secondary, and postsecondary programs during the past decade. According to Witter-Merithew and Dirst (1982), the general responsibilities of interpreters include:

1. Interpreting in educational settings as assigned
2. Interpreting for other activities, conferences, telephone calls, workshops, as assigned
3. Completing paper work as it relates to the interpreting tasks
4. Preparing for interpreting assignments by studying content area, lesson plans, outlines, etc.
5. Establishing a physical setting in conjunction with the classroom teacher to optimize communication interaction
6. Meeting with the classroom teacher on a regular basis in regard to the communication needs of the students
7. Providing information to the classroom teacher, students (particularly the hearing-impaired students), and other staff on how to maximize benefit from interpreting services
8. Serving as a member of IEP teams as they relate to the communication needs of hearing-impaired students
9. Acting as a resource person for others about interpreting
10. Participating in professional improvement activities
11. Interpreting for extracurricular activities when hired to do so

The interpreter should be positioned so that the student(s) can see both the classroom teacher (or an audiovisual aid) and the interpreter easily. If the room has been darkened for the hearing students (to watch a film or to see a live performance, etc.), then it is the responsibility of the interpreter to provide enough light so that the hearing-impaired student(s) can see mouth movement, cues, and/or signing. The interpreter should wear clothing that is a solid, dark color and little or no jewelry. Long hair should be tied back off the face, and moustaches should be kept trimmed. The extent to which the interpreter listens to the message, uses facial expression and body language, and translates the message into signs corresponding to the English just spoken will depend on the age of the student(s) and the system of communication being used at school.

The interpreter works to facilitate communication. However, Moores (1984) stated that most interpreters in mainstream programs are expected to function also as aides or tutors. Unless hired as a teacher-interpreter, this professional is not responsible to teach, counsel, reprimand, or supervise students (Hurwitz & Witter, 1973). The degree to which the interpreter should assist with self-help skills, prepare materials, and so forth, should be negotiated during the employment interview. Interpreters should be hired with the skills needed to be effective communicators in academic contexts. Moores (1984) expressed that it is necessary to systematically evaluate the effectiveness of interpreters. When students are demonstrating problems in mainstream settings, the possibility exists that the problem may be due to the inadequacies of the interpreter, since the interpreter is the link between the teacher and the student. Therefore, interpreters should be evaluated regularly and goals set with them to improve their performance as needed.

We suggest that you might locate a qualified interpreter by:

Contacting the local, state, or national Registry of Interpreters for the Deaf

Contacting other school programs serving hearing-impaired students in your state

Communicating regularly with colleges that train interpreters so that they are aware of the qualifications that you seek

Asking parents and teachers-in-training to provide services

Retooling interpreters who have been trained in one method of communication in the system that is needed in your program

Teachers can increase their effectiveness in teaching hearing-impaired students and the effectiveness of interpreters by:

Taking time before class to orient the interpreter to the topic being discussed, to the general lesson plan, to the key vocabulary or concepts, etc.

Minimizing movement so that the student can view them, the interpreter, and any visual aids simultaneously

Being sensitive to "lag time" between speaking and the hearing-impaired student receiving the message, and making sure that the student has time to respond to questions that are posed (When teachers use slides or overhead projectors, they need to make sure that the student has time to receive both forms of visual information concurrently.)

Providing comprehension checks periodically to make sure the student is understanding the information that is being presented

Being aggressive in expecting students to repeat information or actively participate in class discussions (adapted from Hurwitz & Witter, 1973)

## Notetaker

By approximately the sixth-grade level, students in regular education are expected to listen to a teacher's lecture and take notes. This may be a difficult task for a hearing-impaired student, who must watch an interpreter, the board, and visual aids. Yet, it is important for them to learn the skill of notetaking, and teachers are advised to use caution in employing the services of a notetaker. According to Wilson (1982), the duties and responsibilities of a notetaker include the following:

1. Be on time to class. Notetakers cannot have complete notes if they miss any part of the class. Frequently, specific assignments and dates of tests are announced when class begins.

2. Get feedback from teachers and students. Constant evaluation of the quality of the notes should be exchanged

between the notetaker, teacher, and student.

3. Determine the notetaker's role in class. The notetaker must clarify his or her role with the teacher and the student. It is important to find out if the notetaker should ask questions in class when something is not clear or wait until after class. Does the teacher want a copy of the daily notes? Do the teacher and notetaker need to get together on occasion? Establishing guidelines such as these early in the program will permit each person to function optimally.

4. Be unbiased. Notes should be taken in a clear, objective manner that reflects what was stated by the teacher. The opinions or beliefs of the notetaker should not appear in the notes.

A notetaker may be a student's peer, a volunteer (e.g., parent or older student), or a trained notetaker, who is receiving payment or credit to write information accurately and legibly for a hearing-impaired student. Typically, carbon paper is used by the notetaker so that the copies of the notes can be disseminated immediately. Xeroxing could be utilized also.

Dilka (1984) recommended that the notetaker:

Date the notes
Identify and record all principle points
Determine and record secondary points
Use headings and subheadings
Organize content logically
Define difficult or new concepts and terms
Record references, assignments, and due dates
Be neat and write clearly

For more information on structuring a notetaker program in your school's program, please refer to Osguthorpe (1980).

# THE REGULAR EDUCATION TEACHER

Placing hearing-impaired students in regular classes means that increased instructional and management demands are placed on regular classroom teachers (Reisberg & Wolf, 1986). Several studies have indicated that regular classroom teachers possess negative attitudes toward mainstreaming (Gallagher, 1985; Ryor, 1978). They believe that they lack specialized training to teach exceptional students, as well as access to professional support that will enable them to deal with the student's learning and behavioral needs (Hudson, Reisberg, & Wolf, 1983; Martin et al., 1988). Concurrently, classroom teachers are also concerned about their own accountability for the progress of handicapped students in regular classes (Heron & Harris, 1982).

Teachers of hearing-impaired students work frequently with professionals who lack specific training for working with the hearing-impaired and who rely on the deaf educator for instructional advice (Sass-Lehrer, 1986). Research reported by Martin et al. (1988), indicates that regular education teachers would prefer to teach hearing-impaired students only if substantial support personnel and in-service training were available. Therefore, one of your primary responsibilities is to establish a positive school-wide relationship that promotes an understanding of deaf education and a belief that general classroom instruction can be modified and organized appropriately to meet the needs of hearing-impaired students. Methods that facilitate this relationship include: securing the support of the principal, offering in-service workshops, making brief presentations at faculty meetings, team teaching lessons with regular classroom teachers, and ensuring the involvement of hearing-impaired students in as many school-wide experiences as possible. Exhibit 4.1, which has been adapted from Featherstone and Woods (1986), provides a list of activities that you can do to promote a posi-

**EXHIBIT 4.1.** 50 Suggestions for promoting positive attitudes about working with hearing-impaired students in mainstream settings (adapted from Featherstone & Woods, 1986)

1. Participate in school staff meetings and extracurricular events.
2. Meet with your principal to elicit support for your program.
3. Encourage your principal to include the hearing-impaired students in the total school program.
4. Share lunchroom and recess duties with the regular education teachers.
5. Volunteer to organize and teach hearing and hearing-impaired students during recess.
6. Provide hearing students with in-service activities to explain a hearing-impairment and to eliminate prejudice.
7. Provide regular education teachers with in-service activities.
8. Offer sign language classes to regular classroom teachers, administrators, support staff, and building staff.
9. Obtain books related to sign language, hearing impairments, deaf awareness, and deaf culture for your school library.
10. Elect a hearing-impaired student to represent his or her classmates on the student council.
11. Invite hearing students to participate in viewing captioned films.
12. Arrange for hearing-impaired students to participate in school programs during holidays and special occasions.
13. Encourage hearing students to participate in hearing-impaired students' classes [reverse mainstreaming].
14. Attend school functions and, when possible, socialize with regular education teachers outside of school.
15. Make contributions to the school newspaper about activities occurring within your program.
16. Sponsor a Deaf Awareness Day or a Deaf Awareness Week.
17. Invite regular education teachers to exchange classes occasionally.
18. Establish a "buddy system" in the mainstream classes and on the playground.
19. Implement a tutorial program.
20. Videotape special lessons or activities in your classroom and share them with regular education teachers, students, and parents.
21. Bake "I love you" cookies for the students in your mainstream class to be sold at school bake sales.
22. Volunteer your students to decorate a bulletin board, in the school office or hallway, featuring famous deaf Americans.
23. Encourage parents of hearing students to volunteer in the classroom with hearing-impaired students.
24. Join and participate in your school's parent-teacher association (PTA).
25. Conduct an annual "Appreciation Luncheon" to thank regular education teachers and other staff members for their support for your program and students.
26. Develop an informational packet that includes easy-to-read material on hearing impairment, support staff, mainstreaming, and special equipment.
27. Display pictures of your students captioned with their names and interests.
28. Have the hearing-impaired class present a class play to the school.
29. Set up a pen pal system between a hearing-impaired class and a regular class.
30. Establish an opportunity for a high-functioning, hearing-impaired students to tutor hearing peers.
31. Promote the involvement of hearing-impaired students with sports, clubs, and after-school activities.
32. Arrange for a hearing-impaired student to be a teacher's helper for a regular classroom teacher during free time.
33. Have a sign-and-sing-along with a class of hearing students.
34. Have a spelling bee with hearing and hearing-impaired students.
35. Organize art fairs and cooperative art projects.

*(continued)*

**EXHIBIT 4.1.** (Continued)

36. Provide opportunities for your students to be a part of the management of the school store.
37. Invite building administrators to take part in special activities.
38. Encourage the parents of the hearing-impaired students to participate in the PTA.
39. Bring information about your program to the local Rotary, Kiwanis, Lions Club, or Jaycees.
40. Have your class participate in a science fair.
41. Invite an audiologist to come to school and speak about hearing and hearing aides.
42. Have the regular class tour a residential school for hearing-impaired students.
43. Start or get involved in a boy scout or girl scout troop that includes hearing and hearing-impaired students.
44. Provide an opportunity for the hearing students to listen through a hearing aid or auditory training unit.
45. Team-teach a subject to a group composed of hearing and hearing-impaired students.
46. Bring in some telecommunication devices with which the hearing students can experiment.
47. Have your class contribute to the school literacy magazine or yearbook.
48. Have a group of hearing and hearing-impaired students develop and share personal biographies.
49. Acquire some equipment that would allow you to mask the hearing of some hearing students for a day.
50. Allow the interpreter/tutor to work with hearing students in the regular classroom when students are doing individual work at their desks.

SOURCE: J. B. Featherstone and H. Woods, "Identifying attitudes to encourage change." *Perspectives for Teachers of the Hearing* Impaired, 4(4) (1988), 17–20.

tive attitude about working with hearing-impaired students.

Another one of your responsibilities will be to make time to consult with teachers who are providing services to your students. During the early stages of the integration process, it is extremely important that you establish a nondirective problem-solving climate between the regular classroom teacher and yourself. Consultation processes are more effective when they result from a collaborative undertaking, rather than from a relationship between *expert and nonexpert* (Dinkmeyer & Carlson, 1973; Montgomery, 1980). By fostering cooperative relationships, each professional can function as an equal and can bring unique skills and perspectives to the problem at hand. The consultant and the classroom teacher discuss the hearing-impaired students' strengths and weaknesses; set appropriate instructional objectives for the students; measure students' entry levels; devise appropriate teaching and learning procedures; and arrange for a measurement system that leads to the evaluation of the procedures. There are times when the regular classroom teacher may serve in a consultative role, assisting you in areas such as materials, subject areas, or curriculum goals and objectives.

Your job as a consultant can be viewed best as a *facilitator* rather than as an *implementor*. It is your responsibility to convey the most appropriate adaptive methods and strategies to regular teachers, who in turn accept primary responsibility to implement a learning program for hearing-impaired students.

Initial use of the classroom curriculum as the basis for teaching and learning procedures enhances the potential of the classroom teacher to accept responsibility for the student's program. Some of the primary curriculum modifications that you might want to consider for hearing-impaired students may include:

1. Placing the student in the same curriculum but at a lower reading level
2. Increasing the opportunities for practice in a variety of concrete experiential situations
3. Rearranging the way in which materials are presented

4. Modifying the way in which the student responds in class
5. Modifying test-taking procedures

Some additional areas in which you may need to work with the regular education teachers include, (1) helping them to understand the impact of a hearing loss on the academic, social-emotional, and English language development, (2) showing them how to use an auditory training system and services such as interpreters, tutors and notetakers, (3) teaching specific techniques that are used to make sure that the hearing-impaired student is involved and following the information that is being presented, and (4) providing opportunities for the student to socialize and feel comfortable in class.

The key to successful mainstreaming is ongoing communication between the regular classroom teacher and the teacher of the hearing-impaired (Luckner, 1988). It is essential that consultation services be available to classroom teachers as a means of providing frequent opportunities to discuss students' progress and assistance when necessary. The lack of adequate time for contact among professionals is the primary factor that inhibits active participation in mainstreaming. As a time-saving device, a series of short, written reports or checklists can take the place of daily meetings. The forms should be short and to the point. They are most helpful if they are left in the teacher's mailbox and returned within a short period of time. Arrangements can be made for meetings as required.

**EXHIBIT 4.2.** Student feedback form

Teacher: _____

Date: _____

Student's name: _____

1. Student progress this week:
   a. Academic skills/subject

   | | | | |
   |---|---|---|---|
   | _____ | Excellent | Good | Fair | Poor |
   | _____ | Excellent | Good | Fair | Poor |
   | _____ | Excellent | Good | Fair | Poor |
   | _____ | Excellent | Good | Fair | Poor |

   b. Classroom behavior — Excellent   Good   Fair   Poor
   c. Personal-social skills — Excellent   Good   Fair   Poor
   d. Independent work — Excellent   Good   Fair   Poor

2. Student effort:
   a. Classwork — Excellent   Good   Fair   Poor
   b. Homework — Excellent   Good   Fair   Poor

Comments:

3. Any problems with:
   a. Personal hearing aid or auditory training equipment — Yes   No
   b. Interpreter services — Yes   No
   c. Notetaker services — Yes   No

Comments:

4. Would you like a conference this week? — Yes   No
   If so, when are you free?

5. List any specific material or information that need to be pretaught or reviewed.

Exhibit 4.2 provides an example of a progress form that can be used between you and the regular education teacher (Luckner, 1988).

It is also recommended that you visit the regular classroom periodically to observe the instruction to hearing-impaired students and their ability to socialize and to assess their ability to function in the setting. You then can collect data as a basis for positive feedback for all the teaching/learning/management procedures and establish a foundation that facilitates the smooth implementation of the intervention program. Simultaneously, it is extremely valuable for the regular classroom teacher to visit your class or other programs for hearing-impaired students, in order to observe teachers of the hearing-impaired modeling specific skills and techniques.

## The Audiologist

The roles and responsibilities of the school audiologist should be clarified and communicated to you. These may include evaluation of unaided and aided hearing acuity, recommendations for auditory training objectives and intervention, supply and upkeep of equipment, making of ear mold impressions as needed, teaching teachers, parents, and students about the care of auditory equipment and batteries, and recommendations about alterations in the classroom environment so that optimal listening conditions are possible. If the student is being seen outside the school for auditory training sessions, it may be the responsibility of the school audiologist to communicate with this agency so that delivery of services can be coordinated. It may be that the audiologist will spend time in activities with you and the student being served, so that assessment and intervention in educational routines and activities, as well as noise levels, can be observed. This professional may provide you with auditory training procedures, materials, and suggestions for integrating activities into curricular areas.

## THE SCHOOL PSYCHOLOGIST

Typically, the school psychologist provides students and their parents with professional support, personal guidance, and evaluations of performance, aptitude, or personality (Gerken, Grimes, & Brown, 1978). However, this professional's ability to perform these duties may be hampered by a lack of manual communication skills (e.g., Cued Speech, sign system, ASL). It is your responsibility as the teacher of hearing-impaired students to advise the school psychologist when you feel that communication abilities are affecting student performance. For example, placement of a student should not be based on test results of instruments administered by a professional who cannot sign proficiently in the language or system being used by the student as a first language. The role that you are expected to assume with the school psychologist should be discussed and clarified so that a positive professional relationship persists.

## THE SCHOOL NURSE

The school nurse may collect appropriate medical information regarding hearing-impaired students. You will be responsible for seeing that this professional has copies of all medical documents pertaining to your students and has had an opportunity to review them before staffings occur. The school nurse should be able to provide parents with community-based resources for specific medical problems. Eye screenings, typically conducted by the school nurse, are especially important for hearing-impaired students. You will want to advocate that these are conducted on a regular basis and that follow-up occurs in cases of suspected visual needs.

## THE COUNSELOR

Counselors serving hearing-impaired students are found increasingly at both the elementary and secondary levels of education. These professionals may see students individually or in small groups for self-concept, abuse, sex, or drug information. They may be responsible also for assisting in gathering information for staffings and coordinating findings from various professionals and family members. Counselors may help you set up and implement behavior or emotional management programs or may be responsible for communicating consistently with regular education teachers. Your role in working with this professional will depend on the description of his or her role with regard to the hearing-impaired students being served in your program. If these duties are new to the counselor, your willingness to share methods and materials may help the counselor to develop skills in working with hearing-impaired students and eventually decrease your need to carry out these and similar duties.

## THE SOCIAL WORKER

Typically the school social worker becomes involved with a student when governmental assistance, financial aid, adoption issues or counseling is needed. As in the case with the psychologist, it may be that you will need to assume some of these responsibilities initially because of the communication skills that are needed to perform them effectively. The social worker should be involved with parents and professionals on a regular basis.

## SUPERVISORS, SPECIAL EDUCATION DIRECTORS, AND PRINCIPALS

It is important that the teacher of the deaf interact in an organized, articulate manner with those who administer programs for hearing-impaired students. Often these professionals have duties beyond those involving your program. They need to be kept informed about positive events, as well as your needs. Likewise, you must be willing to learn new skills, set mutual goals, and accept constructive criticism from your superiors. Invite these professionals to visit your classroom, send them copies of information that goes home to parents, request release time from them to attend workshops and conferences, suggest in-service topics, ask to be evaluated, and so on. It is good practice for you to try to approach these busy people with workable solutions to your needs.

## VOLUNTEERS

Your program can benefit greatly from additional adult participation in all aspects of programming. Parents, older hearing or hearing-impaired students, and community adults can be trained to teach specific tasks, gather materials, make community contacts for activities, and develop needed materials. Deaf adults can teach sign classes, be trained to teach specific tasks, assist on field trips, read stories, transmit cultural values, do and mime, and so forth. If you are organized and reinforcing, you can ease your work load, make supportive contacts, and promote deaf awareness in a realistic manner through the constructive use of volunteers.

## TUTORS

Older students and adults may volunteer or receive credit by serving as tutors in your classroom. You need to give these volunteers specific instruction and supervision if they are going to tutor effectively. Several types of tutoring sessions are presented in Exhibit 4.3 (Osguthorpe, 1982). We feel that this is a useful table and can guide you in your role of explanation, reinforcement, and feedback to the tutors who assist you.

**EXHIBIT 4.3.** Types of tutoring sessions (Osguthorpe, 1982)

|  | Procedures Clarification | Test Preparation | Course Content Study | Completing a Project |
|---|---|---|---|---|
| *Sample Sessions* | Student wants to know when a paper is due and what the teacher wants the paper to contain. | Student schedules a session one week before midterm. You help student prepare a practice test, go over it, correct it, discuss answers. | Student wants explanation about chapter in text. You discuss concepts and then ask questions to make certain student understands. | Student unclear about topic for project. Wants your help in choosing one. You ask student for any ideas. You suggest general areas. Then student comes up with topic. You ask student to talk to teacher about it. |
|  | Student asks how much quizzes will count on grade—when they will be given. | Student comes the night before the test. You quiz student with questions you have made up that could be on test. | Student wants to go over your notes for two class periods. You discuss difficult concepts, then ask student to explain those concepts to you. | Student has half finished project and something goes wrong. You encourage student to talk to teacher about it. |
|  | Student asks about due dates for project and term paper. |  |  |  |
| *Hints to the Tutor* | Make certain you understand requirements before communicating them to students. | Do not do the studying *for* the student. | *Diagnose* student needs—find out what the student does not understand. | Help the student, if necessary, to select a good topic—do not select the topic *for* the student. |
|  | If you are uncertain, encourage student to ask teacher. | Help the student learn to predict test questions. | *Teach* the need diagnosed. Guide the student to correct answers. | Encourage the student to talk to the teacher about the project at several points along the way. |
|  | Get as much clarification from teacher on course requirements as possible. | Stimulate the testing situation as much as possible when helping the student prepare. Use *practice tests*. | *Assess* student growth. Ask the student to explain to you the concepts you have been teaching. |  |

SOURCE: R. Osguthorpe, *The Tutor/Notetaker: Providing Academic Support to Mainstreamed Deaf Students*. Washington D.C.: Alexander Graham Bell Association for the Deaf, 1980. Reprinted by permission.

# PARENTS

Since the implementation of PL 94-142, the need for parent participation in educational decisions that affect their children is widely recognized. Therefore, teachers are finding themselves interacting with parents in many different ways. Sometimes the communication process between teachers and parents breaks down. Davis (1983) suggests that many of the reasons for communication problems between parents and teachers are due to the following:

*Teachers lack awareness of the impact of having a hearing-impaired child.* Teachers are not always aware of both the physical and emotional pain suffered by many parents of hearing-impaired students. Therefore, the behavior of many parents often is misconstrued by teachers as indifference or overprotectiveness towards the child or even as an attack upon the teacher.

*Many parents are distrustful of the school's commitment.* Many parents of hearing-impaired students are wary and distrustful of the public school's true commitment to providing their child with an appropriate education because of past procedures adopted by schools toward deaf child and parents. This distrust is often transferred to the child's teacher.

*Parents have had previous negative experiences with professionals.* Parents of hearing-impaired children are often wary and distrustful of any professionals because of past negative experiences.

*Teachers frequently do not actively listen to parents.* The communication process between teachers and parents frequently is severely impeded because teachers sometimes do not listen to the real questions that the parents are asking or simply do not listen at all.

*Teachers fail to make use of the strengths of parents.* Teachers sometimes fail to capitalize upon the real strengths that parents can bring to the teacher-parent-student situation. Parental involvement in the student's educational process is often perceived by the teacher as passive rather than active.

Including parents in the various aspects of your program can promote understanding and communication. The most negative parents might change their perspective when they join you in a regular weekly session at school and witness your sincere desire to help their children despite the numerous demands and problems that confront you on a daily basis. Exhibit 4.4, adapted from Dinkmeyer, McKay, and Dinkmeyer (1980), can be used to inquire about and record the time and areas of interest that your students' parents want to share in your program.

Parents can be partners by sharing information about their child's behavior at home and in the community, by transferring skills from one environment to another, and by monitoring medical and social aspects of the student's life. Parents may be motivated to become well informed on specific methods or materials and may want your cooperation in trying a new approach with their child. Often this can be done objectively by collecting data and discussing behavior based on empirical evidence. You do not want to bias your view toward parents' concerns in a manner that will inhibit the parents from communicating with you and the other professionals who are working with their child. Finally, parents might need your assistance in locating books, professional journals, conferences, newsletters, and so on, to broaden their understanding of deafness. You should be knowledgeable about information that may be of interest to them and organize your references in a useful manner.

**EXHIBIT 4.4.** Parent involvement sheet (adapted from Dinkmeyer, McKay, & Dinkmeyer, 1980)

Name: _____

Relationship to student: _____

Address: _____

Phone: _____

Place of employment: _____

Phone: _____

Occupation: _____

I would like to have students visit me at work. ————

I would like to come to school and talk about my job. ————

I would like to show pictures (slides) of my job. ————

I would enjoy helping students and the school in the following ways:

1. Field trip escort ————
2. Work on school carnival ————
3. Be a class photographer ————
4. Telephoning ————
5. Provide refreshments ————
6. Clerical work ————
7. Arts and crafts ————
8. Help with plays ————
9. Cooking ————
10. Sewing ————
11. Nurse's aide ————
12. Library aide ————
13. Playground supervisor ————
14. Cafeteria helper ————
15. Bus supervisor ————
16. Teacher's aide ————
    a. Grade papers ————
    b. Listen to students read ————
    c. Keep records ————
    d. Locate materials and arrange field trips ————
    e. Tutor ———— Subject(s) _____
       _____
    f. Work with small groups ———— Subject(s) _____
       _____
    g. Teach a special skill ———— What skill?

17. I have slides of interesting areas of the United States or other countries to share. ————
    Place(s)

18. Special interests and hobbies I would be willing to share.
    _____
    _____

Other suggestions and ideas: _____

SOURCE: T. Hurwitz, *Principles of Interpreting*. Rochester, NY: National Technical Institute for the Deaf, 1971.

## Working with Parents as a Part of the Multidisciplinary Process

Parents are mandated by federal law to join with you and other professionals in the team process. They can assist in the assessment phase by allowing assessments to be made in the home or by providing information about certain skills possessed by the student. They can be helpful in setting goals and objectives in all areas of development and implementing procedures and conditions to implement these goals that involve home and community contexts. Parents also can assist with data collection of goals and objectives in environments that extend beyond the school day. When the hearing-impaired student is viewed as a member of a family system and a communication network, the role of the parents assumes paramount importance.

Many of these roles might be new to the parents of your students. While PL 94-142 has been in effect for more than a decade now, parents traditionally have been asked to assist only with speech, audition, and language intervention (Kretschmer & Kretschmer, 1978). For students with behavioral or learning problems, parents have demonstrated their ability to continue behavioral management programs and to act as effective teachers at home (Gearheart & Weishahn, 1984). Although you need to realize that not all parents have the time or the desire to assist in their child's educational program, you should consider their participation on an individual basis and not assume that they will not be willing to work with you to extend educational goals and objectives into their family lives.

Given the advantages of having parents cooperate in the multidisciplinary team process, you should prepare them well for the formal conferences and staffings that occur regularly regarding their child. We suggest the following preconference tips:

Try to make parents physically and psychologically comfortable when they come to school. This is especially important during periods of initial contact. Consider the fact that many parents feel very intimidated and overwhelmed by a cadre of professionals at a meeting concerning their child, in which they may perceive themselves as being truly alone.

Suggest that child care arrangements be made for other children in the family so that the parents can devote their complete attention to the meeting. If the family cannot make these arrangements, try to assist them by locating a spare room in close proximity to the meeting or other staff members to do the actual care.

Apprise the parents of the timetable for the meeting, the basic agenda, and the written names and positions of those who will be in attendance.

Encourage parents to stay on task. Give them examples of acceptable formats of how to state their concerns with regard to others.

Suggest that the parents bring a list of their concerns in writing to the meeting and take notes during the meeting.

Speak to the parents in plain English about information you wish to share. Define and exemplify terms that may be new to them or that may be used by others during the course of the meeting.

Suggest to the parents that they may wish to thank and praise those members of the service team who have been helpful in promoting effective programming for their child.

Help the parents strive for realistic optimism with regard to their child. Ask them to accept responsibility for following through with methods agreed upon and not to expect that the conference will solve all of their needs at that time. Encourage them to view the team as a partnership that can meet whenever it is necessary.

Be aware of cultural differences (e.g., dealing with authority, women's roles) when working with non-Anglo parents. Provide an interpreter for parents who do not have proficiency in English.

## Parent-Teacher Conferences

In addition to formal meetings between parents and service professionals you will most likely meet with parents on a regular basis to discuss their child's progress. When it is time to have a scheduled meeting with the parents, it is essential that you be prepared. We suggest that you prepare a one-page progress report to give the parents when they arrive. The evaluation should include:

1. A summary of the student's progress
2. Areas of concern
3. Areas of strength

It is helpful to have the parents read last about their child's strengths. This leaves them thinking about positive things. Exhibit 4.5, adapted from Spodek, Saracho, and Lee (1984), can be used to provide a framework for structuring parent-teacher conferences. Be sure to schedule time appropriately and allow sufficient time for those parents who have a need to talk or have specific concerns that you know will need to be addressed. If possible, try to encourage both parents to attend. If the parents are divorced and the student is in frequent contact with both, invite both to the conference, provided that both parents are willing to meet together and that you feel that the meeting will be productive. If this is not the case, then try to have them both come in at different times. Decide whether or not to include the student in the conference. If you decide not to, you may want to meet with the student in advance. Explain the purpose of the conference and what you plan to discuss.

**EXHIBIT 4.5.** Guidelines for parent-teacher conferences (adapted from Spodek, Saracho, & Lee, 1984)

### Before the Conference

1. Identify the purposes for the conference (e.g., reporting, information sharing, problem solving).
2. Prepare an agenda.
3. Review the student's record.
4. Prepare specific materials to show the parents (e.g., observation notes, test results, work samples).
5. Set a time for the conference that is convenient for all.
6. Invite both parents, if possible.
7. Find a comfortable, relaxing, quiet place for the conference.

### During the Conference

8. Be friendly—establish a positive atmosphere.
9. Inform parents about the class program, schedule, and routines.
10. Make positive comments about the student; talk about strengths as well as problems.
11. Be specific about the problems you present.
12. Use language that parents can easily understand.
13. Provide opportunities for parents to speak as well as listen; be a good listener.
14. Work cooperatively with parents on specific solutions and activities for the student; identify responsibilities.
15. Summarize the meeting; make sure that you and the parents are clear about the next steps.

### After the Conference

16. Make a brief record of the content of the meeting.
17. Plan any follow-up tasks.

This promotes trust within the student and lets the student know that the idea is to provide help, both at home and in school.

After the introductions and casual conversation, provide the parents with their copy of the progress report. Give them time to read it. Get their reactions. Explain anything that they do not understand. If they are upset, listen to their concerns and attempt to use specific examples to further explain your remarks. If they do not say anything, take the initiative yourself to highlight some of the important information on the progress report.

If there exists a specific problem that needs to be worked on in school, at home, or in both settings, use a problem-solving approach to come up with a plan that can be implemented in each of these settings. Be certain to focus on the student's strengths and use appropriate reinforcers. If you disagree with a proposal that is strongly made by the parents, send an "I-message", such as "I'm

**EXHIBIT 4.6.** Daily report card

## Daily Report Card

Student: _____

Day: _____

Data: _____

| Subject | Behavior | Effort | Homework |
|---|---|---|---|
| Language | | | |
| Reading | | | |
| Math | | | |
| Science | | | |
| Health | | | |
| Social Studies | | | |
| Speech | | | |
| Writing | | | |
| Comments | | | |

Signed: _____

SOURCE: B. Spodek, O. N. Saracho and R. C. Lee, *Mainstreaming Young* Children. Belmont, CA: Wadsworth Publishing Co., 1984.

concerned about that plan because. . . ." Ask for other suggestions and make some yourself. If the parents are resistant or you are having difficulty communicating with them, call in your supervisor or the principal to assist in the communication process. Summarize the conference by discussing specifically what is going to be done at school, what is going to be done at home, how it is going to be evaluated, and how you are going to communicate about the student's progress. Exhibit 4.6 is an example of a form that can be used to communicate with parents on a regular basis.

## WORKING PARENTS

School personnel need to recognize, address, and program with sensitivity because of the increase of families in which both parents are working outside the home (Somers, 1987). For example, child care facilities rarely provide personnel who are capable of caring for a hearing-impaired child. Evening meetings that include appropriate child care workers could increase parental involvement and assist parents in obtaining the information and services that are needed. Such flexibility would solve another problem as well: Meetings, sign classes, counseling sessions, and school activities for parents are often scheduled during working hours, making them unavailable to those parents who cannot leave work.

Teachers need to advocate for flexible scheduling for working parents that is sensitive to their special needs. This may require unusual working hours for a limited period of time for the professionals involved (e.g., a school day that is 1:00 P.M. to 9:00 P.M. so that conferences can be held).

## SINGLE PARENTHOOD

One out of every two marriages in the United States is expected to end in divorce (Fewell & Vadasy, 1986). Therefore, more than one-half of all hearing-impaired children that you may work with might spend part of their childhood being raised by only one parent. Teachers who work with single-family parents should be considerate of the stress placed on this individual. In addition to the considerations that we mentioned in our discussion of working parents, single parents may need assistance in locating qualified personnel for respite care, sensitivity to new relationships that might emerge, acceptance of the father being the primary care taker, and so forth. Sensitivity to the feelings of the child whose life is undergoing transition is warranted also.

Simpson (1982) lists the following roles that educators should take on as they serve single-parent and reconstituted families:

1. Be able to suggest resources
2. Be aware that the priority concerns of these parents may differ from yours
3. Be aware that these parents may have severe time, energy, and financial restrictions placed on them
4. Attempt to include noncustodial parents in conferences and programs
5. Recognize the importance of listening to parents
6. Become familiar with your own family-related values as these affect your relationships with single- and reconstituted families
7. Be able to provide reassurance during times of confusion and uncertainty, and stability in the school programming as transitions occur in the home
8. Expect involved adults to fulfill their roles with regard to school procedures (e.g., attendance at meetings, timelines, etc.)
9. Anticipate atypical behavior from both parents and students as changes occur in the family

## LOW-INCOME FAMILIES

One-third of the parents in this country live below the poverty rate (Sidel, 1986). Many of these parents are recent immigrants to this country and may not have proficiency in English. Women are the heads of households in 48 percent of these poor families in the United States (Billingsley & Giovannoni, 1972). While free child care may be available to poor families so that employment is possible, the difficulties in locating appropriate child care for hearing-impaired children are compounded. The cost of hearing aids, new ear molds, telecommunication devices for the deaf (TDDs), fire alarm systems, and so on, may be a burden for these families. Low-income families have listed transportation, child care, feelings of inferiority in relation to school personnel, and communication problems as special needs (Somers, 1987). Solutions offering a range of support have included home-based conferences, parent meetings in neighborhood facilities, and use of community volunteers.

Teachers of hearing-impaired students from poor families need to be sensitive to the communication difficulties that may arise at formal, as well as informal, meetings. They should advocate for the employment of interpreters if they are not proficient speakers or writers of the parents' language. Cultural awareness may be needed with regard to conduct at staffings, parent participation in school activities, values and rituals of the home, and so forth.

## RURAL PARENTS

Teachers of hearing-impaired rural students may need to provide parents with a range of resources, networking plans, and organizational strategies that might not normally be the responsibility of a teacher in an urban area. In addition, you may need to support parents' interest and willingness to become knowledgeable about specific topics (e.g., upgrading the school FM system, obtaining TDDs for local agencies, etc.). Rural parents might be invited to join itinerant teachers at school in-services and state, regional, or national conferences. Newsletters and telecommunication might be important vehicles of communication for families who are geographically isolated. Again, you will need to be flexible and creative in serving the special needs of rural families.

## SUBSTITUTE TEACHERS

At various times in your teaching career, you may be forced to miss part or all of the school day. When this happens, it is essential that you have a well-articulated explanation of how your class operates. We suggest that you take the time early in the year to write out some of the specific procedures that you use and, if possible, that you invite some of the potential substitute teachers to come into your class for a visit. Exhibit 4.7 provides information on the different materials that you may want to pull together.

### *SUMMARY*

It was not too long ago that the job of a teacher of the deaf was solely to provide educational services directly to hearing-impaired students. With the implementation of well-known legislation, job responsibilities have expanded to include the provision of indirect services via a consultation model to a cadre of other professionals and family members. As a teacher of the deaf, you will need to communicate effectively and coordinate the services that are provided to your students to a large number of *significant others*. Your role now has changed from one of "classroom teacher" to that of "program manager."

**EXHIBIT 4.7.** Contents for a substitute-teacher plan package

---

Student's names and pictures, or a seating chart.

A brief description of each student, including personal characteristics or behavior patterns that are helpful for the substitute teacher to know.

One large chart with the daily schedule, including who comes and goes, where and when, and alternate plans or activities in case some classes or services are canceled.

A brief explanation of your behavior management system, classroom rules, and discipline procedures.

Information about medication needs of students, when and who gives the medication, and procedures to follow if a student becomes sick or gets injured.

Emergency exit locations for the class.

A description of opening activities, if they are normally conducted (i.e., roll call, lunch tickets, morning circle, etc.).

A set of individual folders with sufficient work in different areas and several group activities. Activities that involve practice and skill building in areas in which students have gained initial knowledge will be particularly useful. This will require less formal teaching by the substitute.

Specific information about student grouping (who can work best with whom) and where the groups or individual students work best (e.g., who works best in a particular study carrel).

Location of instructional materials and extra student work.

Names and schedules of teacher aides, volunteers, practicum students or interns and their roles and responsibilities.

Names of other teachers who can be particularly helpful in an emergency.

Names of students who can be relied upon for assistance and those who should be watched closely.

A floor plan of the school building.

Procedures for fire drills or other emergency drills.

Dismissal procedures.

---

Your role with regard to being a member of a multidisciplinary team, working with paraprofessionals, the speech and language pathologist, the interpreter, the notetaker, the regular education teacher, the audiologist, the school psychologist, the school nurse, the counselor, the social worker, your supervisor and principal, volunteers, tutors, and parents is reviewed in this chapter. Background information about each of these team members is given. In addition, many helpful tools are provided to assist you in communicating with others and to help you coordinate the services provided by each team member.

## ACTIVITIES

1. Interview three professionals who work with hearing-impaired students in three different roles (other than the teacher). Clarify the material presented in this chapter and ask them to comment on additional aspects of their roles.

2. Observe as a professional other than the teacher who works with a hearing-impaired student or family. Describe what you see and how it relates to this chapter's material.

3. Volunteer to work in a setting involving hearing-impaired, school-age children. Participate for at least 10 hours. What jobs were you given? Could the teacher have assisted you or made your role easier? Discuss how you might organize activities for a volunteer who is working with hearing-impaired students.

4. Attend a parents' group that is concerned with hearing-impairment issues or observe a multidisciplinary team in action. Integrate your experience with the information from this chapter.

5. Provide child care for a family with a hearing-impaired child for a total of 6 hours. Discuss your experiences.

# PART TWO

## Language, Speech, Audition, and Speechreading

Assessment and Intervention Strategies

# CHAPTER 5

# Language Use

## OVERVIEW

Although language is comprised, as we have seen in Chapter 1, of the *interaction* between use, content, and form, it is sometimes beneficial for us to isolate each of these components so that appropriate assessment and intervention strategies can be decided. We have taken this organizational advantage in the first three chapters of Part Two, defining developmental milestones, listing them, and providing taxonomies for coding language samples for each. Several informal techniques for assessing use, content, and form behaviors, and specific intervention strategies are explained as well. In addition, we highly recommend that you read the *Developmental Language Curriculum: A Comprehensive Guide and Record Keeping System for Hearing-Impaired Students, Infant through Twelve Years* (University of Washington Press, 1988) as a comprehensive language guide, assessment tool, and record keeping system for hearing-impaired students.

We begin the complex task of discussing language with this initial chapter about the functional use of language. Language use or pragmatics involves sharing social rules for correct use of language across a wide variety of contexts. The knowledge of these rules and the ability to apply them has been referred to as "communicative" competencies (Hymes, 1971). So that you can assess each student's ability to use language, we recommend that you sample genuine language use in multiple situations, and we suggest several intervention strategies that would follow logically from this activity.

---

**CHAPTER TOPICS**

Use Assessment
Language Sampling
Coding for Language Use
Setting Priorities for Intervention
Use Intervention

---

## USE ASSESSMENT

Assessment of hearing-impaired students' language traditionally has utilized formalized standard measures of the production of language structures (Cole & Cole, 1988). Not many tests have been developed to evaluate the use acquisition of hearing-impaired children. Instruments by Damico (1985), Simon (1979), and Wiig and Bray (1983) merit inspection. Less formal measures of evaluating language use abilities are dependent on reported information gathered from significant others. It is possible that teachers, parents, relatives, neighbors, audiologists, and speech and language pathologists can provide use information about young children, such as that listed in Exhibit 5.1. For example, the language behaviors provided in this exhibit state that at 10 months, a typical child uses novel means (i.e., new words) to achieve familiar ends (e.g., requests for objects, actions, and attention). The information provided in the exhibit also clarifies that it is important during this stage of development that parents engage frequently in predictable dialogue and repetitive fingerplays, and that they read familiar stories to the child. The idea behind stimulating developmentally appropriate language behaviors at a particular time is to facilitate the emergence of specific use behaviors—in this case requests, com-

**EXHIBIT 5.1.** Infant and toddler's use of language

| Age Level | Caregivers |
|---|---|
| *0–9 months* | |
| Prelocutionary (prior to language use), communicative acts (e.g., crying because of discomfort, etc., is not intentional or goal oriented).<br>Gestural behaviors for social purposes.<br>Child is topic of every conversation. | Parents are highly motivated to try and elicit and maintain child activity-centered dialogues.<br>Dialogues take place within the context of familiar routines.<br>Parents weave utterances around child's smiles, burps, and vocalizations (Coggins & Sandall, 1983).<br>Parents respond as if child's behavior were intentional and establish rudimentary turn-taking (Snow, 1977).<br>Bell and Ainsworth (1972) maintain that caregivers can strengthen social bonds by being responsive to infant vocalizations and by engaging the child in social action and communication games (e.g., peek-a-boo). |
| *9–15 months* | |
| As a precursor (behavior that precedes another behavior) for the development of intentional communication (use for a deliberate purpose), children analyze causal relationships (which brings about an action or a state) and realize adults can intervene on their behalf (Bates, 1976b).<br>Children use novel means to achieve familiar ends (e.g., vocalizations to achieve desired goals), include requests for objects, actions, and attention; comment on objects and actions; and protest against adult actions (Coggins & Sandall, 1983). | Caregivers play social-action games (e.g., peek-a-boo, gonna get you, so big, build and bash, point and name) with toddlers. Bruner (1975) argues that these games are important language learning strategies for the child because:<br>    they limit and familiarize content;<br>    they provide predictable simple and repetitive utterances;<br>    and they allow reversible role relationships.<br>Parents continuously adjust behavior and expectations to increase the likelihood of child's success. |

**EXHIBIT 5.1.** (Continued)

| Age Level | Caregivers |
| --- | --- |
| *16–24 months* | |
| Words and word combinations are used to request information, answer routine questions, and acknowledge prior speakers' utterances (Chapman, 1981). | Adults simplify their input and make modifications that are syntactically and semantically simplified. Their input is simple, short, and grammatically well formed (Nelson, 1973) about present objects, people, and ongoing actions. Chapman (1981) and Slobin (1970) suggest that words occurring at the end of utterances are more salient to the child and allow the child to retain the word in memory long enough to learn its meaning. It appears that a linguistically stimulating environment may be an important variable in accelerating early language acquisition (Chapman, 1981). Adults appear to have a facilitative effect on early language development when their input is contingent on the child's activity or utterances. |
|    Words become multifunctional (serving many social purposes) language for instrumental, regulatory (controlling), and interactional (pragmatic) functions. | |
|    Genuine dialogue can develop. | |
|    Child participates in verbal exchanges in which child's utterances are influenced by the content and communicative intent of the speaker's utterances. | |
|    Child begins to tell listener about events that are not present in the situation. | Adult repeats own utterance. |
| | Adult repeats child's utterance. |
| | Adult expands child's utterance (repeats utterance to include more information). |
| | Folger and Chapman (1978) found that hearing children (19–25 months) were three times as likely to imitate their parent's utterance spontaneously if that utterance was itself a repetition or expansion of the child's own utterance. For example: |
| | C: Daddy drive. |
| | P: That's right; daddy is driving the car. |
| | C: Daddy drive car. |

ments, or protests. These behaviors should be documented by you as reported by the parents and others across various environments.

A glance at Exhibit 5.2 also confirms that information from caretakers is of paramount importance in assessing and intervening in the area of language use. The exhibit provides educators with a developmentally organized guide for both assessing use behaviors and noting, too, the form used to express these abilities. Exhibit 5.2 is based on data from monolingual hearing children and has been adapted for use with bimodal (signing and speaking) children. Goals and objectives based on this assessment would need to be written to include an observable behavior so that a reasonable criterion could be set (see Chapter 2). In addition, the tool can assist you in informing significant others as to which behaviors are appropriate for the hearing-impaired child with whom you are working.

For preschool and elementary-age students, Cazden, Vera, and Hymes (1972) advocate that teachers determine whether their classroom environment nurtures language use. They suggest that you ask yourself questions such as these:

> Are conversations occurring in my classroom? Does talk (and sign) go back and forth between the students and myself, or do I do all the talking?
>
> Do I ask open-ended, divergent questions?
>
> Do I tell students how they should think

**EXHIBIT 5.2.** Language use abilities of children (based on hearing, *monolingual* child data and adapted for *bimodal* (signed and voiced) communication

| | Gesture | Cues or Sign | Sign and Voice | Voice Alone |
|---|---|---|---|---|
| *1/2–1 Year* | | | | |
| 1. Begin to reproduce an event consciously; may try to get others around them to participate (e.g., in order to be picked up, holds arms towards an adult) (Miller, 1981a). | | | | |
| 2. Use sounds and/or gestures to interact with environment (interactional function) (Miller, 1981a). | | | | |
| 3. Use sounds and/or gestures (gazing, crying, touching, grasping, sucking, etc.) to express an awareness of self (e.g., personal feelings of interest, pleasure, disgust, etc.) (personal function) (Bates, 1976a; Miller, 1981a). | | | | |
| 4. Uses sound and/or gestures to satisfy material needs and obtain objects and help from others (instrumental function) (Miller, 1981a). | | | | |
| 5. Uses sound and/or gestures to control the behavior of others (regulatory function) (Miller, 1981a). | | | | |
| 6. Repeat a vocalization or sign upon it being initiated (Miller, 1981a). | | | | |
| 7. Play communication games (e.g., pat-a-cake, peek-a-boo, so-big) (Miller, 1981a). | | | | |
| 8. Vigorously move arms and body to express "do it again" (Cano & Schmidt, 1974). | | | | |
| *1–2 Years* | | | | |
| 9. Manually or orally express requests for object or attention (e.g., point to object with grasping objectives while vocalizing "uh, uh, uh") (Miller, 1981a). | | | | |
| 10. Manually or orally express rejection (e.g., "uh" with gesture indicating pushing away or head shake) (Miller, 1981a). | | | | |
| 11. Manually or orally express comment (e.g., point to object while vocalizing "uh" or "see"; "hi" or "bye") (Miller, 1981a). | | | | |
| 12. Express routine (e.g., ritualized games, such as "down," as knocks blocks down) (Miller, 1981a). | | | | |
| 13. Use signed and/or voiced words more narrowly than adults ("fafa" for one specific picture of a flower) (Miller, 1981a). | | | | |
| 14. Only name (by sign or voice) objects and people that are present unless occurrence is a routine (Miller, 1981a). | | | | |
| 15. Show onset of verbal dialogue (answers speech or sign with speech or sign) (Miller, 1981a). | | | | |
| 16. Increase frequency of talking or signing (Miller, 1981a). | | | | |
| 17. Demonstrate awareness of turn-taking in conversation (e.g., "what's a cow say?") (Corsaro, 1981). | | | | |
| 18. Answer some signed and/or voiced routine questions (Miller, 1981a). | | | | |

**EXHIBIT 5.2.** (Continued)

| | Gesture | Cues or Sign | Sign and Voice | Voice Alone |
|---|---|---|---|---|
| 19. Ask (using voice or sign) "what's that" question as a routine. | | | | |
| *2–3 Years* | | | | |
| 20. Carry on a signed and/or voiced "conversation" with self or toys (Cano & Schmidt, 1974). | | | | |
| 21. Initiate conversations typically by orally and/or manually getting the listener's attention, usually repeating the listener's name over and over, putting forth a topic, seeking acknowledgement of the topic, and adding new information (Kretschmer & Kretschmer, 1980). | | | | |
| 22. Are more concerned with own intent than that of the listener (Bloom & Lahey, 1978). | | | | |
| 23. Participate in conversational *discourse* by using signed and/or voiced utterances that are linguistically related to the topic of someone's previous utterance (Bloom & Lahey, 1978). | | | | |
| *3–4 Years* | | | | |
| 24. Utilize *roles* in play (e.g., "I'm the mom," etc.) (McCune-Nicolich, 1981). | | | | |
| 25. Dramatize, combining signed and/or voiced words and actions for own pleasure (Cano & Schmidt, 1974) | | | | |
| 26. Engage in signed and/or voiced peer conversations (Bloom & Lahey, 1978). | | | | |
| 27. Use signed and/or voiced "motherese" with younger children, simplifying the form (Corsaro, 1981). | | | | |
| 28. Employ signed and/or voiced *queries* to maintain mutual understanding, attention, and rapport in peer interaction (Corsaro, 1981). | | | | |
| 29. Are able to initiate conversations in sign and/or voice (Kretschmer & Kretschmer, 1980). | | | | |
| 30. Use "hints" to make desires known ("My mom lets me have cookies before lunch") (Cano & Schmidt, 1974). | | | | |
| 31. Use slang (Crystal, 1976). | | | | |
| *4–5 Years* | | | | |
| 32. Whisper and increase volume in voice *or* vary signs in signing space (Cano & Schmidt, 1974). | | | | |
| 33. Change voice to faster rate *or* vary signing speed (Cano & Schmidt, 1974). | | | | |
| 34. Request an action in sign and/or voice (Bloom & Lahey, 1978). | | | | |
| 35. Request permission in sign and/or voice (Bloom & Lahey, 1978). | | | | |
| 36. Use words of warning, inviting, or promising in sign and/or voice (Bloom & Lahey, 1978). | | | | |

and feel (i.e., moralizing) instead of accepting their values?

Do I really listen to my students, or do I jump in with a response as soon as I think I've guessed what they mean?

Do I only give answers that fit in with my own preconceptions or need for control?

Is my language production geared to that of my individual students?

Do I know students' levels of the use, content, and form of English?

Do I involve the students in activities that promote verbal (voiced and signed) interactions?

Is there a maximum chance for students to converse with each other?

Are my interactions with the students based on their real world and characters, themes, toys, and so on that are of interest to them? (For example, can I name and sign all the Saturday morning cartoon characters or the names of breakfast cereals that my students eat?)

Does the interaction between each student and myself occur in the context of mutual trust and respect, based on genuine friendliness, acceptance, empathy, and interest?

## LANGUAGE SAMPLING

Another technique for assessing use ability is to take a language sample in several contexts (Bloom & Lahey, 1978) of the student's spontaneous speech, cued speech, or speech and sign. The spontaneous and consistent use of language is a more accurate indicator of the communication ability of an adult or a child than evidence obtained through use of formal tests (Lucas, 1980). However, the value of the information obtained from such a sample depends largely on how the sample was taken, coded, and analyzed. The procedure can be as time consuming as the administra-

tion and interpretation of formal tests (Bloom and Lahey, 1978).

To capture the student's use, content, and form knowledge, the targeted language user should be stimulated to talk about several contexts in various settings. Less structured conversational settings elicit more language and more complex language than structured, task-oriented settings or pictures (Lee, 1971). Planning the observations involves a consideration of a number of factors: context of observations, length of observations, method of transcription and coding of features of interest, and analysis of features of interest. We will discuss each of these characteristics in the next section.

## Context of Observations

It is best to take a language sample with different types of materials in a variety of contexts that are familiar and routine for the student. These settings should be representative of the kinds of routines in which improvement in the language or system is needed. In fact, the closer the parallel between the sampled language and routines that typically occur, the easier will be the transition to intervention goals that might lead to successful acquisition of the desired skills.

Bloom and Lahey (1978) found, too, that a greater number of language behaviors can be obtained when conversations revolve around some concrete activity (e.g., symbolic play, story telling, constructing toys, science experiments, or art projects) and the student is allowed to talk about the activity in an unstructured manner. Questions should be open-ended (e.g., "How do you think this is supposed to work?"). Avoid questions that typically yield one-word responses (e.g., "What is this?"). Lund and Duchan (1988) have provided us with some useful *hints for getting the reluctant talker to want to talk*, which are as follows.

1. Keep the focus off your attempt to get the child to communicate. With students

who are very hesitant to say or sign anything, provide contexts that demand little verbalization for participation, such as drawing pictures or playing a game. This allows the student to become a participant with you in a nonthreatening way. During the event, you should comment on what you are doing and allow for, but not directly request, the student's verbal participation.

2. Do not talk too much, and do not be afraid to allow silent pauses during the conversations. Do not fill up every empty space with a question. This encourages the student to let you take the lead.

3. Select materials appropriate to the student's interest level. For example, students operating at a preschool level tend to be more interested in toys than in books or games. Older students tend to like unusual objects or things that can be manipulated.

4. Toys with detachable or moving parts and broken toys generally stimulate interest. If possible, you might have the student or caretaker bring in one or two of the student's favorite toys. They often have more to say about familiar things than about new ones. When toys become too enrapturing, they tend to inhibit verbal interaction. If this happens, it is best to announce that you will have to put the toy away in a few minutes and do something else or to present an interesting alternative while you quietly remove the distracting toy.

5. Most children are naturally curious. If they know you have something concealed from them, they usually want to find out more about it. Having a big box or bag (or even a pillowcase!) from which you can withdraw objects may prompt conversation about what else it contains. Likewise, noise sources that they cannot see or mechanisms that make toys move stimulate curiosity. It is generally best not to have all of your materials out at once, but you might present alternatives and ask the student which one he or she wants to look at first.

6. If the student will initiate conversation about your materials, let the student take the lead; you can ask questions or comment briefly on what the student is saying. For a more natural and less "testing" atmosphere, insert your own opinions or comments occasionally.

7. If the student does not initiate, make comments yourself about the materials and ask open-ended leading questions such as, "That looks broken. What do you suppose happened to it?" or "Can you figure out what's going on here?" If these prompts do not elicit any verbalization, try more specific questions that require minimum output such as, "Do you . . .?" "Where. . .?" "What is . . . ?" and then build up to more open-ended questions such as, "Tell me . . . "or "What about . . . ?"

8. If statements or questions trigger no reaction, demonstrate what you expect from the student. For example, take a toy yourself and play with it, tell about what you are doing, and personalize your account by using an imaginary situation. Engage the student in the play as soon as possible and begin to prompt indirectly. For example, make your car crash into the student's car and then ask what happens next.

9. If the student is reluctant to talk about pictures or tell stories, do it first and set the stage. A series of sequence pictures provides more story structure than a single picture and therefore is generally easier for creating a beginning story. You can have the student tell the same story after you or create a new story by using different pictures or characters. Unless you are analyzing for storytelling structures, do not ask the student to tell too familiar a story, since it might have been memorized and therefore unlike more natural output.

10. Include another person in the elicitation or collection procedure. This might be a speech clinician or aide who can model the responses you expect from the student, or it might be a parent, sibling, or friend who can be included in the activities. Having a third

party involved tends to take the focus off the student and makes talking more comfortable.

## Length

Several educators suggest that the language sample collected be at least 50–100 utterances in length (Bloom & Lahey, 1978; Lee, 1971). We have found that for samples of adults (used to target signing problems, for example), a 50-utterance corpus yields the same information as a sample of 100 utterances. Our work has demonstrated also that an adequate sample can be collected from a talkative and signative adult in about 15 minutes; students can require up to an hour of sampling time.

## Videotaped Samples

We strongly encourage the use of videotaped language samples. Even in situations in which students might be intelligible on audiotape, the use of a videotape provides additional context, which often is useful in deciding how pragmatically or semantically to code the students' intent. Bimodal communication is so complicated that it is impossible to capture all of the elements of interest without the aid of a pause button, slow-motion option, and replay feature (so that it can be viewed at a later date). Videotapes can be shown to other professionals and sent home for parents' viewing. They serve well to document progress if samples are taken over time, too.

In this day and age, student teachers, teachers, and speech and language pathologists need to know how to operate video equipment. They should feel as comfortable unpacking, loading, and using a portapac as they do accessing a computer terminal.

## Transcription

Standard orthography or international phonetic symbols can record what is said and/or signed by the student. Several transcription conventions have been devised for American

Sign Language (Stokoe, Casterline, & Cronberg, 1965; Sutton, 1976). If the student or significant adult is using one of several English sign systems, we have found that upper- and lower-case print can capture this language accurately. For example:

1. <u>The boys are running.</u>
   THE BOYS ARE RUNNING.
2. <u>The girls are jumping.</u>
   GIRL ARE JUMP

In sentence 1, the sign markers are both signed and spoken and so are transcribed simply as the morphemes that they represent. In sentence 2, one word and two morphemes only were spoken, so their signed counterparts are not written down. We recommend that transcribers study ASL transcription systems in order to incorporate linguistic manual features that might be used by students in an otherwise English sample.

Commonly used transcription conventions are as follows:

F-I-N-G-E-R-S-P-E-L-L-I-N-G

= a fingerspelled word or affix

$$\frac{won}{\text{(waves hand to left)}}$$

= ( ) to explain a gesture

$$\frac{\text{Take it over there}}{\text{TAKE}}$$
(DIRECTIONALITY UTILIZED)

= ASL feature utilized

$$\frac{\text{She is there}}{\text{POINT (over there)}}$$

= Point is used and the referent indicated in ( )

## Coding

Taxonomies or listings of a particular category of use, content, and form behaviors can be used to code the language samples of either children or adults for features of interest. Several use taxonomies appear in this chapter. In addition, the semantic taxonomy of Bloom and Lahey (1978) is provided in Chapter 6, and the form taxonomy of Lee (1974) is provided in Chapter 7. Transcribers should set a limit or criterion before they begin coding as to the number of examples of a particular use, content, or form behavior that will be accepted as evidence that that aspect of language is a productive part of the user's system. Bloom (1974) recommended that a teacher find five different occurrences of a target behavior as evidence that the student has knowledge of a particular linguistic rule.

*Mean-Length-Utterance.* Mean-length-utterance (MLU) is a measure of linguistic length, using the morpheme (the smallest unit of meaning) as a measurement. Information about both the voiced and signed MLUs in a sample have been found to be useful in setting goals for adults and students (Luetke-Stahlman & Moeller, in press). The procedure that is utilized for finding the MLU of the signed portion of manually coded English utterances is based on the spoken English that accompanies it. In our work, the calculation of the MLU has been based on the first 100 utterances that satisfy the following rules (adapted from Brown, 1973):

1. Use transcription that does not involve a recitation of some kind. Do not use utterances that have been read or sung.
2. Use only fully transcribed utterances. If a word in an utterance is unintelligible or the user does not complete an idea, do not use the utterance.
3. Do not use exact repetitions of immediately prior utterances.
4. Stuttering is defined as repeated efforts at a single word or phrase. Count the word or phrase once in the most complete form produced. In the cases in which a word is produced for emphasis (e.g., "No, no, no"), count each word of the phrase only once.
5. Do not count such fillers as "mm" or "ah ha," but do count "oh, no," "yeah," and "hi."
6. All compound words (two or more free morphemes), proper names, and ritualized reduplications count as single words (e.g., *birthday, highway, Mary Pat, quack-quack, night-night, pocketbook, see-saw*).
7. Count as two morphemes all irregular past tenses of a verb (e.g., *got, did, went, saw*).
8. Count as multiple morphemes all derivations of words (e.g., *exactly, happiness, replace*). If the word with a prefix or a suffix is signed as one sign in a particular system, it is credited as the multiple spoken morphemes it represents (e.g., *wonderful* in Signed English).
9. Count as separate morphemes all auxiliaries (*is, have, will, can, must, would*). All catenatives (e.g., *gonna, wanna, hafta*) are counted as two morphemes. Count as separate morphemes all inflections, for example, possessive (s), plural (s), third person singular (s), regular past (d), progressive (ing).
10. Count signs as multiple morphemes that conform to spoken English grammar (e.g., HAVE-TO = 2, DON'T KNOW = 3, A-LITTLE-BIT = 3, etc.) but might be signed with a single sign.
11. If the sign system uses several signs to represent a single English word (e.g., in SEE-1: *motorcycle* = 3 signs; in ASL and Signed English: *today* = 2 signs), count it as one morpheme.

12.  Calculate the MLV by dividing the total number of morphemes by the number of utterances.

***Sign-to-Voice Ratio.*** A sign-to-voice ratio can be calculated to provide information about the amount of what was signed in an English-based system as compared to what was said (using the morpheme as the unit of measurement). To compute the ratio, take the total number of signed morphemes in the sample and divide it by the total number of voiced morphemes in the sample. The equation would look like this:

$$\frac{\text{total signed morphemes}}{\text{total voiced morphemes}} = \frac{130}{150}$$

$$= 86 \text{ percent}$$

The resulting number is a percentage of what was signed as compared to what was said. We would suggest that this ratio should be above 80 percent for adults signers across a variety of contexts. The sign-to-voice ratio of hearing-impaired children has not been studied.

***Semantic Intact Ratio.*** A *semantic intact* ratio provides information about how the meaning that was conveyed through speech is coded with sign in a sign system. To compute the semantic intact ratio, take the total number of utterances in which the meaning that was spoken was also signed (refer to Bloom and Lahey, 1978, Chapter 6, for a useful taxonomy), and divide it by the total number of utterances in the language sample. The equation would look like this:

$$\frac{\text{total number of utterances in which meaning is intact}}{\text{total number of utterances in language sample}} = \frac{x}{100}$$

The result is a percentage. Work by Luetke-Stahlman (in press) has indicated that 50 teachers of hearing-impaired students had a mean semantic intacted ratio of 74 percent. We would recommend that adults try to have

a ratio that is above 80 percent across a variety of contexts. The following are examples of intact utterances:

1.  I need a    little bit    of that
    I NEED    LITTLE-BIT    THAT
2.  I don't know    who   did it
    DON'T KNOW WHO DID
3.  Mommy,  come to    the store
    MOTHER COME TO    STORE
4.  We  need   a lot of hats
    WE NEED MANY HAT HAT HAT

## CODING FOR LANGUAGE USE

A language sample can be coded for both *utterance level* and *conversational level* use skills. An utterance level coding involves deciding how the student was using language to request, respond, describe, and so forth. A coding at the conversational level would involve diverse skills, such as initiating a conversation, maintaining a conversation, and so on. A suggested taxonomy for coding use skills is listed in Exhibit 5.3, which includes an example of coding as well (Luetke-Stahlman, 1987). The example has been coded at the utterance level, using behaviors listed in the taxonomy. This taxonomy (based on the taxonomies of Clark, 1978 and Dore, 1978) has been useful in assessing the English language abilities of young hearing-impaired students (Luetke-Stahlman, 1987). A language sample coded for use, content, and form behaviors appears as Exhibit 5.4. Use taxonomies of Bereiter and Englemann (1966) and Wells (1975) appear in Exhibit 5.5 and are suggested for older students. If a particular student is not using all the possible or expected use behaviors (at both the utterance and conversational levels), then these behaviors could be set as objectives for future intervention.

Applebee (1978) provides useful conversational stages for dialogue assessment. These include "heaps" (a series of unconnected utterances), narratives, unfocused chains (inci-

**EXHIBIT 5.3.** A pragmatic skills taxonomy

## Utterance-Level Skills

*Requests*

1. Makes a yes-no request ("Is this a cake?")
2. Asks a wh- question ("Where's Thomas?")
3. Makes an action request ("Give me milk.")
4. Makes a permission request ("Can I go?")
5. Asks a rhetorical question ("This one?")

*Responses*

6. Answers a yes-no question (affirmatively or negatively)
7. Answers a wh- question ("Kent is here.")
8. Agrees with another's previous statement
9. Disagrees with another's previous statement
10. Complies with a request
11. Refuses to comply with a request
12. Qualifies or clarifies a previous utterance

*Performatives*

13. Establishes a fantasy; role plays (labels a block "a train")
14. Protests
15. Jokes
16. Initiates, continues, or ends a game ("You can't catch me.")
17. Makes a claim ("I'm first.")
18. Gives a warning
19. Teases

*Descriptions*

20. Identifies by labeling ("This is a girl.")
21. Establishes possession ("That's Carmen's.")
22. Represents an event, action, or process ("I'm making a doll.")
23. Represents properties ("That's a blue car.")
24. Represents location ("I live far away.")

## Conversational Skills and Devices

25. Gives new information
26. Varies the communication style (depending on audience or social situation)
27. Selects a topic
28. Introduces a topic
29. Maintains a topic
30. Makes returns ("Oh." "Uh-huh." "Okay.")
31. Changes a topic
32. Terminates a topic
33. Takes turns
34. Repairs a conversation
35. Checks a listener's comprehension of a topic
36. Interrupts a conversation
37. Uses boundary markers ("Hi. . .Bye.")
38. Uses polite markers ("Please . . . Thanks.")

(continued)

**EXHIBIT 5.3.** (Continued)

| Other (Not for Communication) |
| --- |

39. Talks to self

40. Uses "hollow" comments

41. Uses imitation

| An Example of Bimodal Transciption: A Father Talking to His Three-Year-Old Son |
| --- |

Matt
MATT

| Let's get going now and play<br>LET GET GOING NOW AND PLAY<br>    around a little bit<br>    AROUND    LITTLE BIT | request |
| What would you like to do?<br>WHAT WOULD YOU LIKE TO DO? | request |
| Put the people downstairs in<br>PUT THE PEOPLE DOWNSTAIRS IN<br>    the castle hmm?<br>    CASTLE ? | request |
| I found a tractor to drive<br>I FOUND A TRACTOR TO DRIVE | performative |
| | description |
| Just like my tractor at home<br>    LIKE MY TRACTOR AT HOME | |
| My new tractor<br>MY    TRACTOR | description |
| I bumped your lady.<br>I BUMP YOUR LADY | description |
| Will that lady be mad?<br>WILL THAT LADY BE MAD? | request |
| No<br>NO | response |

**EXHIBIT 5.4.** Example of a bimodal language sample

| | V-MLU | V-Semantics | V-Pragmatics |
| --- | --- | --- | --- |
| 1. Brian, Brian your turn | 3 | Notice and Possession | 21, 17 |
| 2. What did you draw? | 5 | Question, Time, Action | 2 |
| 3. Look; good boy, you get a happy face today. | 9 | Notice, Attribution, Action, Time | 3, 22, 23 |
| 4. Thanks | 1 | (none) | 38 |
| 5. Stephan, look. | 2 | Notice | |
| 6. David? Where is David? | 3 | Question and Locative State (or locative action) | 2 |
| 7. Maybe he is sick.<br>MAY BE | 4 | Epistemic and State | 25, 22 |
| 8. I hope not | 3 | State | 9 |

**EXHIBIT 5.4.** (Continued)

|  | V-MLU | V-Semantics | V-Pragmatics |
|---|---|---|---|
| 9. <u>Sit on you bottom.</u><br>       BOT + M | 4 | Action and Possession | 3 |
| 10. <u>Stephan's turn</u> | 3 | Possession | 21, 17 |
| 11. <u>Stephan, what did you draw today?</u> | 7 | Notice, Time, Action | 2 |
| 12. <u>Your picture was of windows.</u><br>    PICT + R    WIND + O + S | 6 | Possession, Time, Action, Quantity | 12 |
| 13. <u>Stephan drew two windows.</u><br>        WIND + O + S | 6 | Action, Time, Quantity | 22, 23 |
| 14. <u>Tell me.</u> | 2 | Action and Dative | 3 |
| 15. <u>Yes, tell me.</u> | 3 | Action | 3, 30 |
| 16. <u>Sheneka, what did you draw today?</u> | 7 | Time, Action, Notice | 2 |
| 17. <u>a robot</u> | 2 | Existence | 12, 20 |
| 18. <u>two robots</u> | 3 | Quantity | 12, 20, 23 |
| 19. <u>Chris, what did you draw?</u> | 6 | <u>Notice</u>, Time, Action | 2, 27 |
| 20. <u>at the fair?</u> | 3 | Locative State | 5, 12, 29 |
| 21. <u>Was it a scary ride?</u> | 6 | Time, Attribution | 1, 12, 29 |
| 22. <u>You were writing something today because</u> <u>you liked the ride?</u> | 12 | Time, Action, Causality | 1, 29, 12 |
| 23. <u>a what?</u> | 2 | Existence | 2, 29, 12 |
| 24. <u>That's right, and Liz has helped you draw</u> a maze<br>    M-A-Z-E | 12 | <u>Specifier</u>, <u>Attribution</u>, <u>Coordination</u>, Time, Action | 29, 22, 30 |
| 25. <u>It's for me?</u> | 4 | Dative | 29, 1, 2 |
| 26. <u>You didn't write the name down.</u> | 8 | Time and Nonexistence | 22, 27 |
| 27. <u>Write it again.</u> | 3 | Action and Recurrence | 3, 29 |
| 28. <u>Thank you for waiting patiently.</u> | 7 | Action, Time, Attribution | 38, 22 |
| 29. <u>Not that!</u> | 2 | Rejection and Specifier | 9, 12 |
| 30. <u>Okay, try one more time.</u> | 4 | <u>Action</u>, <u>Quantity</u>, <u>Time</u> | 3, 30 |
| 31. <u>That's not a pencil?</u> | 5 | Specifier and Denial | 20, 9, 12 |
| 32. <u>Not a pencil</u> | 3 | Denial | 12 |
| 33. <u>ok</u> | 1 | (none) | 30 |
| 34. <u>Sheneka is in her chair.</u> | 5 | Locative State | 22 |
| 35. <u>Sheneka's turn</u> | 3 | Possession | 21, 17 |
| 36. <u>good girl</u> | 2 | Attribution | 29, 9, 23 |
| 37. <u>I want it.</u> | 3 | State | 3 |
| 38. <u>I have it.</u> | 3 | Possession | 21 |
| 39. <u>OK, you can have it, but then give it back.</u> | 10 | Mood, Possession, Antithesis, Time, Dative | 3, 22 |
| 40. <u>You would?</u> | 2 | Mood | 12, 5 |
| 41. <u>I don't know.</u> | 4 | Epistemic | 7 |
| 42. <u>Write your name and give it to me.</u> | 8 | Action, Possession, Coordination, Dative | 3 |
| 43. <u>Yes</u> | 1 | Epistemic | 6 |

(*continued*)

**EXHIBIT 5.4.** (Continued)

| | V-MLU | V-Semantics | V-Pragmatics |
|---|---|---|---|
| 44. <u>Wait.</u> | 1 | Action | 3 |
| 45. <u>I think you are right.</u> | 5 | State and Attribution | 8 |
| 46. <u>No, mom is down the hall.</u> | 6 | Rejection and Locative State | 9 |
| 47. <u>Another one?</u> | 2 | Recurrence and Quantity | 5 |
| 48. <u>His paper is over there.</u> | 4 | Possession and Locative State | 24 |
| 49. <u>That should do it.</u> | 4 | Specifier, Mood, Action | 17 |
| 50. <u>Fine</u> | 1 | Attribution | 30 |

Voiced MLU = __4.3__ semantic intact ratio = __90%__
Signed MLU = __3.8__ sign-to-voice ratio = __89%__

*Note:* Underlining on the left side of the page represents words or parts of words that are both signed and spoken; underlining on the right side of the page represents semantic information that would not be credited for sign.

**EXHIBIT 5.5.** Use taxonomies for older students

Bereiter and Englemann (1966) list the following:

1. *To instruct*: provide specific sequential directions
2. *To inquire*: seek understanding through asking questions
3. *To test*: investigate the logic of a statement
4. *To describe*: tell about, giving necessary information to identify
5. *To compare and contrast*: show how things are similar and different
6. *To explain*: define terms by providing specific examples
7. *To analyze*: break down a statement into its component parts, telling what each means and how they are related
8. *To hypothesize*: Make an assumption in order to test a statement's logical or empirical consequences
9. *To deduce*: arrive at a conclusion by reasoning; infer
10. *To evaluate*: weigh and judge the relative importance of an idea

Wells (1975) describes five communicative functions:

1. *Controlling*: communication acts in which the participant's dominant function is to control behavior (e.g., commanding, offering, suggesting, permitting, threatening, warning, prohibiting, contracting, refusing, bargaining, rejecting, acknowledging, justifying, persuading, arguing)
2. *Feeling*: communication acts that express and respond to feelings and attitudes (e.g., exclaiming, expressing a state or an attitude, taunting, commiserating, tattling, blaming, disagreeing, rejecting)
3. *Informing*: communication acts in which the participant's function is to offer or seek information (e.g., stating information, questioning, answering, justifying, naming, pointing out an object, demonstrating, explaining, acknowledging)
4. *Ritualizing*: communication acts that serve primarily to maintain social relationships and to facilitate social interaction (e.g., greeting, taking leave, participating in verbal games such as pat-a-cake, reciting, taking turns in conversations; participating in culturally appropriate speech modes such as teasing, shocking, punning, praying; and demonstrating culturally appropriate amenities)
5. *Imagining*: communication acts that cast the participant in imaginary situations, and include creative behaviors such as role playing fantasizing, speculating, dramatizing, theorizing, and storytelling

SOURCE: Carl Bereiter/Siegfried Englemann, TEACHING DISADVANTAGED CHILDREN IN THE PRESCHOOL, © 1966. Reprinted by permission of Prentice Hall, Inc., Englewood Cliffs, New Jersey.

dents leading from one to another but not linked cohesively), focused chains (incidents that are sequenced and related to a central idea and joined appropriately), and narrative (a complete, well-formed story). Taxonomies can be adapted to fit your needs, so you should not hesitate to add behaviors to a use listing provided to suit your needs. However, Duchan (1988) stated that, although a functional coding approach to the assessment of pragmatics provides a way to assess opaque communicative acts, includes nonverbal communication in its procedure, and focuses on what the student is trying to accomplish rather than on what the adult deems important (p. 35), the analyses can be time consuming. Duchan cautions that coders should not presume that each utterance has only one intent and should not ignore the context in which each utterance was used. Duchan reminds us, as well, that currently available taxonomies are based on the behaviors of hearing children and should not be taken as exemplary.

## SETTING PRIORITIES FOR INTERVENTION

Once a language sample has been taken and coded, you must decide how to use the information to set goals and objectives for individual students. In Exhibit 5.6, use behaviors are organized in a developmental sequence by phases (based on the information provided in Exhibit 5.2). If a child demonstrates a particular behavior in five different contexts (Bloom & Lahey, 1978), successful use of that behavior can be recorded on the grid. In this way, priorities for intervention can be decided. For example, data for the use abilities of Mary Pattie, a 2-year, 7-month-old deaf girl, is charted on the grid in Exhibit 5.6. Appropriate objectives would be that she answer routine questions and ask "What is that?" Next, objectives would need to be set in all but one of the behaviors listed for a

hearing 2-3-year-old child. Thus, Mary Pattie's teacher could set objectives to facilitate the acquisition of Phase 2, then Phase 3 (etc.) use behaviors as indicated.

Long-range goals for language use might be based on an informal assessment, using the skills listed in Exhibit 5.2. Objectives would be written as subskills of the proposed goals. For example:

### Goal

Kent will demonstrate 2-year-old use abilities by April.

### Objectives

1. Kent will express five requests for objects during a one-week period.
2. Kent will express five comments during "show and tell" in one week.
3. Kent will initiate a dialogue with a hearing peer twice during free play in one week.

## USE INTERVENTION

For more than a century, teachers have struggled with the problem of how to teach English to hearing-impaired students. Unfortunately, there is little research available that indicates the advantage of one language approach over another, and it has been shown that, at best, the effectiveness of each program is limited (Clark & Stewart, 1986; Moores, 1987). We believe that teachers should strive for *communicative competence* as they are planning the facilitation of language goals; that is, students should be able to communicate effectively in a variety of contexts and for a variety of purposes, using language functionally and purposefully to meet their own needs (Goodman, 1986).

The grid provided as Exhibit 5.7 is useful in assessing use competence. It requires that significant adults assess a student's use

**EXHIBIT 5.6.** A developmental sequence of the skills (Luetke-Stahlman, 1987) taken from research compiled by the author and adapted from Bloom and Lahey (1978)

Name: _____

Date: _____

Key
# = Number of times the function was observed used by the student

**Phase 1: ½–1 years** columns:
- Reproduces event, tries to get others to participate
- Interacts with environment
- Expresses awareness of self
- Satisfies material needs and obtains them from others
- Controls behavior of others
- Repeats vocalization or sign
- Plays communication games

**Phase 2: 1–2 years** columns:
- Makes requests
- Expresses rejection
- Expresses comment
- Expresses routine
- Shows onset of dialogue
- Increases frequency
- Awareness of turn taking
- Answers routine questions
- Asks "What is that?" routinely
- Carries on conversations with self
- Initiates conversations
- Concerned with own intent
- Participates in discourse by using linguistically related utterances

**Phase 3: 2–3 years / Phase 4: 3–4 years** columns:
- Uses roles in play
- Dramatizes
- Engages in peer conversations
- Maintains conversations
- Uses "childrenese" with younger children
- Employs queries to maintain conversation
- Initiates conversations
- Uses hints
- Uses signing
- Makes metalinguistic comments

Rows: Phase 1: ½–1 years — Student A, Student B, Student C, Student D, Student E; Phase 2: 1–2 years — Student A, Student B, Student C, Student D, Student E; Phase 3: 2–3 years — Student A, Student B, Student C, Student D, Student E; Phase 4: 3–4 years — Student A, Student B, Student C, Student D, Student E.

Recorded entries:

Student A (Phase 1): #5+ for "Reproduces event...", "Interacts with environment", "Expresses awareness of self", "Satisfies material needs and obtains them from others", "Controls behavior of others", "Repeats vocalization or sign", "Plays communication games".

Student A (Phase 2): #5+ for "Makes requests", "Expresses rejection", "Expresses comment", "Expresses routine", "Shows onset of dialogue", "Increases frequency", "Awareness of turn taking"; #1 for "Answers routine questions"; #2 for "Initiates conversations"; #5+ for "Concerned with own intent".

**EXHIBIT 5.7.** Assessing the environments in which language use skills are used by the student

| | | Environments | | |
| --- | --- | --- | --- | --- |
| | Arrival | Opening | Bathroom | Other School Contexts |
| **Requests** | | | | |
| Yes/No request | | | | |
| Wh-question | | | | |
| Action request | | | √ | |
| Permission request | | | | |
| Rhetorical question or request | | | | |
| **Responses** | | | | |
| Answers Yes/No questions | | √ | | |
| Answers wh-questions | | √ | | |
| Agreement with other's previous statement | | | | |
| Etc. (see Exhibit 5.3) | | | | |

√ = Child demonstrates behavior at least once on five different days

of language in several age-appropriate school contexts. Listed vertically in this grid are the use skills that the target student had not demonstrated. Listed horizontally are environments representative of those experienced by the student. As an example, in Exhibit 5.7 the data for 2;7-year-old Mary Pattie has been charted by her preschool teacher. Significant adults in her environment would each want to evaluate Mary Pattie in these environments and look closely at their own language practices to ensure that they are providing her with opportunities to communicate for a variety of purposes. They would list home, community, or school environments horizontally across the top of the grid and track her use of English.

## Strategies for Intentional Language Intervention

If providing environmental opportunities for language use do not prove to be successful, Fey (1986) suggests techniques that are appropriate for students who are reluctant or unable to use language in interactions with others. He defines *planned intentional* (as opposed to *spontaneous incidental*) language intervention as that in which appropriate goals for each session have been set and the adult arranges the environment to increase the likelihood that opportunities for selected language targets will be provided. For example, you could adapt the free-play time that typically is scheduled into the preschooler's day into a *facilitative play period* during which you deliberately assist in language acquisition. During this time, you would interact with the children, modeling play and language behaviors, suggesting roles, and so on. Your role should be one of a highly accepting, responsive social partner. You would follow the student's lead and play with the toys or materials that the student had chosen, acknowledging or commenting on behavior as the student plays. To use the techniques described next with older students, you would need to let the student control the situation or topic at various times throughout the day.

***Following the Student's Lead.***    In following a student's lead, you would wait for the student to initiate a behavior and then you would interpret that action as meaningful and communicative. Using your knowledge of the child's language use development (determined from the information obtained by language sampling, you would respond to the student's behavior at a level slightly more developmentally advanced than the student's level (i.e., *input + 1*). For example, if a 2-year-old child were offered a toy and shook her head "no" (e.g., rejection), you might say and sign "no, don't want it." If she knocked down blocks, you might say and sign "down," "fell down," or "blocks fell down."

***Self-Talk (and Sign).***    You can use two strategies to encourage the noncommunicator to talk and sign: the strategies of *self-talk* and *parallel talk* are appropriate for both preschool and elementary-age students. *Self-talk* (Van Riper, 1963) is defined as talking (cueing or signing) out loud to oneself and verbalizing what the communicator is seeing, hearing, doing, and feeling. No demands are made on the student to attend to the input, although the intervention will be more successful in that regard if the facilitator uses materials and actions that are age and cognition appropriate and that are of interest to the child. For example, as you play cars with a 2-year-old, you might say and sign, "my car goes," "zoom, zoom," "my car goes fast." Enthusiastic but appropriately paced self-talk can often lead to play or activity interactions (Fey, 1986).

***Parallel Talk (and Sign).***    The significant adult shifts from his or her own thoughts and actions to assertions about the actions and objects of the student when the strategy of *parallel talk* is utilized (Fey, 1986). Again, no demands are made of the student to respond, but when the appropriate (*input + 1*, as explained in Chapter 1) language is paired with the student's play or work, the assumption is that the student will notice the language (Carroll, 1986). Let us contrast self-talk and parallel talk with the 2-year-old just mentioned. You might both play with cars, and as the student moves the blue car quickly up an imaginary hill, you might say and sign, "your car goes fast," "zoom goes that blue one," "up the hill you go." This would be parallel talk.

To model responses, requests, performatives, descriptions, and conversational and device skills, you would need to role play and invent conversations with toys or tasks. For example, you might notice during social studies time that a student forgot his pencil. You could move near the student and ask, "Can I get a pencil?," as if the student were asking the question to your now vacant chair. An important feature of parallel talk is that utterances are produced that are related to the student's own interests or needs and are genuine (see Chapter 1).

***Informative Talk.*** When students are working or playing with peers who do not sign or cue, you will need to use the strategy of *informative talk*. This form of talk may be in the style of interpreting what the other student has said or what the hearing-impaired student has signed or cued. It may be also that you will describe or comment on the actions of the student's peer, much as you would do using self-talk (and sign). For example, let us assume that two students are mixing paint at a science center.

| | |
|---|---|
| **BETTE:** | (hearing) Red and blue make purple—see? |
| **TEACHER:** | (to Sue, who is hearing-impaired) Bette said that red and blue make purple. (informative talk) |
| **SUE:** | Yellow and red make <u>YELLOW AND RED MAKE</u> orange. <u> </u> ORANGE. |
| **TEACHER:** | (to Sue) Bette is painting with the orange you made. |
| **SUE:** | I am painting with <u>I AM PAINTING WITH</u> orange. <u> </u> ORANGE. |
| **TEACHER:** | (to Bette) Sue said she is painting with orange. (informative talk) |

***Expansions.*** *Expansions* are responses that repeat the student's prior utterance and add relevant details. This technique would be a suitable intervention strategy to use if you want to expand utterances within the categories provided for use as well as those of content and form.

## Making Juice (adapted from Constable, 1983)

| | |
|---|---|
| **CHILD 1:** | "No! Put the top on, then shake." |
| **TEACHER:** | (using a sentence completion strategy) "If I don't put the top on. . . ." |
| **CHILD 1:** | "The juice come out." |
| **TEACHER:** | "The juice might come out if I don't put the top on." (expansion) |
| **CHILD 2:** | "We hafta put the top on or the juice will come out." |
| **TEACHER:** | "That's right! Here, you put this top on, then the juice won't spill out when we shake it." |
| **CHILD 2:** | "I put the top on, then the juice won't spill." |

## Saboteur Strategies

Lucas (1980) described the role of "saboteur" as that in which the significant adult changes the organized, predictable environment of the classroom into one that needs constant verbal (spoken or signed) interaction to produce the desired consequences. Lucas suggested that significant adults become saboteurs rather than "doers" for students.

Much of the success of use intervention hinges on the significant adult's ability to create real needs to communicate in routine situations that are familiar to the student. For the toddler, this often means identifying moments in which the child is motivated to use language. In these situations, you have to allow the child time to use the language that he or she is capable of using and not move too quickly to solve a problem or to satisfy the child.

A necessary ingredient to utilizing yourself as a saboteur would be to first establish familiar sequences and routines. These routines begin, progress, and end in essentially the same way each time they occur (Duchan, 1983). They can be manipulated because the student has a *script* or expectation of each routine in mind. Scripts help students organize the environment. They are mental representations of events and the temporally and spatially related acts that typically characterize such events (Fey, 1986). Scripts encode what occurred previously and contain an expectation of what will transpire. Many manipulations of the script can be performed, creating the need for functional language (Fey, 1986). Functional language gives the student control of the environment, as well as continued interaction with adults. Constable (1983) has organized the manipulation of the *nonlinguistic* environment into three areas to set the stage for the saboteur; that is you are manipulating an object, an activity, or the storage of something is being manipulated so that the student will use language functionally.

**Violation of Routine Event** *(Constable & VanKleck, 1985; Lucas, 1980).* In this strategy, a familiar step in an activity is omitted or performed incorrectly. For example, if you were facilitating the use of performatives such as protests, warnings, and teases, you might try to send the students to music class at the wrong time, ask the wrong student to join a reading group, or sit down to a lesson without having on hand the usual, necessary supplies.

**Withholding Objects and Turns.** Here the teacher mischievously excludes a student (from a group, in a line to leave the room, in a game, while handing out materials, etc.) so that the student will have to perform some type of conversational act (e.g., make a request for attention, action, or information) in order to have a turn or obtain an object that is crucial to completing some larger task. Storing materials in view but out of the reach of young children would be a strategy that would fit in this category, also.

**Violation of Object Function or Manipulating and Hiding Objects.** Lucas (1980) has suggested derivations on this theme. She lists "environmental problems," such as scissors that are taped together, plugged glue bottles, empty or dried-up pens, broken pencil leads, coat sleeves turned inside-out (so children

will need help fixing them), not enough chairs, not enough snacks, cups with holes, missing toy pieces, flat balls, short jump ropes, missing colors and paints, water faucets turned off tightly, and so on. Use of these strategies for intervention of meaning will be discussed in the next chapter.

## SUMMARY

Language use has been discussed in this chapter as if it were a separate, rather than interactional, component of language. This contrived organizational scheme allowed for the presentation of information regarding assessment, the setting of goals and objectives, and various intervention strategies that was discussed so that bimodal abilities of preschool and elementary-aged children might be improved. However, in reality, language components interact, and intervention and subsequent acquisition of a skill in one area will affect most certainly the other areas as well. It is our hope that information which we have provided in this chapter will allow significant adults to consider the important area of pragmatic language development as they work with hearing-impaired students. Also in this chapter, language sampling was recommended for assessing genuine language behaviors. Specific information on taking a bimodal language sample—in what contexts, for how long, the use of videotaping, coding procedures, and ways to analyze—were described.

## ACTIVITIES

1. Assess the language use abilities of three children of different ages.
2. Take a language sample and critique it based on the conditions described in the chapter (e.g., representational, length of time, etc.).
3. Calculate MLU and semantic intact ratio on a 50-word bimodal language sample.
4. Using Exhibit 5.6, enter some hypothetical information about an 8-year-old boy, Doug.

Write two use objectives based on this data.

5. Visit a child care program and follow one child. Use a grid, like the one begun in Exhibit 5.7, to chart how language is used in the program. Discuss whether the child is being given sufficient opportunities to use language by his or her teachers.

6. Pick a partner and practice self-talk, parallel talk, informative talk, and expansions.

7. Brainstorm 10 ideas as a saboteur and list the expected language use results for each action or activity.

# CHAPTER 6

# Language Content

## OVERVIEW

*Language content* is defined and discussed in this chapter, and it is separated artificially from use and form so that assessment and *goal* priorities can be explained. Because we believe that there is an advantage in using *informal* measures to assess a student's abilities to comprehend and utilize semantic information, we have not included information regarding formal tests that could be used (please see Moeller, 1988, for a discussion of the disadvantages of using such measures). Our focus here is on informal assessment tools and intervention strategies that have been proven successful with hearing-impaired students. We emphasize the interventions of the teacher as saboteur, visualizations, and semantic mapping.

---

### CHAPTER TOPICS

Content Defined
Content Assessment
Goals and Objectives
Content Intervention

---

## CONTENT DEFINED

Results from research with language disordered students have suggested that attention to content goals should precede concern with form goals. McAnnally, Rose, and Quigley (1987) stated that only after students have conquered the basic components of meaning do they attend to syntactic elements of language. We have ordered our chapters with regard to use (Chapter 5), content (Chapter 6), and form (Chapter 7) with these thoughts in mind.

*Language content* or *semantics* can be subdivided into three areas (Bloom & Lahey, 1978) for assessment and intervention:

1. *object knowledge* (that of particular objects and classes of objects)
2. *object relations* (existence, disappearance, attribution, quantity, action, location, and possession)
3. *event relations* (time, causality, mood, epistemic)

Teachers need to feel comfortable defining, assessing, and intervening with language *content* in each of these areas, since an appraisal of these abilities can provide them with information as to a student's (and not your) intended meaning in communicative utterances or conversations.

## CONTENT ASSESSMENT

Typically, the majority of hearing-impaired students have not had the environmental linguistic advantage discussed in Chapter 1 (Meadow, 1980). Work by Kantor (1977), Lucas (1980), and Newport and Ashbrook (1977) has demonstrated that hearing-impaired students develop content abilities in a similar but slower manner, as compared to peers who have acquired language normally. Given the assumption that hearing-impaired students will develop content abilities in a developmental order, we can use information from normal language research to guide us in our assessment endeavors.

### "Normal Language" Content Development

There is no evidence for assigning meaning to children's behaviors during the *preintentional period* of development, when language is not yet used for a deliberate purpose. (Please refer to the cognitive development stages listed in Chapter 1.) Infants below approximately 8 months of age simply do not understand what significant others are saying or signing (Miller, 1981). When infants do start to encode meaning, the developmental sequence through which they evolve is remarkably similar across various *types of language users* (e.g., monolingual, bilingual, bimodal, etc.). This phenomenon is demonstrated in Exhibit 6.1, which illustrates normal language behavior across children with various language backgrounds. The content taxonomy provided by Bloom and Lahey (1978) (organized in phases of development that become more and more complex) serves as the horizontal axis in this exhibit, and the age of the child serves as the vertical axis. The exhibit allows us to make a comparison of the *expressive language* abilities of hearing bilingual, hearing monolingual (one language), hearing bimodal, and hearing-impaired bilingual/bimodal language users. It illustrates that:

No one type of user evidenced earlier acquisition than another

The sequence of stages provided by Bloom and Lahey (1978) were followed.

Information such as this assists teachers of hearing-impaired students, who must look beyond monolingual (i.e. English) language literature, in defining "normal language development;" that is, the results demonstrate that, when given the necessary linguistic environment (as discussed in Chapter 1) in which to acquire language:

All children begin to express language at about the same age if they have been provided with an appropriate environment and if their ability to do so is not necessarily dependent on their mode of communication or on their ability to hear.

Children exposed to a bilingual or bimodal language environment are neither cognitively advantaged nor cognitively disadvantaged.

Professionals working with hearing-impaired students can benefit from referral to developmental information based on studies using all four types of language acquirers; that is, these four types of students evidence "normal" language acquisition.

### Content Tools

Word comprehension begins to occur for most children at around the end of the first year. Such comprehension is highly dependent on predictable contexts and routines that involve familiar people. Knowing this, we will find that the comprehension strategies provided by Chapman and Miller (1980) are helpful in both assessing young hearing-impaired children or older students with multiple handicaps in the area of language content and in providing significant adults with guidance in facili-

**EXHIBIT 6.1.** Similarity of content across four types of language users

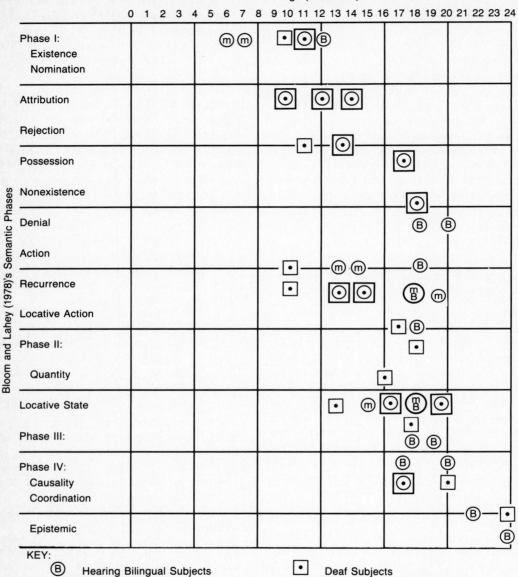

**EXHIBIT 6.2.** Content abilities of young children and guidelines for adults (Chapman & Miller, 1980)

| Child | Significant Adult |
|---|---|
| 1. *Attends to object mentioned*. When the adult says or signs "Where's the X?" the child looks at, that is, attends, to the object mentioned. However, the child will not retrieve an absent object (one that cannot be seen), even if the object is located in a familiar place. | 1. Request the child to attend to objects and events in the "here and now," within predictable contexts and routines that involve familiar people and objects. |
| 2. *Gives evidence of notice*. The child follows adult's line of regard by looking at objects that the adult looks at and, when possible, acts on the objects. | 2. Within predictable contexts and routines, talk about (in voice, cues, or sign) familiar people, events, objects, and wait for the child to give evidence of notice. |
| 3. *Does what adult usually does*. The child responds to a request by attending to an object in a conventional manner. For example, if the child is holding an apple and the mother says or signs, "Take a bite," and the child complies, this is not evidence that the child comprehends the adult's input. We can only be certain that the child comprehends if, when holding the apple, the adult gives an unexpected command such as "Kiss it" and the child gives the apple a kiss. | 3. Make unexpected requests with familiar objects, events, and objects to check the child's comprehension. |

SOURCE: R. Chapman and J. Miller, "Analyzing language and communication in the child." In R. L. Schiefelbusch (Ed.) *Nonspeech, Language and* Communication. Baltimore: University Park Press, 1980.

tating language development (see Exhibit 6.2). You may also want to refer back to Exhibit 1.6 to compare a student's content abilities with other developing behaviors.

A content taxonomy that is useful with children who express two-word combinations appears in Exhibit 6.3. It can be used as an assessment tool. Additional content charts, such as those explained for the area of language use (Exhibit 5.2), appear in Exhibit

**EXHIBIT 6.3.** The nine most prevalent relational meanings expressed in hearing, monolingual children's two-word combinations (Garwood and Fewell 1983)

| | Gesture | Sign | Sign and Voice | Voice Alone |
|---|---|---|---|---|
| 1. *Demonstrative-Entity*: The child names an object or person and may point to or pick up the referent. Examples include: "see boy," "here truck," "there car," "here doggie," and "that chair." | | | | |
| 2. *Negation-Entity*: Negation is signaled by a linguistic marker (e.g., *no, not, all gone*) and accompanied corresponding nonlinguistic evidence of negation in the immediate context. Three semantic categories (nonexistence, rejection, and denial) are consolidated and considered as a single relationship. Negation-entity examples are "no bubble," said after the child has been unsuccessful at blowing a soap bubble, and "no want," said as the child pushed a toy aside. | | | | |

*(continued)*

**EXHIBIT 6.3.** (Continued)

| | Gesture | Sign | Sign and Voice | Voice Alone |
|---|---|---|---|---|
| 3. *Agent-Action*: An *agent* is someone or something, usually, but not necessarily, animate, which is perceived to have its own motivating force and causes an action or process. An *action* involves perceivable movement (e.g., *sleep, drive, eat, sing, go*). Agent and action examples are "daddy eat," as the child watches daddy at the dinner table, and "car go," as the car moves down a ramp. | | | | |
| 4. *Action-Object*: An *object* is someone or something either suffering a change of state or simply receiving the force of an action. An object may be the name of a person or thing or a pronoun like *it* or *that*. Action-object examples are "brush teeth," as the child is brushing his or her teeth, and "eat it," as the child is eating dinner. | | | | |
| 5. *Agent-Object*: The agent and object in this relationship are viewed in direct interaction when the person initiates movement on an entity. Agent-object examples are "doggie bone," where *eat* is implied by the context, and "mommy door," where *open* is implied by the context. | | | | |
| 6. *Action-Locative*: A *locative* is the place or locus of an action. A locative can also mark the spatial orientation of an action. Early locatives almost always omit the obligatory adult preposition. Action-locative examples are "sit bed," as the child places the doll on the bed, and "boy school," as the child pretends to walk a doll to play "school". | | | | |
| 7. *Entity-Locative*: An *entity* is any thing or person having a distinct separate existence in time and space. Entity-locative examples are "mommy home," as the child looks at the mother doll in a playhouse, and "car garage," as the child puts a toy care in a playhouse garage. | | | | |
| 8. *Possessor-Possession*: Possessions name an entity more specifically than its class name can. Two forms of possession appear with high frequency and apparent productivity near the end of the second year: (1) notions of property and (2) part-whole relationships. An example of the first form of possession is "daddy chair," as the child sees daddy sitting in his chair, and an example of a part-whole possession is "mommy nose," as the child points to the mother's nose. | | | | |
| 9. *Entity-Attribute*: An *attribute* specifies some inherent characteristic of an entity that could not be known from the class alone. Examples are "big block," as the child picks up a building block, and "brown bus," as the child points to a picture of a brown van. | | | | |

SOURCE: Garwood and Fewell 1983.

6.4. These, too, are ordered developmentally for assessment and objective-setting purposes. As was obvious with the assessment of the component of language *use*, information provided by significant adults is paramount also in assessing a hearing-impaired student's content abilities. A fuller understanding of language development and the facilitation of language development is possible as adults work together to define and verify a student's abilities in each of these component areas.

As was discussed in Chapter 5, a language sampling procedure is another means of assessing a student's language (i.e., content) abilities (see Chapter 5 for collection procedures). A suggested taxonomy of skills that can be used to code the utterances in such a sample is provided in Exhibit 6.5a (Bloom & Lahey, 1978). A sample, coded for content behaviors appears in Exhibit 5.4. After the sample has been coded, it may be helpful to indicate a student's content development on a graph such as the one provided in Exhibit 6.5b. Here the taxonomy has been sequenced by phases so that priorities for content objectives can be prioritized for intervention.

**EXHIBIT 6.4.** Language content and play abilities of children (based on hearing, monolingual data and adapted for bimodal communication)

| | Gesture | Sign | Sign and Voice | Voice Alone |
|---|---|---|---|---|
| *1/2–1 Year* | | | | |
| 1. Finger or oral babbling occurs. | | | | |
| 2. Uses differential cries or gestures (requests, greeting, surprise, frustration, etc.) (Miller, 1981). | | | | |
| 3. Hands a familiar object upon a voiced and/or signed request (Cano & Schmidt, 1974). | | | | |
| 4. Comprehends several voiced, cued, or signed words (e.g., *no-no, hot*, own name) (Cano & Schmidt, 1974). | | | | |
| 5. Understands the function of a number of household objects (e.g., will demonstrate use of a spoon, cup, toy truck, hammer, etc., out of context) (McCune-Nicholich, 1981). | | | | |
| *1–2 Years* | | | | |
| 6. Utterances contain announcing words (e.g., *mama, papa, baby*, pet's name) (Miller, 1981). | | | | |
| 7. Utterances contain greeting (e.g., *hi, bye*) (Miller, 1981). | | | | |
| 8. Utterances contain existence (e.g., *there milk*) (Miller, 1981). | | | | |
| 9. Utterances contain rejection (e.g., *no*) (Miller, 1981). | | | | |
| 10. Encodes object use or acted on with object name (e.g., *milk*, as child drinks it) (Miller, 1981). | | | | |
| 11. Encodes objects that move and change (Miller, 1981). | | | | |

(*continued*)

EXHIBIT 6.4. (Continued)

| | Gesture | Sign | Sign and Voice | Voice Alone |
|---|---|---|---|---|
| 12. Uses new signed and/or voiced semantic roles (Miller, 1981):<br>a. Agent (*mama*)<br>b. Action (*go*)<br>c. Object (*ball, cup*)<br>d. Recurrence in requests for actions (*more, milk*)<br>e. Cessation (*stop*)<br>f. Disappearance (*all gone*). | | | | |
| 13. Uses signed and/or voiced object—object relations (e.g., *no pocket, there ball*) (Miller, 1981). | | | | |
| 14. Follows simple commands that are signed, cued and/or voiced. | | | | |
| 15. Points to eyes, ears, nose, and so on upon signed, cued and/or voiced request. | | | | |
| 16. Engages in autosymbolic play—the child pretends at *self-related* activities (e.g., simulates drinking from a toy baby bottle, eats from an empty spoon, closes eyes and pretends to sleep, etc.); child seems playful and is aware of pretending (McCune & Carroll, 1981). | | | | |
| 17. Engages in *single-scheme* symbolic games—the child extends symbols to include other actors or receivers of action (e.g., child feeds or grooms mother or doll) (McCune-Nicholich, 1981). | | | | |
| *2–3 Years* | | | | |
| 18. Identifies action in pictures (Cano & Schmidt, 1974). | | | | |
| 19. Understands at least three signed, cued and/or voiced prepositions (Cano & Schmidt, 1974). | | | | |
| 20. Understands signed, cued or voiced basic time words (e.g., *later, now, soon*) (Cano & Schmidt, 1974). | | | | |
| 21. Joins two or more pretend behaviors in a sequence (symbolic play) (McCune-Nicholich, 1981). | | | | |
| 22. Is capable of planning pretend actions and demonstrates this ability by<br>a. Substituting one object for another (e.g., stick acts as a horse)<br>b. Using own body to represent another person or object<br>c. Engaging in planned, realistic scenes (e.g., child puts play food in a pot, stirs, says and signs *soup* or *mommy* before feeding the mother or doll, etc., waits, asks, "more?," etc.) (McCune-Nicholich, 1971). | | | | |
| 23. Uses signs and/or voiced utterances that contain more than one semantic relationship in a single utterance (Bloom & Lahey, 1978). | | | | |
| 24. Uses signed and/or voiced utterances containing "no" to indicate disappearance, nonexistence, or nonoccurrence (Bloom & Lahey, 1978). | | | | |

**EXHIBIT 6.4.** (Continued)

| | Gesture | Sign | Sign and Voice | Voice Alone |
|---|---|---|---|---|
| 25. Uses signed and/or voiced utterances that contain attribution (Bloom & Lahey, 1978). | | | | |
| 26. Uses signed and/or voiced utterances that contain action (Bloom & Lahey, 1978). | | | | |
| 27. Uses signed and/or voiced utterances that contain locative action (Bloom & Lahey, 1978). | | | | |
| 28. Uses signed and/or voiced utterances that contain quantity (Miller, 1978). | | | | |
| 29. Uses signed and/or voiced utterances that contain possession (Miller, 1978). | | | | |
| *3–4 Years* | | | | |
| 30. Uses utterances that contain causality (Bloom & Lahey, 1978). | | | | |
| 31. Uses utterances that contain possessive (Bloom & Lahey, 1978). | | | | |
| 32. Understands use of "it" or, if ASL, POINT for referent, when it is used *anaphorically* (Bloom & Lahey, 1978). | | | | |
| 33. Signs and/or voices full name (Cano & Schmidt, 1974). | | | | |
| 34. Signs and/or voices own sex (Cano & Schmidt, 1974). | | | | |
| 35. Engages in *sociodramatic play*—games that involve two or more children, capacity for sustained interaction with a peer; there is a theme to the play, often including fantasy elements introduced from TV and stories (McCune & Carroll, 1981). | | | | |
| 36. Uses utterances that contain *coordination* (Bloom & Lahey, 1978). | | | | |
| *4–5 Years* | | | | |
| 37. Names *red, blue*, and *green* colors in sign and/or voice (Cano & Schmidt, 1974). | | | | |
| 38. Begins to show interest in signed, cued and/or voiced word meanings (Cano & Schmidt, 1974). | | | | |
| *5–6 Years* | | | | |
| 39. Gives signed and/or voiced connected accounts of recent events or experiences (Cano & Schmidt, 1974). | | | | |
| 40. Carries out more complicated signed and/or voiced three-stage commands (Cano & Schmidt, 1974). | | | | |
| 41. Begins to sign and/or voice some abstract words (Cano & Schmidt, 1974). | | | | |
| 42. Defines simple words using sign and/or voice (Cano & Schmidt, 1974). | | | | |
| 43. Makes many spontaneous corrections of grammar in sign and/or voice (Cano & Schmidt, 1974). | | | | |

(*continued*)

**EXHIBIT 6.4.** (Continued)

| | Gesture | Sign | Sign and Voice | Voice Alone |
|---|---|---|---|---|
| *6–7 Years* | | | | |
| 44. Asks the meaning of abstract words in sign and/or voice (Cano & Schmidt, 1974). | | | | |
| 45. Attempts to verbalize casual relationships in sign and/or voice (Cano & Schmidt, 1974). | | | | |
| 46. Verbalizes about differences in objects using sign and/or voice (Cano & Schmidt, 1974). | | | | |
| 47. Understands differences in time intervals (e.g., minutes compared to hours, weeks to years, seasons, etc.) (Cano & Schmidt, 1974). | | | | |
| *8 Years* | | | | |
| 48. Derivational suffixes (*-er*, *-man*, and *-ist*) understood by 90 percent of children at this age. | | | | |
| 49. Adverbial (*-ly*) produced at this age. | | | | |
| *9 Years* | | | | |
| 50. Acquires contrast. | | | | |
| 51. Depends less on visual input for recall and meaning. | | | | |
| 52. Acquires many dictionary and multiple meanings. | | | | |
| *10 Years* | | | | |
| 53. Acquires more dictionary and multiple meanings. | | | | |
| 54. Develops *temporal concept* of periodicity. | | | | |
| 55. Acquires and understands "ask." | | | | |
| *11 Years* | | | | |
| 56. Uses both reversible and nonreversible *passives* (e.g., *by*). | | | | |

## GOALS AND OBJECTIVES

As we noted in Chapter 5, goals and objectives that are written based on informal assessment tools need to be individualized for particular students and written in a manner such that behaviors are defined observably and a reasonable criterion set. For example:

### Goal

Ward will demonstrate 2-year-old content abilities by April.

### Objectives

1.  Ward will identify 10 actions when he is presented with colored pictures that display activity.
2.  Ward will demonstrate his comprehension of at least three prepositions.
3.  Ward will express from two to three contents in spontaneous utterances.
4.  Ward will express five different types of attribution in five different contexts.
5.  Ward will express three different types of quantity in three different contexts.

**EXHIBIT 6.5a.** The content taxonomy developed by Bloom and Lahey (1978)

**Existence.** The child either looks at, points to, touches, or picks up an object while naming it and pointing out its existence with a single word or question.

**Nonexistence-Disappearance.** The child makes reference to the disappearance of an object or the nonexistence of an object or action in a context in which its existence might be expected ("No." "All Gone").

**Recurrence.** The child makes reference to the reappearance of an object or another instance of an object or event.

**Rejection.** The child opposes an action or refuses an object that is in the context or imminent within the situation and uses forms of negation.

**Denial.** The child negates the identity, state, or event expressed in another's utterance or in his or her own previous utterance.

**Attribution.** The child makes reference to the properties of objects with respect to an inherent state of the object ("broken") or specification of an object that distinguishes it from others in its class ("red").

**Possession.** The child makes reference to objects within the domain of different persons ("Mommy") to indicate the possessor.

**Action.** The child refers to action that affects an object other than to change its location or to movements of actors (persons or things) in events where the movement does not affect another person or object.

**Locative Action.** The child refers to movement where the goal of the movement is a change in location of a person or object.

**Locative State.** The child refers to the relationship between a person or object and its location, where no movement established the locative relations within the context of the speech event.

**State.** The child makes reference to states of affairs usually involving persons or other animate beings.

**Quantity.** The child designates the number of objects or persons by use of a number word, plural, or adjective ("some").

**Notice.** The child refers to attention to a person, object, or event and necessarily includes a verb of notice (such as "see" or "hear").

**Time.** The child makes reference to time (ongoing, imminent, future, or past) by use of grammatical morphemes, adverbs of time, or modals and auxiliary verbs.

**Coordinate.** The child refers to two events or states that are independent of each other but are somehow bound together in space or time.

**Causality.** The child expresses an implicit or explicit cause and effect relationship between two verb relations (that is, one expressed event or state is dependent on the other for its occurrence).

**Dative.** The child designates the recipient of an object or action with or without a preposition.

**Specifier.** The child specifies a particular person, object, or event by contrastive use of the demonstrative pronouns "this" versus "that" or "these" versus "those."

**Epistemic.** The child describes a relationship between two states or an event and a state that refers to certainty or uncertainty about an event or state.

**Mood.** The child expresses an attitude about an event by the use of modal verbs ("can," "should").

**Antithesis.** The child expresses a dependency between two events or states, and the dependency is a contrast between them (e.g. . . . but . . .).

SOURCE: B. S. Bloom and M. Lahey, *Language Development and Language disorders*. New York: Macmillan Publishing Co., 1978. Reprinted by permission.

**EXHIBIT 6.5b.** A sequence of content phases, arranged by order of complexity of semantic acquisition (adapted from the taxonomy of Bloom & Lahey, 1978)

|  |  |  |  |  |  |
|---|---|---|---|---|---|
|  |  |  |  |  | Phase |
|  |  |  |  | X | Existence |
|  |  |  |  | X | Nonexistence |
|  |  |  |  | X | Recurrence |
|  |  |  |  | X | Rejection |
|  |  |  |  | X | Denial |
|  |  |  |  | X | Attribution |
|  |  |  |  | X | Possession |
|  |  |  |  | X | Action |
|  |  |  |  |  | Locate Action |
|  |  |  |  | Locative State |  |
|  |  |  | X | State |  |
|  |  |  | X | Quantity |  |
|  |  |  | Notice |  |  |
|  |  |  | Time |  |  |
|  | X | Coordinate |  |  |  |
|  |  | Causality |  |  |  |
|  |  | Dative |  |  |  |
|  |  | Specifier |  |  |  |
|  | Epistemic |  |  |  |  |
|  | Mood |  |  |  |  |
|  | Antithesis |  |  |  |  |

SOURCE: B. S. Bloom and M. Lahey, *Language Development and Language disorders*. New York: Macmillan Publishing Co., 1978. Reprinted by permission.

## CONTENT INTERVENTION

After goals and objectives have been established, you should make an environmental inventory of those locations experienced by your students where opportunities to facilitate desired content abilities would occur naturally. Using Exhibit 6.4 as an example to fos-

ter the skills typically acquired by 2–3-year-olds, you would need to find opportunities that involved actions, locations of people and objects, time factors, and so on.

Language is best learned when the focus is not on language form but on the meaning being communicated (Goodman, 1986). The strategies of self-talk (cueing and/or sign) and parallel talk (cueing and/or sign) discussed in Chapter 5 can be utilized to promote the student's use of unacquired meaning. For example, the significant adult can talk about things that he or she sees while playing (existence), or might need to act out a particular play theme (nonexistence), or can describe (encoding action, locative action, state, locative state, quantity, possession, time, etc.). These procedures can stimulate the student's formation and testing of hypotheses about the association between word combinations and the relationships among objects, states, and relations in the nonlinguistic world (Fey, 1986).

Repetition is a helpful strategy in facilitating the development of both language content and form. When you say something to a student and the student appears to be particularly attentive, you might repeat it again, stressing the new word or phrase (or the form) that is a target for that child. Here is an example.

> KAREN: It's going fast, Mr. Relly.
>
> TEACHER: Yes, it's going faster and faster—faster and faster.

The use of expansions, in which significant adults repeat the student's initial utterance and supply added *semantic* or syntactic information, is another useful intervention strategy to facilitate content development. Matching expansions to the intents and interests of students should aid in the comprehension of meaning, and teachers who work with older students should find this to be a useful technique in facilitating the development of complex English (e.g., use of coordination, causality, epistemic, mood, and antithesis contents), as well as simpler content. Examples of expansion that utilize the Bloom and Lahey (1978) taxonomy for content (Exhibits 6.5a and 6.5b) are listed in Exhibit 6.6. (Information about using expansions to facilitate form development appears in Chapter 7.)

The role of saboteur, which we discussed in Chapter 5, can be used as an intervention strategy for content goals and objectives also.

Violation of routine events might encourage the student to use forms of negation (i.e., nonexistence, disappearance, rejection, denial), whereas withholding objects and turns would most probably cause the use of possession and action (e.g., "Hey it's my turn" or "You missed me."). Violation of object function or manipulation might cause students to encode attribution, state, and dative contents (e.g., "The scissors are taped! It's hard. Please get it for me."). However, when specific intervention for content acquisition is necessary, the information pertaining to intentional strategies that follows may be helpful.

## Intentional Interventions to Facilitate Language Content

*Scripts.* Scripts that include content targets can be practiced formally by significant adults and students in play or academic contexts. In such situations, the language typically used in a routine context is modeled for the student so that desired meanings are encoded linguistically into the event. Deaf preschoolers have demonstrated their ability to practice speech or language scripts in a contrived situation and then to use the language *targets* (the articulation, use, content, or form skills they need to acquire) spontaneously during play periods. For example, the teacher or speech and language pathologist may role play "breakfast" with a child, focusing on turntaking, two-word replies, and correct labeling of breakfast foods and behaviors. The adult might then play with the child in free-play time and repeats the role play. Later the adult could watch to see if the child uses all or part of the rehearsed script while playing independently with other children. (Scripts can be devised for hearing and hearing-impaired children to practice content and form of speech, cues and/or sign in mainstream situations, too. Later, students will be more apt to communicate in these situations, because they have practiced and rehearsed.)

**EXHIBIT 6.6.** Choices of adult semantic expansion possibilities

| Child | Adult | Semantic Category |
|---|---|---|
| monkey | There is a monkey.<br>It is a monkey.<br>Is that a monkey? | Existence |
| | No more monkey.<br>The monkey went bye-bye.<br>Yes, the monkey is gone. | Nonexistence, Disappearance |
| | Another monkey.<br>Here is the monkey again.<br>More monkeys | Recurrence |
| | No, that's not a monkey.<br>That monkey's not walking . . . she's running. | Denial |
| | A little monkey. | Attribution |
| | I have a monkey book.<br>It's the monkey's paw print. | Possession |
| | He is jumping.<br>Yes, monkeys run. | Action |
| | The monkey is over there.<br>He's on the chair.<br>She's sitting at the feeder. | Locative State |
| | The monkey is going to the feeder.<br>He is running over there.<br>She is on her way to the water dish. | Locative Action |
| | She is cold.<br>The monkey thinks it's funny.<br>I think that hurts him. | State |
| | Two monkeys, yes!<br>There are some monkeys.<br>I see a few of them.<br>I see a group of monkeys.<br>It's a glass of milk for the baby one. | Quantity |
| | Look, a monkey.<br>Watch me, I'm a monkey too. | Notice |
| | The monkeys are jumping.<br>He jumps on the limb.<br>She ate it. | Time |
| | The monkey and the tiger eat.<br>Do you see the bear or the monkey? | Coordination |
| | The monkey jumps because he is playful.<br>If you go like this, then the monkey will too. | Causality |
| | This is for the monkey.<br>The monkey gave it to the zookeeper. | Dative |
| | This monkey is bigger than that one.<br>These little monkeys or the big one over there? | Specifier |
| | I don't know if that's a monkey.<br>That is definitely the baby over there. | Epistemic |
| | Should we get a drink? | Mood |

**EXHIBIT 6.6.** (Continued)

| | |
|---|---|
| We can feed the monkey this?<br>Would you say that again?<br>You have to look here to see the baby. | |
| This is the monkey house, but the monkeys are all outside today.<br>I want to go there, although it looks like the public is not allowed<br>inside yet. | Antithesis |

SOURCE: B. S. Bloom and M. Lahey, *Language Development and Language Disorders*. New York: Macmillan Publishing Co., 1978.

***Listing, Comparing, and Grouping.*** Some teachers of the deaf use a technique of listing, comparing and contrasting, grouping and labeling, temporal sequence, spatial organization, seriation, and/or causality (see Exhibit 6.7) to help hearing-impaired students understand vocabulary or expressions. These strategies can be used in conjunction with *visualizations*.

***Visualizations.*** The use of *visualizations* involves a method used by educators of hearing-impaired students who are in at least the elementary grades, but they can be used with postsecondary students as well. Visualizations are drawings that represent relationships and can serve as a link between written or read information and conversation (void of context) about topics. These schema link old with new information (Johnson, Pittleman, & Heimlich, 1986) and help students organize their thoughts (Wallach & Miller, 1988). For example, if you are discussing the causes of the Civil War, you might use visualizations

**EXHIBIT 6.7.** Vocabulary expansion techniques (Eccarius, 1985)

| Cognitive Skill | Related Academic Task |
|---|---|
| Listing | "Define _____"<br>"Let's think of as many as we can."<br>"Give some examples of _____."<br>"Tell me about _____ _____."<br>"What are some other _____?"<br>(reasons/affects)<br>"What can you think of that fits these criteria (this rule)?" |
| Comparing and Contrasting | "What is the best _____ _____?"<br>"How are they (the same or different)?"<br>"What was the difference in the results of the experimental condition and the control?"<br>Analogies:<br>"_____ is to _____ as _____ is to _____." |
| Grouping and Labeling | "Why do all these go together and belong to a group?"<br>"Which group do these belong in?" "Why?"<br>"What supporting details contributed to that main idea?" |
| Temporal Sequence | "What happened next?"<br>"Explain the life cycle of a _____."<br>"How were these sequences the same or different?" |

*(continued)*

**EXHIBIT 6.7.** (Continued)

| Cognitive Skill | Related Academic Task |
| --- | --- |
| Spatial Organization | "Find _____ on the map. What direction is _____ from that point?" <br> "Where did _____ live?" <br> "What do you see?" <br> "Which is _____." <br> (taller/longer/broader) <br> "Who had the _____?" <br> (most/least) |
| Seriation | "Which of these words best describes _____?" <br> "What do you think is better?" <br> "What was the most important _____? The least important?" <br> "On a scale of _____ _____, rate _____. <br> "What do you think? Why do you think that?" |
| Causality | "What (event) happened? If _____ had happened, how would the story have changed?" <br> "What were the causes of _____?" <br> (event) <br> (condition) <br> "What makes you feel _____?" <br> (emotion) <br> "How did _____ become _____?" |

SOURCE: M. Eccarius, *Personal Communication*. Omaha: Boys Town National Research Hospital, 1985. Reprinted by permission of the author.

such as those depicted in Exhibit 6.8. Part (a) in Exhibit 6.8 might help students to see the relationship between a major event and several subsequent activities that occurred because of that event (e.g., "What happened when the slaves were freed?"). Part (b) of the exhibit could be used to illustrate a relationship between several events and a subsequent major event (e.g., "Why was the Civil War fought?"). It is the content of the pursuant discussion and not the correct form (whether students draw stick figures in the boxes or used abbreviated or full English forms) that is the focus of a teacher-student dialogue such as this. From such discussions, the student is encouraged later to try to express complex meanings that can be formed in proper English. See Exhibits 6.9 and 6.10 for examples of other visualizations (Eccarius, 1982; Jones, Pierce, & Hunter, 1989).

Jones, Pierce, and Hunter (1989) provide a procedure for training students to use visualizations. They suggest that you

1. Present one good example of your use of a visualization to your students. Use cooperative learning strategies (see Chapter 10) to insure that your students examine the visualization closely.
2. Model how to use the visualization by verbalizing your decision-making process and asking yourself questions out. loud.

**EXHIBIT 6.8.** Visualization for the causes of the Civil War (Eccarius, M. 1985)

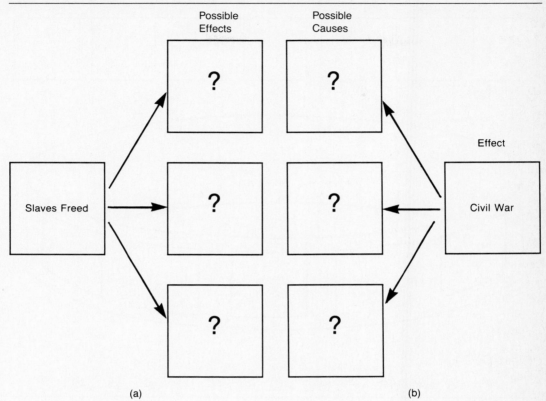

(a)                    (b)

SOURCE: M. Eccarius, *Personal Communication*. Omaha: Boys Town National Research Hospital, 1984. Reprinted by permission of the author.

3. Provide procedural knowledge that will give students a rationale and a motivation for using visualizations to master content.

4. Coach your students, first as a class and then in small groups. Allow them to share and compare their choices for visualizations.

5. Give your students ample time to practice using a visualization and discussing content from it.

*Semantic Mapping.* Hearing-impaired students frequently need to enlarge their English vocabularies. Limited exposure to many English words or teachers' failure to teach words void of context can result in student inability to recognize, use, read, or write age-appropriate lexicon. Semantic mapping, illustrated in Exhibit 6.11, has been shown to be an effective strategy for vocabulary instruction and involves a context-rich categorical structuring of information in graphic form. A

**EXHIBIT 6.9.** Examples of visualizations (Eccarius, M. 1985)

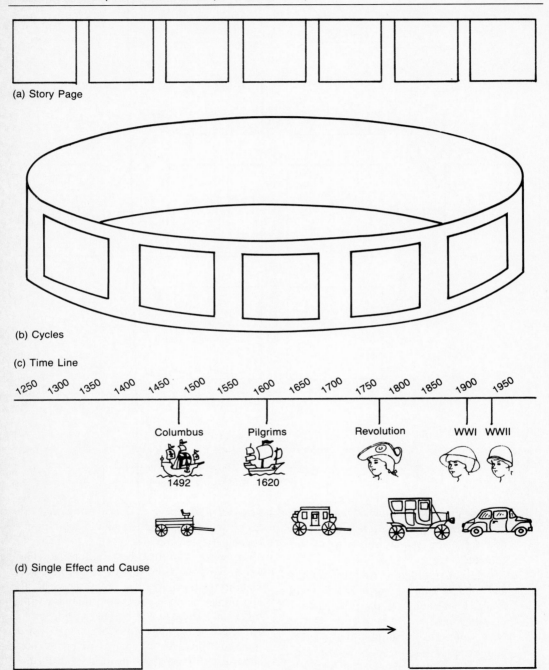

(a) Story Page

(b) Cycles

(c) Time Line

1250  1300  1350  1400  1450  1500  1550  1600  1650  1700  1750  1800  1850  1900  1950

Columbus    Pilgrims         Revolution      WWI  WWII

1492        1620

(d) Single Effect and Cause

**EXHIBIT 6.9.** (Continued)

(e) Multiple Cause and Effect

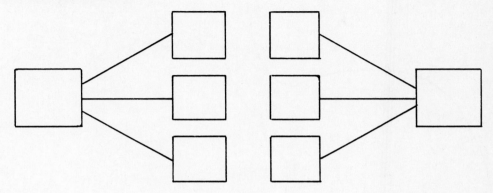

(f) Networks

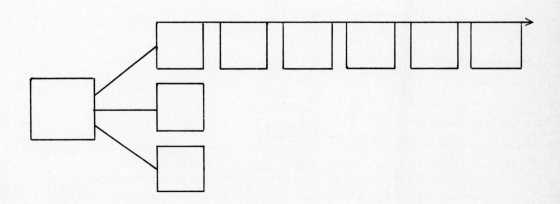

**EXHIBIT 6.9.** (Continued)

(g) Direct Comparison

(h) Comparative Graphs

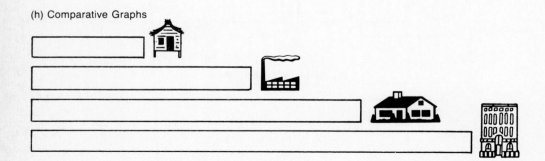

SOURCE: M. Eccarius, *Personal Communication*. Omaha: Boys Town National Research Hospital, 1984. Reprinted by permission of the author.

Graphic representations are visual illustrations of verbal statements. Frames are sets of questions or categories that are fundamental to understanding a given topic. Here are shown nine "generic" graphic forms with their corresponding frames. Also given are examples of topics that could be represented by each graphic form. These graphics show at a glance the key parts of the whole and their relations, helping the learner to comprehend text and solve problems.

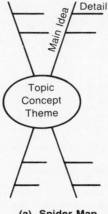

**(a). Spider Map**

Used to describe a central idea: a thing, process, concept, or proposition with support. Key frame questions: What is the central idea? What are its attributes? What are its functions?

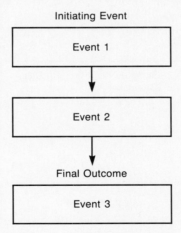

**(b). Series of Events Chain**

Used to describe the stages of something (the life cycle of a primate); the steps in a linear procedure; a sequence of events; or the goals, actions, and outcomes of a historical figure or character in a novel. Key frame questions: What is the object, procedure, or initiating event? What are the stages or steps? How do they lead to one another? What is the final outcome?

**EXHIBIT 6.10.** (Continued)

Low                   High

**(c). Continuum/Scale**

Used for time lines showing historical events or ages, degrees of something, shades of meaning, or rating scales. Key frame questions: What is being scaled? What are the end points?

|            | Name 1 | Name 2 |
|------------|--------|--------|
| Attribute 1 |        |        |
| Attribute 2 |        |        |
| Attribute 3 |        |        |

**(d). Compare/Contrast Matrix**

Used to show similarities and differences between two things (people, places, events, ideas, etc.). Key frame questions: What things are being compared? How are they similar? How are they different?

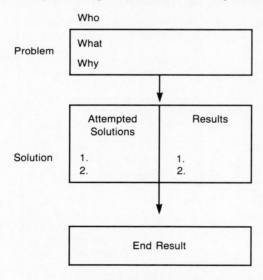

**(e). Problem/Solution Outline**

Used to represent a problem, attempted solutions, and results. Key frame questions: What was the problem? Who had the problem? Why was it a problem? What attempts were made to solve the problem? Did those attempts succeed?

**EXHIBIT 6.10.** (Continued)

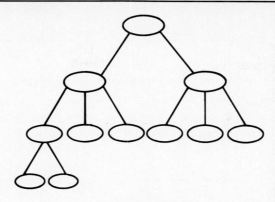

**(f). Network Tree**

Used to show causal information (causes of poverty), a hierarchy (types of insects), or branching procedures (the circulatory system). Key frame questions: What is the superordinate category? What are subordinate categories? How are they related? How many levels are there?

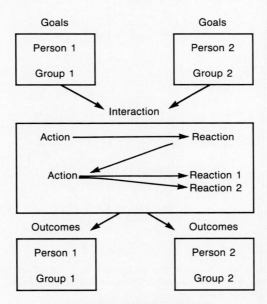

**(g). Human Interaction Outline**

Used to show the nature of an interaction between persons or groups (European settlers and American Indians). Key frame questions: Who are the persons or groups? What were their goals? Did they conflict or cooperate? What was the outcome for each person or group?

**EXHIBIT 6.10.** (Continued)

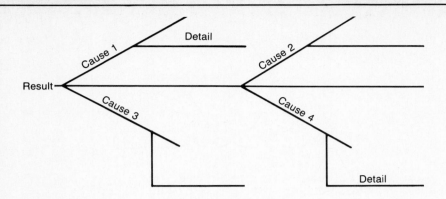

**(h). Fishbone Map**

Used to show the causal interaction of a complex event or complex phenomenon. Key frame questions: What are the factors that cause X? How do they interrelate? Are the factors that cause X the same as those that cause X to persist?

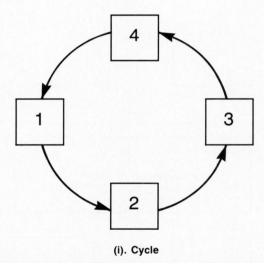

**(i). Cycle**

Used to show how a series of events interact to produce a set of results again and again (weather phenomena, the life cycle). Key frame questions: What are the critical events in the cycle? How are they related? In what ways are they self-reinforcing?

SOURCE: B. Jones, J. Pierce and B. Hunter, "Teaching Students to Construct Graphic Representations," *Educational leadership*, *46*(4) 1989, pages 20–26. Reprinted with permission of the Association for Supervision and Curriculum Development and the authors. Copyright © 1989 by the Association for Supervision and Curriculum Development. All rights reserved.

**EXHIBIT 6.11.** Examples of semantic mapping

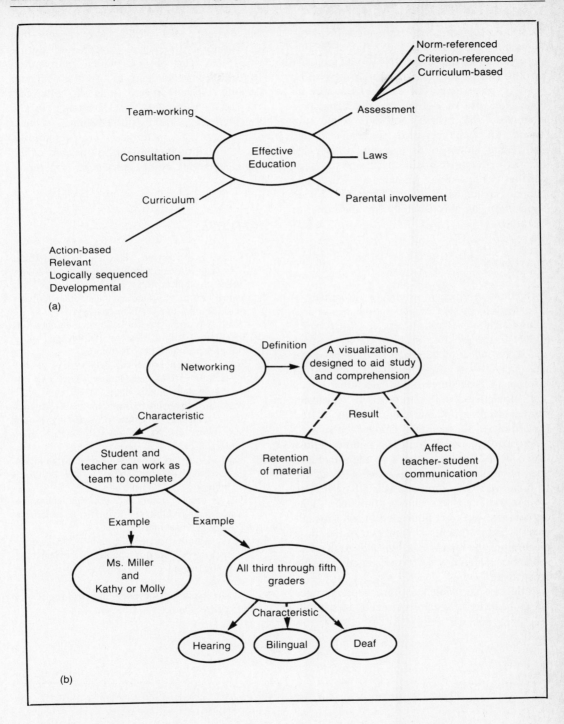

155

specific adaptation of semantic mapping, "networking" is used at the National Technical Institute of the Deaf (NTID) to enhance reading and writing skills. Part (b) of Exhibit 6.11 is an example of *networking* and includes the use of definitions, characteristics, examples, and results. Students relate new words to their personal experiences and knowledge (Johnson & Pearson, 1984). Semantic mapping can aid discussion and expansion of old knowledge in any communication area. (See Chapter 11 for an application of this strategy in the area of reading.)

## SUMMARY

Perfection of speech, sign, or grammar is secondary to the act of generating meaningful communication (Kretschmer & Kretschmer, 1986). In the previous section, the assessment and intervention of language *content* has been presented. It was suggested that after informal assessment procedures have determined goals and objectives for intervention, teachers should inventory student environments to find opportunities to facilitate content behaviors. Approaches in which significant adults follow the students' lead and teach to their interests and intentions were suggested. Next, an *intentional learning* approach was advocated, in which brief, positive interactions that focus on content were recommended. Lastly, strategies to help students organize material in a meaningful manner (e.g., visualizations and semantic mapping) were presented for the practitioner.

Success in using these procedures hinges on your ability to create real needs in natural-istic contexts (Fey, 1986). We suggest that significant adults plan a trial period during which they can observe which intervention strategies cause students to use the semantic contents that are targeted. It is our belief that you should plan activities of interest to the students (e.g., social studies units, science experiments, art activities, problem-solving tasks), in which they might be unaware of the language targets being introduced and monitored.

## ACTIVITIES

1. Assess a 2-year-old child by using Exhibit 6.3, and write several behavioral objectives based on your results.
2. Using Exhibit 6.4, assess the content abilities of three children of different ages.
3. Write two sentences for each of the categories listed in Exhibit 6.5a to demonstrate your comprehension of this taxonomy.
4. Supply some hypothetical data in Exhibit 6.5 for a little girl named Hannie. Write two objectives based on this data.
5. Write a semantic expansion for each category of the semantic taxonomy provided by Bloom and Lahey (1978), using Exhibit 6.5 as a guide.
6. Write a script to target two semantic contents. Have a least two roles and underline the target content.
7. Pick a science topic and use the techniques provided in Exhibit 6.7 to plan the expansion of student vocabularies.
8. Pick a social science unit and four visualizations discussed in this chapter to demonstrate how you would convey key concepts to your students.
9. Map or network one paragraph from a school subject textbook.

# CHAPTER 7

# Language Form

## OVERVIEW

This chapter will focus on the assessment and intervention of language form—specifically that of English form. If teachers are working with students who are exposed to two languages in the home, then assessment and intervention with the form of another language (other than English) would be an important consideration as well. The procedures suggested in this chapter could be adapted accordingly in such a bilingual situation. Within this chapter, informal assessment strategies and intervention techniques are provided, as they were for language use (Chapter 5) and language content (Chapter 6). An eight-step model (Reed & Bugen, 1986) for viewing the process of the development of language form, which provides a step-by-step procedure for maximizing efficiency of language acquisition, is discussed and exemplified in detail.

---

### CHAPTER TOPICS

Form Defined and Assessed
Form Intervention
Communication Games

---

## FORM DEFINED AND ASSESSED

All languages are comprised of several categories of form. For example, both ASL and English have a system of *phonology* (sign or speech articulation), a system of *morphology*, and a system of *syntax*. Terms such as *minimal pair* (two words that differ by only one characteristic), place of *articulation* (the location of production), and *distinctive feature* (a specific, distinguishing characteristic) can be used to describe characteristics of both oral and manual languages. Both modes of communication are also *verbal* in that they are

linguistic and rule governed (Baker, 1979; Stokoe, personal communication, 1982); therefore, educators should reserve use of the term *nonverbal* when they are referring to gestures, body movements, and facial expressions that do not code features of a signed language.

The phonology of English is emphasized in the field of deaf education to the extent that it will be discussed separately in Chapter 8. Morphology comprises two main areas: *lexicon* and *inflection*. Lexicon is defined as a particular vocabulary word (e.g., *run*, *girl*, *disappoint*). Inflection encompasses the morphemes added to a lexical item that change its meaning (e.g., *running*, *girls*, *disappointed*). The syntax of a language provides a way of ordering the lexical items. Examples include subject-verb agreement, coordinate and subordinate clauses, and sentence types (e.g., declarative). Teachers of students with impaired hearing need to be knowledgeable of all of these categories of form (Bloom & Lahey, 1978; Miller, 1981).

Because of the link between cognition and language (as described in Chapter 1), the surface features of language for children who use more than one language usually emerge simultaneously (Bonvillian et al., 1983). Schlesinger and Meadow (1972) and Schlesinger (1978) found that hearing-impaired children of Deaf* parents produce their first signs at about 9–15 months, the same period of de-

velopment during which Nelson (1973) reported that hearing children of hearing parents produce their first spoken words. Likewise, at a time when hearing children are first learning to print their name, deaf children of Deaf parents are learning to fingerspell their names correctly (Akamatsu, 1983; Padden & LaMaster, 1985) (see Exhibit 7.1). Some of the form abilities of hearing-impaired children of Deaf parents appear for reference in Exhibit 7.2 and provide teachers with developmental form data (e.g., MLU, classifiers, use of space, etc.). A language sample, coded for voiced mean-length-utterance (MLU), appears in Exhibit 5.4. Form abilities based on research appear in Exhibit 7.3. This material can be used as an informal assessment tool, as we described previously in Chapters 5 and 6. The *Developmental Language Curriculum* by Cheney, Compton, and Harder (1989) is highly recommended as well.

---

* The convention of capitalizing the word *deaf* denotes cultural affiliation and will be explained in Chapter 14.

**EXHIBIT 7.1.** Acquisition of fingerspelling

| | |
|---|---|
| 2;0 | Displays fingerspelling-like activity |
| 2;9 | Willingly produces fingerspelled items on request |
| | Fingerspelling involves at least three hand configurations (e.g., "U-B-A" when asked for dog's name). Two-letter words were ignored or labeled as mistakes (Padden & LeMaster, 1985). |
| | Distinguishes when fingerspelling is appropriate and when sign is required. Uses name sign (with the "S" sign but spells name "E-U-B") (Padden & LeMaster, 1985). |
| 3;0 | Fingerspells in sequences |
| 3;8-5;3 | Attempts to fingerspell, but words do not resemble English words, yet fingerspelled sequences appear to be analyzed as words (e.g., "LDA" = Trisha; "ALALAL" = "Trisha did it") (Akamatsu, 1983) |
| | Fingerspelled sequences produced in a consistent pattern (Akamatsu, 1983) |
| 4;7 | Consistency between name sign and fingerspelling of name |
| 4;11 | Reverses letters (ignores form), but meaning still intacted (e.g., E-T, T-E to denote movie character used interchangeably) (Padden & LeMaster, 1985) |
| 5;0 | Spells in English consistently (Padden & LeMaster, 1985) |

Boyes-Braem (1973) outlined four stages of fingerspelling movement based on neuro-muscular development of the hand:

STAGE 1:  A, S, G, flat 0, 5, C, L
STAGE 2:  B, F, 0
STAGE 3:  Y, I, D, K, 3, W, U, V
STAGE 4:  8, S, E, X, T, M, N

**EXHIBIT 7.2.** Developmental signed form data

*1 Month*
"One infant (Maestas y Moores, 1980) appears to synchronize FULL* at 25 days, YOU at one month-21 days and GRANDMOTHER at two months-28 days." (p. 9).

*3 Months*
Fingerbabbling and a possible T handshape are reported (Maestas y Moores, 1980; p. 11).

*6 Months*
"Mouthing without vocalization is observed in infants under six months of age" (Maestas y Moores, 1980, p. 9).

*8 Months*
Ann (Schlesinger & Meadow, 1972) expressed "vocalization and gestures which conveyed emphasis and emotions." (p. 57)
Boyes-Braem (1983) found that her subject acquired the pincher grasp ability, L, B0, G, 4 and 5 handshapes.

*10 Months*
Ann (Schlesinger & Meadow, 1972) signed **BYE, **FATHER (hits side of head with heel of open hand), **STUPID (hits side of head with fist), and **EAT (hand in a loose fist). (p. 57)
Flavia (McIntire, 1973) joined signs (i.e., MOTHER SHOW MORE MILK) and had a vocabulary of about 20 signs (1974).
Petitto's subject (1980) looked where her mother pointed and used eye gaze and pointing to direct the mother's attention. The infant also used point to pick or poke at objects a "linguistic point" was also observed only using the left hand with the arm in the opposite direction from the child's head and eyes. The eye gaze was fixed on the addressee as if for comment. Child signed MOTHER, ME, MILK. ME + POINT also occurred.

*11 Months*
Flavia (McIntire, 1973) had an expressive sign vocabulary of the following 16 words: MILK, CAT, SHOE, BIRD, DOG, BALL, BOOK, HORSE, MOUSE, DUCK, FOOD, BATH, MOM, DAD, NO, BYE. She understood the following signs: BEAR, DOLL, SOCK, APPLE, CAN, HOME, ORANGE, ICE CREAM, DRINK, KISS, UNCLE, YES. She also conjoined MA SHOE (all reported by her mother).
Ann (Schlesinger & Meadow, 1972) vocalized negatively after her mother gave a mock scolding with "no."

*13 Months*
Flavia (McIntire, 1973) signed ICE CREAM , HOME, UNCLE, APPLE, SOCKS, DRINK, GIRAFFE, PENGUIN, ELEPHANT, LION, SAND, BANANA, FLOWER, RABBIT, TIME, TURTLE, TREE, HAIRBOW, GRANDMA, HURT, BRUSH, DRESS, CRY, SLEEP, BICYCLE, WET, DIRTY, RED, and HOT. She also fingerspelled, N-O. (This initial appearance of *no* is supported by Lacy, 1972b). She used holistic signs (e.g., CRY had at least five meanings). She combined BABY SLEEP, MOM/DAD WET, and MORE ICE CREAM (reported by her mother)

*14 Months*
Ann (Schlesinger & Meadow, 1972) signed **CAT, **SLEEP, **HAT, **EAT, and the two sign combinations **EYE, **SLEEP. She used head shaking, negative vocalizations, and **NO when unhappy.

*16 Months*
Ann (Schlesinger & Meadow, 1972) answered OLD WRONG, ONE, and OLD ONE to the question of age.
Maestas y Moores' subject (1980) signed "YOU" on her parent's body; another guided her father through the sign for DOG. A child invented the pulling of her hair to indicate WANT and the biting of her arm to mean DISPLEASURE. One infant at 16 months signed **WATER with the proper location and action but with index finger instead of W-handshape. At the same age, another infant produced **CAT, **AIRPLANE, and **FROG with the open hand (5-handshape) instead of the F-, Y-, and bent-V-handshapes, respectively. One infant who also was 16 months old placed her index finger on her other wrist, instead of crossing the H-hand fingers of the adult sign, meaning "sit"

*(continued)*

**EXHIBIT 7.2.** (Continued)

Another child placed the open hand at the back of her head instead of on the forehead to sign FATHER. A 16-month-old infant signed SHOE by tapping together the upper sides of her wrists, instead of the radial sides of the fists, in her multisign phrase MOMMY MORE **SHOE. One child signed **CAT with a downward motion and open hand instead of her usual upward brushing movement with the open hand

*17 Months*

Ann (Schlesinger & Meadow, 1972) asked **HOME, CAR?

*17 Months*

McIntire reported three-sign utterances, (1974). At 19 months, Schlesinger and Meadow reported that Ann's and Karen's vocabulary consisted of well over 100 signs and connected language. Ann used a small set of signs with multiple functions. She used signs for reference, request, comment, and so on (1972).

*22 Months*

Ann (Schlesinger & Meadow, 1972) signed three phrases: BOY GIRL PLAY, ME GIRL, HELLO THANK YOU FOOD. She could discriminate signs that were very close in configurations—WRONG, "Y" PLAY, YELLOW.

---

\* The convention of capitalization is used in this paper to denote sign.
\*\* Indicates "baby signing" where sign phonology is not adult-like.

---

**EXHIBIT 7.3.** Language *form* abilities of children based on hearing *monolingual* child data and adapted for *bimodal* communication

| | Gesture | Sign | Sign and Voice | Voice Alone |
|---|---|---|---|---|
| *1/2–1 Year* | | | | |
| 1. Engages in finger or oral babbling (Cano & Schmidt, 1974). | | | | |
| 2. Moves and uses gestures or vocalizes simultaneously (Miller, 1981a). | | | | |
| 3. Hands a familiar object upon a voiced and/or signed request (Cano & Schmidt, 1974). | | | | |
| 4. Comprehends several voice, cued or signed words (e.g., *no-no, hot*, own name) (Cano & Schmidt, 1974). | | | | |
| 5. Understands the function of a number of household objects (e.g., will demonstrate use of a spoon, cup, toy truck, hammer, etc., out of context). | | | | |
| 6. Uses gesture plus vocalization (Miller, 1981a). | | | | |
| 7. Uses gesture plus word(s) (Miller, 1981a). | | | | |
| 8. Uses signed and/or voiced single-word utterances that contain few function words (*there, no, all gone*). These are persistent from week to week and are used consistently (Miller, 1981a). | | | | |
| 9. Uses a few names that are persistent from week to week and uses them consistently (Miller, 1981a). | | | | |
| 10. Productive use of substantives may drop out from week to week, but comprehension remains (e.g., *milk, cup, dog*) (Miller, 1981a). | | | | |
| 11. Demonstrates rapid signed and/or voiced vocabulary increases (Miller, 1981a). | | | | |

**EXHIBIT 7.3.** (Continued)

| | Gesture | Sign | Sign and Voice | Voice Alone |
|---|---|---|---|---|
| 12. Uses successive signed and/or voiced single-word utterances (chaining) (e.g., *man-coat-hat*) (Miller, 1981a). | | | | |
| 13. Uses signed and/or voiced two-word utterances, but single-word utterances dominate (Miller, 1981a). | | | | |
| *1–2 Years* | | | | |
| 14. Demonstrates object permanence when can no longer see or act on object (Bloom & Lahey, 1978). | | | | |
| 15. Utterances contain announcing (e.g., *mama, papa, baby*, pet name) (Miller, 1981a). | | | | |
| 16. Uses one word (e.g., *dog*) to describe a category of objects (family pet, stuffed dogs, other four-legged animals). | | | | |
| 17. Uses words globally (*cookie* or *mommy* may both refer to mother, cookies, or a desire for a cookie). | | | | |
| 18. Asks (using voice or sign) "What's that" questions as a routine. | | | | |
| 19. Uses basic but consistent word order (Bloom & Lahey, 1978). | | | | |
| 20. Uses gestures (Miller, 1981a). | | | | |
| 21. Uses gestures plus vocalization (Miller, 1981a). | | | | |
| 22. Uses gestures plus word (Miller, 1981a). | | | | |
| 23. Uses signed and/or voiced single-word utterances that contain few function words (*there, no, all gone*). These are persistent from week to week and are used consistently (Miller, 1981a). | | | | |
| 24. Uses a few names that are persistent from week to week and uses them consistently (Miller, 1981a). | | | | |
| 25. Demonstrates rapid signed and/or voiced vocabulary increases (Miller, 1981a). | | | | |
| 26. Uses successive signed and/or voiced single-word utterances (chaining) (e.g., *man-coat-hat*) (Miller, 1981a). | | | | |
| 27. Uses signed and/or voiced two-word utterances, but single-word utterances dominate (Miller, 1981a). | | | | |
| 28. Uses two- and three-word signed and/or voiced phrases (Cano & Schmidt, 1974). | | | | |
| 29. Vocally and/or manually names one color (Cano & Schmidt, 1974). | | | | |
| 30. Vocally and/or manually asks simple questions (e.g., *Where ball? Go bye-bye? where, what, whose, who*) (Ervin-Tripp, 1974). | | | | |
| 31. Uses voiced and/or signed relative pronouns (e.g., *myself*) (Bloom & Lahey, 1978). | | | | |
| 32. Uses voiced or signed adjectives (Bloom & Lahey, 1978). | | | | |
| 33. Uses voiced and/or signed "ing" or *reduplicated signs* (Bloom & Lahey, 1978). | | | | |
| 34. Uses voiced and/or signed conjunctions (Bloom & Lahey, 1978). | | | | |

*(continued)*

**EXHIBIT 7.3.** (Continued)

| | Gesture | Sign | Sign and Voice | Voice Alone |
|---|---|---|---|---|
| 35. Voiced or signed utterances contain *in* and *on*. | | | | |
| 36. Uses signed and/or voiced *uncontractible copula* (e.g., *am*, *is*, *are*, *be*). | | | | |
| 37. Uses signed and/or voiced transitive action verbs (e.g., *ride, put, make, go, get*). | | | | |
| 38. Uses locative action verbs (e.g., *sit chair*, *go home*, *put table*, etc.) (Bloom & Lahey, 1978). | | | | |
| 39. Uses signed and/or voiced *subject-verb-complement* word order. | | | | |
| 40. Uses demonstratives, including *this, these, those, that*, or referential pointing. | | | | |
| 41. Uses articles like *a* and *the*, but not always appropriately. | | | | |
| 42. Uses quantifiers like *some, a lot, two*. | | | | |
| 43. Uses possessives like *hers, his, mine*. | | | | |
| 44. Uses *can, will*, and *am* (Miller, 1981a). | | | | |
| *3–4 Years* | | | | |
| 45. Uses some signed and/or voiced *plurals* (or noun reduplication) if child is an ASL user (Cano & Schmidt, 1974). | | | | |
| 46. Uses some signed and/or voiced *articles* (Cano & Schmidt, 1974). (If child is an ASL user, give credit for item.) | | | | |
| 47. Uses some signed and/or voiced *adverbs* (e.g., *maybe, too*) (Corsaro, 1981). | | | | |
| 48. Uses several signed and/or voiced *pronouns* (Cano & Schmidt, 1974) or referential point if child is an ASL user. | | | | |
| 49. Uses signed and/or voiced utterances containing *contractible copula* (e.g., *I'm, he's, they're*) (Brown, 1973). (If child is an ASL user give credit for item.) | | | | |
| 50. Uses signed and/or voiced utterances that contain past regular (Brown, 1973) or some directional verbs (if child is an ASL user). | | | | |
| 51. Uses utterances that contain third-person irregular (Brown, 1973). | | | | |
| 52. Uses some signed and/or voiced complex sentences (Bloom & Lahey, 1978). | | | | |
| 53. Uses signed and/or voiced conjunctions other than *and* (Bloom & Lahey, 1978). | | | | |
| 54. Asks many signed and/or voiced questions, especially using *how* and *why* (Cano & Schmidt, 1974). | | | | |
| *4–5 Years* | | | | |
| 55. Uses several signed and/or voiced future tenses (Cano & Schmidt, 1974) or verb modulations. | | | | |
| 56. Uses several signed and/or voiced past tenses (Cano & Schmidt, 1974) or verb modulations. | | | | |
| 57. Begins to use signed and/or voiced conjunctions (*but, and, because*) to form *complex sentences* (Cano & Schmidt, 1974) or facial distinctions in ASL. | | | | |

**EXHIBIT 7.3.** (Continued)

| | Gesture | Sign | Sign and Voice | Voice Alone |
|---|---|---|---|---|
| 58. Uses well-established intonation and rhythmic patterns in speaking or signing (Cano & Schmidt, 1974). | | | | |
| *5–6 Years* | | | | |
| 59. Signs and/or speaks in clear, usually complete sentences (Cano & Schmidt, 1974). | | | | |
| 60. Has very few substitutions in sign and/or speech (Cano & Schmidt, 1974). | | | | |
| 61. Has very few misarticulations and/or voice (e.g., uses correct handshapes and place of articulation) (Cano & Schmidt, 1974). | | | | |
| 62. Signs and/or speaks fluently using all grammatical forms (Cano & Schmidt, 1974) of ASL *or* orally or manual English. | | | | |

## FORM INTERVENTION

After you have assessed a student's form abilities in the target language (e.g., English, ASL), you should write your goals and objectives to guide you in the intervention process. We feel that this process has been described adequately in Chapters 5 and 6. As we have suggested (in facilitating the development of use and content), we recommend that an environmental survey be conducted to determine whether strategies such as self-talk, parallel talk, informative talk, repetition, and expansions might produce positive changes in a student's ability to comprehend or produce a desired form. If this does not occur, direct intervention or instruction may be necessary.

When you are planning a language form program for hearing-impaired students, Clark and Stewart (1986) suggest that three principles should guide the instructional process:

> First, instruction should be guided by features related to the normal language acquisition process. (See Chapter 6).
> Second, emphasis should be placed on conversations or interactive communication with a variety of appropriate models.

Third, specific and systematic language experiences should be established.

Reed and Bugen (1986) propose an eight-step model (that is followed through in the balance of this chapter) for viewing the process of language development. This model clearly organizes a step-by-step procedure to maximize efficiency in language acquisition. By using this procedure, you seek to create a natural language environment in the classroom but present individual language *structures* (in parts of the utterance) in formal lessons. Historically, the following basic sentence structures have been taught to deaf children:

1. $N + V$      John ran.
2. $N^1 + V + N^2$      John threw the ball.
3. $N + be + adj.$      John is tall.
4. $N^1 + be + N^1$      John is a boy.
5. $N + be + adv.$      John is outside.

We caution that these structures are not ordered developmentally (Engen & Engen, 1983).

When students have demonstrated a pragmatic and semantic knowledge of a structure (e.g., acknowledging its use and meaning in a conversation), you introduce that structure formally at a *literal, concrete level*. In other words, the initial emphasis is on a sense of the structure, but, as students become familiar with it, the emphasis shifts to correctness of form. You guide experimentation and practice and lead students towards independent and spontaneous use. Lessons are a mix of student-centered lessons, spontaneous student-controlled topics, and conversations; teacher-centered lessons; and hybrids of the two. Reed and Bugen's process approach to developing language is based on the premise that hearing-impaired students can develop linguistic competence if they have the prerequisite pragmatic and semantic knowledge and interact in an *intentional* language environment. This environment includes both spontaneous and carefully planned use of target structures that have been identified through assessment procedures. The language is used for a deliberate purpose: to expose the student to forms that he or she is not using correctly.

Central to the approach is the contention that a language structure should be introduced naturally and not through drill. As students come to understand the form, they will need practice and reinforcement in order to retain it. This support should be reduced gradually until they can use the new structure independently to express their own ideas. We will now look closely at the eight steps of the Reed and Bugen (1986) process approach to developing language with hearing-impaired students.

## Step 1: Assessing Student Needs and Identifying the Target Structures

Skills to be targeted must be determined in a coordinated fashion. Collecting formal and informal diagnostic information, consulting records, reviewing individual education plans (IEPs), and meeting with previous teachers all are a part of completing this step. A good starting point is consulting developmentally based curriculum outlines and scope-and-sequence organizations of language structures.

We have supplied several tools for assessment:

1.  The form skills listed in Exhibits 7.1 through 7.3 are based on research.
2.  Another description of form is found by calculating *mean-length-utterance* or MLU (Brown, 1973). This is possible if a language sample is taken (see Chapter 1). This gross indication of the typical length of a student's voice and/or signed utterance can indicate progress with language form. You will want to know your signed and/or voiced MLU, as well, in order to supply an appropriate MLU to facilitate form acquisition. Rules for calculated voiced MLU are available through Brown (1973). Some suggested rules for the calculation of signed MLU appear in Chapter 5.
3.  Lee's (1974) developmental sentence-scoring procedure is a popular form tool. Fifty utterances containing a subject and a verb relationship are needed for analysis. Words in eight categories are given weighted point values according to developmental complexity (Cole & Cole, 1989). Exhibit 7.4 illustrates the eight categories and specific examples. The column on the left represents the point values given to the student for using that particular construction. A sentence point can be awarded also if the utterance is a complete, mature sentence. The formula for calculating the developmental sentence scoring (DSS) is,

$$DDS = \frac{\text{total points for all sentences}}{\text{total number of utterances}}$$

For a more detailed description of the procedure, see Lee (1974).

**EXHIBIT 7.4.** The developmental sentence scoring (DSS) system SOURCE: L. Lee, *Developmental Sentence Analysis*. Evanston, IL: Northwestern University Press, 1974. Reprinted by permission.

| Score | Indefinite Pronouns or Noun Modifiers | Personal Pronouns | Main Verbs | Secondary Verbs | Negatives | Conjunctions | Interrogative Reversals | WH-Questions |
|---|---|---|---|---|---|---|---|---|
| 1 | it, this, that | 1st and 2nd person: I, me, my, mine, you, your(s) | A. Uninflected verb: I see you. <br> B. copula, is or 's: *It's* red. <br> C. is + verb + ing: He *is coming.* | | it, this, that + copula or auxiliary is, 's, + not: It's *not* mine. This is *not* a dog. That is *not* moving. | | Reversal of copula: *Isn't it* red? *Were they* there? | |
| 2 | | 3rd person: he, him, his, she, her, hers | A. -s and -ed: *plays, played* <br> B. irregular past: *ate,* <br> C. Copula: *am, are, was, were* <br> D. Auxiliary *am, are, was, were* | Five early-developing infinitives: I *wanna see (want to see)* I'm *gonna see (going to see)* I *gotta see (got to see)* Lemme [to] see (let me [to] see) Let's [to] play (let [us to] play) | | | | A. who, what, what + noun: *Who am I? What is he eating? What book are you reading?* <br> B. where, how many, how much, what . . . do, what . . . for *Where did it go? How much do you want? What is he doing? What is a hammer for?* |

*(continued)*

EXHIBIT 7.4. (Continued)

| Score | Indefinite Pronouns or Noun Modifiers | Personal Pronouns | Main Verbs | Secondary Verbs | Negatives | Conjunctions | Interrogative Reversals | WH-Questions |
|---|---|---|---|---|---|---|---|---|
| 3 | A. no, some, more, all, lot(s), one(s), two (etc.), other(s), another<br>B. something, somebody, someone | A. Plurals: we, us, our(s), they, them, their<br>B. these, those | | Noncomplementing infinitives:<br>I stopped *to play.*<br>I'm afraid *to look.*<br>It's hard *to do that.* | | and | | |
| 4 | nothing, nobody, none, no one | | A. can, will, may + verb: *may go*<br>B. Obligatory do + verb: *don't go*<br>C. Emphatic do + verb: I *do see.* | Participle, present or past:<br>I see a boy *running.*<br>I found the toy *broken.* | can't, don't | | Reversal of auxiliary be:<br>*Is he coming? Isn't he coming? Was he going? Wasn't he going?* | |
| 5 | | Reflexives: myself, your-self, himself, herself, itself, themselves | | | A. Early infinitival complements with differing subjects in kernels:<br>I want you *to come.*<br>Let him [*to*] *see.*<br>B. Later infinitival complements: | isn't, won't | A. but<br>B. so, and so, so that<br>C. or, if | | When, how, how + adjective<br>*When shall I come?*<br>*How do you do it?*<br>*How big is it?* |

6

A. Wh-pronouns: who, which, whose, whom, what, that, how many, how much
I know *who* came.
That's *what* I said.
B. Wh-word + infinitive:
I know *what* to do.
I know *who(m)* to take

A. could, would, should, might + verb:
*might come, could be*
B. Obligatory does, did + verb
C. Emphatic does, did + verb

I had *to go.*
I told him *to go.* I tried *to go.* He ought *to go.*
C. Obligatory deletions: Make it [to] go.
I'd better [to] go.
D. Infinitive with wh-word:
I know what *to get.*
I know how *to do it.*

because

A. Obligatory do, does, did: *Do they run? Does it bit? Didn't it hurt?*
B. Reversal of modal: *Can you play? Won't it hurt? Shall I sit down?*
C. Tag question: It's fun, *isn't it?* It isn't fun, *is it?*

*(continued)*

EXHIBIT 7.4. (Continued)

| Score | Indefinite Pronouns or Noun Modifiers | Personal Pronouns | Main Verbs | Secondary Verbs | Negatives | Conjunctions | Interrogative Reversals | WH-Questions |
|---|---|---|---|---|---|---|---|---|
| 7 | A. any, anything, anybody, anyone<br>B. every, everything, everybody, everyone<br>C. both, few, many, each, several, most, least, much, next, first, last, second (etc.) | (his) own, one, oneself, whichever, whoever, whatever<br>Take *whatever* you like. | A. Passive with *get*, any tense<br>Passive with *be*, any tense<br>B. must, shall + verb:<br>*must come*<br>C. have + verb + en:<br>*I've eaten*<br>D. have got:<br>*I've got it.* | Passive infinitival complement:<br>With *get*: I have to get *dressed.*<br>I don't want to get *hurt.*<br>With *be*:<br>I want to be *pulled.*<br>It's going to be *locked.* | other negatives:<br>Uncontracted negatives: I can *not* go. He has *not* gone.<br>Pronoun-auxiliary or pronoun-copula contraction: I'm *not* coming. He's *not* here.<br>Auxiliary-negative or copula-negative contraction: He *wasn't* going. He *hasn't* been seen. It *couldn't* be mine. They *aren't* big. | | | why, what if<br>how come how<br>about + gerund<br>*Why are you crying?*<br>*What if* I won't do it?<br>*How come* he is crying?<br>*How about* coming with me? |
| 8 | | | A. have been + verb + ing<br>had been + verb + ing<br>B. modal + have + verb + en:<br>*may have eaten*<br>C. modal + be | Gerund:<br>*Swinging* is fun.<br>I like *fishing.*<br>He started *laughing.* | | A. where, when, how, while, whether (or not), till, until, unless, since, before, after, for, as, as + adjective + as, as if, | A. Reversal of auxiliary have:<br>*Has he seen you?*<br>B. Reversal with two or three auxiliaries:<br>*Has he been* | whose, which, which + noun<br>*Whose car is that?*<br>*Which book* do you want? |

+ verb +
ing:
*could be*
*playing*
D. Other
auxiliary
combinations:
*should have*
*been*
*sleeping*

like, that,
than
I know
*where you*
*are.*
Don't come
*till* I call.
B. Obligatory
deletions:
I run faster
*than you*
[run].
I'm as *big*
as a man
[is big].
It looks *like*
a dog
[looks]
C. Elliptical
deletions
(score 0):
That's *why*
[I took it].
I know *how*
[I can do it].
D. Wh-words
+ infinitive:
I know *how*
to do it.

eating?
Couldn't *he*
*have*
*waited?*
*Could he*
*have been*
crying?
*Wouldn't he*
*have been*
going?

SOURCE: L. Lee, *Developmental Sentence Analysis.* Evanston, IL: Northwestern University Press, 1974. Reprinted by permission.

## Step 2: Analyzing the Target Grammatically

Analyzing the structures that need to be taught is the next step. You must be able to isolate the specific areas of strength and weakness that students demonstrate and be able to plan activities geared to the students' current needs. For example, after assessing the students' level of functioning, you establish that a student is ready for exposure to pronouns. The objective then becomes: The students will learn to use such words as *I*, *you*, *he*, *she* and later *themselves*, etc. It is not necessary for them to learn the term "pronoun" until much later in their development. However, it is essential that you have a comprehensive knowledge of grammar so that you can pinpoint and intervene with established targets.

## Step 3: Analyzing the Structure for Language Sense—Planning

Developing an understanding of the structure's meaning and a sense of the structure is probably the most crucial step in the whole process, because all teaching activities that follow will depend on your understanding of how the structure is used. Reed and Bugen (1986) list specific steps that you can use to analyze a language structure for its meaning or sense:

1. Write five or more sentences using the target structure.
2. Identify real-life situations in which communication involving this target structure would be employed. Pay special attention to those situations that relate to students' interests and daily life. They will be the source of teaching activities.
3. List verbs that are associated with the target structure or that "trigger" it.
4. Determine which question forms elicit

the target structure or represent the concept of the target structure.

5. Write down a description of the sense of the target structure. Seek to develop insight about how and why the target is used.

By working through these five steps you are attempting to develop a clear understanding of the target structure. This understanding allows you to develop a blueprint for working on the structure in natural and structured ways. An analysis of a structure for its sense by using the target structure of the present progressive follows (adapted from Reed & Bugen, 1986):

1. Five sentences.
   a. I am talking.
   b. Sally is playing baseball.
   c. The baby is sleeping.
   d. The flowers are growing.
   e. Father is working.
2. Real-life situations.
   a. Snack—eating and drinking.
   b. Playground—running, jumping, throwing, talking.
   c. At home—talking, watching, playing, sleeping, eating.
   d. At the store—shopping, walking, buying.
   e. In school—writing, reading.
3. Trigger verbs: eating, talking, signing, writing, reading, listening, running, walking, sleeping, kissing, watching, throwing, catching, jumping, hopping, drinking, cleaning, working, driving, riding, cooking, coloring, carrying, washing, singing.
4. Question forms: what, who, where.
5. Description: Present progressive indicates continuing or ongoing action. It is represented by *be* + _____ *ing*

## Step 4: Designing and Implementing Activities to Develop the Sense of the Target Structure—Teaching

Exposure and comprehension of the structure should precede attempts to have the students produce it. Your responsibility is to arrange events so that the students will experience the sense of the language. It is an evolving progression that begins with your presentation of a target structure and culminates in the students' independent use of the same structure. Within this fourth step, you take the information that was generated in step 3 and use it both to develop appropriate activities and to create natural learning opportunities in order to make the target structure come alive in the classroom. The challenge of this step is to manipulate the environment in a fashion so that you are working with a desired target structure in a natural and effortless manner. It is at this point that the natural and structured approaches to teaching language are most closely meshed. Within this step are four specific methods for imparting a language sense. They are: spontaneous events, action work, dialogues, and "unassumed knowledge." We will now give a short explanation of each method.

*Spontaneous Events.* Spontaneous-event work entails the common practice of turning unplanned incidents into language learning opportunities that use the target structure. For example, if you are developing the sense of the present progressive with verbs such as *playing, eating, talking, writing*, and *reading*, you take every opportunity to use the structure to communicate ideas to the class. If two of the students are playing a game, you might tell the other students, "Sue and Marilyn are playing dominoes." (See also the discussions of self-talk and parallel talk that appeared in chapters 5 and 6). If the class is walking down the hall and two teachers are having a discussion, you might say, "Mrs. Heinze and Mr. Kapperman are talking."

*Action Work.* Action work is a teacher-designed dramatization that is intended to impart a language sense. It is a planned, nonverbal event that can be described by using the target structure. Following each section of the dramatization, you would ask questions in order to be certain that the students understand the context of the dramatization. For example, you are working again on the present progressive. You pretend to be driving your car on the way to a restaurant. You ask the class, "What am I doing?" You accept answers in any form: "the sign DRIVE," "the word *drive*," incomplete sentences, or sentences. You then model the target structure back to the class with the statement: "Right! I am driving the car." Then you might continue and pull up to a McDonalds, walk in, and ask the class, "What am I doing?" Once again, you accept all responses and model the target structure back to the students. This can continue as you order the food, talk to someone at the counter, pay the bill, carry the food to a table, sit down, and eat the food. You stop each time to ask the class what you are doing. Other scenarios (e.g., playing soccer or making popcorn) should be provided to give the students more exposure to the target structure. Students' contributions are not corrected; they are expanded (as discussed earlier in chapters 5 and 6). It is important at this point for you to remember that the goal at this stage is not to get correct forms from the students but rather to give them an intuitive grasp of the language structure or grammatical form that is being taught.

*Dialogue.* Dialogue is a conversation that is directed and controlled by the teacher for the purpose of imparting the sense of the target structure. For example, its content might be

student-recalled experiences that have occurred outside the classroom. You may
choose to recall an experience if it is valid
for the purpose. Your task is to stimulate a
flow of ideas and model back some of those
ideas by using the target structure. This entire
process is best done as you maintain an
awareness of the students' outside activities
and interests. Therefore, you are always
aware of the target structure and can sneak it
in whenever the opportunity for conversation
comes along.

Your direction and control are essential
to the effectiveness of the activity. Having
initiated the discussion of an experience, you
can use questions and statements that could
emerge naturally from the discussion but that
also would put the students in touch with a
sense of the structure. For example, as you
develop the concept of the present progressive, you talk to students about the things that
they are doing while they are doing them.
While walking on the playground during recess, you will ask the students questions
about other students, such as, "What is Bob
doing?" and "Who is playing soccer?" Questions can be asked also about people, pets,
and television programs that are genuinely
important to the student: "Jose, what is your
Dad doing now?" "What do you think your
brother is doing now?" Though these dialogue seem natural, they are examples of intentional intervention; you have manipulated
the environment and have planned goals be-
forehand. Planning is an essential component
of the language process approach to teaching.

*Unassumed Knowledge.* As you intervene
with language form, you can use the strategy
of "unassumed knowledge" and respond only
to the information provided by the student.
For example, you might ask, "How did this
mosquito get in here? Did you bring him in
your lunch box? Did he walk in the door?
How did he get in here?" If a student says,
"Window," then you could ask, "Did he

swim through the window?" By following
this line of questions, you would get to the
sentence, "The mosquito flew in the open
window." Moeller and McConkey (1983) provided another example of this principle. During snack time, a deaf child asked/signed
"peanut butter" with an outstretched hand.
The teacher put the peanut butter on the
child's palm. The student then specified his
request.

Another important point to keep in mind
during the acquisition of language form is the
Cummins model of language proficiency (see
Chapter 1). A teacher could move up the vertical axis, begin with concrete, literal applications of the target structure, and move to
more abstract or figurative levels as students
develop their awareness of the structure. A
good rule to keep in mind is that language
work should always progress from the concrete and literal to the abstract, and from immediate experience to vicarious experience
(i.e., *context embedded*, *cognitively undemanding*, to *context-reduced*, *cognitively demanding*).

## Step 5: Provide Practice and Reinforcement—Teaching

By providing practice in a wide variety of
settings and activities, you can anticipate that
the students are going to begin to produce the
language in some manner. Your responsibility
is to create situations in which students can
use the target structures. It is at this stage
that students will begin to apply the structures
themselves through the use of language-
processing activities and composition work.
You support them throughout this step by using questions and direct suggestions for use.
The transitions from practice-with-support to
practice to independent usage are gradual. As
we discussed in step 4, this can be done by
using the procedures of spontaneous events,
action work, dialogues, and questioning. Additional strategies that can be used are media

(pictures, transparencies, and videotapes) and drill.

*Media.* Because pictures are more abstract than personal experiences, the use of media should not precede earlier language-processing experiences. However, the use of media is an excellent follow-up activity; it helps students to concentrate and review their earlier experiences with the target structure. When using media, you will want to stimulate language expression beyond what is actually portrayed in the media. Through active questioning, you and the students can share ideas that will form the basis for the target structure, and you can guide students to express ideas in the target structure.

*Drill.* Drill is a reinforcement activity; its effectiveness depends on the content of the activity, as well as the knowledge and skills that the students must acquire prior to engaging in any form of drill and practice. The value of drill is in the repetition that it provides. Students will not be able to learn the target structure from drill work; understanding and beginning competence of the target structure must proceed drill. As you will see when you read Chapter 10, use of guided practice and high success rates are essential for promoting gains during individual practice opportunities.

## Step 6: Assessing Progress

Assessment focuses on both the students and the learning opportunities that the students have had so that they can acquire a degree of proficiency with the target structure. At this point, the focus is on whether the students comprehend the structure and whether they have had sufficient exposure to multiple examples of it. If the students are making consistent errors, it may be necessary for you to reteach the structure or for you to provide additional activities in order that they develop a better sense of the structure.

## Step 7: Generalize—Teaching

If the target has been developed both in comprehension and in production, you now need to provide opportunities for its generalization to other contexts. There are many ways to structure this. One way is for you to try to involve all support staff and parents in an ongoing awareness of the language target that students are working on and to try to make a conscious effort to be sensitive to the students' development in that area. A second method for fostering generalization is through various subject areas. You can make a point of using particular structures to express ideas relating to the subject being taught. Also, teacher-led discussions and questions of reading content can be geared to the language concepts on which the students are working.

Another way to promote generalization is through the area of written language. Some specific ways in which you can encourage students to incorporate specific structures into their written work are: (1) Suggest that specific structures be incorporated into compositions; (2) provide support by asking specific questions about student compositions that would draw out their ideas and cause them to use the structures in specific places in their compositions (see also Chapter 12).

## Step 8: Expand Target Structure to Higher Levels of Difficulty—Teaching

In developing a language *sense* of a structure, you deliberately restrict the introduction of too many different examples and too many structures at one time. Once you have laid the foundation, you need to plan ways to broaden the students' understanding and use of the target structure. Different ways of expressing the same structure may be expanded upon. Five general categories in which expansion may occur are: concept expansions, structural expansions, linking expansions, vocabulary expansions, and abstract/metaphorical/idiomatic expansions.

*Structural expansions* focus attention on how students can use a target structure. For example, when you are introducing adjectives at the simple-sentence level, you will likely begin by introducing them following the copula in sentences, such as, "The boy is tall." A structural expansion would be to move the adjective to precede the noun in a sentence, such as, "The tall boy is my friend."

Another type of expansion is one in which the targeted structure belongs within the same structure or a very similar structure. For example, while working with the progressive tense of a verb, you might focus initially on the present progressive. After that has been mastered, you might begin work on the past progressive.

*Linking expansions* is the process of linking one or more target structures with each other. If you are working on possessive nouns and adjectives, students could begin to develop sentences that reflect the linked structures and produce sentences such as, "My father's car is fast."

Another technique is structuring language instruction at this level into lessons that emphasize problem solving (Stone & Fortier, 1984). For example, a student working on relative clauses could be placed in a role-playing situation in which the student has to convince an uncooperative adult to purchase an object, game, or item that is unfamiliar to the adult (e.g., I want to get the game that has a Pacman on it.). The focus of the conversation is on solving the problem, not on the language per se, but the student must have the ability to use English to achieve the goal. What is unique about this suggestion is that, instead of disrupting the exchange by constantly correcting the student's efforts, you wait until the conversation is completed and then reverse roles in order

to model any appropriate language that the student may not have used. Once the conversation is completed and the problem is solved, you and the student reverse roles again in order to provide the student with an opportunity to generate the appropriate language. By providing problems and practicing their solutions, the hearing-impaired student gains multiple exposures to English, but always in a conversational format rather than in isolated sentences or workbooks.

## COMMUNICATION GAMES

Communication games facilitate the use of language content and form in an enjoyable way. There are several different types of games that can be played, four of which are described in the following discussion.

### Barrier Games

Two players have identical sets of stimuli and are separated by a barrier. One player is designated as the leader. The leader's objective is to issue a series of one-step commands to the other player. For example, "Put the balloon under the ball." The leader's challenge is to use prepositions in a manner such that the directions can be followed.

The second player is the partner. This player's objective is to respond correctly to the leader's one-step commands without peeking over the barrier. The partner's goal is to arrange the items in a pattern identical to the leader's.

The teacher may need initially to model the leader's role for the players. After a student has assumed the role of leader and has given the commands, the partner should be permitted to verify directions or check information. Students play until all the objects are placed. The barrier is removed, and displays are checked for accuracy. The teacher can help players by identifying any incorrect placements and by repeating the original requests.

A variation of the game uses street maps or maps of states or countries instead of objects. The leader's assignment is to route the partner from one location to another. As part of the game, the leader tries to use vocabulary words that the teacher has integrated into the game map. (For example, the leader might rename streets by using words from the students' vocabulary list.) Once the leader has directed the partner from a starting to an ending point, the barrier is removed and the results are discussed. Roles are reversed, and the game is repeated.

Another variation of the barrier game is for the teacher to have students decorate identical cookie faces with different colored frostings. They can practice using color words or naming the parts of the face. To encourage students to practice shape words and prepositions, the teacher gives them identical sets of shapes and challenges them to arrange them in identical patterns.

The teacher can offer players a twist in the barrier game by purposely giving them slightly different sets of objects. As a result, opportunities for questioning abound. "What did you say?" "I don't have that," or similar requests are a natural consequence of the alteration and add another dimension to the activity.

## The Hiding Game

The hiding game is also played in pairs. The teacher identifies one player as the "hider" and the other as the "finder." The players use a set of cups under which are hidden small objects or cards. The cups can be similar or can differ in size or color. The cups are placed between the two players. The hider is supplied with a set of items or vocabulary words, or speech sounds on small cards. The object of the game is for the finder to locate the hidden items or cards by asking questions.

To begin, the finder closes his or her eyes while the objects or cards are hidden. The teacher can model the players' roles to explain the procedure. The hider asks the finder to locate an object: "Find the toy car." The finder must determine the hiding place through questioning: "Is the car under the blue cup?" or "Blue cup—car?" However, the finder must use language to question.

Variations of the game can include hiding objects inside other objects, on a person's body, or in a location around the room. In the latter case, the hider must come back and tell the finder where the object is hidden. Then the finder must locate it. If the finder comes back empty-handed, it is obvious that the hider needs to rephrase or reemphasize information. The farther the object is from the finder (i.e., context-reduced), the greater is the demand for language comprehension and communication.

As the ultimate hiding-game challenge, the teacher uses three players. Player 1 hides an object or a vocabulary card while the other players close their eyes. Player 1 then tells player 2 where the object is hidden (while player 3 keeps his or her eyes closed). Player 2 then tells player 3 where the object is hidden, and player 3 is expected to find it. Using written directions that have been created by player 1 and rewritten by player 2 for player 3 adds yet another dimension to this basic hiding game and promotes students' writing skills.

## The Describing Game

The describing game is played in teams. The teacher prepares by drawing some simple pictures that the students can easily redraw and that describe key vocabulary or word relationships (e.g., of a clown in a circle or a shoe on a box by a bed).

To begin the game, teams sit together with pencils and paper at an equal distance from the teacher. One member of each group is designated as the "runner." On signal, the runners rush to the teacher, who shows them a picture and explains its content. When the teacher signals again, the runners rush back to their groups and describe the picture. Runners are not permitted to draw or point; they must use only language to describe the picture. To win, all members of a team must accurately draw the teacher's picture. New runners are chosen, and the game goes on until each student has been a runner.

A variation of the game includes filling a paper bag with various small objects. The runners race to the teacher, who selects one runner to reach in the bag, pick an object (unseen by the others), and describe it to the other runners. Then the teacher signals again, and the runners return to their teams to describe the object. Team members take turns asking questions; the team to name the object first wins.

## The Telephone Game

For this game, students are grouped in several rows. The teacher identifies one player as the leader in each group. The teacher then gives each leader a brief, written message: Leaders read the message and repeat it to the person behind them (without the others watching). That person must then relay the message to the next person in the same manner and so on down the line, until the message reaches the last student in the row. That student writes down the message.

The challenge is for the students to pass an accurate message. The fun is in seeing how much the message changes in the process. If the teacher emphasizes good articulation, whether in sign, speech, or both, students will strive for accurate communication as they pass the message along.

A variation of the game is for students to be divided into several teams. One player from each team stands at the board, ready to write down vocabulary words or short sentences. The other students stand in a row behind the player. The last student in each row is the leader and faces the teacher; all the other students face the player at the blackboard.

To start the game, the teacher simultaneously gives a message to each of the leaders. The leaders can clarify the message if necessary; then they turn to the player who is standing with his or her back to them, tap that person's shoulder, and relay the message. That player clarifies the message, taps the next player's shoulder, and repeats the message. The game continues until the message has traveled down the line of students and has been written on the board. All players continue to face the blackboard until they are tapped. The teacher waits until the leaders in each row have sent a message before sending another message, but teachers can send messages as fast as the teams can handle them. This keeps everyone communicating. After the teacher has sent 8 or 10 sentences, the students compare the words or sentences listed on the board for accuracy.

## *SUMMARY*

Opportunities for practicing syntactic structures or lexical aspects of language should be provided within a meaningful context. Traditional language intervention approaches, which are usually structured in small group settings, create artificial situations designed to enhance the development of isolated linguistic constructs without consideration of the interrelationship of these skills to one another. In addition, many teachers fall into the trap of expecting young hearing-impaired students to use standard adult forms of English from the beginning. This runs counter to research evidence that shows that children learn language through the process of achieving closer and closer approximations to the language to which they are exposed. All children go through stages in the discovery of the rules for the structure of their language, and it is only after assimilation of a number of different rule-governed stages has been completed that the target structure is finally acquired (Rice & Kemper, 1985).

The communication approach that is advocated here closely approximates "normal" patterns of language acquisition. It is a means of (1) developing linguistic constructs at the developmental level of functioning of any particular student, (2) integrating all linguistic areas within the communication framework; and (3) providing meaningful and age-appropriate contexts in which to do so. If structures are to be acquired and not taught, there should be a period of meaningful exposure to them prior to expecting the student to recognize, comprehend, or use them. If you are aware of the language needs of your students and are sensitive to their next stage of development, then almost any subject matter can become the vehicle for introducing new complex structures. Once goals are identified, you should provide tangible experiences with objects and events, linguistic forms, and interpersonal interactions so that linguistic rules can be induced by the students in a sequence that is similar to that of hearing students. When new vocabulary is introduced, each word or phrase should be demonstrated by using several examples to encourage generalization. The challenge for teachers of hearing-impaired students is to have an understanding of the developmental stages of language acquisition, to establish a classroom environment that promotes conversation, and to use facilitative activities and specific systematic experiences so that every hearing-impaired student has the opportunity to develop competence in communication.

## ACTIVITIES

1. Compare and contrast the form of two languages. Discuss at least 10 similarities or differences.
2. Write 5 form goals for a hypothetical hearing-impaired 6-year-old girl, Stacey.
3. Pick a form structure of English to teach to a 10-year-old child and plan lessons by using the 8 steps of the Reed and Bugen process approach to guide you.
4. Using one of the communication games, teach signs or spoken words to at least one child or adult.

# CHAPTER 8

# Speech

## OVERVIEW

In this chapter, information pertaining to the assessment and intervention of speech to hearing-impaired students who have been assessed as capable of benefiting from intervention is provided. The material is based primarily on the work of Ling (1976, 1988). Outlined are nonsegmental aspects of speech, vowel and diphthong, simple consonant, and phonological evaluations. A sequential and systematic intervention approach is recommended, as is the contention that the teacher of hearing-impaired students should be responsible for coordinating the program of those students who are receiving speech services. A collaborative model of intervention, including all significant adults, conducted in an environment that is relaxed and yet challenging, is suggested.

---

### CHAPTER TOPICS

Speech Defined
Methods of Speech Training
Speech Assessment
Phonetic Evaluation
Phonologic Evaluation
Speech Intervention

---

## SPEECH DEFINED

*Speech* is the oral production of language. It is a complex motor behavior that requires precise control and manipulation of the vocal tract and oral musculature. To produce speech, a child must learn to coordinate respiration (inhaling and exhaling), phonation (producing sound), resonation (modifying tone), and articulation (the production of consonants and vowels), in addition to the suprasegmental features of *pitch, rate, rhythm, and loudness* (Lieberth, 1982) that pertain to the overall pattern of speech. A hearing loss is a major impediment to speech development because it severely restricts reception of speech and reduces the ability of the speaker to monitor his or her own speech. A person with a hearing loss will not have an opportunity to develop intelligible speech without a systematic and comprehensive intervention program. Therefore, it is essential that educators have an understanding of how speech is developed and know how to intervene in order to help the hearing-impaired student learn to speak.

Ling (1976, 1988) has described the orderly process of speech development and has suggested a sequential model that can be used in teaching speech to hearing-impaired students, which is based on research with normal, hearing students. Central to his approach is the belief that speech is a motor activity. The development of any given sound pattern demands the presence of previously acquired motor patterns. As each new sound pattern emerges, it interacts with those that have already been established. Ling (1976, 1978) contends that failure to consider the sequence in which sound patterns are taught results in faults that hinder development. According to Ling (1979), normal speech development progresses from (1) simple vocalization through control over voice patterns, to (2) the emergence of a basic vowel system and the coarticulation of consonants, to (3) mastery of the blending process in running speech. In each of these stages students vary in the order of their phoneme acquisition and in their concurrent mastery of several distinctly different speech patterns. Each stage of development provides the foundation for the acquisition of speech patterns in the next and subsequent stages.

Phonetic level skills include the ability (1) to control intensity, duration, and voice frequency during vocalizations and (2) to produce, repeat, and alternate *segmental* patterns within syllables. Phonological skills include the ability to use the segmental and suprasegmental features of speech in meaningful contexts. Without control over vocalization and voice patterns, students will not possess the basic tools of breath and voice control that permit vowel differentiation and consonant production.

Exhibit 8.1 charts the development of speech acquisition; these stages are detailed later in this chapter under the section concerning speech intervention.

**EXHIBIT 8.1.** Major stages of speech acquisition

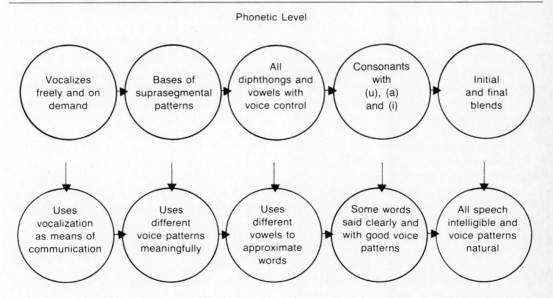

Phonetic Level

Vocalizes freely and on demand → Bases of suprasegmental patterns → All diphthongs and vowels with voice control → Consonants with (u), (a) and (i) → Initial and final blends

Uses vocalization as means of communication → Uses different voice patterns meaningfully → Uses different vowels to approximate words → Some words said clearly and with good voice patterns → All speech intelligible and voice patterns natural

Phonologic Level

SOURCE: Reprinted by permission of the publisher from "Speech development in hearing-impaired children," by D. Ling, *Journal of Communication Disorders*, Vol. 11 (2/3). Copyright 1978 by Elsevier Science Publishing Co. Inc.

## METHODS OF SPEECH TRAINING

The object of speech training is to enable hearing-impaired individuals to communicate with other persons more efficiently than if they used written messages or sign that would not be understood by the majority of hearing people (Marimont, 1974). Several methods for teaching speech to the hearing-impaired have been proposed and used. In general, these methods fall into three categories, depending upon the linguistic level emphasized when new or incorrectly pronounced speech is taught: *phoneme* (smallest unit of language sound), *syllable*, or *word* (Abraham & Stoker, 1984). The use of the phoneme method for teaching speech has become questionable and is rarely advocated. As expressed by Marimont (1974), "the correct pronunciation of each phoneme is not always necessary nor sufficient for comprehensible speech" (p. 225). Syllable methods of teaching speech employ repetitive practice of novel phonemes such as "la, la, la" or "bo, bo, bo" in non-meaningful syllable stimuli prior to their pronunciation within meaningful words. Such methods emphasize the motor aspects of speech production, the movement of the articulators from one placement to the next, and as a result often view misarticulation as a motor speech disorder (Abraham & Stoker, 1984). Word methods use pronunciation of phonemes in the context of meaningful words as the basis of teaching speech.

Little empirical research exists concerning systematically evaluating the relative effectiveness of any method for teaching speech to hearing-impaired students and youth (Abraham & Stoker, 1984; Moores, 1987). The presence of diverse teaching methods in the absence of a substantial research base has resulted in considerable confusion within the field of deaf education. Valid comparisons of different training methods are desperately needed. As a result of this paucity of empirical research, it is difficult to choose objectively and to recommend an approach for teaching speech to hearing-impaired students. In addition, it is beyond the scope of this textbook to provide an in-depth explanation of all the methods that professionals currently use to teach speech to hearing-impaired students. The reader is encouraged to use the resources developed by Calvert and Silverman (1983); Ling (1976); Sanders (1982); and Sims, Walter, & Whitehead (1982) for more comprehensive information on this topic.

Given the limitations cited, we recommend an assessment and intervention approach of speech for those hearing-impaired students who have been assessed as able to benefit from such intervention that draws most heavily on the work of Ling (1976, 1988). While there has been little research to substaniate Ling's work, the approach is the one that has been accepted by the majority of programs in the field of deaf education (Bunch, 1987). We have made specific adaptations as they were necessary for maintaining a systematic yet balanced approach toward teaching speech to hearing-impaired students. Speech development has been defined as "the acquisition of a variety of skills related to the production and reception of meaningful, spoken language. These skills include "linguistic competence, auditory comprehension and pragmatics as well as speech production ability" (Nittrouer & Hochberg, 1985, p. 491). Although there are many diverse philosophies concerning the education of hearing-impaired students, all of the contemporary approaches encourage and advocate the development of oral communication skills to whatever extent is possible (Monsen, 1981). Golf, (1980) presented a list of eight factors that contribute to the attainment of intelligible speech. They are:

A positive attitude toward the value of
　oral communication
Effective and skillful teachers
A systematic speech program
Appropriate amplification and maximal
　development of residual hearing

Adequate experience in the use of speech

Development of an effective auditory-kinesthetic feedback system

Transfer of automatic phonetic skills to the phonological level

Supportive, informed, and cooperative parents

Many of these factors are related directly to the attitude and skill level of the teacher. Therefore, it is recommended that the teacher should be the person who is primarily responsible for the speech training of the students (Ling, 1976; Nittrouer & Hochberg, 1985; Siebert, 1980). This is recommended because hearing-impaired students develop speech patterns whenever communication takes place, and such development should not be restricted to the period or place set aside for speech. Although the speech and language pathologist may assess articulation, set goals, and assist the students in developing the desired phonetic skills and phonologic skills, it is clearly the responsibility of the classroom or itinerant teacher to provide the opportunity for practice throughout the course of a school day. Consequently, it is important that you as a teacher of hearing-impaired students, establish an environment that facilitates the use and practice of speech. Features of that environment include

An expectation that speech is to be used when communication takes place

Appropriate modeling of speech for the students

Goals and objectives written after speech assessment has been completed

Abundant and functional opportunities for using speech

Encouragement and positive (but realistic) feedback for speech use.

## SPEECH ASSESSMENT

Evaluation is essential to effective teaching. Evaluation techniques should be employed to determine the skills already mastered but not consistently used in meaningful speech, as well as to determine the areas that need further development. As stated by Pronovost (1979), "at the present time, the best analyzer of human speech is the human ear and . . . a well-trained, experienced listener could provide more useful and valid descriptive and judgmental information than could be gleaned from acoustical and/or physiological measurements alone" (p. 512). The trained listener, from hearing and observing the hearing-impaired speaker, makes inferences concerning the choice of appropriate intervention strategies. Formal assessment can be accomplished by using Ling's phonetic and phonological evaluation. The results of these evaluations are then used as a basis for setting up specific targets to be developed on phonetic and phonologic levels. If you are hearing-impaired yourself, ask the speech and language pathologist to undertake the evaluation process and then to share with you the specific speech targets to work on with students.

The purposes of a phonetic-level evaluation are (1) to determine what motor speech skills the child has mastered or retained and (2) to specify what targets should be developed next. The tasks that the student is asked to do follow the developmental sequence of spoken English acquisition and represent the abilities needed in order to produce fluent spoken English. The evaluation tool is broken down into eight sections. Each section is then divided into steps. The specific areas that the test examines are: nonsegmental aspects (use of voice, duration, intensity, and pitch), vowels and diphthongs, simple consonants and word-initial blends. For young students, the assessment would need to be given over several days. The test is administered imitatively: You provide the model, and the student repeats it. The criterion is based upon what the student does once he/she understand the procedure. The student's productions are marked ($\sqrt{}$) if they are produced consistently, (+) if

**EXHIBIT 8.2.** Phonetic-level speech evaluation (Ling, 1976)

---

*Nonsegmental aspects*

Indicate whether produced consistently (✔), inconsistently (+), or not at all (−).

(a) Vocalization:     spontaneous _____ on demand _____
(b) Vocal duration:   sustained _____ brief _____ varied _____

*Vowels and diphthongs*

| | S R | | S R | | S R | | S R |
|---|---|---|---|---|---|---|---|---|
| [ba] | – – | [pa] | – – | [wa] | – – | [ʌa] | – – |
| [bi] | – – or | [pi] | – – | [wi] | – – or | [ʌi] | – – |
| [bu] | – – | [pu] | – – | [wu] | – – | [ʌu] | – – |

| | S R | | S R | | S R | | S R |
|---|---|---|---|---|---|---|---|---|
| [fa] | – – | [va] | – – | [θa] | – – | [ða] | – – |
| [fi] | – – or | [vi] | – – | [θi] | – – or | [ði] | – – |
| [fu] | – – | [vu] | – – | [θu] | – – | [ðu] | – – |

*Simple consonants: Step 1*

| | S R A P | | S R A P | | S R A P | | S R A P | | S R A P |
|---|---|---|---|---|---|---|---|---|---|---|
| [a] | – – – – | [i] | – – – – | [u] | – – – – | [aʊ] | – – – – | [aɪ] | – – – – |

| | S R A P | | S R A P | | S R A P | | S R A P | | S R A P |
|---|---|---|---|---|---|---|---|---|---|---|
| [ɔ] | – – – – | [ɔɪ] | – – – – | [ɛ] | – – – – | [ʊ] | – – – – | [ɪ] | – – – – |

---

SOURCE: D. Ling, *Teacher/Clinician Planbook and Guide to the Development of Speech Skills*. Washington, D.C.: Alexander Graham Bell Association for the Deaf, Inc., 1978. Reprinted by permission.

they are produced inconsistently, or (−) if they are not produced at all. Unless the student is at the stage of abundant vocalization or is unable to participate in an imitative test, test through step 4 consonants of the phonetic-level evaluation sheet in order to determine all the productive voice patterns, vowels and diphthongs, and consonants in the child's repertoire. Administration of the phonetic and phonologic evaluations should follow the guidelines that follow. Excerpts of Ling's forms, which can be acquired from the Alexander Graham Bell Association for the Deaf, are found in Exhibits 8.2 and 8.3.

## PHONETIC EVALUATION

### Administration of Nonsegmental Aspects

1. *Vocalization*: It is not necessary to test this directly. Use what you know about the student's spontaneous and elicited speech.

2. *Vocal duration*:
   Sustained: Model one long vowel, sustained with good breath control and stable intensity and pitch.

   Brief: Model one or more short syllables, such as *bi, bi, bi, bi, bi.*

   Varied: Model a string of syllables spoken with English rhythmic characteristics, such as *bi bi ba, bi bi ba, bi bi ba.*

3. *Vocal intensity*:
   Loud: Model a loud voice or shout in a syllable or syllable string, or ask the child to call someone (or pretend to do so) who is far away, or to wake you from a pretend sleep.

   Quiet: It is not necessary to test this if the child has produced the duration tasks in a normal conversational voice. If necessary, model a *bi* or a *hello* in a normal voice.

**EXHIBIT 8.3.** Phonologic-level speech evaluation (Ling, 1976)

### Nonsegmental Aspects

Normal (✔)    Faulty ( − )

Breath control _____ Intensity control _____ Pitch control _____

Intonation _____ Duration of vowels _____

Duration of consonants _____ Phrasing _____ Stress _____

### Segmental Aspects

Indicate if sound is produced consistently (✔), inconsistently ( + ), or not at all ( − ).

*Vowels and Diphthongs*

u _____ ʊ _____ o _____ ɔ _____ ɑ _____ a _____ ʌ _____

ɝ _____ ə _____ ɚ _____ æ _____ ɛ _____ e _____ ɪ _____

i _____ aɪ _____ aʊ _____ ɔɪ _____ eɪ _____ Other _____

*Simple Consonants*

Plosives: b _____ d _____ g _____ p _____ t _____ k _____

Unreleased stops: p̄ _____ t̄ _____ k̄ _____ b̄ _____ d̄ _____ ḡ _____

Nasals: m _____ n _____ ŋ _____

Semivowels: w _____ j _____ ʍ _____

Liquids: l _____ r _____

Fricatives: h _____ f _____ θ _____ ʃ _____ s _____ v _____ ∂ _____ ʒ _____ z _____

Affricates: tʃ _____ dʒ _____

SOURCE: D. Ling, *Teacher/Clinician Planbook and Guide to the Development of Speech Skills*. Washington, D.C.: Alexander Graham Bell Association for the Deaf, Inc., 1978. Reprinted by permission.

Whisper: Model a string of whispered syllables *pipipipipi* or *su su su su su*.

Varied: Model a string of syllables varying between quiet and that replicate the stress patterns of English *wiwiwiwiwiwiwi*. Then, model a string of syllables varying between quiet and whispered.

4. *Vocal pitch*:

Mid: Ask the child to say "hi" to establish his or her normal midpitch.

Low: Model a *hi* or a *ba* several tones lower than the midpitch.

High: Model a *hi* or a *ba* several tones higher than the midpitch.

Continuously varied: Model a sweep on a single vowel from high to low ( ) and another from low to high ( ). You can also model a series of continuously varied sweeps ( ).

Discretely varied: Model a series of discrete pitches: low-mid-high (-¯), low-high-mid (-¯-), high-low-mid (¯-⁻), and so on.

## Administration of the Vowels and Diphthongs

1. *For all simple vowels*:

Single syllables: Model the vowel once in isolation.

Repeated syllables: Model the vowel in a syllable string released with *b* or some other consonant that the student can easily produce at a rate of at least three per second.

Alternated syllables: Model the vowel alternated with another nonadjacent vowel in a syllable string released with *b* or some other easily produced consonant at a rate of at least three per second.

Pitch: Model the vowel released with a consonant in a series of syllables having English-sounding pitch changes.

2. *For all diphthongs*:

Single syllables: Model the diphthong once in isolation.

Repeated syllables: Model the diphthong in a syllable string at a rate of at least three per second.

Alternated syllables: Model the diphthong in a syllable alternated with a nonadjacent vowel or diphthong at a rate of at least three per second.

Pitch: Model the diphthong in a series of syllables having English-sounding pitch changes.

## Administration of Simple Consonants

1. Single syllables: Model the consonant-vowel *CV* or vowel-consonant *VC* syllable as written.
2. Repeated syllables: Model the *CV* or *VC* syllables as written in a string at a rate of at least three per second.
3. Can alternate: Model one syllable set

(e.g., *bama*). Then, model that set repeated at a rate of at least three per second (e.g. bamabamabama.)

4. Can produce in loud voice, quiet voice, and whisper: Model two or three strings of repeated syllables that the student is able to produce in a loud voice and in a whisper.
5. Can vary pitch over range of eight semitones: Model two or three strings of repeated syllables that the student is able to produce with English-sounding pitch changes.

When the student demonstrates considerable mastery of these levels and additional targets are necessary for the student, use similar procedures to assess the student's phonetic speech skills on word-initial blends and word-final blends.

## Planning Phonetic Intervention

After you have administered the Phonetic Level Speech Evaluation, there are some specific procedures that you should follow in order to plan the student's speech treatment programs appropriately (Ling, 1983). The first step is for you to make a list of the student's productive, inconsistent, and non-

---

**EXHIBIT 8.4.**

Student Name _____     Date _____
Teacher _____     School _____

**Productive Speech Patterns**

*Nonsegmentals*

*Vowels and Diphthongs*

*Consonants*

productive speech patterns using forms similar to those found in Exhibits 8.4 and 8.5. Consider the principle of *least intervention* (e.g., If a student can make the /i/ sound in single syllables but the sound cannot be repeated, then this should be one of your first objectives since the student will need a minimal amount of practice to be able to master the repetition task). Work only on targets with which the student needs practice and do not spend time on speech patterns that are already being used. If the student demonstrates limited mastery at the nonsegmental level, then concentrate on achieving abundant vocalization, on establishing a pleasant sounding voice, and on enriching and stabilizing achievable patterns. Voice problems should be given priority attention. For example, Danielle, a 7-year-old, severely hearing-impaired student, demonstrated difficulty in the area of vocal intensity. She was unable to whisper and also had problems using a loud voice. Therefore, we decided to make both of these two of her initial targets. If fundamental pitch is inappropriate, establishing an appropriate pitch should be the first priority. If the student is already using English-sounding suprasegmentals, most vowels, and some consonants, work on some nonsegmentals if necessary, some vowels, and some consonants.

## PHONOLOGIC EVALUATION

The purpose of the phonologic evaluation is to determine what speech skills a student actually uses in spontaneous speech and to evaluate the student's cognitive/linguistic functioning in five aspects of discourse—conversation, description, explanation, narration, and questioning. When you are preparing to administer the phonologic-level evaluation, it is important to gather the appropriate materials for each specific activity in each discourse area. Assemble all the materials you will need and position them so that you can handle them easily. Set up a videotape or a tape recorder. Use a video or tape recorder to record the student's utterances so that you can summarize the data after the assessment has been completed. Be certain to put the machine on pause if you have to talk to the student for any length of time. Exhibit 8.6 is a list of the five areas of discourse and the subtopics that you will want to evaluate. In addition, there are suggestions for procedures that you may want to use to help elicit those target areas.

---

**EXHIBIT 8.5.**

Student Name _____     Date _____
Teacher _____     School _____

### Inconsistent and Nonproductive Speech Patterns

| Inconsistent | Nonproductive |
|---|---|
| *Nonsegmentals* | *Nonsegmentals* |
| *Vowels and Diphthongs* | *Vowels and Diphthongs* |
| *Consonants* | *Consonants* |

**EXHIBIT 8.6.** Suggested procedures and activities for assessing phonologic-level skills (adapted from Long, 1986)

| Discourse | To Evaluate | Procedure |
|---|---|---|
| Conversation | Interaction and relatedness.<br>Use of the conventions or "rules" of conversation. | Engage the student in conversation on a topic of interest to the student. |
| Description | Creativity and colorfulness of language.<br>Ability to code spatial relations. | Ask the student to choose a room in his or her house and to describe it. Ask the student to include information about the furnishings and their specific locations. If the student has difficulty with the demands of this task, you can show the student a dollhouse or a room in a doll house that has been set up and ask the student to describe it. |
| Explanation | Use of imperative statements.<br>Ability to code temporal relationships.<br>Understanding of and ability to code cause. | Set out the ingredients and utensils needed for making a sandwich (perhaps peanut butter and jelly). Ask the student to pretend you do not know what anything is or what it is for and have the student tell you what to do. |
| Narration | Imaginative thinking.<br>Ability to sequence ideas.<br>Use of words that cue time sequence. | Show the student a story in the form of a set of pictures in mixed-up order. Ask the student to put the pictures in correct order and to think of a story. Take the pictures away and have the student tell you the story. |
| Questioning | Curiosity.<br>Broad-to-narrow cognitive processing abilities.<br>Use of open questions.<br>Use of yes/no questions. | Hold a picture so that the student cannot see it. Tell the student to ask you questions to determine what is in the picture. If this is too difficult, have the student ask you questions about yourself or take turns with the student asking questions of one another. |

SOURCE: M. Long, *Phonologic Evaluation*. Rochester, NY: Rochester School for the Deaf, 1986.

## Planning Phonologic Intervention

After completing the phonologic assessment procedures, you will want to analyze the data. The first step is to transcribe the student's utterances, using written English from the recording you have made. While you are listening to the tape, fill out the nonsegmental aspects of the phonologic assessment sheet and note the English phonemes that are present and that have been correctly used. When you are done, you can compare the results of the phonologic evaluation with the results from the student's phonetic-level speech evaluation. In an attempt to offset any bias that you may have because you are familiar with the student's speech patterns, it is a valuable practice to have the speech and language pathologist or another teacher of the hearing-impaired listen to the tape and designate the segmental sounds that he or she feels is being made appropriately. This type of assessment should be undertaken at least twice, if not three times, during the academic school year.

## Other Assessment Methods

There is an additional assessment tool that you may want to become familiar with has been developed by Monsen, Moog, and Geers (1988). It uses pictures as stimuli to provide an estimation of the overall speech intelligibility of hearing-impaired students. It is referred to as the CID Picture Speech Intelligibility Evaluation (SPINE) and was developed at the Central Institute for the Deaf, St. Louis, Missouri. The test materials consist of a test manual, response forms, and a box containing the picture cards. The test requires 20 to 30 minutes to administer and about 10 minutes to score. The pictures used are generally known to students who are age 7 and above. The 100 picture cards are organized into four sets of 25 each. Each set of 25 cards consists of phonetically similar words, such as pie, pig, pin, pen, and pants. The student is given a deck of cards and asked to pick a card without the examiner seeing it. The student then says the name of the picture, still without showing it to the examiner. The student's task is to say the pictured word intelligibly so that the examiner can decide which word from the 25 possible choices the student is trying to say.

After the picture is named by the student and a response is written by the examiner, each card is set aside and carefully stacked in order. Although the examiner knows the set of 25 possible pictures, the examiner does not know which word the student will try to say on any given test item. As a result, the examiner is not evaluating how well a word was said but only if the quality of what was said was functionally good enough to make the word understandable. Keeping the cards in order facilitates the scoring process. After the test has been administered and the student has left the testing area, the responses are checked. The examiner checks the written responses against the picture cards. The number of correct responses is tallied and converted to a percent correct score. Approximate interpretations of the scores are as follows:

| | |
|---|---|
| 100–90 percent correct: | Excellent achievement |
| 89–80 percent correct: | Good achievement in speech intelligibility |
| 79–70 percent correct: | Listener experienced difficulty in understanding the intended message |
| 69–60 percent correct: | Listener experienced great difficulty in understanding the intended message |
| 59 percent and below: | Listener experienced overwhelming difficulty in understanding the intended message |

Copies of the CID Picture SPINE can be obtained from the Central Institute for the Deaf.

A speech intelligibility test that requires less time and can be used with students from ages 8 and older is the Speech Intelligibility Test for Deaf Children, which was developed by Magner (1980). The test correlates highly with the results found in the SPINE (Porter & Bradley, 1985), but it requires a large number of professionals to do the assessment. The test can be obtained from the Clark School for the Deaf in Northampton, Massachusetts.

## SPEECH INTERVENTION

Behaviors that are necessary for speech readiness should be present before actual intervention is begun. *Physical availability* and eye contact are two necessary behaviors. Physical availability is defined as a child's comfort at being close to a teacher; it is related to social-emotional factors. A comfortable rapport needs to be created in which a good relationship and the student's confidence is achieved. This rapport can be achieved through different play exchanges, which are targeted at activities that are of interest to the student. To proceed with speech, the teacher has to obtain eye contact with the student. Playful games like peek-a-boo and blowing bubbles can be helpful, since they force the student to look at the face and eyes of the teacher. The student must also be ready to focus on the planned stimuli for an activity.

Age and cognitively appropriate activities that arouse interest, excitement, and curiosity are beneficial. To exploit a student's interest in teacher-initiated activities, the student should be allowed to make choices and share the "control" of the situation with the teacher. Having a second student join the ac-

tivity could be workable in some cases. You may find the chart in Exhibit 8.7 to be useful for planning and recording the development of some precursory speech behaviors that are essential prior to beginning any form of formal speech training. Examples of activities that can be used to encourage speech behaviors that have been adapted from Long (1981) are found in Exhibit 8.8.

## The Stages of Speech Acquisition

Look again at Exhibit 8.1. The first stage of speech acquisition requires abundant *vocalization*. The basic factor for speech is voice,

---

**EXHIBIT 8.7**

Student Name _____     Date _____
Your Name _____     School _____

### Precursory Behaviors for Speech Intervention

|  | Date of Evaluation | Behavior Emerging | Behavior Consistent |
|---|---|---|---|
| 1. Physical availability |  |  |  |
| 2. Eye contact |  |  |  |
| 3. Imitation of motor activities |  |  |  |
| 4. Abundant vocalizations |  |  |  |
| 5. Vocal duration |  |  |  |
| 6. Vocal intensity |  |  |  |
| 7. Vocal pitch |  |  |  |

List the activities to be used to promote the skills listed above:

1.

2.

3.

4.

5.

6.

7.

**EXHIBIT 8.8.** Activities for encouraging precursory speech behaviors adapted from Long (1981)

I. A. *Physical availability*
   B. *Eye contact*
      1. Peek-a-boo
      2. Put on make-up, shaving cream
      3. Put on or take off wigs, jewelry, glasses, hats
      4. Make and wear Halloween masks and play games with them
      5. Feed each other
      6. Blow bubbles
      7. Blow up balloons

II. *Involvement in teacher-initiated activities*
   A. Teacher offers child choices
   B. Teacher produces activities from different types of surprise bags or boxes, appealing to child
   C. Teacher encourages child's involvement with manipulative toys and blocks
   D. Teacher brings another child to session to serve as model

III. *Imitation of motor activities*
   A. Let child initiate activities; teacher imitates child
   B. Teacher taps parts of body; child imitates
   C. Teacher walks, hops, jumps; child imitates
   D. Teacher and child play ball, throwing ball in characteristic ways
   E. Teacher and child make similar block constructions
   F. Teacher and child do imitative art activities
   G. Child's and teacher's puppets imitate each other
   H. Teacher and child make shadow figures using the overhead light to show one hand or both hands, to wiggle fingers, to show a hand making circles, to show hands as a mouth moving, to make animal faces, and so on.
   I. Teacher and child play get up and sit down
   J. Teacher and child face one another and simultaneously mirror each other's actions
   K. Teacher and child imitate one another's actions in a mirror
   L. Teacher and child sign participation songs

SOURCE: Adapted from M. Long, *Phonologic Evaluation*. Rochester, NY: Rochester School for the Deaf.

which produced by respiration, phonation, and resonation. Vocalization is the first step in developing voice. The student should be encouraged to vocalize in abundance. A creative and imaginative teacher can make the student vocalize through different playful exercises. Exciting and interesting activities will naturally motivate the student to vocalize spontaneously. Always encourage the student to produce a pleasant (not harsh, brief, or shrill) voice. If simple evocation of voice is required, tickle the student to evoke laughter or engage the student in exertion (e.g., by pulling, pushing, or lifting a heavy object). You should use these games prudently, because the student may associate voicing with overall body tension. If the student does not want to be touched, let the student touch or tickle you while voicing.

Breathing has a basic role to play in voicing. The student should learn to take proper breath and maintain it and release it as needed. Prosodic qualities in speech, such as rhythm, stress, phrasing, intonation, and so on, depend on breath. Activities like blowing out candles and making bubbles will help.

Always encourage the student to vocalize, and allow and encourage the student to take risks. Although the pleasure that the student will receive from vocalization could be an intrinsic reinforcement, the student with poor hearing probably will require external reinforcement. Make a point to reinforce the student's vocalizations by repeating the student's utterance, smiling, patting, giving any verbal response, giving stickers, or giving food. Set pragmatic objectives such that the student must use voice to get others' attention, to express emotion, to make comments, or to vocalize in response to a question.

*Voice patterns* are to be considered as the stepping-stone to suprasegmental structure. As a result, the second stage requires voice patterns that vary in intensity, duration, and pitch. The speech of hearing-impaired students is often choppy. What usually is needed is practice holding the breath, sustaining this behavior for a certain time, and vocalizing in chunk phrases according to the situation or message that has been given. Training in vocal duration is a major long-term goal. By *vocal duration* we mean that the student has come to the point at which there is control over duration of voice. In one breath the student is able to imitate groups of up to four distinct vocalizations varying in duration, for example, *papapapa-------------pupupu------pu------pupu* or *fafafa----fufufufu-----fafafa----------fufu*.

*Timing control* is fundamental to further speech development. When a student is able to sustain vocalization for at least three seconds, other aspects (e.g., intensity and pitch) can be attempted. At this level, specific vowels or consonants are not attempted; only vocal duration.

According to Ling (1976), the subskills to be achieved are

1. *Sustain* vocalization *for at least three seconds*. (e.g., *ba----------- >*)
2. *Imitate separate* vocalizations *differing in duration*, each on one breath (e.g., *baba/bababa/ba/*)
3. *Imitate* up to *four separate vocalizations* differing in duration, all on one breath (e.g., *baba-----bababa--------babababa----ba*)

In the following list are some different activities that can be used to increase a stu-

dent's ability to maintain the duration that is necessary for functional speech:

Rock a baby doll smoothly; bounce a baby doll.

Move a car, truck, animal, and so on, smoothly or roughly across the floor.

Play "make me walk glidingly/make me hop or jump" (by having the child move appropriately to your utterances first).

Pull out a measuring tape in a sustained manner or in jerks.

Pull yarn or scarves out of a can that has a hole in the lid.

Finger paint or color

Splash water on a doll; drip and pour water into containers.

Smear toothpaste or shaving cream.

"Paint" with water on a mirror.

Drop or slide objects through a tube.

Turn a faucet on or off; let the water drip.

Walk up the steps of a slide; slide down.

Squeeze glue or water out of a plastic bottle or tube.

*Intensity* is the loudness in one's voice or speech. In everyday speech a hearing person varies loudness according to the need, the environment, the number of listeners, the type of conversation being held, the area or the space, the ambient noise, the distance between the listener and the speaker, and so forth. A hearing-impaired student needs assistance to comprehend these skills.

It is important that the student be able to produce voice at various intensity levels and differentiate them from each other before pitch control is introduced. This will help avoid confusion between intensity and pitch. Whispering will help the student to listen and avoid a falsetto voice.

Some specific activities that can be used to promote an understanding of intensity are:

**Quiet** (if not already developed or to reinforce)

sing or talk to a doll.
Indicate to the child that you want the child to talk louder or more quietly.
Ignore a too quiet voice.
Associate with a quiet drum beat.

## Loud

Associate with a loud drum beat.
Throw things.
Pretend to sleep and have the child wake you up with a loud voice or do this to a doll.
Pop up from behind a barrier on child's production of a loud voice.
Use a toy that lights up to sound.
Set up an angry situation.
Have someone go away from the child and then call that person back.
Go outside and call someone from a distance.
Get excited about something and shout for joy or triumph.

## Whisper

Put a baby doll to bed.
Breath on a mirror and show the condensation that results.
Play with tissues or feathers.
Blow bubbles, rice, and so on, smoothly.
Play a secretive game or tell a secret.

## Varied intensities

Tiptoe up to someone talking quietly and then yell "boo!"

*Pitch* may be very difficult for profoundly deaf students because it cannot be replicated visibly. The goal is to achieve mid, high, and low levels. Tactile cues such as feeling the vibrations of the thyroid cartilage or the chest for a low pitch, repeating central vowels [*ea*, *a(r)*, *aw*] for midpitch, or feeling the vibrations on the forehead for a higher frequency could be employed. If the classroom is alive with exciting and playful activities, it will be an optimum environment for spontaneous utterances in various pitch levels. The student should be reinforced immediately when good pitch is used.

In the initial stage, only gross pitch adjustments are targeted. If the student's utterances demand too much pressure on the larynx and articulators, the student has not come to the point at which it is done automatically or has not achieved a spontaneous reflexive action. Continue with nonmeaningful utterances (elicited with playful situations) at the phonetic level until the utterances become automatic. Here is a list of activities that can be used to promote an understanding and competence in the area of vocal pitch:

Use a blue paper towel roll and a small red tube that fits over the blue roll to represent the larynx. Make associations between your own larynx being up and a high-pitch voice. Move the red tube up and down and have the student produce an associated pitch.
Make three buildings that vary in height: high, medium, and low. Have Superman fly to the top of and off the buildings. The student discriminates or produces an appropriate pitch level to move Superman or while moving him.
Associate the movement of an airplane, bird, car, or roller coaster by fluctuating your pitch level up and down.
Associate body movement (arms up, lowering of head to chest to force larynx down) with production of lower pitch level.
Incorporate pitch into stories like "The Three Bears" giving Papa Bear a low voice, Baby Bear a high voice, etc.)

The third stage focuses on vowel and diphthong production, while the fourth stage attends to consonants and the fifth, to consonant blends. At each stage, there are two levels of acquisition: the phonetic level, in which the primary goal is to establish correct and clearly differentiated motor patterns, and the phonologic level, in which established patterns are used meaningfully and systematically in running speech. Any given speech target behavior may be considered as consisting of a series of component subskills, each of which the student must master before use can be expected in communicative speech. An effective program of speech training should include training on both the phonetic and phonologic levels. At each phonetic level that skill has been acquired, it must be repeated, generalized to a variety of phonetic contexts, and alternated with other segmental patterns. Repetition and alternation in various phonetic contexts at rates required for normal speech (at least three syllables per second) demand levels of automaticity that can be achieved only through overlearning. One advantage in providing a detailed description of the numerous subskills that underlie each speech target is that it provides the teacher with a series of unambiguous objectives. Additionally, the student's progress toward each objective can be incrementally tested at both the phonetic and phonologic level.

## Building Skills

*Fluency* can be achieved only if the neuromotor skills required for producing speech patterns have been acquired. There are four principal components of any motor skill: accuracy, speed, economy of effort, and flexibility (Ling, 1979). All four components are essential to automatization of a speech pattern. Automaticity, production without conscious attention, is required if the student is to be concerned with what to say rather than how to say it. Syllable practice allows the student to proceed in carefully controlled steps, from the easy to the difficult, from the simple to the complex, and from the known

to the unknown, without requiring the student to make quantum leaps in skill acquisition, therefore risking failure. An example of subskill sequence suggested by Ling (1976) is as follows:

SUBSKILL 1:   Production of *b* in single syllables, releasing various vowels, including *i*, *a*, and *u*.

SUBSKILL 2:   Production of *b* in a series of repeated syllables formed with one vowel or another (e.g., *bubububu*, *bibibibi*, etc.).

SUBSKILL 3:   Production of *b* in a series of repeated syllables formed with various vowels (e.g., *bibabu*, *b bi bae*, etc.).

SUBSKILL 4:   Alternation of syllables released with *b* and syllables released with other consonants in subskill 1 (e.g., *bamabama*, *bifibifi*, etc.).

SUBSKILL 5:   Production of *b* in syllables varying in intensity.

SUBSKILL 6:   Production of *b* repeated in intervocalic position with either the first or second vowel stressed.

SUBSKILL 7:   Production of *b* in repeated or alternated syllables varying over at least eight semitones in pitch.

The emphasis in syllable drills is on automaticity, rhythm, and breath control. Producing new words is easy for the student who has already acquired the motor skills demanded by their production. Working on a number of speech objectives concurrently (e.g., four to six) prevents boredom, allows the student to experience success on several patterns even if mastery of one pattern is difficult, permits the student to contrast one sound with another, and allows the student to move ahead at a faster rate. When appropriate, it is suggested that targets be drawn from the nonsegmentals and segmentals on both the phonetic and phonologic levels. In addition, it is suggested that the time devoted to teaching specific speech skills should be allocated to brief blocks of 2 or 3 minutes duration for each student, four or five times a day, rather than to longer, more drawn out lessons. If this type of schedule is not manageable for you, then begin by doing one individual session of 8 to 10 minutes duration and incidental practice during the day. An example of an individual lesson plan for formal practice that was developed by Cole and Paterson (1984) appears in Exhibit 8.9.

One way to structure the incidental practice is to choose targets that a number of students have in common and practice them in various ways. An activity suggested by Cole and Paterson (1984) is to use a "speech pocket." This entails making a pocket out of construction paper and taping it to the back of the classroom door. You then jot down a series of targets for the week on cards that fit into the pocket. An example of such targets could be: (1) *bama*; (2) *bibibi*; (3) *fubufubu*; (4) *1, 2, 3, 4, 5*; (5) *toe, two, tie, tea*. Each time the students leave the room, they line up and, one by one, produce the target chosen from the pocket as they leave the room. In addition, individual objectives can be written on post-its and put on the corner of each student's desk, or goals can be placed on a wall chart and each student's progress marked on it. Ling (1978) has developed a Cumulative Record and Teacher/Clinician Planbook. It provides teachers with a comprehensive and systematic ongoing record of progress, as well as instructional schema for planning future student objectives. An example from the planbook is found in Exhibit 8.10.

The ultimate goal of the speech development program is to have the student use the skills that he/she has mastered during speech practice in his/her spontaneous communication throughout the day. Students need to be encouraged to use correct speech patterns taught at the phonetic level in a broader, more demanding context of meaningful speech. It cannot be expected that skills developed at the phonetic level will automatically transfer to oral communication. There is a need for the teacher to develop and implement specific carry-over activities. Failure to provide such carry-over activities is one reason that students in speech programs who are focusing only on the development of phonemes in isolated syllables may never learn to communicate through spoken language. Consequently, extensive work in fostering the use of phonetic skills in meaningful expression is a very important part of the speech program. The student needs to be taught to incorporate those skills acquired on the phonetic level into words and sentences. Using combinations of consonant-vowel or vowel-consonant words, such as *bye, me, shoe, off, boo, up, no, hi, two*, and so forth, as quickly as possible in meaningful contexts will expedite the teaching and learning process. As progress continues, training should proceed to consonant-vowel-consonant-word, to bisyllabic words, to two-word utterances, and finally to connected speech. Using the Cummins approach to language proficiency, these would be ordered as in Exhibit 8.11.

At the word, phrase, and sentence levels, integrating speech and auditory training with language training will increase the meaningfulness of the speech practice. The vocabulary used may be based on a particular sound, and the items that are introduced may be loaded with the syllable being developed or they may be centered around a particular topic, such as foods, toys, clothes, transportation, units being studied, and so on. (Siebert, 1980). By maintaining a continual awareness of individual student's speech objectives, you can integrate phonologic practice opportunities into all academic subjects. The key is to remember that during a lesson you do not want to spend time remediating one student while the other students sit and wait. This is tantamount to asking students to misbehave. Simultaneously, you do not want to compromise the content of your lesson in order to focus on speech. Finding the blend of the two is a matter of personal style.

**EXHIBIT 8.9.** Sample individual lesson plan (Cole & Paterson, 1984)

Name _____

Date _____

| Target-Stage of Practice | Sense Modality | | Techniques | Activities, Materials |
|---|---|---|---|---|
| 1. /f/—multiple reduplicated syllables, "legato," one breath | Vision Touch | Step 1. | Go from long ʌf and release into vowel ʌf a, slowly with control. | Move hand on table to show how long to hold /ʌf.../; when hand reaches pencil say /a/. |
| fᴗfᴗfa fᴗfᴗfi fuᴗfuᴗfu | Audition | Step 2. | Remove the crutch of /ʌ/. Have child imitate vocalization of f a¹. Check for good coarticulation. | |
| | | Step 3. | Have child self-monitor, maintain, repeat 3 times for today with /a, i, u/. | |
| 2. ba/ma— a. auditory discrimination² | Audition | Step 1. | Auditory discrimination—follow-up from last time, build confidence in ability to differentiate ba-ma. | 2 sets colored blocks |
| b. multiple recursive syllables /baᴗma baᴗma baᴗma/ | (Free variation) | | | |
| /biᴗmi/,etc. /buᴗmu/,etc. | | Step 2. | Syllable practice. Alternate each set 5 times. Student will self-monitor. Do once slowly; then try normal rate. | |
| Then: /biᴗma/ /buᴗmi/ | | | | |
| 3. /p/ meaningful use a. in initial position only b. look for self-correction c. consistent production | Audition Vision Touch | Step 1. | Quickly review production of /p/ with a range of known vowels. | 2 pens, 2 pandas, 2 pans, 2 pennies, 2 pears, 2 pigs. |
| | | Step 2. | Game round the table a. Name objects. Q. What's that? A. It's a _____. b. Take turns giving and following directions for placing objects in strange places. Pass me a\|the _____. Put a\|the _____ in a\|the _____. | |

SOURCE: E. B. Cole and M. M. Paterson, "Assessment and treatment of phonologic disorders in the hearing impaired." In J. M. Cotello (ed.). *Speech Disorders in Children: Recent Advances.* San Diego: College Hill Press, 1984. Reprinted by permission.

**EXHIBIT 8.10.** (Ling, 1978)

| | |
|---|---|
| 5.2 | The Vowel [ʊ] |

*Phonetic Level*

_____ is able to:

| | |
|---|---|
| 5.2.1 | produce the vowel [ʊ] with adequate oral breath stream and satisfactory voice quality. |
| 5.2.2 | repeat 12 syllables containing [ʊ] (e.g., [fʊfʊfʊ]) at a rate of three/second or more. |
| 5.2.3 | alternate 12 syllables containing [ʊ] with syllables containing another vowel (e.g., pʊpɛpʊpɛ]). |
| 5.2.4 | sing 12 syllables containing [ʊ] using high, medium, and low voice pitch. |

*Phonologic Level*

_____ is able to produce /ʊ/ correctly:

| | |
|---|---|
| 5.2.5 | in familiar words such as *look, book, put, foot, could.* |
| 5.2.6 | in commonly met phrases such as: "Look at my book." |
| 5.2.7 | in fluent speech. |

A valuable resource for phonologic level activities is *Messy Monsters, Jungle Joggers, and Bubble Baths* (Sobel & Pluznik, 1987). It is a book of poetry for hearing-impaired students that is enjoyable as well as functional. Also, materials that are personally relevant to the student, such as self-generated sentences or information that is known to be of high interest to the student, should be incorporated whenever possible. For example, the student has asked you for help in pronouncing various designer labels so that she could get assistance from sales clerks. It is important to continually monitor the student's utterances to find out what exists in her spontaneous vocabulary so that practice exercises can be organized to help her produce those utterances correctly and automatically.

Another important aspect of a comprehensive and systematic speech program is the need for collaboration among service providers, such as the teacher of the hearing-impaired, the speech and language pathologist, the regular classroom teacher, and the parents. "The lack of generalization of skills in all areas is a major problem in educating hearing-impaired students" (Fisher & Schneider, 1986, p. 84). Instead of separate and distinct services being provided, there should be a formal coordination of services with overlapping functions and one common goal: improving the student's communication skills. It is essential that everyone work on similar goals and reinforce the use and improvement of speech skills. A breakdown of how to coordinate and delineate responsibilities across different service providers appears in Exhibit 8.12 (Miller, 1981; Nittrouer & Hochberg, 1985).

## Speech Correction

Speech must not only be developed but also improved and maintained in those students who demonstrate speech ability. The quality of speech production when prompted, elicited, or cued by you is likely to be better than when the student has spontaneously initiated speech. Many times, skills that are intact on the phonetic level have not been acquired at the phonologic level because of a lack of practice in a variety of phonetic contexts. If this is the case, then it is not appropriate for you to correct a student's speech in the middle of a lesson or during a conversation. Stopping the flow of classroom dialogue to isolate one student breaks up the continuity of the lesson. If it is done during conversation, the interruption sends the message to the student that how something is said is more important than what is said. Finally, it is confusing, because when you correct a word,

**EXHIBIT 8.11.** Cummins' model of language proficiency adapted for speech articulation

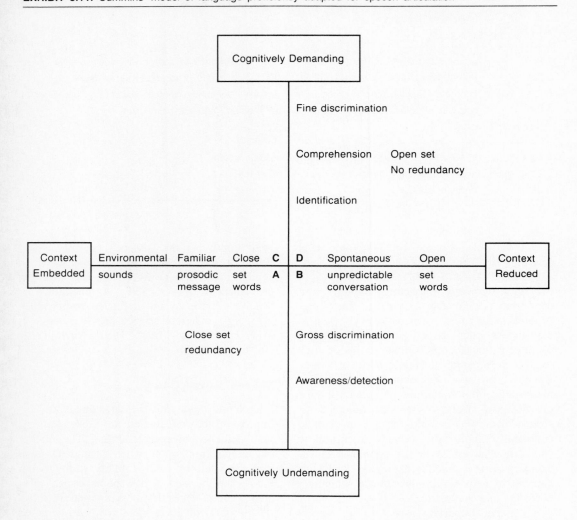

SOURCE: B. Luetke-Stahlman, "Applying bilingual models in classrooms for the hearing impaired." *American Annals of the Deaf*, *128*(7) (1983), 21–29.

phrase, or sentence one time but, due to time constraints, let it go five other times, the student has difficulty understanding why the word, phrase, or sentence was acceptable five times but not one time.

When the necessity does arise for correction, such as when you are introducing new phonologic skills or when you are working on phonologic goals, some modeling, expansion, and repetition of speech patterns are inevitably required in order to ensure optimal performance. You need to maintain a continuing, but not overly intrusive, attitude of awareness of the deviation from acceptable speech. Acceptability will vary according to the skill level of each individual student. Calvert and Silverman (1983) suggest some techniques that teachers can use for correcting speech.

**EXHIBIT 8.12.** Responsibility of each service provider

| Speech Specialist | Classroom Teacher | Parent |
|---|---|---|
| Coordinate speech programs for individual students. | Check the hearing system regularly. | Encourage a positive attitude toward all communication modes and offer consistent family support for all communication efforts. |
| Assess skills in all areas at each level. | Create an environment in which interchanges of thoughts and ideas are frequent and rewarding. | Assist in the maintenance and care of hearing-aids. |
| Provide diagnostic information to other team members and help develop an intervention plan. | Provide opportunities for practice of phonetic- and phonologic-level skills. | Request and participate in training sessions in the areas of manual communication, speech, speechreading, and hearing-aid care and use. |
| Check the hearing system regularly. | Extend carry-over activities for specific skills to the classroom. | Practice speech and auditory training. |
| Develop skills at the phonoetic and phonologic levels. | Provide a good model by simultaneously using signs or cues, and speech. | |
| Initiate carry-over activities. | Inform appropriate team members when difficulties arise, such as changes in auditory response or development of negative attitudes. | |
| Offer advice and support to classroom teachers concerning how to extend carry-over work to the classroom and how to incorporate oral communication into all teaching areas. | | |

One of these is *signaling* (you signal that an error or deviation has been made). Possible expressions for signaling are: "What did you say?" "I did not understand you." "Can you say that again?" Another is *specifying* (you point out that a deviation has been made and specify exactly what it is). Some techniques that you can use to specify are: (1) Communicate the locus of the deviation ("I didn't understand the first part of your sentence."); (2) indicate the type of deviation ("You left out a sound."); (3) describe the nature of the error ("Your voice was too high.").

Another method is to use the process of

*modeling.* When you model an utterance for a student, you give the student an oral model to be imitated. It should not be exaggerated or tense. You also can use the process of *demonstration* with students. Use whatever sensory channels that are necessary to provide the student with an appropriate explanation of what is deviant and what needs to be done to remediate it. Some specific techniques that can be used include:

1. Exaggeration—exaggerate the deviation and then exaggerate the proper way to make the sound

2. Analogies—use easily understood analogies, such as tapping out rhythm or using hands, to demonstrate flicks or the proper pressure of the articulators, or make reference to other examples that are within the same class (e.g., manner of production or placement)
3. Reduction of the variables and focusing on one component of the deviation at a time (e.g., work on *ch* in *chop* and then put it back together as a word)

Another approach for correcting speech mistakes is to *manipulate* the student's articulators. This entails manually shaping the accessible parts of the speech mechanism, such as rounding the lips or pressing the tongue down with a tongue depressor. This should be considered as a last resort in correcting a student's speech.

## SUMMARY

Speech is developed most effectively in an environment that is relaxed yet demanding. (Siebert, 1980). We endorse the use of a systematic approach to teaching speech to hearing-impaired students who have been assessed empirically as capable of benefiting from such intervention. To date, the work of Ling (1976, 1988) seems to provide the practitioner with a strong foundation from which to work. Such a system emphasizes that all skills essential for the production and perception of spoken language are considered, that they are not a series of isolated skills, and that they form an organized framework in which all skills are integrally related. Bear in mind that this is no cookbook formula for teaching speech. The activities and practice words, phrases, and sentences that are used are completely dependent on each teacher's preference, creativity, as well as individual student interests. The hierarchy and compo-

nent skills merely provide the teacher with guidelines within which to work. In addition, it is recommended that training integrate the communication areas of speech, auditory training, and language. This allows for training to occur both expressively and auditorially and permits the opportunity for monitoring and reinforcing these skills in varied contexts.

A student's motivation to improve speech is a very important factor. It is the teacher's attitude of expectation that both speech, cues and/or sign will be used that becomes an important element in developing speech as a communication habit for hearing-impaired students (Herx & Hunt, 1976). If you let your students know that their efforts at using speech are held in high regard, if you provide students with experiences that help them to understand the value of functional speech, then students will be motivated to use speech and to improve their ability to communicate. Finally, speech intervention must begin early. Ling (1976) stated that "to be optimally effective, speech training has to begin early, be undertaken frequently and consistently, and be systematically carried out so that it rapidly enables the student to use speech as an effective means of communication" (p. 49). We challenge you to learn to conduct speech assessment and to intervene appropriately so that your students can have access to the hearing world as much as possible.

## ACTIVITIES

1. Use a suggested speech assessment tool to evaluate the articulation abilities of either a hearing toddler or a hearing-impaired student. Write a report describing this experience and a plan for utilizing the assessment results.
2. Observe the teaching of speech to a hearing-impaired student. Assist with intervention over several sessions.
3. Choose two phonetic-level goals. Then make a list of phonologic-level goals that you can in-

troduce that will complement the phonetic-level objectives.

4. Design an activity that you could use with a hearing-impaired student to help the student understand the difference between intensity and pitch.

5. Visit a teacher of the deaf. Ask how speech goals are coordinated among service providers.

6. Work with a hearing-impaired student and try some of the methods suggested for correcting the student's speech. Which were easiest to use? Which were the most difficult? Why?

# CHAPTER 9

# Audition and Speechreading

## OVERVIEW

This chapter abounds with auditory assessment and intervention material. Within it, three auditory training approaches and four basic auditory tasks (i.e., detection, discrimination, activities for identification, and comprehension) are exemplified. Integration of audition and tips for integrating auditory training into the curriculum are provided also. We believe that hearing-impaired students who can benefit from auditory training should have teachers who are confident with these procedures. In addition, *speechreading* assessment is discussed in a manner that allows intervention to occur systematically. Reported case study data (Swanson, 1986) exemplifies practical uses of the Cummins (1984) model of language proficiency (explained in Chapter 1) with regard to hearing-impaired students who communicate bimodally.

---

**CHAPTER TOPICS**

The Role of Auditory Training
Assessment
Auditory Training Methods
Integrating Speech, Language, and Auditory Training Objectives
Speechreading Defined
Speechreading Assessed
Application of the Cummins Model to Speechreading Assessment of
     Hearing-Impaired Students
Speechreading Intervention

---

## THE ROLE OF AUDITORY TRAINING

The majority of hearing-impaired students have sufficient *residual hearing* so that they can benefit from wearing hearing aids (Ling, 1976; Paterson, 1982). Improvement in hearing-aid technology over the past 30 years has contributed to the acquisition of spoken language well beyond levels traditionally expected for hearing-impaired individuals (Quigley, Power, & Steinkamp, 1977). More sophisticated hearing aids, superior earmolds, the use of mold and tubing adaptations, hearing-aid filters, and upcoming digital aids are constantly changing our expectations of what hearing-impaired students can hear and use to increase their awareness of speech and language. As a result, many hearing-impaired students with unaided severe-to-profound losses learn to communicate through spoken language when their residual hearing acuity is aided. However, research shows that wearing a hearing aid is not a sufficient condition alone to guarantee that students will optimize their auditory capacity (Ross & Giolas, 1978). Beyond fitting students with the most appropriate hearing aids, it is essential to have good audiological management, provide support and education for significant adults, and supply students with auditory experiences of spoken language that are meaningful and appropriate to their age and interests (Bunch, 1987).

Auditory training involves teaching students to *listen* and to make use of their residual hearing. Listening differs from hearing in the degree of understanding and effort involved. Learning to listen occurs when students seek to extract meaning from the acoustic events that surround them all day and every day. Listening takes effort; hearing may not. Auditory training supplements auditory experience, allowing skills that are not learned in a natural way to be presented systematically in a more structured environment. The term *auditory training* is used to describe numerous teaching methods designed specifically for improving students' auditory speech-perception performance (Erber, 1982). Auditory training should include developmental language and speech activities that help the student to

1. Develop a more natural ability to relate and monitor the environment
2. Obtain a more normal voice quality
3. Improve speech reception
4. Improve articulation (Fisher & Schneider, 1986) when these objectives have been assessed as appropriate

It is convenient to think of auditory skills as involving four levels: detecting sounds, discriminating among them, identifying auditory patterns, and comprehending their meaning (Ling, 1986). *Detection* refers to the process of determining whether sound is present or absent. *Discrimination* means the ability to perceive the difference between two sounds. If two sounds are presented, are they the same or are they different? *Identification* refers to the process of recognizing what has been heard when presented with an auditory *stimulus*. Generally, the student is given a stimulus within a specific category and indicates that the stimulus was heard in some manner, such as pointing to a picture, reading the word, or repeating the sentence of the stimuli that was presented. *Comprehension* of speech is the most difficult auditory skill to master. It requires that the student understand the acoustic message and react appropriately. An example of a comprehension task is telling a student, "Put your hand on your head." If the student understands the acoustic signal, the student will complete the directions. A recitation of what was said indicates that the student can identify the stimulus but does not comprehend it. Comprehension is a prerequisite for auditory communication to occur and should be the long-term goal of every auditory training program.

## ASSESSMEMT

In preparation for the assessment of audition abilities, we suggest that teachers plot each student's aided and unaided hearing acuity on an audiogram, such as the one that appears in Exhibit 9.1. This information was gathered by an audiologist, who may have used one of several tests. Possible tests used in this process and the implications of the results are summarized in Exhibit 9.2. You may need to conduct additional formal and informal assessment measures as you attempt to identify areas of need for a particular student (see Exhibit 9.3). To further assist you, Erber

**EXHIBIT 9.1.** Intensity and frequency distribution of speech sounds in the English language (Schowe & Nerbonne 1980). The values given should only be considered as approximations, and are based on data reported by Ling and Ling (1978). Sounds with more than one major component appear in the figure in more than one location.

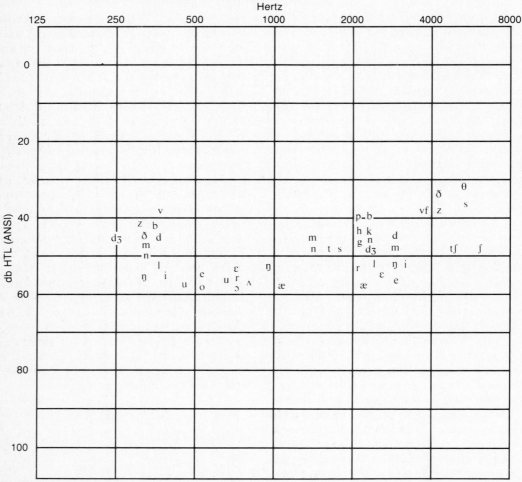

SOURCE: R. Schowe and M. Nerbonne, *Introduction to Oral Rehabilitation*. Austin: PRO-ED, Inc., 1980. Reprinted by permission.

(1982) has developed a matrix that can be used to guide the evaluation and intervention aspects of auditory training. In this matrix, shown in Exhibit 9.4, you can indicate whether a student can respond to speech stimuli as they become longer and linguistically more complex. You can indicate also whether the student can respond to speech stimuli through audition alone at one or more auditory levels.

These Erber response levels are graphed on a Cummins model of language proficiency (1984) (explained in Chapter 1) in Exhibit 9.5. Use of this model can help you to predict which students, who can discriminate familiar sounds in a closed set only (bottom,

**EXHIBIT 9.2.** Audition assessment and related information

*Behavioral observation audiometry (BOA)* (Lloyd & Young, 1974): Observe behavioral changes (e.g., reflex active, greeting, localization, distraction behavior, etc.) following auditory stimulus. Reliant on poststimulus activity being observably different than prestimulus activity. Reflex may be reflexive, such as the Moro response or the Auro-Palpetoral Reflex. Shows only the stimuli to which neonates and infants prefer to respond; does not reveal capabilities of their auditory processing systems. It is difficult, if not impossible, to design BOA procedure to quantify discrete aspects of an infant's auditory capabilities (Hasentab & Horner, 1982). Dependent on high-intensity signals to elicit a response. See specifically Wedenberg Procedure (Wedenberg, 1963), Eisenberg Procedure (Eisenberg et al., 1964), Downs and Sterritt Newborn Procedure (Downs & Sterritt, 1964), Simmons and Russ (1984), and Ewing and Ewing (1947).

*Electrophysiologic audiometry*: Response systems record changes in the electrical properties of the body systems as an indirect result of auditory stimulation. Little success in establishing infant auditory threshold norms, nor much definitive information regarding peripheral processing, transmission characteristics of the eighth cranial nerve, integrative functional naturation of the brain stem, or central processing of complex stimuli (Hasentab & Horner, 1982). Specific auditory response systems currently being employed to obtain auditory responses are the cochlea, the eighth cranial nerve, and the brain stem. The response is electric signals. Absence of a response does not necessarily imply a change in the central nervous system. Interpretation with caution (Hasentab & Horner, 1982).

*Conditioned behavior audiometry (CBA):* Uses auditory stimulus to signal and condition the child to expect a reward within a prechosen time interval after the stimulus onset. The response to the stimulus is verified by a number of trials. Response can be head turn, increased sucking, button pushing, visual reinforcement, or putting rings on a stack toy. Subject must be able to be conditioned. Absence of the acceptable response does not necessarily mean that the child cannot function auditorily. Unsuccessful performance may mean that the child's auditory system is too immature, the performance of the test is not rewarding, and so on. Enables one to have more confidence in thresholds, and discrimination abilities. See specifically, Hardy, Dougherty, and Hardy (1959) and DiCarlo and Bradley (1961).

*Condition orientation reflex audiometry (CORA)* (Suzuki & Ogiba, 1961): Requires the pairing of a sound-field pure tone with a visual stimulus (e.g., eyes in a doll).

*Visual reinforcement audiometry (VRA)* (Liden & Kankkonen, 1969): Colorful slide pictures reinforce a response.

*Tymponometry and stapedial reflex testing:* Relies on an instrument that, through a probe sealed in a person's ear canal, can introduce a known quantity of sound. The amount of sound remaining in the sealed canal and not passing beyond the tympanic membrane into the middle ear can be measured via a microphone and bridge circuit attached to the probe. Presence or absence of an observable reflex in response to stimuli can permit monitoring of the middle-ear status of hearing-impaired children who suffer from middle-ear disease.

*Pure-tone audiometry (PTA):* PT audiometer is located in one room of a two-room, double-walled audiometric test suite. Small children can be held by parents. The child is first conditioned to the pure tone stimuli, and then the test begins. Frequencies are tested in each ear, and silent control periods are interspersed among the tonal presentations to ensure validity of responses.

*Aided testing:* Degree, type, and configuration of hearing loss is of minimum ability to the educator. Behavioral conditioning techniques appropriate during pediatric audiological assessment can be used while evaluating child's responses with hearing aids. Teachers are often more realistic in establishing levels of expectation after being provided with an aided audiogram. With such information, it is possible at the outset to comprehend which segments of the acoustic spectrum of speech will and will not be audible while the child is wearing amplification.

*Auditory discrimination tests:* Administered in quiet listening environment but also in a background of competition for educational planning. The acoustic environment in which the hearing aid will be used will determine in large part the benefits to be derived (Heiber & Tillman, 1978).

**EXHIBIT 9.3.** Formal and informal auditory assessment tools

1. Rhyme tests (e.g., Word Intelligibility by *Picture Identification*; WIPI, Ross & Lerman, 1970).
2. *Sound Effects Recognition Test* (SERT). Finitzo-Heiber et al. (1980) present subtest of environmental sounds, which child identifies through pictures.
3. *GASP!* (Glendonald School for the Deaf Auditory Screening Procedure) Subtest 1, 2, and 3 (Erber, 1982). No unusual test items or unusual response behavior from student. Performance is described based on how many items are perceived correctly and by the type of adaptive strategies needed. The test is not a formal, reliable, standardized instrument. It is valid for reflecting a teacher's speech clarity and the environmental conditions under which the test was administered. It is important that the student's teacher administer the test and that it is administered through the amplification system normally used by the student. It is a brief screening test (less than one hour's duration), intended for teacher use.
4. *The KDES Auditory and Speechreading Skills Development Guide.* (1983). Gallaudet College Press, Washington, DC 20002.
5. *The Five Sound Recognition Test* and the *Ling Speech Evaluation* (Ling, 1983).
6. *The Test of Auditory Comprehension (TAC)*, Foreworks, P. O. Box 9747, North Hollywood, CA 91609.
7. *A picture identification test for hearing-impaired children* (Ross & Lerman, 1970).

left quadrant), will not be able to function without a visual mode of support in an academic situation. A student who can comprehend open-set teacher instructions (quadrant D) should be able to be placed in a hearing classroom on a trial basis (and monitored to see whether simultaneous communication support is needed).

**EXHIBIT 9.4.** An auditory stimulus-response matrix in which the relative positions of the three GASP! subtests are shown: phoneme detection (1); word identification (2); and sentence (question) comprehension (3) (Erber, 1982).

Speech Stimulus

| Response Task | Speech Elements | Syllables | Words | Phrases | Sentences | Connected Discourse |
|---|---|---|---|---|---|---|
| Detection | **1** | | | | | |
| Discrimination | | | | | | |
| Identification | | | **2** | | | |
| Comprehension | | | | | **3** | |

**EXHIBIT 9.5.** Auditory perception ability, adapted from Cummins (1984)

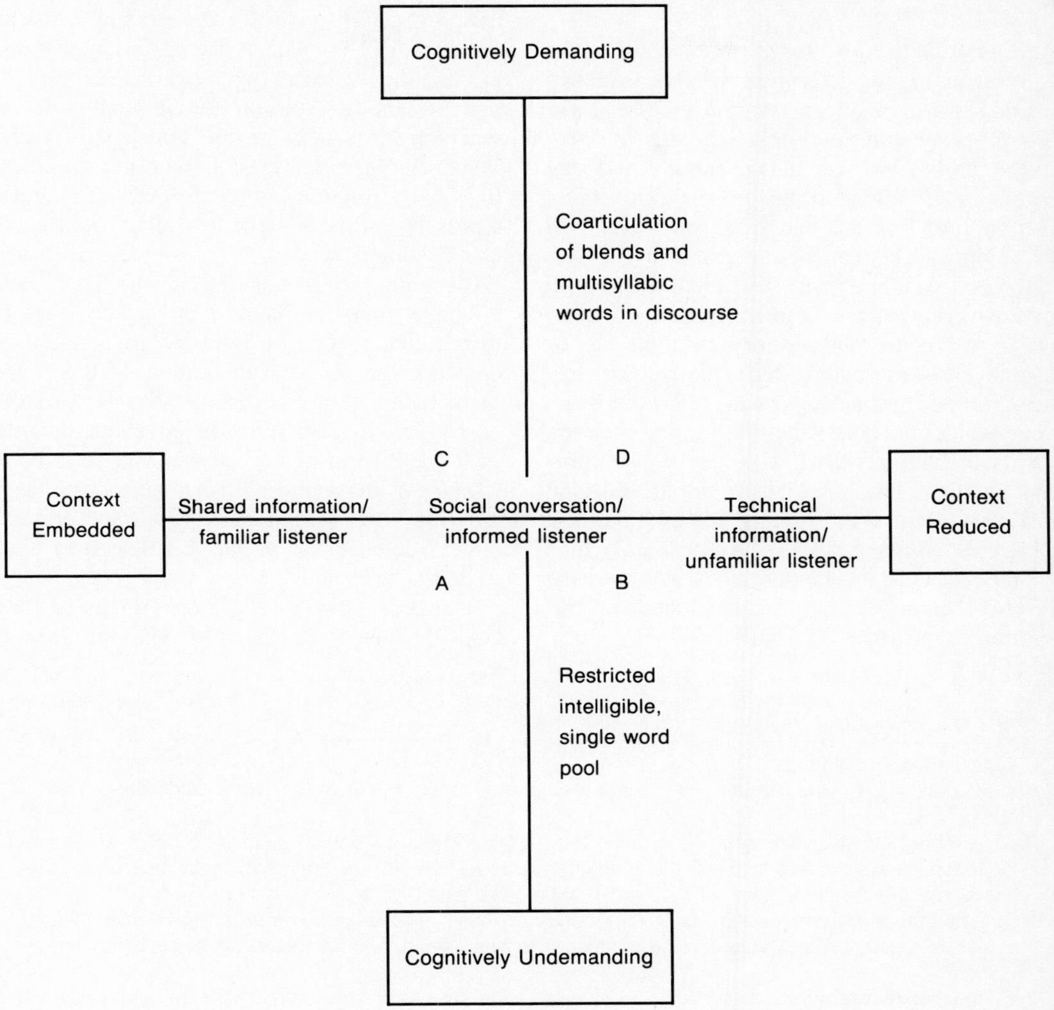

## Specific Auditory Assessment Tasks

It may be that you have assessed that a student needs to practice a specific task. For example, if a student is having difficulty responding to who, what, and where questions, then it may be appropriate for you to work with the student on discriminating these words, then identifying them, and finally working towards providing accurate comprehension responses.

The general progression for this approach is that you preselect a set of acoustic stimuli, preparing relevant materials and sequencing the activities logically in accordance with the needs of a specific student. An explanation of each level of tasks and some specific examples of what you can do to provide practice in that area follow.

***Auditory Detection Tasks.*** Detection tasks can be used to determine if the student's hearing aid or auditory training unit is working properly and to try to increase the student's ability to respond to sound. (If the equipment is not working properly, the information found at the end of this chapter will be helpful.) This can be done in many different ways. Students can raise their thumbs up or down or indicate with the sign for yes or no as to whether an auditory stimulus has or has not been presented. Also, the student may turn around or stand up when he or she hears your voice or takes the five-sound hearing test (see Exhibit 9.6). If you need more information than that provided by the five-sound test, you may want to use a detection task designed by Erber (1982). A form on which to record student responses, as well as the level of intensity required to obtain a response, is provided in Exhibit 9.7.

***Auditory Discrimination Tasks.*** The primary purpose of assessing auditory discrimination is to set goals for the student who can detect sound but who is having difficulty discriminating between two or more stimuli. As you present the stimuli, the student indicates whether the sounds are the same or different. For example, if the class is working on adjectives, you might want to practice vocabulary words by asking a student to discriminate between stimuli such as "The boy is tall," and "The cute girl is walking to the bus," and "What a hard math problem!". The level of discrimination can be adjusted to increase or decrease the length and degree of difficulty. Once again, you can change several variables as you try to gain information about the student's ability to hear. You can talk loud or in a whisper, make the phrasing long or short in duration, use a high or a low pitch, or use either sentences or connected discourse such as songs or poems.

Erber (1982) also recommended the GASP! Subtest 2 (listed in Exhibit 9.3) to

---

**EXHIBIT 9.6.** Five-sound hearing test (after Ling, 1983)

1. Detection of five sounds
   a. Student is requested to clap hands when student first hears one of the five sounds; /a/, /i/, /u/, / /, /sʃ /, /s/.
   b. Teacher sets the volume of the hearing aid to low and stands behind or to the side of the student.
   c. Teacher says the five sounds and gradually increases the volume (older students may adjust the volume themselves).
   d. When student indicates that all of the sounds or those capable of being heard have been heard, this is the "detection" level for the student. The hearing-aid volume should never be below this point.
   e. Teacher moves slowly away from the student, each time saying the sound with the same intensity but from a greater distance. This will demonstrate the maximum distance from the sound source at which the student may function auditorially.
2. Discrimination of five sounds
   a. Student is requested to listen carefully for any one of the five sounds. Student is asked to repeat the sound that is heard with eyes closed.
   b. One sound at a time is presented from normal teaching/therapy distance.
   c. When all five sounds, or those that the student is capable of discriminating or hearing, have been discriminated correctly, the student is ready to function auditorially in a teaching and testing situation.
3. Comparison of audiogram with formats
   a. Comparison of student's audiogram with the chart in Exhibit 9.7 will determine those sounds in the five-sound test that the child is capable of hearing with a properly fitted hearing aid set at the proper volume.

**EXHIBIT 9.7.** A form on which are recorded a student's responses to GASP! Subtest 1 (phoneme detection) (Erber, 1982)

GLENDONALD
AUDITORY
SCREENING
PROCEDURE
!

Child: _____
Teacher: _____
Tester: _____
Date: _____

| | L | Bin | R |
|---|---|---|---|
| How HA | | • | |
| was FM | | | |
| child AT | | | |
| tested V | | | |
| ? | | | |

I. *PHONEME DETECTION* — Place dot(s) in the *yes/no* box(es) to indicate child's response(s).

| | beet | bit | bet | bat | pot | bought | book | boot | but | bird | no sound | nas. | | lat. | | voiced fricative | | | | unvoiced fricative | | | |
|---|---|---|---|---|---|---|---|---|---|---|---|---|---|---|---|---|---|---|---|---|---|---|---|
| | i | ɪ | ɛ | æ | ɑ | ɔ | ʊ | u | ʌ | ɝ | | m | n | r | l | z | ʒ | v | ð | s | ʃ | f | θ |
| yes | ○ | • | • | • | • | • | • | ○ | • | | | • | • | • | • | | ○ | • | | | ○ | | |
| no | • | | | | | | | • | | | •••••••• | | | | | • | • | | • | • | • | • | • |

• = normal intensity; ○ = increased intensity

SOURCE: N. P. Erber, *Auditory Training.* Washington, D.C.: Alexander Graham Bell Association for the Deaf, Inc., 1982.

assess discrimination. To use this test, you ask the student to point to each word that has been said by you in random order. The test allows you to determine whether the student is able to point to the correct picture (by using a strategy based on the number of syllables in a word) or can actually identify specific words. Pictures for the procedure appear in Exhibit 9.8. The scoring guide and an example of a form on which a student's responses have been recorded appear in Exhibit 9.9. The data indicate that this student could discriminate words with various stress patterns, but could identify these words only with a 50 percent accuracy (a perfect identification score would result in the dots being lined up on the horizontal line in Exhibit 9.9). Intervention objectives would include the identification level and would involve stimuli of various syllable constructions (e.g.,

one syllable, two syllable, stressed-unstressed syllables, etc.).

A hierarchy for discrimination tasks that has been suggested by Paterson (1982) involves the technique of selecting one known item from a group of known items. Some examples at the word level are:

1. All items vary in acoustic properties and syllable length (e.g., a *boat*, an *airplane*, a *sheep*, and a *banana*).
2. Pairs of words that rhyme or are acoustically similar (e.g., a *boat* versus a *goat*, *father* versus *brother*, *boy* versus *toy*).
3. Initial consonants are similar, but these are different vowels and final consonants (e.g., *down*, *dime*, *dance*, *door*).
4. Initial consonant differing in how it is

**EXHIBIT 9.8.** Words and pictures representing four different stress pattern categories used to elicit a student's responses to GASP! subtest 2 (word identification) (Erber, 1982)

SOURCE: N. P. Erber, *Auditory Training.* Washington, D.C.: Alexander Graham Bell Association for the Deaf, Inc., 1982.

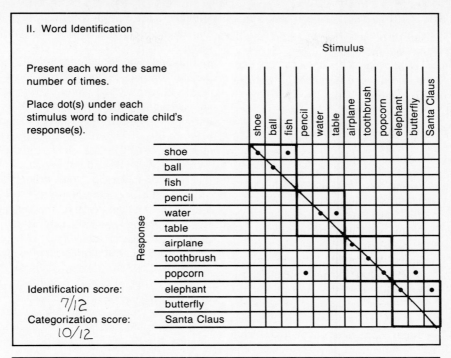

II. Word Identification

Present each word the same number of times.

Place dot(s) under each stimulus word to indicate child's response(s).

Stimulus: shoe, ball, fish, pencil, water, table, airplane, toothbrush, popcorn, elephant, butterfly, Santa Claus

Response: shoe, ball, fish, pencil, water, table, airplane, toothbrush, popcorn, elephant, butterfly, Santa Claus

Identification score: 7/12

Categorization score: 10/12

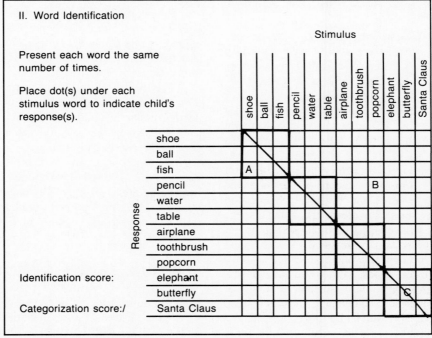

II. Word Identification

Present each word the same number of times.

Place dot(s) under each stimulus word to indicate child's response(s).

Stimulus: shoe, ball, fish, pencil, water, table, airplane, toothbrush, popcorn, elephant, butterfly, Santa Claus

Response: shoe, ball, fish, pencil, water, table, airplane, toothbrush, popcorn, elephant, butterfly, Santa Claus

Identification score:

Categorization score:/

SOURCE: N. P. Erber, *Auditory Training*. Washington, D.C.: Alexander Graham Bell Association for the Deaf, Inc., 1982.

made with the rest of the word rhyming or acoustically similar (e.g., *bean*, *team*, *dream*, *mean*).

5. Initial syllable is the same, but the end of the word is different (e.g., *kick*, *kill*, *kiss*, *king*).

***Auditory Identification Tasks.*** Practice at this level enables students to recognize specific stimuli and is an essential prerequisite skill for comprehending a spoken message. Stimulus materials will depend on the age, interests, and English language abilities of the student. To conduct this assessment, you would provide the student with a specific set of items, such as pictures, written words, or written sentences. You would practice saying the words or sentences to the student until you felt comfortable that the student understood the task. Then you would cover your mouth (without distorting the sound) and say one of the items. The student would listen and indicate which item was presented by pointing to it.

***Auditory Comprehension Tasks.*** When students can identify stimuli but have difficulty demonstrating comprehension of requests or statements, then they may need some additional practice on the comprehension level of auditory training. Erber (1982) has provided a comprehension screening tool and a form on which hypothetical data have been completed (see Exhibit 9.10). To administer this test, you practice the vocabulary in each question and make sure the student understood the task. Then you ask the student each question (or similar ones that are at the student's age and interest level) and record whether or not the student is able to respond to each question appropriately. A student assessed to have comprehension needs would warrant comprehension level objectives and intervention; that is, if a student can understand short and basic stimuli but has difficulty with longer and more complex forms of language, structured activities may be necessary. You might present a set of stimuli to a student or group of students. Perhaps you could use a set of pictures or a collage. You then cover your mouth and say something about one of the pictures or part of the collage. First the student will identify the picture about which you are talking and then will respond to specific questions regarding the picture. For example, you might put pictures of fruit on the board and say, "Where is the picture of the apple?" "What picture is beside the apple?" "Point to the stem of the apple" or "Where do apples grow?" Other comprehension tasks include asking the student to give the opposite of a word or giving a statement to which the student must answer that it is either true or false. Additional activities involve having the student follow a request, such as "Put the pencil in your pocket," using word associations (e.g., you say a word, such as *toy*, and the student must say something that would correspond with that word, such as *ball*). You might tell a brief story and have the student answer questions about it.

Erber (1982) recommended the use of an *audiotape-card machine* to practice all levels of audition (Exhibit 9.11). He recommended also that vibro-tactile aids be used during auditory training sessions.

The use of the telephone is another auditory training activity that should be part of a hearing-impaired student's curriculum. The use of the telephone is universal in our society, and most hearing-impaired students are anxious to use it to the best of their ability. Erber (1982, 1985) has developed a comprehensive auditory program for telephone training for hearing-impaired students. Other resources in this area appear in Exhibit 9.3.

## AUDITORY TRAINING METHODS

Since auditory training involves the training of residual hearing, it is essential that students be fitted with appropriate amplification and that they wear consistently through the

**EXHIBIT 9.10.** A form on which are recorded a student's responses to GASP! (sentence comprehension) (Erber, 1982)

III. *Sentence Comprehension* (*Questions*)

*Practice items* (A-V):

Indicate:

(a) How many fingers do you have?  (A-V)

(b) Where is your mouth?  *Emphasis*

(c) What color is the table?  (Gesture)

| *Test items* (auditory alone): | Response | Comments | number of presentations | ✓ if correct (auditory alone) |
|---|---|---|---|---|
| (1) What's your name? | | | | |
| (2) What color are your shoes? | | | | |
| (3) How many people are in your family? | | | | |
| (4) Where's your hearing aid? | | | | |
| (5) When is your birthday? | | | | |
| (6) What is your teacher's name? | | | | |
| (7) What number comes after seven? | | | | |
| (8) How many legs does an elephant have? | | | | |
| (9) Where do you live? | | | | |
| (10) How old are you? | | | | |
| | | | Score: | |

III. *Sentence Comprehension* (*Questions*)

*Practice items* (A-V):

Indicate:

(a) How many fingers do you have?  (A-V)

(b) Where is your mouth?  *Emphasis*

(c) What color is the table?  (Gesture)

| *Test items* (auditory alone): | Response | Comments | number of presentations | ✓ if correct (auditory alone) |
|---|---|---|---|---|
| (1) What's your name? | Richard | difficult | 4 | |
| (2) What color are your shoes? | blue | shoes→chair | 2 | ✓ |
| (3) How many people are in your family? | 4 | confident | 1 | ✓ |
| (4) Where's your hearing aid? | points to car | | 5 | |
| (5) When is your birthday? | Nov. 22 | confident | 1 | ✓ |
| (6) What is your teacher's name? | Miss Powell | | 2 | ✓ |
| (7) What number comes after seven? | 4, 8, 9 ect. | "comes after?" | 9 | |
| (8) How many legs does an elephant have? | 4 | confident | 1 | ✓ |
| (9) Where do you live? | S. Kingsville | no problem | 1 | ✓ |
| (10) How old are you? | 13 | you → we | 6 | |
| | | | Score: | 6/10 |

SOURCE: N. P. Erber, *Auditory Training*. Washington, D.C.: Alexander Graham Bell Association for the Deaf, Inc., 1982.

**EXHIBIT 9.11.** Examples of general audiotape-card formats for individual listening practice. Tasks of this sort may be applied as part of auditory training at each response level (Erber, 1982).

I. Detection (presence/absence of sound)

a. [ ]  [ ]
   Stimulus    (blank)

b. [ 1 | 2 ]

T: Record stimulus cards and mix with equal number blank cards.

C: Listen: place card in *YES* or *NO* box.

T: Record stimulus on either first or second half of card.

C: Listen; place card in *1* or *2* box.

II. Discrimination (same/different)

a. [ 1 | 2 ]

b. [ ]  [[[[ ]]]]
   ref.        stim.

T: Record the two segments either with same or different stimuli.

C: Listen: place card in *SAME* or *DIFFERENT* box.

T: Record target stimulus on reference card; record various stimuli, including target, on other cards.

C: Listen; compare each stimulus card with reference; place in *SAME* or *DIFFERENT* box.

III. Identification, recognition (labeling)

a. [ 1. ~~~~
      2. ~~~~
      3. ~~~~
      4. ~~~~ ]

b. [ ]

T: Record stimulus on card; write alternatives on front of card, write correct response on back of card or in answer book.

C: Listen; write response; turn card over or look in answer book for correct response.

T: Record categorical stimulus: e.g., pause/ no pause in sentence; male/female talker.

C: Listen; place card into appropriately labeled box.

IV. Comprehension (understanding meaning)

a. [ ]

b. [ ]

T: Record question on card; write correct answer on back of card or in answer book.

C: Listen; write response; turn card over or look in answer book for correct response.

T: Record instruction on card; describe correct behavior in answer book.

C: Listen; perform task as specified; consult answer book for desciption of correct response.

SOURCE: N. P. Erber, *Auditory Training*. Washington, D.C.: Alexander Graham Bell Association for the Deaf, Inc., 1982.

waking day if it is to be beneficial to them. The goal here is that the students desire to wear a hearing aid or auditory trainer (e.g., spontaneously retrieves the assisting listening device), indicates when they hear something or when the equipment is not working, or protest when the hearing aid is removed (Cole & Mischook, 1982). Appendix A contains information about equipment and preventive and troubleshooting procedures.

Auditory training should follow a developmental plan (refer to examples of audition milestones in Exhibit 3.2 in Chapter 1). For infants and toddlers, *significant adults* should engage in turn-taking activities around common routines (e.g., "Do you want this?" The child looks at the rattle. "Oh, you do?") as forms of attention-getting techniques and games that encourage the child to listen and take a turn (i.e., grasp for the rattle). Significant others should enrich the audition opportunities that exist in the natural environment, for students of all ages, by making frequent, conscious efforts to make students aware that sound events are occurring and by reinforcing attention to sound (Cole & Mischook, 1982).

During the preschool years, fingerplays and rhymes are a rich source of auditory stimulation in which the child can engage for 3 to 20 minutes. This kind of cooperation and enjoyment from turn-taking and sharing activities lay a foundation for adult-directed or structured (i.e., school) learning tasks (Cole & Mischook, 1986). Nonverbal activities (e.g., music instruments) should not be chosen over a presentation of spoken stimuli, because the goal of auditory training is to attend to and respond to auditory stimuli in the natural environment. Ling and Ling (1978) list the following reasons for using speech and language stimuli rather than noncommunication-based sounds.

Speech segments are much shorter in duration than nonverbal sounds.
The two types of sounds are processed in different hemispheres of the brain.
Speech patterns provide a greater range of contrast and similarity.
Training involving speech is a direct approach.

However, regularly occurring, meaningful environmental sounds should be included as auditory training stimuli: dog barking, car honking, telephoning, doorbell ringing, etc. The guiding principle is that the student should enjoy the auditory experience rather than be trained to respond every time a bang or a drum is heard (Cole & Mischook, 1982).

We suggest that you eliminate the manual portion of communication systematically with students who typically use it to facilitate audition; that is, you should expect students to begin to respond appropriately via audition to unsigned short, familiar, prosodic messages (e.g., "Good morning," "How are you?" etc.). Using the adapted Cummins' model that appears in Exhibit 9.5, it would be logical for you to progress from quadrant A, to quadrant B, to quadrant C, to quadrant D as you set objectives for intervention.

## Teaching Approaches

Erber (1982) has presented three primarily language-based approaches for teaching auditory training. They are language-based because they emphasize that auditory work cannot be divorced from language development and should be integrated into the context of everyday talk, play, and academic learning. They include the natural conversational approach, the moderately structured approach, and practice on specific tasks. The following is a short explanation of the two approaches.

*Natural Conversational Approach.* This approach requires that the student receive acoustic information without having any opportunity to see the speaker. This method may entail simply talking to the student as normally as possible and providing listening practice without specifically directing attention to the movements and positions of your mouth. This can be done by covering your mouth with a card, not your hand. Another technique is for you to stand behind the student while you talk or to sit beside the student when you work with him or her.

Some specific examples of how this approach could be used in the classroom are:

> Sit behind a student and give directions while the student draws or paints a picture.
>
> Use barrier games (explained in Chapter 7). Put together some beads, Legos, or other manipulable objects on one side of a game board and explain to the student that he or she must try to arrange the objects in the same manner on the other side of the board.
>
> During math class, sit next to the student and have the student point to a problem on the page after you have given the student the auditory stimulus. Have the student open a book to the page number that you say.
>
> In content classes, such as science, social studies, spelling, or health, have the student write down the vocabulary word, key phrases, or sentences that you deliver without any visual stimuli.

The goal of this approach is to improve auditory speech-perception abilities as a result of repeated practice in a low-pressure (low affective filter) communication task.

When you are using the conversational approach, it is valuable for you to bear in mind the matrix found in Exhibit 9.4. Using the matrix allows you to break down comprehension level tasks into their component skills and possibly structure an auditory learning situation that is more successful for the student. For example, if you ask the student to open the math book to page 47, you have asked the student to perform a comprehension level response. If the student is unable to respond accurately, you may want to repeat the message. If the student continues to have difficulty, then it is appropriate to change the task to an identification level response. Giving the student a choice between page 46 and 47, you could say, "Where is page 47." If the student responds incorrectly then you may quickly try a discrimination task, in which you might compare two contrasting phrases: "Did I say open your math book" or "on the bike path." The student should listen and decide if the phrases sound the same or different. If the student continues to have problems with this task, then you may want to provide an auditory-visual cue and let the student use visual cues as well as listen to the acoustic signal. When the student is successful, it is a good practice to move back up through the matrix as much as possible towards the comprehension level.

***The Moderately Structured Approach.*** This approach is a more directed and formal approach to auditory training than the natural conversational approach. First the class participates in a shared activity. Using the activity as the stimulus, the class discusses what was just done. Depending on the amount of time available and the level of the class, the teacher, or the teacher and the students, develop a list of words, phrases, or a set of sentences that differ in length and vocabulary. These will become the stimulus for the students to work with. These stimuli can be used to practice the interdependent areas of language, speech, and auditory training simultaneously. Prior to beginning listening practice, it is important that you make sure that each student is familiar with the content of the material. For younger students, you may need to put a picture next to the word, phrase, or sentence to add clarity.

After the sentences or vocabulary words have been written and discussed, it is time to practice listening. This can be done in a group or individually. If it is done in a group, it is a valuable practice to involve as many students as possible in listening and responding. Specific methods for actively involving students in guided practice activities will be discussed in Chapter 10. When working with a student, you should cover your mouth and say one of the stimuli or say nothing at all. The student then must choose the stimulus that was presented or decide if there was an absence of sound. If the student correctly identifies an auditory stimulus, the teacher may ask for the student to read the word or sentence. If the student's answer is incorrect, then the teacher can choose one of the adaptive techniques discussed later in this chapter in order to make it a positive experience for the student.

## INTEGRATING SPEECH, LANGUAGE AND AUDITORY TRAINING GOALS

Research reported by Novelli-Olmstead and Ling (1984) indicates that *integrating* auditory training with speech production training is more beneficial for both auditory discrimination and speech production than auditory training alone. This is because such integration is a natural process. For example, a typical lesson with an individual student might include: (1) a hearing-aid check, (2) the five-sound test, (3) phonetic-level speech practice, (4) auditory discrimination of syllables related to speech practice, (5) phonological-level speech practice, (6) auditory practice involving the phonologic stimuli, and (7) language experience activities incorporating specific semantic, syntactic, or pragmatic goals (Paterson, 1982).

### Teaching Tips

Asking a student to give an oral response should be a technique that you employ in all parts of your work sessions to encourage spoken interchanges, to verify auditory reception, and to practice speech production. Also, oc-casionally it is valuable to reverse the listening-speaking process—have the student make a sound and then *you* respond. Role reversal allows the student to take a turn playing teacher. For example, you give the auditory stimulus for two blocks, one of which represents the syllable /pa/ and the other of which represents /ta/. The student indicates which syllable was heard. After satisfactorily completing the activity once or twice, you can ask the student to say the syllables while you listen. This puts the responsibility of producing good speech on the student, who has been assessed as possessing this capability. This activity can be expanded to use of word, phrase, sentence, or connected discourse goals.

When a work session with a student is finished, you should not simply remove your materials from the table and go to the next activity. Use this time to reinforce what you have just worked on: Provide the student with an auditory stimuli and ask the student to pick up the appropriate object or material. The demands of this task can be increased by asking the student to place the materials in a specific sequence or in a specific place. For example, you might provide the student with the following series of directions: "Pick up the book. Put it in the brown bag. Now pickup the banana. Place it on top of the book."

When students demonstrate difficulty with an auditory stimulus, specific adaptations may be appropriate. Some suggestions presented by Erber (1982) include:

Repeat all or part of the utterance.
Clarify or emphasize some aspect of articulation.
Decrease the complexity of the vocabulary or language in the message.
Redefine the situational context.
Allow visual perception of part or all of the utterance and reduce the number of alternatives from which the student must choose.

The level of difficulty can be controlled by moving up or down the matrix or by using the adaptive procedures just discussed. To provide reinforcement for the activity, you can simply smile and nod when the student responds correctly. More extrinsic reinforcement may include: moving a marker along a path, using tangible reinforcers such as chips or Cheerios, giving the student the card when he or she is correct, or keeping track of the number correct and displaying it on a chart or graph.

Specific curricula that you may be interested in reviewing are the *Auditory Skills Curriculum* (Stein et al., 1980), the *Kendall Demonstration Elementary School (KDES) Guide for Auditory Skills and Speech Training* (Nussbaum, Waddy-Smith, & Wilson-Favors, 1982), and the *SKI-HI Model* (Clark & Watkins, 1985).

## SPEECHREADING DEFINED

Speechreading refers to the process of understanding a spoken message through the observation of a speaker's face (O'Neil & Oyer, 1981). In the past, this process was referred to as *lipreading*. However, more recently, terms such as *speechreading* and *visual communication* have been used because understanding what people are saying involves more than reading just their lips. Since the speaker's lip positions and movements offer incomplete clues to the message, the importance of recognizing and using supplementary clues is strongly emphasized. In speechreading, one cannot depend upon the acoustic code for understanding, but rather one must rely upon the visually contrastive part of the code. Since some of the difference in the acoustic code depends upon voicing and nasality and since both of these cannot be seen, it is obvious that there are far fewer visually distinctive than acoustically distinctive sounds. As a result, contemporary thinking on this subject takes into consideration more variables than just lip movement. It includes the variables of gestures, facial expressions, and situational cues.

1.  *Gestures*. Gestures are stylized movements, primarily of the hands and arms, but may also involve the head, torso, or other body parts. Gestures may simply supplement the speaker's words to add emphasis or clarity, or they may be quite complex and function as the total but brief and limited message of the speaker. Some examples of universal gestures are shaking the head up and down to indicate that you agree, shaking the head from side to side to suggest disagreement, and the outstretched palm to indicate that something should be given.

2.  *Facial Expressions*. Facial expressions generally offer a clue to a speaker's psychological state and to the speaker's opinions on the subject matter under discussion. Some examples include facial expressions of happiness, sorrow, surprise, and disgust.

3.  *Situational Clues*. Situational clues include the physical location where the conversation is going on, as well as the participants in the conversation and the objects in the environment. For example, the hearing-impaired individual can be reminded to speechread certain questions that will occur when at a restaurant, such as questions by the waitress: "May I take your order?" or "Will you have cream with your coffee?" Other sets of words and phrases can be expected from a speaker who is a grocery clerk, a teacher, or a football player who drops the ball in the end zone.

## SPEECHREADING ASSESSED

Classroom observations occasionally result in apparently contradictory findings related to a student's speechreading performance. For example, a student may speechread the names of familiar objects while working individually with a therapist in the clinic but fail to do so when you incorporate the same words into classroom presentations. Teachers would benefit from using speechreading evaluation tools that assess a student's abilities in several contexts and that, according to Moeller (1982), provide information about a student's strengths as well as weaknesses.

There are, however, few commercially available tests designed for students (Jeffers & Barley, 1971; Moeller, 1982; Yoshinaga-Itano, 1988). When existing speechreading tests are organized by quadrant constraints from the Cummins model, it appears that a complete speechreading evaluation of hearing-impaired students cannot be conducted without additional test development. Further, Montgomery (1988) lists several variables that would need to be considered in an assessment (e.g., ability to integrate, auditory and visual information, differences between speakers, improvement after instruction, etc.).

There have been few attempts made to organize speechreading assessment systematically for use with hearing-impaired students (see Garstecki, 1981, for a review of this literature). Sanders (1977) suggested that auditory training should incorporate the use of visual stimuli and proposed that *linguistic* and situational cues be controlled and ordered. Erber (1977) described such a paradigm for students, which would be used for both speechreading and auditory training (discussed earlier in this chapter). The Erber matrix (see Exhibit 9.4) can assist teachers in adapting communication tasks for the student who is having speechreading difficulty by systematically altering the task demands. For example, you might refine the situational context or require lower-level responses (e.g., discrimination rather than comprehension). Erber (1977) further suggested that teachers could utilize a group of tests constructed to examine performance at a variety of stimulus-response levels and thereby diagnose a student's individual speechreading strengths and weaknesses. Such an adaptive communication process could result in diagnostic findings that would assist teachers in establishing objectives for the student's development in visual communication.

We believe it is again possible to use the Cummins model of language proficiency (explained in Chapter 1) to assess speechreading abilities (see Exhibit 9.12). The Erber (1982) matrix, which was designed for audition assessment, could be used as well. However, an advantage of using the adapted Cummins model over the Erber model is that the former allows for the assessment and placement of bilingual or bimodal students.

### The Context Dimension

In order to understand the fleeting succession of context-varying shapes associated with running speech, the hearing-impaired student must engage in an active, visual search, utilizing whatever cues accompany the message. The student must draw heavily on past experience and training (Ling, 1976). Cues may be provided by giving the speechreader context: background information about the topic, cueing of sounds spoken, or pictorial or written support (see Exhibit 9.12). Ling (1976) has stated that speechreading often fails at the *suprasegmental* level, where there is little visible information. Other factors that would affect context are lighting conditions, distance, and angle of the stimuli to be speechread (Sanders, 1982).

**EXHIBIT 9.12.** The Cummins (1984) model of language proficiency assessment with speechreading tasks incorporated

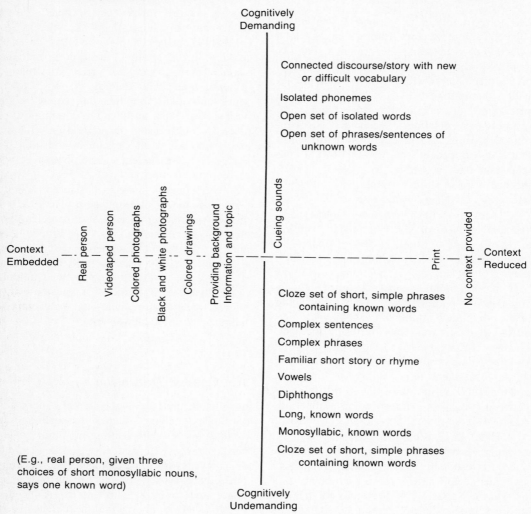

## The Dimension of Cognitive-Linguistic Demand

Within the Cummins model, cognitive-linguistic demand is defined as the syntax and semantic difficulty of the stimulus language. Regarding English, Wozniak and Jackson (1979) found that diphthongs were easier than vowels for hearing-impaired adults to identify visually. Erber (1977) reported that students could usually identify longer words, such as spondees, more easily than shorter words, such as monosyllables. The results of studies by Clouser (1976) and Schwartz and Black (1967) were that students were able to speechread short, syntactically simple sentences more readily than longer, complex ones.

## APPLICATION OF THE CUMMINS MODEL TO SPEECHREADING ASSESSMENT OF HEARING-IMPAIRED STUDENTS

The benefit of using an adapted Cummins model in assessing individual speechreading ability in hearing-impaired students was tested in a tutorial situation by Luetke-Stahlman and her college trainees, who were studying to become teachers of the deaf. Although this situation utilized college-age students, we have included it because it illustrates the value of this type of assessment and exemplifies the predictive advantage of the Cummins' model. These trainees generated three questions to reflect the age and interests of a particular hearing-impaired student who attended weekly clinic sessions. Questions included each of the combinations of high and low context and high and low cognitive-linguistic demand in the Cummins model. Cognitively demanding questions were longer in mean-length-utterance than cognitively undemanding questions and involved higher cognitive processing skills (Bloom & Krathwohl, 1977). Therefore, a set of individualized questions was used with each hearing-impaired student, but all question stimuli conformed to the Cummins quadrant constraints. One such set of questions follows.

QUADRANT A:    *Cognitively undemanding, context embedded*
What color is this table?
What time is it now?
Who is sitting near you?

QUADRANT B:    *Cognitively undemanding, context reduced*
Where is your school?
What color is your bedroom?
What's your Dad's name?

QUADRANT C:    *Cognitively demanding, context embedded*
What do you think this textbook is about?

Why are these shoes made of leather?
How does electricity make this light work?

QUADRANT D:    *Cognitively demanding, context reduced*
How is a tree like a family?
How does a cochlear implant work?
Why are ear level aids better than body aids?

Each hearing-impaired student was asked to speechread a *random ordering* of the questions, which were asked once each without voice. All questions were asked once during weekly sessions. Data were kept and graphed. Each question was asked at least three times over three consecutive sessions.

Results of the speechreading task were:

All but one hearing-impaired student could answer the questions via speechreading that represented the cognitively undemanding, context-embedded (A) quadrant.

Eight of the 12 hearing-impaired students were able to answer questions asked in oral English (alone) when the questions were cognitively undemanding and context-embedded (quadrant A) but not when they exemplified other points along the two continua.

One hearing-impaired student could answer all questions (i.e., representing all quadrants) asked in oral English.

In a variation of the speechread task first explained, two of the oldest girls who were enrolled in the clinic were given the same set of questions (Swanson, 1986). Both students lived on campus, but they exhibited different preferences in terms of communication mode. Marcy had a profound loss, did not use a hearing aid, and signed primarily in ASL. Jane had a profound loss and was a satisfied hearing-aid user. She had good use of her residual hearing and was mainstreamed into a university course of study. She relied on speech to communicate.

The procedure for the two girls included a set of age-appropriate questions that adhered to the Cummins continua. However, the set was multimodal, including three questions for each of three inputs (i.e., ASL, speechreading, and Signed English). These inputs were chosen because they represented the languages and systems used in the linguistic environment on campus. In the ASL condition, questions were signed only and respective of ASL lexicon and grammar. Questions to be speechread were asked in voice alone; no sign or gestures were used. Questions asked in Signed English were communicated simultaneously in corresponding voice and sign and utilized signs described in Bornstein, Saulnier, and Hamilton (1980).

The results were that Jane could answer all of the questions asked in all modes in the cognitively undemanding, context-embedded situation and could comprehend speechreading in the cognitively demanding, context-reduced situation. Her peer, Marcy, could also answer all the questions in all modes in the cognitively undemanding, context-embedded situation but could not comprehend speechreading in the cognitively demanding, context-reduced situation. Cummins (1984) work with hearing bilingual students evidenced this type of behavior also. He found that some Spanish-speaking students perplexed teachers because they could understand English in some conversational situations but not in academic ones (quadrant D).

Cummins suggested that success in one mode within a quadrant could predict eventual success in another mode in that same quadrant; that is, a student who is able to speak and comprehend Spanish in cognitively undemanding, context-embedded tasks would be a good candidate for English intervention on tasks that reflected the same combination of conditions (i.e., constraints of that same quadrant). Likewise, parents and professionals who work with hearing-impaired students might facilitate communication proficiency across various modes within the cognitively undemanding, context-embedded quadrant before they expect performance at tasks that are more difficult and/or in which context is reduced. A hearing-impaired student who could answer questions, for example, from the cognitively undemanding, context-embedded quadrant would seemingly be a better candidate for speechreading work using similar questions than a student who could not respond to such questions in any mode. We could make similar predictions with regard to the cognitive-linguistic demands and context constraints of the other quadrants.

The Cummins model of language proficiency is a useful tool in organizing speechreading assessment material for hearing-impaired students. Teachers might benefit from categorizing speechreading assessment and later, intervention, with regard to context and cognitive-linguistic task demands. For example, you might assess a student and find that the intervention that is needed is highly dependent on context and is familiar and routine (i.e., cognitively undemanding). We recommend that you pick one or more utterances that are characteristic of these constraints (e.g., "Good morning," "Go back to your desk now," "Can I help you?" etc.), first say them, and then repeat them a second time with sign. This strategy will give the student an opportunity to speechread but will not sacrifice the student's comprehension of the situation.

## SPEECHREADING INTERVENTION

There are specific factors that affect an individual's ability to accurately speechread someone. It is important to practice speechreading in optimum conditions but also to include practice opportunities in "real-world type situations." The following variables affect speechreading. When planning speech-reading practice, be certain to vary these factors so that students get training in generalizing outside the confines of the classroom.

1. *Viewing angle of the speaker.* It has been recommended that speechreading be practiced so that the viewing angle of the speaker is at 0 degrees, rather than at 45 degrees, and then at 90 degrees.
2. *How much of the speaker is in view.* The more visible the speaker, the easier it is for the speaker to be speechread. The optimum is that the upper torso be in view.
3. *Rate of speech.* A slower than average rate of speech has been found to be the easiest to speechread. However, people will continue to speak at their normal rates, and we therefore must train hearing-impaired students to meet the challenge of speechreading different rates of speech presentation.
4. *Familiarity with the speaker.* It has been said that knowing the personality of people makes it easier to understand them. Speechreaders typically report that their relatives and close friends are easier to speechread than are persons who are less well known.
5. *Distance from the speaker.* If the individual has good visual acuity, it appears that distances of up to 20 or 24 feet do not have a significant affect on speechreading performance. Training is most meaningful when it is done at distances most representative of typical daily conversational situations (between 4 and 10 feet).
6. *Lighting on the speaker.* Typical classroom lighting is sufficient for optimum speechreading. Special or increased amounts of light on the speaker do not prove to be valuable additions.
7. *Visual distractions.* Certain characteristics of people or the apparel that they wear can affect speechreading. Some specific examples include: a person wearing dark glasses, a male sporting a beard or mustache, a female wearing long, dangling earrings, a female with long, flowing hair that covers part of her face, the movement of a hand in front of the face, a speaker with a pipe, cigar, or cigarette.

Many of the intervention strategies described earlier in this chapter for auditory training could be adapted to facilitate speechreading goals. The communication games that were explained in Chapter 7 can be adapted for speechreading also. Speechreading training should incorporate real-life situations and should be practiced in a nonthreatening environment. Palmer (1988) suggested the following components of speechreading intervention:

1. Identify different situations. Assessing and planning speechreading intervention in authentic situations increases the chances of true behavior change and instills confidence.
2. Practice conversations in small groups so that the rules and routines of everyday dialogues can be learned.
3. Practice situations involving conflict (e.g., returning an undesired item to a store) so that assertiveness and good decision making are integrated with speechreading.
4. Use role playing and simulation in the classroom so that students can gain experiece in handling these situations in the real world. Videotape these for the purposes of self-evaluation.
5. Model expected behavior when communication failure occurs. Use role reversal with students as a method of

practicing speechreading in these situations.

Yoshinaga-Itano (1988) discussed a holistic approach to speechreading for children in which other components of communication were combined with speechreading objectives and practice occurred in authentic contexts. She stated that such an approach:

Enhances student self-motivation
Is a strategy-based instruction
Is an interactive approach focused on meaning
Allows bisensory instruction
Begins with quadrant A Cummins' activities and moves in a systematic direction.

A resource that you may want to review is *Speechreading in Context* by Deyo (1984).

## SUMMARY

Learning to listen for meaning requires that professionals and parents create communicatively appropriate and meaningful learning environments in which acoustic redundancy, repetition, and predictability help the student to focus on acoustic cues (Paterson, 1986). Your task is to ensure on a daily basis that the auditory training equipment is functioning appropriately and that an attitude of helping students to develop listening skills is maintained (see Appendices A-C at the end of this text for more information on these and related topics). Your job is to plan auditory activities that relate to the students' experiences and interests and fall within the range of their cognitive abilities as well.

Information in this chapter has centered on the assessment and intervention of audition and speechreading. It is hoped that educators of hearing-impaired students will assess these abilities in each of their students, set goals and intervention strategies as is appropriate, and strive to incorporate this component of communication into daily lessons in meaningful ways.

## ACTIVITIES

1. Plan an activity that would be appropriate for each level of auditory assessment: detection, discrimination, identification, and comprehension.
2. Try three auditory training approaches with a hearing-impaired student. Write up your procedure, activities, and results. To which approach did the student best respond?
3. Administer all three parts of the GASP! to a hearing-impaired student. Take data and report your results in a professional manner.
4. Using an audiotape-card format (e.g., Language Master), conduct an activity for each level of auditory training.
5. Conduct a speechreading assessment and decide on at least two intervention objectives that you will use.

# PART THREE

# Effective Strategies for Teaching Academics to Students with Hearing Impairments

# Strategies of Effective Instruction

## OVERVIEW

The growing body of research related to instructional techniques, teacher behaviors, and presentation skills is greatly influencing our educational system. Research on effective instruction indicates that certain teacher practices common to instruction in all subjects are correlated positively with student achievement and attitudinal outcomes. This chapter provides a summary of current thinking and successful applications of this research.

Although identified instructional processes make a difference, research indicates that complex instructional problems cannot be solved with surefire prescriptions. It is not possible to follow a "cookbook" sequence for teaching and expect positive outcomes. The real key to instructional effectiveness is wise and informed teachers who make decisions based on the particular student or group of students and on the subject matter that is being mastered. The information that is presented in this chapter and throughout this text is selected so that you can incorporate the techniques and practices into *your* teaching repertoire, understand the reasons why these procedures can promote student development, and rework them to fit your individual style and preferences.

This chapter explains the component behaviors that have been identified in the literature and offers specific examples of how to structure the teaching environment. In addition, methods of teaching concepts and rules and ways to pose questions that encourage development are presented. Finally, a review of teaching strategies such as cooperative learning, conceptual maps, peer tutoring, and learning centers are included so that you have a variety of approaches to choose from as you address the many instructional purposes and the variety of students with whom you will work.

---

**CHAPTER TOPICS**

What is Effective Instruction?
Teaching Concepts
Teaching Rules
Question Prompts
Additional Teaching Strategies

---

## WHAT IS EFFECTIVE INSTRUCTION?

In the past decade our knowledge of successful teaching has increased considerably. The results of the research undertaken on effective instruction (e.g., Brophy & Good, 1985; Brophy et al., 1983; Good, 1983) have demonstrated that, when educators teach more systematically, student achievement improves, frequently with gains in students' attitudes towards themselves and school. Because the findings presented in this chapter are based primarily on research in regular classroom settings or in special education classes for mildly handicapped students, their implications for educating hearing-impaired students are conjectural. However, several researchers and writers in the field of deaf education (e.g., Moog & Geer, 1985; Quigley & Kretschmer, 1982) contend that hearing-impaired children who achieve at levels significantly above the national averages for hearing-impaired students do so as a result of consistent and high-quality educational programs. Until research is undertaken and a knowledge base is developed, it is our position that the effective instruction methods discussed in this chapter have considerable application to teaching basic academic subjects to hearing-impaired students.

### Components of Effective Instruction

According to Rosenshine (1986), researchers have found that when effective teachers teach *concepts* (abstract ideas generalizing particular instances) or *skills* (practical application of knowledge in a given activity), they

> Secure students' attention
> Begin a lesson with a short review of previous, *prerequisite learning*
> Begin the lesson with a short statement of objectives
> Introduce new material in small steps, with student practice sessions after each step

> Give clear and detailed instructions and explanations
> Provide active practice sessions for all students
> Ask many questions, check for their students' understanding, and obtain responses from all students
> Provide systematic feedback and correction
> Provide explicit instruction and practice for seatwork exercises and monitor the students during these exercises
> Continue practice sessions until students are independent and confident

The following is a short explanation of the essential components of effective instruction.

***Securing Student Attention.*** Prior to beginning any lesson it is important that you make sure that all of the students are ready to learn. This is best accomplished by waiting until you have eye contact with each individual student. Simple statements like "Eyes up here" or "It's time to get started." If necessary, you can blink the lights to signal to students that you want their attention.

***Daily Review.*** Effective teachers begin a lesson with a review of previous materials, homework, and relevant prior knowledge. The goal of the review at the start of the lesson is to make sure that the students know the prerequisite skills for the day's lesson. In the review, effective teachers go beyond simply asking, "Remember what we did yesterday?" They actually test student performance by requiring students to explain the meaning of concepts and to apply those concepts to problems.

On occasion, a student may give you a long, involved answer that you do not understand, or a student may give you a response that involves a Deaf-culture–specific example with which you are not familiar. At these times, we suggest that you keep in mind material discussed in Chapter 1—the importance of genuine communication. You may want to apologize to the student for not understanding, and you may want to ask the student to reexplain the response. Another option is to ask another student who has gleaned the essence of the answer to explain it to you and the class. At this point, you can turn back to the student who initiated the response and expand or react to the answer that was provided. The third option is to rephrase your question by using some of the question prompts that we will provide later in this chapter. Remember: treat each interaction as genuine communication; do not nod your head that you understand or agree if you have missed the intent of the message.

*Stating Objectives.* Once the review has been completed, effective teachers engage in purposeful behavior that provides an overview of the lesson, including information concerning what is to be learned, what students will be doing, and why it is important. Effective teachers attempt to establish a link between the new information and previously learned material.

You should begin the lesson by orienting the students to the subject that they are going to learn and its relevance. This is done by specifying the lesson's objective and purpose. For example, you could start out by telling the class, "Today we're going to learn to write compound sentences. By the end of the lesson, you will be able to combine two sentences into one sentence using the connector *and*. It is important for you to learn to write compound sentences, because it is a skill that will help you to improve the quality of your writing. Having good writing skills is important for success in school and later when you work."

*Introducing New Material.* Spending time on presenting new material and guided practice (supervised reinforcement to facilitate the change from short-term memory into long-

term memory) makes teachers more effective. As an effective teacher, you need to provide many examples and to check for student understanding in order to ensure that students can practice independently with minimal difficulty. Effective teachers present one point at a time and use many examples to ensure acquisition (Bickel & Bickel, 1986). Teacher behaviors appropriate to this phase include:

Modeling the concept, rule (defined and explained later in this chapter), or procedure

Focusing attention on the essential points of the presentation

Providing many examples and nonexamples and relevant and nonrelevant characteristics of a concept

Providing guided practice sessions for the concept or skill

Research suggests that teachers who maintain a brisk pace and a high rate of progress through the curriculum produce greater academic gains than teachers who do not. Effective teachers also stop to check for understanding by posing questions and by asking students to make a prediction, to summarize the presentation to that point, to repeat directions or procedures, or to state whether they agree or disagree with another student's answer. An ineffective way to check for understanding is to ask, "Are there any questions?" and, after receiving no response, assume that the students have learned the material. Another error is to ask a few questions, call on volunteers for responses, and then assume based on the feedback from a few students that the entire class understands the information.

*Conducting Guided Practice Sessions.* After the presentation, or after short segments of the presentation, an effective teacher conducts guided practice sessions. The primary purpose of this activity is to supervise the students' initial practice on a skill and provide the active practice, enhancement, and elaboration necessary to move new learning from short-term to long-term memory.

During successful guided practice sessions, a high frequency of teacher-directed questions is important. There are two types of questions that are usually asked: those calling for specific answers (i.e., product questions) and those calling for an explanation of how an answer was found (i.e., process questions). For example, when you are teaching concepts such as regular and irregular verbs, the guided practice session could consist of you giving examples and having the students identify them and explain their answers, and later, having the students generate a list of examples.

At each step, the guided practice session continues until the students are successful. When you feel that they are ready, the students proceed to the next step. If they are not ready to go on, you should give them additional practice sessions. When you are teaching a more elaborate skill, such as mastering the steps involved in solving a long-division problem, you might begin by having the students restate the steps that were taught one at a time until all of the students are fluent. Then you would supervise as the students begin the actual practice, guiding them through each procedure until they can do the steps without errors.

### Checking Student Understanding.
Not only is the frequency of teacher-generated questions important, but also the percentage of correct student responses is important. Effective teachers try to ensure a high success rate of student responses to their frequent questions. The optimal success rate seems to be around 80 percent during guided practice sessions (Stevens & Rosenshine, 1981; Rosenshine, 1983). High success rates are obtained by presenting materials in small steps and by directing initial student practice sessions through the use of questioning and practice. Therefore, it is important for you to prepare many questions prior to beginning the lesson.

There are specific techniques adapted from Rosenshine (1986) that may increase the amount of active participation for all students. Ask all students to:

Tell the answer to a neighbor
Write a summary of the main idea on a piece of paper and share it with a neighbor
Write the answer on an individual chalkboard and then hold it up
Raise their finger if they agree with an answer that someone else gave
Show the manual letter of the alphabet when the answer is *a*, *b*, or *c*.

Not only do these procedures provide active participation, but also they allow you to see how many students have correct answers and exhibit confidence.

### Providing Feedback and Correction.
*Academic feedback* is defined as information given a student about whether his or her answers were right or wrong (Berliner, 1980). The percentage of instructional time during which a student receives feedback is positively related to that student's achievement (Fisher et al., 1978). If a student answers correctly and is confident, you can simply ask another question or give a short statement of praise (e.g., "Very good") while you maintain the momentum of the practice session. However, if the student answers correctly but is hesitant, it is important that you tell the student that the answer is correct and give *process feedback*. Process feedback means that you will say "Yes, that's right, because . . ." and then you will proceed to explain why the answer is right or to describe the process that must be followed to get the right answer. Such reteaching, or process feedback, gives students the additional explanation that is sometimes needed when they are still unsure. When a student has made an error, it is appropriate for you to simplify the question, provide hints that guide the student

to the right answer, give the student the process or rule to be used in determining the answer, or reteach the material. The important point is that errors should not go uncorrected and should not be glossed over by simply giving the correct answer and then continuing the lesson (Stevens & Rosenshine, 1981).

***Conducting Independent Practice Sessions.***
The primary purpose of independent practice sessions is to provide drill and overlearning and to assess if what has been covered is understood by each individual student. Seatwork or computer work provides the additional practice that students need to become fluent in a skill and to enable them to work without the cues given during guided practice sessions. The independent practice sessions should be on the same material as the guided practice sessions. For instance, if the guided practice session was on characteristics of mammals, then the independent practice session should be on the characteristics of mammals or should differentiate between mammals and reptiles. Independent practice sessions should be viewed as a continuum in which the students begin their work under teacher supervision and conclude with homework without supervision.

Seatwork activities often consume from 50 to 70 percent of the school day (Englert, 1984). As a result, there are fewer opportunities for teacher-student interactions, and this all too frequently fosters student off-task behavior. Therefore, a major concern of effective teachers is the proper management of seatwork activities in order to maintain high task engagement and to promote academic learning (Rosenshine, 1980; Stevens & Rosenshine, 1981).

Three management techniques that can be used to enhance performance on seatwork include *monitoring seatwork, accuracy on seatwork tasks,* and *accountability* (Englert, 1984). Investigators have found that students are more engaged during seatwork when the teacher circulates around the room and moni-

tors and supervises their work. However, those contacts should be relatively short, averaging 30 seconds or less (Everston, Emmer, & Brophy, 1980). Lengthy explanations during seatwork indicates that the initial teaching and guided practice were not sufficient. Similarly, accuracy on seatwork has been found to be an important factor contributing to student learning (Rosenshine, 1983). Materials and activities that yield a low success rate for students are consistently and negatively correlated with achievement (Berliner, 1980). Therefore, students need to work at high levels of accuracy in order to receive the full benefit of seatwork practice. There is a great need to be sure that what is taught and what is practiced and measured are congruent. This can be accomplished by making certain that the independent practice is used to consolidate and develop automaticity on previously taught skills rather than being used to teach new skills or to provide practice on tangential skills (Brophy et al., 1983).

***Continuing Practice and Accountability.***
Teachers must hold students accountable for their assignments. Effective teachers keep track of student progress and work completed and require students to complete their work on time, according to specific work standards regarding format, neatness, and accuracy. When work is incomplete, effective teachers require students to redo assignments until they meet acceptable performance criteria (Anderson, Everston, & Emmer, 1980).

As we discussed in Chapter 3, graphing individual students' accuracy on specific seatwork assignments is a method of assuring accountability and monitoring the effectiveness of the intervention and the appropriateness of the seatwork assignments. Involving the students in charting and measuring their seatwork accuracy can further increase students' seatwork performance, as well as their accountability in maintaining high performance levels (Englert, 1884). Again, it is recommended that you review the previous week's

**EXHIBIT 10.1.** Effective Teaching Checklist

| Introduction Phase | Present | Absent |
| --- | --- | --- |
| 1. Secure student attention | | |
| 2. Reviews prior learning | | |
| 3. States objective of the lesson | | |

| Demonstration Phase | | |
| --- | --- | --- |
| 1. Presents information in small steps | | |
| 2. Provides many examples | | |
| 3. Maintains a brisk pace | | |
| 4. Asks frequent questions | | |
| 5. Conducts guided practice sessions | | |
| 6. Provides feedback and correction | | |
| 7. Conducts independent practice sessions | | |

| Follow-up Phase | | |
| --- | --- | --- |
| 1. Provides daily, weekly, and monthly reviews | | |
| 2. Provides frequent practice and assessment of student mastery | | |
| 3. Maintains continuous records of student progress | | |
| 4. Makes instructional decisions based on student performance | | |

work every Monday and the previous month's work every fourth Monday. These reviews and tests provide additional practice for students.

Exhibit 10.1 is a checklist that will help you to plan and then review and evaluate each of your lessons. Lessons may not always include all of these steps or follow them in exactly the same order. Variations in the structure may occur in relation to the type of lesson being taught.

## Additional Considerations

*Academic learning time (ALT)* is defined as the amount of instructional time that students spend actively engaged in relevant academic tasks performed with high success rates (Wilson & Wesson, 1986). There is research evidence that ALT is significantly and positively associated with achievement (Anderson, Evertson, & Brophy, 1979; Rosenberg, Sindelar, & Stedt, 1985). Use the time that students are in school efficiently. Although a major portion of the day is assumed to be spent in instructional activities, this is not al-

ways the case. Thurlow et al., (1983) have reported that up to 50 percent of the school day may be spent in noninstructional activities in special education classrooms. Similar results have been reported in regular classrooms (Good, 1983; Rosenshine, 1980).

Effective teachers schedule generous amounts of time for instruction, whereas they decrease the time spent in noninstructional activities, such as the transition from subject to subject or class to class, task management, socializing, and waiting for teacher assistance. Additionally, they insulate themselves and their students from intrusions into academic learning time by

Establishing rules for working students (e.g., rules for early finishers or stalled students)

Using a wide variety of reinforcers for accurate work completion

Teaching and rehearsing all new lesson procedures and equipment in advance (Berliner, 1984; Bickel & Bickel, 1986)

Specific suggestions for eliminating wasted time are given by Daniele and Aldersley (1988).

1. Treat days just before and after vacations as no different from other class days.
2. Prepare instructional materials and activities for the full allocated time. Endeavor to begin and finish your lessons at the appropriate times.
3. Maintain enough flexibility to allow for student comments to generate learning, but be mindful that such flexibility can deteriorate into excessive off-task discussion.
4. Avoid using class time in activities that could be done outside of class; for example, prepare overheads in advance rather than writing at length on the chalkboard.
5. Avoid using class time for activities that students could do equally well outside of class or during free time, such as running to the library or getting something from the office.

## TEACHING CONCEPTS

*Concepts* are a set of specific objects, symbols, or events that share common characteristics (critical attributes) and can be referenced by a particular name or symbol (Tennyson & Park, 1980). We come to understand our world through concepts. Concepts allow us to organize and store similar pieces of information efficiently. They permit us to treat information in an integrated manner, which allows information to be retrieved efficiently. Concepts are the basic elements that we use in higher thought processes. The acquisition, usage, enlargement, and revision of concepts is a continual process. Concepts also facilitate the communication process. They allow us to discuss ideas, events, or objects without having to explain everything in great detail, because the individuals with whom we are communicating share similar concepts.

Essential to an understanding of concepts is the idea of *categorization*. Concepts are categories into which we group our knowledge and experiences. The criteria that we generally use to sort events or objects into categories are their basic characteristics or critical attributes. Once formed, these categories act as intellectual magnets that attract and order related information or experiences (Martorella, 1986). The categories that we create generally have single or multiword labels or names that are used to identify them, such as "apple" or "World War II." As we have ideas or experience events or objects, we sort them into the various categories that we have created. Illustrations of a concept are referred to as *examples*. *Nonexamples* of a concept are any illustrations that lack one or more of the critical attributes of the concept.

Many of the concepts that we acquire come through informal channels of experience (e.g., *car*, *house*, *television*), while others come through systematic channels of instruction, such as parents or schools (e.g., *square*, *hydrogen*, *government*). The teaching of concepts is an important aspect of working with hearing-impaired students. Whether you are teaching language, reading, health, or social studies, concept instruction is included. Concept learning is regarded as the identification of concept attributes, which can be generalized to newly encountered examples, as well as the ability to discriminate examples from nonexamples (Tennyson & Park, 1980). If a piece of information meets the criteria for a concept category that we hold, then we attach the concept name to the item and begin to relate it to the other information that we have. In general, there are two kinds of concepts: *basic concepts* and *associated concepts* (Archer, Isaacson, & Schiller, 1987).

## Basic Concepts

Basic concepts cannot be adequately explained or defined with words in a way that can clearly be understood by a student. Examples of basic concepts would include: *blue*, *more*, *little*, *door*, and *same*. Associated concepts are related to previously learned concepts and can be explained through language. When you are teaching basic concepts, use examples and nonexamples to demonstrate the concept. Whenever possible, use a full range of examples to avoid overgeneralization of the concept. Also, carefully select nonexamples in order to draw attention to the critical aspects of the concept. For example, if you were introducing the color green, you might want to use a 4-inch green circle as the example. Initially, for the nonexample, it would be best to keep the size and shape the same and only differ the color. Therefore, it would be best to use a 4-inch purple circle as a nonexample rather than a 2-inch purple square. You could then introduce a 2-inch green square as an example and a 2-inch blue square as a nonexample. This demonstration and explanation should continue with several more examples and nonexamples.

Point out to the students the *critical attributes* of the concept while you are presenting them with the examples, and, at the same time, show them those attributes that are not present in the nonexamples. When you feel that the students have an understanding of the concept, you will want to check their understanding of the concept by using other examples and nonexamples.

## Associated Concepts

When you are teaching associated concepts (concepts that can be described with other words that are known to the students), be sure that you teach only one meaning at a time. Teach the most common meaning or the meaning that will be used in instruction or in a reading assignment. Other meanings can be taught after the first meaning has been mastered. In doing so, choose an appropriate synonym or definition. When you are choosing a definition, try to include a *class* and a distinction from other members of the class. For example, the concept *neighbor* can be placed in the class "a person," with the distinction "who lives near you." When you are developing definitions or using synonyms, try to be sure that the words that you are using are known to the students.

After a synonym or definition has been selected, you need to determine the *critical attributes* of the concept—those attributes that distinguish it from the other similar concepts or situations. For example, if you were studying about mammals, there would be some important and some not important (noncritical) attributes of mammals that you would want to share with the students. The class and critical attributes that you could use could include: "A mammal is an animal (class) that has hair, is warm-blooded, and feeds its young with mother's milk (critical attributes)." Some examples that could be used are: *dog*, *cat*, *cow*, *rabbit*, and *horse*. Some nonexamples would be: *fish*, *chicken*, *duck*, *frog*, and *snake*. Some noncritical attributes that may confuse students are: *color*, *two eyes*, *lives on land*, and *eating habits*.

A sequence and examples for teaching concepts that draws from the work of Cole and Cole (1989) and Martorella (1986) follow.

1. Identify the concept. What name is most commonly applied to the concept (e.g., *lake*)?
2. Select an appropriate synonym or definition (e.g., *body of water surrounded by land*).
3. Identify the essential characteristics or critical attributes of the concept. Critical attributes include the characteristics that, when put together, differentiate one concept from another concept. The entire set of attributes must be present

to define a particular concept (e.g., *land*, *water*, *surroundings*).

4. Identify some noncritical attributes that are typically associated with the concept. Noncritical attributes have characteristics that do not differentiate one concept from another. It is best to identify those characteristics that may confuse students (e.g., shape, location, depth).

5. Identify some interesting and learner-relevant examples or cases of the concept that you can use in its explanation. Examples of the concept contain the set of critical attributes (e.g., *local lakes*, *mountain lakes*, *desert lakes*).

6. Identify some contrasting nonexamples of the concept that will help clarify and illustrate the concept. Nonexamples are those that lack the set of critical attributes (e.g., *ocean*, *stream*).

7. Develop some cues, questions, or directions that you can use to call attention to critical attributes and noncritical attributes in the concept examples (e.g., "Look at all the points where the water meets the land.").

8. Choose the most efficient method and the most interesting materials to present examples and nonexamples (e.g., real objects, pictures, slides).

9. Decide the level of concept mastery that you expect students to achieve and how you will measure it (e.g., they should be able to define *lake* and state the similarities and differences this body of water has with other major bodies of water).

10. Present examples and nonexamples. Concept examples teach students to generalize to other cases within the same concept. Nonexamples teach discrimination among differing concepts. Examples and nonexamples should be presented in a manner that entails an increasingly finer level of discrimination by students.

11. Provide guided practice sessions using more examples and nonexamples.

12. Provide independent practice sessions to assess if the students have an understanding of the concept.

## TEACHING RULES

A *rule* is a relationship that can be applied to a large set of examples (Gagne, 1984). Educating of hearing-impaired students involves all types of rules. Students learn rules that enable them to compose sentences (e.g., a period goes at the end of a telling sentence), to perform arithmetic computations (e.g., if the number in the one's column is more than 9, we have to rename it), to behave in certain ways (e.g., when your work is done, find a quiet activity), and for all aspects of their academic and personal life. Rules make it possible for individuals to respond to a class of things with a class of performances. For example, students learn that by adding a particular ending to a word they will make a plural out of the word (*s*) or place it in the past tense (*ed*).

Typically, a rule is composed of several concepts. Concomitantly, rules make it possible for individuals to use concepts (Bigge, 1988). For example, if you explained to students that the first word of every sentence must be capitalized, they must first understand the meanings of the concepts *capitalize* and *sentence*. With an understanding of these two concepts, the students will be prepared to combine the two concepts and to use them in relation to one another (Gagne, 1984). This ability is what constitutes rule learning. It is characterized by the capacity to use symbols and concepts that were previously learned in combination with one another. In essence, when individuals learn a rule, they have learned a new relationship that exists between previously learned concepts.

Rule learning entails the ability to generalize from an example to a large class of instances. When students are able to communicate the words that represent the rule, it does not indicate that they have learned the rule. However, it is important to recognize that linguistic statements usually are crucial in the process of learning new rules (Gagne, 1984). We say that learners have learned a rule when they can "follow it" in their performances. In other words, a rule is a learned capability that makes it possible for individuals to do something by using symbols (most commonly, the symbols of language and mathematics). The capability of doing something should be distinguished carefully from being able to state something. To determine whether the rule has been learned, you must find out whether students can identify the component concepts and demonstrate the relationship between those concepts.

An abstract concept, as previously described, is actually not formally different from a rule and is learned in much the same way (Gagne & Briggs, 1979). A sequence that can be used for teaching rules that draws from the work of Gagne (1984) is as follows:

1. When you teach rules, teach only those rules that have enough application to merit instruction (e.g., "Capitalize the names of people").
2. State the rule clearly, simply, and accurately (e.g., "When we write a person's name, we use a capital letter at the beginning of the name").
3. Determine the critical attributes of the rule (e.g., people's names, capital letters).
4. Establish a list of examples, (e.g., *Steve, Bob Carr, Marion, Sue Marie Rudolph*).
5. Establish a list of nonexamples. Be sure that your nonexamples bring attention to the critical attributes of the rule (e.g., *dog, lunch money, clown, glass of milk*).
6. Present the rule to the students (e.g., "When we write a person's name, we use a capital letter at the beginning of the name").
7. Ask a question about the rule or have students repeat the rule (e.g., "What do we do when we write a person's name?").
8. Model the rule, using examples and nonexamples (e.g., *Steve, Bob Carr, Marion, Sue Marie Rudolph*; nonexamples are *dog, lunch money, clown, glass of milk*).
9. Provide guided practice sessions in discriminating examples from nonexamples.
10. Check the students' understanding of the rule by providing them with independent practice sessions.

## QUESTION PROMPTS

The questions that teachers ask can facilitate student comprehension of concepts and rules. The question prompts in Exhibit 10.2 have been adapted from Moeller, Osberger, and Eccarius (1986) and provide parents and teachers with alternatives to repeating a question that a student has not answered or has not answered correctly. Following are explanations of the types listed in the exhibit.

*Standard focusing phrase with repetition.* Sometimes a teacher asks a student a question, but the student does not realize that an answer is expected. This prompt calls attention to the demands of the situation and is analogous to a "listening set" in auditory training. You are overtly saying, "listen to my question."

*Exaggeration of the interrogative.* In this

category, you use the relevant question word at a place in the interrogative where it can be emphasized.

*Multiple choice*. If a student cannot answer your question, it may be helpful to provide a closed set of possible answers. We suggest that you give at least three different answers from which the student can select an answer. Also, be careful to alter randomly the placement of the correct response so that the student does not depend on its location (e.g., always the last choice) as a clue.

*Relevant comparison*. By using the strategy of relevant comparison, you provide the student with part of a possible listing of information that is needed to answer your question. The information you provide should not always be accurate, as in the math example in Exhibit 10.2.

*Visualization*. As previously discussed in Chapter 5, visualizations can link context to verbal (signed or spoken) description. A visualization provides a student with a cognitive crutch with which to discuss the desired information.

*Model with related content*. A model provides the student with the grammatical form of an answer so that the student can concentrate on the content of what is being discussed. If a student does not answer a question or answers it incorrectly, you can ask an adult or another student the same question. After a model of the desired answer has been given, ask the first student a similar question—one that uses the same grammatical form but that is about slightly different content.

*Analogous example*. When a student cannot respond to your question, it may be helpful to provide the student with an analogous situation. This prompt gives the student an opportunity to think about a concept or process without being told the very information you are trying to ascertain.

These prompts have proven to be helpful in teaching hearing-impaired students of all ages and who possess various degrees of hearing loss. Educators are encouraged to set a goal for themselves to incorporate at least three different prompts into each lesson.

Significant adults can use the prompts to ask both *closed* and *open questions*. Closed questions have a specific answer; open questions could have many answers. Teachers should be cognizant of asking questions of older students that require them to evaluate, judge, synthesize, predict, and so on—the higher Bloom and Krathwohl (1977) skills. (See Exhibit 10.2) For example, a teacher, using a visualization, might ask a student to compare the Civil War with World War I. The student might use descriptions that compare the two events or descriptions that contrast the two events. To require the student to encode more complex meanings, the teacher might then ask the student to make a prediction about a future war or to evaluate what was beneficial about the two wars being reviewed. This open-ended question will stimulate the use of connectives such as *and*, *because*, and *but*. The use of open-ended questions provides opportunities for students to use more complex language (Bloom & Lahey, 1978).

An additional point for you to consider when you are developing and asking questions is the concept of *wait time*. Research indicates that teachers wait approximately 1 second after they ask a question before they call on a student and only 1 second after the student responds before they rephrase the question and redirect it to another student or provide the answer (Rowe, 1974). In general, in order to involve more students in thinking and to give students sufficient time to develop an appropriate response, more wait time

| Question Prompt Type | Strategy Description Preschool | Math |
|---|---|---|
| Standard focusing phrase with repetition | "Listen to the question" signals the student that his/her response was in error. Direct his/her attention to the repetition; highlights. | "Listen to the question." How many boys are in this classroom? <br><br> ------------------------------------------------- <br><br> In all of the examples, the question |
| Sequence | What day is this? <br> Monday, Tuesday, _____? | What number is after 4? <br> 1, 2, . . . |
| Listing | Who is in your family? <br> Mom, Dad, _____? | |
| Exaggeration/ placement of the Interrogative | Which of these coats belongs to Hannah? vs. I have three coats. *Which one* is Hannah's? | "When we keep track of accounts in our check books, we can either add or subtract our money. If I am depositing money, *what operation* do I use?" |
| Multiple Choice | "What animals are near extinction?" No response. "Which is near extinction, a panther, a cow, or a gorilla?" | "How do you find the area of a circle?" No response. "Is the formula, length x width or x radius squared, or x the ? distance? |

**EXHIBIT 10.2.** (Continued)

| Spelling | World History/ Social Studies | Science |
|---|---|---|
| "Listen to the question." How many syllables are in the word buttercup?" | "Listen to the question." What year did Columbus sail? | "Listen to the question." At what degree does water boil? |

was asked first and the student's response was incorrect. The question is repeated emphasizing key words.

| Spelling | World History/ Social Studies | Science |
|---|---|---|
| How do you spell house? h . . o . . . | MacArthur was famous in which war? The Civil War, World War I, . . . | What is the life cycle of a frog? Tadpole . . . |

| Spelling | World History/ Social Studies | Science |
|---|---|---|
| Who knows how to spell cat? *"How* do you spell cat?" | "There are 7 continents in the world. *Which one* does the United States *belong to*?" | "Water boils at a certain temperature? *What* temperature does water boil at"? |

| Spelling | World History/ Social Studies | Science |
|---|---|---|
| "What is a noun?" No response. "Does a noun name a person, place or thing, show an action, or describe a verb? | "What is the name of a communist country?" No response. "Which is communist, the United States, Russia, or France?" | "Name a mammal." No response. "Which is a mammal: a monkey, a frog, or a butterfly? |

*(continued)*

**EXHIBIT 10.2.** (Continued)

| Question Prompt Type | Strategy Description Preschool | Math |
|---|---|---|
| Relevant Comparison Yes/No | "What does a hockey player need?" No response. "Does a hockey player need skates?" "Yes!" "Good!" "What else does he need?" | "What are the multiples of 3, up to 21?" No response. "Is 10 a multiple of 3?" "No." "Good." "What are the multiples of 3?" |
| Visualization of Relationships | "How are an apple and a cookie alike?" No response. Draw a semantic feature chart.<br><br>bakes eat grows on tree<br>apple   +   +     +<br>cookie   +   +     − | $1 + 2 = 3$<br>$\overline{0\ 1\ 2\ 3\ 4\ 5\ 6}$ |
| Model example with related content | Hannah, what color is this? No response. Breeze, what color is this? Good. Hannah, what color is this? (new object) | "Toni, how many inches in a foot?" Respond Incorrectly. "Kap, how many inches in a foot?" "12" "Excellent." "Toni how many inches in 1/2 of a foot?" "6" "Great job!" |
| Analogous Examples | What do people need to live? No response. Plants need food and water. What do people need to live? | |

**EXHIBIT 10.2.** (Continued)

| Spelling | World History/ Social Studies | Science |
|---|---|---|
| "Does jump follow the 1 + 1 + 1 rule?" No response. "Does jump have 1 syllable?" "Yes." "Good." "Does jump have 1 vowel?" "Yes." "Great." "Does jump have 1 final consonant?" "No." "Wonderful." "Does jump follow the 1 + 1 + 1 rule?" | When looking at a map, what states does the Mississippi River touch?" No response. "Does it touch Illinois?" "Yes." "What states does the Mississippi touch?" | "What are the parts of an atom?" No response. "Are electrons parts of atoms?" "Yes" "Good, what are parts of an atom?" |

"Does jump follow the 1 + 1 + 1 rule?" No response.

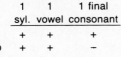

|  | 1 syl. | 1 vowel | 1 final consonant |
|---|---|---|---|
| hop | + | + | + |
| thump | + | + | − |
| stop | + | + | + |

1 + 1 + 1 rule = 1 syllable, 1 vowel, 1 final consonant for doubling the final consonant before -ed and -ing.

"Which states have more people?"

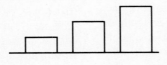

Histogram Graph: *Growing Plants*

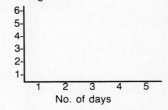

No. of days

"Mark how do you spell receive?" Spells it wrong. "Debbie, how do you spell *receive?*" Spells it correctly. "Good!" "Mark, how do you spell deceive?" Spells it with the ei correct. "Wonderful!"

"John, what are three branches in government?" Wrong response. "Sue, what are the 3 branches?" Sue responds. "Good!" "John, which branch is made up of the laws?" John responds. "Excellent!"

"Art, how can you measure the volume of some solid?" Answers Incorrectly. "Bill, same question." Answers correctly. "Art, what does water displacement measure?" "Volume."

How are decisions made in a democracy? No response. How are decisions made in scouting?

"What powers a hearing aid?" No response. A battery powers a car. "What powers a hearing aid?"

is necessary between asking the question and seeking a response. Research shows that a 3–5 second pause is significantly more effective in stimulating a higher quality and a greater quantity of student thinking (Rowe, 1974). Therefore, it is advantageous for you to try and develop the habit of pausing after you have asked a question and after a student has responded.

## ADDITIONAL TEACHING STRATEGIES

The information that has been presented on effective teaching is valuable for guiding you through all types of teaching-learning opportunities. Because you will be working with a wide variety of students, who will have diverse strengths, needs, and learning styles, you will want to have a repertoire of methods of structuring learning in your educational setting. You quickly will learn that what works for one student does not work for another student and what worked with one student last week is not working with that student this week. Also, you will want to try new and different ways of facilitating learning with your students so that you can personally continue to grow and develop as a teacher. The following section is a compilation of additional teaching strategies that can be used with your students. They are presented with the intent of helping you to develop a large "toolbox" from which you, the artisan, can pull the right tool at the right time.

### Mapping

A technique that can assist students in organizing and remembering information is a procedure referred to as *mapping*. As we mentioned in Chapter 6, mapping is a categorical structuring of information in graphic form. Maps have both a linguistic and nonlinguistic component, with concepts displayed within nodes and links drawn between nodes to represent associations between concepts.

Mapping is based on the research in the area of schema theory. A *schema* "is an organized representation of a person's knowledge about some concept, action or event, or a larger unit of knowledge" (Kintsch, 1974, p. 374). Schema theory, an extension of Piaget's beliefs, attempts to deal with comprehension by proposing that what is comprehended during reading or communication integrates in some conceptual way with what already exists in the mind of the person. A fundamental tenet of schema theory is that messages do not, in themselves, carry meaning. On the contrary, the message provides cues and directives for individuals as to how they should, using their own previously acquired knowledge, construct meaning. This previously acquired knowledge is stored in memory in the form of abstract cognitive structures called *schema*. The purpose of schema is to serve as a cognitive template against which incoming data can be matched. A fundamental application of schema theory is that learning is strengthened when new material is conceptually related to previously stored knowledge.

When you are teaching students a body of knowledge, particularly in a content area subject, there is often a group of related concepts and facts that you would like to introduce. These facts and concepts can be arranged in a "conceptual map." Instruction using a conceptual map can supplement or replace the reading of textbook material. The conceptual map shows the relationship between the concepts and facts. Conceptual maps should generally be organized with the most general, most inclusive idea at the apex of the map, with successively less general, less inclusive concepts in appropriate subordinate positions. The conceptual map's roadways (lines between terms) provide information about the relationships by indicating the connections between concepts.

***Constructing the Conceptual Map.*** A sequence that can be used for constructing a conceptual map that draws from the work of Archer, Isaacson, and Schiller (1987) follows.

1. Determine the concepts and facts that you would like to teach. This can be accomplished by reading the text material and highlighting or outlining it.
2. Select the critical concepts and facts that you would like your students to master.
3. Arrange the concepts and facts in a logical manner that best represents the body of knowledge.
4. When possible, add graphics to provide context, increase interest, and aid retention of information.
5. Prepare a completed map, a partially completed map, and a blank map. Sometimes you will need more than one map in order to cover all of the material that you want your students to master.

Exhibit 10.3 is an example of a conceptual map that was developed for part of a unit on safety.

6. Prepare overheads that can be used during instruction. Making a complete map and using white-out to make your partial and blank maps will save you time and energy.

***Teaching Procedures.*** There are many different ways in which you can use your conceptual map when you are introducing and/or reviewing material. The following is one sequence that you may want to consider.

1. Introduce the new information. Depending on the skill level of your students, you can give them a blank map, a completed map, or a partially completed map for instruction. If your students are

**EXHIBIT 10.3.** Conceptual map

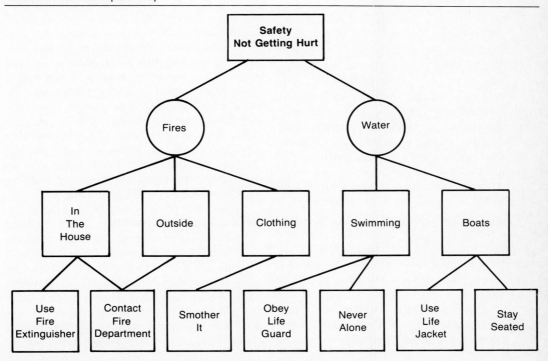

able and can write fairly quickly, use a blank map. Since they will be writing throughout the lesson, active participation will be maximized. If your students have some difficulty copying and organizing their responses, use a partially completed map. If your students have a great deal of difficulty making written responses, give them completed conceptual maps.

2. Present each of the concepts and related facts in order. Teach each concept by using examples and nonexamples (see the section, "Teaching Concepts" in this chapter). Present the definition or synonym for important terms. Ask questions about the definition or synonym or have students repeat the definition. Check the students' understanding, using examples and nonexamples. If appropriate, have your students generate examples of the concept.

3. Present any important facts. When you are introducing the facts, be certain that you tell the students the information rather than have them make guesses. Having students guess what something means does not make optimum use of their time, and on occasion students remember other students' wrong guesses rather than the right information. For example, if you were studying illnesses and you asked what the term *germ* meant, you would want to say that "Germs are small living things that cause people to be sick," rather than "Has anyone ever heard of the word *germ* before?" and risk that a student will start telling the class a story that has nothing to do with the topic of illnesses. Then ask the students questions concerning the factual information or have them repeat the information. Using the preceding example, you would ask, "Who can tell me what a germ is?"

4. After you have introduced the information, discuss it by giving as many practical and age-appropriate examples as possible.

5. Continually review the content of the conceptual map as you add new information.

6. Check the students' acquisition of the concepts. This can be done in several ways. You can put a blank or partially completed conceptual map about the overhead and ask students questions on the missing content. You can give students a blank conceptual map and have them fill in the missing information. This is a good project to have them do cooperatively (discussed later in this chapter). Finally, you can have students answer written questions using the conceptual map as a reference.

## Cooperative Learning

An alternative to group lessons and individual instruction is *cooperative learning*. Lessons can be structured cooperatively so that students work together to accomplish shared goals. Cooperative learning is a systematic model for helping teachers implement and work with groups so that students will consistently learn their subject matter, complete tasks, include all group members in their work, solve group problems with minimal teacher assistance, resolve differences among themselves, and enjoy the process of working together (Johnson & Johnson, 1987).

Research on cooperative learning (e.g., Johnson et al., 1981; Slavin, 1981) has indicated that this approach to teaching and learning has many positive effects on both students and teachers. Studies that have compared cooperative, competitive, and individualistic learning approaches suggest that achievement is higher when learning situations are structured cooperatively rather than competitively or individualistically (e.g.,

Johnson, Skon, & Johnson, 1980; Slavin, 1980).

The cooperative learning approach gives students a great deal of control within the group structure. They become both teachers and students and are taught communication and group process skills, as well as leadership skills. The reward structure promotes group identity and importance. In most cooperative learning models, the students work in small groups and receive a group grade or reward for their efforts. Their grade may be contingent upon a group project or the average of each student's progress towards meeting group objectives. Working for a group grade encourages students to provide support for those members who are having trouble reaching goals, be they academic goals or the performance of cooperative learning skills. As a result of this type of structure, research indicates that cooperative learning experiences promote greater competencies in critical thinking, more positive attitudes towards the subject areas studied, greater competencies in working collaboratively with others, and greater psychological health than competitive and individualistic approaches (Johnson & Johnson, 1987).

The cooperative learning approach can be used with most learning tasks, especially concept attainment, problem solving, categorizing tasks, and skill attainment. Also, the cooperative learning approach has been used with kindergarten students up through adults in college. Supporters of cooperative learning do not advocate that it be used exclusively for all class work but, rather, that teachers begin to integrate this approach into their existing repertoire. It is recommended that you start using cooperative learning in a very limited way at first by implementing it with one subject until the process feels comfortable to you. After you have mastered managing the approach in one subject, then you can begin to use it with different subjects and experiment with some of the many different cooperative learning techniques.

There are several specific approaches for implementing cooperative learning. The type of format used depends on your preference and the students' needs, abilities, and willingness to cooperate with others. Several commonly used cooperative learning methods are:

Learning Together, Student Teams—Achievement Divisions (STAD)
Teams—Games—Tournament (TGT)
Jigsaw 2
Team Assisted Individualization (TAI) (Slavin, 1981).

Regardless of the specific approach that you decide to use, there are four basic elements of cooperative learning that you need to include. They are *positive interdependence, individual accountability, collaborative skills,* and *group processing* (Johnson & Johnson, 1987).

Positive interdependence means that students are linked with others in the group in such a way that one student cannot succeed unless the others do. This can be accomplished by making the group's goal and reward dependent on the group's overall achievement. Individual accountability means that each student will be assessed so that group members know who needs more assistance in completing the assignment and that they must fulfill their individual responsibilities in order for the group to be successful. Many students lack the necessary social skills to work collaboratively. Therefore, those collaborative skills need to be taught just as purposefully and precisely as academic skills. Group processing entails providing students with specific time to discuss how well they are achieving their goals and maintaining effective working relationships among themselves. They need to discuss which actions are helpful and which are not helpful and make decisions about which actions to continue or change.

Implementing cooperative learning involves a series of structured procedures. The following 18 steps and short explanation have been adapted from Johnson et al. (1984).

## Phase I: Planning

1. *Specify instructional objectives.* Both academic and cooperative skill objectives should be established before you begin each lesson.
2. *Decide on the size of the groups.* Depending on the objectives of the lesson and the nature of the learning task, the size of cooperative groups should be determined. Groups should range in size from two to six students.
3. *Assign students to groups.* Decide on making groups of homogeneous or heterogenous ability levels. Separate or group nontask-oriented and task-oriented students.
4. *Arrange the room to accommodate working groups.* You can arrange the students' desks or tables in clusters, placing individual desks in pairs, or blocking off a carpeted corner of the room.
5. *Arrange instructional materials.* Materials should be distributed in carefully planned ways to communicate that the assignment is a cooperative one.

## Phase 2: Preparing Students

6. *Assign roles to ensure interdependence.* Interdependence may be arranged through the assignment of complimentary and interconnected roles to group members.
7. *Explain the academic task.* You set the task so that students understand the assignment and are aware of the objectives of the lesson.
8. *Structure positive goal interdepend-ence.* Emphasize the group goal and make it clear that students must work collaboratively to reach the group goal.
9. *Structure individual accountability.* Each individual will be assessed, as well as the group. Therefore, students know which members need encouragement and help.
10. *Promote intergroup cooperation.* Positive outcomes found within cooperative groups are extended throughout the whole class by structuring intergroup cooperation.
11. *Explain the criteria for success.* At the beginning of the lesson you will want to explain clear criteria by which the students' academic work will be evaluated.
12. *Specify desired social skills behaviors.* You will need to define, discuss, and possibly even model specific social skills behaviors that you have targeted for the group to work on.

## Phase 3: Monitoring and Intervention

13. *Monitor students' behavior.* After group work begins, you will spend your time observing group members to see how they are doing with the assignment and working cooperatively.
14. *Provide task assistance when necessary.* When needed, you can clarify instructions and review procedures and strategies for completing the assignment.
15. *Intervene to teach collaborative skills.* You can remind students of the social skills that you are working on or intervene to suggest more effective procedures for working together as needed.

## Phase 4: Evaluation and Processing

16. *Provide closure to the lesson*. You will want to summarize the major points of the lesson, ask the students to recall ideas, and answer final questions.
17. *Evaluate the quality and quantity of students' learning*. Whatever the product of the lesson, it is best to evaluate it by a criteria-referenced system. (See chapter 2).
18. *Assess how well the group functioned*. Time should be spent discussing how well the group worked together. They should discuss which things were done well and which could be improved.

Cooperative learning is an exciting and effective way to work with students. It provides an avenue for helping students develop those social skills that are necessary to be accepted in our ever changing world while simultaneously mastering academic skills. Because of the small class sizes and the age, ability, and language differences that frequently exist in self-contained classes for hearing-impaired students, you may need to monitor closely which aspects of the cooperative learning environment work or do not work in your educational setting. Starting with groups of two or three may be essential. When the groups begin to demonstrate that they can work together, you may get to the point at which your class becomes one cooperative group working together or a group of five while you work individually with a student who needs a more direct instructional approach. The point is that you must monitor how the program is working and what changes need to be made in order to accommodate the strengths and needs of your students. For more information on cooperative learning, we suggest that you look at the work of Johnson & Johnson (1987) and Kagan (1985).

## Peer Tutoring

If you have a big discrepancy in the abilities of the students in your class or if some of your students need extra practice to master materials, *peer tutoring* may be a valuable program for you to use with your students. The use of students to teach other peers is not a new concept. As early as the first century, Roman teachers indicated that younger students could profit from instruction by older classmates (Gartner, Kohler, & Reissman, 1971). Contemporary research on peer tutoring suggests that, when a program is properly instituted, peer tutoring can: (1) improve academic skills, (2) enhance self-esteem, (3) help students who have problems with authority figures, and (4) promote positive relationships and cooperation among peers (Mercer & Mercer, 1985). Otis-Wilburn (1984) implemented a peer tutoring program with hearing-impaired students. She compared peer tutoring with two methods: sustained silent reading and naturalistic teaching. Her research indicated that peer tutoring was significantly more effective in improving the areas of reading rate, comprehension, and story retelling than to the other two approaches.

Peer tutoring is most effective when *you* introduce the new concepts to be learned and the *tutor* provides the necessary review (Gearheart & Weishahn, 1984). The role of the peer tutor should be limited to carrying out your instructional plan. You maintain full responsibility for the program and carefully and continually monitor it by periodically observing the sessions. You determine the skills to be taught, the materials to be used, and the instructional activities.

When you are using peer tutoring, several conditions suggested by Paine et al. (1983) should be considered. First, *determine the role* of the tutor. Decide what part the tutor can play in the classroom. Some examples include instruction in academic and/or social skills, record keeping, making observations, and providing feedback. Second, *select the tutor*. The tutor should be proficient in the skill that they are assigned to teach. Therefore, it is important that you select a tutor who is capable of demonstrating the task to be performed. In addition, there should be a good fit between the two individuals that work together. Third, *train* the tutor. The tutor should be trained in how to work with your students.

It is beneficial to have tutors participate in a training program so that they will learn how to use instruction, feedback, and reinforcement efficiently. An extensive training program for tutors that involves four 30–45-minute training sessions, which was developed by Deterline (1970), includes the following sequence.

*Session One.* Present tasks, questioning techniques, feedback procedures, demonstration techniques, and positive reinforcement. You should model the guided practice procedure with the peer tutor. The peer tutor should rehearse the procedure with you while you provide feedback.

*Session Two.* Engage in role playing and play both the tutor and the tutee role.

*Session Three.* Familiarize the tutor with day-to-day functions, review of material to be used, and practice with record-keeping forms.

*Session Four.* Answer questions about the student with whom the tutor is going to work. While this may seem like an inordinate amount of time to get things started, it is important that the program begin in a structured manner so that less time is required for monitoring and evaluation and positive results occur.

Fourth, *supervise and reinforce* peer-tutoring arrangements. When the tutor initially works with the student, you should supervise closely to ensure that the actual instruction is consistent with the instructional plan. As the tutor becomes more competent, you may observe less often. The tutor should make frequent reports on the student's progress. Permanent products of the student's work may be the most reliable indicator of this progress. Both the tutor and the student should be reinforced liberally for their cooperative efforts. Reinforce tutors for presenting stimuli, providing feedback, and maintaining pleasant interactions. Reinforce students for following directions and responding to task materials. Tutors who fail to meet deadlines and program standards should be asked to leave the program.

Some additional points you should consider when you are establishing a peer-tutoring program suggested by Allen (1976).

1. Young students prefer a tutor of the same sex, because they tend to have mutual interests.
2. Tutoring sessions that last too long may produce negative effects. Recommended are 20–30 minute sessions held two to three times per week.
3. Tutoring should occur in a place in which there are minimal distractions, for example, the hallway is not an appropriate place.
4. It should be explained to parents that tutoring supplements teacher instruction but does not replace it.
5. You should make sure that the tutor has mastered the instructional content before tutoring occurs.
6. The goals and activities of the tutoring session should be specified. Tutoring sessions should have materials that are easy to use and a set routine.

## Classwide Peer Tutoring

Another approach towards using a peer-tutoring program, suggested by Delquadri et al. (1986), is referred to as *classwide* peer tutoring. Classwide peer tutoring is used as a method for increasing the opportunity for students to participate and respond actively to instructional material. The procedure requires about 30 minutes: 10 minutes for each student to be a tutor, 10 minutes to serve as a tutee, and 5–10 minutes to add and display team points. Each week students are assigned to a different team. Teams are restructured weekly so that everyone has a chance to be a member of the winning team.

Students get together with their tutoring partner, and a timer is set for 10 minutes. The tutee responds to material that the class is working on, such as spelling words, math problems, or reading a story. The tutor observes the tutee doing the work and awards points and corrects errors. Two points are earned for every correct answer. One point is earned for successfully correcting an error that the tutor has identified. For example, if the students are working on spelling words, the tutor would communicate to the tutee the word to be spelled. The tutee would write the word. If it was correct, then the tutor would tell the tutee that it was correct and would give the tutee two points. If it was incorrect, the tutor would tell the tutee that it was incorrect and spell the word correctly from a list for the student. The tutee then writes the word three times, earns one point, and continues on with new material.

While class members are involved in tutoring each other, you move from group to group, providing assistance and awarding bonus points to tutors for correct tutoring and to tutees for working cooperatively with the tutor. This procedure continues for 10 minutes, after which the roles switch and the tutors become the tutees and the tutees become the tutors. Individual points are summed, reported, and recorded on a team chart.

To make this system work efficiently, it is important that students are properly trained before you begin the program. It is best to make use of the procedures of explaining, modeling, and practicing with feedback. You should begin by explaining how the "game" works. You outline the rules of the game and the method for earning points. Then, you model the process by having one student act as the tutee and you act as the tutor. At this time, you can demonstrate how points are earned and how to correct errors. This should be followed by having two students tutor each other, while the other students watch and you give feedback to them. Finally, all students should practice and receive feedback before the system is implemented.

## Learning Centers

A learning center is a designated area where instructional materials in one major curriculum area are located and organized. Learning centers can take many forms and provide many advantages. When they are effectively designed and managed, students can benefit a great deal from the individual instruction for which they are intended. Some advantages to using learning centers are that they (1) provide an alternative to pencil and paper seatwork, (2) allow students to work at their own rate, (3) provide an opportunity to learn through various modes, (4) allow the teacher time to work with students at the learning center, (5) help develop responsibility and self-discipline through accomplishment and success, and (6) provide immediate self-evaluation (Gearheart & Weishahn, 1984).

The learning center may parallel classroom instruction, encourage exploration, reinforce a curriculum area, provide a framework for a theme with curricular linkages, or provide enrichment experiences and activities. Three types of learning centers that you may want to consider using are skills centers, discovery or enrichment centers, and creativity centers. The following is a brief explanation of each.

*Skills center.* A skills center can include activities such as practice sheets, drill cards in mathematics, or sentence completion activities. The center should have an activity card that states the goal, objectives, and pretest and posttest criteria.

*Discovery or enrichment center.* This center might include science activities, brainteasers, or advanced mathematics activities.

*Creativity center*. This center may include art, crafts, mathematics, or language arts activities.

A learning center has several essential components, which will vary, depending on its objectives and the age of the students. Each learning center should have clearly stated objectives that structure the activities. Understandable directions should be provided that specify what should be done, where and which materials should be used, and how the work is to be evaluated. Design of the center itself includes furniture arrangement (or lack of it), student materials, and the method of presentation (i.e., task cards, filmstrips, microscopes, art supplies and/or a combination of the available resources). Methods of student response and additional materials that you will require also need to be considered. You will want to introduce the center in such a way that the students fully understand the directions and how to use the materials, activities, and media that are available. Evaluation procedures and how materials are to be returned should also be explained before students begin using the center. If you carefully demonstrate the use of the center and periodically monitor its use, many problems may be avoided. Clearly, all of these decisions will be based on the topic of the center as well as the individual students and their needs. Exhibit 10.4, which has been adapted from Blackburn and Powell (1976), is a valuable resource that you can use to help you when you are developing learning centers.

One of the most common problems associated with learning centers is the time it may take to develop them. Initially, development does take extra time and effort, but once the learning centers are produced they may be easily modified and used in subsequent years. Some teachers seek assistance from students in setting up learning centers. Also, as we suggested in Chapter 4, asking a paraprofessional or parents to help with this type of project makes optimum use of the resources available to you.

Stephens (1977) and Morlan (1974) provide some excellent examples of centers that organize activities and materials according to instructional objectives. These centers may be expanded by increasing the number of objectives or the types of materials and activities. The following are a few examples to consider using with your students.

## Math Center

ACTIVITY A:

*Purpose*: To discriminate cups, pints, quarts, gallons, and ounces.

*Materials*: Milk and juice cartons, measuring cups, water, recipes.

*Directions*: Use the existent containers and a water basin. Make a list of the things that can be discovered by experimenting (Example: How many cups can fit into a pint?)

*Evaluation*: Keep a record of "What I Discovered." Compare with correct answer sheet.

ACTIVITY B:

*Purpose*: To discriminate inches and feet.

*Directions*: Have different items to measure (Examples: Measure a book by width and length; measure the width and the length of the desk; measure the height of a board). Measure area of a specified part of the room (i.e., blackboard, bulletin board, a desk).

ACTIVITY C:

*Purpose*: To write and say correct answers when given multiplication facts.

*Materials*: Four egg cartons, in each of which the holes are numbered 1 to 12; two bottle caps for each egg carton.

**EXHIBIT 10.4.** Checklist for creating and using learning centers

1. Determine educational goals and decide upon the type of center you need.
   a. Is a learning center appropriate for helping meet the goal?
   b. What purpose(s) will the center serve?
2. Specify your objectives.
   a. What objectives of the curriculum can be accomplished in the center?
   b. How do space allocation and design affect the objective?
   c. How do the objectives relate to the abilities and interests of the students?
   d. What alternatives are available for communicating objectives to students (e.g., posters, objective cards)?
3. Choose the optimum space and decide upon a design for the center.
   a. How much space can be allocated to the center?
   b. Is this the only classroom center or will there be others?
   c. What kinds of furniture and equipment are needed for the center?
   d. How will the location of the center affect other classroom activities?
   e. Does the center need certain environmental conditions (e.g., plants in a science center need to be near light or windows)?
4. Secure needed furniture and materials.
   a. What furniture and equipment are needed?
   b. Are furniture and equipment available in the classroom, school, or school system?
   c. Are there other local sources for obtaining furniture and equipment?
   d. Can students contribute, lend, or make the necessary furniture and equipment?
   e. What instructional materials are needed?
5. Design the learning activities.
   a. Are the activities consistent with the objectives of the center?
   b. Are the activities explained in such a way that the students know:
      (1) What to do?
      (2) Where to find information and what media to use?
      (3) What to do with results or products from the activities?
   c. Is there a wide assortment of activities to accommodate varying abilities, learning styles, and interests?
6. Write instructions for the students' use of the center.
   a. How many students can use the center at one time?
   b. What can students do at the center?
   c. Are assessment procedures clearly established and available to the students?
   d. What will the students do with the products made in the center?
7. Devise a management system.
   a. Is the management system appropriate for the age and ability levels of the students or for self-management activities?
   b. Does the system maximize student self-management and ease of record keeping for the teacher?
8. Set up the center.
   a. Are all materials, furniture, equipment, and other necessary accessories available for the center?
   b. When and how will it be best to put all the parts of the center together?
9. Orient students to the center.
   a. Are students well informed about purposes, procedures, and management of the center?
   b. Do students understand the relation of the center to other instructional activities in the classroom?
10. Evaluate the center.
    a. Did students achieve the objectives establishd for developing the center?
    b. Were the materials, equipment, and activities appropriate?
    c. What adaptations would you make to the center in the future?

*Directions*: Students place the two bottle caps inside an egg carton and close the lid. They shake the carton for a few seconds. Then they open the lid. They look at the two places where the caps landed. These are the numbers that they must multiply. They then write these two numbers on their paper and compute the multiplication. If they are working in pairs, one student may shake the carton and then ask the partner to give the resulting combination. If the partner answers correctly, the student then shakes for the partner. When the student misses, the partner can then shake for the student.

## Reading and Spelling Center

*Purpose*: To improve sight word vocabulary.
*Materials*: Checkerboard, checkers, and index cards.
*Directions*: Students play checkers in the standard manner. As a student moves, the student's opponent draws a card and reads the word. The first student must spell the word correctly in order to complete the move.

## Science and Written Language Center

*Purpose*: To have students identify, classify, and report information.
*Materials*: Cardboard boxes with fold-down flaps and a wide variety of objects.
*Directions*: Make some "touch boxes" from standard boxes. "Touch boxes" are boxes that have one or two holes cut out of them so students can place their hands inside without looking inside. Place one or two objects in each touch box. Students can identify or classify what is inside by naming the objects and/or describing the objects.

You can begin by using familiar objects and gradually make the objects more difficult.

## Theme Centers

As we discussed in Chapter 2, units of study are enjoyable ways in which you can teach students. An addition to your unit would be to include a learning center on the unit theme. For example, if you were studying dinosaurs, you might have a wall chart that listed a series of activities that the students could do. Some activities you might consider are the following:

Draw a picture of a dinosaur egg hatching.
Write a story called "If I met a dinosaur."
Read a book about dinosaurs.
Graph the size of dinosaurs compared with other animals.
Compare two different types of dinosaurs.
View a filmstrip on dinosaurs. List five things that you learned.
Make a book of dinosaur shapes.
Write a poem about dinosaurs.
Read a book to find out how long dinosaurs lived.

## SUMMARY

We have attempted to present information in this chapter that will help teachers organize the presentation of their material to hearing-impaired students in an effective manner. We know that teachers of regular education and of mildly handicapped students have utilized the principles of effective teaching and that the results have been improved student achievement. We are confident that this information can benefit hearing-impaired students as well. Initially, each of the components of effective teaching were defined and exemplified. The skills of teaching a concept and teaching a rule were explained. Several question prompts, developed specifically for use with hearing-impaired students, were introduced. Finally, several styles of teaching—using conceptual maps, cooperative learning, peer tutoring, classwide peer tutoring, and learning centers were explained. We agree with researchers in our field who have found that hearing-impaired children who achieve at levels significantly above the national averages for hearing-impaired students do so as a result of consistent and quality instruction. We believe that all teachers of all types of students are capable of providing effective instruction.

Hearing-impaired students depend more on formal instruction than do hearing students, since they are less likely to have access to the incidental learning that is continuously available to hearing students because of their auditory link to society (Daniele & Aldersley, 1988). What teachers say and do in the classroom has a critical effect on student learning. Englert (1984) pointed out that an important teaching function related to student achievement is the establishment of a classroom environment that is conducive to student learning and student attention to academic tasks. Classroom environments that were characterized as cooperative on academic tasks, warm, democratic, convivial, and with high levels of student responsibility for academic work proved positive predictors of achievement (Berliner, 1980; Fisher et al., 1978).

In addition, research by Wong, Wong, & LeMare (1982) indicates that knowledge of the goal and the criterion for success on an assignment has a critical effect on how much special education students learn. Concomitantly, research reported by Moog and Geer (1985) with hearing-impaired students indicates that intensity of instruction and increased teacher effort can make a significant difference in the academic achievement levels of their students. If hearing-impaired students are to make adequate progress, teachers must use systematic instructional procedures and manage the classroom environment so that students are engaged in academic tasks that are functionally relevant and provide adequate academic practice. Understanding and implementing the components of effective instruction will help you meet the needs of your students and enhance your feelings of accomplishment.

## ACTIVITIES

1. Observe a teacher of the deaf who is teaching a group lesson and discuss how the components of effective instruction were or were not incorporated into the lesson.
2. Plan a lesson that is appropriate for an elementary-level group of hearing-impaired students. Make a videotape of yourself presenting the lesson. Review the tape, using the checklist of effective instruction.
3. Determine the critical attributes and noncritical attributes for teaching the concepts of *tree*, *winter*, *clouds*, *problem*, and *truth*.
4. Choose an associated concept. Make a list of examples and nonexamples.
5. Teach a concept to an elementary-school-age child, employing the sequence of instruction provided in this chapter.
6. Teach a rule to an elementary-school-age child, employing the sequence of instruction provided in this chapter.
7. Plan a lesson that includes academic and social skills, which uses the cooperative learning format.
8. Make a list of academic subjects around which you could structure a peer-tutoring learning environment.
9. Plan and develop a learning center on a topic of your choice.
10. Develop a conceptual map for a lesson that you would like to present.

# CHAPTER 11

# Reading Instruction

## OVERVIEW

Reading is an essential skill for hearing-impaired students to develop. It is their primary means of gaining information from society in general. Yet it is an area of great challenge to teachers of the deaf, since hearing-impaired students all too frequently learn to read at the same time that they are acquiring language. Consequently, your task is a complex one: Can you help your students enjoy reading and simultaneously become proficient in this truly complex skill?

This chapter provides a wealth of information on how to prepare students to read as well as on how to teach them to read. It begins with the assessment of reading. The use of formal tests, both survey and diagnostic, are discussed, and the strengths and limitations of each are presented. In addition, use of criterion-referenced tests are addressed. Informal methods of assessment, including information on how to use observation, informal reading inventories, and teacher-constructed tests, are also reviewed in the chapter. We advocate that you use a variety of methods to determine accurately how well your students can read. The use of readability scales, computer programs, and experienced professionals to help you make reading enjoyable are discussed as well. Prereading considerations are given, and many practical ways to make print come to life for young students are suggested. In addition, many different approaches for planning a reading program are provided. We have attempted to give you lots of tools to use so that you will feel able to structure reading lessons, teach vocabulary, and develop students' comprehension skills. We suggest that you hold reading in high regard, share your enthusiasm for the process with your students, read to them often, and provide lots of time and experiences for them to read to you and others.

---

**CHAPTER TOPICS**

Formal Assessment
Informal Assessment
Determining Reading Levels
Models of Instruction
Preliteracy
Prereading Considerations
Approaches to Beginning Reading
Elementary-Level Reading Approaches
Vocabulary Development
Increasing Comprehension

---

## FORMAL ASSESSMENT

A number of different assessment techniques are commonly used to appraise the reading abilities of hearing-impaired students (La-Sasso, 1987). In many instances, standardized tests are administered, whereas in other settings, observations and informal tests are used in planning appropriate instructional strategies. It is our contention that in most cases the most efficient evaluation process employs a variety of assessment techniques, including both formal and informal assessment.

As we described in Chapter 2, standardized tests constitute one approach towards evaluating how students are performing. The lack of standardization of these formal tools with regard to hearing-impaired students is a major problem (King & Quigley, 1985). According to May (1986), there are four types of standardized reading tests:

1. Group survey tests, that are part of a battery of school achievement tests, such as the Stanford Achievement Test—Hearing Impaired and the California Achievement Test (CTB/McGraw-Hill, 1985)
2. Group survey tests that measure only reading abilities, such as the Gates-

MacGinitie Reading Tests (MacGinitie, 1978)
3. Group diagnostic tests, such as the Doren Diagnostic Reading Test (Doren, 1973) and the Stanford Diagnostic Reading Test (Karlsen & Gardner, 1985)
4. Individual diagnostic tests, such as the Woodcock Reading Mastery Tests-Revised (Woodcock, 1987) and the Durrell Analysis of Reading Difficulty (Durrell & Catterson, 1980).

Survey tests usually provide general scores on vocabulary and comprehension, while diagnostic tests generally provide scores related to more specific skills such as word reading, spelling, reading rate, literal comprehension, and inferential comprehension. A standardized survey test is useful for comparing groups of students or programs, but it lacks the technical characteristics necessary for use in making specific instructional decisions (Salvia & Ysseldyke, 1988). In addition, such standardized survey tests generally require students to respond to multiple-choice questions, which require recognition of the correct answer, while reading itself is a skill that is far more complex.

Standardized diagnostic tests usually

yield a great deal of information about a particular student. The drawback is that they are usually much more difficult and time consuming to administer and in some cases they are difficult to score. However, standardized tests are sometimes valuable because they enable personnel to place students initially and to identify skill areas in need of diagnostic assessment.

Some publishers of *basal readers* (discussed in this chapter) have developed norm-referenced tests that are similar to standardized reading tests and criterion-referenced tests to use for placement of students. By administering and scoring these short skill tests, you can arrive at a score that can be converted into an estimate of the student's instructional reading level. May (1986) points out that some of these tests may lack validity and reliability because they are very brief and have not been normed on large groups of students (and not on hearing-impaired students).

Criterion-referenced testing has recently become a widely accepted alternative to standardized testing. Teachers use criterion-referenced reading tests to determine if a student has mastered specific reading instructional objectives. Test items are presented in a hierarchy so that the student is assessed within a sequence of reading skills. The student's progress is determined by comparing the student's current performance with his or her previous performance. Examples of criterion-referenced tests that may be of value are the Brigance Diagnostic Inventory of Basic Skills (Brigance, 1977) and the Fountain Valley Teacher Support System in Reading (1971).

## INFORMAL ASSESSMENT

Informal assessment is another approach that can be used to appraise the reading skills of hearing-impaired students (King & Quigley, 1985). Some of the most widely used informal assessment techniques in reading are observations, informal reading inventories, and teacher-constructed tests. Informal assessment techniques usually have two advantages: They require less time to administer than formal tests, and they can be used with classroom materials during regular instruction periods (Mercer & Mercer, 1985).

Observations are an excellent additional source of assessment data that may be used in conjunction with other evaluation information. The teacher has many opportunities to observe and obtain information about a student's reading interests, vocabulary level, and comprehension skills by conducting observations during reading activities, seatwork, and recreational reading periods. It is necessary that you have some type of recording system for such observations. Records can be kept as dated observations through the use of anecdotal records or by using a checklist. Several of the diagnostic reading tests mentioned at the beginning of the chapter contain checklists that may be used in observing reading behaviors.

An *informal reading inventory* (IRI) is another technique that can assist teachers in determining a student's strengths and weaknesses, as well as helping to decide what book to use for instruction when choosing a basal reading series. This method focuses on determining three levels of a student's reading: the independent level, or the level at which the student can read easily with no help from others; the instructional level, or the level at which the student can read with some fluency but with enough difficulty to make instruction necessary; and the frustration level, or the level at which the student understands little of what is read and makes many mistakes (May, 1986).

Some textbook publishers provide teachers with an IRI that contains portions of stories that are the same or similar to those in the publisher's basal reading series. There are also IRIs that have been developed independent of publishing companies. Examples of these include the Classroom Reading Inventory by Silvaroli (1979), The Analytical Reading Inventory by Woods and Moe (1985), and the Ekwall Reading Inventory by Ekwall and English (1971). Another alternative is to prepare your own informal reading inventory by using portions of stories. The stories are copied, without pictures, from the basal reader. Generally, it is best to choose portions from the middle third of the book and choose enough words (75 words at the preprimer level to 200 words for the sixth-grade level, with 100 words being the norm for most elementary-level students) to get a clear picture of the students' comfort level with the material.

In order to make this a positive experience for the student, you should begin by having the student read material at a grade level below what you believe the student can read. As the student reads, discretely begin to identify and count mistakes on your copy of the material. In addition, record errors such as omission of words or parts of words, insertion or substitution of words, reversal of words, and repetition of words. If the student comes to a proper noun, help the student with it the first time. After the student has completed the selection, ask the student three literal questions about the story and three inferential questions. Continue testing with more difficult material until the student misses 15 percent of the words or 50 percent of the questions. According to May (1986), many educators, when they were interpreting the IRI, agreed with the following percentages for determining the three reading levels:

| INDEPENDENT READING LEVEL: | 98 percent of the words correct |
| | 90 percent of the questions correct |
| INSTRUCTIONAL READING | 94 percent of the words correct |
| LEVEL: | 60 percent of the questions correct below |
| FRUSTRATIONAL READING | 90 percent of the words correct |
| LEVEL: | below 50 percent of the questions correct |

Although it is time consuming to use IRIs because they are individually administered, these tests are very valuable. They help you to plan needed corrective instruction and to provide the student with reading material that is suited to his or her abilities (Mercer & Mercer, 1985). Some potential limitations that accompany using an IRI is that some professionals feel that the criteria for determining IRI reading levels are arbitrary, rigid, and too high (Wallace, Cohen, & Polloway, 1987).

Teacher-constructed tests are another valuable method for assessing a student's reading skills. They can be designed to measure almost any specific reading skills, from sight vocabulary to comprehension skills, such as identifying the main idea. Teacher-constructed tests can be developed by using items in standardized tests and workbook exercises as guides. Hammill and Bartel (1986) suggest that a good scope-and-sequence chart, which outlines the major reading skill areas in the recommended order of presentation, may be used as the framework for building the test. You should be careful to include enough items to sample the skill adequately. According to Wallace, Cohen, and Polloway (1987), the sequence for constructing an informal reading test is as follows.

1. Decide exactly what information is desired and how you can observe this.
2. Devise test items, materials, or situations to sample the behavior.
3. Keep a record of the student's behavior and responses.
4. Analyze the information.
5. Judge the information for answers to your assessment questions.

A bibliography on how to prepare informal reading tests can be found in King and Quigley (1985).

## DETERMINING READING LEVELS

*Readability formulas* can be used for estimating the reading level of ungraded material. This estimation can then be matched with the test score that has been established through the assessment process. While some experts in the area of reading question this approach, it is presented here as background knowledge that you may find valuable. The one formula that has been shown to be relatively easy and quick was developed by Fry (1968). The steps of the process are:

1. Select three 100-word passages near the beginning, middle, and end of the book. Count proper names, initializations, and numerals.

2. Count the total number of sentences in each 100-word passage. Estimate to the nearest tenth of a sentence. Average these three numbers.

3. Count the total number of syllables in each 100-word sample. Average the total number of syllables for the three samples.

4. Plot on the graph (see Exhibit 11.1) the average number of sentences per 100 words and the average number of syllables per 100 words. The diagonal lines mark off approximate grade-level areas. Where the dot is plotted shows the approximate grade level.

In addition, teachers can use computer software programs to estimate reading levels.

**EXHIBIT 11.1.** Fry readability formula

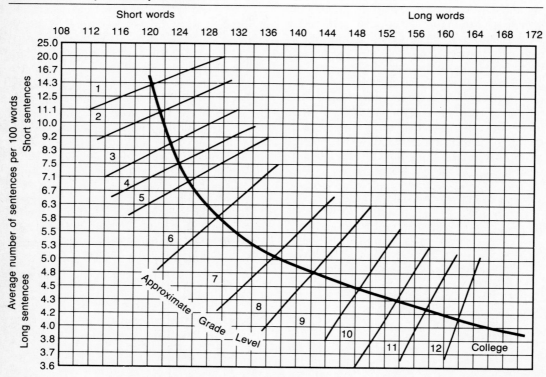

Readability Formulas, produced by Encyclopedia Britannica Educational Corporation, allows the user to choose from seven different readability formulas to simultaneously determine reading levels. Also, the Foxie Systematic Readability Aides (Fox, 1979) has a reference book that lists the readability level for thousands of children's stories and many basal reading series.

Another resource that you can use is a *readability scale*. With this scale you compare a passage from your book, which you have found to be appropriate for your student, with a set of previously prepared graded passages. If the passage that you are using is most similar to that of a second-grade passage, you would rate your book as being a second-grade reading level. A final resource (and possibly the most reliable for determining if a book is suitable for a student functioning on a specific grade level) is to ask an experienced teacher who teaches that grade or confer with the school's reading specialist. Israelite (1988) supports the use of using other professionals and the students themselves to identify appropriate materials. She contends that conventional measures of readability are too limited in scope to account for the complex interacting factors that influence text comprehensibility. She suggests that the most widely recommended alternative to readability formulas is the informed judgment of writers, editors, classroom teachers, and the readers themselves.

In addition to indicating a student's current reading ability, assessment measures can point to specific strengths and areas of concern that help teachers in planning instructional objectives. Both commercially prepared instruments and informal measures are useful. To obtain a valid assessment of a student's reading ability, you should use a variety of assessment procedures that are determined by the type of information that the you want to obtain (King & Quigley, 1985).

## MODELS OF INSTRUCTION

Reading comprises a variety of complex behaviors and processes that serve many functions for individuals and society. Albert Einstein is said to have observed that the task of learning to read is the most complex of all the tasks that humans have devised for themselves (Cramer, 1971). Most models of the reading process can be classified as *bottom-up models*, *top-down models*, or *interactive models*.

In the bottom-up models, reading is basically viewed as a *translating, decoding*, and *encoding* process. In these models, the reader attends to letters, anticipates the words the letters will spell, and identifies the words with further expectations as to how they will be strung together and what they will mean when assembled into phrases and sentences. Reading comprehension in the bottom-up models is essentially viewed as an automatic outcome of accurate word recognition. An underlying assumption of the bottom-up model is that readers predominantly use a speech-based code to access meaning from print.

Most of the top-down models of the reading process are based on psycholinguistic concepts involving interaction between thought and language. The reader's cognitive and language competence plays the key role in the construction of meaning from printed material. Reading, in a top-down model, is not viewed as a precise process in which the reader attends to every letter of every word. Rather, reading is viewed as a dynamic psycholinguistic process by which a reader extracts meaning from a message presented in graphic form. Rather than processing each element of a written message, the reader samples selectively from the text and formulates a hypothesis about the meaning (Goodman, 1986).

Interactive models claim that bottom-up and top-down processes occur simultaneously for skilled readers. Good readers perceive reading as a form of communication; that is, they sense that there is a story or a message being presented to them, and they use searching-type behavior to understand what is happening or what is being expressed (Jones, 1982). The reader's knowledge of syntactic and semantic constraints, along with the natural redundancy of language, help the reader to formulate a viable prediction, which is confirmed or denied as the reader continues to process the written material.

Smith (1978) suggested that two kinds of information facilitate the reading process: the visual information, which is the written word, and the nonvisual information, which is the knowledge already present in the reader's cognitive store. The reader must learn to make full use of both forms of information in order to comprehend written language effectively (Hammermeister & Israelite, 1983). Thus, the graphic information in the text and the information in the reader's mind are both important in describing interactive models. Specific features of the top-down and bottom-

up approaches, as well as suggestions concerning intervention, are presented in Exhibit 11.2. Maxwell (1986) has noted that it seems sensible to adopt both points of view as support for instructional procedures.

## PRELITERACY

The Early Childhood and Literacy Development Committee of the International Reading Association (1987) stated that literacy begins in infancy. They listed several areas of knowledge pertaining to literacy in the preschool years. These include experiences about the functions and uses of oral and written language, a command of the language, an ability to read environmental print, and knowledge about the parts of the book. What strikes us as educators is that, while some deaf children of deaf parents demonstrate knowledge of some of these experiences, as is depicted in Exhibit 11.3, many hearing-impaired preschoolers do not enter kindergarten with this

**EXHIBIT 11.2. Teacher responsibilities in top-down and bottom-up reading approaches**

| Features | You, the Teacher |
|---|---|
| **Top-Down Reading Approach (Gestalt to Analysis; Holistic)** | |
| 1. Hearing-impaired students lack experience with English conversation and stories—experiences that are prerequisites to reading. | 1. Read daily stories and talk about them with hearing-impaired preschoolers and beginner readers. Use the environmental print task checklist that appears in Exhibit 11.4. |
| 2. Hearing-impaired students need to practice higher-level thinking skills by using language to explain what they have read (or what has been read to them). | 2. Use the strategies of participation, prediction, comprehension, and evaluation. Use question prompts to check comprehension (see Chapter 10). |
| 3. Students need to take risks in the areas of language and cognition as they share predictable literature with a more accomplished reader. | 3. Read the same stories more than once. Teach parents to sign at least one favorite story completely and consistently. |
| | Schedule *recreational reading periods*. Let students go to the library and pick their own books. |
| 4. Hearing-impaired students need to integrate into at least two cultures. | 4. Introduce family histories, stories about Deaf adults, ethnic stories for non-Anglo students, etc. Teach simple rhymes, fingerplays, and the words to typical children's songs. |

**EXHIBIT 11.2.** (Continued)

| Features | You, the Teacher |
|---|---|
| **Top-Down Reading Approach (Gestalt to Analysis; Holistic)** | |
| 5. Hearing-impaired students need to be provided with the background of classics for certain aspects of moral development and later responses to fiction and biography (Maxwell, 1986). | 5. Read classics to hearing-impaired students. Show students stories of empowerment from Deaf culture. |
| 6. Hearing-impaired students need to have other communication activities integrated into reading. | 6. Students recite familiar patterns in books for speech practice and locate particular phrases for auditory training. |
| 7. Hearing-impaired students need to see that their experiences (said, felt, thought) can be recorded (genuine communication). | 7. Use language experience approach (see this chapter). Record student's version and standard English both (i.e. be *bilexical*). |
| **Bottom-Up Reading Approach (Focus on Analytical or Subskills)** | |
| 1. Harp (1987) cautioned teachers to be developmental in terms of cognition. Preschoolers cannot typically memorize rules or generalize. | 1. Assess cognitive abilities of preschoolers and beginner readers. Show "A, B, C" stories from Deaf culture. |
| 2. Students need experience with *phoneme-grapheme* concepts. | 2. Help students match lowercase and uppercase, and fingerspelling to print. Play letter-matching games. Find letters in *environmental print*. |
| 3. Students need to learn concepts about print in books, book-handling, parts of the book, etc. | 3. Use a book handling list (see Exhibit 11.5) as an informal assessment to set objectives. |
| 4. Students need to be able to analyze words (e.g., words with similar first letters or first sounds, final letters or sounds, and semantic confusions, words that are signed similarly, etc.). | 4. Capitalize on residual hearing, structured speech, speechreading, and audition activities. Use fingerspelling and cued speech to cue sounds. |
| 5. Students need to be able to distinguish similar words and function words and to break words into syllables. | 5. Separate words, using colored chalk or large print and then small print. Use hangman and computer games. Try shape diagrams: ⌐bus⌐. |
| 6. Students need to be able to find the derivational and inflectional elements of words. | 6. Teach with a sign system, and sign complete and consistent input so students are constantly exposed to root words and affixes. |
| 7. Students need to be able to analyze single words, then phrases, sentences, and larger units of familiar stories (theme, plot, etc.). | 7. Use ideas from item 5 above. Use Signed English and SEE-2 books with Sign Print so students can read signs and fingerspelling. Allow students to read large units of stories without being interrupted. |
| 8. Students need to develop self-monitoring and risk taking. | 8. Keep activities fun and nonthreatening (low affective filter). Facilitate the development of self-monitoring techniques (explained in this chapter). |
| 9. Students need to have analytical skills incorporated into the reading approach. | 9. Use process reciprocal teaching as discussed in this chapter. |
| 10. Students' parents need to know what they can do to help the acquisition of reading. Teachers need to work with families who will need specific ideas to facilitate reading. | 10. Keep parents informed about the skills and activities their child enjoys at school. Provide them with developmentally based, specific suggestions regarding reading. Share the signs you are using for text-specific vocabulary. |

**EXHIBIT 11.3.** A Deaf child, Alice, of Deaf parents learns to read (adapted from Maxwell, 1980).

| | |
|---|---|
| 2;2—2;6 years | Began to fingerspell—no meaning (e.g., *A-ll* for *all*). |
| | Recognized printed and fingerspelled name. |
| 2;7—3;0 years | Focused on sign-print meaning. Skipped signs she did not know. Ignored English print. Could not use arrows for signing clues. |
| 3;1—3;6 years | Fingerspelled short words. Read familiar words (food containers). Copied storytellers expressions and gestures. |
| 4 years | Would guess at words: *M* for *mother* when it was really *Mark*. Began to sign sign-print and vocalize English. Used the English print for meaning. Would align herself with the sign-print. Did not read the sign print in order. Signed the English print words that she knew the meaning of and fingerspelled the others (Ewoldt, 1977). Paid no attention to word boundaries. Sometimes she recognized a word after spelling it and would make the sign. |
| 5 years | Concentrated on form: *Shaped out signs* like hearing children sound out words. Looked carefully at sign-print to decipher it. Frequently used one mode to check her comprehension of another. |
| 6 years | Read much like a hearing child. Learned words from print and then transferred them to fingerspell, speech, and invented signs. |

SOURCE: M. Maxwell, "The development of language in a deaf child—Signs, sign variations, speech and print." in K. E. Nelson (Ed.), *Children's Language (Vol. 3)*. New York: Gardner Press, 1980.

basic knowledge. Yet, these same students are expected to begin the tasks of formal reading and writing instruction without the linguistic foundation on which they can attach the new skills being taught them. As a teacher, you might need to teach preliteracy and early literacy behaviors directly so that students will be ready to learn to read and write.

## PREREADING CONSIDERATIONS

*Functions and Uses of Oral, Signed, and Written Language.* There are many opportunities throughout the day when significant adults can model that knowing how to read and write is useful or pleasurable. A parent might express ideas such as, "I need to make a shopping list so I remember to buy milk and eggs," or "I'm going to write the name of this movie on the VCR box so we remember which one it is." A teacher can model reading for enjoyment or explain the purpose of school correspondence: "This tells your Dad that there is a meeting at school tomorrow" or "The secretary has written a note to

say your lunch money is late." Many of the functions and uses of oral, signed, and written language are absorbed by students simply by virtue of their membership in our literate society. Van Kleeck and Schuele (1987) have labeled this process "literacy socialization."

Reading to students is an obvious literacy event that researchers have found to be linked positively to reading success (Cochran-Smith, 1983; Health, 1982; Taylor, 1984). We recommend that you read daily to hearing-impaired students of all ages for both literacy and language benefits (Ninio & Bruner, 1978; Snow & Goldfield, 1982). Hearing/seeing stories offer hearing-impaired students the opportunity to experience the joys of playing with vocabulary, listening to or seeing rhythmical English patterns, and encountering ideas that stimulate and reinforce imagination and curiosity (Gelzer, 1988).

*A Command of the Language.* Research by Luetke-Stahlman (1988a) has demonstrated that the more closely the sign system input to which hearing-impaired students are exposed corresponds to written English, the better students are able to read. This means that significant adults need to encode completely the vocabulary, figurative English, inflected verb forms, and affixes that are read and written to students who sign. Luetke-Stahlman's work predicted that children who are raised, seeing expressions such as "hair do," "piled in the car," "runny nose" signed in a form that corresponds with spoken or written English will learn to read these forms with comprehension. When novel vocabulary words such as *stool*, *lawn*, and *trot* are fingerspelled, students have the opportunity to learn to comprehend and produce an expanded vocabulary. Luetke-Stahlman's work (1988a, 1988b) has indicated that students who are exposed to Signed/Manual English and Pidgin Sign English (in which words *stool*, *lawn*, and *trot* might be signed as *chair*, *grass*, and *walk fast*) score the lowest on tests of reading and English language because the input system to which they were exposed inconsistently represents the form of English.

Assessment of hearing-impaired students' abilities in terms of the use, content, and form of English would provide knowledge as to their command of that language. Information as to how to conduct these assessments was provided earlier in this text and would help you to decide if preliteracy and literacy activities were appropriate for a particular student.

### An Ability to Read Environmental Print.

Environmental print is the written language children see every day in their communities. For example, safety and informational signs, lettering on food and toy containers, lettering on t-shirts, and names of restaurants and stores are all forms of environmental print. Gillam and Johnston (1985) found that language-delayed children's performance on print awareness tasks was poorer than that of children with normal language development.

Significant others can help hearing-impaired children attach signed, cued, and/or spoken labels to print by taking advantage of daily opportunities to label sounds, letters, words, and phrases in a comprehensible manner that corresponds to spoken English. For example, if you and your students ride by Sears on your way to McDonalds, you should label these places as you would for hearing children and not call them simply a restaurant and a store (if you have used the exact names in your spoken utterance). You may find it useful to use the checklist that was designed to chart students' receptive and expressive knowledge of real objects, labels cut from objects, xeroxed labels, and printed sight words that appears in Exhibit 11.4. These objects, labels, or sight words can be grouped in sets of six in front of the student. As the teacher, you might say something like, "Where is the gum?" The student would point to the correct gum or pictures. Or ask, "What is this?" and the student would attempt to tell you the correct name for the item.

### Knowledge About Books.

While hearing 3-year-olds can name the parts of books (e.g., front page, last page, etc.) and parts of the pages of books (e.g., top, bottom, etc.) hearing-impaired preschoolers typically cannot. This may be because significant others avoid or omit phrases such as "turn the page," "oh, see the _____ at the top there?" or "we've come to the last page of the story—the end." To emphasize this point, we once asked a group of seasoned teachers the sign for *page* and discovered that few knew one. A checklist of book awareness skills for hearing-impaired students appears in Exhibit 11.5 and could be used for both assessment and intervention of print awareness skills.

## Guidelines for Reading to the Hearing-Impaired

Significant adults should read in two different ways to preschoolers. First, when children show an interest in books, you can follow

**EXHIBIT 11.4.** Environmental print task checklist Goodman, Altwerger, and Marek (1989)

Significant adults ask each child (using the expressive task and then the receptive task) to demonstrate knowledge of print typically found in the child's home and community.

| Examples of Stimuli Typical of Child's Environment | Expressive (You ask "What is this?") | | | | Receptive (Child points to object you label.) | | | |
|---|---|---|---|---|---|---|---|---|
| | Real Object | Colored Label | Xeroxed Label | Sight Word | Real Object | Colored Label | Xeroxed Label | Sight Word |
| Bubble gum | 1 | 1 | 1 | 1 | | | | |
| Push sign | 2 | 2 | 2 | 2 | | | | |
| Charmin toilet paper | 3 | 3 | 3 | 3 | | | | |
| Burger King | 4 | 4 | 4 | 4 | | | | |
| Peter Pan peanut butter | | | | | | | | |
| Campbell soup | | | | | | | | |
| Crest toothpaste | | | | | | | | |
| Stop sign | | | | | | | | |
| Legos | | | | | | | | |
| McDonalds | | | | | | | | |
| Kentucky Fried Chicken | | | | | | | | |
| Johnson's baby powder | | | | | | | | |
| Play Doh | | | | | | | | |
| Pull sign | | | | | | | | |
| Coca-Cola | | | | | | | | |
| Push sign | | | | | | | | |
| Wendy's | | | | | | | | |
| Ivory soap | | | | | | | | |
| Exit sign | | | | | | | | |
| Crayola crayons | | | | | | | | |
| Milk | | | | | | | | |
| Potato chips | | | | | | | | |
| Jell-O | | | | | | | | |
| Band-Aid | | | | | | | | |
| Kleenex | | | | | | | | |

1. An acceptable answer would be the child saying/signing *gum* given the indicated stimulus
2. An acceptable answer would be the child saying/signing *push* given the indicated stimulus
3. An acceptable answer would be the child saying/signing *toilet* given the indicated stimulus
4. An acceptable answer would be the child saying/signing *restaurant* given the indicated stimulus

SOURCE: B. Luetke-Stahlman, C. Ewoldt and K. Saulnier, "Environmental print performance of hearing and hearing-impaired preschoolers. (In Progress).

their lead, labeling pictures and describing what is happening. Soon after, you should begin to read simple stories to these children, following exactly what is written in the text. In this way, they will begin to understand that written words (i.e, print) can convey an author's ideas. Students also should be allowed an independent reading time each day. You can roam around the room, asking the children about the stories they are reading, the names of main characters or check vocabulary comprehension.

Gelzer (1988) has provided guidelines for reading to hearing-impaired children. These have been adapted to create the following list.

**EXHIBIT 11.5.** Checklist of book awareness skills

| **Ask Your Child/Student** | **Dates** |
| --- | --- |
| 1. What do you do with a book? (Read it.) | |
| 2. What's inside it? (Pages, pictures, words, etc.) | |
| 3. Show me one page. | |
| 4. Show me the top of this page. | |
| 5. Show me the bottom of this page. | |
| 6. Where should I start to read? (Indicates print on first page) | |
| 7. Show me with your finger exactly where I have to begin reading. (Points to first word on the page) | |
| 8. Show me which way I go when I read this page. (Shows left to right) | |
| 9. You point to the story while I read it. (Does it exactly) | |
| 10. Where do I go to now? (Points to the print on the page) | |
| 11. Can you show me one letter? Two letters? | |
| 12. Can you show me one word? Two words? | |
| 13. Show me the first letter in any word. | |
| 14. Show me a capital letter in any word . . . a lowercase letter. | |
| 15. Show me the name of this story. | |
| 16. Tell me something that happened in the story. | |
| 17. Show me the beginning of the story . . . the end of the story. | |
| 18. Tell me one character in the story. | |
| 19. Why do we use the bookmark? | |

SOURCE: B. Luetke-Stahlman, C. Ewoldt and K. Saulnier, "Environmental print performance of hearing and hearing-impaired preschoolers. (In Progress).

1. Be familiar with the story you plan to read. Determine the major purpose and appeal of the story and be prepared to describe the sequence of events, the characters, and the feelings that are communicated in the story.

2. Be prepared to communicate your interest in the story through the use of voice, cues, sign, gesture and mime, body posture, and facial expression. Try practicing reading the story out loud before sharing it with your students.

3. Practice cuing and signing. Make important decisions in advance.
   a. Choose the signed vocabulary.
   b. Fingerspell or cue the words for which there are no signs.
   c. Cue and sign at a comfortable pace.
   d. Alter the communication frame and center of focus, depending on the visual needs of the group.

4. *English:*
   a. Choose a story to read that is at the right content and form level (see Chapter 1: input + 1).
   b. Use gestures, and ASL Features mime to supplement English.
   c. Label pictures and point to them at appropriate times.
   d. Read the text as it is printed in the book.

5. *Expression:* Communicate important events and changes in moods through devices such as facial expression, body posture, voice, and sign.
   a. Use a steady, quiet voice, but let your voice change to reflect a change in mood.
   b. Slow down the pace of the story at appropriate times and increase the pace when the action in the story is swift.

6. Establish a rapport between yourself and the students and create a climate of ex-

pectancy before you begin to read the story.

 **a.** Look at the cover of the book and the title page together. Encourage the students to predict what the story might be about and what its name might be.

 **b.** Discuss the topic of the story. Point to the characters and name them. Ask questions that relate the students' past experiences to those of the characters.

 **c.** Decide how the book will be held—who will hold the book and who will turn the pages.

**7.** Begin to read the story. Read each page first and then show the pictures.

 **a.** Look directly at the students as much as possible. Avoid staring at the book while you are reading.

 **b.** Give the students ample time to look at the pictures and to respond with thoughts of their own.

 **c.** Allow the students plenty of time to absorb what is happening in the story—to look away and rest their eyes, to shift positions, and to share an occasional thought with the students next to them.

 **d.** Encourage the students to repeat particular phrases or sounds in the story as you read.

 **e.** Reinforce the action in the story with interaction with the students. Have them imitate gestures (such as shaking hands, pretending to climb, or knocking on a door).

**8.** Ask the students questions from time to time to encourage their involvement.

 **a.** Do not ask unnecessary questions for which there are obvious answers.

 **b.** Do not interrupt the flow of the story with frequent explanations or with questions that are too simple for the students.

**9.** Be alert to changes in the students' level of interest.

 **a.** If their attention wanders too much, stop reading until they are ready to continue. Allow the students time to take a break if necessary or wait until another time to finish the story.

 **b.** If short interruptions occur, stop and return to the story. Review a few pages or ask the students what happened before the interruption.

**10.** Use follow-up activities that allow the students to show what they have learned.

 **a.** Discuss the plot, ideas, characters, and related subjects. Cue and sign the exact labels for these concepts.

 **b.** Have the students retell the story.

 **c.** Let the students dramatize the story.

 **d.** Ask the students to write similar stories.

 **e.** Ask the students to draw illustrations for the story.

## Additional Prereading Activities

The following tools are suggested for use in direct, bottom-up readiness activities (see Exhibit 11.6) to prepare young children to read:

1. Puzzles—to practice visual discrimination and matching.

2. Shapes—building cards in which they build a pattern by covering the appropriate squares on a grid.

3. Chain puzzles (shape, letter, or word dominoes).

4. Letter-matching cards with a stimulus on the left and a row of symbols that either match the stimulus or are foils on the right.

5. Configuration puzzles with a word on the left and a picture on the right. The cards have been cut in half and are to be reassembled by the student.

6. Word-building cards—three letter words with one letter per square. The student covers each letter with a matching one.

7. Lotto games.

**EXHIBIT 11.6.** Checklist of book awareness skills

**Word-building Cards** (Johnson & Paulson, 1976)
 *(a) Description:*
A Word-building Card consists of a number of three-letter words grouped according to regularity of patterning. Each letter occupies a one-inch square. An illustration of the meaning of each word is superimposed on the word but illustrated faintly so that the actual word is prominent. An example of Word-building Cards follows:

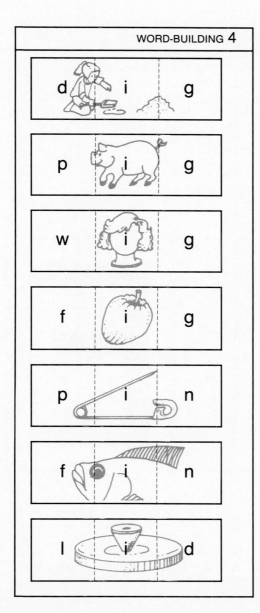

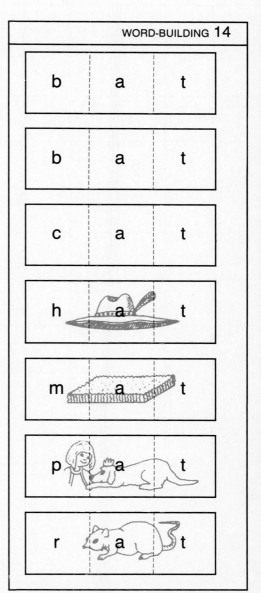

**EXHIBIT 11.6.** (Continued)

**Shape-building Cards**

*(a) Description:*

Shape-building cards are a set of materials which contain

    (1) a blank grid divided into 1-inch squares,

    (2) a pattern grid in which certain of these squares have been colored in, and

    (3) 1-inch squares which can be used to fill in the squares of the blank grid.

The following is an example of a Shape-building Card:

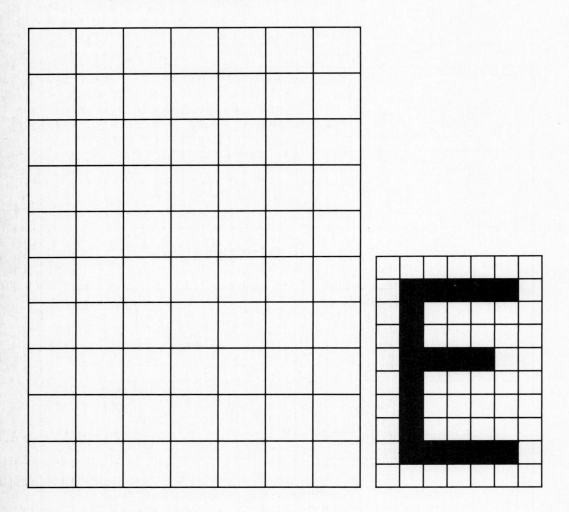

*(b) Uses:*

    A student takes a blank grid, a pattern grid, and a number of 1-inch squares. On the blank grid, the student builds up the pattern that is printed on the pattern grid by covering the appropriate squares on the blank grid with the 1-inch colored chips.

**EXHIBIT 11.6.** (Continued)

### Chain Puzzles

*(a) Description:*

Chain Puzzles are like dominoes. Each puzzle consists of a number of rectangular cards. On each end of each card there is a picture, a symbol, a letter or a word printed. The cards of each puzzle can be fitted together by matching the end of one card with that of another.

In a set of prereading materials, the complexity of Chain Puzzles can be increased gradually; for example, if there are 20 Chain Puzzles in a set, the first 5 puzzles may use picture matching, the second 5 may use symbol matching, the third 5 may use letter matching, and the fourth 5 may use word matching. The following is an example of Chain Puzzles:

| bus —hen |
| --- |

| △  —  🗙 |
| --- |

| o  —  p |
| --- |

| a  —  B |
| --- |

| bag — wag |
| --- |

| girl — man | man — tree | tree — tug |
| --- | --- | --- |

*(b) Uses:*

A student takes a puzzle, spreads its cards out and finds the starting piece (this will be a card with no print on the left-hand side). The student then proceeds to complete the Chain Puzzle by matching the picture on the right side of the first card with that on the left side of another card.

Not only individual, but two-persons and small-group activity, as described under Jigsaw Puzzles, can be used.

Chain Puzzles provide not only visual discrimination and matching of shapes but also practice in left/right direction.

EXHIBIT 11.6. *(Continued)*

### Letter-matching Cards

*(a) Description:*

Letter-matching Cards consist of two parts:

    (1) the 1-inch squares described in the Shape-building Cards above, and

    (2) a card in which on the left side there is a master letter set off from others in a column of a different color.

Along a row next to each master letter there are a number of other letters, some of which are the same as the master letter and some of which are different. (*N.B.,* In addition to letters, other print material could be used—pictures, symbols, groups of letters, words).

The following are examples of Letter-matching Cards:

| | WORD-BUILDING 8 | | | | | | | |
|---|---|---|---|---|---|---|---|---|
| N | N | N | H | N | M | A | Z | N |
| G | O | Q | G | G | C | E | G | C |
| S | Z | S | R | S | X | S | S | X |
| B | B | D | P | E | B | B | D | E |
| Y | V | X | Y | Y | V | Y | P | Y |

| | WORD-BUILDING 8 | | | | | | | |
|---|---|---|---|---|---|---|---|---|
| N | N | N | ■ | N | ■ | ■ | ■ | N |
| G | ■ | ■ | G | G | ■ | ■ | G | ■ |
| S | ■ | S | ■ | S | ■ | S | S | ■ |
| B | B | ■ | ■ | ■ | B | B | ■ | ■ |
| Y | ■ | ■ | Y | Y | ■ | Y | ■ | Y |

| | WORD-BUILDING 12 | | | | | |
|---|---|---|---|---|---|---|
| a | e | a | a | a | d | a |
| a | a | a | a | a | a | a |
| a | l | n | t | x | f | a |
| c | y | | **a** | | w | g |
| a | a | | | | a | a |
| p | o | | | | u | m |
| a | q | z | b | r | j | a |
| a | a | a | a | a | a | a |
| a | h | a | a | a | k | a |

| | WORD-BUILDING 12 | | | | | |
|---|---|---|---|---|---|---|
| a | | a | a | a | | a |
| a | a | a | a | a | a | a |
| a | | | | | | a |
| | | | **a** | | | |
| a | a | | | | a | a |
| a | | | | | | a |
| a | a | a | a | a | a | a |
| a | | a | a | a | | a |

**EXHIBIT 11.6.** *(Continued)*

*(b) Uses:*

A student takes a card and, using the 1-inch squares, covers those letters which are not the same as the master letter.

There are many variations of this that can be used. One is to print letters on the other side of the 1-inch squares. A student could then, instead of covering the letters that are not the same as the master letter, find examples of the master letter in the 1-inch squares and cover those letters so that the row would be a line of all the same letter.

In addition, small group games of a Bingo type can be played with these materials.

### Configuration Puzzles

*(a) Description:*

A Configuration Puzzle consists of a number of rectangular cards in an envelope. Each card has two parts to it: an illustration on the left, and a word on the right. Each card in a puzzle is then cut to separate the word from the picture, with the configuration of each cut being different. In this way. the two pieces of each card will be the only ones that fit together. The following is an example of a Configuration Puzzle:

 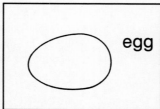 

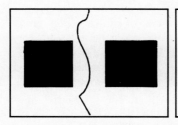 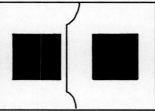 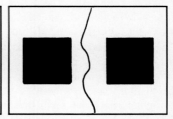

*(b) Uses:*

A student takes an envelope and puts all the pieces in front of him or her. The pieces are then matched by matching the cutting edge. This exercise trains students to associate pictures and words. At the prereading stage, we would not ask students to read aloud the words. However, exercises such as this do help students to make associations of printed words and their meanings.

# APPROACHES TO BEGINNING READING

Because hearing-impaired children do not typically begin the task of learning to read with a language base comparable to that of their hearing peers, we will describe several approaches that integrate language acquisition and learning with reading. These approaches have been highlighted here because they have proven to be successful with hearing-impaired or bilingual students. It is expected that educators in deaf education would assess systematically the benefits of these approaches should they try one or more of them with their students. An attempt has been made to describe the procedures so that they could be adapted to nonreaders of any age.

## Phonics Approach

At issue in the field of deaf education is whether a *phonics* approach to teaching reading is appropriate. Many hearing-impaired students do not have sufficient *aided hearing acuity* to use speech as a *decoding* tool, therefore a phonics approach does not seem to be a logical one. Yet, evidence from the hearing literature suggests strongly that reading acquisition is dependent upon decoding into sound (Conrad, 1979; Hochberg, 1970; Kleitman 1975). While no evidence exists to suggest that students who do not use phonics cannot learn to read (Hirsk-Pasek, 1981), it seems reasonable to recommend that hearing-impaired students who are assessed as capable of benefiting from a phonetic decoding and recoding approach be so instructed. Students assessed as using a whole-word or finger-spelling approach to decoding words should be instructed in nonphonics methods.

### Interactive Language Development Teaching (ILDT). Each ILDT lesson (Lee, Koeningsknecht, & Mulhern, 1975) consists of three basic parts. First, the teacher presents a teacher-written story especially designed for the children in the group (i.e., input + 1

content). In writing the story, Lee, Koeningsknecht, & Mulhern, (1975) suggest that the theme of the story, its characters, and the events in which they play a role be familiar to the students. Secondly, the narrative should be designed so that the important events in the story are repeated and restated, giving the students sufficient exposure to aid comprehension (see Chapter 3 regarding optimal input). Third, target responses to questions are required from the students only after sufficient information has been provided so that inferences about the correct answer would be unnecessary.

It is suggested that student form objectives be incorporated into the ILDT story at least five times. These structures would be modeled by you or another reader several times before the students would be expected to reproduce them. Secondary targets that would become primary targets in future stories should be incorporated in the story about three times. The teacher is expected to ask both closed- ("Can you point to John?") and open-ended questions ("What do you think John will do next?") pertaining to the content of the story. The students' responses to these questions would either include the target form or not. If it does, reinforcement is provided (e.g., as an expansion or repetition of what the student has said). If the form is not used, you would use one of the strategies presented in Chapter 7 to facilitate the use of the target form (e.g., parallel talk, informative talk, expansion, etc.). However, students' spontaneous comments about the story content should not be discouraged, since it is this type of contribution that would make the story relevant and interesting to them.

Following the story and a short break, the students take part in an activity that focuses on the theme, characters, concepts, vocabulary, or grammatical forms contained in the story. These might be artistic, dramatic, or real-life events (e.g., washing windows after discussing a story that included that task). During this second part of the lesson, language samples can be taken to assess the students' progress. [This entire description is based on Lee, Koenigsknecht, & Mulhern (1975) and Fey (1986).]

## Comprehensible Input and the Language Experience Approach

The Language Experience Approach (LEA) (Lee & Allen, 1963; Stauffer, 1970; Veatch et al., 1979) was developed to teach both native readers to read their language and nonnative readers to read in a second language. The technique has proven to be successful for bilingual students assessed to have the English language abilities of 3- and 4-year-olds. Many professionals in the field of education of hearing-impaired students contend that the language experience approach is a beneficial method for teaching reading (Ewoldt & Hammermeister, 1986; Johnson & Roberson, 1988; LaSasso, 1983; Gormley & Geoffrion, 1981). The teacher activates the students' interest about the topic, writes down what students' dictate verbatim, and then reads back to them what they have said and signed. An assumption of the method is that the text is comprehensible and of genuine interest to the students because they have chosen the words.

There are many variations of the LEA (Ekwall & Shanker, 1983). Moustafa and Penrose (1985) utilized naturally repeated, comprehensible input (CI) (structures at the children's language level) prior to LEA lessons (CI + LEA) to facilitate students' use of complex content and form in the target language. Their CI + LEA stories used contextualized items that could be referenced as they discussed and read, such as slides, large pictures, models, and so on. (These would be located on the left-hand side of the Cummins model. See Chapter 1.) The steps in the CI + LEA procedure are as follows.

*Prerequisite behavior:* Students should have an English language base of 2.6 years.

1.  Given a picture of a familiar situation (e.g., eating), ask an array of *wh*-questions. Reinforce student responses with expansions that utilize the correct forms of English. Supply answers yourself only after you have allotted students sufficient time to think and formulate answers. (Utilize the question prompts provided in Chapter 10.) Point and label all items in the picture as students respond to your queries.

2.  Teach your students to read vocabulary sight word labels. As you read, point to each person, process, or object picture in the print. You can ask students to match the written words to the referent in the print.

3.  Using the picture as contextual support, allow your students to dictate sentences about the picture. As you write these on large paper, say each word. Then ask the students to read the sentences back to you while you point to each word. Continue this way, using six to eight sentences. Next, read the story with your students in unison as you move your finger under each word.

4.  Choral read as a group using an overhead projection of the story.

5.  Give your students a copy of each story and allow them to keep these copies in a file folder. Have students read the stories to each other.

6.  Require your students to learn to spell all the words in the stories.

Teachers would need to make decisions about how to record nonstandard, ungrammatical English when they are using the LEA approach with hearing-impaired and hearing bilingual students. Gormley and Geoffrion (1981) recommended that both versions be written. This bilexical approach would seem advantageous because the students' self-esteem would not be endangered and yet a correct English form model would be provided.

The *group experience chart approach* usually involves having an entire class or group of students develop a story that the teacher prints on a large chart or a chalkboard. The content of the story derives from the students' experiences as they share information through group discussion. The charts may be developed around topics such as narrative descriptions of experiences, news events, reports of experiments, or fiction stories made up by the students. During the writing of the story the teacher guides the students' suggestions and discusses word choice and sentence structure. Specific skills such as capitalization, punctuation, spelling, and correct sentence structure can be taught during the composing or editing phase of the story's development (Mercer & Mercer, 1985). Students subsequently read the story as a group or individually with the teacher or the paraprofessional.

Ewoldt and Hammermeister (1986) advocate a process that makes use of *individual dictation*. In this approach, the teacher does not plan a common experience for all the students, but, rather works individually with each student to write a story that can be read by the target child. A strength of this approach is the one-to-one interaction between the student and the teacher. The student receives individual attention and also gets to watch as his or her words are being turned into written language. The steps of the individual dictation approach are:

1.  The student chooses an experience. Each student draws from his or her own unique experiences. If students have difficulty generating their stories, drawing or discussion prior to dictation can help facilitate the development of the story. Some examples of topics that can be used for LEA stories if students have difficulty choosing a topic, are:
    a.  What they have learned about Thanksgiving or Halloween
    b.  What places they would like to visit
    c.  What stories they enjoy and why they enjoy them
    d.  How they like to spend their free time
    e.  What Deaf adults they know
    f.  What they liked about a school art exhibit or a trip
    g.  What they dream about
    h.  Who their favorite television characters are
    i.  How to make a kite or paper airplane
    j.  What there is to see at a zoo
    k.  What ideas puzzle them
    l.  What jobs their parents have
    m.  How they learned to ride a bicycle or to swim
    n.  What to look for on a walk through the woods
    o.  What kinds of transportation they see in the neighborhood
    p.  What outdoor games they enjoy
    q.  Which foods they prefer and which ones are good for them
    r.  Admired cartoon characters
    s.  Why and when they should wash their hands or brush their teeth
    t.  What riddles they like

2.  The student dictates the story. Using whatever mode of communication that the student is comfortable with, the student dictates the story to the teacher.

3.  The teacher records the student's story. The primary emphasis of this step is on retaining the meaning of the story; therefore, the form of the message is less important than the content.

4.  The teacher reads back the story to the student. By reading the story back to the student, the student is able to make sure that the story contains the intended content and is able to make

corrections and additions to the story.

5. The student reads the story to the teacher. The student attempts to read the story to the teacher and gets help when necessary. This step is practiced for the next few days.

6. The student adds the story to his or her collection of stories to be read repeatedly with the teacher, students, and other significant adults. The stories that each student writes can be illustrated and bound in an attractive folder.

An alternative to using the chalkboard or charts for recording the students' stories is using a microcomputer. The student or students whose story is being dictated can watch their story unfold on the screen. Their story can be stored on the disk for future use and printed whenever necessary. Students can edit their own stories as they dictate them by asking the teacher to make the appropriate changes, or the stories can be edited at a later date after a discussion has been held about ways to improve them. A valuable piece of software that some teachers use is called the Language Experience Recorder Plus (Mason, n.d.). The program allows you to develop stories that are either 20, 40, or 80 columns wide. This permits you to change the size of the print, contingent on the purpose and age level of the students that you are working with. It also furnishes you with a record of students' language development by providing a summary of the average word length, average sentence length, number of sentences, and individual cumulative word lists.

One potential limitation of the LEA is that it does not provide a structured, systematic method of teaching sequential reading skills. In addition, a method of evaluation or determination of grade equivalence does not exist. As a result, parents and school administrators may be resistant to a reading program that seems less structured than basal readers. Therefore, it is suggested that educators make use of other approaches to teaching reading to their hearing-impaired students as well as using the LEA.

## Reciprocal Teaching

Reciprocal teaching consists of modeling the desired reading behaviors for students, leading them through the reading task, and then fading out of the process so that the students themselves can control all parts of the task (Andrews & Mason, 1986). The procedure, which has been shown to be successful with hearing-impaired students, utilizes the concept of self-monitoring. Self-monitoring encourages students to stay on task even when there is no one around to assist them. Clay (1979) presented a number of appropriate self-monitoring strategies to aid young children. Instead of correcting the student, she suggested that the teacher should ask the student to reread and point to each word, look at the picture, and think about what happened in the story. The teacher can guide the student via clues, asking, and signing: "Does it make sense?" "Does it look right?" "Is that a correct English sentence?" In the Andrews and Mason (1986) strategy, the teacher follows these basic steps:

1. The teacher reads a teacher-made book to the students. Each book contains from three to five new printed words in a picture context with manual sign illustrations. Each book is from seven to eight pages long.

2. The teacher discusses the new vocabulary words with the students to see if they use these words in their own communication.

3. Following the discussion, the students receive their own copies of the storybook. The students hold and read the book to themselves and to their peers with the assistance of the teacher. The

sign-to-print correspondence is made explicit in the storybooks.

4. Using the storybooks as a script, the students playact the story. One student holds the book for the others so that the play resembles the story line.

5. The students return to their seats and one student retells the story without the aid of the storybook. Peers are prompted as needed.

6. Students practice fingerspelling the words with the aid of the storybook, print them on the chalkboard, and read and retell the stories to each other.

7. The teacher provides praise and feedback specific to the students' level of participation (by describing what specific students are doing). Following this feedback, the teacher models any activity on which the students need improvement.

8. The students take the storybooks home to read with family members. Andrews (1988) suggested that 20 such books might be read in a school year.

## Delayed Reading Instruction

Within this model of language proficiency, Cummins (1984) suggested that formal literacy instruction be delayed until the student has an age-appropriate language base on which such instruction can be built. This stance is in line with the theory of Clay (1979), also. While language learning through reading (as just described) might be a partial solution, teachers should assess the reading readiness of nonreaders before they attempt to actually teach children to read.

## ELEMENTARY-LEVEL READING APPROACHES

One of the major differences between the education of a hearing-impaired child and that of the hearing child is that the hearing-

impaired child begins reading acquisition at almost the same time as he or she begins formal progress in language acquisition (Blackwell et al., 1978). Another difference can be found in the manner that print is coded. Ewoldt (1978) found that, although hearing-impaired and hearing children recode graphic symbols into different internalized language systems, they still use essentially similar strategies for processing written information. Hirch-Pasek (1981) found that deaf students could be taught to decode and recode by using fingerspelling. Work by Ewoldt (1978) supports this contention, also. Deaf children seem to use fingerspelling to "sound out" new words, just as hearing children use phonics (Ewoldt, 1978). However, Hirch-Pasek (1981) noted also that teachers need to assist students in making a connection between fingerspelled words and printed words. As Chall (1967) observed, hearing children are more likely to benefit from phonics if the relationship between spelling and sound is taught explicitly. It can be inferred from the work of Hirch-Pasek that you should fingerspell often with your students so that the strategy of fingerspelling as an acceptable and comprehensible form of communication is modeled. Therefore, many of the methods and approaches to reading instruction appropriate for hearing children may also be applicable to hearing-impaired students.

## Predictable Books

Prediction plays a vital role in reading comprehension. It involves a three-step cycle: *sampling, predicting,* and *confirming* (Goodman, 1986; Smith, 1979). In the first step, sampling, students select the most useful syntactic, semantic, and visual information from the text in order to make a prediction. Through sampling, they exclude the unlikely alternatives. Then in the second step, predicting, students hypothesize the most probable meaning of the text based on the information they selected during sampling. In the third step, confirming, students ask themselves if their hypotheses make sense based on the feedback they receive from the text. This feedback allows them to confirm or reject their hypotheses. This three-step cycle is repeated as students read, and the outcome is reading comprehension (Tompkins & Webeler, 1983).

It is only through practice in reading that students learn to be efficient predictors of meaning and economical users of visual information. Using literature as part of a reading program provides natural motivation. Genuine literature, which has not been modified and appears as it was written by the author, is pleasurable and exciting to children. Students are more likely to become skillful readers if they are given many opportunities to read real books, which enable them to experience literate behaviors from the beginning. To help beginning readers practice reading, the task should be made as easy as possible for them. The key to making reading easier for the beginning reader lies in finding materials for initial reading instruction that are easy and meaningful, thus predictable. Selections with repetitive structures enable readers to anticipate the next line or the next episode. The reader's familiarity with the repetitive pattern and dependable line makes it possible to predict what is coming next.

Predictable texts share the following characteristics:

1. They meet reader's expectations about textual cohesion.
2. They build the story through naturally patterned repetition of English and events.
3. They use story lines, sequences, and concepts that are familiar to the reader.
4. They contain illustrations that support the content and English of the text (Israelite, 1988).

Predictable books are especially effective in promoting young students' use of the pre-

diction cycle. They have repetitive language patterns or repeated or cumulative story events. For example, *Bears on Wheels* (Berenstain, 1969) begins with:

> One bear, one wheel.
> One bear on one wheel.
> Two bears on one wheel.
> Three on one.
> Four on one.
> Four bears on one wheel.

The major value of using predictable books during initial reading instruction is that they enable the beginning reader to process the printed page in the same way as the mature reader does, employing the predicting, sampling, confirming, and disconfirming strategies. Numerous experiences with patterned books also facilitate the development of sight vocabulary through repeated exposure to the vocabulary in dependable contexts (Bridge, 1979). Many of the books have a repeatable stem or phrase comprised of high-frequency structure words, such as *the*, *a*, *an*, and *of*. The student is able to read these words successfully as the phrase is repeated over and over again in meaningfully patterned structures. Gradually these words become incorporated into their sight vocabulary.

You can use predictable books to help students and promote automatic use of the prediction cycle by adapting the questions and steps presented by Stauffer (1980) and Tompkins and Webeler (1983). You can use variations of the following steps, either when you are reading to a group of students or when you are helping an individual student to read.

1. Read the title and show the picture on the cover of the book to the students and ask, "What do you think this book will be about?" Encourage students to use both word and picture clues as they make their predictions.
2. Begin reading the book and continue

through the first set of repetitions and into the second set. As soon as the students have enough information, stop reading and ask more of the following questions to encourage the students to predict what will happen: "What do you think will happen next?" "What do you think will happen this time?" "What do you think (character) will say next?" "What do you think (character) will do next?"

3. After the students have made their predictions, ask them to explain why they made those predictions, using one or more of the following questions: "Why do you think that will happen next?" "Why do you think that idea is a good one?" "Why do you think (character) will say that next?" "Why do you think (character) will do that next?" The purpose of these questions is to help the students realize that they are basing their predictions on the book's repetitive patterns.

4. Read through the next set of repetitive patterns to enable students to confirm or reject their predictions.

5. Continue reading and have the students repeat steps 2, 3, and 4. For students who are reading individually, encourage them to finish reading the book using the prediction cycle.

6. On the second day, read the story again, allowing plenty of opportunity to join in, as well as some opportunity for them to say the next line before you read it.

7. Using large print or individual dittoed books, have the students take turns or use their own booklets to read along with you.

8. After they have had sufficient exposure following along, ask for a volunteer to read parts of the story.

9. When they have learned the story well, let the students take the booklets home and read them to their parents.

After students learn to use the three-step prediction cycle with predictable books, they should be encouraged to apply this strategy to all of their reading activities. Teachers are encouraged to select well-written stories for instructional and independent reading activities with hearing-impaired students. A comprehensive bibliography of predictable books is provided by May (1986), McClure (1985), and Rhodes (1981).

## Basal Reading Series

*Basal readers* are a sequential and interrelated set of books and supportive materials designed to teach developmental reading skills systematically (Harris & Sipay, 1985). Recent research reported by LaSasso (1987) indicates that basal readers are the primary approach used for reading instruction with hearing-impaired students. Most series include a sequential set of reading texts and supplementary materials, such as workbooks, flash cards, and achievement tests. In addition, a comprehensive teacher's manual provides precise plans and suggestions for skill activities. A basal reading series generally consists of graded readers that gradually increase in difficulty, typically beginning with preprimers and going through the eighth-grade level. The books increase in difficulty in vocabulary, story content, and skill development.

A disadvantage of using a basal reading series is that its structured, comprehensive nature may limit a teacher's creativity and contribute to an inflexible method of teaching. Some potential negative outcomes of the structure that frequently accompany the use of basal readers are decreased individual instruction for students and an overreliance and misuse of the teacher's manual and student workbooks (Wallace, Cohen, & Polloway, 1987).

The basal reader has been the target of continual criticism in the field of education of hearing-impaired students for quite some time now (Gormley, 1982; King & Quigley, 1985). General criticisms relate to the unfamiliarity of textual material, the need to rewrite stories to accommodate for grammatical and lexical limitations, and syntactical complexity (Bunch, 1987). However, we believe that many basal reading series can be used effectively with hearing-impaired students. We want to qualify this statement with an additional point. We strongly feel that teachers should be flexible in their use of this approach. Readers should not be used from start to finish in a routine manner. Selections should be analyzed by the teacher for appropriateness in building skill areas, in providing reading in areas of student interests, and being within the experiential and linguistic ranges of the students (Browns & Arnell, 1981). In addition, judicious use of workbook activities and the use of a great deal of supplementary materials and activities should be integrated when basal readers are used. Also, basal readers should be viewed as a component of a reading program, rather than the reading program itself.

The basal reading series that currently are the most frequently used with hearing-impaired students are *Reading Milestones* (Quigley & King, 1981), Reading Systems and Systems Unlimited (Scott Foresman), Ginn 360 and Ginn 720 (Ginn & Co.) and Houghton-Mifflin Readers (Houghton-Mifflin) (LaSasso, 1987). Of these reading series, *Reading Milestones* is the only one written specifically for hearing-impaired students. The series was designed as a set of readers with controlled syntax and controlled vocabulary. It consists of 8 levels, each of which has 10 readers, 10 workbooks, and a teacher's guide. Each level is color-coded and introduces or reinforces new vocabulary and a new syntactic structure.

## High Interest-Low Vocabulary Method

High interest-low vocabulary books have been produced in greater quantities during the last decade. They allow students to read books that are geared to their interest level and contain a relatively easy vocabulary and style. These books can be used individually or with small groups. As indicated in Appendix A, materials covering a wide variety of topics are available. A more extensive list of books and their publishers is provided by Harris and Sipay (1985). Teachers can estimate the reading level of these materials by following the procedures that were recommended in the assessment section of this chapter.

## Individual Reading Approach

In an individualized reading program, students select their own reading material according to their interests and ability and progress at their own rate. After students choose their own book to read, they read independently and keep records of their own progress. You work with students individually on vocabulary and comprehension as each student needs, and you meet with each student several times during the week to read with the student and to check for the student's understanding of the material. During the conferences, you observe, diagnose, and record reading strengths and weaknesses. From the conference you plan activities in order to develop specific skills.

Whether you choose to use this approach as the primary method of teaching reading or as an additional component to your reading program, there are some specific factors that you might consider when you are organizing individualized reading opportunities. They include the following:

1. Provide sufficient time for students to read. Reading should not only happen during reading time or when students finish their work. Time for free reading should be included in weekly lesson plans.
2. Provide a wide variety of books from which students can choose.
3. Help students find books that are not too difficult for them to read. Students will become easily discouraged if one book after another is hard for them to understand.

4. Suggest books to students based on their hobbies, interests, and personal problems.
5. Establish a method by which students can share their impressions of a book with other students. These can be done through the avenues of drama, arts and crafts, stand-up reports, or written reports.
6. Use extrinsic forms of positive reinforcement. This can be done by having each student keep a personal record or by the use of a class record of the different books that the class has read (May, 1986).

A limitation of this type of approach is that it requires a large number of books. In addition, no provision is made in advance to deal with unknown words or difficult concepts if they surface while the students are reading and the teacher is working with an individual student.

## Whole-Language Approach

The whole-language approach has been adapted from many of the principles developed by language theorists in New Zealand, Australia, Canada, and Great Britain (Goodman, 1986). Whole-language programs are developed with the contention that students should be immersed in meaningful, language-rich environments. Advocates of this approach question the notion that reading is a precise process involving exact, detailed, sequential perception and identification of letters, words, and sentences. Rather, they view reading as a "psycholinguistic guessing game" (Goodman, 1986) and advocate teaching reading as a holistic activity.

Within the whole-language approach, reading is treated as an integrated behavior and is never broken into separate skills. The emphasis is on meaning, and materials are expected to be genuine and relevant. The whole-language approach opposes the current practice of using basal readers, workbooks, skills sequences, and practice materials that fragments the process. The teaching of skills occurs as teachers observe that students are developmentally ready and have a functional need for them in reading and writing (Shanklin & Rhodes, 1989).

In the whole-language classroom, teachers surround students with language in meaningful context. The print-rich environment includes children's literature in all its variety; enlarged texts for shared reading; curriculum science and social studies projects; reading and writing material related to all curriculum areas; and books in reading and special interest areas (Goodman, 1986). Reading is integrated with conceptual learning in a rich, literate environment in which students read, write, and share poems, big books, little books, stories, songs, notes, maps, recipes, charts, messages, graphs, plays, newspapers, and lists. Eventually, these meaningful literary events are linked together in thematic units (see Chapter 2). For example, students studying fish life observe fish, take notes, make sketches, write descriptions in their journals, read poems, articles, and stories about fish, trace the history of fish through folklore, visit an aquarium, and interview a fisherman. Throughout their immersion in this area of study, students interact with each other as they share information, solve problems, read, write, ask questions, and observe and emulate adults who demonstrate literacy in the school setting.

Whole stories, poems, and songs form the basis of reading experiences in whole-language programs. It is contended that the use of a whole text enables students to learn important structural patterns in fiction and nonfiction material. Students, realizing that narratives have a beginning, middle, and end, begin to internalize a story. As students mature, they develop a more detailed framework for organizing story information that includes the concepts and vocabulary of characters, setting, problems, events, and resolutions. These understandings enable students to read new material with an organizing framework that aids in their comprehension.

In a whole-language classroom, there are books, magazines, newspapers, directories, signs, packages, labels, posters, and every other kind of appropriate print (Goodman, 1986). Students bring in all kinds of written language materials appropriate to their interests and the curriculum. Lots of recreational books are needed—fiction and nonfiction—with a wide range of difficulty and interest, as well as resource materials of all kinds, such as beginners' dictionaries and encyclopedias, phone books, and TV guides. Students communicate, read, and write as they need to. If a puppet show is developed to dramatize a story, then the story will be read, an outline or script will be written, and various class members will participate as actors, stagehands, or the audience.

Currently, there is a great deal of excitement among teachers who are using the whole-language approach (Shanklin & Rhodes, 1989). The enthusiasm of the teachers and the students towards reading and writing is wonderful to experience. However, to date there is a paucity of research that substantiates this approach in comparison to other methods of teaching reading. Hopefully, in the next few years research will verify that what appears to be a viable and exciting way to teach reading and writing is also an effective method.

## Story Mapping

To help students define the elements contained in typical stories, the technique of story mapping is recommended. Having explained the necessary elements of the story (e.g., the title, setting, characters, problem, goal, episodes, resolution, etc.), you assist students in analyzing stories around these parts. Begin with stories that have one main plot, clearly defined episodes, one major solution, and so forth (Bergenske, 1987). Next, allow students to create their own stories by using these identified elements (see Exhibit 11.7 for an example of a narrative story guide). After students have rewritten or word processed their stories, peers can be challenged to find the story elements in their classmates' work.

## Paired Reading

Research has shown that it is advantageous for parents to be involved as children begin to read (Hewison & Tizard, 1980; Topping, 1987). In the Paired Reading Approach, the student chooses the reading material. The technique allows students to be supported through texts of high readability levels. The student reads independently with the parent until a difficult section is reached. At this point, the parent and student both read all the words out loud, signing together. The parent adjusts the reading speed to achieve synchrony, and the student must say and sign every word. The parent repeats any word that the student says or signs incorrectly until it is read correctly. When encountering easier sections of the text, the student makes some prearranged signal that indicates a desire to read alone. A knock, squeeze, or nudge signals the parent to be quiet until the student makes a mistake. Parents should praise for correct reading, self-correction, and signaling to read alone. (Topping, 1987.)

Paired reading has been shown to be effective with students of all levels of assumed ability and potential. Students between the ages of 6 and 13 have been studied, and the results are very positive (Topping & Wolfendale, 1985). Some other points that ensure success with reading that involve the home environment are listed below:

The quality of parental verbal (voiced, cued or signed) interaction with the student is positively related to reading achievement (Moon & Well, 1979).

Parents who display an interest themselves in reading contribute both to students' confidence and interest in reading (Moon & Well, 1979). A considerable body of evidence shows that students who are good readers have parents who spend leisure time reading

**EXHIBIT 11.7.** Narrative story guide

_____

(Author)                                                    (Title)

_____ lived in  _____.
(Character)                                                 (Location)

He had a problem. The problem was that _____
                                                            (Problem)

_____

So what he wanted to do was _____.
                                          (Goal)

In order to accomplish his goal, he did three different things.

He _____

He _____

He _____

When he had finished doing these things (episodes) he had solved the problem. So the resolution was that

_____

_____
                                    (Resolution)

(Clark, 1976; Durkin, 1966; Morrow, 1983).

Exposure to a variety of reading materials in the home is related to reading proficiency (Hess & Holloway, 1984).

Noisy conditions and overcrowding in the home can adversely affect reading achievement (Wachs, 1979). Greaney (1986) reported that over one-half of all leisure reading takes place in bed. Evidence from Southgate, Arnold, and Johnson (1981) shows that the majority of children read more at home than they do at school. Parents need to be reminded to provide a conducive atmosphere and time for their children to read.

Parents who read to the child can help to stimulate their childrens' imagination and help them to understand written words before they can recognize them (Morrow, 1983; Ninio & Bruner, 1978): "It's read to me now and I'll read to you later!"

## Getting Over the Hump

Students often can master the written English that is presented in basal readers if they are given opportunities to personalize and utilize novel vocabulary. The approach of "getting-over-the-hump" reading skills (Bersgal, personal communication, 1983) has proven to be successful in adapting basal readers for hearing-impaired students.

1. The teacher might tell the student (depending on the story) the basic story

line, the period in history in which the story takes place, or that it is fiction and not fact, and so on. There is *genuine communication* between teacher and student; this is not a *lecture*.

2. The teacher allows the student to read the story silently with no interruption (Ewoldt, 1979).

3. The teacher probes for the student's general comprehension of the story: Does the student know the story line, main characters, cause and effect, ending (often using the pictures in the book)? The student may be asked to act out the story.

4. The student reads the story a second time, recording words and phrases that are unknown, and later compares the list to one that has been made by the teacher. (This approach allows multiple meanings and idioms to be addressed in the context of a comprehensible story.) Each new vocabulary word or phrase is written by the student on a 3 × 5 card. Later the words are defined on the back of the card (with either a picture or a written definition). It is very important that the definitions be the student's and not be supplied by the teacher. The teacher checks the cards when the student has finished making them.

5. The teacher and the student read the story together (group work is possible at this point). A *network* (see Chapter 6) is done, focusing on the content of the story, not the English grammar. The network is later used by each student to answer questions about the story. A written vocabulary test is given. If the student is not successful, the cards and the network are reviewed and a retest is given.

6. After many cards have been filled out, a test can be given as a separate review activity.

## Functional Reading

According to Smith (1985), teachers can also make frequent use of print whether it is in the form of a play, keeping a store, publishing a newspaper, or the daily routine. Printed materials and products that make sense to students in the outside world should be brought into the classroom. Menus from restaurants and computer menus constitute meaningful print, as do posters, notices, direction signs, maps, catalogs, timetables, and telephone books. These can be reproduced in a format that students can handle, using print that they can discriminate and language that they can understand. Give your students opportunities to experience the power of reading. Arrange your room so that students are reading to find needed or desired materials. Here is a list of what second-grader Breeze encounters:

Lunch menu
Letters from grandmas and friends
Labels "Handmade by Breeze" on things that she makes
Captions in coloring books
Directions for school and play-school (at home) worksheets
Software in her organizer at home
Labels under snapshots in the family photo album
Simple stories that she reads to her little sister
Labels on food products in the grocery store
Food coupons that she uses in the grocery store
The grocery list
The television schedule
Labels on her audiotapes and VHS tapes that she wants to use
Verses in the greeting cards that she is sent
Toys that are available on a flyer inside the box of the toy she has just received
Directions on board games
Computer screen, computer directions
Words on cereal boxes

## Echoic Reading

The teacher reads sections of print, and individuals reread those sections. In this approach, the teacher models proper vocabulary, fluency, and expression. Each passage should be long enough to prevent the student from recalling it from memory without looking at the print and short enough to allow the student to hold the words and expression in memory (Swaby, 1982).

## Choral Reading

Some stories lend themselves to being read aloud by a group. The entire group can read the repetitive segments, and individual students can read the nonrepetitive text.

## Writing Student Stories

Mothner (1980) used a technique to help develop an interest in reading in a student who was consistently unmotivated to read. He wrote stories about a superhero and named the superhero after the unmotivated student. The stories were developed with the purpose of entertaining and arousing the student's curiosity. They included information that related to the student's personality and gave credence to the student's predicaments in her life. Stories that are geared to the student's own life keep students highly motivated and demonstrate gains in both writing and reading.

## Computer Applications

Computers can be a valuable addition to a classroom's reading program. Computers provide individual instruction, give nonthreatening feedback, have infinite patience, and give large amounts of skills-oriented practice (Lerner, 1985). We recommend computer activities that are drill and practice, problem solving, tutorial, and simulation formats. Computer instruction provides students with a supplement to other forms of reading instruction and can help them to integrate previously learned material.

# VOCABULARY DEVELOPMENT

Knowledge of words is a critical factor related to success in reading (Johnson, Toms-Bronowski, & Pittelman, 1982). Comprehension of a passage cannot occur until the reader identifies the author's chosen words, recognizes interrelationships among those words, and attaches meaning to the word combinations (Johnson & Pearson, 1984). Research reported by LaSasso and Davey (1987) indicates that hearing-impaired students' vocabulary skills are an effective predictor of their reading comprehension. Therefore, one of the major tasks facing teachers of hearing-impaired students is the expansion of students' knowledge of words and their meanings. Learning to read will be a difficult process for students if *significant others* limit the vocabulary that they sign to them. Students must *be exposed* to new words in a meaningful context, they must *discuss* the words so that expressive vocabulary develops, and then they must *read and write* the new words. Students should come to understand that they are learning new words, not as an end in itself, but as a means of becoming more capable in communicating.

## Sight Words and Phrases

*Sight words* are those words that are recognized instantly without any additional analysis. An individual's sight vocabulary refers to the ever expanding pool of words that a reader recognizes as they are encountered. These words have been stored in a visual memory bank and can be recognized easily. They occur in such high frequency that they are deemed essential to fluent reading. In order to be effective readers, students must be proficient in word and phrase recognition skills; they cannot stop to analyze every word or figure of speech that they encounter if they want to read fluently (Simms & Falcon, 1987).

Several published word lists have been

developed by various writers and researchers, such as those by Dolch (1955), Fry (1980), and Johnson (1971), and they are available for instructional purposes. It has been found that the Dolch word list, which contains 220 sight words that make up 50–65 percent of the words that students encounter in elementary basal readers (Mercer & Mercer, 1985), and the Johnson word list, which is composed of 306 words, consist of words that are found in 87–93 percent of basal reading series (Johnson & Pearson, 1984). Therefore, it is important to gradually and carefully introduce sight words to hearing-impaired students and to make use of constant review. In addition, we would recommend expanding the concept of teaching sight words to hearing-impaired children so that the approach includes teaching phrases of figurative language as well.

**Two Approaches.** The first of the approaches that we have found useful was developed by Simms and Falcon (1987). The Dolch Basic Sight Word List (Dolch, 1955) has been divided into 27 semantic categories, based on a "best fit" approach. See Exhibit 11.8 for the categories and words. Each new category is introduced with an extended discussion. An example of a discussion is: "Today we are going to begin learning some action words. Who can give me an example of an action? The first word is *push*. Can someone stand up and show us how to push something? Can someone use *push* in a sentence?" As each new word within a category is presented, its meaning is discussed and a sentence is generated. In addition, its relationship to both the category name and the other words in the category are stressed. Each

---

**EXHIBIT 11.8.** Word categories

*Action Words* (Acts upon an object): pick, put, pull, buy, carry, open, use, show, start, stop, wash.

*Away Words*: away, down, far, out, there, from.

*Connecting Words*: because, but, and, with, too.

*Feeling Words*: want, hurt, kind, laugh, thank, wish, like, funny.

*Little Words*: if, of, or, so, to, as, for.

*Number Words*: one, two, three, four, five, six, seven, eight, nine, ten.

*Question Words*: who, which, where, why, how, can, may, what, when, could, would, shall.

*Sharing Words*: let, gave, give, get, bring, take, help, together.

*Temperature Words*: cold, warm, hot.

*Amount Words*: a, all, an, both, every, many, much, some, the, only, just, any.

*Be Words*: be, an, are, been, is, was, were.

*Do Words*: do, did, does, done, make, made, try, must, will, sleep, sit.

*Good Words*: fast, best, better, clean, yes, good, pretty, well, very, please, new.

*Moving Words*: came, come, play, jump, go, goes, ran, going, run, walk, ride, fly, went, fall.

*Other People Words*: he, her, him, she, his, their, them, they, you, your

*School Words*: draw, know, word, write, sing, read, think.

*Size Words*: round, big, light, little, long, small.

*When Words*: before, after, once, again, old, soon, first, about, always, then, today, now.

*Anything Words*: that, it, this, these, its, those.

*Color Words*: black, blue, brown, green, red, white, yellow.

*Eating Words*: ate, cut, drink, eat, full.

*Life Words*: live, see, look, saw, grow.

*No Words*: don't, never, no, not.

*Possession Words*: had, found, got, has, have, hold, keep, own, find.

*Self Words*: I, me, my, myself, our, we, us

*Talk Words*: call, say, tell, said, ask.

*Where Words*: at, around, by, in, into, on, over, right, under, up, upon, here, off.

---

SOURCE: R. B. Simms and S. C. Falcon, "Teaching sight words." *Teaching Exceptional Children*, 20(1), 1987, 30–33.

word should be written on the board or on a large word card as it is introduced. Individual or group practice can continue by means of word drills; for example, students can be asked to develop sentences or solve scrambled word sheets.

When you are using this approach remember to:

1. Pretest students on the word list prior to beginning teaching sight words. If the students know few or none of the first 20 words, discontinue testing.
2. Transfer the results to a recording sheet that also lists the words by categories.
3. Use various techniques to practice and reinforce the words.
4. Make a progress chart for each student by listing the categories and making a box for each one. Let each student mark off or place a sticker next to each category that has been mastered.

This method is applicable to any sight word list. Phrases of figurative language could be included also. The important point is to divide the list into logical categories such as size words and color words. You will find that some words do not fit into any category. Call them "other words" Remember that it is important that you introduce each new category and discuss the words and phrases. Making words and phrases meaningful to students enhances learning.

A second method for teaching sight vocabulary was developed by Johnson and Pearson (1984). They use a five-step plan:

1. *Seeing*. The word or phrase is written on the chalkboard, flash card, or piece of paper and is expressed to the students.
2. *Discussing*. After the word or phrase has been written, it should be read by the teacher and students. Whenever

possible, the word or phrase should be discussed.
3. *Using*. Students are asked to use the word or phrase in a sentence or two or to suggest a synonymous word or phrase.
4. *Defining*. Whenever possible, students should try to define the word or phrase by using their own words to explain what it means to them.
5. *Writing*. Students should be encouraged to practice writing the word or phrase both alone and in various contexts.

Research (Dickerson, 1982) indicates that the use of games to reinforce sight vocabulary is a very effective activity for promoting retention. The communication games discussed in Chapter 7 could be adapted for a sight vocabulary emphasis. Excellent resources for vocabulary games were developed by Humphrey and Sullivan (1970) and Wagner and Hosier (1970)

*Self-selected Vocabulary Words.* Another technique that you can use to help students increase their reading vocabulary is to have them select the words and phrases that they want to learn to read. Key vocabulary words are drawn from the students' expressive language. Learning to read these words and phrases is not difficult for most students, because they have been involved in the selection process and have chosen vocabulary words that carry a high personal-interest value. The following procedures, developed by Johnson and Pearson (1984), can be used when you are implementing the self-selected vocabulary approach:

1. Motivate students prior to word and phrase selection through exposure to books, movies, or discussions.
2. Elicit meaningful words through discussion and the use of probing questions.

3. Print words and phrases on personal word cards.
4. Read the words or phrases and have the students read the words or phrases.
5. Practice using the words or phrases in a sentence.
6. File the words or phrases in a personal word bank.
7. Review words or phrases as often as possible by using games or activities.

*Vocabulary Preinstruction.* In a study by Johnson, Moe, and Baumann (1983), it was found that, on a list of 9,000 words of great importance to elementary school students, 72 percent of them were words that had more than one meaning. In addition, they found that most stories contained unfamiliar vocabulary words. Preteaching of these potentially difficult items, in meaningful contexts, will help students be able to read selections independently. Prior to beginning any reading selection, pull out the words or phrases that may cause comprehension problems. Instruction should include discussing the concepts and using the words that are found in the selection.

In stories that have many vocabulary words, there may be more difficult words or phrases than there is time to teach or than the students have the ability to learn at one sitting. In such cases, be pragmatic and choose the most useful words in terms of frequency of use and necessity of concepts to promote understanding of a particular selection (Swaby, 1982). Be realistic about the number of words or phrases that you introduce. Eight to ten words or phrases may be adequate for preinstruction. To develop vocabulary understanding, you should present difficult words or phrases in a meaningful context. Instructional methods that relate readers' personal experiences to the acquisition of new vocabulary words or phrases are recommended extensively in the literature (Johnson & Pearson, 1984). By using the new words and phrases in sentences and by asking a series of questions about their semantic and structural elements, you can make the meaning of words and phrases more memorable and relevant.

Another approach that can be used for introducing vocabulary to hearing-impaired students has been adapted from May (1986). It is composed of the following seven steps:

1. Introduce the word or phrase in context. Write sentences containing the word or phrase on the board or overhead. Underline the word or phrase that you are emphasizing. Read the sentence to your students and have them read with you whenever possible. Discuss the meaning of the word or phrase whenever possible; the context clue should be *explicit*. For example, if you were introducing the word *homicide*, an explicit context clue would be: "The judge decided that the death of the man was not an accident. It was a homicide because the murderer wanted to kill him."
2. Have students enhance their memory of the word or phrase. Have them look at the word or phrase and spell it to themselves. Have them close their eyes and imagine writing the word or phrase. Ask them to look at the board and see if they are correct.
3. Ask them to write the word or phrase from memory. Have them look at the word or phrase and spell it to themselves. After they have done this, cover the word or phrase and ask them to write it on their papers. Uncover the word or phrase and ask them to see if they have written it correctly. Check their papers to make sure that they have it right.
4. Repeat Steps 1, 2, and 3 for each of the words or phrases.
5. Have students practice recognizing the words or phrases in isolation. Write

the words or phrases on flash cards and expose each to the students for about one second. Then ask them to read each one for you.

6. Have the students use the words or phrase in context. Using the sentences that you have developed earlier, ask the students to read them to you without your help. Whenever possible, have them explain the word or phrase to you. Give them the page number and have them search for the word in their stories.

7. Practice by using different games and activities spread out over the next few days and weeks.

***Semantic Mapping.*** Cues or strategies employed directly or indirectly in teaching vocabulary should relate new knowledge to what is already known (Johnson, Toms-Bronowski, & Pittelman, 1982). *Semantic mapping* is a categorical structuring of information in graphic form (an example appears in Chapter 6). It is an individualized content approach in which students are required to relate new words to their own experiences and prior knowledge. Using a semantic mapping approach, the schema is constructed on the chalkboard or overhead, where new concepts, different story parts, and new vocabulary words are introduced during the readiness stage (Sinatra, Berg, & Dunn, 1985). The advantage of the semantic mapping approach is that it enables a student not only to visualize relationships but also to categorize them.

According to Johnson and Pearson (1984), semantic mapping follows an eight-step process:

1. Select a word or topic central to the story or selection that will be read.
2. Write the word on the chalkboard, overhead, or large sheet of chart paper.
3. Ask students to think of and to write down on paper as many words as they

can that in some way are related to the target word or topic. Write these words down in categories if possible.

4. Have students share the words that they have written while you write them on the board, overhead, or chart paper, and arrange them in broad categories. You may wish to add words to categories that you know will be critical to their understanding of the reading selection.

5. Number the categories, identify the categories, and name the categories that appear on the map.

6. Discuss items as they are entered onto the map and when the map is completed. Discussion is the most important component of semantic mapping. Through this process, students learn the meanings and uses of new words and new meanings for known words. In addition, they see the relationships among words.

7. Focus attention on the one or two categories that are appropriate for your reading selection.

8. Use the semantic map for review and reinforcement of key vocabulary words and concepts.

***Context Analysis.*** *Context analysis* refers to a reader's attempt to figure out the meaning of a word by examining the way in which it is used. May (1986) contends that context analysis is probably the most important tool for learning new words. During regular reading instruction, there are many opportunities for you to demonstrate to students how to make intelligent guesses about a word's meaning. Start off by explaining to students that authors often provide clues or signals to the meanings of difficult words. Read a passage with your students that provides good cues for a specific word that you are going to try and figure out. Go through the paragraph and underline words or phrases that help to identify the meaning of the key word. Discuss the cues that have been identified and generate an explanation for the word.

After you have modeled this technique, put a new word on the board and provide the students with the page number on which it appears in the story. Challenge them to discover what the word means by reading the words around it. When the students do this correctly, ask them to explain how they figured it out. This type of activity can be done with words and passages that you have created in order to provide them with additional practice. Using various activities to promote this type of skill helps students learn independently to derive meaning for an unknown or target word by understanding the words or phrases that surround it.

A second activity for improving contextual analysis skills is the use of the *cloze* procedure. The cloze procedure is a method of systematically deleting every fifth or eighth word from a passage and replacing it with a blank line. This can also be done with specific aspects of grammar such as nouns. The student's task is to read the passage and examine the surrounding context. The student must then supply the missing words in the passage. The words that are supplied do not need to be exactly the same as the ones that you have deleted, but they should make sense to the reader. Here is an example taken from the *Little Chick's Story* by Kwitz (1978), in which every eighth word was deleted.

> Broody Hen laid five eggs. She laid _____ egg in the hen house for the _____ son. She laid one egg in the _____ for the farmer's daughter. She laid one _____ in the meadow for the ring-tailed raccoon.

A computer program, M_ss_ng L_nks (Chomsky & Schwartz, 1983), provides teachers with many deleted variations of children's literature and has been used successfully with exceptional learners.

A third method that can be used with students to focus on context clues is the use

of riddles, in which the missing word is supplied by the students. Write the clues on the chalkboard or overhead and have the students write down what they think the answer is. After someone has correctly responded, have the student explain how he or she figured it out. For example:

> I am round.
> I am hot.
> I am far away.
> I am bright.
> I am the __(sun)__.

**Using Additional Resources.** A sound program of vocabulary development must expose students to many new words and also help them to learn techniques for independent vocabulary acquisition (Johnson & Pearson, 1984). Two resources that encourage vocabulary development are the dictionary and the thesaurus. One important consideration when you are assigning work with these resources is to avoid assigning tasks that the students do not have the prerequisite skills to complete. Learning from a dictionary requires considerable sophistication. As a result, it is extremely important that direct instructions on how to use these resources occurs prior to assigning any work with them.

The dictionary is of little or no help as an aid for spelling. When students cannot spell a word, they will have extreme difficulty looking it up. In addition, we caution teachers concerning use of the dictionary as part of a drill type activity. Many skill-building exercises that use the dictionary and thesaurus are dull and uninspiring. The practice of looking up a word and copying the meaning generally is viewed by students as punitive rather than as an opportunity to learn. In addition, research reported by Miller and Gildea (1987) indicates that having students look up a word in the dictionary and write a sentence incorporating that word is of limited educational value. Johnson and Pearson (1984) provide a series of activities, and Archer and Gleason (1988) present lessons and exercises that can be used to assist students in becoming competent users of these resources. A dictionary that we have used and find to be very helpful for working with hearing-impaired students was developed by Baker and Bettino (1988).

## INCREASING COMPREHENSION

### Reading Comprehension

The knowledge that readers bring to the text is a significant factor in both the quality and quantity of their recall and retention (Paratore & Indrisano, 1987). Classroom applications have revealed that students who prepare for reading by relating background knowledge to both specific content and structure of the reading material improve their comprehension (Hansen & Pearson, 1982). A logical implication for teachers of hearing-impaired students is that reading instruction should place an emphasis on developing the necessary background for all reading. The importance of the prereading stage of an instructional lesson cannot be overemphasized. In this stage, background information is provided, new knowledge is related to existing knowledge, purposes for reading are determined, and significant vocabulary terms are pretaught (Wood & Robinson, 1983). Gormley and Franzen (1978) expressed a concern that insufficient time was being allocated for prereading activities when they stated that "the poor reading performance of the deaf may be a failure of the educational process to teach the meaning of reading—making sense of written information in terms of the reader's experience" (p. 543).

### Inferential Questions

An author never states *everything* that happened in a story. Information that can be logically assumed may be omitted. The reader uses information from the explicit text, plus knowledge of the world, to infer the missing information or the implicit text base. The ability to draw inferences is a prerequisite to reading development. Investigations of text grammar indicate that inference is perhaps the most important comprehension subskill (Strange, 1980). However, Pikulski (1983) noted that "most of the questions we ask in the name of comprehension do little to stimulate thought or to teach reading comprehension. Most tend to test children's memory for facts contained in the materials they have read" (p. 111). Practice in answering inferential-type questions before, during, and after reading can improve students' reading ability (Holmes, 1983; Hansen & Pearson, 1980). In addition, probing questions elicit nearly three times the number of inference statements than are revealed in free recall (Carr, 1983). May (1986) recommends that you consider the following categories and types of questions when you are discussing a story:

| | |
|---|---|
| **SETTING:** | Where is it taking place? When? If it happened at another place or time, would it make a difference? |
| **CHARACTER:** | What kind of person is she? What makes you think so? Why do you think that she did what she did? |
| **THEME:** | What does she learn in this story? |
| **CONFLICT:** | What problems does she face? How do you think that she will solve it? |
| **REACTION:** | What are her feelings about the problem? |
| **ATTEMPTS:** | What does she do first? What do you think that she will do next? Why did the first attempt fail? |
| **RESOLUTION:** | How was the problem solved? |
| **REACTION:** | How did she feel about the way it was solved? What are some other ways in which it might have been solved? What do you think she will do now that the problem has been solved? |

Some question prompts that may be helpful in asking inference questions appear in Chapter 10 of this text.

## Story Frames

Fowler (1982) presented a technique, referred to as "story frames," for helping students organize information in order to identify important ideas, analyze characters and their problems, make comparisons, and summarize the content of a passage. A "story frame" is a sequence of spaces hooked together by key language elements (see Exhibit 11.9). After reading a story with a group, the teacher displays a story frame. The students read the first line or set of key words of the frame and then discuss possible responses. The frames are relatively open, so there are no specific words or answers for each space. Next, the teacher moves the discussion to the subsequent lines of the frames. The students are asked to think back to the first line and to select information that will make the different lines relate to one another.

This process continues for each line of the frame, so that the students can make as many connections as possible. Once students can use story frames effectively as a group, they can begin to use the story frames indi-

---

**EXHIBIT 11.9.** Story frame: identifying problems and main ideas (Fowler, 1982)

The problem was that _____

_____

It started when _____

_____

After that _____

_____

Then _____

_____

The problem is solved when _____

_____

The story ends _____

_____

vidually. According to Fowler and Davis (1985), there are four steps that are involved in constructing story frames:

1. Read the story and identify the problem that you want the students to focus on. It may be the plot, the sequence of events, or a comparison of characters.
2. Write out a paragraph that addresses the problem.
3. Take the completed paragraph and delete all words, phrases, and sentences, except those that are needed to sustain the purpose of the paragraph.
4. Try the story frame with other stories that have a similar theme. Modify the story frame so that it can be used in several situations.

## Metacomprehension

In attempting to understand new material, skilled readers elaborate and transform the material in order to construct a coherent representation of it. As discussed earlier, students use their stored knowledge to help generate hypotheses about the best possible interpretation of a passage; they attempt to integrate new material into this interpretation; and they make inferences to fill in the gaps or to tie the material together. They also continually evaluate how well their interpretation fits the material, and they revise or replace their working hypotheses when necessary. According to such a perspective, comprehension monitoring is an integral part of the comprehension process itself (Capelli & Markman, 1982; Rumelhart, 1984). There is evidence that suggests that poor readers do not integrate text as well as good readers. Less proficient readers are not adept at monitoring their understanding of what they have read (Kendall & Mason, 1982). They generally lack an awareness of when they understand a passage and when they do not understand it. Poor monitoring of comprehension often results from a failure to process the material actively, by failing to formulate a hypotheses, generate

expectations, or relate and integrate the material (Capelli & Markman, 1982).

Most students are capable of performing certain cognitive activities, such as making inferences or generating hypotheses, but may fail to do so spontaneously in appropriate situations. One way to improve a student's comprehension is to increase the student's awareness by having the student work to improve self-monitoring skills and by providing intervention strategies that the student can use while reading (Fitzgerald, 1983). Chamot and O'Mallery (1984) found that metalinguistic strategies were beneficial to hearing bilingual students who were able to compare elements of their first language with those of the dominant language. Some specific questions suggested by Paratore and Indrisano (1987) that ask students to help foster a personal awareness of reading include:

How do you get ready to read?
When you come to a word that you cannot read, what do you do?
When you have a question that you cannot answer, what do you do?
What do you do to help remember what you have read?
How do you check your reading?
If a young child asked you how you read, what would you tell the child?

We encourage teachers to use explicit instruction to teach students comprehension strategies. One technique is to model comprehension monitoring. In this activity, the teacher reads a selection to the class, explaining his or her own monitoring and hypotheses testing while reading. An example, using a short passage taken from *Fievel's Boat Trip* by Teitelbaum (1986), would be:

Once there was a little mouse named Fievel Mousekewitz. He was a curious little mouse with a big floppy hat that fell down over his eyes. Today was a special day for Fievel. His family was leaving their home in Russia to start a new life in America. Fievel was going on a great big boat for the first time in his life.

You could begin the lesson by saying, "When we begin to read something, it is important to make a picture in our mind of what we think the story is going to be about. It is also important that we think about what we are reading and realize what we understand and do not understand. When I read, I try to think about what I understand and do not understand, and I try to make guesses about what I am reading. Let me show you what I mean."

After reading one or two sentences, you might ask questions such as, "Where is Fievel?" and "What is this story going to be about?" and then make guesses such as, "I think that he's in a city" and "I think that he is going to get into some trouble because he is curious and because his hat might fall and block his vision." Then you may want to state all the things that you do know and identify the things that the author has not told you yet. Using the first two sentences from the example, we do know that Fievel is a mouse, that he is curious, and that he has a hat that falls down over his eyes. The information that we do not know is where he is, who he is with, or what he is doing. You may want to place this information on the blackboard to show graphically what is going on in your mind.

This procedure is repeated for the next group of sentences. At this point, you will want to add to and move things from the "know" and "do not know" columns as the new information is interpreted. In follow-up lessons, you can gradually involve the students in self-monitoring procedures by repeating the first lesson with a different passage. This should be followed by having the students work in groups of two with a different text and finally working individually with new material (Fitzgerald, 1983).

A similar procedure was presented by Capelli and Markman (1982). They found that students who were taught to answer ques-

tions as they read were able to improve their comprehension skills. They suggested that questions about inferences, forming hypothesis, and tying information together are the most effective. The four steps that they recommend are:

1. The teacher and students read a short story. After each sentence has been read, the teacher makes hypotheses and models the answers for the following set of questions:
   a. Who are the characters?
   b. What is going on?
   c. Why did the characters do what they did?
   d. When and where did the story take place?
2. The students read the next story to themselves and answer the same questions.
3. The teacher models the questions and answers for the story that the students have just completed.
4. The explicitness of the questions are gradually diminished until the students simply describe their interpretations as completely as possible while keeping the questions in mind.

These teaching sequences provide a framework for constructing a better understanding of how to ask and answer questions. By using these steps, students learn that posing questions or problems as they read may be helpful. They also learn to formulate, think about, and evaluate through further reading the possible answers. Use of these types of strategies should be viewed as a transition step that attempts to assist students in making reading and comprehension of what they read an automatic process. Long-term use of these strategies may make reading too complex, too slow, and too laborious. Therefore, we recommend only a temporary use of these comprehension exercises. Some students will need more than modeling and application in order to be able to use a particular strategy effectively. For these students, you may need to break the strategy into smaller steps and provide guided practice with each step. Once each step has been learned, students will need many opportunities to read and interpret what they have read so that they can integrate the steps into an automatic process.

## SUMMARY

Despite the seemingly poor performance of hearing-impaired students in reading, research (North & Stevenson, 1975) indicates that reading is the most efficient and effective method of obtaining information for this population. In order to learn to read, students must see ways of employing reading to further their own aims and interests. It is essential that you make reading a meaningful, enjoyable, useful, and frequent experience for your students.

We are in agreement with most authorities in the field of reading who believe that there is no one best method of teaching reading. Therefore, information regarding a variety of reading methods and materials has been provided in the chapter. The successful teacher is one who analyzes selections and decides on appropriate instructional strategies based on the demands of each.

Knowledge of vocabulary, along with basic comprehension strategies, is the key to understanding written language (Johnson & Pearson, 1984). The acquisition of new vocabulary words is based, in part, on the fact that comprehension is building bridges between the new and the known; that is, for new concepts to be learned, they must be related to concepts already known (Johnson, Toms-Bronowski, & Pittelman, 1982). Taking the time to preteach and review vocabulary in reading lessons provides a bridge between ideas that are unfamiliar to students and knowledge that they have already acquired.

A final point of concern is that, to date, there is a dearth of research that demonstrates that isolated tests and workbooks on single isolated subskills will not help students to read better. On the other hand, there does seem to be evidence showing that comprehension can be improved when teachers use corresponding input (Luetke-Stahlman, 1988a, 1988b) and teach comprehension in an integrated, interactive way, with an emphasis on inferential thinking (Carr, 1983; Hansen & Pearson, 1980).

## ACTIVITIES

1. Administer a formal and/or informal reading assessment to a student. Summarize your results and plan a reading program for the student.
2. Determine the reading level of a children's literature book.
3. Plan and teach a reading session by using one of the strategies discussed in this chapter.
4. Videotape yourself teaching a reading lesson. Critique your performance in a positive manner integrating information from this chapter.
5. Read a story to a preschool child. Keep track of the different techniques that you need to use to keep the child interested and involved.
6. Take out a children's book from the library that would be appropriate for an elementary school student. Examine the story and decide what vocabulary you would need to preteach. Use one of the methods of teaching vocabulary discussed in this chapter to plan your lesson.
7. Familiarize yourself with some computer software that you could use to augment a reading program for hearing-impaired students.
8. Compare the metacomprehension skills of a good and a poor reader. Plan a demonstration lesson for the poor reader.

# CHAPTER 12

# Prewriting and Writing Instruction

## OVERVIEW

Writing is an essential skill in our contemporary society. Within most educational programs, writing is a primary means by which students demonstrate their knowledge. It is also an effective method for recording ideas and exploring thought. In addition, writing increasingly has become a critical occupational skill (Graham & Harris, 1988). Yet, written language is an area of skill acquisition that provides great frustration and difficulty for most hearing-impaired students (Quigley & Paul, 1984).

The objectives for assessing written language parallel those for assessing all academic areas: to identify students' strengths and weaknesses, to determine instructional objectives, to monitor student progress, and to provide feedback. In order to become comfortable with the process of evaluating student writing, you must approach the assessment process with a positive attitude, believing that it is possible for you to judge the quality of written composition and to plan instruction accordingly. In this chapter, we provide you with extensive information regarding the assessment of written language. Additionally, we look at the area of intervention. We advocate that students begin to write early in their educational program and that an important responsibility that you will have is to model reasons for writing to your students. In addition to such modeling we suggest that you model and teach students to use the process approach to writing. The process approach places equal attention on the planning, transcribing, and revision stages of the writing effort.

One important suggestion that is made in the chapter concerns the use of a two-path approach to teaching writing. In this parallel tracks approach, one track focuses on the writing process, while the second track is geared towards helping students develop the basic skills of writing. Five aspects of writing are presented—fluency, content, conventions, vocabulary, and syntax—and information on how to structure learning in each of these aspects is provided. Finally, some activities that you can use to motivate students and diversify your writing program are presented.

---

### CHAPTER TOPICS

Assessment of Written Language
Prewriting: Suggestions for Intervention
Teaching the Writing Process
Instructional Strategies
The Editing Stage: Towards the Final Draft
Publishing
Teaching Related Skills
Writing Activities

---

## ASSESSMENT OF WRITTEN LANGUAGE

Writing abilities can be assessed directly by both holistic (a general impression of the written product), and *atomistic* (direct countable measures of a single language feature) measures, and indirectly by norm-referenced tests. *Direct* assessments require writing samples from the students. *Indirect* assessments typically involve a series of multiple-choice, machine-scorable items. Norm-referenced tests are standardized on large groups of students and, in general, can be used to locate significant problem areas. However, the nature of standardized tests makes them insensitive to very specific gradual gains that occur as a result of instruction.

Norm-referenced tests are indirect in that, with few exceptions, they require recognition, not production, of correct writing conventions. The major limitation of indirect measures is the difficulty, if not impossibility, of measuring several aspects of composition by means of multiple-choice responses. In other words, multiple-choice tests measure students' ability to recognize standard English usage but not actual composition skills. Cooper and Odell (1977) argue that these standardized achievement tests measure only such editorial skills as choosing the best sentence and recognizing correct usage, punctuation, and capitalization, and do not judge the students' actual writing. In fact, little evidence suggests that there is a relationship between the multiple-choice editing and selecting skills measured by group standardized tests and the ability to write and edit one's own work (Grant, 1982; Poplin, 1983). The limitations of standardized tests have been succinctly stated by Salvia and Ysseldyke (1988): "Commercially prepared tests have doubtful validity for planning individual programs and evaluating the progress of individual pupils" (p. 411). Exhibit 12.1 provides a list of some commercial standardized tests and some of the specific aspects of the written product that they evaluate.

### Direct Measures

Direct product evaluation involves examining samples collected in natural settings, such as classroom assignments, or samples elicited specifically for assessment purposes. When employing direct product measurement, evaluators may choose between holistic or analytic scoring procedures (Moran, 1987).

Holistic assessment assigns values to a group of students' writing samples by determining the ranking of the students' work using a scale of 1–4 or 1–9 points and a set of predetermined criteria or standards. Assigning values to the writing samples yields a judgment of quality relative to other papers of the same group and is used as a quick method of determining which students fall below a minimum proficiency level and should, therefore,

**EXHIBIT 12.1.** Tests of written language

| Test | Publisher | Age Levels | Focus of Assessment |
|------|-----------|------------|---------------------|
| Picture Story Language Test | Western Psychological | 7–17 | Productivity, syntax, meaning |
| Iowa Test of Basic Skills | Riverside | 6–16 | Word usage, mechanics |
| Stanford Achievement Test—Hearing-Impaired | | 8–21 | Mechanics, grammatical structure |
| Metropolitan Achievement Tests | Harcourt Brace Jovanovich | 3.5–9.5 | Punctuation, capitalization, usage |
| California Achievement Test | McGraw-Hill | 5–21 | Mechanics, word usage, syntax, paragraph organization |
| Test of Written Language (TOWL) | Pro Ed | 7–18.11 | Word usage, punctuation, spelling, handwriting, capitalization, vocabulary, sentence production |
| Brigance Diagnostic Inventory of Basic Skills | Curriculum Associates | 5–13 | Vocabulary, handwriting, grammar, mechanics, spelling |

have beginning level instruction. A primary limitation of holistic evaluation centers on its inability to provide any information for instructional planning (Moran, 1987; White, E. 1984).

Analytic scoring, on the other hand, attempts to take into account discrete countable features of the written product. The advantage of the analytic scoring approach is that a complex task is rendered manageable so that teachable components can be isolated. Identified subskills then can be taught individually so that teachers and students do not have to try to deal with all of the aspects of a complex task simultaneously. The primary evaluation procedure presented in this chapter is of an analytical nature and is designed to help you evaluate and identify levels of performance in students' writing. The procedure is based on the work of Luckner and Isaacson (In press). The major advantage of this approach is that, if implemented thoughtfully, it can be a relatively efficient way to provide diagnostic information about the strengths and weaknesses of each student and can also provide you with specific direction for planning instruction and monitoring student progress (Mullis, 1984).

## An Informal Assessment Procedure

Five aspects of written products have been delineated by several researchers and writers as being essential components of the written product (Howell & Morehead, 1987; Isaacson, 1985; Isaacson & Luckner, 1988). They are:

*Fluency*: the number of words written
*Syntax*: complexity of sentences
*Vocabulary*: originality and maturity in the student's choice of words
*Content*: organization of thought, originality, and maturity of style
*Conventions*: the mechanical aspects of writing, such as grammar, spelling, and punctuation

The first task in conducting a written language assessment is to collect a sample of students' work that can be used to determine strengths and areas of concern. There are a number of ways in which you can obtain samples of written work. Whenever possible, it is best to allow students to choose a topic that they feel most comfortable writing about (Graves, 1983). It is in this way that students become interested in the subject, find their "voice," and enable their thoughts to flow more easily and in greater quantity. If students seem to be stuck, then you can discuss with them possible topics of interest or use a writing sample that the students have completed recently. A picture or series of pictures, a description of an age-appropriate situation, or a question can be used to suggest a topic. Since a student's prior knowledge and current interest in the topic are critical, it is important that you consider stimuli that require little previous experience or permit wide variations in experience.

After the sample has been collected, you should go through and evaluate the students' writing in each of the following areas (Isaacson, 1988; Luckner, 1989):

Fluency
Syntactic maturity
Vocabulary
Conventions
Content

*Fluency.* Fluency, the number of words written, is an indicator of maturity in written expression. More words are written as the student grows older (Deno, Marston, & Mirkin, 1982; Moss, Cole, & Khampalikit, 1982). Research has indicated that there is a significant correlation between fluency and other measures of writing skills (Daiute, 1984). Deno, Mirkin, and Wesson (1984) suggest that you obtain three writing samples in order to establish an individual baseline on fluency. Objectives are then set by estimating an average rate of increase for each individual student based on the student's current level of functioning.

| | |
|---|---|
| **METHOD:** | Count the total number of words written. |
| **EXAMPLE:** | An 8-year-old student writes compositions of 16, 12, and 20 words. Deno, Mirkin, and Wesson (1984) have suggested that it is best to use the median score (16) as the baseline score. |

| | |
|---|---|
| **CORRESPONDING OBJECTIVE:** | The student will write original compositions of _____ words or more. |

*Syntactic Maturity.* Skilled writers usually write longer and more complex sentences (Hunt, 1965; Morris & Crump, 1982). Assessing syntactic maturity requires measuring the degree to which a student uses expanded, more complex sentences. One way to judge syntactic maturity is to use terminable units, (T-unit). These are the shortest, grammatically complete segments that a passage can be divided into without creating fragments (Hunt, 1965). T-units may have subordinate clauses, phrases, or modifiers attached to or embedded within them. It is most conveniently conceptualized as a "thought unit." Any main clause, and all dependent clauses, comprise a thought unit.

### Example

> My sister loves cats. (1 T-unit)
> The parrot, with the yellow and green feathers, flew away early this morning. (1 T-unit)

In contrast, a compound sentence, however, is composed of two or more T-units, since either part can stand alone as a sentence.

### Example

> He likes soccer but prefers to play football.
> He likes soccer. (1 T-unit)
> (He) prefers to play football. (1 T-unit)

The T-unit has been used and advocated as a method of judging syntactic maturity by many writers and researchers (e.g., Hunt, 1977; Polloway & Smith, 1982). Increases in the mean length of T-units illustrate increases in syntactic maturity.

### Method

To calculate the mean length of a T-unit follow these procedures:

1.  Count the total number of words in the sample.
2.  Count the total number of T-units in the sample.
3.  Divide the total number of words by the total number of T-units. The quotient will be the mean length of T-unit.

### Example

I watched a very scary movie last night./ It was dark in our house/ and I did not like that./ So I turned on the light./

T-units = 4
Words = 26

**26 words**

4 T-units = 6.5 words / T-unit.

### Corresponding Objective

The student will increase sentence complexity to an average of _____ words per T-unit in original compositions.

*Vocabulary.*  Skilled writers use mature, interesting words and fewer commonplace, high-frequency words (Chatterjee, 1983; Deno, Marston, & Mirkin, 1982). You can assess a student's written vocabulary by judging the uniqueness or maturity of the words used in the composition (Isaacson, 1985). Using a list of the 100 most frequently used words (see Exhibit 12.2) as a reference, calculate the proportion of mature words. Lists are available for the 100 most common nouns, verbs, adjectives, and adverbs (Hillerich, 1978), which more sophisticated writers can use.

### Method

1.  Count the number of words in the composition that are not on the list of frequently used words.
2.  Divide by the total number of words.
3.  Multiply by 100 to get the percentage of mature words used.

### Example

Here is a quick example to help you see how this procedure is done.

Mary and I went shopping yesterday. We had a good time. While we were at the mall we saw a few friends and ate some popcorn. I think that we will go back there next Saturday.

Number of words not on the list of frequently used words = 11
Total number of words = 36
11/36 = .30 x 100 = 30 percent

### Corresponding Objective

The student will increase written vocabulary to a proportion of _____ mature words per composition.

*Conventions.*  "Good writing implies a knowledge of the conventions of the written code" (Rivers & Temperley, 1978, p. 264). Skilled writers are better at the mechanics of writing, such as spelling, punctuation, and correct verb endings (Videen, Deno, & Marston, 1982). Evaluations of student writing are influenced heavily by spelling, punctuation, handwriting, and grammatical errors (Graham, 1982). Videen, Deno, and Marston (1982) validated a quantitative measure of several convention factors that they referenced to as the Correct Word Sequence (CWS). Correct word sequences are two adjacent, correctly spelled words that are acceptable grammatically within the context of the phrase. In some instances, there are several ways to mark a sequence of words correct. When this occurs, you will need to decide what the intended meaning is, based on the surrounding written content. The surrounding content will need to be relied upon specifically to establish sentence tense and article usage. Therefore, each sequence should be scored as a part of the overall composition, not as an unrelated entity. Capitalization and punctuation also can be considered within the sequence.

To calculate the proportion of CWS in a writing sample do the following:

**EXHIBIT 12.2.** 100 most frequently used words

| | | |
|---|---|---|
| a | have | saw |
| about | he | school |
| after | her | see |
| all | here | she |
| am | him | so |
| an | his | some |
| and | home | that |
| are | house | the |
| as | how | their |
| at | I | them |
| back | if | then |
| because | in | there |
| but | is | they |
| by | it | this |
| came | just | time |
| can | like | to |
| come | little | two |
| could | make | up |
| day | me | us |
| dear | mother | very |
| did | my | was |
| do | not | we |
| down | now | well |
| for | of | went |
| friend | on | were |
| from | one | what |
| get | or | when |
| go | our | well |
| going | out | with |
| good | over | would |
| got | play | write |
| had | put | you |
| has | said | your |

SOURCE: From R. L. Hillerich, *A Writing Vocabulary of Elementary Children*, 2978. Courtesy of Charles C. Thomas, Publisher, Springfield, Illinois.

1. Place a caret (^) over every correct sequence between the two words that form the sequence.

2. Place an inverted caret (ˇ) under every incorrect sequence. Include inverted carets before and after misspelled words.

3. The first sequence is not comprised of two words but marks how the sentence was begun. (In the following example, the sentence beginning with the first word *the* is marked as an incorrect sequence because the "T" is not capitalized.) The last sequence is the last word before the punctuation mark. (*Example:* ˇthe ˇdog ˇlike ˇeat ˇmeet.) An omitted word makes the sequence between *like* and *eat* incorrect. The sequences on either side of the misspelled word are counted as incorrect.

4. Divide the number of correct word sequences by the total number of sequences (correct and incorrect), which gives the proportion of CWS. In the example, there is one correct and five incorrect sequences. Therefore, 1/6 gives us a proportion of 16 percent.

*Corresponding objective*: The student will increase his or her use of conventions to a proportion of _____ correct word sequences per composition.

**Content.** Skilled writers produce compositions that are rated higher in terms of the quality of ideas, awareness of audience, cohesiveness, and organization (Cooper, 1977; Robinson, 1984). In evaluation of written expression, the area of content has been acknowledged to be important and difficult to assess objectively (Hall, 1988; Moran, 1987). Beginning writers often lack strategies for generating or discarding ideas to the constraints of the writing task and for constructing discourse that conforms to accepted text structures (Scardamalia & Bereiter, 1986). The success with which writers manage these cognitive processes is evident in the unity, clarity, and coherence of the final composition. Several researchers and writers (e.g., Cartwright, 1969; Coop et al., 1983) have developed analytic scoring guides in order to address this area of writing. To assess content, therefore, we turn to the use of an analytic scale. Although this approach is not completely objective, it does provide foundational guidelines for the evaluation of content in writing.

### Method

Rate the student on the aspects of content using the scale. Total the score to calculate the final rating.

### Main Idea

3 = The main idea is clearly stated.
2 = The main idea is implied in the paragraph or may be indicated in the title.
1 = The main idea is not discernible.

### Supporting Details

3 = Two or more supporting details are evident, or one supporting detail is evident and has been expanded.
2 = One supporting detail is evident and has not been expanded.
1 = One or more details are evident but are not related to a main idea.

### Unity

4 = All sentences relate to the topic.
3 = More than half the sentences relate to the topic.
2 = At least one sentence relates to the topic.
1 = None of the sentences relate to the topic.

### Coherence

3 = All sentences flow logically.
2 = There is some evidence of cohesiveness.
1 = There is no evidence of cohesiveness; sentences are disjointed.

Total Score: _____

### Corresponding Objective

The student will improve the quality of his or her writing by achieving a score of _____ or better on his or her compositions when evaluated using the content evaluation sheet.

## Analyical Scoring Guides

Analytic scoring guides and checklists also can be used to evaluate students' writing skills. Scoring each writing sample involves making a number of passes through each paper in order to examine specific subskills. This procedure generally takes about 15 minutes per paper (Mishler & Hogan, 1982). Several instruments that you may find helpful include the Checklist of Written Expression Skills (Poteet, 1980) and the Tiedt Analytical Checklist for Compositions (Tiedt, 1983). A copy of the analytical scoring guide developed by Coop et al. (1983) can be found as Exhibit 12.3. In addition, Exhibit 12.4 provides a developmental scope-and-sequence list

**EXHIBIT 12.3.** Analytic scoring guide

_____ 1.  *Paragraph Format*

4 = The student has a title on the top line, has skipped a line between the title and body, has indented the first sentence, and has maintained adequate margins.

3 = The student has failed to perform one of the functions listed in the criteria for writing a paragraph.

2 = The student has failed to perform two of the functions listed in the criteria for writing a paragraph.

1 = The student has failed to perform three or more of the functions listed in the criteria for writing a paragraph *or* has simply listed sentences.

_____ 2.  *Main Idea*

3 = The main idea is clearly stated.

2 = The main idea is implied in the paragraph or may be indicated in the title.

1 = The main idea is not descernible.

_____ 3.  *Supporting Details*

3 = Two or more supporting details are evident, *or* one supporting detail is evident and has been expanded.

2 = One supporting detail is evident and has not been expanded.

1 = One or more details are evident but are not related to a main idea.

_____ 4.  *Unity*

4 = All sentences relate to topic.

3 = More than half the sentences related to the topic.

2 = At least one sentence relates to the topic.

1 = None of the sentences relate to the topic.

_____ 5.  *Coherence*

3 = All sentences flow logically.

2 = There is some evidence of cohesiveness.

1 = There is no evidence of cohesiveness; sentences are disjointed.

_____ 6.  *Sentence Structure*

4 = All sentences are complete.

3 = The student has written two or more sentences, and *only one* sentence is incomplete.

2 = The student has written two or more sentences; two or more, but not all of the sentences, are incomplete.

1 = The student has attempted one sentence and it is incomplete, *or* all sentences are incomplete.

_____ 7.  *Usage*

4 = There are no errors in usage.

3 = There is one error in usage.

2 = There are two to three errors in usage.

1 = There are four or more errors in usage.

*Check appropriate description:*

_____ Subject-verb agreement

_____ Verb forms

_____ Verb omissions

_____ 8.  *Mechanics* (Score is an average of capitalization, punctuation, and spelling)

_____ (Capitalization)

4 = The first word in every sentence and all proper nouns and "I" are capitalized, and no other words are capitalized.

3 = The first word in every sentence is capitalized, but there are *one or two* capitalization errors.

2 = The student has failed to capitalize or has inappropriately capitalized three or more words, which may include the first word in a sentence, or capitalization error(s) occur only in the first word of a sentence.

**EXHIBIT 12.3.** (Continued)

_____

1 = The student has failed to capitalize any words that require capitalization.

_____ (Punctuation)

4 = The student correctly uses end punctuation.

3 = The student writes two or more sentences and fails to put end punctuation on one sentence or uses the incorrect end punctuation.

2 = The student fails to put end punctuation on two or more sentences, or uses the incorrect end punctuation on two or more sentences, or writes only one sentence and fails to punctuate that sentence correctly.

1 = The student uses no end punctuation.

_____ (Spelling)

4 = All words are spelled correctly.

3 = One or two words are misspelled.

2 = Three or four words are misspelled.

1 = More than four words are misspelled.

Total score _____

---

**EXHIBIT 12.4.** (Adapted from Poplin, 1983) Developmental scope-and-sequence list to guide assessment and intervention of writing

1. Students observe others involved in written language activities.
2. Students begin to scribble and draw.
3. Students begin to differentiate drawing from writing and begin to "read" their scribbles to others.
4. Students request that adults write words or phrases for them.
5. Students begin to copy letters, words, or phrases.
6. Students attempt to write letters, words, or phrases on their own.
7. Students, using invented spellings, dictate more lengthy messages and stories.
9. Students, using invented spellings, continue to practice writing messages and stories.
10. Students continue to increase frequency and fluency of production and complexity of syntactic structures.
    a. Simple sentences are joined by connectors such as _and_, as well as present- and past-tense verb forms.
    b. Adjectives, adverbs, prepositional phrases, and conjunctions such as _because_ and although are introduced.
    c. Grammatical transformations are used to form _who_, or _what_ questions, conjunctions, indirect objects, and comparatives.
    d. Use of infinitives, gerunds, and participle structures are introduced.
    e. Use of clauses begins.
    f. Use of free modifiers begins.
11. Individuals continually use more complex vocabulary and express more abstract meaning.
12. Penmanship, punctuation, capitalization, and complexities of word usage gradually improve.
13. Writers spend more time writing, reading, reflecting, and editing.
14. Styles mature; whole products improve and mature.

that has been adapted from Poplin (1983), which can be used as a guide for the assessment and intervention of the writing abilities of hearing-impaired students.

## Using Assessment Data

The purpose of assessing writing is to gain diagnostic information that will enable you to plan appropriate instruction and to monitor student progress throughout the process of instruction. Teachers who work with hearing-impaired students must know how to assess accurately a student's written language skills and to write corresponding instructional objectives. Although holistic scoring and standardized tests have been used traditionally to evaluate written language abilities, they are not as useful to a classroom teacher as simple, direct measures using samples of the student's writing. Simple, direct measures can be used with each of the five product components: fluency, content, conventions, syntax, and vocabulary.

After completing the initial assessment of each student's writing, you should develop a list of specific skills that need to be targeted for remediation and introduction. You should list skills by priority in sequence for instructional planning. The most important skills should be taught first, and they should be the major instructional objectives on the student's individualized education program (IEP). Once a diagnostic assessment has been completed, you do not need to score every aspect of writing to monitor student progress. After the initial assessment, you only need to take data on the factors relevant to the student's objective(s). It is also important to note that marking a paper with a lot of red marks is not a wise practice. It is recommended that analytical notations be made on a xerox copy of the student's paper. Feedback should stress the positive aspects of the composition and limit itself to only one or two points of correction.

## PREWRITING: SUGGESTIONS FOR INTERVENTION

Early writing (printing) occurs in conjunction with early reading. Students move though various stages of writing, including scribbling, multiple letter use, reversals, filling a page, and so on, as they progress towards actual printing. There is thought to be no predictable sequence to these activities (Goelman, Oberg, & Smith, 1984; Shuy, 1981). Yet, utilizing various formats can serve several purposes (Conway, 1985):

To organize personal information (e.g., self-portraits, pictures of home, etc.)

To organize general information (e.g., names, alphabet, calendar cards)

To interact with a specific audience (e.g., letters delivered to school friends or sent to grandparents)

To entertain (e.g., One child draws a blob, saying "HOOHOH," which reads back as "hohoho" and say it is funny)

To practice skills (e.g., One child writes a lot of *ms*, *es*, and *rs*, to "work on letters")

To explore creative writing

Preschool is not the time for you to worry about the form of print. Rather, you should provide a time for drawing and writing so that the students can experiment and discover things. When a student attempts to convey a message with pictures, you should view them as transitions to words. You should attend to the function and meaning of what your students are trying to express through their work. Teachers need to utilize opportunities that occur in school routines to model various functions of literacy (e.g., completing attendance forms, recording milk money, making a list of needed supplies, etc.). You should encourage genuine reasons for reading and writing.

Giordiano (1984) has suggested that students make a pictorial outline as an activity that will assist them in producing more formal written products. In pictorial outlining, students record illustrations to remind them of an episode. Suppose a teacher and a group of children leave the classroom. They pass through the hallway, cross over the parking lot that surrounds the school building, walk around the block, and return. After they return, the teacher requests that the students individually draw three pictures, each of which will represent an incident that transpired while they were on their walk. If students have difficulty recalling experiences, they can make an illustration outline while they are participating in the activity. Exhibit 12.5 is an example of a pictorial outline. This outline tells a story of a student who left her second-story classroom, walked down a flight of stairs, and crossed over the parking lot. A large dog barked at her while she was walking around the block.

## TEACHING THE WRITING PROCESS

Current research on the teaching of writing suggests that there is a major shift in the instruction of written expression (Calkins, 1983; Graves, 1983). In the past, the focus was on the final product created by the student. Writing was assigned, corrected, and graded by the teacher, who paid particular attention to surface-level errors. The corrected paper was then returned to the student, and the student was expected to learn and improve writing skills from these grades and corrections. The result of this type of writing instruction was that most people learned to dislike writing.

In contrast, the recommended shift focuses on three aspects of writing: the *purpose*, the *process*, and the *product*. Therefore, your responsibility as a teacher of hearing-impaired students involves three components. The first is to structure opportunities for students to write for real audiences and across different purposes. The second is to establish a classroom environment that holds writing in high regard and works with students to actively be involved in the writing process. The third is to provide direct instruction on all aspects of the written product.

Most authors (Hayes & Flower, 1980; Isaacson & Luckner, 1988; Nold, 1981) agree to variations of a three-step model, which begins with a *planning* stage, includes a *writing* or a transcribing stage, and ends with a *rewriting* or revision stage. Writers do not move through each stage in a straight line that goes from planning to transcribing to revision, but, rather, they move back and forth through each of these subprocesses (Humes, 1983). Each of these components requires careful planning and instruction in order to ensure student success. Exhibit 12.6 provides a schematic depiction of the stages and the recursive process.

**EXHIBIT 12.5.** Sample of an Illustration Outline

**EXHIBIT 12.6.** The writing process

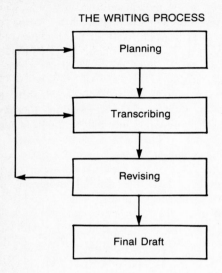

THE WRITING PROCESS

## Planning

In the planning process, writers form an internal representation of the knowledge that will be used in writing. Planning involves a number of subprocesses, the most obvious of which is the act of generating ideas. You can help students by providing time and suggesting ways in which they can activate these processes before pencil touches paper. Initially, you can help the students discover interests, narrow the topic, and develop a flexible writing plan. Discussing the subject, exchanging parallel experiences, observing objects and events, jotting down descriptive words that apply, outlining, and mapping key words and thoughts help to generate and shape substance and suggest structural possibilities. The visualizations that appear in Chapter 6 could be useful in stimulating organizational strategies for writing.

Graves (1983) recommended a series of short (three-minute) topic conferences in which students choose their own topic. You ask *open-ended questions* about their ideas and experiences. The first conference should not include writing and should focus solely on the students' ideas rather than on a rough draft or written outline.

The act of goal setting is another important part of the planning process. It provides the structure from which the writer will operate. This goal setting is addressed in two ways. First, it is procedural and helps the writer to plan the steps that are going to be followed throughout the writing task. Second, there is a product goal that focuses attention on the length of the product, the timelines for its completion, and the audience for whom the product is geared and with whom it will be shared.

## Transcribing

The act of transcription entails the transformation of relevant information, under the guidance of a writing plan, into written English. Just as students learn to read by reading, so they learn to write by writing. As important as practice is to learning to write, the act of writing, in and of itself, does not necessarily improve writing quality (Graham, 1982). The careful development of a limited number of papers under your guidance is better than independent production of many frequent compositions (Glatthorn, 1981). It is important for you to encourage students to focus initially on ideas rather than on mechanics, so that they will first feel comfortable with writing before they try to achieve perfection with mechanical skills.

The students need feedback on their work. Helpful responses come during, not after, the composing. These are possible both from peers and from you, who consistently models the kind of thoughtful, appropriate restatements and questions that help the students reflect on and rethink the content of their writing. Teaching students how to read and respond to a piece of writing in progress is one of your central tasks (Perl, 1983). Robinson (1984) found that probing (i.e, asking the student from six to seven questions about the passage being written) improves significantly the quality of written expository tasks.

## Reviewing and Revising

The function of the third process, reviewing and revising, is to improve the quality of the material written. Students must be taught specific steps to follow in reviewing their own written work samples in order to develop a positive concept of reviewing. Revision is a thinking process that can occur at any time that the students choose to evaluate or revise their text or plans. These periods of reviewing frequently lead to new cycles of planning and composing. Because students are least experienced and comfortable with revision, they need more help with this than with other phases of the composing process.

To improve students' revision skills, you will have to adopt a role of a working editor who is responding to drafts in progress rather than that of a grader who is looking for mistakes. The traditional practice of marking every error on students' papers often does more harm than good. It is discouraging to the students and too much for them to deal with at one time. A more effective practice is *selective feedback*. By identifying one or two specific target areas, you should provide correction only for those aspects of the composition (Graham, 1982). Another point to remember is that not all writing needs to be taken through the revising stage. Permit students to set aside occasional pieces of writing that they do not want to carry through to a finished product.

## Final Draft

The final draft is the students' last attempt at improving their compositions. This does not mean that the product is error-free. In fact, for many students it will contain some grammatical errors, syntactical mistakes, or misspelled words. What the final draft does mean is that the students no longer want to work on the piece and that they either want to put it away for a while or have it published (which is discussed in detail later in the chapter).

The point is that we want students to feel proud of the work that they have created. In doing so, we have to view the writing process as just that, a process. Only through multiple opportunities to write will students improve their skills and develop an appreciation for the joys of written communication. Within this process approach, students will complete a final draft of one piece, return to revise an old piece, and simultaneously begin planning a new piece.

## INSTRUCTIONAL STRATEGIES

### Planning Instruction

Graves' (1983) research revealed that students think of themselves as authors when they are consistently engaged in writing. Writers need regular chunks of time—time to think, write, confer, and write some more; they need time on which they can depend. Writing once a week does not allow students to feel like authors and fosters an overreliance on the teacher to suggest topics. However, when they are writing daily, students learn to think independently about writing and are able to explore self-selected topics (Dahl, 1985).

Allocated writing time allows students to get in touch with their personal world of interests, experiences, and adventures as sources of material for their writing. We recommend that students write at least four times per week for 30-minute periods. However, the importance of short assignments when students are first beginning to write cannot be overstated. By presenting students with lengthy tasks or by setting aside an inordinate amount of time for them to write, you may inadvertently create an association in the students' mind between writing and boredom, thus generating disinterest and destroying the purpose of the assignment. You can structure time for writing by integrating it into related areas (e.g., reading, handwriting, spelling, and language). Writing produces gains in all of these subject areas (Graves, 1983).

In addition to planning time for writing, you should provide opportunities for students to write for different purposes. Britton (1978) believed that the starting point for developing content should be expressive writing that focuses on the writer's experiences and feeling. A comprehensive curriculum, however, requires that writing include attention to each of the areas of narration, description, exposition, and persuasion. Therefore, hearing-impaired students should receive specific instruction and opportunities to write personal and business letters, biographical sketches, directions, book reports, cartoon strips, creative writing, editorials, and scripts for a class play.

## Establishing a Writing Climate

An appropriate climate for writing includes a teacher who has an open and friendly, rather than rigid, demeanor about writing activities. Student motivation can be developed if the teacher shows a basic interest and respect for students' expression, by establishing a real purpose to writing, and by endowing writing with a special sense of importance and enjoyment. Interest is increased through an accurate assessment of the students' current level of functioning and the provision of tasks geared to the students' present skill level. Assisting students in identifying their personal interests and structuring a writing program that capitalizes on these interests is essential.

Students need to take risks when they write in order to improve their present level of writing. Graves (1983) contended that there are some specific teacher behaviors that stifle student development. They include:

1. An overabundance of attention to mechanics at the expense of information
2. A lack of understanding of the writing process; a teacher who attends only to the finished product
3. Providing students with a general response on their papers that is limited to one or two words, such as "Good" or "Rewrite"

## Motivating Students

Keep in mind that a strong relationship exists between the quantity of input experiences and the quality of output in the form of writing (Lerner, 1985). You should provide rich input experiences, such as trips, stories, discussions, and visual stimuli so that students can develop an interest in a topic as well as a degree of familiarity or the experience necessary to desire to communicate about it. Research has indicated the importance of familiarity of topic and text in working with hearing-impaired students (Gormley, 1981). Writers with very little knowledge about a topic tend to produce descriptive sequences that lack logical coherence (Stein, 1983).

## Providing Structure

Create a classroom atmosphere that provides students with a consistent structure for writing. It is important to establish a place where paper, pencils, and crayons can be found. Students can be supplied with manila folders to hold all of their writing samples. Inside the folder, they can record the nature of the writing task, the dates that it was undertaken and completed, and comments by peers and by you about weaknesses to be addressed and strengths to be maintained. You can keep a record of skills that students master on one side of their writing folder. All of the writing folders can be kept in one box, from which students can retrieve and return them as needed. Also, an initial discussion and agreement of rules should be undertaken that gives students guidance as to what to do if they cannot spell a word, are stuck for a topic, do not know what to say next, or do not know what to do if they are finished writing for the day.

## Providing Models

Models of good writing are important in providing students with opportunities to examine the structure of written language (Ewoldt, 1985). Models also provide positive examples of appropriate styles and text structures. Selections from children's books and magazines, autobiographies of Deaf adults, or your own writing can serve as models. More important than models of written language are *process* models. The process that is modeled should begin with the planning stage. You can share with students some topics of personal interest. Then, narrow the list down to one. Jot down words and phrases, and add necessary information. You should also model operations of composition to demonstrate the translation of idea material, outlines, or patterned notes into acceptable written sentences. You can model self-instructions by "thinking aloud" while performing the task. Finally, you should model reviewing and revising strategies.

## Conferencing

To progress as writers, hearing-impaired students need to pursue goals that are slightly beyond their current capabilities. One procedure that has been used to help young writers carry out more sophisticated composing processes is conferencing (Graham & Harris, 1988; Graves, 1983). During conferences, teachers act as collaborators, giving hints and prompts on what to say or do. During the conference, it is important to set an atmosphere in which the student does most of the communicating. Let the student provide the lead during the conference. Ask the student what the story is about. Give the student some time to formulate a response prior to your beginning to ask for answers. Ask questions that follow what the student has said or reflect back on what has been shared with you. In addition, you can ask process questions that will help the student extend his or her thinking. Such a question may be phrased as, "What do you think you'll do next?" or "What other information can you add to this?" When going over the student's work, you should point out the student's strengths before noting any weaknesses. Find something positive to say, whether it be about the choice of topic, the vivid details, or the selection of words. Then, depending on the writing skill being looked at during the con-

ference, you can focus on the difficulties that the student is having with that skill and suggest solutions.

Graves (1983) contended that a conference should adhere to specific characteristics. These include:

1. *Predictability*. The student should be able to predict most of what will happen during the conference, including the conference setting, the timing, and the structure. The most important component of this predictability, though, is your interest in the student and the student's writing.

2. *Focus*. You should not center attention on more than one or two features of the student's writing. Three factors should guide your interaction with the student: the intention, the frequency of the targeted skill, and the place of the writer in the draft. A sequence that may be used during conferences is focus on questions that help discover the subject during the first conference; attend to the organization of the story during the second; and focus on one or two mechanical errors during the third.

3. *Demonstrated solutions*. You need to show what you mean rather than tell the student what to do. You can show how this is done by using a story that you are writing and showing a student how you move information, rewrite endings, insert information, or change terms. This can also be done by forming a small group of students who are having similar problems and demonstrating to them how to make changes. (Use an example that you have developed or one of the students' papers.)

4. *Reversible roles*. Students should be free to initiate questions and comments and demonstrate their own solutions. An important component of reversing roles is allowing enough waiting time for students to respond or rephrasing a question for them.

5. *Playful structure*. There should be a combination of experimentation, discovery, and humor. Writing should not be viewed as a grueling task that avoids error at all costs but, rather, as a joyful pursuit that helps the writer communicate what he or she desires to share with others.

Keeping conference records is another vital component to a good writing program. After each individual conference, make an entry into a writing notebook. Include information such as the title and content of the story that the student is working on, what skills need to be reinforced or need direct teaching, and a summarizing statement about how the conference went.

## Peer Interaction

Peer interaction can be used as a way for students to share their written work and to provide and receive helpful criticism (Johnson, 1988). Students can share the topics that they have decided on in small groups or pairs, discuss some of the problems that they are having writing, or read parts of what they have written. Another option is to have students exchange papers with a partner and complete the evaluation for homework. When reviewing a student's piece in a group setting, you should establish a structure in which peers first give compliments about the composition, focusing on specific strengths. After a round of positive compliments, the group can ask questions about things that were unclear to them and make suggestions about how to revise the composition. Writers also can identify trouble spots and ask the group for some assistance. Johnson (1988) suggests that initially you lead the questioning process to direct the students' responses. Such questions as, "Which part did you like best?" "Was there anything more that you wanted to know?" "What would you like to ask the author?" help to phrase the questions in a positive manner. A guide that can be used for

comments and suggestions can be displayed to aid in the transition towards asking good questions themselves. Such a chart was presented by Johnson (1988):

1. How does the writing make me feel?
2. Can I identify with the characters? Have I had a similar experience?
3. What do I especially like about this topic?
4. What else would I like to know about this paper?
5. Was anything in this paper unclear or confusing?

With peer interaction, students write for a real audience, and their work receives more immediate, concentrated, and energetic feedback than an individual teacher could provide.

## Working with Parents

Some parents may not understand your view of the writing process or your acceptance of student errors. Parents need to be shown how your students are improving in order to gain an understanding of how you could publish a piece of writing that is not grammatically error-free. Making use of the students' writing files is one way of demonstrating progress. An additional method to facilitate this understanding is to invite parents to come in to school and observe various components of your writing program, which will allow them to see the writing process in action, as well as the educational benefits of your writing program.

## Use of Word Processors

The environment for effective writing also requires an adequate supply of reference material and equipment, from dictionaries and high-interest reading books to typewriters and word processors. Word processor programs not only remove a lot of drudgery from revising, editing, and proofreading but also provide students with an opportunity to practice writing in situations that they will increasingly find in the world of work. Word processing allows the writer to quickly and easily type over what has previously been typed, to insert new text within the old, to erase sections, and to print a final copy that is legible and professional looking. Teachers report that students who use word processors for the various stages of writing have an improved attitude towards  writing in general, tend to make more revisions, write longer papers, and pay more attention to detail (Smith, 1985).

## THE EDITING STAGE: TOWARD THE FINAL DRAFT

It is important to help students become editors of their own work. Concomitantly, you should not take on the responsibility of trying to make a perfect product for them. If something that they have written is not clear to you, then they need to be informed of this. However, it is not possible or desirable to correct everything. A common instructional practice that should be avoided is overemphasizing student errors. As stated earlier, when you are examining students' compositions, only one or two types of errors should be pinpointed at any one time. Furthermore, priority should be given to errors that occur frequently and that obstruct the reader's understanding of the text.

Spelling and handwriting are subjects that must be taken into consideration when you are working with the students' writing. If their handwriting has a poor appearance or there are multiple spelling errors, the writing will not be judged well. However, handwriting and spelling should not be emphasized at the expense of content (Graham & Harris, 1988). You will want to help students gain experience in speculating which words are spelled incorrectly. If they are having difficulty trying to figure out which words may be misspelled, you may want to provide some more specific information. For example, you could say, "There are six words that are spelled wrong. I want you to circle the six that you think may be incorrect" and then go over the words together. Students also can maintain a list of high-frequency words that writers often misspell. In addition, you can teach students to put boxes around places where punctuation may be needed: Students place punctuation marks where they know that punctuation should go and then put boxes where they are not sure.

In order to provide feedback throughout the writing process, it is best to collect drafts and scribble reactions, questions, and suggestions. When papers are returned to students, you should discuss the targeted problems and reteach those items in which the students are deficient. You cannot assume that marking errors will enable students to understand why improvement is needed. Students often need direct instruction in order to correct their errors. Another technique that can be used during the editing phase is for you and the student to edit a piece of writing by using a plastic overlay and marker. After the two of you have agreed on some essential changes, the student can then go back to his or her desk and make the changes on his or her own hard copy.

One additional technique that can be used to help students overcome their resistance to revising is to make first drafts different from the completed product. One method for doing this is to use colored paper for first drafts (Raphael, Kirschner, & Englert, 1986). Students can be instructed to write on every other line, leaving a space between lines to make corrections and insertions. Another approach is to have students compose their first draft by writing each sentence on a separate slip of paper (Crealock et al., 1985). After a conference, the sentence strips can be taped to a larger sheet of paper and space can be left between each sentence in order that additional changes can be made. When the students feel that their papers have been revised and edited and are ready for the final draft, then they can make their final copy.

## PUBLISHING

Providing a designated audience for writing transforms a required exercise into a purposeful activity. Having students work on their product until the best possible paper emerges deserves an outlet and recognition that goes beyond a grade. Rather than reserving publishing for only the best writers, it should the experience of every writer (Dahl, 1985). Within two to three weeks of first working with writing, it is desirable for every student to have some type of publication. This provides students with a sense of accomplishment and evidences progress to be shared with parents. By posting papers on bulletin boards, sharing them with class members to read, giving them to students in lower grades to read and discuss, making booklets to circulate around school, sending them home for parents to read, submitting them to the school paper for publication, producing a class literary magazine to be distributed, or sending them for publication in an age-appropriate periodical, students become recognized for their writing and are motivated to continue to improve.

After a student publishes his or her writing, you can establish a section of the bulletin board that has been designated "Author of the Week." In this area, a student author displays his or her work (and possibly some first drafts) for others to see. In addition, a picture of the student can accompany the work. As the school year continues, you can add to this display by posting a list of other pieces that the student has written, as well as the picture of his or her latest piece.

## TEACHING RELATED SKILLS

A writing program should address all aspects of the written product as it evolves through each stage of the writing process. Skilled writers are not judged by the process that they use but, rather, by the good composi-

tions that they produce. Therefore, in addition to establishing a writing studio in your classroom, students will need direct instruction in the five aspects of the written product (fluency, content, vocabulary, syntax, and conventions). This approach, which is the development of parallel skills—concept development pertaining to the process of writing and basic writing skills necessary for an unacceptable product—taught *concurrently* rather than sequentially is advocated by various researchers and writers (Roit & McKenzie, 1985; McAnally, Rose, & Quigley, 1987; Schloss & Sedlak, 1986; Wallace, Cohen, & Polloway, 1987).

Exercises should be used regularly for short periods of time in conjunction with time allotted for writing. As students develop an understanding of each of these skills, they should be shown how and when to apply them to specific writing that they are undertaking. Examples of some specific activities that can be undertaken to promote development in each of the areas that we have studied in this chapter's discussion of assessment are provided. Bear in mind that these are only examples. Your own imagination and knowledge of your students' needs and interests will provide ideas for you to use.

### Fluency

Your first goal is the aspect of fluency. This entails helping students write simple sentences and elaborate their thoughts into compositions of gradually increasing length. Students' first writing attempts may only consist of scribbling or labeling the people or objects portrayed in their drawings (Dyson, 1982). In fact, it may be necessary for you to begin this process by having students dictate ideas and stories to you that you read together. To encourage fluency, many teachers recommend "free writing"—a technique in which a writer sets down the words, phrases, and sentences suggested by a topic in a continuous stream, uninterrupted by attention to mechanical or grammatical errors.

Beginning fluency also develops as students write simple messages to each other and the teacher, reinforcing the function of written communication. The importance and effectiveness of practicing these initial skills with hearing-impaired students have been expressed by Blackwell et al. (1978) and Ewoldt (1985). One technique that can be used to foster this exchange of writing is to put a mailbox in your room and on a daily basis exchange messages to each other.

Alvarez (1983) suggests an activity that has students writing for an allotted amount of time and counting the number of words that have been written in sentence form. The total number of words are counted and placed at the top of the page and then plotted on an individual graph by the students themselves. It is important that students know that they are not competing with their classmates, but only with themselves. Students are not penalized for errors in spelling, grammar, or sentence structure. You can spell any word for the students that they ask or write it on the chalkboard. For the purposes of this activity, students can write on a topic of their choice or you could provide them with open-ended topics such as, "If I were a fish. . . .," "If I were a flower. . . .," or "If I were a teacher. . . ." Research has demonstrated that students can significantly increase the total number of words in their compositions through the use of social recognition, data collection, and public display based on the number of words that they wrote (Van Houten, Morrison, Jarvis, & MacDonald, 1974).

Other activities for increasing fluency that have been suggested by Klansek (1983) include the following: making inventories and lists of things, such as classroom objects or street signs that you pass while on a class trip; using scrapbooks of students in class or school or famous people such as sports stars, movie stars, or politicians; keeping a class diary or a ledger of current events; arranging for pen pals with other classrooms or schools; and writing captions for cartoons or pictures.

Dialogue journals (discussed later in this chapter) also have been a popular instructional tool that can be used to promote a positive attitude about writing and to increase fluency. Information about the use of dialogue journals can be found in the "Writing Activities" section of this chapter.

## Syntax

Sentence syntax can be taught to beginning writers through sentence maps or patterned guides, such as *Sentences and Other Systems* (Blackwell et al., 1978), *Apple Tree* (Anderson et al., 1980), the *SIMS Written Language Program* (Minneapolis Public Schools, 1977), or the *Phelps Sentence Guide Program* (Phelps-Terasaki & Phelps, 1980). Research reported by Akamatsu and Armour (1987) indicates that having hearing-impaired students transcribe videotapes of short, signed passages in English word order can improve their understanding of syntactic word order. Scrambling sentences is another technique that can be used to assist students in developing an understanding of proper word order. This activity can be done with sentences from students' writing or from content material in other subject areas. Sentence-combining exercises are also an effective way to increase students' syntactic maturity. The purpose of sentence-combining exercises is to make students more conscious of the transformational choices available to them for expressing their ideas (Mellon, 1981). Nutter and Safran (1984) reported that the use of sentence-combining exercises with students in grades one through nine resulted in definite gains in the syntactic maturity of their writing. An example of a simple sentence-combining exercise would be:

The girls are busy.
The girls are making popcorn.
The girls are busy making popcorn.

Cooper (1973) has devised a systematic outline to help teachers write their own exercises, and Perron (1976) describes a number of sentence-combining games and activities that can be used with elementary school students.

## Vocabulary

The primary objective of instruction in vocabulary is to expand the lexical options available to students. Such expansion should include efforts to increase the variety of words used while enhancing the complexity and descriptiveness of their writing. Since vocabulary is woven into every phase of our lives, new words can be drawn from any aspect of the students' experience: television, sports, newspaper, advertising, science, and so on. Having students develop a new word book to which they add new words daily is a technique that can be used to address this problem. In addition, you can teach synonyms for overused words, using the procedures presented in the reading vocabulary section. Synonym and antonym charts can be hung in the room for reference during writing periods. Mercer and Mercer (1985) recommend giving students a short passage in which several words are underlined. You then ask the students to substitute the underlined word for a more colorful or interesting word or phrase. The cloze method that was discussed in the preceding chapter also can be used to foster vocabulary development. As we suggested in the fluency section, students can be reinforced through recognition and data display to increase significantly the number of new and different words (Brigham, Graubard, & Stans, 1972) and different adjectives and action words used (Maloney & Hopkins 1973).

Students also can be taught to develop and use attribute guides such as the one that follows, which has been adapted from Alley and Deshler (1979) for describing objects, places, and people.

### Object to be described

Color:
Shape:
Height:
Weight:
Feel:
Temperature:
Movement:
Smell:
Taste:

Such a guide structures students' observations and directs their attention to salient features. To use the guide, students first record details relevant to the dimensions that are presented on the attribute guide. Then the dimensions and the related details are used as a framework for writing the text. You can train students in using the guide by modeling its use, assisting students in completing one, and guiding them to use it independently (Stewart, 1985). After your students have become skilled at using teacher-made guides, they should be taught to make their own. This helps them to develop self-questioning skills that are essential for becoming skilled writers.

## Content

One of the basic rules for writing appropriate compositions is that the writer of the message must provide enough information for the reader of the message to understand what is being conveyed. *Content* refers to the ideas, concepts, and overall integrity of the written product (Wallace, Cohen, & Polloway, 1987). It is essential that writing instruction focus on content and organization, because, once the content of the paper is appropriate, then its form can be improved; the opposite is not necessarily true (Stewart, 1985). As we mentioned earlier, peer evaluation is an extremely valuable technique. Perl (1983) recommended an "active listening" procedure, whereby one student would respond to another's shared composition by paraphrasing what he or she thought the author intended to communicate. The listener's interpretation helps the author evaluate his or her writing and make necessary revisions to accommodate the audience. Students also can exchange their papers and indicate to each other where clarification or more information is needed.

An activity that can be used to promote an understanding of developing main ideas with supporting statements is presenting students with mixed-up literary passages or pieces that have been written by their classmates. The students must arrange the sentences in logical order. Also, students may be given a topic sentence and a closing sentence and asked to write two detailed sentences that would form a paragraph. Another way to help students to organize the sequence of events or actions is to use a flow diagram (Exhibit 12.7). The flow diagram is useful because it provides students with a simplified structure within which they can organize their thoughts by using the visual diagram as

a memory aid throughout the transcribing stage.

## Conventions

Spelling, punctuation, correct word usage, and handwriting are the writing factors most frequently taught: They are also factors that should be approached most cautiously in the context of composition. This is not to say that you should not teach spelling, punctuation, and handwriting; they are among the factors that most influence judgments of quality (Brown, 1981). Initially, however, they should be taught separately, on a parallel track, and not interfere with or discourage beginning writers in their composition attempts.

During composition, the mechanical concerns should not compete with ideas for the writer's attention. As fluency develops, conventions should be introduced as an editing task. Editing for writing conventions should begin with structured materials provided by the teacher and then, as editing skills become proficient, applied to the student's own work in the reviewing and evaluating stage. The use of an editing checklist, such as the one developed by Schumacher et al. (1981) can be developed and introduced to help students through this arduous process:

**EXHIBIT 12.7.** Sample flow diagram for building a bird house

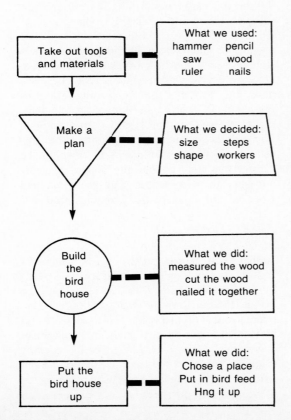

1. Read each sentence separately.
2. Ask yourself the "COPS" questions:
   a. C Have I capitalized the first word and proper names?
   b. O How is the overall appearance (spacing, neatness, complete sentences)?
   c. P Have I put in commas and end punctuation?
   d. S Have I spelled all the words correctly?
3. When you find an error, circle it and put the correct form above the error if you know the correct form.
4. Ask for help if you are unsure of the correct form.
5. Reread the story as a final check.

## WRITING ACTIVITIES

### Question Sets

You can devise a set of questions so that the students' responses to these questions are an outline. The simplest type of questions to generate are ones that reflect narrative elements. Some questions should be open-ended. Questions may have to be written out with specificity at first, but later an abbreviated set of questions can be substituted. If the students have difficulty sorting out the key and incidental information, you should structure an incident about which they will write, such as a film, and supply them with the outline before the viewing of the film. You should ask the students to respond to only one type of question, such as a question about characters, if the task is too complex. You can add another question about a different narrative element as students become adept at responding to the one type of question.

### Question Generation

Question generation can be a suitable exercise with which to proceed from question set outlining (see example below). Instead of responding to an organized group of questions, students *create* the questions. Eventually, students may be able to form question sets based on narrative elements or a taxonomy of question types. However, a method of forming questions that is simpler than question sets is likely to be needed initially. As they attempt to write about an incident, students make a list of questions that they can answer in their written messages. Some examples of question sets are:

> Who is the main character?
> Where was Little Red Riding Hood going?
> Why was she going there?
> What happened at grandma's house?

### Interviewing

An activity presented by Graves (1983) that can be fun as well as very meaningful is to structure interviews with classroom visitors.

This procedure helps students learn to develop questions and to take those questions and produce a piece of writing from them. The object of this activity is for the students to find out as much as they can about the visitors and about their interests. The interviews can be done individually or in small groups. After the interview has been completed, the students then write their stories about the visitors. To help structure this learning opportunity, visitors should be asked to adhere to two guidelines: (1) Only provide information based on the questions that will be asked, and (2) observe a 10-minute time allotment.

### Collaborative Writing

Collaborative writing is another method that can be used to enhance students' writing skills. Collaborative writing restructures the writing process, transforming it from an individual activity into a shared, cooperative experience. In peer collaboration, students become coauthors of a shared product. When students share the task of planning, composing, and revising a piece of writing, they see how other students use the writing strategies presented in class. In this way, students model the writing process for one another. The process encourages students to communicate about writing itself, as well as about the subject that they are writing about. Students are able to share ideas and problems and work towards a mutually satisfying product.

### Dialogue Journals

As has been seen in other areas of communication, students acquire and learn new skills by performing them with more experienced people (Staton, 1985). Dialogue journals are interactive, written conversations carried out by students and their teacher frequently and continuously over an extended period of time (Staton, 1985). They permit writing about real life, with a real audience. They provide the opportunity for students to state ideas and describe events. Dialogue journals are more like face-to-face conversations than formal writing assignments. Yet, they provide practice in the three levels of language: the surface forms, the syntactical rules of transforming word meanings into comprehensible statements, and the deep structure or semantic level (Staton, 1980). Another benefit of using dialogue journals is that they provide an avenue for teachers to model sentence structure, introduce and reinforce vocabulary, and expand concepts when responding to students' writing.

To begin using dialogue journals, give each student a personalized notebook to be used exclusively as a private journal. At least once a day, each student writes a message to you in the journal. By the next day, you respond to each student in writing and return the dialogue journal to the students. The students read your comments and write another entry to continue the dialogue. Abrams (1987) provides some guidelines that you can use: She encourages teachers to

1. Use natural, conversational language.
2. Do not write in letter format.
3. Make your entries about as long as the students'.
4. Respond directly to the students' entries.
5. Share your personal feelings and experiences.
6. Be as honest as possible.
7. Whenever possible, allow students to introduce most of the topics.

According to Staton (1985, p. 132), dialogue journals are defined by the following characteristics:

1. Writers are free to express their own purposes and to communicate about real concerns and issues, introducing their own topics and commenting on another's topics.
2. There is a focus on meaning and on understanding rather than on correct form. Unclear statements require clarifying questions or statements rather than correction.
3. The communication between writers is kept private.
4. There is a time period for reading and writing prior to responding.
5. The communication exchange is kept in a tangible form, such as a bound notebook, that is portable and accessible to both parties.

We would add that you should aim your responses at a level slightly above that of the students in the areas of English content and form.

Dialogue journals have been used with hearing-impaired students of all ages. The reports by both teachers and the students themselves (Staton, 1985) consistently are favorable. One of the by-products of using dialogue journals is that they allow you to have an active interchange with your students. This avenue permits you to gain an understanding of the interests of students and to get to know each other in a very direct way. If students are reluctant to start a dialogue journal, graffiti boards, note writing to peers, and the writing of cartoon captions are techniques that might get them started (Giordiano, 1984). Another valuable resource for helping you to structure a dialogue journal program in your class is *It's Your Turn Now* by Bailes et al. (1986).

An alternative to using dialogue journals has been presented by Mettler and Conway (1988). They have reported about a program that used dialogue journals between two students and the teacher. The students wrote to each other on a daily basis about books that they were reading outside of class. The role of the teacher shifted to that of a monitor—clarifying terms, expanding concepts, and praising their efforts. The authors reported positive gains with the program and have expanded the use of journal writing to other subject areas, such as history. The students took the roles of early American settlers and kept a journal incorporating the locations, dates, and events of that period but presented them through their own feelings and opinions. This type of activity could be integrated into many other content areas.

## SUMMARY

For many hearing-impaired persons, acquiring a reasonable degree of facility in written language may contribute substantially to self-sufficiency and independence in the community, vocational flexibility, and success in higher education.

Assessment is an essential part of a writing program. In this chapter, several different ways to assess students' writing have been described. One method is to use standardized tests, which tend to use an indirect approach to assessment, whereby students are asked to edit material rather than to compose their own. A second method, referred to as a *direct measure*, involves collecting writing samples from students and then analyzing them. Some of the different procedures that can be used to examine students' writing directly include an informal procedure that looks at the five aspects of the written product, an analytical scoring guide, and a developmental scope-and-sequence chart.

If written English is to be a meaningful, useful form of communication for hearing-impaired students, they must experience it as being a representation of their thoughts and those of others and as a practical tool for communicating (Dahl, 1985). Students learn about writing by writing (Calkins, 1986; Graves, 1983). However, simply having students write will not result in improved writing performance (Graham, 1982). The development of writing skills is not only dependent on the opportunity to write but also requires motivation, properly designed and sequenced instruction, and guidance and practice in developing relevant skills and strategies (Graham & Harris, 1988). The traditional pedagogy of (1) select the topic, (2) correct

the error, and (3) expect improvement is still widely practiced today. In contrast, the process approach to writing emphasizes a high degree of student involvement, attention to planning in the prewriting stage, direct instruction in the skills of writing, and assistance in writing through direct coaching. Proponents of this method regard writing as an ongoing, multistage process in which equal emphasis is given to each of the stages.

As stated by Graves (1983), "Teaching writing well is no different than teaching any other subject. The teacher has to know the subject, the process, the students, and the means for the children to become independent learners" (p. 11). The cornerstone of promoting good writers is to establish an environment that builds students' confidence, provides instruction in specific skill areas, and assists students in understanding how the process of written communication works.

## ACTIVITIES

1.  Ask a preschool teacher to save you 20 samples of his or her students' drawing and writing. Write a paper discussing the samples with regard to the information provided by Conway (1985) concerning why children write, which was presented in this chapter.
2.  To practice the principles of using dialogue journals, obtain an elementary school pen pal. Respond to each letter as you would to a journal entry.
3.  Teach an elementary school student to outline by using four of the strategies discussed in this chapter. Discuss the results in a short paper.
4.  Acquire a writing sample from an elementary school student and assess his or her writing skills in several ways as discussed in this chapter. Set instructional objectives for the student.
5.  Teach a peer a related skill (as presented in this chapter). Evaluate your lesson.
6.  Write a short story about a personal experience. Using your story and the technique of modeling, plan a lesson for teaching the writing process to a group of students.

# CHAPTER 13

# Math and Science

## OVERVIEW

Both math and science research and intervention have been labeled repeatedly as neglected areas in the education of hearing-impaired students (Bunch, 1987; Fridriksson & Stewart, 1988). In an effort to effect positive change in all curriculum areas, material is presented in this chapter with regard to assessment and the scope-and-sequence of these two areas. While the content of these subject areas does not differ greatly among hearing and hearing-impaired students, we have chosen them to exemplify curricular considerations in general for hearing-impaired students. We remind you that the principles underscored in the chapter on effective instruction (see Chapter 10) and in this chapter would be relevant in the teaching of social studies, history, art, Deaf culture, physical education, or any communication area, that is part of your school's curriculum. We believe, as well, that the ability to communicate proficiently in the language or system that functions as the students "first language" is a critical skill in teaching subjects effectively.

There are a number of factors that have hindered learning in academic areas (from Fridriksson & Stewart, 1988, unless otherwise indicated) that you will need to face and seek to overcome when you work with hearing-impaired students.

The heterogeneity of academic and communication abilities in classes of hearing-impaired students

The need to individualize when working with students

The lack of resources and materials

A focus on the teaching of speech rather than school subjects (Watts, 1979)

Teachers who possess neither the appropriate knowledge of the content nor the confidence to teach it (Johnson, 1977)

A focus on paper-and-pencil learning rather than on hands-on experiences and use of physical capabilities (Silvia, 1983)

Language difficulties that interfere with comprehension of higher-level thinking skills (Watts, 1979)

Lack of specific signs to encode specific concepts (e.g., ratio, reciprocal, factor, prime number, maximal value, etc.)

A variety of curriculum sources used as guides; failure to use the series of one company throughout the elementary grades (Johnson, 1977)

Teachers' low expectations of student abilities

The need for early introduction into basic concepts and vocabulary (Ling, 1978)

Lack of technology use and types of software suitable for visual learners

---

### CHAPTER TOPICS

Mathematics Defined
Assessment of Early Mathematics Skills
Mathematics Assessment for Older Students
Curricula and Materials to Monitor Progress
Early Mathematics Intervention
Elementary Mathematics Intervention
Science for Young Children
Elementary Science Intervention

---

## MATHEMATICS DEFINED

Mathematics is a symbolic language that enables human beings to think about, record, and communicate ideas about elements and the relationships between quantities (Lerner, 1985). Mathematics encompasses more than arithmetic, because mathematics is the study of numbers and their relationships, while arithmetic involves computational operations. The National Council for Teachers of Mathematics (1980) recommended that a mathematics curriculum include 10 basic skill areas. These are:

1. Problem solving
2. Applying mathematics in everyday situations
3. Alertness to the reasonableness of results
4. Estimation and approximation
5. Appropriate computational skills
6. Geometry
7. Measurement
8. Reading, interpreting, and constructing tables, charts, and graphs
9. Using mathematics to predict
10. Computer literacy

## ASSESSMENT OF EARLY MATHEMATICS SKILLS

Piaget (1965) described several cognitive concepts that are basic to understanding numbers and need to be assessed prior to math instruction with hearing-impaired preschoolers. We have outlined these in Chapter 1 and now define them here in their relationship to preschool mathematics.

*Classification* is the study of relationships (i.e., likenesses and differences) and involves categorizing objects according to a specific property. Copeland (1979) found that most 5- to 7-year-old students can sort objects by the attributes of color, shape, texture, and function.

The concept of order is not understood by many children until they are 6 or 7 years old (Copeland, 1979). *Ordering* involves counting in sequence, counting each object only once, identifying patterns (e.g., XOOX-OOXOO. . .), knowing who is first and last in line, and so forth. To seriate and order, students must focus on the systematic change of a property. Six and 7-year-old students can complete ordering tasks such as arranging various lengths from shortest to longest (Copeland, 1979).

*One-to-one correspondence* involves understanding that one object in a set is the same number as one object in a different set, whether or not characteristics are similar (Mercer & Mercer, 1985). Given two sets of objects, students who understand this concept can tell if there are more or less objects or how many objects there are in one set. Sometimes students who do not understand one-to-one correspondence think sets of objects are similar based on sensory cues (e.g., length of two unequal rows, height of objects in dissimilar containers, etc.). One way to test one-to-one correspondence is to ask a student to match a set of napkins to a set of apples at snack time.

The concept of *conservation* can involve either conservation of quantity or conservation of number. Conservation means that the quantity of an object or the number of objects in a set remains constant, regardless of spatial arrangement (Mercer & Mercer, 1985). In traditional tasks of conservation, students might be asked whether the amount of water in a tall, thin glass is identical to that in a short, fat glass or if the mass of a clay ball is equal to that of a long roll of clay. Most students master this concept between the ages of 5 and 7 (Copeland, 1979)

In addition to the cognitive abilities suggested by Piaget, researchers Karnes et al. (1985) believe that preschoolers must also develop *task persistence* in preparation for mathematics (and science). This is the ability to persevere when presented with a difficult problem. Research has shown that students who demonstrate task persistence accomplish more at school. Hamilton and Gordon (1978) found that improvement in task persistence was linked to problem-solving abilities.

Some researchers have been able to enhance preschoolers' task persistence by developing the metacognitive thinking skills of the students; that is, students have been taught to solve problems by analyzing, gathering information, developing a plan, and monitoring progress. To initiate step 1, students were taught first to employ the strategy of self-talk (see Chapter 5) for motor activities (e.g., "I am touching my head. Now I am. . . . ). Next, they repeated what a puppet said (signed) as they completed a short project (e.g., "I want to build a bird house. Let's see, I need some wood. I need a hammer and nails."). Finally, students were taught to attach verbal labels to their teacher's actions as they completed a project. Sometimes students told a peer what the teacher was doing. Supplying students with the exact language to encode each problem was a unique component of the process.

When students began to work on their own projects, materials were withheld until the next step of the task was verbalized (in speech and/or sign) by the students. Decision points were monitored by teachers, at which time either the teacher or the students would evaluate their performance thus far and provide overt feedback. All appropriate student verbalizations were reinforced by the teacher. At the end of the project, students were encouraged to mention what they had accomplished.

Benefits of the model for teaching task persistence were that task-engaged time increased across all students, and some children continued to be systematic in their approach to new problems. One student, who had initially looked at a block design and had given up, attempted the same task later. He looked at the picture he was to copy repeatedly and then said, "I'm starting with the bottom."

We suggest that you assess both the cognitive and task persistence abilities of your students as you begin premath activities. Informal tests should be used to assess whether the students can use the following concepts in mathematical situations: one-to-one correspondence, sorting, classifying with one or more attributes, conservation of quantity or number, and seriation (Gruenewald & Pollack, 1984).

## MATHEMATICS ASSESSMENT FOR OLDER STUDENTS

Learning mathematics tends to follow a sequence that includes the understanding of concepts, the development of computational skills, and the application of computation skills (Evans, Evans, & Mercer, 1986). There are numerous tests available for conducting evaluation of elementary school students' comprehension of mathematic concepts and computational skills. Standardized, or formal, mathematical tests are classified usually into two categories: survey and diagnostic.

Survey tests cover a broad range of mathematical skills and provide general information on students' performance. Most of the survey tests in math are part of a general battery of achievement tests. They provide a single score that can be compared to standardized norms or converted into a grade or age-equivalent score. Survey tests are useful for screening students, so that those students who need further assessment can be identified or long-term goals can be established. Among those that are used widely are the Stanford Achievement Test—Hearing Impaired, the California Achievement Test, the Woodcock Johnson Achievement Test, and the Metropolitan Achievement Test. These types of tests tend to be group tests, but they can be administered to individuals as well.

There also are a wide variety of diagnostic tests that can be used to assess students' mathematical skills and conceptual knowledge. As with other academic areas discussed in this book, diagnostic tests in mathematics provide information on specific areas and tend to provide more information for planning instruction. Several of the most frequently used tests include the Key Math Diagnostic Arithmetic Test, the Stanford Diagnostic Arithmetic Test, the Brigance Diagnostic Mathematics Inventory, the Sequential Assessment of Mathematics Inventory, and the Diagnostic Mathematics Inventory/Mathematics Systems.

Supervisors, teachers, and parents should be aware of the role that English proficiency might play in a student's ability to perform on some of these test items. Gruenewald and Pollack (1984) have provided a curricular sequence for math skills that include the English vocabulary necessary to comprehend each skill (see Exhibit 13.1).

### Informal Mathematics Assessment

Informal mathematics assessment involves examining the students' work or administering a teacher-made test. Informal assessment is an important tool that can be used to monitor the progress of students. It allows you to sample specific skills that are directly related to the curriculum. When you are giving students informal assessments, it is important for you to analyze student error patterns so that you can plan appropriate intervention. *Error analysis* can be used to identify systematic error patterns that underlie the students' mathematics performance. Four error patterns have been identified by Roberts (1968). They include: (1) wrong operation, (2) computational error, (3) defective algorithm, and (4) random response. When students add when they should have subtracted, they have undertaken the *wrong operation*. If they apply the correct operation to add 15 plus 9 but come up with 23, they have made a *computational error*. An algorithm includes the specific steps that are used to compute a math problem. For example, when Saba responds to the problem "27 + 38 = ?" with the answer 515, she

**EXHIBIT 13.1.** Curricular sequence for math skills (Gruenewald & Pollack, 1990)

| C.A. | Grade Level | Cognitive Period | Math Skills | Concepts/Operations | Instructional (Vocabulary) | Math Sentences |
|---|---|---|---|---|---|---|
| 6 | 1 | Late preoperational (4–7) according to Copeland (1980). During this period the student is developing mathematical concepts, which include:<br><br>Topological space<br>Simple classifications<br>Seriation and ordering<br>Number conservation<br>Length conservation<br>Area conservation | I. Sets<br>1. Inserts missing sets, such as a set of 3 between a set of 2 and a set of 4<br>2. Uses physical objects to demonstrate renaming a number<br>3. Joins sets to define addition<br>4. Separates sets to define subtraction<br>5. Selects the number of objects associated with a given number up to 20 | I. Sets<br>A. Seriation<br>B. Comparatives<br>C. Class inclusion<br>D. Class exclusion<br>E. Association<br>F. Conservation | *Between, more than, join, separate, member, empty set, same, greater than, less than* | Choose the correct set<br>• is a member of: b<br>△ △<br>a ▲<br>○ ○<br>b ○ ●<br><br>6 > 5 or<br>5 < 6 |
|  |  |  | II. Number theory and numeration systems<br>1. Demonstrates numeral/number association to 20<br>2. Is able to sequence a set of numerals through 20 | II.<br>A. One-one correspondence<br>B. Seriation<br>C. $=, +, -,$ conservation number, cardinal number | *before, after, next to, all, one, two, three equals, addition (plus) subtraction (minus) take away*<br>*Six plus one = seven*<br>*Six and one is seven* | $6 + 1 = 7$<br>$6 - 1 = 5$ |

*(continued)*

**EXHIBIT 13.1.** (Continued)

| C.A. | Grade Level | Cognitive Period | Math Skills | Concepts/Operations | Instructional (Vocabulary) | Math Sentences |
|---|---|---|---|---|---|---|
| | | | 3. Recognizes and uses symbols for equality (=), addition (+), and subtraction (−). | | | |
| | | | III. Mathematical sentences and properties<br>1. Understands the use of +, −, and = | III. Comprehends written symbols | | |
| | | | IV. Whole number computation<br>1. Recalls addition facts through sums of 10<br>2. Is able to add numerals less than 10<br>3. Recalls subtraction facts through 10<br>4. Is able to subtract numerals less than 10 | IV. Class inclusion Class exclusion | conjunction *and* | 6 + 1 = 7 (Class inclusion)<br>6 − 1 = 5 (Class exclusion) |
| | | | V. Decimals and fractions<br>1. Demonstrates an understanding of *whole* and *half* | V. Part/whole relationship | Ring shapes that show one-half | |
| | | | VI. Geometry<br>1. Identifies squares, | VI. Spatial, discrimination sorting | Attributes of shapes— round, square, rectangle, long, | |

rectangles, circles, triangles, and gives a distinguishing characteristic of each

short, and circle
*Put an × on the shapes that are the same.*
*Circle the object that has the same shape.*

VII. Measurement
1. is able to order 5 objects by size

VII.
Seriation
Ordinal number

Complete the pattern
△ △ △
Number the pictures from *smallest* to *largest; big, bigger, biggest;* and *first, second, third*

VIII. Integers
IX. Graphing and statistics

has an understanding of the correct operation, such as a recall of the basic addition facts, but she lacks an understanding of the place value and the steps to take to properly answer this problem. When a *defective algorithm* is the only error, the students are using the correct operation and recalling the basic facts. Finally, a *random response* indicates that there is no apparent relationship between the answer and the problem and that the students are taking wild guesses.

When you are doing an error analysis, Howell and Kaplan (1980) suggest that you use the following guidelines:

1. Collect an adequate sample by having the students do several problems of each type in which you are interested.
2. Encourage the students to work but do nothing to influence their responses.
3. Record all the responses that the students make, including comments.
4. Look for patterns in the responses.
5. Look for exceptions to any apparent pattern.
6. List the patterns that you have identified as causing problems in the students' computations.

## Clinical Interview

In order to help you understand the types of mistakes that the students are making, you may want to use a technique called the *clinical interview* (Piaget, 1963). In this technique, students are presented with a math problem and are asked to solve the problem. The students express their thought processes while solving the math problem. Your focus as a teacher should be on the meaning that the students are expressing and not the form of English (see Chapter 6). Here is an example. You give Mike three subtraction problems, and you say to him, "Please do the following problems and explain to me what you are doing while you are doing them."

Mike has solved the problems in the following manner:

$$
\begin{array}{ccc}
23 & 46 & 31 \\
-15 & -28 & -16 \\
\hline
12 & 22 & 25
\end{array}
$$

While he was doing the first problem, Mike explained that 5 is bigger than 3, so he took 3 from 5, which left 2; and 2 is bigger than 1, which meant that he should take 1 from 2, which is 1. The explanations for the next two problems were similar. Through the use of the clinical interview, you have learned that Mike does not understand the concept of regrouping. This procedure allows you to understand his error patterns and to make a plan for teaching the right algorithmic procedure, such as providing him with concrete work on regrouping problems.

Evans, Evans, and Mercer (1986) have suggested that you use the following guidelines when you are conducting the clinical interview:

1. Establish rapport with the student. Begin with items that are easy for the student to do.
2. Focus on the student's problem area that is lowest on the skill sequence. Limit each session to one area of difficulty (e.g., two-column addition with regrouping).
3. Allow the student to solve the problem in his or her own way.
4. Record the student's thinking processes and analyze them for error patterns and problem-solving techniques.
5. Once you have discovered an error pattern or a faulty problem-solving technique, introduce diagnostic activities for assessing the student's level of understanding and provide intervention activities appropriate to the student's level of functioning.

## CURRICULA AND MATERIALS TO MONITOR PROGRESS

Most basal math programs include a variety of placement tests, chapter tests, specific skills tests, and review tests to monitor student performance. Many of these also include a scope-and-sequence skills list for several grade levels; these can be used as a guide for developing test items that follow the skills sequence presented in the text.

*Kendall Demonstration Elementary School Mathematics* (KDES) (MacKall et al. 1982) and the *Mathematics Curriculum: Basic Level* (Addison et. al. 1985) provide scope-and-sequence charts that are very valuable for developing goals and objectives. The KDES, an especially valuable resource, is comprehensive in nature and emphasizes a developmental perspective that makes use of many hands on activities. The curriculum also provides evaluation procedures that are appropriate for hearing-impaired students. According to Bunch (1987), the most commonly found math kits in elementary school classes for hearing-impaired students are:

> SRA Math Lab (Scientific Research Associates)
> ADLM Math Lab (Developmental Learning Materials)
> PAL Math Program (Project Life)
> Key Math Teach and Practice (American Guidance Service)
> Key Math Early Steps (American Guidance Service)
> Oregon Math Computation (Dormac)
> Veri Tech (for Versa Tiles)

Another technique that can be used to assess student mastery of the facts is referred to as "probes." Probes include a variety of items that are presented to students to measure their performance in relation to any math objective (Evans, Evans, & Mercer, 1986). Examples of probes that are frequently used are flash cards or math facts sheets. The students are presented with the flash cards or facts sheets and given a designated time period, such as two minutes, to see how many problems they can answer correctly. The total number of correct and incorrect responses are then recorded in some manner. As students continue to develop and move through the curriculum, the type of probe can be changed to meet the students' current level of functioning. Since proficiency in facts occurs over a period of time and overlaps or parallels the development of other computational skills, it is a good practice to test facts proficiency through the use of timed probes.

## EARLY MATHEMATICS INTERVENTION

Teachers of preschoolers face the challenge and responsibility of initiating positive feelings about mathematical inquiry and activity in young minds (Stone, 1987). We recommend that preschool math programs be concrete, filled with play and uninterrupted exploration, and include specific language labels for the key cognitive concepts (one-to-one correspondence, conversation, classification, etc.). We caution that worksheets and workbooks have no place in the preschool curriculum; yet, they are often found in these classrooms. Some of the reasons frequently given by teachers for using workbooks and worksheets are listed below. Counterstatements are provided in favor of using manipulative materials (based on Stone, 1987):

> Manipulative math materials are more expensive over time than workbooks (numerous manipulative math materials can be teacher-made by using low-cost or free materials; see Baratta-Lorten, 1972).
> Worksheets are more convenient (although manipulative math materials are more motivating).

There is need for accountability and to send a product home to parents. (While manipulative math materials focus on process rather than on product, supervisors and parents can be educated about the value of these activities through newsletters, journal articles, and conferences. Data sheets that outline progress can be shared with parents in lieu of worksheets.)

Worksheets provide a more controlled and "academic" environment. (Proponents of manipulative math materials would argue that observation and handling are essential to comprehension and that the room is alive and active with learning when manipulative math materials are utilized.)

In planning math content for young students, you should consider the following concerns for providing an effective curriculum:

1. Problems of students' readiness for a task may form the basis for failure in learning later math tasks. Do not skip over the cognitive groundwork that is needed for future work. For example, borrowing requires skill in class inclusion, regrouping, and conservation (Gruenewald & Pollack, 1984). Prerequisite skills need to be assessed before instruction with new concepts is initiated (see Exhibit 13.1).

2. Significant adults should be aware of the linguistic demands of mathematical tasks (See Gruenewald & Pollack, 1984 in this regard) and should try to cue and sign comprehensible and complete input.

3. The syntax in written math (e.g., story problems) for each student should match the student's verbal (oral or signed) ability.

4. A researched-based symbolic play curriculum (Westby, 1980) should be employed with preschool children (see Chapter 1).

5. Professionals should advocate an activity-based approach to teaching math concepts to hearing-impaired students (Fridriksson & Stewart, 1988). Two highly recommended reference books are those by Barratta-Lorten (1976) and Barratta-Lorten (1977a and b).

6. Teachers should not complicate the directions given with other verbalizations that may confuse the student (Gruenewald & Pollack, 1984).

7. The teacher's questions are important. Language concepts, as well as comprehension, can be monitored through the strategy of asking relevant questions. We suggest using the question prompts provided in Chapter 10 to discern if the student understands and can apply his or her knowledge of the target objective.

8. Math lessons should be task analyzed by varying context and cognition. (See the Cummins model, Chapter 1).

9. Lessons should be taught by using the principles of effective teaching (see Chapter 10).

## Sample Preschool Mathematics Activities (adapted from Stone, 1987)

The math activities described below can help you plan appropriately for preschool aged, hearing-impaired children:

*Sizes.*   Collect pairs of objects that differ by size (e.g., a big square block and a little square block; a tennis ball and a beach ball, etc.). Put all of the items in a bag and have the students either match or sort them by size. Bring in cards and envelopes and let the students match them. Allow the students to fit lids to various size containers.

*One-to-one Correspondence.*   Have the students place a shoe in a shoe bag; repeat this for 10 shoes. Allow students to paste a pebble in each compartment of an egg carton.

***Matching Pairs.***  Gather typical pairs (e.g., shoes, mittens, dice, etc.) and place them in a bag. Students must match the contents of the bag. Having traced and cut their hand-shapes out of wallpaper samples, students paste a pair of paper mittens on their hands.

***Short/Long.***  Children roll snakes of clay, line them up along a baseline, and compare their lengths. Rearrange the snakes from shortest to longest, then from longest to shortest. Have the students attach all of the snakes together and make a long snake. The students take long spaghetti and snap it into shorter pieces. Help them to cut drinking straws into various lengths. Short pieces can be glued on one side of a paper, and long pieces can be glued on the otherside. Different size tubes can be collected (e.g., from toilet paper, gift wrapping, tin foil, etc.), painted, and compared at a baseline.

***Height.***  A student stacks blocks to match the height of a partner's blocks. Have them change places and repeat this procedure. Place tape on the classroom wall to indicate the heights of the students. Pile blocks to match the marks on the wall and compare heights. The students watch as you burn candles to various heights. The students put them in order in clay birthday cakes or on a Chanukah menorah by height. (See Stone, 1987, for additional activities for measuring, shapes, sets, halves, etc.)

Another valuable resource in teaching math concepts to hearing-impaired students is children's books. Several educators (Matthias, Platt, & Thiessen, 1980; Radebaugh, 1981; Smith & Wendelin, 1981) have discussed the importance of books that emphasize counting, comparison, geometry, measurement, time, money, ordinal numbers, fractions, and math operations. Burke (1986) has stated that books can form a bridge between manipula-

tive materials and semiconcrete (and later concrete and abstract) concepts. Preschoolers can benefit from books that deal with prenumber skills such as classification, ordering, conservation of number, cardinal numbers, or number recognition. Ballenger, Benham, and Hosticka (1984) have cautioned parents and teachers that not all books are appropriate for teaching math to young children, usually because the illustrations are unclear or the content is too advanced. Examples of recommended books appear in Appendix C.

Harsh (1987) used the book *Freight Train* by Crews (1978) to illustrate opportunities for learning a wide variety of prenumber skills:

*Classification*. The colors and types of train cars lend themselves to sorting activities by color and type of car.

*Comparison*. Children can move train cars in positional relationships (e.g., by, across, through, etc.) to tunnels, trees, and rivers, as depicted in a story.

*Ordering and ordinal numbers*. Children can seriate the order of the types of cars and use such terms as *first*, *second*, and *last* with paper trains.

*One-to-one correspondence*. Children can match and count the different types of cars pictured. Train cars could be matched to paper cup terminals in a learning center (given an equal and unequal number of terminals). Children could count the trains parked in the block area.

*Cardinal numbers*. Children can be asked the quantity of train cars pictured, the number of pieces of coal found in the coal box, and so on. The skills focus on the final counted number, not on each number as in rational counting.

*Number recognition*. Children can choose plastic or magnetic numbers that represent objects counted in the book.

*Conservation of numbers.* The teacher plans a follow-up activity, in which children can experiment with conservation by comparing rows of different pieces of coal.

We recommend the use of preschool literature to expose hearing-impaired students to the written language that is needed to express mathematical concepts and to provide them with a motivating context for the comprehension of such terminology. Books provide significant others with a scripted content that encourages the use of novel vocabulary words and phrases (e.g., signs and affix markers) as mathematics vocabulary is utilized.

## ELEMENTARY MATHEMATICS INTERVENTION

There is a shortage of mathematics curricula designed specifically for use with hearing-impaired students (Bunch, 1987; Fridriksson & Stewart, 1988). Modifications usually involve controlling the vocabulary and syntax that are used to present the material and an increased use of manipulative and visual aids. For the most part, mathematics curricula and activities for hearing-impaired students have followed the trends established in the regular educational system (Bunch, 1987). Two available curricula are:

Mechall, Dayoub, Frye, Concoran-Horn, Mann, Long, & Baldine. (1982). *Kendall Demonstration Elementary School Mathematics.* Washington, D.C.: Pre-College Programs, Gallaudet College.

Addison, Arkley, Lalond, Lavoie, Mac-Donald, McKenna, & Wren. (1985). *Mathematics Curriculum: Basic Level.* Toronto, Ontario: Ontario Ministry of Education, Provincial Schools.

Many teachers view teaching mathematics in terms of four basic operations: addition, subtraction, multiplication, and division. An examination of the amount of time and the types of instructional materials used in classrooms for hearing-impaired students shows an overwhelming focus on the computational aspects of mathematics, almost to the exclusion of other areas (Daniele, 1982; Johnson, 1977).

The work of Piaget (1965) has greatly influenced the teaching of mathematics. According to Reisman (1981), Piaget's work has the following implications for instruction in mathematics:

1.  Intellectual development takes place through a series of stages that occur in the same order.
2.  Stages are defined by clusters of mental operations (seriating, conserving, classifying, hypothesizing, inferring) that underlie intellectual behavior.
3.  Movement through the stages is accomplished by *equilibration*, which is the process of development that involves the interactions between experience (*assimilation*) and growing cognitive structures (*accommodation*).

This means that it is inappropriate to teach a mathematics skill or concept before the necessary stage of cognitive development has been reached by the student. Another important point that has been gleaned from Piaget's work is the need to use concrete materials to facilitate mathematics learning (Thorton, Tucker, Dossey, & Bazik, 1983).

Additional points for you to consider when you are planning and implementing mathematics lessons can be gained from the work of Driscoll (1983), who has identified five factors that correlate with effective mathematics instruction:

1.  *Questioning*. Effective    teachers    ask

more process (explanations) and product (short answer) questions.

2. *Encouragement*. Effective teachers are encouraging and receptive to student input, focusing on the meaning being expressed and not on the form of English.

3. *Modeling*. Effective teachers demonstrate and communicate the importance of problem-solving behaviors.

4. *Clarity*. Effective teachers systematically explain vocabulary.

5. *Expectations*. Effective teachers set firm and appropriate expectations for high academic achievement.

## Levels of Learning

There are three levels of learning that you should consider when you assess and plan mathematics instruction. According to Underhill, Uprichard, and Heddens (1980), these levels are the *concrete*, *semiconcrete*, and *abstract*. The concrete level involves the manipulation of objects. It is at this level that students learn to relate manipulative and computational processes. For example, in instruction of addition problems involving sums of 8, a concrete activity would be to have the students group tiles into all combinations of 8 (6 + 2, 5 + 3, etc). Concrete-level experiences are necessary so that students can learn skills at all levels of the mathematics hierarchy.

The semiconcrete level involves working with illustrations of objects in order to perform mathematics tasks. These illustrations can be pictures of real objects, such as cars or balls, or the use of tallies, such as making markings on the page. For example, circles could be used and presented in this manner: "00 + 0000 = 6." At this level, the focus is on developing associations between visual models and the symbolic processes.

The abstract level refers to the use of numerals. This tends to be the focus of most mathematics programs. They tend to move quickly to the abstract level of instruction and limit the number of activities that are undertaken using the concrete and semiconcrete levels. As a result, many students demonstrate problems, because they lack the necessary understanding of basic concepts in beginning mathematics instruction (Reisman, 1982; Underhill, Uprichard, & Heddens, 1980).

It is beyond the scope of this chapter to provide detailed strategies for teaching concepts in each of the mathematics curricular strands. Rather, we will address selected areas—such as number concepts, number usage, computation, problem solving, calculator usage, microcomputers, money, time, fractions—and discuss the critical components of the teaching process for these areas. The reader is referred to Reys, Suydam, & Lindquist (1984) and Baratta-Lorten (1977) for more information on this subject.

## Number Concepts

The concept of numbers is based on an abstraction related to quantity. Because of this, classification and grouping of objects is a prerequisite skill. Therefore, the concept of sets should come early in the instructional sequence. In order to be able to group things together, students must be able to discriminate objects. Shapes and sizes are two discriminating features that can be used. Students should be provided with opportunities so that they can learn to discriminate objects on several variables. It is also important to help students develop a numerical vocabulary early. Words like *most, few, many, long, short, top*, and *bottom* should be introduced and used frequently so that students can internalize their meaning. Gearheart, DeRuiter, and Sileo (1986) presented a sequence that can be used to help students understand grouping and numerical symbols:

1. Students assemble groups of concrete objects (buttons, pennies, beans) and

match their object groups with pictorial representations (dot cards) of various quantities.

2. Once students are successful in matching concrete objects with pictorial representations, the printed numerical symbol may be introduced for each group.

3. Students then match the group of objects with the appropriate pictorial representation and the printed numerical symbol.

4. Students are then presented with groups of objects in random order and asked to match the appropriate symbol card with the correct group of concrete objects that are replaced gradually with the pictorial representation.

## Number Usage

Rote counting is usually the first step that is used to teach students to use numbers. Students should be requested to count familiar objects within the classroom environment, such as the number of chairs or the number of crayons on a desk. Once students are able to count concrete objects, they can progress to counting pictures. The next skill generally is to match or write numbers that indicate how many objects are within a set. After they have learned to count objects, they are taught to count and compare. Relationships between sets, such as "equal to," "greater than," and "less than" are topics of instruction. Also, students need to learn to count by 2s, 5s, and 10s, and master ordinal numbers as well.

## Computation

There are four computational areas: addition, subtraction, multiplication, and division. Each of these can be further divided into two general types of problems: facts and process problems. The facts are those problems that need to be committed to memory (3 + 2;

4 × 8). The process problems need to be solved by utilizing the facts and by following specific operational rules (28 − 19; 13/4). As we have stated earlier, students can best understand mathematics concepts when teaching progresses from the concrete to the semi-concrete to the abstract. Too often, instruction in mathematics centers only on the semi-concrete and abstract stages. Many students lack an understanding of concepts that are basic to achieving proficiency in computation (Evans, Evans, & Mercer, 1986). Most mathematics programs do not provide adequate activities for teaching mathematics concepts. For this reason, we are presenting an approach to teaching mathematics that attempts to ensure that students have adequate exposure to mathematics concepts prior to being asked to do abstract level computation.

*Addition.* Piaget (1963) pointed out that addition—the union of groups into a larger group—is the basic operation around which all other computational operations are constructed. Therefore, it is important that the concept is well understood and that facts are well learned by students. Fridriksson and Stewart (1988) have presented a sequence for teaching computation that draws from the work of Barrata-Lorten (1976) and Barrata-Lorten (1977). With this approach, a great deal of emphasis is placed on dialogue, as well as the concrete manipulation of objects from which the use of mathematics symbols and computation is evolved. Students are encouraged to explore mathematics concepts as teachers guide them through independent work. Here is an illustration of the process.

Present each student with a set number, (e.g., 8) of popsicle sticks or tiles. Have the students make two piles, and you do the same on a overhead. When everyone has finished, an interaction such as the following should take place:

**T:** Can anyone describe what you have just done with the eight popsicle sticks?

**S:** I made two piles of sticks.

**T:** Can you use some math words to describe what you have done?

**S:** I took the eight sticks and made a pile of three and a pile of five.

**T:** Good. Now let's write this down (writes 3 + 5 = 8 on the overhead; students do the same on their papers). Can anyone think of another way to make two piles?

**S:** I made a pile of two and a pile of six.

**T:** That's good. And how would you write that?

**S:** (writes 2 + 6 = 8)

**T:** Good. I want all of you to think of as many different ways of making two piles as you can. Each time you finish making two piles, write down how many sticks you used in each pile and then start again. When you are done, we will make a list of all the ways in which you can make piles of eight sticks.

Continue this process by using different numbers of objects and different objects, such as beans, blocks, and cubes. When the concept of two piles has been mastered, you should introduce the idea of using several piles.

When teaching two-digit addition, you should try to avoid calling the digit in the "tens" place a single-digit number. Instead, you should call it a two-digit number such as 20 or 30 during the regrouping process. Additionally, when you are working with the symbol, it is best to introduce the expanded form, such as:

$$35 = 30 + 5$$
$$14 = 10 + 4$$
$$49 = 40 + 9$$

**Subtraction.** The procedures for exploring the concept of subtraction are similar to those for addition, with one exception: The piles are shown as taking away from a whole number instead of adding up to a whole number.

To start, present the students with a set number of beans, and have them make two piles while you do the same on the overhead.

Then have each student place a styrofoam cup over one of the piles. A discussion similar to the following should then be initiated.

**T:** Can anyone describe what you have just done?

**S:** I put eight beans into piles of six and two and then covered up the bigger pile.

**T:** Good. Now let's show how we can write this in arithmetic (on the overhead the teacher recreates the student's piles, along with placement of the cup over the pile of six beans. Writes under this, 8 − 6 = 2; students do the same on their paper). Does anyone have two different piles from the one we have?

**S:** I have a pile of three and five, and I have covered the pile of three.

**T:** Very good. And how can you write that?

**S:** (writes 8 − 3 = 5)

Have the students move the beans around and write as many equations as they can that show what they have covered.

Eventually, progress from two piles to three and more. At this point, you can introduce the concept of zero, although by this time the students will likely have discovered this on their own. This is best done by placing a styrofoam cup on the desk so that it is covering nothing. For example, leave all eight beans in one pile and place the styrofoam cup off to the side of the pile. The arithmetic equation would therefore be, 8 − 0 = 8.

**Multiplication.** Multiplication is best understood as repeated addition. It should be introduced as a shortcut for adding the same number over and over again. Therefore, the initial assignment is to expose the students to repeated addition.

Distribute 12 popsicle sticks to each of the students. Have them make different piles so that at least two of the piles contain the same number. An interaction like the following should occur:

**T:** Would someone tell us what addition equation they created?

**S:** I made a pile of four, another pile of four, and a third pile of four.

**T:** Wonderful. Could you show me an arithmetic statement to describe what you did?

**S:** (writes 4 + 4 + 4 = 12)

**T:** How many piles of four did you make?

**S:** Three.

**T:** I will show you a shortcut for writing that (writes 3 × 4 = 12).

By continuing this activity, the students will create many statements in which they have derived multiplication equations. Students also should develop problems that include both addition and multiplication symbols. For example, if a student is given 13 popsicle sticks, the student could make piles of sticks and then write the following equation 6 × 2 + 1 = 13.

***Division.*** In the same manner that the concept of multiplication flowed from that of addition, the concept of division comes quite naturally from that of multiplication. Division should be presented as the process of breaking up a large group into a number of equal smaller groups. Students should work on manipulative materials or counters until the idea of equal groups is established. Start by giving each student 14 popsicle sticks

**T:** Take your 14 sticks and separate them into two different piles. We can pretend that one pile is for you and the other pile is for a friend. A simple way to do this is to start dealing one stick to each person—one for you and one for me. Let's do this together. Are there any left?

**S:** No.

**T:** Right. We are able to divide 14 by two and we have none left over. One way of writing this is 14/2 = 7. Even at this first step, some of the students might make the connection between multiplication and division. They will realize that

what they have done to the sticks is the same for both operations and that only the language and symbols have changed.

Continue the exercise, this time dividing 14 by different numbers. For example,

**T:** Let's do the same thing, except that we will divide the 14 sticks by 3 because we need a pile for you, a pile for your friend, and a third pile for another friend: one for friend number one, one for friend number two and one for you. Now look what we have here. We have two sticks left over. We will record it as the number remaining. This is how you record it: 14/3 = 4  r2.

***Mastering Basic Facts.*** Many students have difficulty in computational arithmetic, not because they do not know how to solve complicated problems, but because they are not proficient at answering basic facts problems. Most cognitive scientists now believe that as basic skills are practiced, their execution requires less cognitive processing and attention and becomes automatic. This refers to the concept of automaticity that was discussed in the chapters on speech and effective instruction. Success in higher-level mathematical skills is directly related to the efficiency with which lower-level processes are executed (Hasselbring, Goin, & Bransford, 1987). Therefore, it is important to help hearing-impaired students develop rapid, effortless recall of basic mathematics facts.

Hasselbring, Goin, and Bransford (1987) present a series of steps to help you develop a relational network between mathematics problems and their answers. These steps include:

1. Assessing current level of automaticity.
2. Building on existing knowledge.
3. Focusing on small sets of facts.
4. Using "challenge times."
5. Drill and practice.

***Assessing Current Level of Automaticity.*** The purpose of this step is to find out which facts the student has automatized and which need more practice. This can be done through the use of computer programs or flash cards. If the student takes more than two seconds, or uses a counting strategy to solve the problem, the problem should be considered to be a nonautomatized fact. After the assessment has been completed, a matrix such as the one in Exhibit 13.2 can be constructed; an explanation of its use is offered.

***Building on Existing Knowledge.*** New facts are selected by building on those facts that the student has automatized and by gradually increasing the difficulty of the facts presented. Selection of facts is based on the size of the minimum addend. For example, once all of the facts that have an addend of 1 have been automatized, then you can begin work on those with the minimum addend of 2, and so on.

***Focus on Small Sets of Facts.*** It is best to work on a small set of facts, such as two or three facts and their reciprocals, at a time. This set of facts becomes the set for the day or the week. Instruction of this set continues until the student can retrieve the answer without using counting strategies.

***Use Challenge Times.*** Students use challenge time to practice newly learned facts with those that have already become automatized. By using flash cards in random order, students are presented with the stimulus and must respond automatically within the challenge time, which ranges between one and three seconds, depending on the student and how you believe they need to be challenged. The student must respond within the chal-

**EXHIBIT 13.2.** Fast facts matrix

|   | 0 | 1 | 2 | 3 | 4 | 5 | 6 | 7 | 8 | 9 |
|---|---|---|---|---|---|---|---|---|---|---|
| **0** | 0 + 0 | 0 + 1 | 0 + 2 | 0 + 3 | 0 + 4 | 0 + 5 | 0 + 6 | 0 + 7 | 0 + 8 | 0 + 9 |
| **1** | 1 + 0 | 1 + 1 | 1 + 2 | 1 + 3 | 1 + 4 | 1 + 5 | 1 + 6 | 1 + 7 | 1 + 8 | 1 + 9 |
| **2** | 2 + 0 | 2 + 1 | 2 + 2 | 2 + 3 | 2 + 4 | 2 + 5 | 2 + 6 | 2 + 7 | 2 + 8 | 2 + 9 |
| **3** | 3 + 0 | 3 + 1 | 3 + 2 | 3 + 3 | 3 + 4 | 3 + 5 | 3 + 6 | 3 + 7 | 3 + 8 | 3 + 9 |
| **4** | 4 + 0 | 4 + 1 | 4 + 2 | 4 + 3 | 4 + 4 | 4 + 5 | 4 + 6 | 4 + 7 | 4 + 8 | 4 + 9 |
| **5** | 5 + 0 | 5 + 1 | 5 + 2 | 5 + 3 | 5 + 4 | 5 + 5 | 5 + 6 | 5 + 7 | 5 + 8 | 5 + 9 |
| **6** | 6 + 0 | 6 + 1 | 6 + 2 | 6 + 3 | 6 + 4 | 6 + 5 | 6 + 6 | 6 + 7 | 6 + 8 | 6 + 9 |
| **7** | 7 + 0 | 7 + 1 | 7 + 2 | 7 + 3 | 7 + 4 | 7 + 5 | 7 + 6 | 7 + 7 | 7 + 8 | 7 + 9 |
| **8** | 8 + 0 | 8 + 1 | 8 + 2 | 8 + 3 | 8 + 4 | 8 + 5 | 8 + 6 | 8 + 7 | 8 + 8 | 8 + 9 |
| **9** | 9 + 0 | 9 + 1 | 9 + 2 | 9 + 3 | 9 + 4 | 9 + 5 | 9 + 6 | 9 + 7 | 9 + 8 | 9 + 9 |

lenge time. If the student is too slow or the answer is incorrect, then you give the student the answer and present the fact again.

*Drill and Practice.*   After the student can answer facts within the challenge time, the facts should be added to a set of drill-and-practice facts. It is important that facts be included in this set until they have been automatized. Therefore, if you use a computer program, try to make sure that the program is appropriate or one that can be adapted accordingly. If you are using paper-and-pencil worksheets, you can easily control the set of facts that you use.

## Calculators

Research (Channell, 1978) indicates that the development of basic facts is enhanced by the use of calculators. Reys, Suydam, and Lindquist (1984) suggest that there are a series of steps for introducing calculators to students. They include:

1. *Free play time.* This permits students to have a short opportunity to experiment with their calculators prior to instruction.
2. *Explanation of keys.* Provide a brief description, of the keys and how they are used. Be sure to include a reminder that the " = " key is needed to find the sum of a product.
3. *Counting.* Counting provides the foundation for many mathematical concepts. Students can begin to count by ones by pressing " + ", "1", " = " and stopping at a designated number such as 50. This activity can be extended to counting by 2s, 3s, and so forth. Counting backwards, which is often a difficult skill for young students, can be introduced and practiced. This activity can be extended to counting forward or backward from a particular number, such as starting at 7 and

counting forward by 5s. Helping students to count with their calculators will promote learning many problem-solving skills.

*Overloading.*   Calculators can become overloaded in many ways. Helping students become aware of their limitations allows them to recognize the overload signal, understand its importance, and learn how to deal with it. Therefore, specific examples need to be provided so that each student experiences this aspect of computer literacy and does not believe that the calculator is broken.

## Computers

According to Reys, Suydam, and Lindquist (1984), teachers should have a basic understanding of computers. You should be able to:

Discuss different uses of computers in homes, businesses, and schools
Explain the basic operations of a computer
Use common computer terms
Run prepared programs on microcomputers
Understand the strengths and limitations of computers for classroom instruction

If you do not feel competent in any of these areas, it is important that you find an avenue to acquire these skills prior to beginning your work with hearing-impaired students.

Microcomputers are not a panacea or a substitute for good teaching, but they do provide a valuable tool to help you teach students mathematical skills (Reys, Suydam, & Lindquist, 1984). Some important instructional uses of microcomputers include:

*Drill and Practice.*   Drill-and-practice programs help students develop automatic recall of concepts that have been previously taught. The programs provide many opportunities for practicing specific skills and numbering correctly in order to monitor progress. Computer-based drill and practice should be used only after students are able to retrieve answers automatically. If the students do not have an association between a problem and its answer prior to using the computer drill-and-practice activity, then the time essentially has been wasted (Hasselbring, Goin, & Sherwood, 1986).

***Tutorial.*** Tutorial programs provide direct instruction on specific topics. Good programs simulate a teacher by introducing, explaining, illustrating, questioning, evaluating, and providing feedback.

***Learning games.*** Currently, there are hundreds of computer-based games related to mathematics available. Through the use of these games, students can develop a basic awareness and understanding of concepts such as graphing, basic facts, and consumer-related skills.

## Money

Money is an aspect of the mathematics curriculum that should be taught in short, frequent, and interspersed lessons. Whenever possible, real money should be used (Silvia, 1983). The manipulation of real coins tends to aid the learning process. After students have mastered use of the real objects, then replicas can be used in order to help them progress from actual coins to using an abstract symbol system. A sequence for teaching money that has been adapted from Gearheart, DeRuiter, and Sileo (1986) is as follows:

1. Discuss the use of money. Help students understand that it is used as an exchange for goods and services.
2. Students learn the names of the coins and can recognize them on sight.
3. Introduce the cent sign and have students learn the value of each coin.

4. The equivalence of value of coins should be undertaken next so that students understand that $.05 equals five pennies, and so on.
5. Teach students to count groups of coins that total less than $1.00.
6. Give students totals that are less than $1.00 and have them match them with coins. They should be able to do this using several different coin combinations.
7. Teach them to make change for amounts of money up to $1.00.
8. Introduce bills larger than $1.00.
9. Teach students to write amounts more than $1.00 and to count these amounts.
10. Teach them to add amounts of money that have sums greater than $1.00.
11. Make change for amounts over $1.00.

An activity that you can set up in your class is to have students become waiters and waitresses. They can write down orders taken from each other by using the menus that you have provided. They can look up the items ordered, compute the cost of the order, and write the total on the order pad.

## Time

Instruction in time should initially focus on the concept of time as a unit and as a sequence of events. Digital watches and clocks have changed the way in which students learn to tell and write time notations. There is a greater tendency to state the time according to the hours and minutes, for example, 10:20 or 9:50. As a result, digital clocks have eliminated the translation step in stating and writing time notation. A sequence that can be used to teach this concept has been suggested by Gearheart, DeRuiter, and Sileo (1986):

1. Students need to understand the ordering and sequence of the day. A discus-

sion of what they do from the time that they get up in the morning until the time that they go to bed at night will help to develop this concept.

2. Use activities that students are familiar with and discuss large blocks of time, such as a week, a month, and a year.

3. Students need to develop an understanding of the passage of time. The concept of "how long" can be developed by using familiar activities, such as the length of classroom activities or television shows. Short time intervals can be understood by using such activities as bouncing a ball or standing on one foot for 1 minute and then 2 minutes.

4. Students should then estimate the duration of time in a variety of activities, such as sitting and reading or playing on the playground. Begin with a 1-minute block of time and increase it to larger blocks, such as 5 or 10 minutes.

5. After students understand the concept of time and the vocabulary associated with it, they are ready to learn to tell time and to use a calendar.

One method for teaching how to tell time is to begin with a number line that goes from 1 to 60. Have the students count using the number line. Then take another number line that is the same length as the first one but only goes from 1 to 12. Take the second number line and place it over the first one. Then count off every five units and mark them in a different color. This number line is placed on a large clock or teacher-made clock face without hands.

The 1 to 60 number line will correspond with the minute markings on a clock, and the 1 to 12 number line will correspond with the hour markings. The minute hand is then attached and used to indicate the passage of time in minutes. This should be tied as much as possible with the passage of time that exists for classroom activities. When students begin to understand the concept of minutes, the hour hand can be attached and used to indicate how many times the minute hand has gone around. It should be pointed out to students that on standard clocks the hour hand does not jump from one hour to the next after 60 minutes have passed but, rather, moves slowly between the hour designations as the minute hand moves around in a full turn.

Some activities that you may want to use when you are teaching time can be found in Exhibit 13.3. Others can be deduced by using the Cummins' model (see Chapter 3) to task analyze activities.

**EXHIBIT 13.3.** Time activities

Paste pictures of various events (breakfast, riding to school on the bus etc.) on cards and shuffle them. Have students arrange the cards to show the order in which events occur.

Post a series of clocks on the wall or bulletin board. Mark the correct time on the clocks for each school activity, such as mathematics, gym, library, lunch, recess, and so on. Have students be responsible for letting you know when it is time to make a transition.

Provide the students with blank clock faces and a variety of schedules (such as those for television, a movie, or a bus). Have them record schedule times on the clock faces.

Provide the students with a calendar and a worksheet with numerous questions. Ask the students to respond to questions like these:

1. How many days are in a week?
2. On what day is the 27th of May?
3. List the dates of all the Wednesdays in January.
4. How many months are there in a year?
5. Which months have the fewest days?
6. List the months that have 31 days.

## Problem Solving

Problem solving is an inquiry process in which students make observations, organize information, and express mathematical ideas as a basis for understanding their environment (Gearheart, DeRuiter, & Sileo, 1986). Problem solving allows students to use their mathematical skills to find answers to questions that they want to know about. Problem-solving activities let students integrate separate skills into the most important mathematical skill of all—thinking (Baratta-Lorten, 1977a). To gain skill in solving problems, students must have many experiences in solving problems. Research (Pace, 1961; Suydam, 1982) indicates that students who are given many problems and taught strategies to solve problems score higher on problem-solving tests than students who are given few problems and are not taught strategies. Many of the best problem-solving situations come from everyday occurrences. For example, you might ask, "How many cookies will we need if everyone is going to have two?" or "What time will we go out for recess if we leave in 10 minutes?" Word problems should incorporate anything that relates to the students' environment or interests. Whenever possible, the use of props, student's names, and actions are valuable. They should be consistent with the students' cognitive abilities and should help them to organize and integrate mathematical concepts and applications. Problem-solving activities at first should rely on the use of concrete manipulative materials, such as cars, dolls, balls, and cookies and then progress to those that can represent the information, such as beans or blocks. Once the students have acted out the word problem, you can introduce the mathematical symbols and equations for each problem.

***Stages of Problem Solving.***   Polya (1973) proposed a four-stage model of problem solving:

1.   Understand the problem.
2.   Devise a plan for solving it.
3.   Carry out the plan.
4.   Look back and examine the solution.

As a result, students are taught to see, plan, do, and check. There are some specific strategies that you can introduce to students to help them understand the problem. A strategy that helps students to utilize what is involved in a problem is to act it out. Such an approach allows students to become active participants rather than passive spectators, and it also helps them to see and understand the meaning of the problem (Sobel & Maletsky, 1988). Many real-life situations can be acted out, giving students opportunities to use English to label mathematical concepts. For example, "Eight students are in our class. Three leave to go to speech class. How many students are left in the room?" Another strategy that you can teach students to do is to make a drawing or a diagram. An example that you could use with this strategy is the following: "A restaurant has eight tables. There are four chairs at each table. How many chairs are there in the restaurant?"

Often students will need to restate a problem in a manner that uses their own words. This will help them to understand what the problem means and requires. In addition, it will help you find out if the students actually understand the problem and what needs to be done. Also, students will need instruction breaking problems down into smaller parts so that they can learn to answer one part of the problem in order to answer the entire problem.

***Teaching Problem Solving.***   Schloss and Sedlak (1986) recommend the following procedures for instruction in problem solving:

1.   Start teaching word problems in the primary grades.
2.   Start with pictures and manipulative materials to create the problems.
3.   Focus on the process of solving a problem, not on the mechanics. (There

is more than one correct approach for solving a problem.)

4. Keep both the language and the mathematics simple initially; then gradually increase the complexity of the language but keep the mathematical aspect simple.
5. Create problems that contain extraneous information.
6. Gradually withdraw the pictures and manipulative materials.

Van de Walle and Thompson (1981) contend that problem-solving instruction involves carefully guided discussion, interaction among students, and an examination of strategies employed. Research reported by Suydam and Weaver (1981) suggests that time spent discussing and reconsidering ways in which to solve a problem may be the most important strategy in helping students become better problem solvers. There are many different ways in which you can provide opportunities for students to be involved in problem-solving activities.

*Activities.* Exhibit 13.4 is a list of problem-solving activities that have been adapted from Baratta-Lorten (1977a). In addition, Van de Walle and Thompson (1981) suggest using several different formats for presenting problem-solving activities.

They include the use of the following:

1. *Shoebox problems.* Package manipulative objects, such as Cuisenaire rods, blocks, strings, rulers, or beans in shoe boxes. Assemble the shoe box problems, along with a card explaining the problems, and place them where the students can work with them during math periods. This type of activity also can be done with tanagrams that are placed in envelopes. It is valuable to number each shoe box and envelope and rotate problems on a weekly basis.
2. *Folder problems.* File folders can be used for problems that require only a pencil and paper. You can place a drawing or map on the inside of the file folder and then cover it in acetate.

---

**EXHIBIT 13.4.** Group problem-solving activities

Plan a trip. Where would you go? How much would it cost?

What is the average height of students in our classroom?

Make a map of the school.

Make a map of the neighborhood. Show all the houses.

How fast does your hair grow?

How much food does our pet hamster eat each day? Each week? How much weight does it gain each week?

What is the temperature outside each day at noon?

How many letters come to your house each day? Each week?

What's the best way to fold a newspaper for throwing?

How fast is your pulse? When does it speed up? Slow down? Does everyone's pulse beat the same?

How far can you throw a ball? Does practice increase the distance?

How many times do you breathe each day?

How much milk do they use in the cafeteria each day? Each week? Each year?

What is the average age of our class in years, months, and days?

How much weight can a string hold before it breaks?

How many times can you bounce a ball in one minute? In a day?

---

Students then can write on the folder with a magic marker and wipe the plastic clean when they finish and have checked the answer. Problems can be collected from many sources and stored in a file according to several different categories, such as geometry, measurement, or logic. Also, they can be sorted according to their level of difficulty, ranging from easy to hard.

3. *Bulletin board problems*. The bulletin board can be used to present problems for everyone to solve at the same time during the week. You can establish a section of the bulletin board to post problems.

Students can work on these problems independently or in small groups. We suggest that you set aside a short period of time at the end of the week to discuss the problems and the different ways in which they can be solved. Some specific materials that can be used include graphs, maps, charts, travel brochures, sports statistics, and timetables.

In summary, there are some things that you can do to promote students' interest in problem solving. First, make use of problems that students spontaneously propose. Second, use games and computer programs, in which students will have opportunities to use problem-solving strategies. Third, where possible, personalize the problems by using the names of students in your class and their interest in the problems that you develop. Fourth, establish an environment that is encouraging and promotes enjoyment of problem solving (Reys, Suydam, & Lindquist, 1984).

## Fractions

The initial concept of fractions is that of a fractional part of a whole, which is a geometric concept. If students lack this concept and are asked to do computations, success may be difficult to achieve (Sobel & Maletsky, 1988).

The concept of fractions should be developed slowly through the use of familiar situations. Whenever possible, a variety of concrete materials should be used, including things that vary in size, shape, and the way in which they are grouped. An essential prerequisite to working with fractions is that students understand the concept of conservation. A sequence for learning fractions suggested by Gearheart, DeRuiter, and Sileo (1986) is separating the fraction into equal parts and naming those parts, reading and writing fraction symbols, comparing and ordering fractions, finding equivalent parts, and relating mixed fractions and improper fractions.

You can begin introducing fractions by having students cut a variety of objects into equal parts. Halves, thirds, and fourths should be presented first. Students indicate that they understand the concept of fractions when they know that fractions are divided into equal parts. The naming of the parts indicates the number of parts taken (the first number) and how many equal parts make up the whole of the fraction (the second number). Therefore, they know that "one-half" means one part out of two equal parts. Squares are easier to cut into equal parts than circles. Therefore, we suggest that students begin by using square shapes. It is valuable for you to have on hand a classroom kit that uses circles so that students can use it to generalize the concept of equivalency. After students have demonstrated mastery by cutting up concrete objects into equal parts, they should move on to coloring parts of pictured objects.

After students have learned the vocabulary that designates the parts, they should be introduced to the written symbol. One way to introduce the bar in a fraction is to explain it as meaning "out of" (Gearheart, DeRuiter, & Sileo, 1986). Therefore, they can make statements such as 2/3 means 2 out of 3 parts. Practice should be provided with a variety of fractions and cut-up materials. Students should be shown the objects and then asked to write the fraction for each group.

Students can make their own fraction kits in an effort to help them understand the concept of equivalent fractions. As stated earlier, squares are a good starting point. Students can use an uncut sheet of paper to designate the unit of 1. They should be given equal size pieces of paper divided into halves, fourths, eighths, sixteenths; and thirds, ninths, and twelfths. You want to have students write the symbol of each fractional part on the parts as they make them. This kit can then be used when students are writing equivalencies such as 1/4 = 2/8. Whenever possible, students should be asked to make predictions before they check with the kit.

To help students develop a concept of computation of fractions, you may want to present them with some story problems prior to doing any actual computing. For example, if you say to them, "If you have one-half of a candy bar and I have one-half of a candy bar, how much do we have all together?" or "If you have one-half of a pizza and I have one-fourth of a pizza, how much do we have all together?" After discussing problems such as these and having many experiences with their own fraction kits and with the classroom circle kit, the students can be introduced to addition of the written equation. By using the kits as a reference point, students can do the computation and then check their answers. Rewriting equivalent fractions should be introduced, and regrouping procedures should be presented and practiced. Whenever possible, you should expose students to both the horizontal and vertical manner of expressing fractions.

## Adapting Mathematics Instruction

On occasion, you will work with students who demonstrate difficulty in working independently. Adaptations will be necessary to assist these students so that they can complete their work and learn to become more independent. Lambie and Hutchens (1986) provided information on adaptations that can be made to help students overcome their difficulties.

1. Cut the page of problems into fourths and give the students one-fourth at a time. After all the problems have been completed, tape the page together so students can see that they did it all.
2. Fold the page of problems like an accordion and have the students work on one line at a time.
3. Assign half of the problems to be completed in class and half to be completed as homework.
4. Graph the percentage correct each day and post this on a board or desk.
5. Provide a checking center in the room with answer keys.
6. When students demonstrate difficulty lining up mathematical problems, have them use graph paper and write one number per square or use different colored markers for the one's, ten's, and hundred's columns.

## SCIENCE FOR YOUNG CHILDREN

The assessment of science abilities in young children would be highly similar to those discussed previously for mathematics. Again, educators advocate for tangible experience related to science for young children (Flavell, 1963; Greenberg, 1975; Hawkins, 1965; Hochman & Greenwald, 1963). A contemporary framework for a preschool science curriculum promotes active, child-oriented action on objects and observations about change that are organized developmentally. Iatridis (1981) found that exposing students to specific science experiments using carefully selected materials increased their child-initiated exploration (as opposed to aimless handling of materials) and verbal curiosity.

Your role with regard to science is to capitalize on daily experiences that might involve science concepts. For example, painting (Lasky & Mukerji, 1980) and cooking (Wanamaker, Hearn, & Richarz, 1979). You can use the strategies of self-talk and parallel talk (see

Chapters 5 and 6) to supply the vocabulary and phrases needed to encode concepts as students pursue their own curiosities or initiatives (Kamii & DeVries, 1978). You can encourage your students to observe more closely by your use of questions and the question prompts suggested in Chapter 10. Finally, you can help the students compare and classify their own discoveries (Iatridis, 1981). Your job is to use materials that are of interest to your students and to display them in a manner that is accessible and encourages exploration. You can gradually add to this collection so that new discoveries can be made (Forman & Kuschner, 1983). Be flexible with your objectives so that student self-discovery is not sabotaged.

## Activities

Smith (1987) explained how science can be incorporated into the traditional activities for young children.

*Painting.* Encourage children to match the colors that they are using to those that they are wearing. When colors are mixed (either purposefully or accidentally), call attention to the change that has occurred (not necessarily to the colors produced). Reinforce student observational development. Tactile experiences with dried, bumpy, or smooth paint can call attention to different types of surfaces or textures. Appropriate language (i.e. *smooth, rough, bumpy, scratchy,* etc.) can be introduced as required. Such properties are necessary to the students' development, and the use of novel words should not be avoided.

*Sounds.* Preschool classrooms should include a sound corner where a variety of sound-producing materials are available for experimentation (McIntyre, 1981). Students may be able to detect, discriminate, or identify different sounds (see Chapter 9), and these opportunities should be afforded them. You can supply your students with musical instruments, as well as mechanical toys that light or move to sound. Students can be encouraged to list sounds that they like or dislike, compare the differences of what they hear with and without the use of their personal hearing aids or FM systems, and associate various properties with sound (e.g., loud, soft, high/low pitch, pleasant/unpleasant, etc.).

*Foods.* Cooking and preparing foods are a traditional part of most preschool programs, and they provide opportunities to engage children in developing sight, touch, taste, and smell (Smith, 1987). Properties such as color, texture, taste, odor, size, and shape can be explored either at snack time or during a special activity period (Christenberry & Stevens, 1984; Parents Nursery School, 1974; Wanamaker, Hearn, & Richarz, 1979). The shape of a given fruit can be used to explore movement and to compare the movement of other fruits. Cooking experiences give children opportunities to observe change. Colors, textures, and tastes often change when foods are heated, providing stimuli for new science concepts and language tags. Your role is to exploit snack time for possible science experiences, encourage your students to focus on food properties other than taste, and use questions and question prompts to label emerging concept development.

*The Playground.* Ziemer (1987) suggested that the playground offers rich science resources, in which teachers and students can "joyfully investigate together." She reminds us that children love to name clouds and to learn that a swing acts as pendulum and that slides are an inclined plane. The opportunities inherent in playground physics and kitchen chemistry can be a bridge to planned classroom activities. As a teacher of students using bimodal communication, you and your colleagues will need to make decisions about vocabulary for signs that are not available. However, whether you decide to invent (having checked written resources, Deaf adults, other teachers and parents, etc.), fingerspell, or cue, do not avoid vocabulary. Your students need to be exposed to essential subject area vocabulary, and it is your job to label specifically the concepts that these words and phrases represent.

You are encouraged to read the work of Kamii and DeVries (1978) for ideas pertaining to water play and science; of Hill (1977) for discoveries with sand; Hirsch (1984) for science using toys; Holt (1977) for ideas about children's investigation of themselves; and of McIntyre (1981) for science involving animals. Experiences with these types of activities enable children to link language labels and physical knowledge and to construct relationships between and among objects better (Smith, 1987).

Science for young children can be interwoven into the activities that are experienced normally in early childhood programs if teachers are knowledgeable of their curricular goals. What makes science special for teachers of hearing-impaired children is the need to facilitate the use of specific language labels with their exploration and cognitive growth and to provide an environment in which children can manipulate objects and develop skills of observation. Science books for young children are recommended in Outstanding Science Trade Books for Children (1987).

## ELEMENTARY SCIENCE INTERVENTION

### Curriculum

Like mathematics curricula, science curricula have received scant attention in the field of deaf education. When new emphasis in study emerged from the Sputnik era and placed an emphasis on the process of science rather than on specific bodies of content (American Association for the Advancement of Science, 1963), analogous major change did not permeate science education for hearing-impaired students. Sunal (1984) lamented the paucity of science curricula and support materials available for hearing-impaired students of all ages in both residential and mainstreamed en-

vironments. Educators need to ensure that hearing-impaired students are exposed to science, despite the need for curriculum adaptations with regard to English language and methods. Lang and Propp (1982) and Battaglia, Scouten, and Hamil (1982) have voiced a strong and consistent message that hearing-impaired students can be successful science students when they are given the necessary tools and competent instruction.

Often the pace of the science curriculum is too rapid for hearing-impaired students (Bunch, 1987). If student goals emphasize the process of inquiry and the experience of finding a solution to a problem through problem solving, then the number of particular units covered is not an issue. It is most important that the intellectual curiosity of the students not be affected by a pace that does not allow for adequate comprehension of unit objectives. According to Bunch (1987), the most commonly used science materials in elementary school classes for hearing-impaired students are those listed below. Some strategies listed in these sources are paramount to effective instruction in general; others give specific science information.

1. The Clarke School for the Deaf Science Curriculum (1975)
2. The St. Mary's School for the Deaf Science Curriculum (1985)
3. Science for the Hearing-Impaired (Sunal & Sunal, 1981).

It is our recommendation that teachers of the Deaf follow a contemporary process-oriented science curriculum. This approach requires that students be actively involved in discovery. Use science curricula that were designed by experts, who had adequate time and money to develop the scope and sequence required (Sunal, 1984).

Scouten (1979) suggested a method of teaching science to hearing-impaired students. The students:

1. Preread about a particular experiment in a text
2. Develop a personalized plan for conducting the experiment (the teacher uses question prompts and visualizations to help the student order their work)
3. List procedural steps; language is modeled and used as necessary
4. Perform the experiment following the plan (either independently or with another interactional peer partner)
5. Write a report of the procedure and results.

Bunch (1987) reported that use of this procedure increased confidence, promoted a positive change in the quality of student questions, resulted in increased student time on the task, and heightened independence in the science laboratory.

## Strategies

The strategies used to teach science to hearing-impaired students would include all of the components of effective instruction (see Chapter 10). For example, task directions may need to be spoken, signed, or cued, as well as written. They may need to be restated in simpler English and given one step at a time. Your demonstration of a science task procedure will further clarify student requirements. We would expect teachers to employ basic principles that make learning any subject area possible for hearing-impaired students: developmental scope-and-sequence, task analysis, prescriptive teaching, and so on.

You may need to use prompts as you teach a science lesson. Repeating important verbal information or circling key words in written information to stress their importance can signal to hearing-impaired students that this is information of which they should take note. Whatever verbal or visual prompts are used, they should be withdrawn gradually as students demonstrate that they are no longer necessary.

You may find that hearing-impaired students require additional presentation of science material, additional practice, or a slower pace of instruction than what might be used with hearing students. The most radical of instructional adaptations for hearing-impaired students in mainstreamed classrooms would be to change the criteria for successful performance as compared to that required of hearing peers. These changes may involve requirements for grading, permission to use aids for material that others must memorize, or completion of a smaller set of tasks than typically required of hearing students (Lewis & Doorlag, 1987). However, by providing students with compensatory aids for science assignments, the teacher may be able to pass basic skill deficits in order to facilitate instruction in the content of science.

Teaching science requires the signing of technical signs to students exposed to bimodal communication. For example, Lang and Cacamise (1980) found that teachers in the same school were using the same sign to symbolize different concepts (e.g., current and circuit). If teachers do not communicate in close correspondence with their speech, problems arise for students in understanding information and in test situations. To alleviate these problems, a Technical Signs Project was initiated at the National Technical Institute for the Deaf in 1975. Materials produced include videotaped lists of technical signs and instruction manuals. Technical signs for numerous areas are now available.

## SUMMARY

Two neglected curricular areas were highlighted in this chapter. The considerations discussed are relevant to many other subject areas, and we hope that teachers will be able to apply the principles to the teaching of social studies, art, music, and so forth.

Teaching school subjects should begin

with the belief that it is important for each student to experience success. Ashlock (1982) and Underhill, Uprichard, and Heddens (1980) contend that immediate and continuous success for students are basic to effective mathematics instruction. Some important beliefs underlie our thinking on teaching mathematics. They include: (1) computational skills are more easily learned when drawn from concrete experiences; (2) logical thinking is a key element in learning mathematics and involves the ability to recognize patterns; and (3) students learn best in an environment that is free of the fear of failure (Baratta-Lorten, 1977). It is critical that you teach using a low affective filter in a nonthreatening manner. In addition, it may be essential to help students develop mathematical, science (etc.) vocabulary and key phrases as prerequisites to organizing and sequencing information needed for problem solving and computation.

It is important to remember that individual lesson plans should not be equated with drill-and-practice seatwork or with working through a computer-based mathematics or science program. There is a desperate need to incorporate activity-based teaching strategies (Fridriksson & Stewart, 1988) into lessons with hearing-impaired students. We suggest that, if you use more hands-on exploration in your lessons, then students will be better able to grasp concepts. Progression through the curriculum should include work on the concrete, semiconcrete, and abstract levels. It is important to stress problem-solving opportunities and strategies in all academic instruc-

tion. We believe that teachers of the deaf would benefit from reading journals and textbooks in the disciplines of early childhood education, learning disabilities and general education so that they can obtain relevant curricular research, methods, and materials pertinent to teaching students with impaired hearing. Finally, we have stressed our belief in the creativity of the knowledgeable teacher who enjoys the excitement of discovery that is possible when the curriculum is based on a sound philosophy, assesses individual student needs, prescribes goals and objectives, and develops action-based lessons.

## ACTIVITIES

1.  Make a list of household items and objects that you can get for free, which could be used as manipulative materials for structuring pre-math and science learning activities.
2.  Evaluate several children's books that might be used to facilitate mathematics or science concepts for young children.
3.  Develop a series of daily occurrences that could be used as stimuli for mathematical word problems.
4.  Use the clinical interview procedure with an elementary school student. Plan an intervention based on what you discover.
5.  Choose a science unit that you are interested in teaching. Plan a lesson using the components of effective instruction. Determine the vocabulary that you will preteach and use one of the methods to teach vocabulary presented in the reading section.

# PART FOUR

# Nonacademic Components of Instruction

## Deaf Culture, Self-Esteem, and Behavior Management

# CHAPTER 14

# Deafness and Deaf Culture as Curriculum Components

## OVERVIEW

We believe that all hearing-impaired students should be offered a bicultural curriculum in public, private, and residential contained or mainstreamed classes. Our premise for this approach is that, through the study of Deaf culture, hearing-impaired students will develop an affinity for both their hearing and Deaf cultural and linguistic linkages with people throughout the world and will appreciate more fully the value and relevance of their educational experience. Omaggio (1984) stated that cultural study prepares students to understand, accept, and live harmoniously in the target-language (e.g., hearing) community. While information regarding such Deaf culture curriculum is scant, we are hopeful that, within the next several years, concrete suggestions, activities, procedures, and resources will become available to teachers of the deaf so that they will be able to integrate Deaf culture into daily discussions with their students. The ideas provided in this chapter are presented as harbingers of comprehensive curriculums authored by Deaf adults that we expect to see available in the future.

---

**CHAPTER TOPICS**

Curriculum Components
Teaching Culture

---

## CURRICULUM COMPONENTS

In an effort to help hearing-impaired students understand and accept their hearing loss and simultaneously develop an understanding of Deaf culture, we suggest a program of study that centers on two distinct routes. One track focuses attention on the science of hearing and the impact of a hearing loss on learning and living. This information is what has been taught traditionally to hearing-impaired students and has been criticized as focusing on the deficient (rather than different) aspects of deafness. However, we believe that this material should be taught directly to students so that they have a basic understanding about their hearing ability and can explain it as needed to others.

The second path of study investigates and promotes involvement and understanding of the world through the eyes of Deaf people and the unique contributions that they have made (and are making) to society.

## What Is a Hearing Impairment?

Helping hearing-impaired students to understand and accept their hearing loss is considered by many teachers to be an important goal in Deaf education (Scott, 1983). One way to address this concept is to develop a unit on hearing and hearing impairment. Possible resources to obtain in starting such a unit include:

> Foppiani, V., & Talbot, M. (no date). *Communication and lifeskills curriculum*. Unpublished curriculum. Fairport, NY: Monroe BOCES.
>
> Gragg, V. (1985). *What is an audiogram?* Washington, D.C.: Gallaudet University Pre-College Programs.
>
> *Introduction to communication*. (1986). Washington, D.C.: Gallaudet University Pre-College Programs.
>
> Simko, C. B. (1986). *Ear gear*. Washington, D.C.: Gallaudet University Press.
>
> Stone-Harris, R. (1988). *Let's learn about deafness*. Washington, D.C.: Gallaudet University Pre-College Programs.

A sequence that you may want to consider includes the following topics and activities:

1. Knowledge of the hearing mechanism
   a. How we hear
   b. Hearing problems
      (1) Types of losses
      (2) Etiology of a hearing impairment
   c. Testing hearing
      (1) Audiometers
      (2) Audiograms
      (3) Degrees of hearing loss
   d. Personal hearing aids
      (1) Components of a hearing aid
      (2) Types of personal hearing aids
      (3) Hearing-aid care
      (4) Trouble shooting for hearing aids
   e. Educational amplification systems
      (1) FM systems
      (2) Induction loops
      (3) Hardwire systems
   f. Assistive devices
      (1) Telecommunication devices for the deaf (TDD)
      (2) Telephone amplifiers
      (3) Signaling devices
         (a) Wake-up alarms
         (b) Smoke alarms
         (c) Sound-sensing devices (doorbell, baby crying, telephone ring)
      (4) Television caption decoder
2. Impact of a hearing loss
   a. Effect on audition
   b. Effect on speech development
   c. Effect on language development
3. Communication methods
   a. Oral/aural
   b. Cued speech
   c. Manual communication
      (1) Fingerspelling
      (2) Seeing Essential English
      (3) Signing Exact English
      (4) Signed/Manual English
      (5) Pidgin Signed English
      (6) American Sign Language (ASL)
4. Modifications for hearing-impaired individuals
   a. Speechreading
      (1) One-to-one communication
   b. Group situations
      (1) Using an interpreter
      (2) Notetakers
      (3) Hearing-ear dogs
5. Organizations and agencies (see Exhibit 14.1 for examples)
   a. International organizations and agencies
   b. National organizations and agencies

   c. State organizations and agencies
   d. Local organizations and agencies
6. Projects
   a. Personal hearing record (see Exhibit 14.2 for example)
   b. Interview with a hearing-impaired adult
   c. Research and report on a famous hearing-impaired person
   d. A bulletin board about famous deaf people
   e. Interview with a parent or sibling of a hearing-impaired person

## What Is Deaf Culture?

Deaf culture includes:

People who share a common means of communication (e.g., manual communication), which provides the basis for group cohesion and identity (Schlesinger & Meadow, 1972)

Members bound by attitudinal deafness, which means that the persons identify themselves as members, regardless of degree of hearing acuity

People who have may come to be members of the Deaf culture or community in different ways (e.g., audiological, political, linguistic, social, etc.) and may be accepted at different levels (Baker & Cokely, 1980)

Hearing people and hearing-impaired people who use a sign system to communicate and may be considered members of the Deaf community at some level

**EXHIBIT 14.1.** Organizations and agencies for hearing-impaired individuals

Alexander Graham Bell Association for the Deaf
3417 Volta Place, NW
Washington, DC 2007

Captioned Films for the Deaf
5000 Park Street North
St. Petersburg, FL 33709

Deafpride, Inc.
2010 Rhode Island Avenue, NE
Washington, D.C. 20018

Hearing Dog Programs
American Humane Society
5351 Roslyn Street
Englewood, CO 80110

National Captioning Institute
P.O. Box 598
Ridgely, MD 21681

National Technical Institute for the Deaf at
Rochester Institute of Technology
One Lomb Memorial Drive
P.O. Box 9887
Rochester, NY 14623

Self-Help for Hard of Hearing People
4848 Battery Lane, Suite 100
Bethesda, MD 20814

Telecommunications for the Deaf
814 Thayer Avenue
Silver Spring, MD 20910

American Speech-Language-Hearing Association
10801 Rockville Pike
Rockville, MD 20852

Consumers Organization for the Hearing Impaired
P.O. Box 8188
Silver Spring, MD 20907

Gallaudet University
Kendall Green
800 Florida Ave, NE
Washington, D.C. 20002

National Association of the Deaf
814 Thayer Avenue
Silver Spring, MD 20910

National Fraternal Society of the Deaf
1300 W. Northwest Highway
Mt. Prospect, IL 60056

Organization for the Use of the Telephone
P.O. Box 175
Owings Mills, MD 21117

Suzanne Pathy Speak-Up Institute
525 Park Avenue
New York, NY 10021

World Federation of the Deaf
Congress Office
SF-00171 Helsinki, Finland

**EXHIBIT 14.2.** Personal hearing record

Name _____

Birthdate _____

1. My parents first noticed my hearing loss when I was _____ years old.

2. I have a _____ hearing loss.

3. I became hearing-impaired as a result of _____.

4. I have relatives that also have a hearing impairment.

   Yes _____ No _____

   If yes, list them.



5. My hearing was amplified with a _____

   when I was _____ years old.

6. The best hearing I have is in my _____ ear.

7. I have difficulty hearing the sounds _____.

8. The most difficult thing for me to hear is _____.

9. I use a _____ for amplification of sound.

10. Some things that I would like to learn about deafness or Deaf people are:

   _____

   _____

   _____

Membership based on characteristics of Deaf culture and community that are complex and changing

***Ethnic Deaf Adults.*** We have chosen to use the term *ethnic Deaf adult* in this chapter because it denotes people who view themselves as members of the Deaf community and who are active in that community, despite their degree of hearing loss. Capitalizing the word *deaf* signifies membership in the Deaf community.

Ethnic Deaf adults need to be hired in all types of school programs and in a variety of job roles. Special education directors and supervisors must realize the advantages of hiring these adults as directors and supervisors, itinerant teachers, classroom teachers, assistant teachers, reading specialists, home-parent teachers, and creativity specialists (Rutherford, 1987). There could be no better way to integrate the ethics and values of Deaf culture into the curriculum than to have it transmitted by its members.

Ethnic Deaf adults also need to be hired in university deaf education training programs. Presently some Deaf adults are so employed, primarily teaching sign classes. We believe that Deaf adults should be hired into positions of leadership in the training of future teachers of the deaf and that this degree of participation parallels Black involvement in Black studies and Hispanic inclusion in bilingual education. Even the most well-intended hearing people cannot transmit Deaf culture to future teachers of the deaf as can ethnic Deaf adults.

***Deaf Identity.*** Teachers of the deaf must envision their Deaf students as healthy, Deaf people who will access both the hearing and Deaf cultures as adults. This goal is in contrast to that of viewing these students pathologically as people who cannot hear or of viewing them as members of one culture versus another. Deaf students, like other students, have both strengths and weaknesses. We, as significant adults in the lives of these students, need to facilitate the development of self-esteem by identifying and recognizing their strengths and unique qualities. Deaf adults hold jobs as doctors, lawyers, university professors, fire fighters, librarians, coaches, and so on. Almost every issue of the *NAD Broadcaster* boasts of another "first" in careers held by Deaf adults. We, as teachers, need to provide role models of Deaf adults with a strong sense of identity for our students. We can do this by arranging opportunities for actual contact with Deaf members of our communities, taking our students to the job sites of Deaf adults, accessing secondary training institutions that serve hearing-impaired students, and so forth. We should not let our own prophecies limit the possibilities for future and successful employment of our students.

*Deaf Literature.* Deaf literature consists of a wealth of materials in a variety of genres, including works of Deaf history, ASL history, stories, poetry, plays, and folklore in print, videotape, and film formats (Rutherford, 1988). These materials should be available in all programs that serve hearing-impaired students. Understanding the richness of the folk tradition, and providing opportunities and the environment for its nurturing and self-development are important activities in the educational system (Rutherford, 1985). Examples of available materials are provided in Appendix B.

Rutherford (1988) reported that the folkloristic tradition of Deaf Americans is over 175 years old and abounds with legends, naming practices, tall tales, folkspeech, jokes, sign play, games, folk poetry, stories of empowerment, customs, ritual, and celebrations (Carmel, 1980; Rutherford, 1987). You could incorporate examples of the Deaf tradition in each unit that you plan. Published works by Deaf playwrights that reflect the Deaf experience include *A Play of Our Own* by Dorothy Miles, *Sign Me Alice*, by Gilbert Eastman, and *Tales from a Clubroom* by Bernard Bragg and Eugene Bergman. There

are also Deaf novels, publishing houses, and producers of videotaped programs and productions. The National Theater of the Deaf tours the country each year. Silent Network, the nation's only television network designed for hearing-impaired viewers, is the winner of many awards for fine programming. As a teacher of deaf students you should read and see these examples of Deaf literature.

*Visual Arts.* The Deaf community has a long history in the visual arts (Rutherford, 1988). Artists such as John Brewster (1766–1854) and C. L. Washburn (1866–1965) are world famous. Deaf art has been displayed in the Metropolitan Museum of Art in New York, The National Gallery in Washington, D.C., the Boston Museum of Fine Arts, Carnegie Institute, and the San Francisco Palace of Fine Arts (Gannon, 1981). Deaf Artists of America is a recently formed group that has held several national conferences.

*Deaf Studies.* We have advocated for a bilingual and bicultural perspective throughout this text (as do Stewart and Akamatsu, 1988), believing that hearing-impaired students can be members of more than one culture, just as can hearing bilingual students. Our goal should be that students have autonomy over their lives (Rutherford, 1985). Because the majority of deaf children are born to hearing parents, the culture of deafness is not included naturally in family activities as it may be in families with Deaf parents. Many hearing-impaired children grow up without access to Deaf culture, its values, or knowledge of American Sign Language. Therefore, it is highly likely that it will be your responsibility to teach units or conduct activities to foster deaf awareness.

To begin to understand Deaf culture and it's relevance to their lives, your students may need to investigate various aspects of the concepts "culture" and "community." We have compiled a list of themes that have been field-tested with hearing and hearing-impaired students to enhance their awareness of deaf-

**EXHIBIT 14.3.** Suggested topics for deaf students

1. What is sound, and how is it made? What is an audiogram? What is an aided and unaided audiogram?
2. How did I become deaf?
3. What are the parts of the ear? What causes deafness? What caused my deafness?
4. How does a cochlear implant work?
5. What are the different types of hearing aids, and which works the best for different types of hearing losses? Why does mine work best for me?
6. Caring for hearing aids and auditory training devices.
7. What is Deaf culture and Deaf community?
8. A mime group, signing song group, or Deaf theatre group is invited to perform.
9. Types of manual languages and systems and the various systems used to transcribe them.
10. Abilities, attitudes, and accomplishments of Deaf artists.
11. Famous Deaf people and Deaf history.
12. Folkstories of empowerment for Deaf people.
13. Talent show for the school (showing the special talents of the Deaf students).
14. Interaction with Deaf adults (regular contact with Deaf adults from the community).
15. Making communication work. What can we tell our hearing friends so that they can improve their communication with us?
16. Deaf Awareness Week at school.
17. Jobs and higher education opportunities.
18. Visits to businesses (students see a range of occupational possibilities where Deaf adults are employed).
19. Sign classes by hearing-impaired students for hearing students.
20. Visits or pen pal programs with other hearing-impaired students in other programs, states, or countries.

ness (see Exhibit 14.3) and should be helpful. This list (based on *Deaf in America* by Padden and Humphries, 1988) is not all inclusive but should provide you with ample additional themes for initial study:

Who participates in the Deaf community?

Do the majority of individuals join the Deaf community from birth?

Is residential school the typical avenue for introduction into the Deaf community?

Some people say that ASL is merely made up of gestures. How does this compare with the statement that oral English is made merely of noises?

How is the morphology of ASL similar and dissimilar to that of signed English? Of spoken English?

Can ASL, Signed/Manual English, and ASL each be used to communicate fully (e.g., with various people about various topics, easily and fluently)?

How were you affected by viewing a signed theater performance?

When Deaf friends tell you anecdotes about their lives, can you relate to these experiences in your own life? Does it make you feel good to know that your Deaf friends have similar experiences and feelings?

Are there things that you feel society thinks about Deaf people that are not true?

How did you discover that you could not hear sound or speech? What are your first memories of this? Was it a positive or a negative feeling? (Read Padden and Humphries, 1988, for some positive and negative reactions.)

What are some ways in which you can

decide if someone is hearing or deaf?

How can you tell if someone has been signing for a long time or is a relatively new signer? How can you tell whether someone signs ASL or English or a foreign sign language?

Some people have written that they felt a powerful sense of loss when they were left at a residential school for the first time. Did you feel this way? How did you feel? Have there been other times in which you felt lonely or abandoned that you associate with deafness?

What sorts of dependencies do you experience in your family? (For example, can you tell by yourself that someone is calling on the TDD or telephone or that the doorbell is ringing?) How would these dependencies be different if you lived in a hearing or a Deaf home? How can you arrange your home and school life so that you are less dependent on others?

A Deaf folktale is a story about what it means to be deaf in our society. Retelling these stories can help deaf and hearing people understand the values of the Deaf Community. Read or watch some Deaf folktales. Tell one to your class. Invent a folktale that you would tell to your children.

Sometimes Deaf folktales are "instructions" (Padden & Humphries, 1988). Read or watch a folktale that gives important information about how to live or do something. Tell the story to a Deaf friend and to a hearing friend or family member. Compare their reactions.

Do you have a Deaf teacher? How would your life be different if you did or did not have a Deaf person to talk to at school?

Does the pace of someone's signing tell you anything about them?

What are some of the national, regional, state, and local organizations to which Deaf people belong?

Do you have a "public image"; that is, are there things that you like to mention about yourself or like people to know about you when you first meet them because you think that they might value these qualities? (For example, would you tell someone that you became deaf by accident or through illness because you felt that it was a better way to become deaf than by heredity?)

Would you rather be deaf or hard-of-hearing or hearing? Why?

How do people describe signs in sign language? What are the ways in which people have learned to write signs so that others could learn them? Read about William Stokoe's (Stokoe, Casterline, and Croneburg, 1976) dictionary or how foreign sign languages have been described.

What are some magazines and newspapers that Deaf people read? Consider reading one of these and writing a letter or article to the editor. What television programs are designed for Deaf viewers?

Try to describe in words the sounds that you might hear (e.g., *pop, click, buzz, swish, roar, whir*) (Padden & Humphries, 1988).

Imagine a town, state, or country in which only Deaf people lived, worked, and attended school. Would you like it there? Would you allow hearing parents, brothers, sisters, and friends to visit?

Watch a professional mime. How could mime help you tell better stories and portray poetry?

Knowledge and appreciation of Deaf culture is only one aspect of Deaf studies. It is beyond the scope of this text to describe and exemplify Deaf culture, yet we would expect that you would have studied this culture as part of your formal college education and have a sensitivity to and understanding of it. It is expected that college students who are taking courses in Deaf studies would have a working proficiency of American Sign Language, have studied the linguistics of ASL and sign systems, read Deaf literature, and have become familiar with Deaf values, humor, heritage, and so on. It is now possible to join a Deaf studies special interest group within many of the major professional groups in the United States. We would expect that teachers of the deaf would read updates regarding the progress of Deaf studies, subscribe to publications of Deaf organizations (see Exhibit 14.1), and purchase curriculum and materials as they become available for use with your students.

## TEACHING CULTURE

Both hearing teachers of the deaf and teachers of foreign languages often feel inadequate in their knowledge of the foreign culture (Crawford-Lange & Lange, 1984). Typically, both of these groups of teachers have been trained to teach language, but not culture. Yet, educators of foreign-language instruction recommend that culture not be taught as a body of facts, but be approached as a process (Nostrand, 1974). We agree and suggest that you utilize a systematic model to integrate culture into your curriculum. A process of hypothesis refinement about culture proposed by Jorstad (1981) enables students who are studying foreign languages to achieve outcomes such as those listed. We believe that a plan such as this would be workable in designing units for your students about deafness. Your role is to facilitate students to:

Perceive a cultural aspect about the Deaf Community
Make a statement about that aspect
Gather information from sources related to the aspect
Examine the information and describe, report, and analyze their findings

Modify and refine their original statement as needed
Examine a related aspect in the other culture (e.g., hearing)
Compare refined statements about Deaf and Hearing cultures

## A Sample Model

A process of interactive language and culture has been promoted by Crawford-Lange (1981), Freire (1973), and Jorstad (1981) in the foreign-language classroom. The process is interactive in that the target and native languages, cultures, and cultural perceptions are related for study. As the teacher, you would plan both affective and cognitive goals for units concerning Deaf and Hearing cultures. Of the eight basic stages in the model, you would direct the first five, and the last three would be student directed. Each of these stages is defined and exemplified below:

*Stage 1: Identification of a Cultural Theme.* Cultural themes are provocative and perhaps emotionally charged concerns or issues that can motivate students (Brooks, 1968). It is very likely that a stimulating topic could emerge from the investigation of topics listed previously in this chapter.

For example, in the study of Deaf culture, the study of employment in and of itself may not be a stimulating theme for your students, but the issue of underemployment, ability in occupational situations to use the telephone, and the socializing aspect of employment may well be. The stronger the relationship to the students' experience, the more powerful the theme will be for language and cultural studies. Further development of the theme becomes the responsibility of the teacher and the students. For example, given a unit theme of underemployment, older elementary school students and their teacher might work together to write conversational scripts dealing with job interviews, proficiency on the job, job layoffs, Deaf adults holding unique jobs, and so forth.

**Stage 2: Presentation of Cultural Phenomena.** Cultural phenomena are presented to students via pictures, photographs, displays, slides, overhead transparencies, videotape, software, written text, stimulations, role playing, pen pals, biographies, minidramas, and so on. The target language (i.e., English) is integrated into these presentations (Crawford-Lange & Lange, 1984). For example, newspaper clippings advertising various jobs and personal resumes could be used as phenomena relating to the theme of underemployment.

**Stage 3: Dialogue.** In using the dialogue process, you and your students focus on your perceptions of the phenomena being presented (e.g., "Is the prospective employee qualified for the job as it is listed in the ad?" "What can the employee do if the employee feels he or she is being dismissed from a job for a reason other than job performance?" "What is the relationship between underemployment and the use of the telephone?"). You then engage in an analysis of the thematic features (e.g., "How is discrimination related to employment?") and reaction to the situation in terms of cultural patterns ("How does success in obtaining a particular job relate to other Deaf adults holding that type of job?"). Following this model from foreign-language instruction, hearing-impaired students would use ASL, PSE, or a system of English to express their perceptions and reactions about various situations (that is, the focus of discussion would be on problem solving and not the form of English). You can guide students with questioning techniques, but you should not criticize student comments as correct or incorrect. You are also not required to have a "right" answer for the situations that may arise in discussion.

**Stage 4: Transition to Language Learning.** Students might now be able to examine the language (e.g., language functions, semantics, syntax, registers, and vocabulary) (Crawford-Lange & Lange, 1984) needed to

learn more about the unit theme. For example, if you were job interviewing, what tone would you use to communicate—polite, curt; with an understanding of what the job required? With a knowledge of some of the key terms that describe the demands of the job and demonstrate that you are capable of completing the work? If you were fired unfairly from a job at which you had a high level of performance, what would your tone of communication be with your employer? How might telephone training help some Deaf people at work? What assistive listening devices may be beneficial in the work place?

**Stage 5: Language Learning.** The needed language is now supplied so that students can practice dialogue in the context of the unit theme (e.g. English to interview; ASL to socialize on break). Many of the activities described in the section on form intervention in Chapter 7 would be useful during this stage.

**Stage 6: Verification of Perceptions of the Two Cultures.** Having a sufficient command of the necessary target language, students would now be ready to verify their initial perceptions of the theme by examining materials made available to them. Students can work independently or in groups but eventually bring their information back to the class as a whole to be described, analyzed, and compared with that of their peers. This stage utilizes a second opportunity for dialogue and, because of prior language learning, should involve increased use of the target language. In this stage, changes in the perceptions of both the target and native cultures (i.e., English and Deaf) are noted specifically and described, as are positive and negative reactions (adapted from Crawford-Lange & Lange, 1984).

**Stage 7: Cultural Awareness.** Students work to summarize their findings (e.g., "Why are there cultural differences in this situation of employment?" "What effects do hearing loss, personalities, etc., have on this situation?" "Are there different patterns in different regions of the country for these situations?" "If your perceptions of culture changed during this unit, what caused them to change?") This stage is one of generalization and is an important component of effective instruction.

***Stage 8: Evaluation of Language and Cultural Proficiency.*** Students engage in a culminating activity for the unit and use the target language to demonstrate their understanding of the unit theme. Possible activities are minidramas, simulations, dialogues, and so on. For example, students studying the theme of underemployment may contrast a job interview in a hearing company with one with the National Association of the Deaf. Students create these activities themselves and are evaluated on both their use of the target language and their demonstration of cultural knowledge.

The components described could be adapted to students of various age levels by increasing or decreasing teacher participation and by choosing a theme that is cognitively matched to the abilities of your students. The process is workable both for students studying American Sign Language as the target language, English. Use of resources from bilingual education and foreign-language instruction for this section serve to exemplify that educators in deaf education can look outside their own specific field for information that is useful to promote an awareness and understanding of Deaf culture.

## SUMMARY

We hope that information provided in this chapter will enable teachers of the deaf to integrate Deaf culture into daily lessons with their hearing-impaired students. A responsibility for understanding and respecting Deaf people is expected of all those who teach them. Information centering on both the science of hearing and the impact of hearing loss, as well as involvement and understanding of Deaf culture have been included in this chapter with the expectation that motivated teachers can use the lists of examples to begin integration of material into classroom curriculum. A systematic model for integrating culture into curricular units was explained and exemplified. It should be possible for teachers of the deaf to adapt this example to other relevant areas of study and to share the units with colleagues so that others can begin to include Deaf culture in their curriculum. You are reminded that a wealth of helpful resources for such study are provided in Appendix B.

## ACTIVITIES

1. Compare and contrast Deaf culture with Hearing culture.
2. Develop a unit on the science of hearing or the impact of a hearing loss on learning and living that utilizes the outline provided in the chapter and that is appropriate for elementary school students.
3. Gather literature from major organizations and agencies in this country. Read a year's worth of newsletters or newspapers of two organizations (e.g., *The NAD Broadcaster, Silent News*, etc.).
4. Compile a booklet of newspaper articles about jobs held by Deaf people.
5. Add five resources to the list provided in Appendix B.
6. Devise a unit of study, appropriate for elementary school students that utilizes the eight basic steps to the interactive language and culture model explained and exemplified in this chapter.

# CHAPTER 15

# Self-esteem and Behavior Management

## OVERVIEW

This chapter explores strategies for the classroom that do not relate to specific instructional content but impact on the entire teaching process. First, it provides information on how to help students develop positive self-esteem. We suggest that, when students feel accepted and good about who they are, there is less of a need for them to act out and seek attention via disruptive behavior. Five conditions for developing positive feelings of self-esteem are presented. Suggestions for actions and activities that you can use to facilitate students' self-esteem in each of those areas are provided.

In order to succeed in school, students must also behave relatively well and have a good rapport with classmates and teachers. *Behavior management* refers to any procedure or practice that has the purpose of influencing, changing, or controlling behavior (Gloeckler & Simpson, 1988). There are two primary goals of behavior management procedures. One is to establish a classroom climate that invites and motivates students to learn. The second is to provide the structure and opportunities for students progressively to learn to manage their own behavior.

Finally, this chapter develops further our view that communication occurs within all interchanges between you and your students. It is important to remember that language learning also occurs when you discipline students. Therefore, attention should be directed to the *quality of your interactions* and the *diversity of language* that you use.

---

| CHAPTER TOPICS |
|---|
| Self-esteem |
| Classroom Behavior Management |
| Additional Behavior Management Techniques |
| Behavior Management and Teachers' Language Input |

## SELF-ESTEEM

Self-esteem is a judgment about one's self-worth, one's competence and value, based upon the process of gathering and conceptualizing information about oneself and one's experiences (Johnson, 1979). What individuals believe about themselves vitally affects every aspect of their behavior and their life. A substantial and growing body of empirical evidence (Beane, Lipka, Ludewig, 1980; Hansford & Hattie, 1982; Rosenberg, 1979) suggests the link between positive self-perceptions to personal development.

Next to the home, schools exert the single greatest influence on how students see themselves and their abilities. Any educator plays a major part in students' perceptions of themselves. Research reported by Grissom and Cochran (1986) and Sass-Lehrer (1986) indicates that teachers of hearing-impaired children consider enhancing the self-esteem of their students to be one of the most important competencies that they can possess.

### Conditions of Self-Esteem

A number of writers and researchers have proposed various factors as necessary for individuals to develop positive feelings of self-esteem. Five areas that have been identified as being important for developing positive feelings of self-worth are presented (Luckner, 1987).

Drawing from the work of Coopersmith (1967), Anderson, Redman, and Rogers (1984), and Clemes and Bean (1980) we present the following conditions as essential for the development and maintenance of a high level of self-esteem. Practical suggestions for promoting development of each will also be given in the following discussion.

1. *Connection.* This results when individuals feel loved and cared for; when the student believes that what he or she thinks, communicates, or does matters to others; and, when the people and things that are held in high regard by the student are appreciated also by others.
2. *Uniqueness.* This occurs when an individual knows that he or she is separate and different from other people and when the student receives respect and approval from others for those qualities.
3. *Power.* This comes from being given the opportunity to make choices and decisions and being able to have some control over what happens in one's life.
4. *A sense of models.* This develops from being exposed to other individuals' personal values, goals, and ideas.
5. *Accomplishment.* This comes from placing value on tasks or goals and working successfully to the point of completion.

### Implications for Practitioners

An individual's perception of self develops gradually and is learned as the individual experiences life. Since it is learned, its direction and importance can be altered as other learning experiences and interactions with significant others are encountered. There are many things that you can do to nurture the self-esteem of your students—some simple and perhaps obvious. The following suggestions keep a focus on the importance of establishing an educational environment that promotes positive feelings of self-worth in students. (Luckner, 1987).

### Promoting a Sense of Connection

Send a postcard to each of your new students before school begins. Let them know that you look forward to working with them.

Show affection in what you communicate and do.

Try to meet with each student for even a brief time on a daily basis.

Actively communicate with students by focusing, clarifying, accepting, and encouraging them.

Know and use students' preferred names and name signs.

Notice nonverbal indicators that the student is happy, sad, glad, tired, and so on, and communicate these observations.

Learn about students' personal interests and activities outside of school.

Write positive comments on papers in addition to grades.

Maintain personal contact after school hours in noncurriculum related areas.

Give attention to a student when it is needed or set up a designated time to meet if the present circumstances do not permit.

Make positive personal contact with parents.

Promote student involvement in clubs, teams, and appropriate organizations.

Rotate the seating in the classroom so that each student has the opportunity to sit close to you.

Each week contact a parent with some positive information about his or her child.

Make an effort to understand the fads, fashions, popular heroes, latest films, and television programs that presently motivate your students. Using them as an example while you are teaching can be very effective.

Make use of daily dialogue journals to communicate with each student about personal concerns and interests.

Organize group discussions for students to communicate about particular issues and feelings that affect them.

## Promoting a Sense of Uniqueness

Acknowledge and promote students' special skills and interests.

Be specific in your praise.

Have students develop and share their autobiographies.

Provide individual cubicles or sections of the room for students to decorate and store their personal things.

Have students interview each other.

Accept the fact that students are not adults and that there is a great deal to be learned through experimentation and inappropriate behavior.

Encourage students to express ideas that may be different from yours or other class members.

Increase opportunities for students to express themselves creatively.

Ask students to make a list or draw pictures of their favorite things and activities.

Invite students to talk about their families and some of the things that make their families special.

Use praise privately so as not to embarrass students in front of their peers.

Obtain a full-length mirror and place it somewhere in the classroom where students can see themselves as they pass by.

Take note of positive things that students do, and then describe them to the class without mentioning the students' names.

Put together a costume closet, composed of old hats, uniforms, masks, and unusual clothing. These can be used during free time, role-playing activities, or class plays.

Choose a student of the week or month and display his or her photograph with some background information on a bulletin board.

## Promoting a Sense of Power

Encourage personal responsibility.

Avoid ridiculing or shaming students.

Reward good performance.

Help students find acceptable ways to express themselves.

Whenever possible, use democratic practices when you are planning policies or activities.

Make a classroom suggestion box available.

Help students become aware of the decision-making process.

Teach students how they can influence people in positive ways.

Let each student have a section of the bulletin board for his or her own use.

Provide sufficient time for students to complete their assignments.

Provide opportunities for students to make choices, especially when they are of minor concern to you.

Help students to understand the consequences of their behavior.

Use self-correcting materials.

Communicate clearly about responsibilities, limits, and consequences.

Provide methods for students to handle their own grievances.

Make use of contracts for behavior and academics.

Have students of lower ability tutor children in lower grades.

Encourage students to take risks.

When feasible, let students choose who they want to work with and where to sit.

Help older students plan learning experiences for younger students.

Rearrange the way in which the classroom is decorated. Ask students to assist in the planning and rearranging.

## Promoting a Sense of Models

Remember that you are a primary model for your students.

Share your personal feelings and goals with your students.

Allow students to interview you.

Share your interests, hobbies, activities, and experiences with the students.

Eat lunch or share lunch with a different student on a weekly basis.

Encourage participation in cultural programs and community events.

Model self-praise. Let students know when you feel proud about something that you have done so that they can do the same.

Read and discuss stories and books about other hearing-impaired individuals.

Share with the class when you make a mistake.

Expose students to people whom you hold in high regard, either through personal contact, the media, or literature.

Make use of cooperative learning procedures and techniques.

Invite parents and members of the community to come to school to discuss their interests and careers.

Share laughter and joy with your students.

Phrase directions in a positive manner by focusing on what should be done, rather than on what should not be done.

Avoid responding to a situation while you are angry or upset. It is important to let your temper cool down a little before you act.

Be willing to express your own lack of knowledge on a particular subject, and ask students to work with you to get more information.

## Promoting a Sense of Accomplishment

Plan activities and seat work so that a students' chances of experiencing success are increased.

Let the students evaluate their work and decide what they would like displayed on the bulletin board.

Preserve student work in a three-ring binder rather than throwing it out or sending it home one piece at a time.

Make use of individual charts and graphs

that promote and demonstrate mastery of areas of study.

Provide sufficient opportunities for guided practice and group review prior to having students do individual work.

Relate present learning to future goals of students.

Maintain a balanced attitude towards competition.

Provide opportunities for student self-evaluation of their work.

Help hearing-impaired students broaden their range of experiences.

Encourage students to write goals for themselves for the next day, week, or month and to follow through on them.

Provide incentives for good performance rather than punishment for poor performance.

Assign homework that you know the students can do.

Encourage students to begin collections—cans, rocks, stamps, dolls, matchbox covers, or coins. Invite them to display their collections in school.

Make individual chalkboards for each child to work on. Each student works on his or her own board, then holds it up for the teacher to check. The teacher then knows who needs extra help while others are doing independent seat work.

Look for objects such as broken clocks, radios and simple mechanical devices that can be taken apart and put back together during free time.

What students believe about themselves vitally affects every aspect of their behavior and learning. Creating a classroom atmosphere that is challenging without being threatening and planning activities and procedures that focus on specific ways to promote quality relationships are often the keys to better learning climates, higher levels of academic achievement, and enhanced self-esteem.

# CLASSROOM BEHAVIOR MANAGEMENT

Since there is no one method or approach that meets the needs of all students, you will need to learn and develop skills in various management procedures and to develop a personal philosophy about behavior management in your classroom. This will provide you with a flexible repertoire for meeting the many diverse and challenging behaviors that are often exhibited by students. An understanding of the multiple aspects of classroom behavior management is a vital starting point. Kindsvatter, Wilen, and Ishler (1988) suggest that behavior management can be broken down into four phases: *prevention, maintenance, intervention*, and *adjustment*.

## Prevention

There are several effective ways to structure a classroom to prevent or at least minimize the occurrence of discipline problems. The consistent themes or attitudes that are conveyed in presenting classroom rules, activities, and assignments contribute to the development of a general atmosphere or climate. Stainback, Stainback, and Froyen (1987) identified some characteristics of teachers who foster a positive learning climate. They include the following:

1. Expectations and plans for success, rather than failure

2. A positive, pleasant personality that conveys the attitude that the teacher enjoys the students as worthwhile members of the group

3. Recognition of appropriate rather than inappropriate behaviors and achievements rather than deficits

4. Recognition and understanding of each member as an individual with his or her own unique set of characteristics, needs, past experiences, and home environment

5. An expectation of productive work habits

Classroom order also depends on you providing clear, explicit rules. As much as possible, the students should be involved in developing the rules so that they feel some ownership in the way in which the class will be run. The visualization techniques presented in Chapter 6 may be useful in providing visual support as rules are discussed. It is best to develop a few general rules, with input from your students if possible, and to state them in a positive manner. Such rules might include:

1. Start your work quickly and quietly.
2. Keep your hands, feet, and objects to yourself.
3. Take turns communicating.
4. Raise your hand when you need help.
5. Try to complete all your work.
6. Keep your work and work area neat.

The rules should be displayed where they can be seen and referred to as needed. For students who cannot read, stick-figure illustrations can be placed next to the written rule.

An important part of developing and displaying the rules is to be certain that students understand each of the rules. Therefore, we suggest that you have a discussion about each rule and act out what is acceptable and what is not acceptable behavior regarding each one. Students should feel that you are an ally in these discussions and that success will be mutually shared. Your role is one of facilitator and listener. As you explain the consequences of the behavior that you seek to change, you also need to respect your students' opinions. We suggest that the problem solving that might occur in teacher-student discussions such as this could be of the conversationally based, genuine nature recommended in Chapter 1. By knowing what is acceptable and

unacceptable in the classroom, you and the students are in a better position to communicate clearly about improving behavior.

Another area of importance is the management of routines that are associated with the rules. These include daily routines such as sharpening pencils, checking auditory-training equipment, going to the bathroom, using learning centers, getting a drink of water, as well as what to do when work has been completed. Developing guidelines for doing these types of activities and explicitly discussing them with your students is necessary if your classroom is to run smoothly.

You can prevent inappropriate behavior by monitoring students and providing feedback (Hipple, 1978; Lewis & Doorlag, 1987). Learn to position yourself so that you can see all students and activities and can visually scan the classroom constantly. Give eye-contact or physical proximity to students who are having difficulty staying on task. Directly teach students a hand signal or facial expression that you will use when dissatisfied with present behavior. Be sure to give clear and consistent linguistic (sign/voiced) and nonverbal messages as you monitor their behavior.

Sometimes students become so frustrated that they need your assistance in seeking a different way to handle a situation (Hipple, 1978). Perhaps you can limit the options inherent in the activity or divert their attention elsewhere. For example, you may need to give a student only two choices of materials for an art activity or lead the student to a particular area for free play.

Maybe a student needs an advanced notice or *cue* that things are about to change. A flick of a light switch or an upraised hand can allow a moment of preparation for the student who needs time to make necessary transitions. Another way to prevent inappropriate behavior is to model desired behavior. You, other teachers, parents, or peers can serve as role models of the behavior that you wish the student to exhibit. The target student should be reinforced when he or she imitates this model.

## Maintenance

Maintenance behaviors are those that you will undertake, along with instructional behaviors that are intended to keep students on task. They include moving around the room during the lesson, maintaining eye contact with students, actively involving as many students as possible in the learning activity, and giving positive feedback for good behavior.

## Intervention

An important question to ask when you are planning a strategy to deal with a discipline problem that continues to occur despite prevention and maintenance strategies is this: "What are the internal and external conditions that are causing this situation?" This question can provide the impetus for productive problem solving.

A guiding principle that you should use when you are intervening with students should be to use the least intrusive intervention that is likely to be effective and to use more stringent forms only as necessary. Examples of mild forms of intervention would be to involve the student in the lesson by asking him or her a question. At times, simply having direct eye contact will bring the student back on task. If this does not work, you may need to move yourself physically in the proximity of the student. If these subtle procedures do not work, then a verbal (spoken or signed) reminder may be necessary. It may be possible to get the student's attention and to simply shake your head. If the behavior continues, you may need to redirect the student to the appropriate task. Should this not be successful, then it is essential to approach the student and direct him or her to another seat or a time-out site, remove the

student from the room, or do whatever is appropriate for the situation. It is best to avoid a confrontation with the student, because you will only lose, both emotionally and educationally. Whenever possible, the consequences of the behavior should be related to the misbehavior.

According to Sabatino (1987), *punishment* is a poor deterrent to unwanted behaviors for four reasons. First, fear of punishment generates anger, which produces greater conflict. Second, punishment does not address the initial question related to all inappropriate behaviors: Does the student know that he or she is breaking the rules? Third, punishment does not teach appropriate behavior; therefore, while it may modify a given behavior quickly, rarely is the effect permanent. Fourth, punishment is a negative means of gaining attention from adults. Consequently, punishment may inadvertently reinforce the very behaviors that you are trying to eliminate. Specific intervention methods that can be used as alternatives to punishment are presented later in this chapter.

## Adjustment

The purpose of this step is to diminish and hopefully to eliminate student behavior problems. We are trying to help students realize that their behaviors have certain consequences. It is also a time period in which you can help students gain insight into the reasons for their behavior. This can be done through the use of a brief conference, in which you discuss with the student the behavior and make a commitment to more appropriate behavior in the future. If this does not work, then you may need to sit down with the student and develop a contract. Should this be ineffective, then it may be necessary to involve other individuals, such as a parent, counselor, or administrator to help develop a more comprehensive program to change the behavior.

## ADDITIONAL BEHAVIOR MANAGEMENT TECHNIQUES

### Increasing Appropriate Behavior

It is important to focus on the positive behaviors that students demonstrate, as well as the behaviors that you want to decrease or eliminate. Praise is one of the most effective and convenient *reinforcers* that you can use to manage student behavior. Paine et al. (1983) state that effective praise has several important characteristics:

1. Good praise adheres to the "if-then" rule. This means that, if the student is behaving in the desired manner, then (and only then) do you praise the student.
2. Good praise usually includes the students' names.
3. Good praise is descriptive.
4. Good praise conveys that you really mean what you are saying to the students.
5. Good praise has varied formats.
6. Good praise does not disrupt the flow of individual or class activities.

Exhibit 15.1 provides a list of suggestions that you can use to give students positive feedback.

In some cases, praise will not be a sufficient reinforcer for students, and alternatives involving objects or activities will have to be discovered. It is important to remember that a reinforcer must have a positive effect on the student's behavior. If it does not increase or maintain a desired behavior, then it is not truly a reinforcer. Finding effective and appropriate reinforcers will present a continual challenge for you. Some points to keep in

---

**EXHIBIT 15.1.** Suggestions for giving positive feedback to students

*Physical:*

| | |
|---|---|
| Hug | Smile |
| Pat on head or shoulder | "Thumbs up" sign |
| Arm around student's shoulder | Wink |

*Verbal:*

"I like it when you _____ "

"It's nice when you _____ "

"Thanks for _____ "

"That was terrific when you _____ "

"Great!"

"Nice going!"

"Good job!"

"Super!"

"Fantastic!"

"My, you sure act grown up when you _____ "

"Wow!"

"Beautiful!"

"You did that all by yourself when you _____, and I didn't have to remind you."

"I am really impressed by the way you _____ "

"I am very proud of you when you _____ "

"It makes me very happy to see you _____ "

"I always enjoy it when you _____ "

mind are that: (1) no two students will react equally to the same reinforcers; and (2) items and events that were once reinforcing may lose their effectiveness, therefore, you must continue to search for new, alternative reinforcers (Westling & Koorland, 1988). Exhibit 15.2 is an example of a reinforcement survey that has been adapted from Blackham and Silberman (1975), which you may want to use with your students. Exhibit 15.3 provides examples of potential reinforcers for students. It is valuable always to provide social and/or verbal reinforcement in addition to any other tangible reinforcer that you can use with a student. Frequently, praise alone may be sufficient. If it is effective, then there may be no need to use other objects or activities.

When you are delivering reinforcers, it is best that you try to catch the student while he or she is being good or is performing the target behavior. Whenever possible, the reinforcement should be immediate (Lewis & Doorlag, 1987). Also, when delivering the reinforcer, you should communicate to the student the reason for the reinforcer. A final point is that it is essential that you always deliver a reinforcer that has been promised if it has been earned by the student (Westling & Koorland, 1988).

Behaviors that are being learned initially should be reinforced each time that they occur. This helps to develop a foundation for your behavior program. As the students' behavior increases favorably, you can gradually reduce reinforcement. This helps to avoid the possibility that the reinforcer will lose its effect and also establishes a reinforcement schedule that is *intermittent*, which research has demonstrated to be the most powerful form of reinforcement (Alberto & Troutman,

**EXHIBIT 15.2.** Reinforcement survey

Name: _____ Age: _____ Date: _____

1. The things I like to do after school are: _____
2. If I had $10.00, I would: _____
3. My favorite television programs are: _____
4. My favorite game at school is: _____
5. My best friends are: _____
6. My favorite toys are: _____
7. My favorite subject at school is: _____
8. I like to read books about: _____
9. The places I like to go in town are: _____
10. My favorite foods are: _____
11. My favorite activities inside are: _____
12. My favorite activities outside are: _____
13. My hobbies are: _____
14. My favorite animals are: _____
15. The three things I like to do most are: _____
_____
_____
_____

16. The three things I like to do least are: _____
_____
_____
_____

**EXHIBIT 15.3.** Possible reinforcers for students

Decorating the classroom

Assisting another student

Working with a friend

Being first in the lunch line

Running errands

Playing with toys or games (e.g., playing marbles, coloring, playing with clay, educational toys and games, etc.)

Reading a magazine

Taking a longer recess

Being a team captain

Caring for the class pet

Cutting out magazine pictures

Washing the chalkboard

Having a positive note sent home

Stickers

Having lunch with the teacher

Use new markers

Extra art class

Extra gym class

Library pass

Choose where to sit

Gum chewing

Choose class game

1982). When you change your schedule of reinforcement, make sure that it is gradual enough so that the desired behavior does not disappear. Also, you will want to try and convey to students that they are continuing to grow and improve and that the reduction of reinforcers is not negative but, rather, a positive event. This can be done by making statements similar to the following: "Yesterday, you worked by yourself for five minutes without getting out of your seat. Let's see if you can work today for seven minutes without getting out of your seat."

## Time-Out

Time-out refers to the removal of stimulation from a student (Westling & Koorland, 1988). It is a technique that is often used to decrease inappropriate behavior. There are many varia-

tions of time-out. The feature that is common to all of them is that they change the student's surroundings in such a way that he or she has limited access to the stimulation of whatever is going on. For time-out to be effective, students must *want* to return to what the other students are doing. If the activities are not interesting or if the student can view them from the time-out spot, then it will be a limited success. Another concern when you are considering using time-out is whether the student will go to the time-out area on his or her own. If it is necessary to have a physical confrontation, it may be prudent not to get involved in such a disruptive incident or to seek the help of another adult, such as an aide, to assist in confrontation.

A time-out area can be arranged in a corner of the room or by setting up a divider, bookcase, or filing cabinet so that a three-sided space is created. The opening should face into a part of the class where activity is unlikely to occur. Some suggestions for setting up a program that uses time-out procedures have been delineated by Westling and Koorland (1988). They include:

1. Placing the time-out area away from the majority of class activities.
2. Putting a chair or carpet in the area.
3. Using a small but not confining area.
4. Setting a timer to remind you when the time-out period is over.
5. Using a brief (5- to 10-minute) time-out period.
6. Informing the student of the specific rule broken when you place the student in the time-out area. No further conversation should take place until you and the student are both calm.
7. Not allowing play activity in the time-out area. Time-out should not be fun.
8. Allowing a student to stay for a while longer in the area if he or she does not want to come out.
9. Keeping a log of who goes in, when, and how often. If it seems that a stu-

dent enjoys going to the time-out area, try another approach.

10. Reexamining your rules and activities if you find that you use time-out very often. Students may be avoiding class activities.

## Behavioral Contracts

Behavioral contracts are written agreements between you and a student, which state a contingent arrangement between the student's behavior and specific agreed-upon consequences. Behavioral contracts are based on the Premack principle (Premack, 1959). This principle states that the frequency of a less preferred activity increases when it is followed by an opportunity to engage in a more preferred activity. The important elements of the contract are the statement of what the student will or will not do and what you will do if the student complies. Exhibit 15.4 is an example of a behavioral contract that has been adapted from Idol, Paolucci-Whitcomb and Nevin (1986) for use with a student who demonstrates difficulty in completing seat work.

Behaviors, consequences, and the amount time for compliance can be individually designed. Whenever possible, it is best that you involve the students in the development of the contract. Getting their input on the behavior to be modified, the consequence for the change, and the timelines helps them to understand the problem and to develop some ownership in finding a solution. As new contracts are prepared, they should attempt to shape the student to make steady, gradual improvement in his or her behavior with the long-term goal of discontinuing the use of the contract as the student demonstrates improved behavior.

Steps for developing a behavioral contract suggested by Westling and Koorland (1988) are:

1. Determine the target behaviors that need to be reduced or increased. Exhibit 15.5, which has been adapted from Evans, Evans, and Mercer

---

**EXHIBIT 15.4.** Procedural steps and sample form for writing a contingency contract (adapted from Idol, Paolucci-Whitcomb, & Nevin, 1986)

A. Procedural Steps:
1. Define the task (what must be done).
2. Specify time period (when).
3. Establish criteria (how it must be done).
4. Identify reinforcer (what will be earned).
5. Define penalty clause (what happens if criteria is not met).
6. Describe bonus clause (extra reinforcement for consistency).

B. Sample Form

| | |
|---|---|
| Task: | I will finish my math seat work on Monday, Tuesday, Wednesday, and Thursday. |
| Time: | During math class. |
| Criteria: | Get at least 80 percent correct. |
| Reinforcer: | 20 minutes of free time during math class on Friday. |
| Penalty clause: | If less than 80 percent, I will come in after school to make corrections. |
| Bonus: | 90 percent correct for four days = free time during math class on Friday. |

Signed: Student _____

Teacher _____

Date _____

**EXHIBIT 15.5.** Behavior network (adapted from Evans, Evans, & Mercer, 1986)

| Inappropriate Amounts of Behavior | Conditions Influencing the Behavior (Task, Teachers, Peers, Parents, Community, etc.) | Appropriate amounts of Behavior |
|---|---|---|
| Fails to begin tasks | | Begins task promptly |
| Does not attend to task | | Attends to task |
| Fails to complete tasks | | Completes task |
| Does not follow directions | | Follows directions |
| Does careless or sloppy work | | Completes neat work |
| Is often out of seat | | Remains in seat |
| Interrupts others | | Speaks when appropriate |
| Talks out | | Talks with permission |
| Lies | | Tells the truth |
| Uses abusive language | | Speaks appropriately |
| Tattles | | Does not tattle |
| Appears to be shy | | Interacts with others |
| Is hypersensitive | | Accepts criticism |
| Needs constant reassurance | | Participates without constant reassurance |
| Makes self-deprecating statements | | Does not make self-deprecating statements |
| Cries when inappropriate | | Cries when appropriate |
| Engages in inappropriate age play | | Engages in age-appropriate play |
| Fails to initiate contact with others | | Initiates contact with others |
| Fails to engage in group activities | | Initiates contact with group |
| Has few friends | | Has friends |
| Refuses to share with others | | Shares with others |
| Appearance of mood does not fit setting | | Appearance of mood fits setting |
| Claims illness without apparent physical cause | | Is ill with apparent cause |
| Runs away | | Accepts consequences of behavior |
| Is uncooperative | | Cooperates with others |
| Is disorderly in class | | Follows class rules |
| Is disorderly in school | | Follows school rules |
| Is assaultive | | Resolves problems without violence |
| Destroys property | | Respects property |
| Exhibits temper tantrums | | Responds appropriately |
| Steals | | Takes things with permission |
| Cheats | | Completes work on own |

(1986), can be used to identify and quantify behaviors that are in need of remediation.

2. Determine potentially effective reinforcers.
3. Decide on a suitable length of time for the behavior to be omitted or the number of occurrences that you will allow within a designated period of time.
4. Write a simple statement that specifies the arrangement between the behavior and the reinforcement.
5. Both you and the student sign the contract.
6. Observe the student's behavior and keep a record of it.
7. Provide the agreed-upon positive reinforcer if the student achieves the goal.
8. Rewrite a new contract based on the student's performance. If the goal was achieved, extend the time requirement or reduce the tolerance level. If the goal was not achieved, reduce the time requirement, allow more behavior, or change the positive reinforcer.

## Exaggeration

Sometimes an effective way to change an unwanted behavior is to have the student repeat the single action continuously until it loses its attraction. If a student who spits has to fill a cup with saliva or a student who throws objects must throw 100 pencils in a pail instead of playing at recess, these types of behaviors might soon cease.

## Behavior Modification

The basic premise of behavior modification is that behavior is learned and that, through the use of a highly systematic approach, behaviors can be strengthened, weakened, or maintained. A step-by-step management system that was developed by Paine et al. (1983), which can be used with individual students,

combines the use of positive reinforcement, a warning technique, and *response cost*. The eight steps of the system are as follows:

1. If a student is misbehaving, give praise to nearby students who are demonstrating appropriate behavior. Wait a brief period—30 seconds or so—and see if the misbehaving student responds. If the student responds with more appropriate behavior, praise the student.
2. If the student does not respond positively, communicate to the student in an unemotional manner that he or she is receiving a warning and should continue to work. It is best to deliver the warning near the student and to try to make sure that you have eye contact while you are issuing the warning. If the student begins to improve his or her behavior, provide acknowledgement and praise.
3. If the student does not respond to the warning, calmly remind the student about the warning and write his or her name on the chalkboard and put a check mark next to it.
4. If the student does not comply, put another check mark next to his or her name. It is best to do this without commenting. Also, continue to praise those students who are exhibiting appropriate behavior.
5. If the student continues to misbehave, repeat step 4.
6. For those behaviors that are not acceptable, use predetermined consequences that have been established and discussed at the beginning of the school year.
7. Let each mark after a student's name represent the loss of some type of privilege. For example, one check mark could stand for 5 minutes and

two marks could stand for 10 minutes being lost from play time. The consequences can be similar for all students or varied for different students. The important point is that the system is only effective if students lose privileges that they value.

8. Be certain not to give the student extra attention during the time that he or she is missing an activity. The consequences of the system should not be reinforcing in any manner.

## Group Behavior Modification

Group-oriented behavior modification systems have been used successfully in a variety of settings to modify a wide range of behaviors (Gresham & Gresham, 1982). This type of system uses the group's influence to promote appropriate behavior and to decrease disruptive behavior. One example of a group management program is a procedure referred to as the group *response-cost* system (Salend, 1987). In a group response-cost system, the group is given a predetermined number of tokens. The tokens are placed in full view of the students and within easy access of the teacher. Check marks on the chalkboard, marbles in a jar, or paper strips on an easel are examples of tokens that can be used for implementing the program. Each time a class member displays an inappropriate behavior, a token is removed. If any tokens remain at the end of a designated time period, the agreed-upon reinforcement is delivered to the entire group. As the group becomes more successful and improves their behavior, the number of tokens provided at the beginning of the day should be decreased.

The procedures suggested by Idol, Paolucci-Whitcomb, and Nevin (1986) for implementing a behavior management program focus on the entire class:

1. Define the problem areas. Then convert these areas into measurable behav-

iors (e.g., "Students are often out of their seats during independent practice.").

2. Obtain a baseline measurement. If possible, this should be taken over the course of a few days (e.g., "Students average being out of their seats 11 times per hour.").

3. Decide whether the behaviors being measured are disturbing enough to warrant an intervention program. If they are not, then redefine the target behavior and obtain a new baseline measurement (e.g., "Yes, a change in the plan is needed.").

4. Select reinforcers that will be used to reinforce appropriate behaviors (e.g., "For every 5-minute block of time during seat work that students stay in their seats, they will earn 1 minute of time to play games at the end of the day.").

5. Explain to students the contents of the management program.

6. Implement the program and continue to measure the target behavior. The program should continue for at least five days before you make any changes (e.g., "At the end of five days, students averaged being out of their seats four times per hour and earned 9 minutes of play time.").

7. Evaluate the effects of the program on the target behavior and the students' academic progress (e.g., "It appears that the program is positively modifying the students' behavior.").

8. Decide whether the program should be (1) continued as is; (2) changed so that management is less cumbersome or reinforcers are less frequent or tangible; (3) systematically faded out (e.g., "The program will be continued with blocks of time extended from 5 minutes to 10 minutes.").

## Good Behavior Game

Another technique that can be used to manage groups of students is the "good behavior game" (Harris & Sherman, 1973). The goal of the good behavior game is to reduce disruptive classroom behavior through the use of a game involving competition for privileges natural to the classroom setting other than teacher attention. The procedures for implementing the good behavior game are:

1. Select target behavior and define in observable, measurable terms.
2. Collect baseline data.
3. Determine criterion performance level (a minimal acceptable number of demerits for winning).
4. Select potential reinforcers—natural to the classroom when possible (e.g., extra free time, time to play games at the end of the day).
5. Divide the class into teams.
6. Implement the game. Explain the target behavior in specific terms with the class. Record a demerit for a team each time any member of the team demonstrates the target behavior. Tally the demerits for each team. Use a visual recording system for younger children. The team with the fewest number of demerits wins. If neither team exceeds the criterion level, then both teams are winners.
7. Modify as needed by gradually lowering criterion number of points or extending timelines.

Variations of the game can be to make the entire class the team rather than having competition between two teams. You can also give students points at the beginning of the game and erase the points each time that the target behavior is exhibited. You can shift this around and give students merits for demonstrating a positive behavior. After a desig-

nated number of merits have been earned, the students receive the reinforcer. If there are certain students who are ruining the game for other members of the class, you may want to place them on a team by themselves or revert to some of the procedures discussed earlier in this chapter.

## BEHAVIOR MANAGEMENT AND TEACHERS' LANGUAGE INPUT

Research by Elliott and Luetke-Stahlman (submitted) has revealed that teachers of hearing-impaired students use a very restricted set of types of behavioral reprimands with their students as compared with teachers of hearing, bilingual students. This information appears in Exhibit 15.6 and is based on videotaped language sample analysis of 50 teachers (representing SEE-1, SEE-2, Signed/Manual English, and PSE). Results were that teachers using all types of input relied primarily on a direct form of reprimand (e.g., "Get your book.").

Teachers should consider expanding their use of simple, polite (e.g, "Please get your book."), rhetorical (e.g., "It's time to take out our reading books now, isn't it?"), evaluative, future trade-off (e.g., "Read this now, and later we can read that new book you brought."), group conforming (e.g., "Let's all get our books out now."), and self-referent (e.g., "I like it when you all have your books out.") types of utterances. In doing so, teachers not only expand the semantic and grammatical richness of their utterances of disapproval to students but also expose students to forms of behavioral utterances experienced typically by hearing students.

Furthermore, these researchers found that teachers using bimodal input need to continue to sign when they reprimand. At most, teachers in the sample conveyed the meaning of the direct form of disapproval 34 percent of the time in their signs, compared to their

**EXHIBIT 15.6.** Use of each category of disapproval as compared to the total number of disapproving utterances across 50 teachers of the deaf (Elliott & Luetke-Stahlman, submitted)

| Category | Use of Type/Total Disapproving Example | Utterances | Percent |
|---|---|---|---|
| 1. Direct Form | Sit! Shut up! | 113/170 | 66% |
| 2. Simple polite | Please sit down. | 21/170 | 12% |
| 3. Evaluative | You're not in the right place. | 12/170 | 8% |
| 4. Group conformity | We are paying attention to Mark. | 6/170 | 4% |
| 5. Volition | Would you sit down? | 7/170 | 4% |
| 6. Rhetorical | Can you sit down? | 5/170 | 3% |
| 7. Future trade-off | Sit down now. You can do that later. | 2/170 | 1% |
| 8. Self-referent | If I'm boring you, I'm sorry. | 2/170 | 1% |
| 9. Threat | Sit down if you want to go out for recess. | 2/170 | 1% |

speech, and only conveyed the meaning of their voiced disapproval an averaged 36 percent across all categories. When a student does not comply with your reprimand, the variable of comprehension of input must be considered. Even when you are angry, tired, or frustrated, you can enhance the quality of your interaction with your students by signing in close correspondence to your speech.

## SUMMARY

As a teacher of hearing-impaired students, an integral part of your job is to facilitate the development of the cognitive and affective domains of your students. Within the affective domain, the cultivation of positive feelings of self-esteem is an important goal. By facilitating students' positive feelings of self-worth, you are helping them to believe in themselves, and hopefully they will strive to continue to improve themselves. As a result, you will avert behavior problems before they occur. When students' behavior patterns are ingrained, you will need more specific interventions.

There is no single method or approach that will be appropriate for managing the be-

sential that you become knowledgeable and comfortable using many diverse techniques. You should keep in mind that you are the person responsible for the class and that you should employ behavior management procedures that are beneficial to your students. Behavior management should be viewed as a four-phase process—prevention, maintenance, intervention, and adjustment. Many behavior problems can be prevented. Therefore, the conditions of being prepared, making the topic personally relevant, varying the activities, promoting successful experiences, being enthusiastic, and conveying your spoken meaning in sign or cues all help to cut down on discipline problems.

## ACTIVITIES

1. Make a list of characteristics and behaviors that you might experience from a student who has poor self-esteem. Then make a list of activities and behaviors that you could do to help foster more positive feelings of self-worth.

2. Develop a list of rules that you would want to use in your classroom.

3. Administer the reinforcement survey that is

provided in this chapter to two elementary school students.

4. While observing in a classroom, choose a specific behavior and a particular student and document the number of occurrences of that behavior.

5. Develop a sequence of steps for intervention, and write down exactly what you would say to a student who you have witnessed hit another student but who blatantly denies the action when questioned by you.

6. Ask a teacher of the deaf to share his or her behavior management system and strategies with you.

# APPENDIX A

# The Learning Environment

---

**APPENDIX TOPICS**

Managing the Learning Environment
The Care and Feeding of Equipment
Social, Emotional, Self-Help Behaviors of Children, 5-11 Years of Age
High Interest-Low Vocabulary Reading Materials

---

## MANAGING THE LEARNING ENVIRONMENT

As the teacher, it is your responsibility to manage the physical learning environment of your students. To be effective at this job, you must coordinate time, people (both students and staff), materials, and equipment. Stephens (1980) has outlined six elements that need to be considered:

The composition of the people involved
The use of the room and its furnishings
The amount of time available
Student reinforcement
Provisions for student-to-student and student-to-teacher interactions
Differentiating instruction

Lewis and Doorlag (1987) compiled a teacher survey (presented in Exhibit A.1) that can help you determine the conditions you favor for learning. We suggest that you complete this survey and compare the results with your present teaching style and environment that reflects your preference for learning. However, it may be that this approach will not be successful because of the specific learning needs of your students or the resources available to you.

### Arranging the Physical Environment

A basic survey that you can use to evaluate your physical learning environment is provided by Smith, Neisworth, and Greer (1978) in Exhibit A.2.

You need to keep your learning environment safe. Clutter may cause a serious injury to the student with poor vision or balance problems. Visual fire alarm detectors and signals for tornados, and so forth, will need to be installed. Signal-to-sound modifications are discussed later in this appendix.

You need to make your learning environment accessible. Some of your students may require ramps, modification of rooms, doorways, and drinking fountains.

Your learning environment should be comfortable. Work areas should not be hot and stuffy or cold and damp. They should be free from glare and be well lit. Weinstein (1979) found that attractive rooms improve attention, participation, and positive attitudes towards instruction. Furnishings, bulletin boards, pictures, posters, mobiles, and educa-

**EXHIBIT A.1.** What is your learning style? (Adapted from Lewis and Doorlag, 1987)

Because your goal as a teacher is to meet the needs of your students, you might need to evaluate the learning environment you provide. Is it the one you prefer or does it meet your students' needs? You might find it beneficial to ask you students the following questions and modify your instruction based on these results.

| Factor | Preference |
|---|---|
| Noise | Do you work best in absolute silence, in a quiet room, with music playing, with television on, or with others talking? Are you distracted by the sounds you can hear, or do you not hear these noises? |
| Distractions | Are you able to work with visual distractions (e.g., interesting pictures, bulletin boards, objects)? Does it bother you to work near a window or with people moving about? Do you work best with your desk or table clear? |
| Physical surroundings | Do you work best sitting upright in a straight-backed chair, an easy chair, or on the floor? Can you work anywhere at all? Do you work best if it is warm or cool? Are the best conditions those in which you can eat, drink, or move about as you wish? |
| Time of day | Do you learn best in the early morning, midmorning, midday, afternoon, evening, or late at night? When are you are most alert? |
| Attention span | Are you able to concentrate only a few minutes, about a half hour, for long periods of time, or until the work is done? How often do you need to take a break? Are you able to get back to work immediately after a break? |
| Closure | Do you want to finish a task once you have started it, or can you stop working at any point in the task? Do you like to take breaks in the middle of tasks? Does it bother you to have work interrupted before it is completed or to have to stop before you have finished? |
| Rate | Are you a fast or a slow worker? Do you spend the most time planning, doing the task, or checking your work? |
| Other learners | Do you like to work alone, with others, or with peers or adults? If you work one-to-one, should the other person be the teacher or another student? Do you enjoy working in small groups, teams, committees, or large groups? |
| Structure | Are you most comfortable when all task requirements are clarified for you, when you can make some choices, or when you have complete freedom? |
| Presentation mode | When you are learning about something new, would you rather read about it; have someone talk, cue, sign; see it with pictures; watch a film or videotape; watch someone demonstrate it; try it yourself; or try explaining it to someone else? |
| Activities | Which of the following instructional activities help you learn: lecture, discussion, projects, drill, peer teaching, independent study, games, simulation, or role playing? |
| Response mode | Do you like to show what you have learned by writing reports, taking exams, telling others, demonstrating how to do it, or expressing it artistically? |
| Reinforcement | Do you need incentives, peer approval, praise, and recognition from the teacher, tangible rewards, grades, or pay to do a good job? Is the satisfaction that you did your best a strong motivation for you? |

tional displays all contribute to visual appeal (Lewis & Doorlag, 1987).

Your learning environment should utilize furniture that is attractive, durable, functional, and safe. It is your responsibility to order equipment and adjust furniture to student heights as needed.

The space in your learning environment should be divided into performance areas or zones that accommodate routine activities

**EXHIBIT A.2.** Physical Environment Checklist (Smith, Neisworth, & Geer, 1978)

*Physiological Effects*

Illumination

- Are there at least 100 A-candles of light at the surface for reading and other demanding visual tasks?
- Is the lighting throughout the classroom varied and home-like?
- Is lighting used to help define the different activity areas of the room?
- Is the lighting warm yet not glaring?

Temperature

- Can adequate air movement be obtained when needed?
- Is there an adequate supply of fresh air?
- Are temperatures controlled within a comfortable range (68-74°)?
- Are children assisted in making necessary clothing adjustments for the room temperature?
- Is humidity adequate year round?

Noise

- Can windows be opened without interference from outside noise?
- Is the noise level of each classroom controlled so that the activities of the other classrooms are not disturbed?
- Is the teacher rarely asked to repeat what he/she has said?

Color

- Are the colors in the classroom pleasantly varied?
- Is color used to define areas of the room and to attract attention to important educational displays?
- Are the colors in the room subdued, mellow, and pleasing?

Materials

- Does the classroom contain furnishings, materials, and displays in addition to typical institutional furnishings?
- Do teachers and students bring in a variety of materials and displays related to current assignments?
- Are learning materials and displays well organized by topics or learning area?
- Have excessive, unorganized materials been removed to eliminate confusion or distraction?

*Spatial Effects*

- Are related compatible activities arranged together and unrelated, incompatible activities separated within the classroom?
- Have an appropriate time and place been designated and assigned for all activities?
- Is there a variety of places where different-sized groups can meet and work?
- Are there special places that individual children can go (a) for isolation, (b) for rest and quiet, (c) to let off steam, (d) to reward themselves, (e) for private instruction, (f) to work independently, (g) to be disciplined privately?
- Can children enter, leave, clean up, and dress, etc. without disturbing others?
- Can children space themselves as they need or desire?
- Do the relative amounts of space allocated to various activities reflect their importance in the teaching program?

*Physical Effects*

- Is the environment kept clean?
- Are the furnishings (desks, displays, etc.) movable to provide a variety of groupings and areas within the room for different learning tasks?
- Can the teacher control visual distractions between groups of children (by separating groups, raising room dividers, etc.)?
- Are storage facilities accessible to the students for getting out and putting away materials which they are allowed access to?
- Have high physical barriers been eliminated so that the teacher has visual access to the entire room?

*Setting Effects*

- Can the teacher identify an "overcommitted" setting (one in which most children are observers rather than performers and leaders) and then attempt to create new, smaller work or activity groups?
- Have physical barriers to handicapped children been removed?
- Does the teacher periodically change the environment to improve the teaching program?
- Does the teacher systematically observe and evaluate the effects of the environment and the social behaviors and learning of the class?

(Berdine & Cegelka, 1980). You should arrange your room based on student groupings, storage needs, and distribution and collection of materials and student work. Typically, you will need a group work space and an area for small group or individual work. Typical patterns for working with students whose hearing is impaired are curved rows, clusters of desks, and configurations in the shape of horseshoes or crescents. You may want to set up learning centers or divide a large space by subject areas (e.g., grammar, literature, free reading, and so on—Mercer & Mercer, 1985). Each student should also have an individual work and storage space. These areas should be quiet and private. No room would be complete without a teacher's desk and a storage area. The desk should be arranged so that you can observe as many ongoing activities in the learning environment as possible. You also may need an area for recreational and educational games and a time-out spot. Areas chosen should be considered on the basis of sound, convenience, movement efficiency, flexibility, and density (personal space preserved) (Lewis & Doorlag, 1987). When you have your room arranged, you should not consider the arrangement permanent. You should feel free to experiment periodically in an ongoing attempt to increase the effectiveness of the learning environment.

You need to assign productive seating. Weinstein (1979) found that students who sit in the front center participate more, are more attentive, and spend more time on task than do students who are not. This finding is related to work by Doyle (1986), who found that teacher eye contact correlated to student participation. If you want your students to interact more among themselves, try seating them close to each other or opposite each other. Heron and Harris (1982) found that communication tends to move across tables rather than around them. They recommend setting a talkative/signative student across from a quiet one (who can then see the peer language model).

You should purchase materials and activities that your students have demonstrated are of interest to them. Communication will be enhanced if you store things out of reach but visible to your students.

You should utilize a well-planned schedule. This allows you, the student, and significant others working with the student to predict what will happen throughout the day. Eight guidelines for devising a classroom schedule have been suggested by Smith (1985).

Seek student input

Post schedules in a highly visible location

Alternate pleasant and unpleasant activities

Schedule time intervals that reflect age and ability

Reinforce both attention to task and task completion

Send a copy of the schedule home to parents

Word process a copy of your schedule so that changes or multiple copies are obtainable easily

## References

Berdine, W., & Cegelka, T. (1980). *Teaching the trainable retarded*. Columbus, OH: Charles E. Merrill.

Doyle, W. (1986). Classroom organization and management. In M. C. Witrock (Ed.), *Handbook of researching on teaching*. New York: Macmillan.

Heron, T., & Harris, K. (1982). *The educational consultant: Helping professionals, parents, and mainstreamed students*. Boston: Allyn & Bacon.

Lewis, R., & Doorlag, D. (1987). *Teaching special students in the mainstream*. Columbus, OH: Charles E. Merrill

Mercer, C., & Mercer, A. (1985). *Teaching students with learning problems*. London: Merrill.

Smith, M. (1985). Scheduling for success. *Perspectives for Teachers of the Hearing Impaired*, *3*(4), 14–16.

Smith, R., Neisworth, J., & Greer, J. (1978). *Evaluating educational environments*. Columbus, OH: Charles E. Merrill.

Stephens, T. (1980). Teachers as managers. *The Directive Teacher*, 2(5), 4.

Weinstein, C. (1979). The physical environment of the school: A review of research. *Review of Educational Researcher*, 49, 577–610.

## THE CARE AND FEEDING OF EQUIPMENT

Hearing-impaired students come with equipment. As an effective teacher of these students, it is your responsibility to be knowledgeable about the equipment that your students are using and about devices that could benefit them. Making sure equipment is working could be the most important thing you do each day! It is your job to see that equipment is upgraded regularly and operating at its best capacity and that your supervisors are aware of your needs in this area.

### Hearing Aids

There are several different types of hearing aids, but all require an earmold, microphone,

**EXHIBIT A.3.** Basic troubleshooting for the hearing aid

| Symptom | Possible Cause | Test | Solutions |
|---|---|---|---|
| Hearing aid dead | 1. Dead or run down batteries.<br>2. Battery reversed in compartment such that "+" end is where "−" end should be.<br>3. Earmold plugged with wax or water (from cleaning).<br>4. Batteries oozing liquid (resulting in poor battery connections).<br>5. Telephone circuit switched on by mistake. | 1. Check batteries with voltmeter or substitute new batteries.<br>2. Examine battery.<br>3. Inspect earmold and blow through it to determine whether passage is open.<br>4. Examine battery and battery holder for evidence of leakage in the form of liquid or corrosion.<br>5. Examine switching device. | 1. Replace worn-out batteries.<br>2. Insert batteries correctly.<br>3. Disconnect earmold from hearing aid. Wash in lukewarm soapy water, using pipe cleaner to open blocked canal of earmold. Rinse in clear water and dry.<br>4. Replace batteries before they run down completely. If leakage does occur, remove battery, clean terminals with dampened cloth to remove battery fluid.<br>5. Select M or microphone input. |
| Working but weak | 1. Dead or run down batteries.<br>2. Battery reversed in compartment such that "+" end is where "−" end should be.<br>3. Earmold plugged with wax or water (from cleaning).<br>4. Batteries oozing liquid (resulting in poor battery connections). | 1. Check batteries with voltmeter or substitute new batteries.<br>2. Examine battery.<br>3. Inspect earmold and blow through it to determine whether passage is open.<br>4. Examine battery and battery holder for evidence of leakage in the form of liquid or corrosion. | 1. Replace worn-out batteries.<br>2. Insert batteries correctly.<br>3. Disconnect earmold from hearing aid. Wash in lukewarm soapy water, using pipe cleaner to open blocked canal of earmold. Rinse in clear water and dry.<br>4. Replace batteries before they run down |

**EXHIBIT A.3.** (Continued)

| Symptom | Possible Cause | Test | Solutions |
|---|---|---|---|
| | | | completely. If leakage does occur, remove battery, clean terminals with dampened cloth to remove battery fluid. |
| Works intermittently | 1. Dead or run down batteries.<br>2. Battery reversed in compartment such that "+" end is where "−" end should be.<br>3. Earmold plugged with wax or water (from cleaning).<br>4. Batteries oozing liquid (resulting in poor battery connections). | 1. Check batteries with voltmeter or substitute new batteries.<br>2. Examine battery.<br>3. Inspect earmold and blow through it to determine whether passage is open.<br>4. Examine battery and battery holder for evidence of leakage in the form of liquid or corrosion. | 1. Replace worn-out batteries.<br>2. Insert batteries correctly.<br>3. Disconnect earmold from hearing aid. Wash in lukewarm soapy water, using pipe cleaner to open blocked canal of earmold. Rinse in clear water and dry.<br>4. Replace batteries before they run down completely. If leakage does occur, remove battery, clean terminals with dampened cloth to remove battery fluid. |
| Feedback or whistles | 1. Punctured or cracked tubing.<br>2. Earmold not properly inserted in ear.<br>3. Earmold plugged with wax or water (from cleaning).<br>4. Receiver close to wall or other sound-reflecting surface. | 1. Examine tubing.<br>2. Press earmold firmly into the ear.<br>3. Inspect earmold and blow through it to determine whether passage is open.<br>4. Observe student's placement in the room. | 1. Replace tubing.<br>2. Insert earmold properly.<br>3. Disconnect earmold from hearing aid. Wash in lukewarm soapy water, using pipe cleaner to open blocked canal of earmold. Rinse in clear water and dry.<br>4. Avoid sitting with the aided side of the head near a wall or other reflective surface. |
| Poor tone quality or distortion | 1. Punctured or cracked tubing.<br>2. Earmold not properly inserted in ear.<br>3. Earmold plugged with wax or water (from cleaning).<br>4. Receiver close to wall or other sound-reflecting surface.<br>5. Microphone opening is clogged. | 1. Examine tubing.<br>2. Press earmold firmly into the ear.<br>3. Inspect earmold and blow through it to determine whether passage is open.<br>4. Observe student's placement in the room.<br>5. Examine the hearing aid. | 1. Replace tubing.<br>2. Insert earmold properly.<br>3. Disconnect earmold from hearing aid. Wash in lukewarm soapy water, using pipe cleaner to open blocked canal of earmold. Rinse in clear water and dry.<br>4. Avoid sitting with the aided side of the head near a wall or other reflective surface.<br>5. Clean, using dry cloth. |

Taken From: Consultation: A recourse for educators, (n.d.).

speaker, and battery. A troubleshooting table such as the one provided in Exhibit A.3 can assist you in determining whether each student's hearing aid is working properly. You may need to remind your school audiologist that it is time for new earmolds for Sarah or that Stacey's tubing is cracked and squeaking. Keeping a behind-the-ear-aid on a preschooler can be a challenge, but whether you use tape adhesive, a small roll of surgical tape, velcro, an elastic strap, or another creative solution, your assistance with problems such as these will be appreciated by the student and the significant adults who are working with that student. You should teach your students, beginning at the preschool age, to check their own batteries, take in and out or on and off their personal aids and auditory trainers, wash their earmolds correctly, and view this equipment as an integral part of every day (see Exhibit A.4). You may need to devise a unit concerning telephone use for hearing-aid wearers, instructing interested and capable students about the "T" switch on their aid, as well as strategies to aid communication over the telephone (Erber, 1985). You may work with students and parents to compile a kit for hearing-aid maintenance (see Exhibits A.5 and A.6).

**EXHIBIT A.4.** A kit for hearing-aid maintenance

Helpful and inexpensive materials to be kept in your room for hearing aid maintenance might include:

A battery tester
Hearing-aid stethoscope and adaptor
Forced-air earmold cleaner
Pipe cleaners
Small, soft brush
Lighted magnifying glass
Individual packets of alcohol-saturated swabs
Packets of silica gel and a zip-loc plastic bag
Toothpicks
Wax removal tool
Moisture guard (e.g., Moisture Guard or Super Dri-Aid)
Extra batteries
Pencil eraser (to clean battery contacts)
Tweezers

You should ensure also how each student is benefiting from an FM system as compared with a personal hearing aid. Formal and informal testing with both these pieces of equipment can be used as a means of deciding whether hearing aids or auditory training equipment should be worn. Your job is to be knowledgeable and helpful with needs related to the use of assistive listening devices (see Exhibit A.7).

## Infants, Toddlers, and Preschoolers with Hearing Aids

The difficulties of keeping on hearing aids that are larger than small ears has just been discussed. Additionally, teachers should assist parents in precautions involving the tiny components of the hearing aids that by necessity are constantly near or on children who are touching, pulling, chewing, or salivating on them. Therefore, you should advise parents that:

Controls be covered so that they remain properly set
The case be kept clean
The equipment not be immersed in water
The equipment be kept away from extreme heat
The aid be kept in the same location when not on the child and that this location be out of the reach of children and pets
Siblings realize that the aid is not a toy
The cords should not be chewed or twisted
The receiver is fragile and should not be dropped
The earmold should be cleaned in warm, soapy water and dried thoroughly (alcohol will crack it)

(A good reference for parents and first-year teachers is *Hearing Aids and You* by Craig, Sins, and Rossi (1976).

***Listening Environment.*** Hearing-impaired students who benefit from amplification re-

**EXHIBIT A.5.** Hearing-Aid Checklist—Objectives (South Metropolitan School District, undated).

1. Given the student's hearing-aid harness, the student will put it on
   a. Unassisted
   b. Assisted
2. Given the student's hearing aid, the student will place it in the harness
   a. Unassisted
   b. Assisted
3. Given the student's earmolds(s), the student will place it/them in his/her ears(s)
   a. Unassisted
   b. Assisted
4. Given the student's hearing aid (s), the student will turn it/them off and on
   a. Unassisted
   b. Assisted
5. Given the student's hearing aid(s), the student will adjust the volume settings(s)
   a. Unassisted
   b. Assisted
6. Given the student's hearing aid(s), the student will readjust the volume setting(s) to accommodate for environment changes
   a. Unassisted
   b. Assisted
7. Given the student's hearing aid with feedback, the student will recognize and correct the feedback
   a. Unassisted
   b. Assisted
8. Given the student's hearing aid(s), the student will change the battery
   a. Unassisted
   b. Assisted
9. Given the student's hearing aid(s), the student will change the cord(s)
   a. Unassisted
   b. Assisted
10. Given the student's earmold(s), the student will clean it/them
    a. Unassisted
    b. Assisted

quire a quiet classroom in which to attend to speech (Finitzo-Heiber & Tillman, 1978). When the speech signal is reflected off hard surfaces such as a chalkboard, uncarpeted floors, windows, and walls, hearing-impaired students have difficulty comprehending it. Your responsibility as the teacher of these students is to advocate for changes and upkeep of the environment in which the students spend the majority of their school day. These might included heavier windows and doors, carpeting, and changes in the landscape. Proper acoustic treatment can often be attained by proper use of curtains, rugs, and acoustic tile (Beranek, 1954; Leavitt, 1984).

Significant adults who are working with hearing-impaired students must advocate also for a favorable signal-to-noise ratio. This ratio can be affected by children who are passing noisily in the halls outside your work area, by the students themselves in your classroom, or by noises from traffic in the street outside your windows. Site location of classrooms for hearing-impaired students should consider both external and internal noise levels. Open classrooms are not suitable for students who are dependent to some degree on their aided hearing ability to comprehend academic instruction. Fourcin et al. (1980) suggested that teachers in noisy situations

1. Increase the distance between the teaching area and the noise source
2. Interpose nonteaching areas or dead space between the source of the noise and the teaching area (e.g. storage rooms, corridors, and libraries)
3. Treat corridors with carpet

**EXHIBIT A.6.** Guidelines for hearing-aid management by parents*

*Earmold*

The earmold should fit snugly so that it will not fall out without some stress. It is difficult to make ear-molds to fit very young children, but it can be done. Ask to have another mold made if you feel that your child's mold does not fit properly or if the hearing aid whistles constantly. Your child will also need a new set about every six months because of the growth process.

Keep the earmold clean. Use a pipe cleaner to clean out the canal hole. Unsnap the mold from the receiver and wash it with lukewarm soapy water at least weekly, but make sure that it is dry before resnapping it to the receiver. The hearing aid will appear not to work if the earmold is clogged with wax.

If the earmold is broken, it should be remade. If rough spots appear on the mold, these can be buffed. Sometimes you can eliminate the problem yourself with an emery board.

If your child gets an ear infection, do not put the earmold in your child's ear. Also notify school officials as soon as possible since this may change your child's hearing levels. All infections should be closely followed by a physician.

*Receiver*

If the receiver is broken, a raspy sound may result. You may need to purchase a new one from a hearing-aid dealer.

If the earmold does not fit snugly to the receiver, a whistle, or feedback may result. If you can put your thumb over the receiver hole and stop the whistle at volume settings 4-5, then put your thumb over the earmold hole when it is snapped to the receiver. If the whistle stops, then the contact between the cord, receiver, and earmold is a good one. If you have a good contact and feedback continues, the earmold may not fit properly or the hearing aid is being used at too loud a volume. All hearing aids will squeal or whistle periodically. For example, this will occur if your child puts the ear with the mold next to a wall, bends over and gets the mold too near the microphone, or sometimes even if your child turns his or her head.

*Cord*

*Always keep a spare cord.* A faulty cord will make the hearing aid appear not to work or to have a raspy sound. Do *not* tie knots in the cord. This will cause breakage as will a yank or snag. To determine whether or not a cord is faulty, put the receiver in your ear and wiggle the cord. You may find where the break occurred. Cords can be purchased from a hearing-aid dealer in various lengths.

*Battery*

*Always keep spare batteries.* In placing the battery in its compartment, match the positive or "+" ends. If the hearing aid does not work, always try a fresh battery first. It will last 1-2 weeks. Take it out of the hearing aid when not in use—at night, for example. If it is left in the compartment for a long period of time, it will corrode. You can purchase batteries from any hearing-aid dealer nearest you.

*Hearing Aid Body*

Avoid excessive heat or moisture. Be gentle with the hearing aid. It is a mechanical device and like an appliance, will break down and need repairs. If the microphone case is loose, the hearing aid may rattle when shaken. If there are broken parts, such as a receiver, they must be replaced.

The tone control switches are different for different hearing aids. Ask your audiologist or teacher at what setting it should be worn. In most cases, the volume control should be about midway. If you are not sure where your child should wear his controls, ask the audiologist. If your child has the hearing aid turned up louder than usual, the battery may be low.

A "T" position means telephone. The child will get no sound in a normal speaking situation if the hearing-aid control is on "T."

Do not ever open the case of the hearing aid. Only an expert should do this and doing so may void your service guarantee. It may also cause expensive damage. If you wish to see inside the inner workings of the instrument, ask your hearing-aid dealer to show them to you.

---

*Prepared by project audiologists Ann Sitton and Elizabeth Wildman, Bill Wilkerson Hearing and Speech Center, Nashville, Tennessee. From McConnell, F., & Horton, K. B., *A home teaching program for parents of very young deaf children.* Experimental Form 114, Final Report, Bureau of Education for the Handicapped. USOE, Bethesda, MD: Educational Resources Information Center Document Reproduction Service (1970).

**EXHIBIT A.7.** Troubleshooting of auditory trainer

*Auditory Training* is the structuring of an individual's environment to facilitate the development and use of sound perception.

To be aware of problems that might arise from auditory trainers, it is vital to become familiar with the student's individual trainers. This includes the following: make and model, gain at conversational level, suggested volume by the audiologist, and how often batteries are replaced.

The principal advantages of a group-amplifying system over a personal hearing aid for classroom use, are:

1. The microphone can be located close to the teacher's mouth.
2. A variety of inputs can be used, including tape, phonograph, television, radio, and so on.
3. Amplification provided by group hearing aids is of somewhat higher quality than that provided by personal hearing aids.

*Auditory Trainer Care*

As the teacher of students who are using auditory trainers, you should:

Ensure that each unit has been set for each individual student, as indicated by each personal audiogram

Label trainers so that students always wear the trainer that has been set for them

Do not leave the units in excessive heat

Avoid rough handling

Remove the batteries of the unit when storing it during vacations and holidays

Keep battery terminals and contacts clean

Inspect the cords and connections frequently and have them replaced as needed

Know how to connect the FM system to audiovisual devices used at school and which students could benefit from such use

Be responsible for transferring the teacher microphone to the adult who is most directly working with the student(s)

Use data-based assessment to compare each student's benefit of the auditory trainer as compared with his or her personal hearing aid.

*Trouble Shooting for the FM System*

The most frequently encountered signs of trouble with phonic ear units are: no sound, weak sound, intermittent sound, and distorted speech.

1. *No sound*
   a. Check to see that the plug has been removed from the bottom of the unit.
   b. Make sure both "Power" and "Micro" switches are on. If these conditions are met, and there is still no sound, it is likely that the battery is dead. If, after recharging the battery, the unit still does not work, it should be turned over to the audiology technician.
2. *Weak sound.* This is also generally due to a run-down battery.
3. *Intermittent sound.* This usually results from a defective receiver cord. If replacement of the cord has no good effect, the unit should be turned in to the technician.
4. *Distorted speech* from
   a. Teacher's microphone and environmental microphones.
   b. Environmental microphones.
   c. Teacher's microphone only.
   d. Loop system.

In all cases requiring the replacement or dismantling of equipment, and where all of the above are found to be useless, the audiology technician should be consulted.

(list adapted from Berg, 1987)

## References

Beranek, L. (1954). *Acoustics*. New York: McGraw-Hill.

Berg, F. (1987). *Facilitating classroom listening*. San Diego, CA: College-Hill Press.

Craig, H., Sins, V., & Rossi, S. (1976). *Hearing aids and you*. Beaverton, OR: Dormac.

Erber, N. (1985). *Telephone communication and hearing-impairment*. San Diego, CA: College-Hill Press.

Finitzo-Heiber, T., & Tillman, T. (1978). Room acoustic effects on monosyllable word discrimination ability for normal and hearing-impaired children. *Journal of Speech and Hearing Research, 21*, 440–448.

Fourcin, A., Joy, D., Kennedy, M., Knight, J., Knowles, S., Knox, E., Martin, M., Mort, J., Penton, J., Poole, D., Powell, C., & Watson, T. (1980). Design for educational facilities for deaf children. *British Journal of Audiology*, Supplement No. 3.

Leavitt, R. (1984) Hearing aids and other amplifying devices for hearing-impaired children. In R. Hull & K. Dilka (Eds.), *The hearing-impaired child in school*. New York: Grune and Stratton.

## SOCIAL, EMOTIONAL, SELF-HELP BEHAVIORS OF CHILDREN 5-11 YEARS OF AGE

### 5-Year-Old

*Motor Characteristics*. Stays in one location for longer periods of time but changes often from standing, sitting, and squatting positions. Likes to climb and jump. Likes to march to music. Holds adult's hand when unsure, such as when descending stairs.

*Eating*. Begins to clean plate more. Refuses to eat cooked root vegetables, gravies, casseroles, and puddings. Prefers to eat meat, potatoes, raw vegetables, milk, and fruit. Is able to feed self, but may need help with eating certain foods. Poor table manners.

*Sleep*. Many nap once or twice per week for one hour or more. Sleeps from 7-8 P.M. until 7-8 A.M. May have frightful dreams and awake screaming.

*Elimination*. Fairly responsible. Many need help with wiping. There are a few daytime accidents. May need reminding during the day.

*Bath and Dressing*. With encouragement and reminding, can wash face and hands before meals. Cannot bathe self or cut fingernails. Can dress self completely except for back buttons and shoelaces. Lacks motivation for dressing self. Discards old clothes messily.

*Tensional Outlets*. Nose picking, nail biting, thumb sucking, sniffling, and twitching of nose, stuttering, and hair twisting.

*Emotional Expression*. Dependent on adult company and support. Cooperative. Likes and invites supervision. Friendly, sympathetic, affectionate, and helpful. Likes to be with family. Proud of own appearance. Curious and eager for information. Initiates slapstick humor. Enjoys being read to. Likes to talk and will talk to anyone. Begins name calling. Less crying and gets over it quickly when does cry. Less whining than at 4 years of age. Stamps feet, slams door, and has occasional tantrums.

*Fears and Dreams*. Animals in dreams chase the child. Confusion over dreams and own waking imagination. Talks in sleep.

*Interpersonal Relations*. Parents are center of child's world. Likes to obey. Takes punishment better from mother than from father. Usually good with other siblings. When alone, may tease younger siblings. Enjoys family outings. When reminded, says "please" and "thank you."
and "thank you."

*School*. Prefers playmates of same age. Needs some assistance from teacher with dressing and undressing. Needs to know teacher is there. Enjoys routine. Class enjoys directed activity for about 20 minutes. Child works in short bursts of energy.

## 6-Year-Old

*Motor Characteristics.* In many performances, child makes a good start but needs assistance and direction to complete actions. Child is now sometimes clumsy and deliberate. Child attempts to use tools.

*Eating.* Eats a lot, especially between meals. Likes to snack before bed, and usually takes more than can handle. Always wants the biggest piece. Breakfast is poorest meal. When eating, child may prefer to use a fork to a spoon and is sometimes awkward when spreading foods. Table manners are poor. The child stuffs too much food into mouth, spills, and may chew with mouth open.

*Sleeping.* Does not nap at six P.M., though may appreciate a quiet hour of playing. Bedtime is between 7:30 and 8 P.M. When go to bed, child enjoys being with an adult so that he or she can relay the day's activities. Usually sleep through the night, and if does wake up, it is for toileting, which child can do alone. Can get up alone at 7 to 7:30 A.M. Can dress self if clothes are laid out, but is apt to dawdle.

*Elimination.* Can go to toilet alone. If has an accident, is disturbed by this. It may be a good idea to remind the child to go to the bathroom before going out to play and going to bed.

*Bath and Dressing.* Needs some help while bathing. Can usually wash own arms and legs. Does not like taking baths. Likes to dawdle once in the tub and may refuse to get out until all the water is down the drain. Will wash hands before dinner if reminded. Can dress self, except for very difficult buttons and tying laces. If does tie laces, laces are usually too loose. Dawdles while dressing. Boys will comb their own hair, while girls need some help. Messy with clothes once clothes have been worn. Mom or dad needs to select and lay out the clothes.

*Emotional Expression.* Is very emotional. Tends to brag and know "everything." Likes to be with family and is probably very proud of mother. Tends to be curious and eager for new information. Enjoys slapstick humor, and loves to talk. May throw temper tantrums. Can usually brave real injuries, but cries at the minor ones. Is verbally and physically aggressive. Will hit both adults and other children. Is destructive with both animate and inanimate objects.

*Fears and Dreams.* Realizes an increase in fears, especially from authority. Experience the fear of the supernatural—ghosts and witches. Also fears large animals, insects, and the elements, such as wind, fire, and rain. Loud noises such as sirens and thunder may also be scary. Fears strangers.

*Interpersonal Relations.* Likes family outings and family secrets such as holiday gifts. Likes to have a parent home when gets home from school. Does not like formal social situations. Likes to be in social situations with people known very well. Not good at shaking hands. Forget to say "Please" and "Thank you." May behave rather rudely before company but is not doing this on purpose. Can use the telephone. Has a great interest in having friends. Argues often and needs supervised play. Is a great deal of tattletaling. Is some exclusion of a third player. May prefer an older playmate.

*School.* Usually anticipates the first grade. Loves to bring home products to share with parents. Usually likes teacher and tries to please teacher. Teacher's word is law to the 6-year-old student. Looks for the teacher immediately upon arriving at school to be assured that teacher is there. Brings things to teacher at school.

## 7-Year-Old

*Motor Characteristics*. Shows more caution. Is more variable—active one moment, inactive the next. Great desire for a bicycle. Maybe interested in baseball, dancing.

*Eating*. Moderate appetite. Begins to accept disliked foods but still dislikes strongly flavored cooked vegetables or cheeses. Is able to use silverware with little difficulty. Manners improve, but still spills, stuffs mouth, and talks with mouth full.

*Sleep*. Bedtime still 7–8 P.M. Gets ready with little adult help. Sleeps soundly with fewer nightmares. Wakes up about 7 A.M. and needs reminding to get dressed.

*Elimination*. Few accidents at this age. Only a few need to get up at night and can care for themselves.

*Bath and Dressing*. Washes face and hands at parent reminder. Some bathe with little help and only a little supervision. Dawdle in tub. Girls prefer to be cleaner than boys. Can dress self and is beginning to select for self. Still careless about clothes and leave them about. Can tie shoes, but do not like to.

*Tensional Outlets*. When fatigued, will suck thumb, pick nose, bite nails, or stutter. Try to control these. Poor posture—tilts chair back, only partially sets on chair.

*Emotional Expression*. More serious, absorbed, thoughtful, empathic. Sets goals too high. Self-protection by withdrawal from situations ("deaf" ear). Gets angry with self. More moody, sulky, and unhappy. Sensitive to praise and blame. Jealous of privileges or abilities of siblings. Sense of humor decreases. Uses language more to complain. Less crying, less aggressive behavior.

*Fears and Dreams*. Deeper and more worrisome fears. Afraid of spatial things: shadows, ghosts, and creatures in attic or cellar. Fears war, spies, burglars, people hiding in closet or under bed, new situations, and being late for school. Fears are stimulated by reading, television, and movies. Begins to resolve fears by getting someone to precede self into feared places or by using a flashlight. Less dreaming and fewer nightmares. Dreams about self as the central figure. Dreams consist of animals, flying, swimming, diving into ocean, floating through air, and walking above ground.

*Interpersonal Relations*. Gets along well with parents, but begins to argue and question them. Relationships more companionable and less intense than before. Easier to discipline, since is more sensitive to praise and blame. Father's role seems slight at this stage. Some boys, however, "worship" father and confide their thoughts in him. Girls may be jealous of father's attention to mother. Gets along better with siblings. Protects younger ones and boasts about older ones. Jealous at times of things other siblings are allowed to do. Manners improve. Can greet people easily and behaves better in front of company. Can make social telephone or TDD calls to friends.

*School*. More personal relationship with teacher. Crushes can develop. Child still depends heavily on teacher. Begins to do "forbidden" things when teacher leaves the room. Demands teacher attention and assistance. Begins to prefer older playmates. Does not want to be accompanied by parent when going to school. Looks to other classmates for help and may copy. Class becomes disorganized more easily, especially when teacher leaves the room.

## 8-Year-Old

*Motor Characteristics*. Body movement is more rhythmic and graceful. Is more aware of posture. Gestures become more dramatic and descriptive. Increased eye-hand performance. Turns eyes away to escape situations.

*Eating*. Increased amounts of food eaten. Refusals become fewer. Uses fingers less frequently. Begins to use knife more often. Table manners are variable. Much spilling and playing with food.

*Sleeping*. Bedtime is 8-8:30 P.M. Getting to bed begins to be difficult. Night is usually quiet. Wakes up at about 7 A.M. Most get up within half an hour.

*Elimination*. Few problems at this age. Can manage well alone.

*Bath and Dressing*. Begins to be lazy in washing face and hands. Is able to keep fingernails clean. About half can bathe themselves, but most dawdle in the tub. Can dress without assistance. Some can choose what they will wear during day. Clothes are thrown about and are torn, dirty, and not tucked in. Can keep shoelaces tied without reminders.

*Tensional Outlets*. May still suck thumb during illness and fatigue. May cry when tired and make faces at unwelcome commands. In school, may grimace, scowl, roll eyes, raise eyebrows, hum, and smack lips. Also jiggles legs, but may control it by pressing legs against furniture or by crossing knees.

*Emotional Expression*. Thinks self knows everything, but recognizes that others may know more. Is critical of self and of others. Is also selfish and demands much attention. Very curious about the personal activities of others, such as phone calls and conversations. Has a good sense of humor. Likes to talk, especially about self; likes to exaggerate. May raise voice when angry or tired.

*Fears and Dreams*. Fears fighting, failure, and not being liked. Is shy of the dark, but does like being out with parents. Compulsively repeats fear situations in an attempt to resolve them. Has dreams of being hurt, shot, or kidnapped. Likes to dream and may want to go back to sleep to continue a dream. Is aware that dreams may be affected by television, radio, or movie.

*Interpersonal Relations*. Wants all of mother's attention. Has strong verbal and physical admiration and affection for mother. Is very sensitive to what mother says; if her facial expression changes, may have tears well up. May be jealous of parents' relationship. Relationship with father is less intense than relationship with mother, but is a smoother one. There is less expression of affection for father, but also demands less of father than mother; father is allowed to make a mistake. Respects and obeys father's commands. Does not get along well with siblings. Is selfish and argues about possessions. A few are protective and thoughtful about siblings. Is able to verbalize proper greetings and goodbyes. May have very good manners away from home, but in the home may monopolize mother's attention in front of company.

*School*. Wants to be part of a group and

considers the teacher to be less important. Likes it when the teacher makes a mistake. Is better able to wait for the teacher's attention.

## 9-Year-Old

*Motor Characteristics.* Works and plays hard. Does one thing (riding bike, running) until exhausted. Interested in own strength. More interest in team games and in learning to be more skillful. Better control of own speed and abilities. Possibly interested in contact sports.

*Eating.* Is almost eating a normal adult meal. Frankly refuses certain foods and does not like an old food cooked in a new way. Looks forward to dessert. Good control of implements. Tends to "saw" with the knife and cuts pieces that are too big. Table manners continue to improve.

*Sleeping.* Knows own bedtime, which is now 8 P.M. or later, but still may need to be reminded. Gets ready by self. The night is usually quiet, with only a few nightmares.

*Elimination.* Under control. Only a few still need to be reminded.

*Bath and Dressing.* Bathes two or three times per week and is not resistant. Is independent, but likes to have an adult around. Still needs reminding to brush teeth and wash hands. Does complete job of dressing. Interested in doing own hair. Still careless with clothes and throws them around. Not concerned about how clean clothes are.

*Tensional Outlets.* Individual differences become very evident. Some mutter, sulk, find fault, stamp feet, or may even destroy things. Fewer habits—cry, pick at self, suck thumb, pick at nails. Begins to gesture more when upset.

*Emotional Expression.* Becomes more independent. Impressionable, reasonable, explosive, empathic. More responsible, cooperative, and dependable. Evaluates own behavior. Wants things done right and disgusted with those who deviate from own standards. Gets mad at parents, but is also proud of them. Responds well to compliments. May complain while doing a task. Enjoys humor. Uses language to express emotions, such as disgust, self-criticism, pity, and envy. More physical fighting (mostly with boys), but most aggression is still verbal.

*Fears and Dreams.* Few fears, however, they vary greatly from child to child. Worry most about school failure. Upset by own mistakes. Enjoys frightening other children and spying and hiding. May dream horrid, scary dreams of being hurt, shot, or kidnapped. Parents or friend may be victim instead of self. Motion dreams: whirling, swimming, flying. Dreams of natural events: storms, fires. Some like to go back to sleep in morning to finish a dream.

*Interpersonal Relations.* Wants to be on own and demands less from parents. Child may be demonstrative, affectionate, and anxious to please. May react against demands to be neat and clean. Do not like to be reminded by parents. Begins to "put things over" on them. Boys grow much closer to father. Thinks highly of father and is sensitive to his criticism. Feels proud about parents' occupation. Competes more with siblings, especially if siblings are close in age. Can be embarrassed by actions of siblings. Differences in manners becomes evident. Some are naturally polite. Some enjoy hand shaking. Most have a "best" friend. Gangs and clubs are very important. May run around shouting, giggle, and whisper.

*School*. Most like teacher, but have either a strong feeling of teacher being "wonderful" or "terrible." Less talk at home about teacher. Child wants to be more independent of teacher in both work and play. Blames teacher for low grades. Still prefers teacher's assistance when needed in work. Tends to forget materials unless reminded. Talks about home activities at school. Quieter while at work, more competitive, and is afraid of failure. Becomes self-conscious when reciting before group. Knows when is "sure" or "not sure." Works for longer periods of time. Likes to compare grades.

## 10-Year-Old

*Motor Characteristics*. Very active, with bodily wriggling and fiddling with objects close by. Pushes chair around on floor, and swings and kicks legs.

*Eating*. Loves food and eats constantly. Breakfast continues to be smallest meal. Eyes sparkle if something is good; gestures of vomiting if something is bad. Likes meat, potatoes, raw vegetables, cake and ice cream. Dislikes liver, fish, eggs, cooked vegetables, and stew. About half have good table manners. Children do better when parents are there.

*Sleep*. Average bedtime is 8:30 P.M. and needs to be reminded. This is resisted as much as possible by stalling. Most sleep through the night with no problems. Nightmares equal good dreams. Average waking is at 7 A.M. Most get up right away with no problems.

*Bath and Dressing*. Most bathe once a week, and under protest. Dislikes washing hands or face and brushing teeth. Sometimes sent back from meals to wash up. Little concern for hair appearance. More active role in shopping for clothes; does not have a lot of say but shops willingly with parents. Most select own clothes in morning. Clothes are still treated with no care and flung about room.

*Emotions*. Is direct, matter-of-fact, simple, clear-cut, childish, easygoing, and balanced. Is less anxious, exacting, and demanding. Anger is not frequent but is violent, immediate, and expressed physically. Begins to plot revenge, but seldom remembers to carry it out. When hurt, either goes away or cries. Humor does not seem funny to adults. Jokes are told badly. Can't take a joke about self.

*Worries and Fears*. Fewer worries than fears. Worries include school, lessons, being late, and some worry about family finances. Fears include animals, the dark, high places, fires, and criminals.

*Interpersonal Relationships*. Is straightforward with mother. Mother is final authority. Resistance is beginning, and some may start to yell back at mother. Most get on very well with father. Fighting is more prominent, especially with younger siblings. Picks on younger siblings and aware of it. Relationships with older siblings are better, yet siblings feel like a nuisance at times. Family unit is still very important. Is satisfied with both parents. Sibling fighting upsets family harmony, however. Friendships are close and last longer. Tends to be less fighting than at younger ages. Friends of opposite sex are not very frequent.

*School*. School is "okay." Attention span is short, and is restless. Likes to memorize, but does not like to correlate facts or to use knowledge. Teacher is respected, sometimes more than parents. Critical analysis of teacher is beginning at end of this age. Criticism from teacher can be upsetting.

## 11-Year-Old

*Motor Characteristics.* Much movement, and postures vary extremely. Hands are constantly active; moves legs often (kicks desk, swings legs, fools with shoes).

*Eating.* Eating is becoming a real pleasure. Notices the relationship between amount eaten and increase in size of self. Very definite tastes have formed. Snacks between meals. Table manners still vary, but those with good outnumber those with bad. The main complaints at this age are poor posture, elbows on table, eating with fingers, criticizing food, knocking things over, eating too fast, and talking too much.

*Sleep.* Average bedtime is 9 P.M. Most are reminded or forced to go to bed and then stall or make a fuss. Good dreams are more frequent and of greater length, yet nightmares still occur and are violent. Average waking time is 7 A.M. and getting up can be very difficult for some.

*Bath and Dressing.* Most bathe twice per week and need to be reminded, but less frequently than at age 10. Boys do not care about hair. Girls don't use cosmetics at this age. Gets more involved in buying clothes. About half decide what to wear each day. Refuses to wear certain clothes. Care of clothes is still poor. Clothes are dropped and left on floor.

*Emotions.* Can be penetrating, sensitive, proud, selfish, competitive, belligerent, jealous, resentful, argumentative, contrite, rude, and uncooperative. Expressions are exaggerated (worst mother in the world). Frequent response to anger is violent, physical, emotional, and verbal. Humor is "corny." Physical and emotional violence is more prominent. Verbal retorts are common: yelling, swearing, calling names, and talking back. Report themselves as happy and seldom feel sad. Crying is still evident, with the cause being anger and disappointment.

*Worries and Fears.* This is the most worried and most fearful age. Worries are school, homework, lessons, money, parent's welfare, and own health. Fears include animals (snakes, bugs, cows, or bulls), being left alone in the dark, and high places.

*Interpersonal Relationships.* Tends to be rude and resistant to parents. Argues about everything to prove them wrong. This can include verbal and physical strikes. Child tends to exaggerate and dramatize confrontations. Admiration of father continues. Father's role becomes more of a disciplinarian, and because of this, less is said of father. May be afraid of father. Much fighting occurs with siblings. Becomes critical of younger siblings. Relationships are better with older siblings. Is afraid that is not liked as well as other siblings. Has a strong family feeling, even though behaves negatively toward certain members. Family activities (movies, picnics, zoo, etc.) are enjoyed and are even demanded. Is unaware how quarreling interferes with family harmony. Usually has two or three close friends at this age. Sleepovers are very important. Most parties are just for girls or just for boys. Clubs and secret organizations are still very important at this stage.

*School.* School behavior usually takes a turn for the worse. This can manifest as fatigue, uneven performance, and frequent illnesses. Also become restless, careless, forgetful; may daydream, dawdle, and be boisterous. Much interaction between students: notes, spitballs, teasing, chasing, hitting, and so on. More seem to be interested in their standing among the group and push for grades and self-satisfaction. Most are still excited about learning but have less organization. Homework is left until the last moment and causes more trouble. Rebellion and resentment against teacher increase. Class becomes more difficult to manage.

## References

Fosler, R., Bryski, D., & Melfi, J. (1987) Class project for EPSE 467 at Northern Illinois University, DeKalb, IL 60115.

## HIGH INTEREST—LOW VOCABULARY READING MATERIALS

Publishers' addresses are listed at the end of this section.

| Title | Publisher | Reading Grade Level | Interest Grade Level |
|---|---|---|---|
| Ablest | Fearon | 1–3 | 7–12 |
| Action Libraries | Scholastic | 2–3.9 | 7–12 |
| American Democracy | Garrard | 4 | 7–12 |
| Avon Illustrated Novels | Avon | 2 | 7–12 |
| Basic Illustrated History of America* | Pendulum | 4 | 7–12 |
| Beginner Books | Random House | 1–2 | 1–3 |
| Beginning Science Series | Follet | 2–3 | 2–6 |
| Beginning-to-Read Books | Follett | 1.9–2.6 | 2–6 |
| BesTellers | Fearon | 1.8–4.0 | 6–12 |
| Books for Young Explorers | National Geographic | 2–3 | 3–6 |
| Bright and Early Books | Random House | 1 | 1–3 |
| Career Awareness Program* (out of print) | King Features | 3–4 | 9–12 |
| Checkered Flag Series | Addison–Wesley | 2–4 | 6–12 |
| Classics Illustrated Comics* | Not in print | 4–5 | 7–12 |
| Comics Reading Library* (out of print) | King Features | 3–4 | 4–8 |
| Consumer Education Series | EMC | 3 | 7–12 |
| Contemporary Motivators* | Pendulum | 4 | 7–12 |
| Cowboy Sam Series | Benefic Press | Pre-Primer–3 | 1–6 |
| Crisis Series | Fearon | 2.3–4.5 | 6–12 |
| Dan Frontier Series | Benefic Press | Pre-Primer–4 | 1–7 |
| Deep Sea Adventures | Field Educational Publications | 2–5 | 3–11 |
| Discovery Books | Garrard | 2–3 | 4–6 |
| Disney's Wonderful World of Reading | Random House | 2 | 2–4 |
| Double Action Libraries | Scholastic | 3–4.4 | 7–12 |
| Early Childhood Series | Bowmar | K–2 | 2–4 |

*(continued)*

| Title | Publisher | Reading Grade Level | Interest Grade Level |
|---|---|---|---|
| Easy Readers | Grosset & Dunlap | 1–2 | 2–4 |
| Encounters Series | EMC | 3–4.5 | 7–12 |
| Family Life Education Books | Follett | 2–3 | 4–8 |
| Famous Animal Stories | Garrard | 3 | 4–6 |
| Gallaudet Preschool Signed English Series | Gallaudet | K–1 | K–3 |
| Gallery of Great Americans | Creative | 3 | 4–8 |
| Gemini Books | Childrens | 2–3 | 3–12 |
| Getting Along Series | Pitman Learning | 3–5 | 4–8 |
| Gold Dust Books | Bowmar | 2–2.9 | 4–6 |
| Hardy Boys Mystery Series | Grosset & Dunlap | 4 | 7–12 |
| I Can Do It Series | Bowmar | K–1 | K–2 |
| I Can Read Books | Harper & Row | 1–2 | 1–4 |
| Illustrated Biography Books* | Pendulum | 4 | 7–12 |
| Illustrated Shakespeare Series* | Pendulum | 4 | 7–12 |
| The Hip Reader | Annmaur Corp. | 1–3 | 4–9 |
| I Want to Be–Series | Santillana Publishing | 2–4 | 4–6 |
| Indians | Garrard | 3 | 4–6 |
| Interesting Reading Series | Follett | 2–3 | 7–12 |
| International Folktales Series | Fearon | 2.9–3.7 | 4–8 |
| Jim Forest Readers | Addison–Wesley | 1.7–3.2 | 2–8 |
| Jimmy and Joe Books | Garrard | 1–2 | 2–6 |
| Just Beginning-to-Read Books | Follett | K | K–2 |
| King Classics Library* (out of print) | King Features | 3–4 | 7–12 |
| Let's Find Out Series | Franklin Watts | 2–4 | 5–6 |
| Mania Books | Children's Press | 1 | 1–5 |
| Monsters | Crestwood | 3–5 | 3–8 |
| The Morgan Bay Mysteries | Addison-Wesley | 2–4 | 4–11 |
| Morrow's High Interest/ Easy Reading Books | William Morrow | 1–8 | 4–10 |
| Mystery Adventure Series | Benefic Press | 2–6 | 4–9 |
| NFL Today | Creative | 4 | 4–12 |
| Nancy Drew Mystery Series | Grossett & Dunlap | 4 | 7–12 |
| New True Books | Children's Press | 2–3.4 | 2–4 |
| New Age Illustrated Classics Series* | Pendulum | 4 | 7–12 |
| On the Move | Children's Press | 4 | 7–12 |
| Our Book Corner | Addison–Wesley | 1–3 | 1–3 |
| Pacemaker Classics | Fearon | 2.1–2.9 | 7–12 |
| Pacemaker Story Books | Fearon | 1.9–2.6 | 4–8 |
| Pacemaker True Adventure | Fearon | 2–3 | 5–12 |
| Pacemaker Vocational Readers | Fearon | 1.2 | 7–12 |
| Pal Paperbacks | Xerox | 1.5–5.5 | 4–12 |
| Parks for People | Children's Press | 4 | 4–12 |

| Title | Publisher | Reading Grade Level | Interest Grade Level |
|---|---|---|---|
| Picture Story Biographies | Children's Press | 2 | 2–5 |
| Pilot Books | Whitman | 2.4–5.5 | 7–12 |
| Preprimary Readers | Modern Curriculum | K–1 | K–2 |
| Racing Wheels Series | Benefic Press | 2–4 | 4–9 |
| Reading Incentive Program | Bowmar | 3 | 4–12 |
| Reading Skill Builder | Reader's Digest | 1–4 | 2–5 |
| Ready, Get Set, Go Series | Children's Press | 1–3 | 1–6 |
| Real People at Work | EMC | 2–6 | 4–12 |
| Sailor Jack Series | Benefic Press | PP–3 | 1–6 |
| Scarry's Golden Look-Look Books | Western | K–1 | 1–3 |
| See and Read Biographies | Putnam | 2–3 | 4–8 |
| Space Science Fiction Series | Benefic Press | 2–6 | 4–9 |
| Sparrow Books | Troll | 3 | 7–12 |
| Specter | Fearon | 2–3 | 6–12 |
| Sport Stars | Children's Press | 3 | 4–12 |
| Sports Mystery Stories | Benefic Press | 2–4 | 4–9 |
| Sprint Libraries | Scholastic | 2–3.9 | 7–12 |
| Sprint Starter Libraries | Scholastic | 1.5–1.9 | 4.6 |
| Step Up Books | Random House | 2–3 | 2.5 |
| Super Bowl Champions | Children's Press | 4 | 7–12 |
| Talespinners | Fearon | 2.6–4.5 | 7–12 |
| Target Books | Garrard | 3–4 | 7–12 |
| Tom Logan Series | Benefic Press | PP–1 | 1–6 |
| Triumph Books | Watts | 1.9–4.6 | 4–12 |
| TV and Movies Tie-ins | Creative | 4 | 4–12 |
| Ready, Get Set, Go Books | Children's Press | 1–3 | 1–6 |
| Venture Books | Garrard | K–2 | 1–5 |
| What Is It Series | Benefic Press | 1–4 | 1–8 |
| Wonder Starters | Grosset & Dunlap | 1–2 | 1–3 |
| Young People's Stories Our States | Children's Press | 3 | 2–6 |

*Books in "comic" book format.

## Publishers' Addresses

Addison-Wesley Publishing Company
1 Jacob Way
Reading, MA 01867

Bowmar
1901 North Walnut Street
Oklahoma City, OK 73125

Classics Illustrated
No current address is available

Crestwood House, Inc.
P.O. Box 3427
Highway 66 South
Mankato, MN 56002-3427

Fearon Education
19 Davis Drive
Belmont, CA 94002

Gallaudet University Bookstore
Gallaudet University
800 Florida Avenue
Washington, D.C. 20002

Education Division
Grosset & Dunlap
51 Madison Avenue
New York, NY 10010

King Features
Educational Division
Department 1254
235 East 45th Street
New York, NY 10017

National Geographic Society
Educational Services
Department 85
Washington, D.C. 20036

Putnam Publishing Group
200 Madison Avenue
New York, NY 10016

Avon Books
1790 Broadway
New York NY 10019

Children's Press
1224 West Van Buren Street
Chicago, IL 60607

Creative Education, Inc.
P.O. Box 227
Mankato, MN 56001

EMC Publishing
300 York Avenue
Saint Paul, MN 55101

Follett Library Book Co.
4506 Northwest Highway
Route 14 and 31
Crystal Lake, IL 60014

Garrard Publishing Co.
1607 North Market Street
Champaign, IL 61820

Harper & Row Publishers
10 East 53rd Street
New York, NY 10022

Modern Curriculum Press
13900 Prospect Road
Cleveland, OH 44136

Pendulum Press, Inc.
The Academic Building
Saw Mill Road
West Haven, CT 06516

Random House
201 East 50th Street
New York, NY 10022

Scholastic, Inc.
730 Broadway
New York, NY 10022

Troll Associates
320 Route 17
Mahwah, NJ 07430

Western Publishing Company
850 Third Avenue
New York, NY 10022

Xerox Education Publications
1250 Fairwood Avenue
P.O. Box 2639
Columbus, OH 43216

Sterling Publishing Co.
2 Park Avenue
New York, NY 10016

Franklin Watts
Sherman Turnpike
Danbury, CT 06816

Albert Whitman & Co.
5747 West Howard Street
Niles, IL 60648

# APPENDIX B

# Literature

## BOOKS BY HEARING-IMPAIRED AUTHORS

Balis, S. C. (1902). *From far and near: Graded stories for little folks*. Toronto: MacMillan.

Ballin, A. (1930). *The deaf mute howls*. Los Angeles: Grafton.

Batson, T. W., & Bergman, E. (1972). *The deaf experience: An anthology of literature by and about the deaf*. South Waterford, MN: Merriam-Ebby.

Beard, T. V. (1944). *Poems*. Washington, D.C.: Gallaudet College Press.

Bearden, C. E., & Potter, J. F. (1973). *A manual of religious signs*. Atlanta, GA: Home Mission Board.

Bennett, H. P., (1973). *Road girl*. Long Beach, CA: Collins Printing.

Berg, A. (1944). *Deaf in the profession, art and trades*. (pamphlet: available at Gallaudet College Library).

Booth, E. (1953). *Forty-niner: The life story of a deaf pioneer*. Stockton, CA: San Joaquin Pioneer and Historical Society.

Bove, L. (1980). *Sign language fun*. New York: Random House/Children's Television Workshop.

Bowe, F. (1978). *Handicapping America*. New York: Harper & Row.

Bowe, F. (1980). *Rehabilitating America: Toward independence for disabled people*. New York: Harper & Row.

Bowe, F. (1981). *Comeback: Six remarkable people who triumphed over disability*. New York: Harper & Row.

Bowe, F. G., & Sternberg, M. (1973). *I'm deaf too: Twelve deaf Americans*. Silver Spring, MD: National Association of the Deaf.

Braddock, R. G. (1975). *Notable deaf persons*. Washington, D.C.: Gallaudet College Alumni Association.

Bragg, B., & Bergman, E. (1981). *Tales from a clubroom*. Washington, D.C.: Gallaudet College Press.

Brooks, G. (1976). *The cracked tune*. Torrence, CA: AFP Publication.

Brown, C. A. (1946). *Forty years of silence*. Francestown, NH: author.

Calkins, E. E. (1924). *Louder please*. Boston: Atlantic Monthly Press.

Calkins, E. E. (1946). *And Hearing not—: Annals of an Adman*. New York: Charles Scribner.

Cavanaug, E. (1895). *The deaf poet's sure mount-*

*ing, mute immortal strains*. Omaha, NB: author.

Clark, B. (1865). *An account of St. Ann's church for deaf mutes, and articles of prose and poetry by deaf mutes*. New York: John A. Gray and Green.

Collingwood, H. W. (1923). *Adventures in silence*. New York: The Rural New Yorker.

Dalton, A. C. (1910). *Marriage of music*. Vancouver, British Columbia: Evans and Hasting, Printers.

Dalton, A. C. (1924). *Flame and adventure*. Toronto: MacMillian.

Dalton, A. C. (1926). *The ear trumpet*. Toronto: Ryerson Press.

Dalton, A. C. (1926). *The silent tone*. Vancouver, British Columbia: Evans and Hastings, Printers.

Dalton, A. C. (1931). *Lillies and leopards*. Toronto: Ryerson Press.

Dalton, A. C. (1931). *Neighing north*. Toronto: Ryerson Press.

Davidson, S. G. (1892). *Discussion and Results of Oral Work*. Philadelphia: author.

Duthie, J. (1978). *I cycled into the artic*. London: Eyre-Methven.

Eastman, C. (1974). *Sign me Alice*. Washington, D.C.: Gallaudet College.

Feret, L., & Newman, R. (1946). *American Signs: 1946 anthology of college poetry*. Los Angeles: National Poetry Association.

Fitzgerald, E. (1926). *Straight language for the deaf*. Washington, D.C.: The Alexander Graham Bell Association for the Deaf.

Fitzgerald, E. (1963). *Teaching language to the deaf: The straight language system*. Washington, D.C.: The Alexander Graham Bell Association for the Deaf.

Gannon, J. (1974). *The Gallaudet almanac*. Washington, D.C.: Gallaudet College Alumni Association.

Gannon, J. (1981). *Deaf heritage: A narrative history of deaf America*. Silver Spring, MD: National Association of the Deaf.

Goldman, R. L. (1935). *The good fight*. New York: Coward McCann.

Goldman, R. L. (1942). *Even the night*. New York: MacMillan.

Gustason, G. (1972). *Signing exact English*. Rossmoor, CA: Modern Signs Press.

Hackman, H. E. (1928). *My life transformed*. New York: Scribners.

Heiner, M. H. (1949). *Hearing is believing*. Cleveland, OH: World Publications.

Hicks, C. (1946). *The little lion*. New York: Island Press.

Hodgson, E. A. (1891). *Facts, anecdotes and poetry relating to the deaf and dumb*. New York: author.

Holcomb, R. (1977). *The hazard of deafness*. Northridge, CA: Joyce Media.

Holt, H. (1923). *Garrulities of an octogenarian editor with other essays somewhat biographical and autobiographical*. Boston: Houghton Mifflin.

Illinois School for the Deaf. (1969). *This is just to say: A book of short poems by Mark Johnson and others*. Jacksonville, IL: Illinois School for the Deaf.

Israelson, O. W. (1968). *Forty years of sound, forty years of silence*. Salt Lake City, UH: Utah Printing Company.

Jacobs, L. M. (1980). *The deaf adult speak out*. Washington D.C.; Gallaudet College Press.

Jacobus Jackson County, GA. (1855). *The big bull in a court house: A tale of horror*. Athens, GA: John Jacobus Flournoy.

Jennings, A. (1880). *Heart echoes*. Boston, MA. (Available at Gallaudet College Library).

Jones, H. M. (1969). *The miracle of love*. New York: Vantage Press.

Keller, H. A. (1914). *The world I live in*. New York: The Century Company.

Keller, H. A. (1920). *Out of the dark: Essays, letters and physical and social vision*. Garden City, NY: Doubleday, Page, and Company.

Keller, H. A. (1926). *The key of life: Optimism*. New York: Thomas Y. Crowell.

Keller, H. A. (1929). *Midstream, my later life*. Garden City, NY: Doubleday, Doran, and Company.

Keller, H. A. (1932). *Peace at eventide*. London: Methuen.

Keller, H. A. (1933). *Helen Keller in Scotland: A personal record written by herself*. London: Methuen.

Keller, H. A. (1938). *Helen Keller's journal, 1936–1937*. Garden City, NY: Doubleday Doran and Company.

Keller, H. A. (1941). *Let us have faith*. Garden City, NY: Doubleday, Doran and Company.

Keller, H. A. (1952). *Light-bearer to the world of darkness*. American Foundation for the Blind.

Keller, H. A. (1954). *The story of my life*. New York: Doubleday.

Keller, H. A. (1955). *Teacher, Annie Sullivan Macy: A tribute by the foster child of her mind*. Garden City, NY: Doubleday.

Keller, H. A. (1957). *The open door*. Garden City, NY: Doubleday, Doran and Company.

Keller, H. A. (1967). *Helen Keller: Her socialist years*. New York: International Publishers.

Kent, A. (1911). *Around the world in silence*. New York: Greaves.

Knox, E. (1891). *Gems from the field of thought*. Utica, NY: Author.

Leader, P. (1931). *And no bird sing*. New York: Vanguard Press.

Leisman, A. G. (1919). *Old Wisconsin and other poems*. Merril, WI: Merril Publication.

Leisman, A. G. (1947). *Out of the silence*. Milwaukee, WI: Jackson Printing Company.

Lillie, H. (1970). *The listening silence*. New York: Hawthorne Books.

LinWeber, R. (1961). *American deaf softball guide*. Printed privately by the author.

Long, J. S. (1908). *Out of the silence*. Council Bluffs, IA: Monarch Printing Company.

Long, J. S. (1962). *Sign language*. Washington D.C.: Gallaudet College Press.

Lowman, R. (1964). *Bitterweed*. Bentonville, AR: Bella Vista Press.

Madsen, W. J. (1972). *Conversational sign language II: An intermediate advanced manual*. Washington, D.C.: Gallaudet University Press.

Madsen, W. J. (nd). *You have to be deaf to understand*. Silver Spring, MD: National Association of the Deaf.

Mann, E. J. (1836). *The deaf and dumb*. Boston, MA: Author.

McGreevy, G. G. (1968). *I'm thirsty too!* South Brunswick, NJ. (Available at The Alexander Graham Bell Association for the Deaf).

McVan, A. J. (1942). *Spanish dwarfs*. New York: Order of the Hispanic Trustees.

McVan, A. J. (1953). *Tryst*. New York: Hispanic Society of America.

Merchant, J. (1954). *The greatest of these . . .*

*Poems and prayers*. Nashville, TN: Abingdon Press.

Merchant, J. (1957). *Halfway up the sky*. Nashville, TN: Abingdon Press.

Meyers, L. (1967). *Law and the deaf*. Washington, D.C.: United States Government Printing Office.

Michaels, J. W. (1923). *Sign language: A handbook of the sign language of the deaf for ministers, Sunday school workers, theological students and friends of the deaf*. Atlanta, GA: Home Mission Board.

Michaels, J. W. (1923). *Handbook of the sign language of the deaf*. Atlanta, GA. (Available at Gallaudet College Library).

Miles, D. (1976). *Gestures: Poetry in sign language*. Northridge, CA: Joyce Motion Picture Company.

Miller, B. (nd). *Conditions for survival*. New York: Amazing Stories Press.

Murphy, G. B. (1954). *Your deafness is not you: New design for deafness*. New York: Harper & Row.

Muse, H. E. (1961). *Green pavilions*. New York: Carlton Press.

Nack, J. (1839). *Earl Rupert and other tales and poems*. (Contact the San Francisco Public Library).

Nack, J. (1850). *The immortal, a dramatic romance and other poems*. New York: Stringer and Townsend.

Nack, J. (1859). *The romance of the ring and other poems*. New York: E. Conrad.

Nack, J. (nd). *Writings of James M. Nack, the deaf and dumb poet*. New York: Gordon Press.

Nack, J. (1872). *Legend of the rocks and other poems*. New York: E. Conrad.

O'Connor, J. (1879). *The works of James O'Connor the deaf poet*. New York: N. Tibbal.

Ogden, W. P. (1982). *The silent garden: Understanding the hearing impaired child*. New York: St. Martin's Press.

Orman, J. M. (nd). *Salt spray*. (Available at Gallaudet College Library).

Panara, T. R. F., & McFarland, J. F. (1960). *The silent muse*. Washington, D.C.: Gallaudet College Press.

Parsons, F. M. (1971). *Sound of the stars*. New York: Vantage Press.

Patterson, R. M. (1907). *Success among the deaf.* (Contact the San Francisco Public Library).

Peet, M. (1900). *Gertrude, the story of a beautiful life.* New York: J. T. Taylor.

Peet, M. (1903). *Verses.* Fanwood Press. (Contact the San Francisco Public Library).

Pertersen, D. O. (1952). *American signs: 1952 anthology of college poetry.* Los Angeles, CA: National Poetry Association.

Redden, L. C. (1874). *Sounds from secret chambers.* Boston: J. K. Osgood.

Riddell, F. (1914). *Silent world.* Philadelphia: Lippincott.

Riddell, F. (1932). *Perilous love.* Philadelphia: Lippincott.

Riddell, F. (1933). *Dream island.* Philadelphia: Lippincott.

Roen, R. (1981). *A handful of stories: Thirty-seven stories by deaf storytellers.* Washington, D.C.: Division of Public Services, Gallaudet College.

Rosenstein, L. E. (nd). *Poems.* Boston: Horace Mann School for the Deaf.

Schowe, B. M. (1978). *Identity crisis in deafness: A humanistic perspective.* Temple, AZ: Scholar Press.

Searing, L. C. (1921). *An autobiographical drama.* San Francisco, CA: Harr Warner Publishing.

Searing, L. R. (1865). *Idylls of battle and poems of the rebellion.* New York. (Available at The Alexander Graham Bell Association for the Deaf).

Smith, L. (1973). *Silence, love and kids I know.* Washington, D.C.: International Books.

Sollenberg, E. (1914). *Handful of quietness.* New Jersey: Gayren Press.

Sollenberger, E. (1937). *Alone with me.* New Jersey: Gayren Press.

Sowell, J. W. (1948). *To her I love.* Omaha, NB: Printed privately.

Stephens, P. F. (1936). *Skinning the snake and other poems.* New York: Alexander Press.

Stephens, P. F. (1937). *Teller of stars, a sonnet sequence.* New York: Alexander Press.

Stephens, P. F. (1971). *Songs to my heavenly father.* New York: Horseheads.

Sternberg, M. (1980). *American Sign Language: A comprehensive dictionary.* New York: Harper & Row.

Stout, H. H. (1929). *Sunshine and shadow.* Texas. (Contact the San Francisco Public Library).

Sullivan, J. A. (1964). *Valley forge.* Philadelphia, PA: Dorance.

Teegarden, G. M. (1896). *Stories old and new.* Western Pennsylvania Institution for the Deaf.

Teegarden, G. M. (1915). *In the silent hours.* Philadelphia. (Contact the San Francisco Public Library).

Teegarden, G. M. (1936). *Personal and holiday poems.* Philadelphia. (Contact the San Francisco Public Library).

Terry, H. L. (1898). *A tale of Normandy and other poems.* St. Louis, MO: (Contact the San Francisco Public Library).

Terry, H. L. (1909). *Waters from an ozark spring.* Boston: Gorham Press.

Terry, H. L. (1912). *The dream: A drama in two acts.* Los Angeles: Philocopus Press.

Terry, H. L. (1914). *Voice from the silence.* Santa Monica, CA: Palisades Press.

Terry, H. L. (1917). *California and other verses.* Santa Monica, CA: Palisades Press.

Terry, H. L. (1929). *Sung in silence.* (Contact the San Francisco Public Library).

Thompson, Z. B. (n.d.). *It does not pay.* Council Bluffs, IA: Deaf Hawkeye Press.

Tilden, D. (1887). Articulation in the new light. *American Annals of the Deaf, 32,* 98–103.

Tilden, D. (November 23, 1889). Notes of an idle morning. *The Weekly News.*

Tilden, D. (January 1891). *The silent educator.* (Contact the San Francisco Public Library).

Tilden, D. (1893). *Art education of the deaf.* Paper presented at the World's Congress of the Deaf, Chicago, IL.

Tilden, D. (February 23, March 23, May 11, June 15, and October 15, 1905) *The Deaf-Mutes Journal.*

Tilden, D. (November 1929). California and Theophilus d'Estrella. *The California News.* Fremont, CA: California School for the Deaf.

Tilden, D. (nd). Art among the deaf in France. *American Annals of the Deaf, 34,* 30.

Ulmer, T. A. (1942). *The badge of honor, an anthology of poems.* New York: Author.

Warfield, F. (1948). *Cotton in my ears.* New York: Viking Press.

Warfield, F. (1957). *Keep listening.* New York: Viking Press.

Wiggins, J. (1972). *No sound*. New York: The Silent Press.

Wright, D. (1958). *Monologue of deaf man*. London: Deutsch.

Wright, D. (1969). *Deafness*. New York: Stein & Day.

## FILMS BY DEAF PRODUCERS AND DIRECTORS

Edison, A. E. (Producer). (1913). *The deaf mute*. West Orange, NJ: Edison Library.

Jarashow, D. (Producer), & Wolf, P. (Director). (1979). *Think me nothing*. Signscope.

Marshall, E. (Producer). (nd). *The neighbor*. Bronx, NY. Available from Gallaudet College Library.

Marshall, E. (Producer). (nd). *The debt*. Bronx, NY. Available from Gallaudet College Library.

Marshall, E. (Producer), & Romero, E. (Director). (no date). *A cake of soap*. Bronx, NY. Available from Gallaudet College Library.

*The touch*. (1977). Available from Gallaudet College Media Distribution Center.

Weshsberg, P. W. (Producer). (nd). *Deafula*. Captioned Films for the Deaf, Inc.

## BOOKS WITH DEAF CHARACTERS

Andrews, J. (1989). *The flying fingers club*. Washington, D.C.: Gallaudet University Press.

Andrews, J. (1989). *The mystery of the disappearing newspapers*. Washington, D.C.: Gallaudet University Press.

Batson, A., & Bergaman, E. (Eds.) (1985). *Angels and outcasts. An anthology of deaf characters in literature*. Washington, D.C.: Gallaudet University Press.

Bowen, E. (1968). *Eva Trout, or changing scenes*. New York: Alfred A. Knopf.

Clemens, S. L. (1912). *The adventures of Huckleberry Finn*. New York: P. F. Collier and Son.

Defoe, D. (1720). *The history of the life and adventures of Mr. Duncan Campbell*. London: W. Meers.

Dickens, C. (nd). Doctor Marigold. In T. W. Batson and E. Bergman (Eds.), *The deaf experience*.

Faulkner, W. (1956). Hand upon the wasters. In *Knight's gambit*. New York: Random House.

Faulkner, W. (1959). *The mansion*. New York: Random House.

Hugo, V. M. C. (1973). *The hunchback of Notre Dame*. New York: Dutton.

Melville, H. (1949). Fragment from a writing desk. In *Complete stories of Herman Melville*. New York: Random House.

Musset, A. D. (1907). Pierre and Camille. In *Complete writing of Alfred De Musset*, (Vol. 7). New York: Edwin C. Hill.

Scott, S. W. (1943). *The talisman*. New York: Dodd, Mead & Company.

Turgenev, I. (1904). Mumu. In *Novels and stories of Ivan Turgenev* (Vol. 11). New York: Charles Scribner's Sons.

## DEAF AWARENESS WITH THE YOUNG

### Books and Articles

Glazzard, M. H. (1978). *Meet Camille and Danille, They are special persons*. Lawrence, KS: H & H Enterprises.

Golder, S. (1989). *Buffer's orange leash*. Washington, D.C.: Gallaudet University Press.

Marie, A. (1989). *The day we met Cindy*. Washington, D.C.: Gallaudet University Press.

Peter, D. (1977). *Claire and Emma*. New York: John Day.

Peterson, J. W. (1977). *I have a sister, my sister is deaf*. New York: Harper & Row.

Stone-Harris, R. (1988). Supermachine, a play—Five sketches from the lives of deaf people. *Perspectives for Teachers of the Hearing Impaired, 6*(4), 8–10.

Tabuena-Bogatz, L. (1987). A unit on deaf awareness for the very young. *Perspectives for Teachers of the Hearing Impaired, 5*(5), 9–12.

### Videos and Films

*An evening on deafness* (film). (5 films: 16 mins. each).

*It's okay to be deaf, Denise* (16 mm film). Los

Angeles: David T. Siegel Institute for the Communicative Disorders of Michael Reese Medical Center and the Ear Institute. (28 mins.; color; sound; captioned).

*My third eye* (video). (1973). Washington, D.C.: Gallaudet Media Distribution. (58 mins.; color; sound/signed).

*See what I say* (16mm. film). (1981). Silver Spring, MD: Special Materials Project. (24 mins.; color; captioned).

*The silent world of Jim* (16mm film). (1976). Burbank, CA: Informational Materials, Inc. (14 mins.; color; captioned).

*The only thing I can't do is hear* (video, 16mm film). (1976). Washington, D.C.: Gallaudet Media Distribution. (27 mins.; color; sound/signed).

*The ears and hearing* (16mm film). (1969). Silver Spring, MD: Special Materials Project. (22 mins.; black and white; captioned).

## TRANSLATING CLASSICS INTO SIGN LANGUAGE

### Books and Articles

Anonymous. (1982). Sign unto the Lord: A hymnal for the deaf. *Sign Language Studies*, 36, 226.

Heymont, G. (1983). Singing opera . . . Signing opera. *The Deaf American, 35*(5), 2–6.

Kilma, E., & Bellugi, U. (1979). Poetry in the palm of your hand: A conference. *The Deaf American*, *31*(5), 9–13.

Klima, E., & Bellugi, U. (1980). Wit and poetry in American Sign Language. In *Sign and culture*, pp. 105–132. Silver Spring, MD: Linstoke Press.

Klima, E., Bellugi, U., & Lentz, E. (1979). Wit and plays on signs. In *The Signs of Language*. Cambridge, MA: Harvard University Press.

Maxwell, M. M., & Boster, S. (1982). Interpreting hymns for deaf worshippers. *Sign Language Studies, 36*, 217–226.

Rios, C. R. (1979). Poetry in the palm of your hand: A conference. *The Deaf American, 31*(5), 9–13.

## Films and Video

*Beauty and the beast* (videocassette). (1981). Fairmont, CA: Fairmont Theatre for the Deaf. (60 mins.; color; sound; signed).

*Creative interpretation of literature in sign* (videocassette). (1981). Rochester, NY: National Technical Institute for the Deaf. (48 mins.; color; signed; captions).

*Dark of the moon* (videocassette). (1976). Rochester, NY: National Technical Institute for the Deaf. (120 mins.; color; signed; sound).

*The death of Minnehaha* (16mm film). (1976). Joyce Motion Picture Company. (6 mins.; color; sound; signed).

*A festival of hands: A silken tent* (videocassette). (1980). WGBH Educational Foundation. (30 mins.; color; sound; partially signed).

*Jabberwocky* (16mm film). (1975). Joyce Motion Picture Company. (10 mins.; color; sound; signed).

*Moses* (16mm films). (1975). Joyce Motion Picture Company. (45 mins.; color; sound; signed).

*Oedipus Rex (Oedipus the King)* (16mm films). Washington, D.C.: Gallaudet Media Distribution. (20 mins.; color; signed; silent).

*Romeo and Juliet* (videocassette). (1979). Rochester, NY: National Technical Institute for the Deaf. (120 mins.; color; sound; signed).

*Sing mime: The art of visual imagery*. (1981). Rochester, NY: National Technical Institute for the Deaf. (60 mins.; color; captioned; signed).

*The tragedy of Hamlet, prince of Denmark* (16mm film). (1958). Washington, D.C.: Gallaudet College Dramatics Club. (45 mins.; black and white; silent; signed).

*Tormented pathways* (videocassette). (1976). Rochester, NY: National Technical Institute for the Deaf. (77 mins.; color; sound; signed).

## DEAF FOLKLORE

### Books and Articles

Carmel, S. J. (1982). American deaf folklore. *Communicating with hearing people*. (Available from SFPL, Deaf Services).

Lane, L. G., & Pittle, I. B. (Eds.). (1981). *A handful of stories: Thirty-seven stories by deaf storytellers*. Washington, D.C.: Gallaudet College, Division of Public Services.

Hagemeyer, A. (Ed.) (in press). *Life in deaf America*. Washington, D.C.: Library of Deaf Action.

Holcomb, R. (1977). *The hazards of deafness*. Northridge, CA: Joyce Media.

Huston, C. (1973). *Deaf Smith: Incredible Texas spy*. Waco, TX: Texian Press.

Rutherford, S. (1983). Funny in deaf–Not in hearing. *Journal of American Folklore*. (Available from SFPL, Literature Dept. and Deaf Services).

Schwanke, A. A. (1914). *Schwanke uber schwerhorige menchen, eien verglichende untersuchung*. (Available from University of California, Berkeley, CA.

## Video and Films

Carmel, S. (1981). *American Folklore in the Deaf Community* (videocassette). Washington, D.C.: Gallaudet Media Distribution Center. (56 min.; color; sound; signed).

*Deaf Folklore* (videocassette). (1980). Washington, D.C.: Gallaudet Media Distribution Center. (80 mins.; color; sound; signed).

*Handful of Stories* (parts 1–9) (videocassette). (1980). Washington, D.C.: Gallaudet Media Distribution Center. (Color; sound; signed).

*Legend of Old Bill* (16 mm film). (1975). Joyce Motion Picture Company. (9 mins.; color; sound; signed).

*Memories of Old Hartford* (videocassette). (1913). National Association of the Deaf Historical Collection. (16 mins.; black and white; signed).

*Mother's Bumblebee* (16 mm). (1975). Joyce Motion Picture Company. (4 mins.; color; silent; signed).

*The Professor of Signs* (videocassette). (1976). Washington, D.C.: Gallaudet Media Distributions. (40 mins.; color; silent; signed).

*Simon Carmel: Deaf Folklore/Deaf Culture* (videocassette). (1982). Freemont, CA: Ohlone College. (90 mins.; color; sound; signed).

*Supergrandpa* (16 mm film). (1975). Joyce Motion Picture Company. (12 mins.; color; sound; signed).

Train Ride to Grandfather's (16 mm film). (1975). Joyce Motion Picture Company. (3 mins.; color; silent; signed).

*Yankee Doodle, The Irishman's Flea and the Lady and the Cake*. (1920). National Association of the Deaf Historical Collection. (6 mins.; black and white; silent; signed).

## BOOKS AND TAPES

American Association to Promote the Teaching of Speech to the Deaf. (1892). *Report of the proceedings*. Rochester, NY. (Available at the University of California, Berkeley).

Auerbach, L. (September 1978). The national association of the deaf—Then and Now. *Deaf American*.

Burnes, B. B., & Jones, U. C. (1937). *National association of the deaf needs you* (videotape). Gallaudet College Media Distribution Center.

Celebrating a centennial: The national association of the deaf—1800–1980. (Fall 1980). *Gallaudet Today*.

*Convention of American instructors of the deaf*. (1914). (videotape). Gallaudet College Media Distribution Center.

Dobbins, C. R. (1940). *National association of the deaf day at the New York World's Fair* (videotape). Gallaudet College Media Distribution Center.

Elmer, L. A. (1940). *Nineteenth triennial convention* (videotape). Gallaudet College Media Distribution Center.

Maslic, F. (1955). *World congress of the deafmutes*. Zagreb, Yugoslavia. (Available at the University of California, Berkeley).

National Association of the Deaf. *Proceedings of the fourth, seventh, and ninth conventions, including the proceedings of the world's congress of the deaf, 1893, 1907, and 1910*. (Available at University of California, Berkeley).

PBS Video. (1975). *World congress of the deaf* (VHS cassette). Author.

Royal Commission on the Blind, Deaf and Dumb. (1889). *Report of the Royal Commission on the blind, the deaf and dumb of the United Kingdom*. (Available at the University of California, Los Angeles).

Shaposka, B. (1965). *The NAD story*. Washington, D.C.: Gallaudet College Student Body Government Chapter of the District of Columbia Association of the Deaf.

# APPENDIX C

# Resources and Further Reading

```
┌─────────────────────────────────────────────────────────┐
│                    APPENDIX TOPICS                       │
│                                                          │
│   Education                                              │
│   Sign Language                                          │
│   The Deaf Community                                     │
│   Hearing-Impaired Individuals                           │
│   Parents of Hearing-Impaired Children                   │
│   Hearing Children of Deaf Parents                       │
│   Employment                                             │
│   Also of Interest                                       │
└─────────────────────────────────────────────────────────┘
```

## EDUCATION

### General

Addison, W. H. (1907). *Report on a visit to some of the American schools for the deaf*. London: Moseley Commission.

Andrews, H. (1919). The Wright oral school: A sketch. *Volta Review*, April and May.

Arnold, T. (1881). *A method of teaching the deaf and dumb speech, lip reading, and language*. London: Smith, Elder.

Arrowsmith, J. P. (1819). *The art of instructing the infant deaf and dumb*. London: Taylor and Hessey.

Beggs, R. (1976). *A history of residential schools for the deaf in Canada*. National Leadership Training Program, National Center on Deafness.

Bender, R. E. (1970). *The conquest of deafness: A history of the long struggle to make possible a normal living by those handicapped by lack of normal hearing* (rev. ed.). Cleveland: Case Western Reserve University.

Benderly, B. L. (1980). *Danding without music: Deafness in America*. New York: Anchor Press/Doubleday.

Brill, R. G. (1974). *The education of the deaf: Administrative and professional developments* (2nd ed.). Washington, D.C.: Gallaudet College Press.

Chaves, T., & Soler, J. (1974). Pedro Ponce de Leon, first teacher of the deaf. *Sign Language Studies, 5*.

Chaves, T., & Soler, J. (1975). Manuel Ramirez de Carrion (1579–1652?) and his secret method of teaching the deaf. *Sign Language Studies, 8*.

*Convention of American instructors of the deaf* (3/4" videocassette). (1914). Washington, D.C.: Gallaudet College Media Distribution Center.

Crammatte, F. B. (Ed.). (1975). *Notable deaf persons*. Washington, D.C.: Gallaudet College Alumni Association.

de L'Epee, C. M. (1776). *Institution des sourds et muets, par la voie des signes methodiques*. Available: University of California, Los Angeles.

DeFoe, D. (1720). *The history of the life and adventures of Mr. Duncan Campbell*. London: W. Meers.

Degerando, A. (1827). *De l'education des sourds-muets denaissance*. Available: University of California, Los Angeles.

Fay, E. A. (Ed.). (1893). *Histories of American*

*schools for the deaf 1817-1893*. Washington, D.C.: The Volta Bureau.

Gallaudet, E. M. (1875). *Report on deaf-mute instruction*. Washington, D.C.: U.S. Government Printing Office.

Gordon, J. C. (1892). *Notes and observations upon the education of the deaf with a revised index to education of deaf children*. Washington, D.C.: The Volta Bureau.

Hodgson, K. W. (1929). *The deaf and their problems: A study in special education*. London: Watts and Co.

Holder, W. (1967). *Elements of speech with an appendix—concerning persons deaf and dumb*. (Available from University of California, Santa Cruz).

Love, J. K. (1896). *Deaf mutism: A clinical and pathological study*. Glasgow: J. MacLehose and Sons.

Montague, M. P. (1915). *Closed doors: Studies of deaf and blind children*. Boston: Houghton Mifflin.

*More than one way: Chris* (16mm film). (no date). New York: Rochester Institute of Technology.

National Association of the Deaf. (1885). *Proceedings of the meeting held in the Senate chamber, Madison, Wisconsin, Wednesday, July 16, 1884, to consider the subject of deaf-mute instruction in relation to the work of the public schools*. Washington, D.C.: Gibson Brothers, Printers and Bookbinders.

National Association of the Deaf. (1914). *Methods of educating the deaf, and opinions about the sign language by educators of the deaf, by orally educated deaf, and others competent to speak on the subject*. Author. Washington, D.C.: Gibson Brothers, Printers and Bookbinders.

Orellano, J. (1930). *Reduccion de las letra y arte para ensenar a hablar los mudos*.

Portafilms. (no date). *Understanding the deaf* (15mm film). Perennial Education, Inc., 1825 Willow Road, P.O. Box 236, Northfield, IL 60093.

Porter-Barnard, F. A. (1834). *Observations on the education of the deaf and dumb*. Boston: Office of the North American Review.

*The works of George Dalgarno of Aberdeen*. (1834, 1971). New York: AMS Press.

Thornton, W. (1793, 1917). Teaching the deaf, or consequently dumb, to speak. *Columbia Historical Society Record, 20*.

Tilden, D. (May 1885). Deaf mutes and their education. *Overland Monthly,* 504–510.

Upshall, C. C. (1929). *Day schools vs. insitutions for the deaf*. New York: Teachers College, Columbia University.

Wright, D. (1969). *Deafness*. New York: Stein & Day.

Yale, C. A. (1931). *Years of building: Memories of a pioneer in a special field of education*. New York: L. MacVeagh, the Dial Press.

## Gallaudet University

Atwood, A. W. (1964). *Gallaudet College: Its first one hundred years*. Lancaster, PA: Intelligencer Printing Company.

Bortner, J. (Summer 1979). New life for "Ole Jim. *Gallaudet Today.*

*Dom Pedro's visit to Gallaudet College* (3/4" video-cassette). (1913). Washington, D.C.: Gallaudet College Media Distribution Center.

Edington, W., Peikoff, D., Baumert, H., & Gannon, J. (Eds.). (1974). *The Gallaudet Almanac*. Washington, D.C.: Gallaudet College Alumni Association.

Gallaudet College Alumni Association. (1964). *Our heritage 1864–1964: Gallaudet College Centenial*. Washington, D.C.: Graphic Arts Press.

*Gallaudet College Announcements*. (no date). Washington, D.C.: Gallaudet College.

Gallaudet, E. M. (1983). *History of the college for the deaf: 1857–1907*. Washington, D.C.: Gallaudet College Press.

Fusfeld, I. S. (1956). *Successful careers out of Gallaudet College*. Washington, D.C.: Gallaudet College Press.

Historically speaking. On the green. (Fall 1977). *Gallaudet Today.*

Merrill, E. C. Jr. (June 1981). Edward Miner Gallaudet: A man with a will and way. *Deaf American.*

Ogoke, A. (Spring 1980). The greeks at Gallaudet. *Gallaudet Today.*

*The Gallaudet Story* (16mm film). (1915). Washington, D.C.: Gallaudet College Media Distribution Center.

*The signing of the charter of Gallaudet college* (3/4" videocassette). (1915). Washington, D.C.: National Center on Deafness Media Distribution Center.

*Thomas Gallaudet* (1/2" open reel videotape). (1964). National Center on Deafness Media Center.

Weinstock, R. (Summer 1979). Living with history. *Gallaudet Today*.

## California School for the Deaf

Brill, R. G. (1954). The California school for the deaf. *Volta Review, 56*.

Burnes, C., & Ramger, C. (1960). *A history of the California school for the deaf, 1860–1960*. Berkeley, CA: California School for the Deaf.

California Association of the Deaf. (1967). *The deaf at work*. Berkeley, CA: California School for the Deaf.

California School for the Deaf. (1955). *The California palms*. Author.

California School for the Deaf. (nd). *California news*. Fremont, CA: Author.

*First annual report of the California institution for the instruction of the deaf and dumb and the blind*. (1861–1906). (Available at the University of California).

## Educating Multihandicapped Hearing-Impaired Students

Andrews, J. (1987). How to use the microcomputer with multihandicapped hearing impaired students: Teaching suggestions. *Perspectives for Teachers of the Hearing Impaired 5*(3) 15–19.

Arkell, C. (1982). Functional curriculum development for multiply involved hearing-impaired students. *Volta Review, 84*(4), 198–208.

D'Zamko, M. E., & Hampton, I. (1985). Personnel preparation for multi-handicapped hearing-impaired students: A review of the literature. *American Annals of the Deaf 130*(2), 9–14.

D'Zamko, M., & Hampton, I. (1985). Personnel preparation for multihandicapped hearing impaired students. *American Annals of the Deaf, 131*(1), 9–14.

Egan, K. (1985). Software adaptions for the multihandicapped: A case study. *American Annals of the Deaf, 130*(4), 421–423.

Garwood, S. G., & Fewell, R. R. (1983). *Educating handicapped infants: Issues in development and intervention*. Rockville, MD: Aspen.

Haag, R. F. (1978). A residential program for deaf multi-handicapped children. *American Annals of the Deaf, 123*, 475–478.

Jones, T. W. (1984). A framework of identification, classification, and placement of multihandicapped hearing-impaired students. *Volta Review, 86*, 142–151.

Jones, T. W., & Dunne, M. T. (1988). The CHARGE association: Implications for teachers. *American Annals of the Deaf, 133*(1), 36–39.

Kibler, C. (1986). Board games for multihandicapped players. *Perspectives for Teachers of the Hearing Impaired, 4*(4), 21–23.

Klein, C. (1978). Variables to consider in developing and selecting services for deaf-blind children. Part 2. *American Annals of the Deaf, 123*, 430–433.

LaSasso, C. (1985). "Learning Disabilities"—let's be careful before labeling deaf children. *Perspectives for Teachers of the Hearing Impaired, 3*(5), 2–4.

Levine, L., & Pearson, J. (1985). From schoolroom to living room: Teaching independent living skills to multi-handicapped adults. *Perspectives for Teachers of the Hearing Impaired, 3*(4), 17–19.

Long, M. (1984). The meaning of independence. *Perspectives for Teachers of the Hearing Impaired, 2*(4), 22–23.

Morrow, L. (1985). Helping multihandicapped students remain on task. *Perspectives for Teachers of the Hearing Impaired, 3*(4), 14–16.

Morrow, L. W. (1985). Teaching self-control to dually diagnosed deaf students: Promising procedures. *American Annals of the Deaf, 130*(5), 502–506.

Prickett, H. T., & Duncan, E. (Eds.). (1988). *Coping with the multihandicapped hearing impaired: A practical approach*. Springfield, IL: Charles C. Thomas.

Rice, J. (1973). *A comprehensive facility for multiply handicapped deaf adults: Final report*. Fayetteville, AR: Arkansas Rehabilitation Research and Training Center.

Schein, J. D. (1979). Multiply handicapped hearing-impaired children. In L. J. Bradford &

W. G. Hardy (Eds.), *Hearing and hearing impairment* (pp. 357–363). New York: Grune and Stratton.

Schloss, P. J., Smith, M. A., Goldsmith, L., & Selinger, J. (1984). Identifying current and relevant curricular sequences for multihandicapped hearing-impaired learners. *American Annals of the Deaf*, *129*(4), 370–374.

Shroyer, E. H., & Tweedie, D. (Eds.). (1979). *Perspectives on the Multihandicapped Hearing Impaired child*. (Monograph 2). Washington, D. C.: Gallaudet College Press.

Signorat, M., & Watson, A. (1981). Orientation & mobility training for the multihandicapped deaf. *Teaching Exceptional Children*, *14*(3), 110–115.

Snell, M. E. (Ed.). (1978). *Systematic instruction of the moderately and severely handicapped*. Columbus, OH: Charles E. Merrill.

Stewart, L. G. (1978). Hearing-impaired/developmentally disabled persons in the United States: Definitions, causes, effects, and prevalence estimates. *American Annals of the Deaf*, *123* 488–495

Tweedie, D., & Shroyer, E. (Eds.). (1982). *The multihandicapped hearing impaired: Identification and instruction*. Washington, D.C.: Gallaudet College Press.

## SIGN LANGUAGE

### Books and Articles

Abernath, E. R. (1959). An historical sketch of the manual alphabet. *American Annals of the Deaf, 104*(2).

Baker, C., & Battison, R. (Eds.) (1980). *Sign Language and the deaf community: Essays in honor of William C. Stokoe*. Silver Spring, MD: National Association of the Deaf.

Baker, C., & Paden, C. (1978). *American Sign Language: A look at its history, structure, and community*. Silver Spring, MD: T. J. Publishers.

Bellugi, U., & Klima, E. (1972). The roots of language in the sign talk of the Deaf. *Psychology Today*, *6*.

Charlip, R. (1974). *Handtalk: An ABC of finger spelling and sign language*. New York: Four Winds Press.

Cokely, D., & Baker, C. (1980). *American Sign Language: A teacher's resource text on curriculum, methods, and evaluation*. Silver Spring, MD: T. J. Publishers.

Cokely, D., & Baker, C. (1980) *American Sign Language: A teacher's resource text on grammar and culture*. Silver Spring, MD: T. J. Publishers.

Costello, E. (1983). *Signing—How to speak with your hands*. New York: Bantam Books.

Fant, L. (1983). *The American Sign Language phrase book*. Chicago, IL: Contemporary Books.

Green, L., & Dicker, E. (1981). *Sign Language*. New York: Franklin Watts.

Klima, E., & Bellugi, U. (1979). *The signs of language*. Cambridge, MA:. Harvard University Press.

Lane, H. (September 1977). Notes for a psychohistory of American Sign Language. *Deaf American*.

Lane, H., & Grosjean, F. (Eds.) (1980). *Recent perspectives on American Sign Language*. Hillsdale, NJ: Lawrence Erlbaum Associates.

Long, J. S. (1962). *The sign language*. Washington, D.C.: Gallaudet College Press.

Lytle, J. (1974). *Sign talk*. Washington, D.C.: Gallaudet College Press.

Madsen W. (1972). *Conversational sign language II*. Washington, D.C.: Gallaudet College Press.

Mallery, G. D. (1972). *Sign language among the North American Indians compared with that among other peoples and deaf mutes*. New York: Mouton.

Markowicz, H. (1977). *American Sign Language: Fact and Fancy*. Washington, D.C.: Public Services Programs, Gallaudet College.

Moser, H. M. (1960). Historical aspects of manual communication. *Journal of Speech and Hearing Disorders, 25*(2).

National Technical Institute for the Deaf. (1978). *Principles of interpreting*. Rochester, NY: Author.

Niesser, A. (1983). *The other side of silence: Sign language and the deaf community in America*. New York: Alfred A. Knopf.

Poter, S. H. (1894). Suppression of signs by force. *American Annals of the Deaf, 39*.

Riekehof, L. (1978). *The joy of signing.* Springfield, MD: Linstoke Press.

Sandager, O. K. (1986). *Sign language around the world.* North Hollywood, CA: OK Publishing.

Wilbur, R. (1979). *American Sign Language sign systems.* Baltimore, MD:. University Park Press.

Wilcox, S. (Ed.) (1988). Academic acceptance of American Sign Language (special issue). Sign Language Studies, *59.*

Woodward, J. C. (1976). Signs of change: Historical variations in American Sign Language. *Sign Language Studies*, 10.

## Video and Films

*ASL is a language / Continuum of communication systems* (VHS). Northridge, CA: California State University. (52 mins.; black and white; sound; signed).

*Basic course in American Sign Language* (VHS). (1985). Silver Spring, MD: T. J. Publishers. (3 vol.: 60 mins. each; color; signed).

*Dactylology: Words on your hands (VHS). (1985).* Rochester, NY: National Technical Institute for the Deaf. (8 vols.: 60 mins. each; color; sound; signed).

*Deaf Historical Series* (³/₄″ in videocassette and beta). National Interpreter Training Center. (90 mins.; color).

*Developing the spoken language skills of hearing impaired children* (VHS 55 min.). (1985). Southport, England: Birkdale School for Hearing Impaired Children.

*Feast for the eyes.* Deaf Media, Inc.

*History of sign language* (³/₄″ videocassette and beta). National Center on Deafness. (90 mins.; color).

*Language landscape* (VHS). (1988). San Francisco: San Francisco Public Library. (27 mins.; ASL/English voiceover).

*Signing exact English: Curriculum A* (4 vol.) (VHS). (1984). Los Alamitos, CA: Modern Signs Press.

*Speechreading* (VHS). (1980). Washington, D.C.: Gallaudet University, Pre-college Program.

*The professor of signs* (VHS). (1976). Washington, D.C.: Gallaudet Media Distribution. (40 mins.; color; sound/sign).

*Towards the preservation of sign language* (³/₄″ videocassette). Gallaudet College Media Distribution Center. (16 mins.; black and white).

# THE DEAF COMMUNITY

## General

*A plea for a statue of De l'Eppe in America* (³/₄″ videocassette). (1913). Washington, D.C.: Gallaudet College Media Distribution Center.

Albronda, M. (1977). Tilden's admission day statue returns to Market Street. *California News.* Fremont, CA: California School for the Deaf.

Bernard, R. (1941). *Surdite, surdi-mutite et mustisme dans le Theatre Francais.* Available: University of California, Santa Cruz.

Butler, J., & Gilbert, L. (Ed.) (1981). *Deaf heritage: A narrative history of deaf America.* Silver Spring, MD: National Association of the Deaf.

Deafness Research Foundation (Producer). (no date). *Silent world, muffled world* (³/₄″ videocassette).

First theatre for the hard of hearing. (February 1934). *Volta Review*, 36.

Foppiani, V., & Talbot, M. (no date). *Communication and lifeskills curriculum.* Unpublished curriculum. Fairport, NH: Monroe BOCES.

Gannon, J. R. (Winter 1980–1981). Americans in Paris: Conveying a message of gratitude and paying homage to a friend. *Gallaudet Today.*

*Gettysburg* (³/₄″ in videocassette). (1915). Washington, D.C.: Gallaudet College Media Distribution Center.

Gragg, V. (1985). *What is an audiogram?* Washington, D.C.: Gallaudet University Pre-College Programs.

Hubbard, W. (1913). *An address at the tomb of Garfield* (VHS cassette). Washington, D.C.: Gallaudet College Media Distribution Center.

*Introduction to communication.* (1986). Washington, D.C.: Gallaudet University Pre-College Programs.

Mann, J. E. (Ed.). (1836). *The deaf and dumb.* Available: University of California, Los Angeles.

Montague, H. A. (1941). Things I wish they wouldn't do: A collection of faux pas committed by the normally hearing. *Volta Review, 45.*

O'Neill, J. J., & Oyer, H. J. (1961). *Visual communication for the hard of hearing: History, research, methods.* Englewood Cliffs, NJ: Prentice-Hall.

Padden, C., & Humphries, T. (1988). *Deaf in America. Voices from a culture.* Silver Springs, MD: National Association for the Deaf.

Schuchman, J. (Winter 1982). Oral history and the deaf community: Deaf senior citizens as historical resources. *Gallaudet Today.*

Simko, C. B. (1986). *Ear gear.* Washington, D.C.: Gallaudet University Press.

Stone-Harris, R. (1988). *Let's learn about deafness.* Washington, D.C.: Gallaudet University Pre-College Programs.

Supalla, D. (Director). (1981). *World games of the deaf* (VHS cassette).

*The cracked tune: Based on 5 years of Gregg Brooks' writings on deafness.* (1976). Torrence, CA: AFP Publications.

Tilden, D. (nd). Art among the deaf in France. *American Annals of the Deaf, 34.*

Tilden, D. (May 1982). Art and what California should do about her. *Overland Monthly, 509–515.*

Woods, W. H. Sr. (1973). *The forgotten people.* St. Petersburg, FL: Dixie Press.

*World congress of the deaf* (VHS cassette). (1975). PBS Video (Distributor).

## Minority Groups

Anderson, G. (nd). Vocational rehabilitation services and the black deaf. *Journal of Rehabilitation of the Deaf.* Available at University of California, Berkeley.

Anderson, G. B., & Bowe, F. G. (1971). Racism within the deaf community. *American Annals of the Deaf, 26,* 357–361.

Anderson, T. L. (1944). Postwar and the adult deaf. *American Annals of the Deaf,* 89(4).

Annual Survey of Hearing Impaired Children and Youth, Office of Demographic Studies. (1975). *Ethnic background in relation to other characteristics of hearing impaired students in the United States.* Washington, D.C.: Gallaudet College.

Bachman, J. J., & Hairston, E. E. (1967). *A study of a segment of the negro deaf population in the Los Angeles area.* Northridge, CA: California State University, National Leadership Training Program.

Beggars' symposium. (1949). *The Frat.* Available: Gallaudet College Library and The Alexander Graham Bell Association for the Deaf.

Being deaf . . . being a woman. (nd). *Gallaudet Today, 4*(3).

Benderly, B. (1980). *Dancing without music.* Garden City, NY: Anchor Press/Doubleday.

Billescas, C. M. (1979). *Survey of communication methods and problems of Spanish-speaking parents of hearing impaired children.* Northridge, CA: California State University, National Leadership Training Program.

Bowe, F. (1974). Deafness and ethnic minorities. *Education and rehabilitation of deaf persons with other disabilities* (pp. 34–38). New York: New York University, Deafness Research and Training Center.

Christianson, K. P. (1980). Utilization of videotape programs as educational enrichment for Spanish-speaking families and their deaf children: Focus on parent-child-teacher interaction. *American Annals of the Deaf, 125*(6), 841–843.

Cinelli, P. (Spring 1981). People plus. *Gallaudet Today* 29.

Crammate, F. B. (Ed.). (1975). *Notable deaf persons.* Washington, D.C.: Gallaudet College Alumni Association.

Crist, L. M. (1974). *Through the rain and the rainbow: The remarkable life of Richard Kinney.* New York: Abingdon Press.

*Deaf women: Ambitious dreams, emerging dreams* (videocassette). (1979). Available: SFPL, Deaf Services.

DeLaTorre, T. (1974). *Audio-visual documentary on Chicano families with deaf children—An exploration of feeling attitudes, and experiences related to social, educational, and vocational concerns.* Northridge, CA: California State University, National Leadership Training Program.

Delgado, G. L. (Ed.). (in press). *The Hispanic deaf, issues and challenges* (working title). Washington, D.C.: Gallaudet College Press.

Department for the Colored Blind and Deaf.

(1896). *Report from the Maryland School for the Blind and Deaf*. Baltimore, MD: Author.

Ebel, M. L. (1974). Agatha Tiegel Hanson—Class of 1893. *Gallaudet Today*, 4(3).

Faganism rampant. (March 1949). *The Frat*. (Available at Gallaudet College Library; The Alexander Graham Bell Association for the Deaf).

Gallaudet College Drama (Producer). (1977). *The touch*. Washington, D.C.: Gallaudet College Media Distribution Center.

Gallick, J. (January 1981). The deaf gang, Part 1. *Deaf American*, 4–10.

Gallick, J. (February 13–15, 1981). The deaf gang, Part 2. *Deaf American*.

Gannon, J. (Summer 1979). And finally . . . Douglas Craig. *Gallaudet Today*, 33.

Gannon, J. R. (Ed.). (1974). *The Gallaudet Almanac*. Washington, D.C.: Gallaudet College Alumni Association.

Gannon, J. R. (1981). *Deaf heritage: A narrative history of deaf America*. Silver Spring, MD: National Association of the Deaf.

Germany, J. (1973). *A census of black deaf adult population of Los Angeles County, California*. Northridge, CA: California State University, National Center on Deafness.

Goodlett, C. B., & Greene, V. R. (1940). *The mental abilities of 29 deaf and partially deaf negro children*. Charleston, WV: Jarrett Printing Company.

Gottlieb, L. (1976). The Jewish deaf community. *Second Jewish Catalog*. Philadelphia: Jewish Publication Society of America.

Green, R. E. (1974). *A report of the proceedings: 'The working conference on minority deaf'*. Northridge, CA: California State University, National Leadership Training Program.

Greenmun, R. M. (June 1946). Peddlars. *The Frat*. (Available at Gallaudet College Library; The Alexander Graham Bell Association for the Deaf).

Hairston, E. (1973). To be black and deaf. In *I'm deaf too: 12 deaf Americans*. Silver Spring, MD: National Association of the Deaf.

Hairston, E., & Smith, L. (1983). *Black and deaf in America*. Silver Spring, MD: TJ Publishers.

Hammerman, S. (1981). The deaf in the third world, neglected and apart. *Assignment Children, 53-54*, 91–191.

Hearing levels of adults by race, region, and area of residence. (1972). *Vital Health and Statistics*, 11(114), 72.

Higgins, F. C. (1965). *On the accomplishments of some deaf men and women*. Riverside, CA: California School for the Deaf, Junior National Association of the Deaf Chapter.

Higgins, P. (1980). *Outsiders in a hearing world: A sociology of deafness*. Beverly Hills, CA: Sage Publications.

Higgins, P. C. (1977). *The deaf community: Identity and interaction in a hearing world*. Unpublished doctoral dissertation, Northwestern University, Chicago, IL.

Hurley, O. L. et al. (1979). Predictive validity of two mental ability tests with black deaf children. *Journal of Negro Education, 48*(1), 14–19

Kelly-Jones, N. (1974). Where are our deaf women? *Gallaudet Today, 4*(3).

Leamon, E. (Winter 1983). Illinois's first deaf juror: Deborah Varraros '72. *NTID Focus*, 3–5.

Lexington School for the Deaf. (1963). *Vocational status and adjustment of deaf women*. New York: Author.

Lopez, J. R. (1973). *An analysis of significant factors related to the education and rehabilitation of the Mexican-American deaf*. Northridge, CA: California State University, National Leadership Training Program.

Luetke-Stahlman, B., & Weiner, B. F. (October 1982). Assessing language and/or system preferences of Spanish-deaf preschoolers. *American Annals of the Deaf*, 789–796.

Markowicz, H., & Woodward, J. (1978). Language and the maintenance of ethnic boundaries in the deaf community. *Communication and Cognition, 11*(1), 20–38.

McChord, W. (December 1977). The role of women in the history and development of the Kentucky school for the deaf. *The Kentucky Standard*.

*Minority group needs of the deaf: A follow-up report to the governor and legislature of New York state*. (1969). Temporary State Commission to Study and Investigate the Problems of the Deaf. Albany, NY.

Moorese, D., & Oden, C., Jr. (June 1977). Educational needs of black deaf children. *American Annals of the Deaf*.

Murray, J. R. (1973). *A parent education program for Spanish-American parents of deaf children*. Northridge, CA: California State University, National Leadership Training Program.

Nelson, L. K. (1979). Minnesota's first deaf women's conference. *Deaf American, 31*(5), 15–16.

Nickoloff, E. (January 16–21, 1983). Vocational rehabilitation of the hearing impaired native American. *Journal of Rehabilitation of the Deaf*.

Nickoloff, E. G., & White, J. (1971). *The hearing impaired Indian in Los Angeles—Where is he?*. Northridge, CA: California State University, National Leadership Training Program.

Peterson, R., & Pelarski, J. (19??). The deaf woman as wife and mother. *Gallaudet Today, 4*(3).

Post, R. H. (1964). Hearing acuity variation among negroes and whites. *Eugenics Quarterly,* 11, 65–81.

Rarus, N. (1973). The deaf woman. In *I'm deaf too: 12 deaf Americans*. Silver Spring, MD: National Association of the Deaf.

*Report from Texas Institute for the deaf, dumb and blind colored youths*. (1888). Austin, TX.

Rudner, W. A., & Butowsky, R. (1981). Signs used in the deaf gay community. *Sign Language Studies, 30*, 36–48.

Schein, J. D., & Delk, M. T., Jr. (1974). *The deaf population of the United States*. Silver Spring, MD: National Association of the Deaf.

Schein, J. D., & Ries, P. W. (1970). *Special meeting on the identification of black deaf persons*. Silver Spring, MD: National Association of the Deaf.

Smith, L. D., Jr. (1972). The hardcore deaf negro adult in the Watts area of Los Angeles, California. *Journal of Rehabilitation of the Deaf, 6*(1), 11–18.

Stokoe, W., Bernard, H. R., & Padden, C. (1976). An elite group in deaf society. *Sign Language Studies, 12*, 189–210.

Strobridge, M. L. (1972). *The deaf in the far east*. Northridge, CA: California State University, National Leadership Training Program.

Stump, J. (1976). *Guidelines for non-English speaking parents of deaf children*. Northridge, CA: California State University, National Leadership Training Program.

*The deaf of Minnehaha* (videocassette). (1913).

Available: Gallaudet College Media Distributing Center.

Tidyman, E. (1974). *Dummy*. Boston: Little, Brown.

Tony Brown's Journal. (1978). *Ain't ain't right* (videocassette). New York: Tony Brown Productions.

Trujillo, L. T. (1972). *The deaf Chicano: How his culture affects his education*. Northridge, CA: California State University, National Leadership Training Program.

Vernon, M., & Makowsky, B. (1969). Deafness and minority group dynamics. *Deaf American, 21*(11).

Williams, L. (Winter 1983). Wendy Maruyama '80: Critically acclaimed artist. *NTID Focus,* 15–18.

Woodward, J. (1979). *Signs of sexual behavior: An introduction to some sex-related vocabulary in American Sign Language*. Silver Spring, MD: TJ Publishers.

Woodward, J. C. (1976). *Black southern spring*. Washington, D.C.: Gallaudet College, Linguistics Research Laboratory.

Yoken, C. (1979). *Living with deaf-blindness: Nine profiles*. Washington, D.C.: National Academy of Gallaudet College.

Yoken, C. (1980). Living with deaf-blindness. *Gallaudet Today* 10(3) 9–12.

## HEARING-IMPAIRED INDIVIDUALS

*A lay sermon* (3/4″ videocassette). (1913). Washington, D.C.: Gallaudet College Media Distribution Center.

Albronda, M. (no date). *The magic lantern man: Theophilus Hope d'Estrella*. Unpublished manuscript.

Albronda, M. (1980). *Douglas Tilden: Portrait of a deaf sculptor*. Silver Spring, MD: TJ Publishers.

Albronda, M., & Dreyfus, R. B. (no date). *Theophilus Hope d'Estrella, 1851–1929* (Pamphlet).

Armes, W. D. (February 1898). Douglas Tilden: Sculptor. *Overland Monthly*.

Ballin, A. (1930). *The deaf mute howls*. Los Angeles, CA: Grafton Publishing Co.

Bland, H. M. (November 1906). Two representative men of California, Benjamin Ide Wheeler and Douglas Tilden. *Overland Monthly*.

Booth, E. (1953). *Forty-niner: The life story of a deaf pioneer*. Stockton, CA: San Joaquin Pioneer and Historical Society.

Bowe, F. (1970). The incredible story of Cadwallader Washburn. *Deaf American*, 23(3).

Bowe, F., & Sternberg, M. (1973). *I'm deaf too: 12 deaf Americans*. Silver Spring, MD: National Association of the Deaf.

Braddock, G. C. (1975). *Notable deaf persons*. Washington, D.C.: Gallaudet College Alumni Association.

Brown, D. (Spring 1982). To whom did he tell his dreams? *Disabled USA*.

Calkins, E. E. (1946). *And hearing not—: Annals of an adman*. New York: Charles Scribner's Sons.

*Chapter from the life of Thomas Hopkins Gallaudet* (3/4" videocassette). (1920). Washington, D.C.: Gallaudet College Media Distributing Center.

DEAF Media, Inc. (Producer). (1978). *Rainbow's end* (segments 3 & 4) (3/4" videocassette).

*Discovery of chloroform*. (1913). Washington, D.C.: Gallaudet College Media Distribution Center.

Doctor, P. V. (1957). Amos Kendall: Nineteenth century humanitarian. *Gallaudet College, 7,* Bulletin no. 1.

Earnest E. (January 1923). Louder please! *Atlantic Monthly*.

Gallaher, J. (1898). *Representative deaf persons of the United States of America*. Chicago, IL: Author.

Higgins, F. C. (1965). *On the accomplishments of some deaf men and women*. Riverside, CA: Junior National Association of the Deaf Chapter, California School for the Deaf.

Huston, C. (1973). *Deaf Smith: Incredible Texas spy*. Waco, TX: Texian Press.

Kowalewski, F. (1971). The art of Frederick La Monto. *Deaf American*, 23(7).

Kowalewski, F. (1973). Hillis Arnold: American deaf sculptor. *The Deaf American,* 25(3).

Kowalewski, F. (1973). Robert Freiman, artist of two worlds. *The Deaf American,* 26(3).

Kowalewski, F. (Summer 1981). Profiles of selected deaf artists. *Gallaudet Today*.

*Memories of old Hartford* (3/4" videocassette).

(1913). Washington, D.C.: Gallaudet College Media Distribution Center.

National Center on Deafness (Producers). (1979). *Distinguished deaf Americans: T. Mayes and R. Rosen* (beta videocassette). Northridge, CA: National Center on Deafness Media Center.

Panara, R. F., & Panara, J. (1983). *Great deaf Americans*. Silver Spring, MD: TJ Publishers, Inc.

Powers, H. (1972). *Signs of silence: Bernard Bragg and the National Theatre of the Deaf*. New York: Dodd, Mead.

Runde, W. S. (December 1952). Douglas Tilden, Sculptor. *The Silent Worker*.

Schein, J. D. (1981). *A rose for tomorrow: Biography of Frederick C. Schreiber*. Silver Spring, MD: National Association of the Deaf.

Shklofsky, B. (1936). Eugene O'Neill and deafness. *Volta Review, 38*.

*Silent perspectives: Douglas Tilden* (3/4" videocassette). (1975). (Available from San Francisco Public Library, Deaf Services videotape #247).

Swain, R. L., Jr. (1968). John Brewster, Jr., 18–19th century deaf artist accorded recognition. *Deaf American, 20*(5).

*The Lorna Doone country of Devonshire, England* (3/4" videocassette). (1910). Washington, D.C.: Gallaudet College Media Distribution Center.

Toole, D. (1980). *Successful deaf adults*. Beaverton, OR: Dormac.

Toole, D. K. (1979). *Successful deaf Americans*. Beaverton, OR: Dormac.

Toole, T. (1980). *Courageous deaf adults*. Beaverton, OR: Dormac.

WETA-TV (Producer). (1964). *Thomas Galaudet* (1/2" open-reel videotape). Northridge, CA: National Center on Deafness, Media Center.

# PARENTS OF HEARING-IMPAIRED CHILDREN

## Books and Articles

Ferris, C. (1980). *A hug isn't enough*. Washington, D.C.: Gallaudet College Press.

Freeman, R. D., Carbin, C. F., & Boese, R. J. (1981). *Can't your child hear? A guide for those who care about deaf children*. Baltimore, MD: University Park Press.

Glick, F., & Pellman, D. (1982). *Breaking silence: A family grows with deafness*. Scottdale, PA: Herlad Press.

Griffith, B. F. (Ed.). (1980). *Family to family*. Washington, D.C.: The Alexander Graham Bell Association for the Deaf.

John Tracy Clinic. (1972). *John Tracy Clinic correspondence course for parents of preschool deaf children*. Los Angeles, CA: Author.

Katz, L., Mathis, S. L., & Merril, E. C. (1978). *The deaf child in the public schools: A Handbook for parents of deaf children*. Danville, IL: Interstate Printers and Publishers.

LaSasso, C., & Bodner-Johnson, B. (1983). Parents groups—Are they meeting the needs of the deaf adolescents? *Perspectives for Teachers of the Hearing Impaired*, *1*(4), 20–22.

McArthur, S. H. (1982). *Raising your hearing impaired child: A guide for parents*. Washington, D.C.: The Alexander Graham Bell Association for the Deaf.

Mendelsohn, J. Z., & Fairchild, B. (1981). *Years of challenge: A guide for parents of hearing impaired adolescents*. Silver Spring, MD:. National Association of the Deaf.

Mindel, E. D., & Vernon, M. (1971). *They grow in silence: The deaf child and his family*. Silver Spring, MD: National Association of the Deaf.

Naiman, D. W., & Schein, J. D. (1978). *For parents of deaf children*. Silver Spring, MD: National Association of the Deaf.

Nix, G. W. (Ed.). (1977). *The rights of hearing impaired children*. Washington, D.C.: The Alexander Graham Bell Association for the Deaf.

Ogden, P. W., & Lipsett, S. (1982). *The silent garden: Understanding the hearing impaired child*. New York: Saint Martin's.

Simmons-Martin, A. (1975). *Chats with Johnny's parents*. Washington, D.C.: The Alexander Graham Bell Association for the Deaf.

Spradley, T. S., & Spradley, J. P. (1978). *Deaf like me*. New York: Random House.

# HEARING CHILDREN OF DEAF PARENTS

## Books and Articles

Benderly B. L. (1980). *Dancing without music*. Garden City, NY: Anchor Press/Doubleday.

Brother, M. (November 1983). CODA file. *CODA Newsletter*, 2–3.

Brother, M. (1984). CODA Cudos. *CODA Newsletter*, *1*(3), 3.

Brother, M. (1984). Editorial. *CODA Newsletter*, *1*(2), 1.

Bunde, L. T. (1979). *Deaf parents—Hearing children: Toward a greater understanding of the unique aspects, needs, and problems relative to the communication factors caused by deafness*. Minneapolis, MN: Ephphatha.

Corbett, E. E., & Jensema, C. J. (1981). Hearing impaired among teachers. *Teachers of the deaf: Descriptive profiles*. Washington, D.C.:. Gallaudet College Press.

Day, C. (January 1975). Growing up with deaf parents. *The Deaf American,* 39–42.

Falconer, J. A. (1978). *Expressive non-verbal communication by hearing children of deaf parents*. Ann Arbor, MI: University Microfilms International.

Feldman, D. D. (1974). *A comparative examination of the language ability of pre-school hearing children of deaf and of hearing parents*. Ann Arbor, MI: Xerox University Microfilm.

Fletcher, L. (May 20, 1982). Growth through parents' courage. *The Boston Globe*.

Furth, H. G. (1973). *Deafness and learning: A psychosocial approach*. Blemont, CA: Wadsworth Publishing.

Greenburg, J. (1970). *In this Sign*. New York: Holt, Rinehart and Winston.

Hardy, R. E., & Cull, J. G. (1974). Deafness and family planning. *Educational and Psychosocial Aspects of Deafness*. Springfield, IL: Charles C. Thomas.

Higgins, P. C. (1980). *Outsiders in a hearing world: A sociology of deafness*. Beverly Hills, CA: Sage Publications.

Holland, G. (1969). A school of children of deaf parents. *The Deaf American, 21*(7), 9–12.

Howard, C. (May 24, 1973). Son of deaf parents 1973 teacher of the year. *The Deaf American*.

Jones, M. L., & Quigley, S. P. (1979). The acquisition of question formation in spoken English and American Sign Language by two hearing children of deaf parents. *Journal of Speech and Hearing Disorders*, 44, 196–208.

Litchfield, A. (1980). *Words in our Hands*. New York: Alber Whitman and Company.

Maestas y Moores, J. (1981). Early linguisic environment: Interactions of deaf parents of their infants. *Sign Language Studies, 26,* 1–13.

Marshall, K. G. (1979). *A comparison of the self-concepts of normally hearing offspring of deaf parents with those of normally hearing offspring of normally hearing parents.* Ann Arbor, MI: University Microfilms International.

Mathis, S. L. (1977). Hearing children of deaf parents. *Proceedings of the third Gallaudet symposium on research in deafness,* pp. 135–138.

Mayberry, R. (1976). An assessment of some oral and manual skills of hearing children of deaf parents. *American Annals of the Deaf, 121,* 507–512.

Meadow, K. P. (1968-1969). Self-image, family climate and deafness. *Social Forces,* 47, 428–438.

Perez, L. E. (1985). *A sign of love.* Privately printed by author.

Robinson, L. D., & Weathers, O. D. (1974). LA family therapy of deaf parents and hearing children: A new dimension of psychotherapeutic intervention. *American Annals of the Deaf, 119,* 325–330.

Royster, M. A. (1981). Deaf parents: A personal perspective. *The Deaf American, 34*(3), 19–22.

Schein, J. D. (1968). *The deaf community: Studies in the social psychology of deafness.* Washington, D.C.: Gallaudet College Press.

Schiff, N., & Ventry, I. M. (1976). Communication problems in hearing children of deaf parents. *Journal of Speech and Hearing Disorders, 41,* 348–358.

Schlesinger, H. S., & Meadow, K. P. (1972). *Sound and sign: Childhood deafness and mental health.* Berkeley, CA: University of California Press.

Tendler, R. (1975). *Maternal correlates of differentiation in hearing children of the deaf.* Ann Arbor, MI: University Microfilms International.

Von der Lieth, L. (1978). Social-psychological aspects of use of sign language. In I. M. Schlesinger and L. Namir (Eds.), *Sign Language and the Deaf: Psychological, linguistic, and sociological perspectives,* pp. 315–332. New York: Academic Press.

Wiggins, J. (1980). *No sound* (2nd ed.). New York: The Silent Press.

## Video and Film

*Helping my parents* (video). (in press). Lynnette Taylor (color).

*Mom and dad can't hear.* (1978). Time-Life. (47 mins.; color; sound).

*Sunday and Monday in silence* (l6mm film). (1974). Toronto, Canada: Heritage Visual Sales. (55 mins.; color; sound).

## EMPLOYMENT

### Books and Films

Crammatte, A. B. (1968). *Deaf persons in professional employment.* Springfield, IL: Charles C. Thomas.

*No whistles, no bells, no bedlam* (16mm film). Rochester, NY: National Technical Institute for the Deaf.

Schowe B.M. (1969). *Deaf workers on the home front.* Silver Spring, MD: National Association of the Deaf.

Talcove, A. (1981). *Resource guide for hearing-impaired students.* Washington, D.C.: Pre-College Programs Gallaudet College.

## ALSO OF INTEREST

Andersson, Y. (Winter 1979). Stamp collecting—with a special interest. *Gallaudet Today.*

Bell, A. G. (1884). *Memoir upon the formation of a deaf variety of the human race.* Washington, D.C.: National Academy of Sciences.

Bell, A. G. (1917). *Graphical studies of marriages of the deaf.* Washington, D.C.: The Volta Bureau.

Birdwhistle, R. L. (1952). *Introduction to kinesics.* (Available at the University of California, Davis).

Boatner, M. T. (1959). *Voice of the deaf.* Washington, D.C.: Public Affairs Press.

Bruce, R. V. (1973). *Alexander Graham Bell and the conquest of solitude.* Boston: Little, Brown.

Clark, H. T. (1917). *Talking gloves for the deaf and blind: Their value to men injured in the present war.* Cleveland, OH: Author.

Clark, M. G. (1980). *Who stole Kathy Young?*. New York: Dodd, Mead.

Corcoran, B. (1974). *A dance to still music*. New York: Atheneum.

Davies, D. G. (1986). Bringing other cultures into the classroom. *Perspectives for Teachers of the Hearing Impaired, 5*(1), 15–17.

*Deaf and bright* (16mm video). (1975). Washington, DC: Gallaudet Media Distribution Center.

*Deafness and communications* (16mm). (nd). Rochester, NY: Media Services, National Technical Institute for the Deaf.

*Deaf in a hearing world* (16mm film). (nd). Sun Valley, CA. Media Guild.

*Deaf like me* (16 mm). (1981). Washington, D.C.: Gallaudet Media Distribution Center.

DeGering, E. (1964). *Gallaudet: Friend of the deaf*. Washington, D.C.: Review and Herald Publishing Association.

Fay, E. A. (1898). *Marriages of the deaf in America*. Washington, D.C.: Gibson Brothers.

Fletcher, L. (1989). *Ben's story: A deaf child's right to sign*. Washington, D.C.: Gallaudet University Press.

Frisina, R. (November/December 1976). A place and time of opportunity. *NTID Focus*. (Available from Public Information Office, National Technical Institute for the Deaf, Rochester Institute of Technology, One Lomb Memorial Drive, Rochester, NY 14623).

Garnett, C. B., Jr. (1967). *The world of silence*. New York: Greenwich Book Publishers.

Groce, N. (1985). *Everyone here spoke sign language: Hereditary deafness on Martha's Vineyard*. Cambridge, MA: Harvard University Press.

Harper, P. (1983). Understanding deafness. *Perspectives for Teachers of the Hearing Impaired, 2*(1) 17–19

Hayes, F. C. (1957). *Gestures: A working bibliography*. Los Angeles: University of California.

Hyman, J. (1980). *Deafness*. New York: Franklin Watts.

Johnson, R. C. (1987). Bilingual, bicultural education for deaf students: A deaf researcher's perspective. *Perspectives for Teachers of the Hearing Impaired, 5*(5), 6–8.

Lane, H. (1976). *The wild boy of aveyron*. Cambridge: Harvard University Press.

Leigh, C. W. E. (1932). *Catalogue of the Library for the deaf education*. Manchester: Manchester University Press.

MacIntyre, E. (1975). *The purple mouse*. Nashville, TN: Nelson Publisher.

Margulies, N., & Howard, D. (producers). (nd). *A quiet time*. (Available from Nancy Margulies, 7121 Pershing Avenue, University City, Missouri 63130).

Mindel, E., Vernon, M. (1971). *They grow in silence*. Silver Spring, MD: The National Association of the Deaf.

National Archives and Records Service, United States Department of the Interior (Producer). (1930). *Indian sign languages* ($3/4''$ videocassette). National Center on Deafness Media Center.

Neimark, A. E. (nd). *A deaf child listened*. New York: William Morrow.

Norris, C. B. (1981). *Signs unseen, sounds unheard*. Eureka, CA: Arlinda Press.

*Our priceless gift*. (film) (1982). Washington, D.C.: Gallaudet Media Distribution.

Spence, E. (1972). *The nothing place*. New York: Harper & Row.

*Telephone equipment for the deaf*. (Information module). (Available from Public Information Office, National Technical Institute for the Deaf, Rochester Institute of Technology, One Lomb Memorial Drive, Rochester, NY 14623).

Terry W. (1917). *The William Terry touch alphabet for use by the deaf and the deaf-blind with a brief sketch of the achievements of Dr. William Terry during 15 years of total blindness and deafness*. Cleveland, OH: Author.

# References

Abrams, M. (1987). Learning on paper: Dialogue journals build language skills. *Perspectives for Teachers of the Hearing Impaired*, 5(4), 11–13.

Abraham, S., & Stoker, R.G. (1984). An evaluation of methods to teach speech to the hearing impaired using a simulation technique. *The Volta Review, 86*(7), 325–335.

Addison, N., Arkley, C., Buligan, M., Lalonde B. Lavoie R., MacDonald, D., McKenna, N., Taylor, V., & Wren, N. (1985). *Mathematics curriculum: Basic level*. Ontario, Canada: Ontario Ministry of Education.

Akamatsu, T. (1983). Fingerspelling formulae: A word is more or less the sum of its letters. *Sign language Studies*, 126–132.

Akamatsu, C. T., & Armour, V.A. (1987). Developing written literacy in deaf children through analyzing sign language. *American Annals of the Deaf, 132* (1), 46–52.

Alberto, P. A., & Troutman, A. C. (1982). *Applied behavior analysis for teachers: Influencing student performance*. Columbus, OH: Merrill Publishing Co.

Allen, V. L. (Ed.). (1976). *Children as teachers: Theory and research on tutoring*. New York: Academic Press.

Alley, G., & Deshler, D. (1979). *Teaching the learning disabled adolescent: Strategies and methods*. Denver: Love Publishing Co.

Alvarez, M. C. (1983). Sustained timed writing as an aid to fluency and creativity. *Teaching Exceptional Children, 15*(3), 160–162.

American Association for the Advancement of Science (1983). *Science—A process approach*. Washington, D.C.: American Association for the Advancement of Science.

Anastasi, A. (1976). *Psychological testing* (4th ed.). New York: Macmillan.

Anderson, E., Redman, G., & Rogers, C. (1984). *Self-esteem for tots to teens: Five principles of raising confident children*. Deephaven, MN: Meadowbrook.

Anderson, L. M., Evertson, C. M., & Brophy, J. (1979). An experimental study of effective teaching in first-grade reading groups. *The Elementary School Journal, 79*, 193–222.

Anderson, L. M., Evertson, C. M., & Emmer, E. T. (1980). Dimensions in classroom management derived from recent research. *Journal of Curriculum Studies, 12*, 343–346.

Anderson, M., Boren, N. J., Caniglia, J., Howard, W., & Krohn, E. (1980). *Apple tree*. Beaverton, OR: Dormac, Inc.

Andrews, J. (1988). Deaf children's acquisition of prereading skills using the reciprocal teaching procedure. *Exceptional Children, 54*(4), 349–355.

Andrews, J. F., & Mason, J. M. (1986). How do deaf children learn about prereading? *American Annals of the Deaf*.

Anthony, D. (1971). *Seeing essential English manual*. Anaheim, CA:

Applebee, A. N. (1978). *The child's concept of story*. Chicago, IL: University of Chicago Press.

Archer, A., & Gleason, M. (1988). *Skills for school success*. North Billerica, MA: Curriculum Associates.

Archer, A., Isaacson, S., & Schiller, E. P. (1987). *Teaching mildly handicapped students in elementary school*. Reston, VA: Council for Exceptional Children.

Ashlock, R. B. (1982). *Error patterns in computation: A semi-programmed approach* (3rd ed.). Columbus, OH: Charles E. Merrill.

Bailes, C., Searls, S., Slobodzian, J., & Staton, J. (1986). *It's your turn now*. Washington, D.C.: Gallaudet University.

Baker, C. (1979). *On the terms "verbal" and "non-verbal."* Paper presented at the First International Symposium on Sign Language Research. Stockholm, Sweden (Swedish National Association of the Deaf).

Baker, C., & Cokely, D. (1980). ASL: *A teacher's resource text on grammar and culture*. Silver Springs, MD: TJ Publishers.

Baker, D., & Bettino, C. (1988). *Dormac easy English dictionary*. Beaverton, OR: Dormac, Inc.

Baldwin, S. C., Nielsen, J. B., Ochs, R. M., & Porter, S. L. (1975). *Listening skills curriculum*. Ogden, UT: Utah School for the Deaf.

Ballard, J., Ramirez, B., & Zantal-Wiener, K. (1987). *Public Law 94-142, Section 504, and Public Law 99-457: Understanding what they are and are not*. Reston, VA: Council for Exceptional Children.

Ballenger, M., Benham, N., & Hosticka, A. (1984). Children's counting books: Mathematical concept development. *Childhood Education, 61*(1), 30–35.

Baratta-Lorten, M. (1972). *Workjobs*. Menlo Park, CA: Addison-Wesley.

Baratta-Lorten, M. (1976). *Mathematics their way*. Don Mills, Ontario: Addison-Wesley.

Baratta-Lorten, M. (1977a). *Workjobs II*. Menlo Park, CA: Addison-Wesley.

Baratta-Lorten, R. (1977b). *Mathematics . . . A way of thinking*. Menlo Park, CA: Addison-Wesley.

Bates, E. (1976a). *Language and context: The acquisition of pragmatics*. New York: Academic Press.

Bates, E. (1976b). Pragmatics and sociolinguistics in child language. In D. M. Morehead & A. E. Morehead (Eds.), *Normal and deficient child language*. Baltimore: University Park Press.

Battaglia, M., Scouten, E., & Hamil, F. (1982). A teaching strategy for the science laboratory. *Volta Review, 84*, 34–38.

Beane, J.A., Lipka, R.P., & Ludewig, J.W. (1980). Synthesis of research on self-concept. *Educational Leadership, 38*, 84–89.

Bell, S., & Ainsworth, M. (1972). Infant crying and maternal responsiveness. *Child Development, 43*, 1171–1190.

Bereiter, C., & Englemann, S. (1966). *Teaching disadvantaged children in the preschool*. Englewood Cliffs, NJ: Prentice-Hall.

Berenstain, S., & Berenstain, J. (1969). *Bears on wheels*. New York: Random House.

Bergenske, M. D. (1987). The missing link in narrative story mapping. *The Reading Teacher, 41*(3), 333–335.

Berliner, D. C. (1980). Using research on teaching for the improvement of classroom practice. *Theory into Practice, 19*(4), 302–308.

Berliner, D. C. (1984). The half-full glass: A review of research on teaching. In P. L. Hosford (Ed.), *Using what we know about teaching* (pp. 51–77). Alexandria, VA: Association for Supervision and Curriculum Development.

Bersgal, R. (1983). Personal communication. Omaha, NB.

Bickel, W. E., & Bickel, D. D. (1986). Effective schools, classrooms, and instruction: Implications for special education. *Exceptional Children, 52*(6), 489–500.

Bigge, J. (1988). *Curriculum based instruction for special education students*. Mountain View, CA: Mayfield Publishing Company.

Billingsley, A., & Giovannoni, J. (1972). Child neglect among the poor: A study of parental adequacy in families of 3 ethnic groups. *Child Welfare, 19* 496–504.

Blackburn, J. E., & Powell, W. C. (1976). *One at a time all at once: The creative teacher's guide to individualized instruction without anarchy*. Pacific Palisades, CA: Goodyear Publishing Co.

Blackham, G. J., & Silberman, A. (1975). *Modi-*

*fication of child and adolescent behavior*. Belmont, CA: Wadsworth.

Blackwell, P. M., Engen, E., Fischgrund, J. E., & Zarcadoolas, C. (1978). *Sentences and other systems: A language and learning curriculum for hearing-impaired children*. Washington, D.C.: The Alexander Graham Bell Association for the Deaf.

Bloom, L: (1974). Talking, understanding, and thinking. In R. L. Schiefelbusch & L. Lloyd (Eds.), *Language perspectives—Acquisition, retardation, and intervention* (pp. 285–312). Baltimore, MD: University Park Press.

Bloom, L., & Krathwohl, D. (1977). *Taxonomy of educational objectives. Handbook 1: Cognitive domain*. New York: Longman.

Bloom, L., & Lahey, M. (1978). *Language development and language disorders*. New York: Wiley.

Bochner, J. H. (1982). English in the deaf population. In D. G. Sims, G. G. Walter, & R. L. Whitehead (Eds.), *Deafness and communication* (pp. 107–123). Baltimore, MD: Williams & Wilkins.

Bolte, A. (1987). Our whole language routine: Reading together and loving it. *Perspectives for Teachers of the Hearing Impaired, 5*(5), 3–5.

Bonvillian, J., Nelson, K., & Charrow, _____. (1976). Languages and language-related skills in deaf children. *Sign Language Studies, 12* (12), 211–250.

Bonvillian, J., Orlansky, M., Novack, L., & Folven, R. (1983). Early sign language acquisition and cognitive development. In D. Rogers & J. Stoboda (Eds.), *The acquisition of symbolic skills*. New York: Plenum.

Boomer, L. (1980). Special education paraprofessionals: A guide for teachers. *Teaching Exceptional Children, 12*(4) 146–149.

Boothroyd, A. (1988). Linguistic factors in speechreading. *Volta Review, 90*(5) 77–88.

Bornstein, H., Saulnier, K., & Hamilton, L. (1983). The Comprehensive Signed English Dictionary. Washington, D.C.: Gallaudet University Press.

Bornstein, H., Saulnier, K., & Hamilton, L. (1980). Signed English: A first evaluation. *American Annals of the Deaf, 126*(4), 467–481.

Boyes-Braem, P. (1973). A study of the acquisition of DE2 or ASL. Working Paper. Salk Institute for Biological Studies, Lajolla, CA.

Bridge, C. (1979). Predictable materials for beginning readers. *Language Arts, 56*(5), 503–507.

Brigance, A. (1977). *BRIGANCE diagnostic inventory of basic skills*. North Billerica, MA: Curriculum Associates.

Brigance, A. (1980). *BRIGANCE diagnostic inventory of basic skills*. North Billerica, MA: Curriculum Associates.

Brigham, T., Graubard, P., & Stans, D. (1972). Analysis of the effects of sequential reinforcement contingencies on aspects of composition. *Journal of Applied Behavior Analysis, 5*, 421–429.

Britton, J. (1978). The composing process and the functions of writing. In C. R. Cooper & L. Odell (Eds.), *Research on composing: Points of departure* (pp. 13–28). Urbana, IL: National Council of Teachers of English.

Brooks, N. (1968). Teaching culture in the foreign language classroom. *Foreign Languaqe Annals, 1,* 204–217.

Brophy, J., & Good, T. L. (1985). Teacher behavior and student achievement. In M. C. Wittrock (Ed.), *Handbook of research on teaching* (3rd ed., pp. 328–375). New York: Macmillan.

Brophy, J., Rashid, H., Rohrkemper, M., & Goldberger, M. (1983). Relationships between teachers' presentation of classroom tasks and students' engagement in those tasks. *Journal of Educational Psychology, 75*, 544–552.

Brown, M. T. (1982). *Dinosaurs beware: A guide to safety*. Boston: Little, Brown.

Brown, R. (1973). *A first language: The early stages*. Cambridge, MA: Harvard University Press.

Brown, R. (1981). National assessments of writing ability. In C. H. Frederiksen & J. F. Dominic (Eds.), *Writing: The nature, development, and teaching of written communication* (Vol. 2, pp. 31–38). Hillsdale, NJ: Lawrence Erlbaum.

Browns, F., & Arnell, D. (1981). A guide to the selection and use of *reading instructional materials*. Washington, D.C.: The Alexander Graham Bell Association for the Deaf.

Bruner, J. S., Oliver, R., & Greenfield, P. (1966).

*Studies in cognitive growth*. New York: Wiley.

Bruner, J. S. (1966b). *Toward a theory of instruction*. Cambridge, MA: Harvard University Press.

Bruner, J. (1975). The ontogensis of speech acts. *Journal of Child Language, 2*, 1–19.

Bruner, J. S. (1978). *Human growth and development*. Oxford: Clarendon Press.

Bunch, G. O. (1987). *The curriculum and the hearing-impaired student: theoretical and practical considerations*. Boston: Little, Brown.

Burke, E. M. (1986). *Early childhood literature— For love of child and book*. Boston: Allyn & Bacon.

Bursuck, W. D., & Lessen, E. I. (1987). Curriculum-based assessment: Benefits to handicapped and nonhandicapped learners and their teachers. *Learning Disability Focus 3*(1), 17–29.

Calkins, L. (1983). *Lessons from a child. On teaching and learning of writing*. Exeter, NH: Heinemann.

Calkins, L. (1986). *The art of teaching writing*. Portsmouth, NH: Heinemann.

Calvert, D. R., & Silverman, S. R. (1983). *Speech and deafness*. Washington, D.C.: The Alexander Graham Bell Association for the Deaf.

Cano, E., & Schmidt, B. (1974). *An individualized curriculum*. San Antonio, TX: Early Childhood Education for the Handicapped, Edgewood School District.

Capelli, C. A. & Markman, E. M. (1982). Suggestions for training comprehension monitoring. *Topics in Learning and Learning Disabilities, 17*, 145–149.

Carlsen, J. M. (1985). Between the deaf child and reading: The language connection. *The Reading Teacher, 38*(4), 424–426.

Carmel, S. (1980). *Deaf folklore*. Video produced by Gallaudet University Television.

Carr, K. S. (1983). The importance of inference skills in the primary grades. *The Reading Teacher*, 36(6), 518–521.

Carroll, J. (1986). *Second language in cognition and instruction*. New York: Academic Press.

Cartwright, G. P. (1969). Written expression and spelling. In R. M. Smith (Ed.), *Teacher diagnosis of educational difficulties* (pp. 95–117). Columbus, OH: Charles Merrill.

Cartwright, G. P., Cartwright, C. A., & Ward, M. E. (1985). *Educating special learners*. Belmont, CA: Wadsworth.

Cazden, C., Vera, J., & Hymes, D. (1972). *Functions of language in the classroom*. New York: Teachers College Press.

Chall, J. (1967). *Learning to read: The great debate*. New York: McGraw-Hill.

Chamot, A. U. (1982). Second language learning model. *Focus, 8, 5*.

Chamot, A. U., & O'Mallery, J. (1984). Using learning strategies to develop skills in English as a second language. *Focus*, September, 1–6.

Channell, D. D. (1978). *The use of hand calculators in the learning of basic multiplication facts*. Columbus, OH: Ohio State University.

Chapman, R. (1981). Mother-child interaction in the second year of life. In R. Schiefelbusch & D. Bricker (Eds.), *Early language: Acquisition and intervention*. Baltimore, MD: University Park Press.

Chapman, R., & Miller, J. (1980). Analyzing language and communication in the child. In R. L. Schiefelbusch (Ed.), *Non-speech, language, and communication* (pp. 159–196). Baltimore, MD: University Park Press.

Charrow, V., & Fletcher, J. (1973). *English as the second language of deaf students*. Report 208. Stanford, CA: Institute for Mathematical Studies in the Social Science.

Chatterjee, J. B. (1983). A comparative analysis of syntactic density and vocabulary richness in written language of learning-abled and learning-disabled children at third- and fifth-grade levels. *Dissertation Abstracts International, 44*, 2436A. (University Microfilms No. 83–28234).

Cheney, H., Compton, C., Harder, K. (1987). Developmental language curriculum. Seattle: Univ. of Washington Press.

Chomsky, C., & Schwartz, J. (1983). *M ss ng L nks*. Pleasantville, NY: Sunburst Corporation.

Christenberry, M., & Stevens, B. (1984). *Can Piaget cook?* Atlanta: Humanics Limited.

The Clark School for the Deaf. (1977). *Speech development*. Northhampton, MA: The Clark School for the Deaf.

Clark, B. R., & Stewart, D. A. (1986). Reflections on language programs for the hearing impaired. *The Journal of Special Education, 20*(2), 154–165.

Clark, E. (1978). Awareness of language: Some

evidence from what children say and do. In A. Sinclair, R. Jarrello, & W. Levelt (Eds.), *The child's conception of language*. New York: Springer-Verlag.

Clark, M. (1976). *Young fluent readers*. London: Heinemann.

Clark, M. (1984). *An auditory/oral proqram for hearing-impaired children*. Miniseminar presented at the International Convention of the Alexander Graham Bell Association, Portland, OR.

Clay, M. (1979). *The early detection of reading difficulties*. Auckland, New Zealand: Heinemann.

Clark, T. C., & Watkins, S. (1985). *The SKI-HI model*. Logan, UT: Utah State University.

Clemes, H., & Bean, R. (1980). *How to raise children's self-esteem*. Los Angeles: Price/Stern/Sloan Publishers.

Clouser, R. A. (1976). The effect of vowel consonant ratio and sentence length on lipreading ability. *American Annals of the Deaf, 121*, 513–518.

Cochran-Smith, M. (1983). *The making of a reader*. Norwood, NJ: Ablex.

Cochran-Smith, M. (1984). *The making of a reader*. Norwood, NJ: Abex.

Coggins, T. E., & Sandall, S. (1983). The communicatively handicapped infant: Application of normal language and communication development. In S. Garwood & R. Fevell (Eds.), *Educating handicapped infants*. Rockville, MD: Aspen.

Cokely, D. (1983). When is pidgin not a pidgin? *Sign Language Studies*, *38*, 1–24.

Cole, E., & Mischook, M. (1982). Auditory learning and teaching of hearing-impaired infants. In E. Cole, & H. Gregory (Eds.), Learning auditory training. *Volta Review, 88*(5), 67–82.

Cole, E. B., & Paterson, M. M. (1984). Assessment and treatment of phonologic disorders in the hearing impaired. In J. M. Cotello (Ed.), *Speech disorders in children: Recent advances* (pp. 94–127). San Diego, CA: College-Hill Press.

Cole, M., & Cole, J. (1988). *Effective intervention with the language impaired child*. Rockville, MD: Aspen.

Cole, M. L., & Cole, J. T. (1989). *Effective intervention with the language-impaired child*. Rockville, MD: Aspen.

Collins-Ahlgren, M. (1975). Language development of two deaf children. *American Annals of the Deaf, 120*, 524–539.

Connolly, A., Nachtman, W., & Prichett, E. (1976). *Manual for the key math diagnostic arithmetic test*. Circle Pines, MN: American Guidance Service.

Conrad, R. (1979). *The deaf school child*. London: Harper & Row.

Constable, C. M. (1983). Creating communicative context. In H. Winitz (Ed.), *Treating language disorders: For clinicians by clinicians*. Baltimore, MD: University Park Press.

Constable, C., & VanKleck (1985). *From social to instructional uses of languages: Bridging the gap*. Paper presented at the American Speech & Hearing Association, Washington, D.C.

Conway, D. (1985). Children (re)creating writing: A preliminary look at the purpose of free-choice writing of hearing-impaired kindergartners. In Kretschmer (Ed.), *Learning to write and writing to learn*. Washington, D.C.: The Alexander Graham Bell Association for the Deaf.

Coop, R. H., White, K., Tapscott, B., & Lee, L. (1983). A program to develop basic writing skills in grades 4–9. *The Elementary School Journal, 84*(1), 76–88.

Cooper, C. (1973). An outline for writing sentence combining problems. *English Journal, 62*, 96–102, 108.

Cooper, C. (1977). Holistic evaluation of writing. In C. R. Cooper & L. Odell (Eds.), *Evaluating writing: Describing, measuring, judging*. Buffalo, NY: National Council of Teachers of English.

Cooper, C. R., & Odell, L. (Eds.). (1977). *Evaluating writing: Describing, measuring, judging*. Buffalo, NY: National Council of Teachers of English.

Coopersmith, S. (1967). *The antecedents of self-esteem*. San Francisco: Freeman.

Copeland, R. W. (1979). *How children learn mathematics*. New York: Macmillan.

Cordor, S. P. (1967). The significance of learner errors. *International Review of Applied Linguistics, 5*, 161–170.

Corsaro, W. (1981). The development of social cognition in preschool children: Implications for language learning. In K. Butler (Ed.), *Topics in language disorders* (Vol. 2, No. 1).

Cramer, R. L. (1971). Dialectology: A case for language experience. *The Reading Teacher, 1*(1), 33–39.

Crandall, K. E. (1982). Reading and writing instruction for young deaf adults. In D. G. Sims, G. G. Walter, & R. L. Whitehead (Eds.), *Deafness and communication* (pp. 107–123). Baltimore, MD: Williams & Wilkins.

Crawford-Lange, L. M. (1981). Redirecting second language curricula: Paulo Freire's contribution. *Foreign Language Annals, 14,* 257–268.

Crawford-Lange, L. M., & Lange, D. (1984). Doing the unthinkable in the second-language classroom: A process for the integration of language and culture. In J. V. Higgs (Ed.), *Teaching for proficiency*. Lincolnwood, IL: National Textbook Company.

Crealock, C. M., Sitko, M. C., Hutchinson, A., Sitko, C., & Marlett, L. (1985, April). *Creative writing competency: A comparison of paper and pencil and computer technologies to improve writing skills of mildly handicapped adolescents.* Paper presented at the Annual Meeting of the American Educational Research Association (ERIC ED 259 11531).

Crews, D. (1978). *Freight train*. New York: Greenwillow.

Crystal, (1976). *The grammatical analysis of language disability: A procedure for assessment and remediation*. London: Edward Arnold.

CTB/McGraw-Hill. (1985). *California achievement test*. Monterey, CA: CTB/McGraw-Hill.

Cummins, J. (1979). Cognitive academic language proficiency, linguistic interdependence, the optimum age questions and some other matters. In M. Swain & B. Hurley (Eds.), *Working papers in bilingualism* (pp. 197–205). Ontario, Canada: Modern Language Center, The Ontario Institute for Studies in Education.

Cummins, J. (1981). The entry and exit fallacy in bilingual education. *National Association for Bilingual Education*, 4, 25–60.

Cummins, J. (1984). *Bilingualism and special education: Issues in assessment and pedagogy*. England: Short Run Press.

*Curriculum Guide Bank*. (1987). Washington, D.C.: Gallaudet University Press.

Dagenais, D. J., & Beadle, K. R. (1984). Written

language: When and where to begin. *Topics in Language Disorders*, *4*(2), 59–85

Dahl, K. (1985). Research on writing development: Insights from the work of Harste and Graves. *Volta Review, 87*(5), 35–47.

Daiute, C. A. (1984). Performance limits on writers. In R. Beach & L. S. Bridwell (Eds.), *New directions in composition research* (pp. 205–224). New York: Guilford.

Damico, J. S. (1985). Clinical discourse analysis. In C. S. Simon (Ed.), *Communication skills and classroom success*. San Diego, CA: College Hill Press.

Daniele, V. A. (1982). *A naturalistic study of intermediate and junior high school level mathematics classes in schools of the deaf, with emphasis on time-on-task*. Unpublished dissertation, Syracuse University, Syracuse, NY.

Daniele, V. A., & Aldersley, S. P. (1988). Implications of time-on task research for teachers of the hearing impaired. *American Annals for the Deaf, 133*(3), 207–211.

Davis, W. E. (1983). *The special educator: Strategies for succeeding in today's schools*. Austin, TX: Pro Ed.

Day, P. S. (June, 1985). *Methods for enhancing efficiency of interdisciplinary team decision making*. Paper presented at the Convention of CAID/CEASD, St. Augustine, Florida (ERIC Document Reproduction Service No. ED 266 621.

DeFillippo, C. (1988), Tracking for speechreading training. *Volta Review, 90*(5), 215–240.

DeFillippo, C., & Scott, B. (1978). A method for training and evaluating the reception of ongoing speech. *J. Acoust. Soc. Am.*, *63*, 1186–1192.

Delquadri, J., Greenwood, C. R., Whorton, D., Carta, J. J., & Hall, R. V. (1986). Classwide peer tutoring. *Exceptional Children*, *2*(6), 535–542.

Deno, S. L. (1987). Curriculum-based measurement. *Teaching Exceptional Children, 20*(1), 41.

Deno, S., Marston, D., & Mirkin, P. (1982). Valid measurement procedures for continuous evaluation of written expression. *Exceptional Children*, *48*, 368–371.

Deno, S. L., Mirkin, P. K., & Wesson, C. (1984). How to write effective data-based IEPs. *Teaching Exceptional Children, 16,* 99–104.

Deterline, W. C. (1970). *Training and management of student tutors: Final report*. Palo Alto, CA: General Programmed Teaching (ERIC Document Reproduction Service No. ED 048–133).

*Developmental language curriculum comprehensive guide and record keeping system for hearing-impaired students, infant-12 years*. (1988). University of Washington Press, P.O. Box 50096, Seattle, WA 98145.

Deyo, D. (1984), *Speechreading in context*. Washington, D.C.: Gallaudet Pre-College Programs.

DiCarlo, L. M., & Bradley, W. H. (1961). A simplified auditory test for infants and young children. *Laryngoscope, 71, 628–646*.

Dickerson, D. P. (1982). A study of the use of games to reinforce sight vocabulary. *The Reading Teacher 36, 46–49*.

DiFrancesca, S. (1971). *Academic achievement test results of a national testing program for hearing-impaired students*. Washington, D.C.: Gallaudet College.

Dilka, K. (1984). Professionals who work with hearing-impaired in school. In R. Hull & K. Dilka (Eds.), *The hearing-impaired child in school*. New York: Grune & Stratton.

Dinkmeyer, D., & Carlson, J. (1973). *Consulting: Facilitating human potential and change processes*. Columbus, OH: Merrill Publishing Company.

Dinkmeyer, D., McKay, G. D., & Dinkmeyer, D. (1980). *Systematic training for effective teaching*. Circle Pines, MN: American Guidance Service.

Dolch, E. W. (1955). *Methods in reading*. Champaign, IL: Garrard Press.

Dore, J. (1978). Requestive systems in nursery school conversations: Analysis of talk. In R. Campbell & P. Smith (Eds.), *Recent advances in psychology of language: Language development and mother-child interaction*. New York: Plenum Press.

Doren, M. (1973). *Doren diagnostic reading test of word recognition skills* (2nd ed.). Circle Pines, MN: American Guidance Service.

Downs, M. P., & Sterritt, G. M. (1964). Identification audiometry for neonates: A preliminary report. *Journal of Auditory Research, 4, 69–80*.

Doyle, W. (1986). Classroom organization and management. In M. C. Wittrock (Ed.), *Handbook of research on teaching*. New York: Macmillan.

Driscoll, M. (1983). *Research within reach: Secondary school mathematics*. St. Louis, MO: Research and Development Interpretation Service.

Duchan, J. (1983). Autistic children are non-interactive: Or so we say. *Seminars in Speech and Language, 4, 53–63*.

Duchan, J. (1988). Assessing communication of hearing-impaired children: Influences from pragmatics. In R. Kretschmer & L. Kretschmer (Eds.), Communication assessment of hearing-impaired children: From conversation to classroom. *The Journal of the Academy of Rehabilitative Audiology, 22, 19–40*.

Durkin, D. (1966). *Children who read early*. New York: Columbia University, Teachers College Press.

Durrell, D., & Catterson, J. (1980). *Durrell analysis of reading difficulty*. San Antonio, TX: The Psychological Corporation.

Dyson, A. H. (1982). Talking with young children writing. *Childhood Education, 59, 30–35*.

Early Childhood and Literacy Development Committee of the International Reading Association. (1987). *The Reading Teacher*, 39(8), 819–821.

Eccarius, M. (1982). Personal communication.

Eccarius, M. (1985). Personal communication.

Eccarius, M., & Schroeder, K. (1986). Personal communication.

Eisenberg, R. B., Griffin, E. J., Coursin, D. B., & Hunter, M. A. (1964). Auditory behavior in the human neonate: A preliminary report. *Journal of Speech and Hearing Research, 7, 245–269*.

Ekwall, E. E., & English, J. (1971). *Use of the polygraph to determine elementary school students' frustration level*. Final Report, Project #0G078. Washington, D.C.: U.S. Department of Health, Education and Welfare.

Ekwall, E. E., & Shanker, J. L. (1983). *Diagnosis and remediation of the disabled reader* (2nd ed.). Boston: Allyn & Bacon.

Elliott, C., & Luetke-Stahlman, B. (submitted). Communication with deaf students: A comparison of the form and content of academic and behavioral input. *Exceptional Children*.

Emmer, E., Everston, C., Sanford, J., Clements, B., & Worsham, M. (1984). *Classroom management for secondary teachers*. Englewood Cliffs, NJ: Prentice-Hall.

Engen, E., & Engen, T. (1983). *Rhode Island test of language structure*. Baltimore, MD: University Park Press.

Englert, C. S. (1984). Measuring teacher effectiveness from the teacher's point of view. *Focus on Exceptional Children, 17*(2), 1–14.

Erber, H. (1977). Developing materials for lipreading evaluation and instruction. *Volta Review, 79*, 35–42.

Erber, N. P. (1982). *Auditory training*. Washington, D.C.: The Alexander Graham Bell Association for the Deaf.

Erber, N. P. (1985). *Telephone communication and hearing impairment*. San Diego, CA: College-Hill Press.

Ervin-Tripp, S. M. (1974). Is second language learning like the first? *TESOL Quarterly, 8*, 111–128.

Evans, S. S., Evans, W. H., & Mercer, C. D. (1986). *Assessment for instruction*. Boston: Allyn & Bacon.

Evertson, C. M., Emmer, E. T., & Brophy, J. E. (1980). Predictors of effective teaching in junior high mathematics classrooms. *Journal of Research in Mathematics Education, 11*, 167–178.

Ewing, J. R., & Ewing, A. G. (1947). *Opportunity and the deaf child*. London: University of London Press.

Ewoldt, C. (1977). *A psycholinguistic description of selected deaf children reading in sign language*. Unpublished doctoral dissertation, Wayne State University.

Ewoldt, C. (1978). Reading for the hearing or hearing impaired: A single process. *American Annals of the Deaf, 123*, 945–948.

Ewoldt, C. (1979). Teaching new vocabulary: Skip it! In J. Price (Ed.), *Teaching handicapped students in the English classroom*. Washington, D.C.: National Education Association.

Ewoldt, C. (1981). A psycholinguistic description of selected deaf children reading in sign language. *Reading Research Quarterly, 17*(1), 58–89.

Ewoldt, C. (1985). A descriptive study of the developing literacy of young hearing-impaired children. *Volta Review, 87*(5), 109–126.

Ewoldt, C., & Hammermeister, F. (1986). The language-experience approach to facilitating reading and writing for hearing-impaired students. *American Annals of the Deaf, 131*(4), 271–274.

Featherstone, J. B., & Woods, H. (1986). Identifying attitudes to encourage change. *Perspectives for Teachers of the Hearing Impaired, 4*(4), 17–20.

*Federal Register*. (January 19, 1981). Washington, D.C.: U.S. Government Printing Office.

Ferguson, C. (1959). Diglossia. *Word, 15*, 325–340.

Fewell, R., & Vadasy, P. (1986). *Families of handicapped children*. Austin, TX: Pro-Ed.

Fey, M. (1986). *Language intervention with young children*. San Diego, CA: College-Hill Press.

Filmore-Wong, L. W. (1978). Individual differences in second language acquisition. In C. J. Filmore (Ed.), *Individual differences in language ability and language behavior* (pp. 203–228). New York: Academic Press.

Finitzo-Heiber, Gerling, Matkin, & Skalka. (1980) *Sound effects recognition test (SERT)*. St. Louis, MO: Auditec.

Fisher, C. W., Berliner, D. C., Filby, N. N., Marliave, R., Cahen, L. S., Dishaw, M., & Moore, J. E. (1978). *Teaching and learning in the elementary schools*. San Francisco: Far West Laboratory for Educational Research and Development, Report VII-1, Summary of the beginning teacher evaluation study.

Fisher, E., & Schneider, K. (1986). Integrating auditory learning at the preschool level. *Volta Review, 88*(5), 83–92.

Fitzgerald, J. (1983). Helping readers gain self-control over reading comprehension. *The Reading Teacher, 37*(3), 249–253.

Flavell, J. H. (1963). *Developmental psychology of Jean Piaget*. New York: Van Nostrand.

Folger, J., & Chapman, R. (1978). A pragmatic analysis of spontaneous imitations. *Journal of Child Language, 5*, 25–38.

Forman, G. E., & Kuschner, D. S. (1983). *The child's construction of knowledge: Piaget for teaching children*. Washington, D.C.: NAEYC.

*Fountain Valley teacher support system in reading*. (1971). Huntington Beach, CA: Richard L. Zweig Associates.

Fowler, G. (1982). Developing comprehension skills in primary students through the use of story frames. *The Reading Teacher, 36*(2), 176–179.

Fowler, G., & Davis, M. (1985). The story frame approach: A tool for improving reading comprehension of EMR children. *Teaching Excep-*

*tional Children, 17*(4), 296–298.

Fox, A. C. (1979). *The Foxie systematic readability aides.* Coeur d'Alene, ID: Fox Reading Research.

Frank, A. R. (1973). Breaking down learning tasks: A sequence approach. *Teaching Exceptional Children, 6,* 16–29.

Freire, P. (1973). *Education for critical consciousness.* (Translated by M. Bergman Ramos). New York: Seabury Press.

Fridriksson, T., & Stewart, D. A. (1988). From the concrete to abstract: Mathematics for deaf children. *American Annals of the Deaf, 133*(1), 51–55.

Fry, E. (1968). A readability formula that saves time. *Journal of Reading, 11*(7), 513–516.

Fry, E. B. (1980). The new instant word list. *The Reading Teacher, 34,* 284–289.

Fuchs, L. S. (1987). Curriculum-based measurement: Program development. *Teaching Exceptional Children, 20*(1), 42–44.

Fuchs, L., & Fuchs, D. (1986). Effects of systematic formative evaluation: A meta-analysis. *Exceptional Children, 53*(3), 199–208.

Furrow, S., Nelson, K., & Benedict, H. (1979). Mother's speech to children and syntactic development: Some simple relationships. *Journal of Child Language, 2,* 423–424.

Gagne, R. M. (1984). *The conditions of learning.* New York: Holt, Rinehart and Winston.

Gagne, R. M., & Briggs, L. J. (1979). *Principles of instructional design.* New York: Holt, Rinehart and Winston.

Gallagher, P. (1985). Inservice! A mandated special education course and its effects on regular classroom teachers. *Teacher Education & Special Education, 8,* 115–120.

Gannon, J. (1981). *Deaf heritage.* Silver Spring, MD: National Association of the Deaf.

Garstecki, D. C. (1981). Auditory-visual training paradigm for hearing impaired adults. *ARA, 14,* 223–237.

Gartner, A., Kohler, M. C., & Reissman, F. (1971). *Children teach children: Learning by teaching.* New York: Harper & Row.

Gavelek, J. R., & Raphael, T. E. (1982). Instructing metacognitive awareness of question-answer relationships: Implications for the learning disabled. *Topics in Learning and Learning Disabilities, 2,* 69–77.

Gearheart, B., DeRuiter, J., & Sileo, T. (1986). *Teaching mildly and moderately handicapped students.* Englewood Cliffs, NJ: Prentice-Hall.

Gearheart, B., & Weishahn, M. (1984). *The exceptional student in the regular classroom.* St. Louis, MO: C. V. Mosby.

Gelzer, L. (1988). Developing reading appreciation. *Perspectives for Teachers of the Hearing Impaired, 6*(4), 13–16.

Gerken, K., Grimes, J., & Brown, J. (1978). A step forward:. Psychological services to children who are hearing impaired. *American Annals of the Deaf, 123,* 448–451.

Gessell, J. K. (1983). *Diagnostic mathematics inventory/mathematics system.* Monterey, CA: CTB/McGraw-Hill.

Gilkerson, L., Hilliard, A., Schrag, E., & Shonkoff, J. (1987). *Report accompanying the education of the handicapped act amendments of 1986* (House Report #99-860.) Washington, D.C.: National Center for Clinical Infant Programs.

Gillam, R., & Johnston, J. (1985). Development in print awareness in language-disordered preschoolers. *JSHR, 28,* 521–526.

Giordiano, G. (1984). *Teaching writing to LD students.* Rockville, MD: Aspen.

Glaser, W. (1965). *Reality therapy: A new approach to psychiatry.* New York: Harper & Row.

Glatthorn, A. A. (1981). *Writing in the schools: Improvement through effective leadership.* Reston, VA: National Association of Secondary School Principals.

Gloeckler, T., & Simpson, C. (1988). *Exceptional students in regular classrooms: Challenges, services, and methods.* Mountain View, CA: Mayfield.

Goelman, H., Oberg, A., & Smith, F. (Eds.). (1984). *Awakening to literacy.* Portsmouth, NH: Heinemann.

Golf, H. (1980). Summary comment: Principles, objectives, and strategies for speech training. In J.D. Subtelny (Ed.), *Speech Assessment and Speech Improvement for the Hearing Impaired.* Washington, D.C.: The Alexander Graham Bell Association for the Deaf.

Good, T. L. (1983). Classroom research: A decade of progress. *Educational Psychologist, 18,* 127–144.

Goodman, K. (1967). Reading: A psycholinguistic guessing game. *Journal of the Reading Special-*

*ist, 6,* 126–135.

Goodman, K. (1976). Reading: A psycholinguistic guessing game. In H. Singer & R. Ruddell (Eds.), *Theoretical models and processes of reading* (2nd ed.). Newark, DE: International Reading Association.

Goodman, K. (1986). *What's whole in whole language.* Portsmouth, NH: Heinemann.

Goodman, Y. M., Altwerger, B. and Marek, A. Print awareness in preschool children: The development of literacy in preschool children. Research and review. Occasional Paper #4, Program in Language and Literacy, Arizona Center for Research and Development, College of Education, University of Arizona, October 1989.

Gormley, K. (1981). A functional strategy for writing: A case study of Tom. *Volta Review, 83,* 5–13.

Gormley, K. A. (1982). The importance of familiarity in hearing-impaired readers' comprehension of text. *Volta Review, 84,* 71–80.

Gormley, K. A., & Franzen, A. M. (1978). Why can't the deaf read? Comments on asking the wrong question. *American Annals of the Deaf, 123*(5) 542–547.

Gormley, K. A., & Geoffrion, L. D. (1981). Another view of using language experience to teach reading to deaf and hearing impaired children. *The Reading Teacher, 34*(5), 519–525.

Gormley, K., & Sarachan-Deily, A. B. (1987). Evaluating hearing-impaired students' writing: A practical approach. *Volta Review, 89*(3), 157–169.

Graham, S. (1982). Composition research and practice: A unified approach. *Focus on Exceptional Children, 14,* 1–16.

Graham, S., & Harris, K. R. (1988). Instructional recommendations for teaching writing to exceptional students. *Exceptional Children, 54*(6), 506–512.

Grant, G. (1982). Testing vs. writing: A critique of contemporary composition curricula. *Claremont Reading Conference 46th Yearbook.*

Graves, D. H. (1983). *Writing: Teachers and children at work.* Portsmouth, NH: Heinemann.

Greaney, V. (1986). Parental influences on reading. *The Reading Teacher, 10*(1), 813–818.

Greenberg, P. (1975). *Bridge-to-reading comprehensive preschool curriculum: Discovery science.* Washington, D.C.: Acropolis.

Greenfield, P. (1984). A theory of the teacher in the learning activities of everyday life. In B. Rogoff & J. Cave (Eds.), *Everyday cognition.* Cambridge, MA: Harvard University Press.

Greenfield, P., & Smith, J. (1976). *The structure of communication in early language development.* New York: Academic Press.

Gresham, F. M., & Gresham, G. N. (1982). Interdependent, dependent and independent group contingencies for controlling disruptive behavior. *Journal of Special Education, 16,* 101–110.

Grissom, B. W., & Cochran, S. W. (1986). Critical competencies for teachers of hearing-impaired students: The practitioners' view. *American Annals of the Deaf, 131*(4), 267–270.

Gruenewald, L., & Pollack, S. (1984). *Language interaction in teaching and learning.* Austin, TX: Pro-Ed.

Gustason, G., Pfetzing, D., & Zawolkow, E. (1973). *SEE supplement II.* Rossmoor, CA: Modern Signs Press.

Hall, J. K. (1988). *Evaluating and improving written expression.* Boston: Allyn & Bacon.

Hamilton, V., & Gordon, D. (1978). Teacher-child interactions in preschool and task persistence. *American Educational Research Journal, 15,* 459–466.

Hammermeister, F. K., & Israelite, N. K. (1983). Reading instruction for the hearing impaired: An integrated language arts approach. *Volta Review, 85*(3), 136–148.

Hammill, D. D., & Bartel, N. R. (1986). *Teaching students with learning and behavior problems* (4th ed.). Boston: Allyn & Bacon.

Hammill, D. D., & Larsen, S. (1983). *The test of written language.* Austin, TX: Pro-Ed.

Hansen, J., & Pearson, P. D. (1980). *The effects of inference training and practice on young children's comprehension* (Technical Report No. 166). Urbana, IL: Center for the Study of Reading, University of Illinois.

Hansen, J., & Pearson, P. D. (1982). *An instructional study: Improving the inferential comprehension of good and poor fourth-grade readers.* Urbana, IL: Center for the Study of Reading, University of Illinois.

Hansford, B. C., & Hattie, J. A. (1982). The relationship between self-esteem and achievement/performance measures. *Review of Educational Research, 52*, 123–142.

Hardy, J. B., Dougherty, A., & Hardy, W. G. (1959). Hearing responses and audiologic screening in infants. *Journal of Pediatrics, 55*, 382–390.

Haring, N. G., Liberty, K. A., & White, 0. R. (1980). Rules for data-based decisions in instructional programs: Current research and instructional implications. In W. Sailor, B. Wilcox, & L. Brown (Eds.), *Methods of instruction for severely handicapped students* (pp. 159–192). Baltimore, MD: Paul H. Brooks.

Harp, B. (1987). Why are you doing Piagetian tasks? *Reading Teacher, 41*(2), 212–214.

Harris, A., & Sipay, E. R. (1985). *How to increase your reading ability* (8th ed.). New York: Longman.

Harris, V. W., & Sherman, J. A. (1973). Use and analysis of the "good behavior game" to reduce disruptive classroom behavior. *Journal of Applied Behavior Analysis, 6*(3), 405–417.

Harsh, A. (1987). Teaching mathematics with children's literature. *Young Children*, 24–29.

Hasentab, M. S., & Horner, S. (1982). *Comprehensive intervention with hearing-impaired infants and preschool children*. Rockville, MD: Aspen.

Hasselbring, T. S., Goin, L. I., & Bransford, J. D. (1987). Effective mathematics instruction: Developing automaticity. *Teaching Exceptional Children, 19*(3), 30–32.

Hasselbring, T. S., Goin, L. I., & Sherwood, R. D. (1986). *The effects of computer-based drill-and-practice on automaticity*. Technical report. Nashville, TN: Vanderbilt University, Learning Technology Center.

Hatfield, N., Caccamise, F., & Siple, P. (1978). Deaf students' language competency: A bilingual perspective. *American Annals of the Deaf, 123*, 847–851.

Hawkins, D. (1965). Messing about in science. *Science and Children, 2*, 5–9.

Hayes, J. R., & Flower, L. S. (1980). Identifying the organization of writing process. In L. W. Gregg & E. R. Steingberg (Eds.), *Cognitive process in writing* (pp. 3–30). Hillsdale, NJ: Lawrence Erlbaum.

Health, S. (1982). What no bedtime story means: Narrative skills at home and school. *Language in Society, 11*, 49–76.

Heiber, T. F., & Tillman, T. (1978). Room effects on monosyllabic word discrimination ability for normal and hearing impaired children. *Journal of Speech and Hearing Research, 21*, 440–458.

Heron, T. E., & Harris, K. D. (1982). *The educational consultant: Helping professionals, parents, and mainstreamed students*. Boston: Allyn & Bacon.

Herx, M. A., & Hunt, F. E. (1976). A framework for speech development within a total communication system. *American Annals of the Deaf, 121*(6), 537–540.

Hess, L. (1972). *The development of transformational structures in a deaf child and a normally hearing child over a period of 5 months*. Unpublished master's thesis, University of Cincinnati.

Hess, R., & Holloway, S. (1984). Family and school as educational institutions. In R. Parke (Ed.), *The family*. Chicago: University of Chicago Press.

Hewison, J., & Tizard, J. (1980). Parental involvement and reading attainment. *British Journal of Educational Psychology, 50*, 209–215.

Hill D. (1977). *Mud, sand, and water*. Washington, D.C.: NAEYC.

Hillerich, R. L. (1978). *A writing vocabulary of elementary children*. Springfield, IL: Charles C. Thomas.

Hipple, M. (1978). Classroom discipline problems? 15 humane solutions. *Childhood Education*, February, 183–187.

Hirsch, E. S. (1984). *The block book* (rev. ed.). Washington, D.C.: NAEYC.

Hirsch-Pasek, K. (1981). *Phonics without sound: Reading acquisition in the congenitally deaf*. Doctoral dissertation.

Hirsch-Pasek, K., & Treiman, K. (1982). Recoding in silent reading: Can the deaf child translate print into a more manageable form? *Volta Review, 84*, 71–82.

Hiskey, M. S. (1966). *Hiskey-Nebraska test of learning aptitude*. Lincoln, NB: Marshall S. Hiskey.

Hochberg, J. (1970). Components of literacy: Speculations and exploratory research. In H. Levin, & J. P. Williams (Eds.), *Basic study of reading*. New York: Basic Books.

Hochman, V., & Greenwald, M. (1963). *Science experiences in early childhood*. New York:

Bank Street College of Education.

Hoffmeister, R. (September 1978). *Word order in the acquisition of ASL*. Paper presented at the Third Annual Boston University Conference on Language Development.

Holmes, B. C. (1983). A confirmation strategy for improving poor readers' ability to answer inferential questions. *Reading Teacher, 37*, 144–148.

Holt, B. G. (1977). *Science with young children*. Washington, D.C.: NAEYC.

Howell, K. W. & Morehead, M. K. (1987). *Curriculum-based evaluation for special and remedial education*. Columbus OH: Charles E. Merrill.

Howell, K. H., & Kaplan, J. S. (1980). *Diagnosing basic skills: A handbook for deciding what to teach*. Columbus, OH: Charles E. Merrill.

Howell, K. W., Kaplan, J. S., & O'Connell, C. Y. (1979). *Evaluating exceptional children: A task analysis approach*. Columbus, OH: Charles E. Merrill.

Huberman, M. (1983). Recipes for busy kitchens. *Knowledge, Creation, Diffusion, Utilization, 4*(1), 478–510.

Hudson, F., Reisberg, L., & Wolf, R. (1983). Changing teachers' perceptions of mainstreaming. *Teacher Education & Special Education, 6*, 18–24.

Humes, G. (1983). Research on the composing process. *Review of Educational Research, 53*, 201–216.

Humphrey, J. H., & Sullivan, D. D. (1970). *Teaching slow learners through active games*. Springfield, IL: Charles C. Thomas.

Hunt, K. W. (1965). *Grammatical Structures at three grade levels* (Research Report No. 3). Urbana, IL: National Council of Teachers of English. (ERIC Document Reproduction Service No. ED 113 735).

Hunt, K. W. (1977). Early blooming and late blooming syntactic structures. In C. R. Cooper & L. Odell (Eds.), *Evaluating writing: Describing, measuring, judging* (pp. 91–106). Urbana, IL: National Council of Teachers of English.

Hurwitz, T. (1971). *Principles of interpreting*. Available from the National Technical Institute for the Deaf, 1 Lomb Memorial Drive, Rochester, NY 14623.

Hurwitz, T., & Witter, A. (1973). Principles of interpreting in an educational environment. In W. Northcott (Ed.), *The hearing-impaired child in a regular classroom: Preschool, elementary, and secondary years*. Washington, D.C.: The Alexander Graham Bell Association for the Deaf.

Hymes, D. (1971). Competence and performance in linguistic theory. In R. Huxley & E. Ingram (Eds.), *Language acquisition models and methods*. New York: Academic Press.

Iatridis, M. (1981). Teaching science to preschoolers. *Science and Children, 19*(2), 25–27.

Idol, L., Paolucci-Whitcomb, P., & Nevin, A. (1986). *Collaborative consultation*. Rockville, MD: Aspen.

Isaacson, S. L. (1985). *Assessing the potential syntax development of third and fourth grade writers*. Unpublished doctoral dissertation, Arizona State University, Tempe, AZ.

Isaacson, S. (1988). Assessing the writing product: Qualitative and quantitative measures. *Exceptional Children, 54*(6), 528–534.

Isaacson, S. L., & Luckner, J. L. (1988). A model for teaching written language to hearing impaired students. *Teaching English to Deaf and Second-Language Students, 6*(1), 8–14.

Ispa, J., & Matz, R. (1978). Integrating handicapped preschool children within a cognitively oriented program. In M. J. Guralnick (Ed.), *Early intervention and the integration of handicapped and non-handicapped children*. Baltimore: University Park Press.

Israelite, N. K. (1988). On readability formulas: A critical analysis for teachers of the deaf. *American Annals of the Deaf, 133*(1), 14–18.

Jackson, N., & Beimiller, A. (1985). Letter, word, and text reading times of precocious and average readers. *Child Development, 56*, 196–206.

Jeffers, J. & Barley M. (1971). *Speechreading*. Springfield, IL: Charles C. Thomas.

Johnson, D. D. (1971). The Dolch list reexamined. *The Reading Teacher, 24*, 449–457.

Johnson, D. (1987). Personal communication. Boys Town National Institute, Omaha, NB.

Johnson, D. W., & Johnson, R. T. (1987). *Learning together and alone: Cooperative, competitive, and individualistic learning*. Englewood Cliffs, NJ: Prentice-Hall.

Johnson, D. W., Johnson, R. T., Holubec, E., &

Roy, D. (1984). *Circles of learning: Cooperation in the classroom*. Alexandria, VA: Association for Supervision and Curriculum Development.

Johnson, D. W., Maruyama, G., Johnson, R., Nelson, D., & Skon, L. (1981). Effects of cooperative, competitive, and individualistic goal structures on achievement: A meta-analysis. *Psychological Bulletin, 89*, 47–62.

Johnson, D. D., Moe, A., & Baumann, J. (1983). *The Ginn workbook for teachers: A basic lexicon*. Lexington, MA: Ginn & Co.

Johnson, D. & Pearson, P. (1984). *Teaching reading vocabulary* (2nd ed.). New York: Holt, Rinehart and Winston.

Johnson, D., Pittelman, S., & Heimlich, J. (1986). Semantic mapping. *The Reading Teacher, 39*(8), 778–783.

Johnson, D. D., Toms-Bronowski, & Pittelman, S. D. (1982). Vocabulary development. *Volta Review, 84*(5), 11–24.

Johnson, D. W., Skon, L., & Johnson, R. (1980). The effects of cooperative, competitive, and individualistic goal structures on student achievement on different types of tasks. *American Educational Research Journal, 17*, 93–93.

Johnson, D. W. (1979). *Educational psychology*. Englewood Cliffs, N.J.: Prentice-Hall.

Johnson, E., & Johnson, A. (1984). *The Piagetian language nursery*. Rockville, MD: Aspen.

Johnson, F., & Paulson, C. (1976). *Individualizing the lanquage classroom*. Cambridge, MA: Jacaranda Press.

Johnson, K. (1977). A survey of mathematics programs, materials and methods in schools for the deaf. *American Annals of the Deaf, 122*, 19–25.

Johnson, K. (1987). Improving reading comprehension through prereading and postreading exercises. *Reading Improvement, 24*(2), 81–83.

Johnson, M. A. & Roberson, G. F. (1988). The language experience approach: Its use with young hearing-impaired students. *American Annals of the Deaf, 133*(3), 223–225.

Johnson, M. J. (1988). "Helping circles": Giving high school students a helping hand with writing. *Perspectives for Teachers of the Hearing Impaired, 6*(4), 2–4.

Jones, B., Pierce, J., & Hunter, B. (1989). Teaching students to construct graphic representations. *Educational Leadership, 46*(4), 20–26.

Jones, L. L. (1982). An interactive view of reading: Implications for the classroom. *The Reading Teacher, 35*(7), 772–777.

Jorstad, H. (1981). Inservice teacher education: Content and process. In D. Lange & C. Linder (Eds.), *Proceedings of the National Conference on Professional Priorities*. Hastings-on-Hudson, NY: ACTFL Materials Center.

Kagan, S. (1985). *Cooperative learning: Resources for teachers*. Riverside, CA: University of California.

Kamii, C., & DeVries, R. (1978). *Physical knowledge in preschool education: Implications of Piaget's theory*. Englewood Cliffs, NJ: Prentice-Hall.

Kantor, R. (1977). *The acquisition of classifiers in ASL*. Unpublished master's thesis, Boston University.

Karlin, R. (1980). *Teaching elementary reading* (3rd ed.). New York: Harcourt Brace Jovanovich.

Karlsen, B., & Gardner, E. (1985). *Stanford diagnostic reading test* (3rd ed.). San Antonio, TX: The Psychological Corporation.

Karnes, M. B., Johnson, L. J., Cohen, T., & Shwedel, A. (1985). Facilitating school success among mildly and moderately handicapped children by enhancing task persistence. *Journal of the Division for Early Childhood, 9*, 151–161.

Kendall, J. R., & Mason, J. M. (1982). Metacognition from the historical context of reading. *Topics in Learning and Learning Disabilities, 2*(2), 82–89.

KDES (Kendall Demonstration Elementary School) faculty and staff (1989). Preschool Curriculum Guide. Washington, D.C.: Pre-College Programs.

Kerr, M. M., & Nelson, C. M. (1983). *Strategies for managing behavior problems in the classroom*. Columbus, OH: Charles E. Merrill.

Kindsvatter, R., Wilen, W., & Ishler, M. (1988). *Dynamics of effective teaching*. New York: Longman.

King, C., & Quigley, S. (1985). *Reading and deafness*. San Diego, CA: College-Hill Press.

King, R., Wesson, C., & Deno, S. (1982). *Direct and frequent measurement of student performance: Does it take too much time?* (Research Report No. 67). University of Minnesota Institute for Research on Learning Disabilities.

Kintsch, W. (1974). *The representation of meaning in memory*. Hillsdale, NJ: Erlbaum.

Kirby, A. M. (Ed.). (1980). Curriculum: Content & change. *Volta Review, 82*(6), 325–446.

Kirk, S. A., & Gallagher, J. J. (1986). *Educating exceptional children*. Boston: Houghton Mifflin.

Klansek, V. (1983). Writing with a purpose. *Perspectives for Teachers of the Hearing Impaired, 2*(2) 14–15.

Kleitman, G. (1975). Speech recording in reading. *Journal of Verbal Learning and Verbal Behavior, 14*, 325–339.

Kluwin, T., & Moores, D. (1987). Factors predictive of literacy in deaf adolescents with deaf parents; factors predictive of literacy in deaf adolescents in T. C. programs. Final report to the Nat'l Institute of Neurological & Comm. Disorders & Stroke. Washington, D.C.: Gallaudet University.

Kluwin, T. (1981). The gramaticality of manual representations of English in classroom settings. *American Annals of the Deaf, 126*(4), 417–421.

Knight, L., & Hargis, C. (1977). Math language ability: its relationship to reading in math. *Language Arts, 54*, 423–428.

Krashen, S. (1982). *Principles and practice in second language acquisition*. New York: Pergamon.

Kretschmer, R. R., & Kretschmer, L. W. (1978). *Language development and intervention with the hearing impaired*. Baltimore, MD: University Park Press.

Kretschmer, R., & Kretschmer, L. (1980). Pragmatics: Development in normal-hearing and hearing-impaired children. In J. D. Sublteny (Ed.), *Speech assessment and speech improvement for the hearing impaired*. Washington, D.C.: The Alexander Graham Bell Association for the Deaf.

Kretschmer, R. R., & Kretschmer, L. W. (1986). Language in perspective. In D. M. Luterman (Ed.), *Deafness in perspective* (pp. 131–166). San Diego, CA: College-Hill Press.

Kwitz, M. D. (1978). *Little chick's story*. New York: Harper & Row.

Lacy, R. (1972). Development of Sonla's negotiations. Unpublished manuscript. Salk Institute for Biological Studies, LaJolla, CA.

Lambie, R. A., & Hutchens, P. W. (1986). Adapting elementary school mathematics instruction. *Teaching Exceptional Children, 18*(3), 185–189.

Lang, H. G., & Cacamisse (1980). One on one with the hearing-impaired. *Science Teacher, 47*(8), 20–25.

Lang, H., & Propp, G. (1982). Science education for hearing-impaired students: State-of-the-art. *American Annals of the Deaf, 127*, 860–869.

Lange, D. (1977). Thoughts from Europe about learning a second language in the classroom. *Modern Language Journal, 30*, 265–267.

Lange, D. (1979). Suggestions for the continuing development of pre- and in-service programs for teachers of second languages. In J. Arenat & P. Myers (Eds.), *Foreign language learning, today and tomorrow: Essays in honor of E. M. Birkmaier*. New York: Pergamon.

Langer, J. A., & Applebee, A. N. (1986). Reading and writing instruction: Towards a theory of teaching and learning. In E. Rothkop (Ed.), *Review of Research in Education, 13*.

LaSasso, C. (1983). Using the language experience approach with language-handicapped readers. *Journal of Reading, 27*(2), 152–154.

LaSasso, C. (1987). Survey of reading instruction for hearing-impaired students in the United States. *Volta Review, 89*(2), 85–98.

LaSasso, C., & Davey, B. (1987). The relationship between lexical knowledge and reading comprehension for prelingually, profoundly hearing-impaired students. *Volta Review, 89*(4), 211–220.

Lasky, L., & Mukerji, R. (1980). *Art: Basic for young children*. Washington, D.C: NAEYC.

Lee, D., & Allen, R. (1963). *Learning to read through experience*. New York: Appleton-Century-Crofts.

Lee, L. (1971). *Northwestern syntax screening test*. Evanston, IL: Northwestern University Press.

Lee, L. (1974). *Developmental sentence scoring*. Evanston, IL: Northwestern University Press.

Lee, L., Koenigsknecht, R., & Mulhern, S. (1975). *Interactive language development teaching*. Evanston, IL: Northwestern University Press.

Lerner, J. (1985). *Learning disabilities: Theories, diagnosis, and teaching strategies*. Boston: Houghton Mifflin.

Levine, E. S. (1981). *The ecology of early deafness: Guides to fashioning environments and psychological assessments*. New York: Columbia University Press.

Lewis, R., & Doorlag, D. (1987). *Teaching special students in the mainstream*. Columbus, OH: Charles E. Merrill.

Liden, G., & Kankkonen, A. (1969). Visual reinforcement audiometry. *Acta Otolaryngologica* (Stockholm), *67*, 281–292.

Lieberth, A. K. (1982). Functional speech therapy for the deaf child. In D. G. Sims, G. G. Walter, & R. C. Whitehead (Eds.) *Deafness and Communication* (pp. 245–257). Baltimore, MD: Williams & Wilkins.

Lieberth, A. K. (1988). Teaching functional writing via telephone. *Perspectives for Teachers of the Hearing Impaired, 7*(1), 10–13.

Lindholm, K. (1980). Bilingual children. In K. Nelson (Ed.), *Children's language* (Vol. 2). New York: Garner Press.

Ling, D. (1976). *Speech and the hearing-impaired child: Theory and Practices*. Washington, D.C.: The Alexander Graham Bell Association for the Deaf.

Ling, D. (1978a). Speech development in hearing-impaired children. *Journal of Communication Disorders, 11*(2/3), 119–124.

Ling, D. (1978b). *Teacher/clinician planbook and guide to the development of speech skills*. Washington, D.C.: The Alexander Graham Bell Association for the Deaf.

Ling, D. (1979). Principles underlying the development of speech communication skills among hearing-impaired children. *Volta Review, 81*(4), 211–223.

Ling, D. (1983). *Speech and the hearing-impaired child*. Washington, D.C.: The Alexander Graham Bell Association for the Deaf.

Ling, D. (1986). Devices and procedures for auditory learning. *Volta Review, 88*(5), 19–27.

Ling, D. (1988). *Foundations of spoken language for hearing-impaired children*. Washington, D.C.: The Alexander Graham Bell Association for the Deaf.

Ling, D., & Ling, A. H. (1978). *Aural rehabilitation*. Washington, D.C.: The Alexander Graham Bell Association for the Deaf.

Lloyd, L. L., & Young, C. E. (1969). Pure-tone audiometry. In R. Fulton & L. Lloyd (Eds.), *Audiometry for the retarded with implications for the difficult-to-test*. Baltimore, MD: Williams & Wilkins.

Loban, W. (1973). The green pastures of English. *Elementary English, 50*, 683–690.

Loban, W. (1978). Language arts is unique internal, not external instruction. *Thrust, 7*, 11–12.

Loban, W. (1979). Relationships between language and literacy. *Language Arts, 56*, 485–486.

Loew, R. (October 1980). *Learning sign language as a first language: Voles and reference*. Paper presented at the Third National Symposium on Sign Language Research and Teaching, Boston.

Long, M. (February 1986). *Phonologic evaluation*. (Available from Rochester School for the Deaf, Rochester, NY).

Lowenbraun, S., Appleman, K. I., & Callahan, J. L. (1980). *Teaching the hearing impaired: Through total communication*. Columbus, OH: Charles E. Merrill.

Lucas, E. (1980). *Semantic and pragmatic language disorders: Assessment and remediation*. Rockville, MD: Aspen.

Luckner, J. L. (1987). Strategies for building student's self-esteem. *Perspectives for Teachers of the Hearing Impaired, 6*(2), 9–11.

Luckner, J. L. (1988). Communication is the key to providing effective support services for mainstreamed students. *Perspectives for Teachers of the Hearing Impaired, 65*, 2–4.

Luckner, J. L. (1989). Suggestions for improving the expressive writing of hearing-impaired students. *The Association of Canadian Educators of the Hearing Impaired Journal, 15*(2) 57–72.

Luckner, J. L., Isaacson, S. L. (in press). A method of assessing the written language of hearing-impaired students. *Journal of Communication Disorders*.

Luckner, J. L., Rude, H., & Sileo, T. W. (1989). Collaborative consultation: A method for improving services for mainstreamed students who are hearing impaired. *American Annals of the Deaf, 134*(5) 301–304.

Luetke-Stahlman, B. (1982). *Training receptive language response abilities to assess language and/or system preference of pre-school hearing-impaired children from Spanish-speaking homes*. Unpublished doctoral dissertation, Pennsylvania State University.

Luetke-Stahlman, B. (1983a). Applying bilingual

models in classrooms for the hearing impaired. *American Annals of the Deaf, 128*(7), 21–29.

Luetke-Stahlman, B. (1984). Second-system switching in a hearing two-year old. Sign Language Studies, 42, 13–22.

Luetke-Stahlman, B. (1987a) Efficient uses of single subject design in hearing-impaired classrooms. *American Annals of the Deaf, 131*, 349–355.

Luetke-Stahlman, B. (1987b). A method of assessing the language development of students who use signed and spoken English. *Perspectives for Teachers of the Hearing Impaired, 6*(1), 11–14.

Luetke-Stahlman, B. (1988a). The benefit of oral English-only as compared with signed input to hearing-impaired students. *Volta Review*, 349–361

Luetke-Stahlman, B. (1988b). SEE-2 in the classroom: How well is English represented? In Gustason (Ed.), *Signing English in total communication*. Los Alamitos, CA: Modern Sign Press.

Luetke-Stahlman, B. (1988c). Documenting syntactically and semantically incomplete bimodal input to hearing impaired subjects. *America Annals of the Deaf, 133*(3), 230–234.

Luetke-Stahlman, B. (1988d). The benefit of using CAI to a six-year-old hearing-impaired boy learning previously unknown vocabulary and spelling words. *Early Childhood Development and Care, 32*, 1–4.

Luetke-Stahlman, B. (1989). A framework for assessing speechreading performance in H. I. children. *The Association of Canadian Educators of the Hearing Impaired*, 15(1), 27–37.

Luetke-Stahlman, B. (in progress). *Teacher's consistency of signing using various forms of simultaneous communication.*

Luetke-Stahlman, B., & Luetke-Stahlman, K. (1988). Does computer software help hearing-impaired students learn? *The Educational Treatment of Children, 11*(3).

Luetke-Stahlman, B., & Moeller, M. P. (in press). Teaching parents to sign SEE-2: Progress and retention. *American Annals of the Deaf.*

Lund, N., & Duchan, J. (1988). *Assessing language in natural contexts* (2nd ed.). Englewood Cliffs, NJ: Prentice-Hall.

Lund, K., Schnaps, L., & Bijou, S. (1983). Let's take another look at record keeping. *Teaching Exceptional Children, 15*, 155–159.

MacGinitie, W. (1978). *Gates-MacGinitie reading tests*. Chicago: Riverside.

Mackall, P., Dayoub, I., Frey, R., Cocoran-Horn, K., Mann, K., Long, L., & Baldini, A. (1982). *Kendall demonstration elementary school mathematics*. Washington, D.C.: Gallaudet University.

Madden, R., Gardner, E. F., Rudman, H. C., Karlsen, B., & Merwin, J. C. (1972). *Stanford achievement test: Special edition for hearing impaired students*. Washington, D.C.: Gallaudet College Office of Demographic Studies.

Maestas y Moores, J. (1980). Early linguistic environment. *Sign Language Studies*, 26, 1–13.

Maez, L. (March 1984). Tempe, AZ: Center for Bilingual/Bicultural Education, Arizona State University.

Mager, R. F. (1984). *Preparing instructional objectives*. Belmont, CA: Fearon.

Magner, M. E. (1980). *A speech intelligibility test for deaf children*. Northhampton, MA: The Clarke School for the Deaf.

Mahoney G. & Weller, E. L. (1980). An ecological approach to language intervention. *New Direction for Exceptional Children, 2*, 17–31.

Maktin, N. (1977). Assessment of hearing sensitivity during the preschool years. In F. H. Bess (Ed.), *Childhood deafness: Causation, assessment, and management*. New York: Grune & Stratton.

Maloney, J. B., & Hopkins, B. L. (1973). The modification of structure and its relationship to subjective judgments of creative writing. *Journal of Applied Behavioral Analysis, 6*, 425–433.

Marimont, R. B. (1974). How can the deaf learn to speak? *Volta Review, 76*(4), 223–230.

Marmor, G., & Petitto, L. (1979). Simultaneous communication in the classroom: How well is English grammar represented? *Sign Language Studies, 23*, 99–133.

Martin, F. N., Bernstein, M. E., Daly, J. A., & Cody, J. P. (1988). Classroom teachers' knowledge of hearing disorders and attitudes about mainstreaming hard of hearing children. *Language, Speech, and Hearing Services in Schools, 19*(1), 83–95.

Martorella, P. H. (1986). Teaching concepts. In J. M. Cooper (Ed.), *Classroom teaching skills* (pp. 179–223). Lexington, MA: D.C. Heath.

Mason, G. E. (no date). *Language experience recorder plus*. Gainesville, FL: Teacher Support Software.

Matthias, M., Platt, M., & Thiessen, D. (1980). Counting books: The children's choice. *Teacher, 97*(5), 103–104.

Maxwell, M. (1980). The development of language in a deaf child—Signs, sign variations, speech, and print. In K. E. Nelson (Ed.), *Children's language* (Vol. 3). New York: Gardner Press.

Maxwell, M. (1986). Beginning reading and deaf children. *American Annals of the Deaf.*

May, F. B. (1986). *Reading as communication: An interactive approach*. Columbus, OH: Charles E. Merrill.

McAnally, P. L., Rose, S., & Quigley, S. (1987). *Language learning practices with deaf children*. San Diego, CA: Little, Brown.

McClure, A. A. (1985). Predictable books: Another way to teach reading to learning disabled children. *Teaching Exceptional Children, 17*(4), 267–273.

McCormick, L., & Schiefelbush, R. L. (1984). *Early language intervention*. Columbus, OH: Charles E. Merrill.

McCracken, R., McCracken, M. (1986). *Stories, songs, and poetry to teach reading and writing*. New York: Teacher's College Press.

McCune-Nicholich L., & Carroll, S. (1981). Development of symbolic play: Implications for the language specialist. In K. Butler (Ed.), *Topics in language disorders* (Vol. 2, No. 1).

McIntire, M. (1973). *Assessing language production in children*. Baltimore, MD: University Park Press.

McIntire, M. (1974). *A modified model for the description of language acquisition in a deaf child*. Unpublished master's thesis, California State University.

McIntyre M. (1981). The sounds of music. *Science and Children, 18*(5), 34–35.

McNamee, G. D. (1979). The social interaction origins of narrative skills. *Quarterly Newsletter of the Laboratory of Comparative Human Cognition, 1*(4). LaJolla, CA: University of California.

Meadow, K. P. (1980). *Deafness and child development*. Berkeley, CA: University of California Press.

Mellon, J. (1981). *Sentence-combining skills: Results of the sentence combining exercises in the 1978–1979 National Writing Assessment* (Special Paper No. 10-W-65 prepared for the National Assessment of Educational Progress). (ERIC Document Reproduction Service No. ED 210–696).

Mercer, C. D., & Mercer, A. R. (1985). *Teaching students with learning problems* (2nd ed.). Columbus, OH: Charles E. Merrill.

Mettler, R., & Conway, D. F. (1988). Peer reading journals: A student-to-student application of dialogue journals. *Perspectives for Teachers of the Hearing Impaired, 7*(1), 20–22.

Meyen, E. L. (1981). *Developing instructional units for the regular and special education teacher*. Dubuque, IA: William C. Brown.

Miller, G. A., & Gildea, P. M. (1987). How children learn words. *Scientific American, 1*, 94–99.

Miller, J. (Ed.). (1981a) *Assessing language production in children*. Baltimore, MD: University Park Press.

Miller, M. S. (1981b). A model for providing comprehensive speech services within a total communication program for the deaf. *American Annals of the Deaf, 126*(7), 803–805.

Mishler, C., & Hogan, T. (1982). Holistic scoring of essays. *Diagnosticque, 8*, 4–16.

Mitchell, J. (1985). *Buros ninth mental measurements yearbook*. Lincoln, NB: University of Nebraska Press.

Moeller, M. P. (1982). Hearing and speechreading assessment with the severely hearing-impaired child. In D. Sims, G. Walter, & R. Whitehead (Eds.), *Deafness and communication*. Baltimore, MD: Williams & Wilkins.

Moeller, M. P. (1988). Language evaluation strategies for hearing-impaired students.

Moeller, M. P., & Luetke-Stahlman, B. (1990). Parents' use of Signing Exact English: A descriptive analysis. *JSHD, 55*(2), 327–338.

Moeller, M. P., & McConkey, A. (1983). *Evaluation of the hearing-impaired infant: What constitutes progress?* Paper presented at ASHA, Cincinnati, OH.

Moeller, M., McConkey, A., Hixson, P., & Confal, K. (November 1983). *The DELP project.*

Poster session at American Speech-Language-Hearing Association, Cincinnati, OH.

Moeller, M., Osberger, M., & Eccarius, M. (1986). Cognitively based strategies for use with hearing-impaired students with comprehension deficits. *Topics in Language Disorders, 6*(4), 37–50.

Moeller, M. P., Osberger, M. J., and Morford, J. in J. G. Alpiner and P. A. McCarthy (eds) (1987). *Rehabilitative Audiology: Children and Adults*, Williams and Wilkins, Baltimore, MD.

Moerk, E. (1980). *Pragmatic and semantic aspects of early language development*. Baltimore, MD: University Park Press.

Monsen, R. B. (1981). A usable test for the speech intelligibility of deaf talkers. *American Annals of the Deaf, 126*(7), 845–852.

Montgomery, A. (1988). Issues and developments in the evaluation of speechreading. *Volta Review, 90*(5), 193–214.

Montgomery, M. D. (1980). The special educators as a consultant: Some strategies. In N. J. Long, W. C. Morse, & R. G. Newman (Eds.), *Conflict in the classroom* (4th ed.). Belmont, CA: Wadsworth.

Moog, J., & Geer, A. (1985). EPIC: A program to accelerate academic progress in profoundly hearing-impaired children. *Volta Review, 87*(6), 259–277.

Moon, C., & Well, G. (1979). The influence of home on learning to read. *Journal of Research in Reading, 2*, 53–62.

Moore, M. (1974). Training professionals to work with paraprofessionals. *Personnel and Guidance Journal, 53*, 308–312.

Moores, D. (1984). Interpreting in the public schools. *Perspectives for Teachers of the Hearing Impaired*, 3(2), 13–15.

Moores, D. F. (1987). *Educating the deaf: Psychology, principles, and practices* (3rd ed.). Boston: Houghton Mifflin.

Moran, M. R. (1987). Options of written language assessment. *Focus on Exceptional Children, 19*(5), 1–10.

Morine-Dershimer, G., & Pfeifer, J. (1986). Instructional planning. In J. M. Cooper (Ed.), *Classroom teaching skills*. Lexington, MA: D.C. Heath.

Morlan, J. E. (1974). *Classroom learning centers*. Belmont, CA: Lear Siegler, Inc./Fearon Publishers.

Morris, N. T., & Crump, D. T. (1982). Syntactic and vocabulary development in the written language of learning disabled and non-learning disabled students at four age levels. *Learning Disability Quarterly, 5*, 163–172.

Morrow, L. (1983). Home and school correlates of early interest in literature. *Journal of Educational Research, 76*, 221–230.

Moss, P., Cole, N., & Khampalikit, C. (1982). A comparison of procedures to assess written language skills at grades 4, 7, and 10. *Journal of Educational Measurement, 19*, 37–47.

Mothner, H. (1980). A technique for teaching the unmotivated reader. *American Annals of the Deaf, 125*(4), 551–553.

Moustafa, M., & Penrose, J. (1985). Comprehensible input plus the language experience approach: Reading instruction for LES students. *The Reading Teacher, 38*, 640–647.

Mullis, I. V. (1984). Scoring direct writing assessment: What are the alternatives? *Educational Measurement: Issues and Practices, 14*, 16–18.

Muma, J. R. (1981). Language: A new era. *Journal of Childhood Communication Disorders, 5*(2), 83–89.

Murley, J. (March 1988). *Appilication of the High Scope curriculum in special education early childhood classrooms*. Paper presented at the Illinois Division for Early Childhood, Springfield, IL.

Myklebust, H. (1965). *Development and disorders of written language: Picture story language test*. New York: Grune & Stratton.

National Council for Teachers of Mathematics. (1980). *An agenda for action: Recommendations for school mathmatics for the 1980's*. Reston, VA: Council of Teachers of Mathematics.

Nelson, K. (1973). Structure and strategy in learning to talk. *Monographs of the Society for Research and Child Development, 38*, 149.

Newcomer, P., Nodine, B., & Barenbaum, E. (1988). Teaching writing to exceptional children: Reactions and recommendations. *Exceptional Children, 54*(6), 559–564.

Newport, E. (1977). Mother I'd rather do it myself. In C. Snow & C. Ferguson (Eds.), *Talking to children: Language input and acquisition*. New York: Cambridge University Press.

Newport, E., & Ashbrook, E. (1977). The emergence of semantic relationship in American sign language. *Papers and Reports on Child*

*Language Development, 13*, 16–21.

Newport, E. L., Gleitman, H., & Gleitman, L. R. (1977). Mother I'd rather do it myself: Some effects and non-effects of maternal speech styles. In C. E. Snow & C. A. Ferguson (Eds.), *Talking to children: Language input and acquisition.* London: Cambridge Press.

Nickerson, R. S. (1975). Characteristics of the speech of deaf persons. *Volta Review, 77*(6), 342–359.

Ninio, A., & Bruner, J. (1978). The achievements and antecedents of labeling. *Journal of Child Language, 5*, 1–15.

Nittrouer, S., & Hochberg, I. (1985). Speech communication for deaf children: A communication based approach. *American Annals of the Deaf, 130*(6), 491–495.

Nold, E. W. (1981). Revising. In C. H. Fredericksen & J. F. Dominic (Eds.), *Writing: The nature, development, and teaching of written communication: Vol. 2. Process, development and communication* (pp. 67–79). Hillsdale, NJ: Lawrence Erlbaum.

North, A., & Stevenson, V. (1975). The effects of total communication, manual communication, oral communication, and reading on the learning of factual information in residential school deaf children. *American Annals of the Deaf, 120*, 48–57.

Nostrand, H. L. (1974). Empathy for a second culture: Motivations and techniques. In G. Jarvis (Ed.), *Responding to new realities.* Skokie, IL: National Textbook Company.

Novelli-Olmstead, T., & Ling, D. (1984). Speech production and speech discrimination by hearing-impaired children. *Volta Review, 86*(2), 72–80.

Nussbaum, D. B., Waddy-Smith, B., & Wilson-Favors, V. (1982). *KDES guide for auditory and speech training.* Washington, D.C.: Gallaudet Pre-College Program.

Nutter, N., & Safran, J. (1984). Improving writing with sentence combining exercises. *Academic Therapy, 19*(4), 449–455.

Ogletree, E. J., Gebauer, P., & Ujlaki, V. E. (1980). *The unit plan: A plan for curriculum organizing and teaching.* Washington, D.C.: University Press of America.

Omaggio, A. (1984). The proficiency-oriented classroom. In T. V. Higgs (Eds.), *Teaching for proficiency: The organizing principle.* Lin-colnwood, IL: National Textbook Co.

O'Neil, J., & Oyer, H. (1981). *Visual communication for the hard of hearing: History, research, methods* (2nd ed.). Englewood Cliffs, NJ: Prentice-Hall.

Osguthorpe, R. (1980). *The tutor/notetaker: Providing academic support to mainstreamed deaf students.* Washington, D.C: The Alexander Graham Bell Association for the Deaf.

Otis-Wilburn, A. K. (1984). *The evaluation of the effects of four reading instructional procedures on the achievement of hearing-impaired children.* Unpublished doctoral dissertation, University of Kansas, Lawrence, KS.

Outstanding Science Trade Books for Children. (September 1987). *Young Children*, 52–56.

Pace, A. (1961). Understanding and the ability to solve problems. *Arithmetic Teacher, 8*, 226–233.

Padden, C., & Humphries, T. (1988). *Deaf in America, voices from a culture.* Cambridge, MA: Harvard University Press.

Padden, C., & LaMaster, B. (1985). An alphabet on hand. *Sign Language Studies, 47*, 161–172.

Paine, S. C., Radicchi, J., Rosellini, L. C., Deutchman, L., & Darch, C. B. (1983). *Structuring your classroom for academic success.* Champaign, IL: Research Press.

Palmer, L. (1988). Speechreading as communication. *Volta Review, 90*(50), 33–44.

Paratore, J., & Indrisano, R. (1987). Intervention assessment of reading comprehension. *The Reading Teacher, 40*(8), 778–783.

Parents Nursery School. (1974). *Kids are natural cooks.* Boston: Houghton Mifflin.

Paterson, M. (1982). Integration of auditory training with speech and language for severely hearing-impaired children. In D. G. Sims, G. G. Walter, & R. L. Whitehead (Eds.), *Deafness and communication* (pp. 261–270). Baltimore, MD: Williams & Wilkins.

Paterson, M. (1986). Maximizing the use of residual hearing with school-aged hearing-impaired students—A perspective. *Volta Review, 88*(5), 93–106.

Paul, P. V., & Quigley, S. P. (1990). *Education and deafness.* New York: Longman.

Perl, S. (1983). How teachers teach the writing process: Overview of an ethnographic research project. *Elementary School Journal, 84*, 19–24.

Perron, J. (1976). Beginning writing: It's all in the mind. *Language Arts, 53*(6), 652–657.

Petitto, L. (1980). In the acquisition of anaphoric reference in ASL. Unpublished manuscript. The Salk Institute for Biological Studies, LaJolla, CA.

Phelps-Terasaki, D., & Phelps, T. (1980). *Teaching written expression: The Phelps sentence guide program*. Novato, CA: Academic Therapy Publications.

Piaget, J. (1963). *The child's conception of the world*. Paterson, NJ: Littlefield, Adams.

Piaget, J. (1965). *The child's conception of numbers*. New York: W. W. Norton.

Piaget, J., & Inhelder, B. (1969). *The psychology of the child*. New York: Basic Books.

Pikulski, J. J. (1983). Questions and answers. *Reading Teacher, 37*, 111–112.

Polloway, E. A., & Smith, J. E. (1982). *Teaching language skills to exceptional learners*. Denver: Love Publishing Co.

Polya, G. (1973). *How to solve it*. Princeton, NJ: Princeton University Press.

Poplin, M. (1983). Assessing developmental writing abilities. *Topics in Learning and Learning Disabilities, 3*(3), 63–75.

Porter, K., & Bradley, S. (1985). A comparison of three speech intelligibility measures for deaf students. *American Annals of the Deaf, 130*(6), 514–525.

Poteet, J. A. (1980). Informal assessment of written expression. *Learning Disability Quarterly, 3*(4), 88–98.

Prelutsky, J. (Ed.). (1983). *The random house book of poetry for children*. New York: Random House.

Prelutsky, J. (Ed.). (1986). *Read-aloud rhymes for the very young*. New York: Alfred A. Knopf.

Premack, D. (1959). Toward empirical behavior laws: I. Positive reinforcement. *Psychological Review, 66*, 291–333.

Prescott, G. A., Balow, I. H., Hogan, T. R., & Farr, R. C. (1984). *Metropolitan achievement tests 6: Survey battery*. San Antonio, TX: The Psychological Corporation.

Prinz, P., & Prinz, E. (1981). Acquisition of ASL and spoken English by a hearing child of a deaf mother and a hearing father: Phase II, early combinational patterns. *Sign Language Studies, 30*, 78–88.

Pronovost, W. (1979). Speech assessment and speech improvement for the hearing impaired. *Volta Review, 81*(7), 511–514.

Quigley, S. P., & King, C. (1981). *Reading milestones*. Beaverton, OR: Dormac.

Quigley, S. P., & Kretschmer, R. R. (1982). *The education of deaf children*. Baltimore, MD: University Park Press.

Quigley, S. P., & Paul, P. V. (1984). *Language and deafness*. San Diego, CA: College-Hill Press.

Quigley, S., Power, D., & Steinkamp, M. (1977). The language structure of deaf children. *Volta Review, 79*, 73–83.

Radebaugh, M. R. (1981). Using children's literature to teach mathematics. *The Reading Teacher, 34*(5), 902–906.

Ramirez, A. (1980). Language in bilingual classrooms. *National Association for Bilingual Education Journal, 4*, 61–80.

Raphael, T. E., Kirschner, B. W., & Englert, C. S. (1986). *Text structure instruction within process-writing classrooms: A manual for instruction*. Occasional Paper No. 104. East Lansing: Michigan State University, Institute for Research on Teaching.

Reed, R. D., & Bugen, C. T. (1986). *A process approach to developing language with hearing-impaired children*. Columbia, MO: General Printing Service.

Reisberg, L., & Wolf, R. (1986). Developing a consulting program in special education: Implementation and interventions. *Focus on Exceptional Children, 19*(3), 1–16.

Reisman, F. (1981). *Teaching mathematics: Methods and content*. Boston:. Houghton Mifflin.

Reisman, F. (1982). *A guide to the diagnostic teaching of arithmetic* (3rd edition). Columbus, OH: Charles E. Merrill.

Reys, R. E., Suydam, M. N., & Lindquist, M. M. (1984). *Helping children learn mathematics*. Englewood Cliffs, NJ: Prentice-Hall.

Rhodes, L. K. (1981). I can read! Predictable books as resources for reading and writing instruction. *Reading Teacher, 34*, 11–518.

Ribovich, J. (1979). A methodology for teaching concepts. *The Reading Teacher, 33*(3), 285–289.

Rice, M., & Kemper, S. (1985). *Child language and cognition*. Baltimore, MD: University Park Press.

Rivers, W., & Temperley, M. (1978). *A practical guide to the teaching of English as a second or foreign language*. New York: Oxford University Press.

Roberts, G. H. (1968). The failure strategies of third grade arithmetic pupils. *The Arithmetic Teacher, 15* 442–446.

Robinson, S. F. (1984). *Coherence in student writing*. Unpublished doctoral dissertation, Harvard University, Cambridge, MA. (University Microfilms International No. DA 84212211)

Roit, M. L., & McKenzie, R. G. (1985). Disorders of written communication: An instructional priority for LD students. *Journal of Learning Disabilities, 18*, 258–260.

Rosenberg, M., Sindelar, P., & Stedt, J. (1985). The effects of supplemental on-task contingencies on the acquisition of simple and difficult academic tasks. *Journal of Special Education, 19*, 189–203.

Rosenshine, B. V. (1980). How time is spent in elementary classrooms. In C. Denham & A. Lieberman (Eds.), *Time to learn* (pp. 107–126). Washington, D.C.: National Institute of Education.

Rosenshine, B. (1983). Teaching functions in instructional programs. *The Elementary School Journal, 83*(4) 335–351

Rosenshine, B. V. (1986). Synthesis of research on explicit teaching. *Educational Leadership, 43*(7), 60–69.

Ross, M., & Giolas, T. (Eds.). (1978). *Auditory management of hearing-impaired children*. Baltimore, MD: University Park Press.

Ross, M., & Lerman, J. (1970). A picture identification test for hearing-impaired children. *JSHR*, 44–53.

Rowe, M. B. (1974). Wait time and reward as instructional variables, their influence on language logic and fate control: Part one—wait time. *Journal of Research on Science Teaching, 11*, 81–94.

Rumelhart, D. D. (1984). Understanding understanding. In J. Flood (Ed.), *Understanding reading comprehension* (pp. 1–20). Newark, DE: International Reading Association.

Rutherford, S. (1985). The traditional group narrative of deaf children. *Sign Language Studies, 47*, 141–159.

Rutherford, S. (1987). *A study of American deaf culture*. Unpublished doctoral dissertation. Berkeley, CA: University of California.

Rutherford, S. (1988). The culture of American deaf people. *Sign Language Studies, 59*, 130–143.

Ryan, T., Johnson, J., & Lynch, V. (1977). So you want to write objectives (or have to). In N. G. Haring (Ed.), *The experimental education program: an inservice program for personnel serving the severely handicapped* (Vol. 1). Seattle, WA: University of Washington.

Ryor, J. (1978). 94–142—The perspective of regular education. *Learning Disability Quarterly, 1*, 6–14.

Sabatino, D. A. (1987). Preventive discipline as a practice in special education. *Teaching Exceptional Children, 19*(4) 8–11.

Saint Mary's School for the Deaf (1985) Science Curriculum. Buffalo, N.Y.

Salend, S. J. (1987). Group-oriented behavior management strategies. *Teaching Exceptional Children, 20*(1), 53–55.

Salvia, J., & Ysseldyke, J. (1988). *Assessment in special and remedial education* (4th edition). Boston: Houghton Mifflin.

Sanborn, J. (1986). Grammar: Good wine before its time. *English Journal, 75*(3), 72–80.

Sanders, D. A. (1977). Speech perception and reading. *Auditory perception of speech: An introduction to principles and problems* (pps. 219–229). Englewood, NJ: Prentice-Hall.

Sanders, D. A. (1982). *Aural rehabilitation: A management model*. Englewood Cliffs, NJ: Prentice-Hall.

Sanders, D. M. (1988). *Teaching deaf children: Techniques and methods*. Boston: Little, Brown.

Sass-Lehrer, M. (1986). Competencies critical to teachers of hearing-impaired students in two settings: Supervisors' views. *American Annals of the Deaf, 131*(1), 9–12.

Sattler, J. M. (1982). *Assessment of children's intelligence and special abilities*. Boston: Allyn & Bacon.

Sattler, J. M. (1988). *Assessment of children's intelligence*. San Diego, CA: Sattler.

Scandary, J. (1981). What every teacher should know about due process hearings. *Teaching Exceptional Children, 13*, 92–96.

Scardamalia, M., & Bereiter, C. (1986). Research

on written composition. In M. C. Wittrock (Ed.), *Handbook of research on teaching* (3rd ed.). New York: Macmillan.

Schein, D., & Delk, M. T. (1974). *The deaf population of the United States*. Silver Springs, MD: National Association of the Deaf.

Schlesinger, H. (1978). The acquisition of bimodal language. In M. Schlesinger (Ed.), *Sign language of the deaf: Psychological, linguistic, and sociological perspectives*. New York: Academic Press.

Schlesinger, H., & Meadow, K. (1972). *Sound and sign: Childhood deafness and mental health*. Berkeley, CA: University of California Press.

Schloss, P. J., & Sedlak, R. A. (1986). *Instructional methods for students with learning and behavior problems*. Boston: Allyn & Bacon.

Schowe, R., & Nerbonne, M. (1980). *Introduction to oral rehabilitation*. Baltimore, MD: University Press.

Schumacher, J. B., Deshler, D. D., Nolan, S., Clark, F. L., Alley, G. R., & Warner, M. M. (1981). *Error monitoring: A learning strategy for improving academic performance of LD adolescents*. Lawrence, KS: University of Kansas Institute for Research in Learning Disabilities. (ERIC Document Reproduction Service No. 217 644).

Schwartz, J. R., & Black, J. W. (1967). Some effects of sentence structure on speechreading. *Central States Speech Journal, 18*, 86–90.

Scott, P. L. (1983). Have competencies needed by teachers of the hearing-impaired changed in 25 years? *Exceptional Children, 50*(1), 48–53.

Shanklin, N. L., & Rhodes, L. K. (1989). Transforming literacy information. *Educational Leadership, 44*(6), 59–63.

Shuy, R. (1981). A holistic view of language. *Research in the Teaching of English, 15*, 101–111.

Sidel, R. (1986). *Women and children last: The plight of poor women in affluent America*. New York: Viking Penguin.

Siebert, R. (1980). Speech training for the hearing impaired: Principles, objectives, and strategies for preschool and elementary levels. In J. D. Subtelny (Ed.), *Speech assessment and speech improvement for the hearing impaired* (pp. 102–110). Washington, D.C.: The Alexander Graham Bell Association for the Deaf.

Silvaroli, N. J. (1979). *Classroom reading inventory*. Minneapolis, MN: William C. Brown.

Silvia, E. (1983). A money unit for deaf children. *American Annals of the Deaf, 128*(4), 479–482.

Simmons, F. B., & Russ, F. N. (1974). Automated newborn hearing screening, the Crib-o-gram. *Archives of Otolaryngology, 100*, 107.

Simms, R. B., & Falcon, S. C. (1987). Teaching sight words. *Teaching Exceptional Children, 20*(1) 30–33.

Simon, C. (1979). *Communicative competence: A functional-pragmatic approach in language therapy*. Tucson, AZ: Communication Skill Builders.

Simpson, R. (1982). *Conferencing parents of exceptional children*. Rockville, MD: Aspen.

Sims, D. G. (1982). Hearing and speechreading evaluation for the deaf adult. In D. G. Sims, G. G. Walter, & R. L. Whitehead (Eds.), *Deafness and communication: Assessment and training* (pp. 141–154). Baltimore, MD: Williams & Wilkins.

Sims, D. G., Walter, G. G., & Whitehead, R. L. (Eds.). (1982). *Deafness and communication*. Baltimore, MD: Williams & Wilkins.

*SIMS written language program*. (1977). Minneapolis, MN: Minneapolis Public Schools.

Sinatra, R. C., Berg, D., & Dunn, R. (1985). Semantic mapping improves reading comprehension of learning disabled students. *Teaching Exceptional Children, 17*(4), 310–314.

Skypek, D. (1981). *Teaching Mathematics: Implications*.

Slavin, R. E. (1980). Cooperative learning. *Review of Educational Research, 50*, 315–342.

Slavin, R. E. (1981). Synthesis of research on cooperative learning. *Educational Leadership, 38*(8), 655–660.

Slobin, D. (1970). Universals in grammatical development in children. In G. B. Flores D'Areais & N. J. M. Levelt (Eds.), *Advances in psycholinguistics*. New York: American Isevier.

Smith, B. (1987). *PL 99-457 the new law*. Reston, VA: Council for Exceptional Children.

Smith, F. (1978). *Understanding reading: A psycholinguistic analysis of reading and learning to read* (2nd ed.). New York: Holt, Rinehart and Winston.

Smith, F. (1979). *Reading without nonsense*. New

York: Teachers College Press.

Smith, F. (1985). *Reading without nonsense*. New York: Teachers College Press.

Smith, N. J. (1985). The word processing approach to language experience. *The Reading Teacher, 38*(6), 556–559.

Smith, N. J., & Wendelin, K. H . (1981). Using children's books to teach mathematical concepts. *Arithmetic Teacher, 29*(3), 10–15.

Smith, R. (1987). Theoretical framework for preschool science experiences. *Young Children* 34–40.

Snow, C. (1977). The development of conversation between mothers and babies. *Journal of Child Language, 4*, 1–22.

Snow C., & Goldfield, B. (1982). Building stories: The emergence of information from conversation. In D. Tannen (Ed.), *Analyzing discourse: Text and talk* (pp. 127–141). Washington, D.C.: Georgetown University Press.

Sobel M. A., & Maletsky, E. M. (1988). *Teaching mathematics: A sourcebook of aids, activities, and strategies*. Englewood Cliffs, NJ: Prentice-Hall.

Sobel, R., & Pluznik, N. (1987). *Messy monsters, jungle joggers, and bubble baths*. Potomac, MD: Elan Publishing House.

Somers, M. (1987). Parenting in the 1980s: Programming perspectives and issues. *Volta Review, 88*(5), 68–77.

Southgate, V., Arnold, H., & Johnson, S. (1981). *Extending beginning reading*. London: Heinemann.

Spodek, B., Saracho, 0. N., & Lee, R. C. (1984). *Mainstreaming young children*. Belmont, CA: Wadsworth.

Staab, C. F. (1983). Language functions elicited by meaningful activities: A new dimension in language programs. *Language, Speech and Hearing Services in Schools, 14*(3), 164–170.

Stainback, W., Stainback, S., & Froyen, L. (1987). Structuring the classroom to prevent disruptive behaviors. *Teaching Exceptional Children, 19*(4), 12–16.

Staton, J. (1980). Writing and counseling: Using a dialogue journal. *Language Arts, 57*(5), 514–518.

Staton, J. (1985). Using dialogue journals for developing thinking, reading, and writing with hearing-impaired students. *Volta Review, 87*(5), 127–154.

Stauffer, R. (1970). *The language experience approach to the teaching of reading*. New York: Harper & Row.

Stauffer, R. G. (1980). *The language-experience approach to teaching reading*. New York: Harper & Row.

Stein, D., Benner, G., Hoverstein, G., McGinnis, M., & Theis, T. (1980). *Auditory skills curriculum*. North Hollywood, CA: Foreworks.

Stein, N. L. (1983). Methodological and conceptual issues in writing research. *Elementary School Journal, 84*, 100–108.

Sternberg, R. (1979). The nature of mental abilities. *American Psychologist, 34*, 214–230.

Stevens, R., & Rosenshine, B. (1981). Advances in research on teaching. *Exceptional Education Quarterly, 2*, 1–9.

Stewart, D., & Akamatsu, T. (1988). The coming of age of ASL. *Anthropology and Education Quarterly, 19*, 225–252.

Stewart, S. R. (1985). Development of written language proficiency: Methods for teaching text structure. In C. S. Simon (Ed.), *Communication skills and classroom success: Therapy methodologies for language-learning disabled students* (pp. 341–361). San Diego, CA: College-Hill Press.

Stokoe, W. (1982). Personal communication.

Stokoe, W., Casterline, C., & Cronberg, C. (1965). *A dictionary of ASL on linguistic principles*. Silver Springs, MD: Linstock Press.

Stone, J. (September 1987). Early childhood math: make it manipulative. *Young Children*. 16–23.

Stone P. (1980). Developing thinking skills in young hearing-impaired children. *Volta Review, 82*, 345–352.

Stone, P. (1988). *Blueprint for developing conversational competencies*. Washington, D.C.: The Alexander Graham Bell Association for the Deaf.

Stone, P., & Fortier, G. (1984). *Developing conversational competence: A planning/instruction model*. Miniseminar presented at the International Convention of the Alexander Graham Bell Association, Portland, OR.

Strange, M. (1980). Instructional implications of a conceptual theory of reading comprehension. *The Reading Teacher, 33*, 391–397.

Strong, M., & Charleston, E. (1988). Simultaneous communication: Are teachers attempting an impossible task? *American Annals of the Deaf, 132*(5), 376–382.

Sullivan, P. M., & Vernon, M. (1979). Psychological assessment of hearing impaired children. *School Psychology Digest, 8*(3), 271–290.

Sunal, D. (1984) Without reinventing the wheel. *Perspective for Teachers of the Hearing Impaired, 2*, 16–18, 28.

Sutton, (1976). *Sutton movement shorthand: The sign language key.* Irvine, CA: The Movement Shorthand Society Press.

Suydam, M. N. (1982). Update or research on problem solving: Implications for classroom teaching. *Arithmetic Teacher, 29*, 56–60.

Suydam, M. N., & Weaver, J. F. (1981). *Using research: A key to elementary school mathematics.* Columbus OH: ERIC Clearinghouse for Science, Mathematics and Environmental Education.

Suzuki, T., & Ogiba, T. (1961). Conditioned orientation reflex audiometry. *Archives of Otolaryngology, 78*, 84–150.

Swaby, B. (1982). Varying the way you teach reading with basal stories. *The Reading Teacher, 35*(6), 676–680.

Swain, M. (1972). Bilingualism as a first language. Unpublished doctoral dissertation. Irvine, CA: Univ. of CA at Irvine.

Swanson, S. (1986). *Case study data from a speechreading task.* Completed as a part of the course requirements for LDSE 469 at Northern Illinois University; DeKalb, IL 60115.

Taylor, R. (1984). *Assessment of exceptional students.* Englewood Cliffs, NJ: Prentice-Hall.

Teitelbaum, M. (1986). *Fievel's boat trip.* San Diego, CA: McDonald's Corporation.

TenBrink, T. D. (1986). Writing instructional objectives. In J. M. Cooper (Ed.), *Classroom teaching skills.* Lexington, MA: D.C. Heath.

Tennyson, R. D. & Park, O. (1980). The teaching of concepts: A review of instructional design research literature. *Review of Educational Research, 50*(1), 55–70.

Thibault, J. P., & McKee, J. (1982). Practical parenting with Piaget. *Young Children,* 18–27.

Thorton, C., Tucker, B., Dossey, J., & Bazik, E. (1983). *Teaching mathematics to children with special needs.* Menlo Park, CA: Addison-Wesley.

Thurlow, M. L., Ysseldyke, J. E., Graden, J., & Algozzine, B. (1983). Instructional ecology for students in resource and regular classrooms. *Teacher Education and Special Education, 6,* 248–254.

Tiedt, I. (1983). *The language arts handbook.* Englewood Cliffs, NJ: Prentice-Hall.

Tompkins, G. E., & Webeler, M. (1983). What will happen next? Using predictable books with young children. *The Reading Teacher, 36*(6), 498–502.

Topping, K. (1987). Paired reading: A powerful technique for parent use. *The Reading Teacher, 40*(7), 608–614.

Topping, K., & Wolfendale, S. (1985). *Parental involvement in children's reading.* New York: Nichols Publishing.

Tough, J. (1979). *Talk for teaching and learning.* London: Ward Lock Educational.

Treiman, R., & Hirsh-Pasek, K. (1983). Silent reading: Insights from second-generation deaf readers. *Cognitive Psychology, 15*(1), 39–65.

Trybus, R., & Karchner, M. (1977). School achievement scores of hearing-impaired children: National data on achievement status and growth patterns. *American Annals of the Deaf, 122,* 66–69.

Underhill, R. G., Uprichard, A. E., & Heddens, J. W. (1980). *Diagnosing mathematical difficulties.* Columbus, OH: Charles E. Merrill.

Urey, J. R., & Biasini, F. J. (1989). Evaluating the "difficult" child. *Teaching Exceptional Children, 21*(3), 10–13.

U.S. Office of Education, Department of Health, Education, and Welfare. (1977). Pt. 2. Education of handicapped children, implementation of Part B of the Education of the Handicapped Act. *Federal Register, 42*(163), 42474–518.

Van Houten, R., Morrison, E., Jarvis, R., & MacDonald, M. (1974). The effects of explicit timing and feedback on compositional response rate in elementary school children. *Journal of Applied Behavior Analysis, 7,* 547–555.

Van de Walle, J. A., & Thompson, C. S. (1981). Fitting problem solving into every classroom. *School Science and Mathematics, 81*(41), 289–303.

Van Etten, G., Arkell, C., & Van Etten, C. (1980). *The severely and profoundly handicapped: Programs, methods and materials.* St.

Louis, MO: C.V. Mosby.

Van Kleeck, A., & Schuele, C. M. (1987). Precursors to literacy: Normal development. *Topics in Language Disorders, 7*(2), 13–31.

Van Riper, C. (1963). *Speech correction: Principles and methods* (4th ed.). Englewood Cliffs, NJ: Prentice-Hall.

Veatch, J., Sawicki, F., Elliott, G., Flake, E., & Blakey, J. (1979). *Key words to reading: The LEA begins.* Columbus, OH: Charles E. Merrill.

Videen, J., Deno, S., & Marston, D. (1982). *Correct word sequences: A valid indicator of proficiency in written expression* (Research Report No. 84). Minneapolis: Institute for Research in Learning Disabilities, University of Minnesota.

Vogl, C. G. (1983). *The dangers of strangers.* Minneapolis, MN: Dillon Press.

Vygotsky, L. (1978). *Mind in society: The development of higher psychological processes* (M. Cole, V. John-Steiner, S. Scribner, & R. Souberman, Trans). Cambridge, MA: Harvard University Press.

Wachs, T. (1979). Early experience and early cognitive development: The search for specificity. In I. Uzigiris & J. Hunt (Eds.), *Research with scales of psychological development in infancy.* Urbana, IL: University of Illinois Press.

Wagner, G., & Hosier, M. (1970). *Reading games: Strengthening reading skills with instructional games.* New York: Macmillan.

Wallace G., Cohen, S. B., & Polloway, E. A. (1987). *Language arts: Teaching exceptional students.* Austin, TX: Pro-Ed.

Wallach, G., & Miller, L. (1988). *Language intervention and academic success.* Boston: College-Hill Press.

Walter, G. G. (1982). English skill assessment with the severely hearing-impaired. In D. G. Sims, G. G. Walter, & R. L. Whitehead (Eds.), *Deafness and communication* (pp. 177–186). Baltimore, MD: Williams & Wilkins.

Wanamaker, N., Hearn, K., & Richarz, S. (1979). *More than graham crackers: Nutrition education and food preparation with young children.* Washington, D.C.: NAEYC.

Warren, J. (Ed.). (1983). *Piggyback songs and more piggyback songs.* Everett, WA: Totline Press.

Watts, W. J. (1979). Deaf children and some emotional aspects of learning. *Volta Review, 81*(7) 491–500.

Wechsler, D. (1974). *Manual for the Wechsler intelligence scale for children—revised.* New York: Psychological Corp.

Wedenberg, E. (1963). Objective audiometric tests on noncooperative children. *Acta Otolaryngologica, 175,* 32. (supplement)

Wells, G. (1975). Learning to code experience through language. *Journal of Child Language, 1,* 243–269.

Wertsch, J. (1981). *The concept of activity in Soviet psychology.* Armont, NH: Sharpe.

Westby, C. (1980). Assessment of cognition and language abilities through play. *Language, Speech, and Hearing Services in the Schools, 11,* 154–168.

Westling, D. L., & Koorland, M. A. (1988). *The special educator's handbook.* Boston: Allyn & Bacon.

White, E. (1984). Holisticism. *College Composition and Communication, 35,* 400–409.

White, R. (1984). Paraprofessionals in special education. *Social Policy, 14*(4) 44–47.

Wiig, E., & Bray, C. (1983). *Let's talk inventing for children.* Columbus, OH: Charles E. Merrill.

Wilbur, R. (1979). *American sign language and sign systems.* Baltimore, MD: University Park Press.

Wilbur, R. B., & Jones, M. (1974). Some aspects of bilingual/bimodal acquisition of sign language and English by three hearing children of deaf parents. In M. Lagaly, R. Fox, & A. Bruck (Eds.), *Papers from the 10th Regional Meeting, Chicago Linguistic Society.* Chicago Linguistic Society.

Williams, L. (Spring-Summer 1984). Throwing back the pages. *NTID Focus,* 5–8.

Wilson, J. J. (1982). Tutoring and notetaking as classroom support services for the deaf. In D. G. Sims, G. G. Walter, & R. L. Whitehead (Eds.), *Deafness and communication: Assessment and training* (pp. 407–415). Baltimore, MD: Williams & Wilkins.

Wilson, R., & Wesson, C. (1986). Making every minute count: Academic learning time in LD classrooms. *Learning Disabilities Focus, 2*(1), 13–19.

Winograd, P., & Paris, S. (1989). A cognitive and motivational agenda for reading instruction. *Ed-*

*ucational Leadership, 46*(4), 30–36.

Witter-Merithew, A., & Dirst, R. (1982). Preparation and use of educational interpreters. In D. G. Sims, G. G. Walter, & R. L. Whitehead (Eds.), *Deafness and communication: Assessment and training* (pp. 395–406). Baltimore MD: Williams & Wilkins.

Wong, B., Wong, R., & LeMare, L. (1982). The effects of knowledge of criterion task comprehension and recall in normal achieving and learning disabled children. *Journal of Education Research, 76*, 119–126.

Wood, D., Bruner, J., & Ross, G. (1976). The role of tutoring in problem solving. *Journal of Child Psychology and Psychiatry, 17*, 89–100.

Wood, K. D., & Robinson, N. (1983). Vocabulary, language, and prediction: A prereading strategy. *The Reading Teacher, 36*(4), 392–395.

Woodcock, R. (1987). *Woodcock reading mastery tests-revised*. Circle Pines, MN: American Guidance Service.

Woods, M. L., & Moe, A. J. (1985). *Analytical Reading Inventory*. Columbus, OH: Charles E. Merrill.

Woodward, J. (1973). *Implication lects on the deaf diglossic continuum*. Unpublished doctoral dissertation, Georgetown University.

Woodward, J., Allen, T., & Schildroth, A. (1985). Teachers and deaf students: An ethnography of classroom communication. In S. Delancey &

R. Tomlin (Eds.), *Proceedings of the first annual meeting of the Pacific Linguistics Conference* (pp. 479–493). Eugene, OR: University of Oregon.

Wozniak, V., & Jackson, P. (1979). Visual vowel and diphthong perception from two horizontal viewing angles. *Journal of Speech and Hearing Research, 22*, 354–365.

Yaylor, V. (1986). *A review of math curricula for hearing-impaired students*. Unpublished manuscript.

Yoshida, R., Fenton, K., Maxwell, J., & Kaufman, M. (1978). Group decision making in the planning team process: Myth or reality? *Journal of School Psychology, 16*(3), 237–244.

Ysseldyke, J., Thurlow, M., Graden, J., Wesson, C., Algozzine, B., & Deno, S. (1983). Generalizations from five years of research on assessment and decision making: The University of Minnesota Institute. *Exceptional Education Quarterly, 4*, 75–93.

Ziemer, M. (September 1987). Science and the early childhood curriculum: One thing leads to another. *Young Children*, 44–51.

Zieziula, F. R. (Ed.). (1983). *Assessment of hearing-impaired people: A guide for selecting psychological, educational, and vocational tests*. Washington, D.C.: Gallaudet College Press.

# Glossary

**Abstract/metaphorical/idiomatic expansion.** Using a target structure that has multiple meanings or is used figuratively, such as, "His car has seen better days."

**Accommodation.** The mental process through which an organism's existing cognitive repertoire changes and modifies in accordance with new and different information.

**Acquisition.** The act of gaining a new characteristic, skill, or ability.

**Affective education.** Teaching self-concept, positive attitudes, self-control, problem solving, communication, and interpersonal skills.

**Affective filter.** A filter of emotion that can block language acquisition or learning if it is too high. A low affective filter keeps students from being self-conscience or embarrassed and allows them to take risks.

**Age-appropriate.** Consistent with norms of monolingual, bilingual, and/or bimodal language development, in which children are in a stimulating environment.

**Aided hearing acuity.** Ability to hear while wearing a personal hearing aid.

**American Sign Language (ASL).** A language used by many deaf people that consists of visual-gestural units or signs. The grammar of ASL differs from that of signed English.

**Analytic evaluation.** Examination of selected components of the writing task in order to isolate skills for instruction.

**Anaphoric.** The use of a word or phrase that refers back to another word or phrase that was used earlier in the text or conversation; for example, "Yona likes Toni. Gaylen doesn't like her." *Her* is anaphoric.

**Annual goals.** Activities or achievements that are to be completed or attained within one year. Annual goals are required to be stated for hearing-impaired students in individualized education programs (IEPs), as directed in Public Law 94-142.

**Articulation.** The production of speech sounds, particularly consonants and vowels, in the mouth and throat. The production of signs in terms of movement, handshape, and palm orientation.

**Assessment.** Measurement of the ability of a person, the quality of a course, and so on. May occur by test, interview questionnaire, observation, and so on.

**Assimilation.** The process, complementary to accommodation, through which new information and new experiences are incorporated into an organism's existing cognitive repertoire.

**Atomistic measures.** Direct, countable measures of single language features, such as number of words per clause or proportion of words spelled correctly.

**Audiogram.** Graph on which results of an audiometric evaluation are charted to indicate the person's ability to hear each tone at each of the presented frequencies.

**Audiotape-card machine.** (e.g., a Language Master). A machine that looks like a tape recorder. Quality machines can be heard by some hearing-impaired children and can be used for auditory training.

**Audition.** Reception of information by listening alone.

**Auditory training.** Teaching methods designed specifically for improving a student's auditory speech-perception performance.

**Auditory functioning level.** A hierarchy of listening abilities, Erber (1982).

**Auditory clues.** Time, intensity, and frequency information available in speech; in addition to the acoustic properties of vowels and consonants, includes the effects of coarticulation, natural boundaries, and suprasegmental features.

**Aural.** Reception of information through a combination of audition and speechreading.

**Automatic response.** An accurate response performed at a high rate with distractions present. Automatic responses are often thought to occur without conscious thought. Automaticity is generally considered to be the highest level of proficiency.

**Balanced.** Having equal amounts. When pertaining to bilingualism, it means having equal ability in two languages.

**Basal reader approach.** Highly structured sequence of tasks presented in a series of textbooks with teacher manuals and workbooks.

**Baseline data.** The natural level of occurrence of a behavior before intervention. Baseline data serve a purpose similar to a pretest; they provide a level of behavior against which the results of an intervention procedure can be compared.

**Behavior management.** Any procedure or practice that influences, changes, or controls behavior.

**Behavior modification.** Particular technique of behavior management; procedures used to change behavior that are based on operant conditioning. Manipulation of the environment and consequences are used to bring about desired behaviors or to eliminate undesired behaviors.

**Behavioral objectives.** Specific statements of what is expected to be learned, written in observable terms, with conditions and criteria for measuring achievement.

**Bicultural.** Belonging to two cultures.

**Bilexical.** Written in two languages or dialects.

**Bilingual.** Knowledge and use of two languages (e.g., oral English and oral Spanish; American Sign Language and Manual English).

**Bilingualism.** Using two languages with some degree of proficiency.

**Bimodal.** Knowledge and use of two modes of language (e.g., written and signed English; signed and spoken English, etc.).

**Causal relationships.** A relationship that brings about or causes an action or state; for example, "Peter killed the rabbit." *Killed* is a causal verb. In "The rabbit died," *died* is not a causal verb. "I am going because I need to" shows a causal relationship.

**Classification.** Separating into logical groups, sets, ranks, and so on, based on some characteristic.

**Code/coding.** A system of signals used to code a taxonomy.

**Code-switch.** Using one code of a language and then switching to another code (i.e., talking formally and then talking to peers; signing in English and then speaking).

**Cognition, cognitive.** The act or process of knowing; the various thinking skills and processes are considered cognitive skills.

**Cognitively demanding.** Difficult materials; new; unknown. Academic content should be cognitively demanding to students.

**Cognitively undemanding.** Easy material; reviewed; known. Cognitively undemanding material allows the student to focus on other skills besides the content of the topic.

**Collaboration.** To cooperate and work jointly on an intellectual endeavor.

**Command of the language.** Use of a language for communication such that wants and desires can be expressed successfully.

**Communication.** The act of transmitting, imparting, or interchanging thoughts or information by speech, sign, writing, listening, and so on.

**Communicative competence.** The ability to use

language in dialogues in order to communicate effectively.

**Complex sentence.** A sentence that contains one or more dependent clauses in addition to the independent or main clause; for example, "When it rained (dependent clause), we went inside (independent clause)."

**Comprehensible input.** Input that has been assessed empirically (e.g., single subject design) to be comprehensible to the person in learning new, unknown information.

**Comprehension.** The process by which the meaning of a written or spoken language is understood.

**Computation.** The act of calculating an answer to a mathematical problem.

**Concept.** An abstract idea generalized from particular instances.

**Concept formation.** Mental activity of interpreting, transforming, organizing, and comparing selected sensory information into nonlinguistic and linguistic categories.

**Concept expansion.** Giving additional characteristics, descriptions, or examples to the meaning associated with a word or symbol in a person's mind.

**Confidentiality.** The process of not sharing private information with others.

**Congenital.** Present at birth.

**Conservation.** The cognitive principle that the total energy of a system or a mass is constant, regardless of a change in the form.

**Consultation.** A voluntary, problem-solving relationship between two professionals who have somewhat different bodies of expertise.

**Content.** Meaning of a word or words; semantics.

**Context reduced.** Little or no context that is helpful in determining the meaning of a word or a concept.

**Context embedded.** That which occurs before or after a word or concept that clarifies the meaning. Context can be linguistic or nonlinguistic.

**Contextual clues.** Linguistic information inherent in the message, which facilitates comprehension of the subject matter or topic.

**Continuum of services.** Range of services available to students with special needs.

**Continuum of alternative placements.** Full spectrum of services that may be tailored to the individual needs of each student at any given time during the student's educational career.

**Contractible copula.** Reduction of a form of the *be* verb; for examples: *I'll, they're*.

**Conventions.** Punctuation and capitalization to mark sentences, commas and other internal marks of clarity, spelling, handwriting, segmenting with subheadings, and paragraphing.

**Conversational level, skills, and devices.** Abilities that allow a conversation to be successful in transmitting the speakers' intentions.

**Cooperative learning.** An approach to teaching that promotes peer interaction, cooperation, and communication.

**Coordination.** Phrases that are joined by words linking the two equal parts of the sentences (e.g. *and, or*).

**Criterion-referenced tests.** Tests that compare students with their own mastery level. They measure specific objectives to determine what a person can and cannot do.

**Critical attributes.** The basic characteristics of a concept.

**Criterion (criterion for acceptable performance, or CAP).** The standards in an objective. The criterion tells how well (accurately, frequently, or to what quality) a behavior should be carried out by a student who has finished instruction on a task. See *Objective*.

**Critical age.** An important period of time when child development in one of many areas should be facilitated and enhanced; for audition and speech skills, usually thought to be from 0 to 3 years; for language, from 0 to 12 years.

**Curriculum.** The overall plan in which subject content is specified and organized sequentially; the "what" of teaching.

**Curriculum-based assessment.** Assessment that uses materials and procedures that are directly tied to the objectives being taught.

**Decoding tool.** An instrument or strategy that helps someone try to understand the meaning of a word, phrase, or sentence.

**Delayed reading instruction.** Introducing formal

reading instruction after a language base has been established. This base would be assessed to be equivalent to a 5-year-old hearing child.

**Demonstrative.**   A word that refers to something in terms of whether it is near to or distant from the speaker, for example, *this, that, these, those*.

**Derived score.**   Taking test scores and making calculations to transform them into the form of a normal curve. Examples of derived scores include developmental scores, percentiles, and stanines.

**Detection.**   The ability to detect the presence or absence of sound. At this level, the student knows a sound is there, yet does not know what the sound is or if it differs from any other sound.

**Developmental sequence.**   A series of behaviors that follow those expected in the typical development of young children.

**Developmental milestones.**   A behavior or growth in young children that marks a typical stage or phrase of development for that child's age level.

**Diagnostic.**   In-depth information that is collected to help the practitioner develop an intervention plan for a student.

**Diagnostic assessment.**   The process of obtaining information about students' abilities and needs.

**Diagnostic procedures.**   Procedures to determine what students are capable of doing with respect to given learning tasks.

**Dialogues.**   A model of conversation used to practice language; a conversation in which turn taking is involved.

**Direct instruction.**   The systematic, explicit teaching of academic strategies to students.

**Direct evaluation.**   Evaluation that measures the performance of students in the materials that they are using or on the tasks that they are learning.

**Directional verb.**   A signed verb that can change in directional movement based on the meaning being conveyed, for example, I *gave* it to you. You *give* it to me." *Give* is signed in opposite directions in these two sentences.

**Discipline.**   Consistent and continued organization of behavior.

**Discourse.**   Refers to large units of language use, such as paragraphs, conversations, or interviews.

**Discrimination.**   The ability to perceive similarities and differences. When referred to in the context of auditory training, it is at this level that a student can indicate whether two or more sounds are the same or different yet cannot tell what the sounds are.

**Distinctive feature.**   A particular characteristic that distinguishes one sound or sign from another one; for example, *boat, float* in speech; *thing, child* in sign.

**Divergent questions.**   Questions or queries that do not have an anticipated single, correct answer. "Why is Helen Keller famous?" is an example of a divergent question.

**Domain-referenced tests.**   See *Criterion-referenced tests*.

**Dominant bilingualism.**   Having more proficiency in one language than in another.

**Due process.**   Used in an educational context, the term refers to procedures and policies established to ensure equal educational opportunities for all children. PL 94-142 contains due process procedures specific to handicapped children.

**Duration.**   The length of time of a sound. Duration is affected by stress, rate of utterance, and voicing of adjacent phonemes.

**Duration recording.**   A behavioral assessment procedure used to measure the length of time a target behavior occurs; data may be reported in seconds, minutes, or percentages.

**Effective teacher.**   One who is able to bring about intended learning outcomes.

**Elicit.**   A technique to get learners to produce speech, sign, or writing.

**Encode.**   Convert into a code; reflect ability in one mode (speech can reflect or encode a student's language competence).

**Encode meaning.**   Different systems use different types of symbols to represent the meaning being communicated.

**Environmental print.**   Print that appears in a community, such as lettering on foods, clothing, and restaurants.

**Error analysis.**   The process of examining incorrect responses in order to gain insight into a student's use of inappropriate strategies.

**Evaluation.**   Mean procedures used to determine

whether a child is handicapped and the nature and extent of the special education and related services that the child needs; procedures used selectively with an individual child that do not include basic tests administered or procedures used with all children in a school, grade, or class.

**Event relation.**   Relationship between two things that occur.

**Expand utterance/expansion.**   Mature language user repeats what child has said and signed, adding grammatical words that the child did not use; for example, child says, "Doggie eat." The adult says, "Yes, the dog is eating."

**Expressive language.**   User actively says or signs in order to communicate. Opposite of *receptive language*, in which the child passively demonstrates an ability to understand speech or sign.

**Facilitative play period.**   A play time in which adults are using self-talk and parallel talk strategies to assist in the child's acquisition of language.

**Facilitator.**   An individual whose primary purpose is to promote and to guide the development of others.

**Feedback.**   Information about the effects or consequences of actions taken.

**First language.**   The language of most benefit in learning new and difficult information.

**Fluency.**   In evaluation, fluency is a proficiency dimension defined by the rate of student response. Fluency may also refer to the instruction used to improve a student's skills from accuracy to mastery.

**Form.**   The structure of language; grammar; the way in which linguistic units are combined to produce utterances.

**Formal tests.**   See *Norm-referenced tests*.

**Formant.**   Measured concentrations of energy in the frequency spectrum during production of vowel sounds. Formants are related to the size and shape of the vocal tract and thus vary for different vowels.

**Formative data.**   Evaluation that occurs as skills are being developed. Formative data are considered dynamic because they indicate movement.

**Fossilized input.**   Content and form of input that do not represent proficient use; the learning of the form of the language or system has ceased.

**Forward analysis.**   A task analysis procedure that uses the student's current level of functioning and then identifies each subsequent step of instruction in order to establish what the long-term goal will be.

**Free appropriate public education.**   Used in PL 94-142 to mean special education and related services that are provided at public expense, which meet requirements of the state educational agency and which conform to the individualized education program (IEP) requirements of PL 94-142.

**Frequency data.**   The number of times a behavior occurs during a time interval.

**Function word.**   Words that have little meaning on their own but show grammatical relationships in and between sentences. Opposite of content word or words that refer to a thing, quality, state, or action.

**Functional (language).**   Language viewed as an instrument of social interaction; teaching children language skills that allow them to interact with the people in their community.

**Genuine communication.**   Communication that is sincerely interesting to the student.

**Goals.**   Long-term plans written in terms of a student, an observable verb, specific condition, and a criterion of success.

**Grammar.**   A theory or hypothesis, about the organization of language in the mind of speakers of that language—the underlying knowledge that permits understanding and production of language.

**Group test.**   A test that may be administered to several individuals at the same time by one examiner.

**Guided practice.**   Providing students with opportunities to practice new skills or to use new information in a supervised manner.

**Hearing-impaired.**   Individuals with hearing problems, including deaf and hard-of-hearing persons.

**Holistic evaluation.**   The impressionistic reaction to a written product without an attempt to account for the contributions of the individual components.

**Iconic symbol.**   A word, gesture, sign, or picture that closely resembles that which it refers to or represents.

**Identification.**   The ability to recognize a direct

representation of a stimulus. When referring to auditory training, it is at this level that a student can label an exact representation of a sound by pointing, repeating, signing, drawing, and so on, yet cannot respond appropriately to that sound in the natural environment.

**Implementor.** The professional who provides direct service to hearing-impaired students.

**Incidental.** Occurring by chance or without intention. Spontaneously, unplanned.

**Indirect measures.** Assessment of written language that focuses on students' ability to edit a piece of writing rather than on an evaluation of the students' composition.

**Individual Educational Plan (IEP).** A plan for each special-needs child that is mandated by law.

**Individual test.** A test that can be administered to only one person at a time.

**Inferential.** Relating to deduced meaning. In English, a group of words may have an infered meaning unrelated to each single word comprising the phrase or expression.

**Inflection.** The process of adding an affix to a word or changing it in some way, according to the grammar of a language.

**Informal assessment.** Measurement conducted by teachers, parents, and others without formal testing instruments. Includes observation and anecdotal information.

**Input.** The language that is used around and to the child or student.

**Input + 1.** Supplying a language model and stimulus to the child or student that is slightly more complex or difficult than the use, content, and/or form level of a particular child or group of children.

**Instructional programs.** Those activities that provide the principal elements of the exceptional child's educational development at any given time. These activities may include any or all of the following: (1) evaluation of the nature of the child's educational needs; (2) amelioration of and compensation for visual, auditory, physical, speech, or other impairments; (3) development of language concepts and communication skills; (4) educational experiences that are adjusted in content, emphasis, rate, or location; and (5) modification of social skills or emotional adjustment.

**Instructional objectives.** See *Behavioral objectives*.

**Instrumental function.** Proposed by Halliday, this function of language is used for satisfying material needs; for example, "I want."

**Integrate.** To become a part of the mainstream. Implies joint effort on behalf of special and general educators.

**Intelligence.** The imparted or acquired ability to comprehend and to reason with facts.

**Intensity.** The measurable volume of a sound (in decibels).

**Intentional learning.** Planned teaching and learning based on the student's assessed needs in a particular area.

**Intentional communication.** Communication that is based on a predecided plan (i.e., assessment); a function of language in which language is used for a deliberate purpose.

**Interactive language development teaching.** Facilitating language through communication, conversation, and interest in the same topic (or object of interest).

**Interactive function.** Proposed by Halliday, this function of language is used for other people; for example, "me and you."

**Interdisciplinary team or multidisciplinary team.** Team of professionals from various backgrounds, such as teachers, psychologists, speech and language pathologists, health professionals, and administrators.

**Internal language.** The thoughts used to think about ideas and concepts.

**Interval recording.** A behavioral assessment procedure in which the observation period is divided into equal time intervals; it permits relatively precise measurement of low and medium rates of responding.

**Intervention strategies.** Methods and manners of teaching that are used to modify a student's behavior (e.g., language).

**Intervention.** Teaching so that behavior (e.g., language) can be modified.

**Itinerant services.** Services provided to hearing-impaired students by professionals who travel from school to school.

**Knowledge about books.** Ability to locate the

parts of a book, how a book is held, the order in which a story is read, and so on.

**Language.** Knowledge of a code for representing ideas about the world through a conventional system of arbitrary signals for communication.

**Language acquisition.** The natural process of gaining language, as opposed to learning language in which someone attempts to teach language to a student.

**Language content.** Meaning or semantics of what is conveyed.

**Language experience approach (LEA).** A method of teaching reading and other language skills, based on the experiences of students. The method frequently involves the generation of experienced-based materials that are dictated by the student, written down by the teacher, and then used in class as the material for teaching reading.

**Language intervention.** Directly facilitating the acquisition of a use, content, or form skill.

**Language intervention learning.** To gain understanding of language via teaching.

**Language sample.** A representation of a person's linguistic ability. The all-specific procedures for taking, coding, and analyzing language samples.

**Learning center.** A designated area where instructional materials in one major curriculum area are located and organized.

**Least restrictive environment.** Educational setting as near as possible to a regular class that will meet individual needs; level of placement is based on severity of handicapping condition.

**Legislation.** Laws enacted by state legislators and the United States Congress.

**Lesson plan.** A description of the basic information concepts and skills emphasized in each lesson.

**Lexicon.** The set of all of the words and idioms of any language.

**Linguistic.** Pertaining to language, the study of language, the development of language, and so on.

**Literacy.** The ability to read, formally write, and formally speak a language. Illiteracy is the inability to perform these skills.

**Literal, concrete level.** A level upholding the exact meaning of a word or words of a text; verbatim translation.

**Litigation.** State and federal court cases.

**Long-term goals.** Elements of the IEP that identify major concepts to be learned and skills to be achieved.

**Mainstreaming.** The process of integrating handicapped children into regular educational programs, implementing the least restrictive environment concept.

**Mainstream setting.** The integration of hearing-impaired students with hearing peers.

**Manner of articulation.** The way in which speech sounds are made; for example, fricative, plosive, continuant.

**Mean-length-utterance (MLU).** A measure of linguistic complexity of a person's utterances, especially in children who are acquiring a language. It is measured by counting the average length of the utterance that a child produces, using a morpheme rather than a whole word as a unit of measure.

**Metacognition.** Knowing about knowing. Knowing how to go about the process of learning.

**Milestone.** A developmental event worth noting in a lifetime.

**Minimal pair.** Two words in a language that differ from each other by only one distinctive feature (e.g., by one sound, by palm orientation in a sign only, etc.).

**Modeling.** Observing, then imitating the desired behavior of another person.

**Monolingual.** A person who knows or uses only one language.

**Morpheme.** The smallest meaningful unit in a language. A morpheme cannot be divided or altered without destroying its meaning (e.g., *unkindness* has three morphemes).

**Morphology.** The study or description of morphemes, which are the smallest unit of grammatical structure and meaning.

**Motherese, parentese.** A simpler form of language that someone would use with a mature user. Typically, this caretaker speech or sign has shorter utterances, fewer abstract words, lots of repetition, and clearer pronunciation.

**Multidisciplinary conference.** A deliberation among appropriate persons for the purpose of determining eligibility for special education, developing recommendations for special education placement, reviewing educational progress, or considering the continuation or termination of special education for an individual child.

**Multidisciplinary evaluation.** Using several disciplines or areas of professional expertise and instruments to evaluate a student.

**Native language.** When used with reference to a person of limited English-speaking ability, it means the language normally used by that person, in the case of a child, the language normally used by the parents of the child.

**Negative reinforcement.** The contingent removal of an adverse stimulus immediately after a response. Negative reinforcement increases the future rate or the probability of occurrence of the response, or both.

**Networking.** A graphic visualization in which students relate new words to past experiences to determine definitions, characteristics, examples, results, and so forth.

**Nondiscriminatory assessment.** Assessment of handicapped persons that is not biased by racial, cultural, or socioeconomic factors.

**Nonexamples.** Used when introducing concepts or vocabulary. It is an illustration that lacks one or two of the critical attributes of the concept or term being explained.

**Nonlinguistic.** Apart from the language itself; for example, play or cognitive behaviors, nonlinguistic body movements, or miming.

**Nonsegmental.** Characteristics of speech that include duration, intensity, and pitch.

**Nonverbal.** Gestures, body movements, and facial expressions that do not code features of a signed language. Mime or body movements accompanying speech, which are not linguistic. To say that signing is nonverbal is a misuse of the term.

**Norm-referenced tests.** Commercially prepared tests administered to large groups of students; contain a manual to determine norms, scaled scores, and ranks. They enable users to compare scores with a normative sample.

**Norm/normed.** The scores or typical performances of a particular group as measured in some way. Norms are then used to compare the performance of an individual or group with the norm group. If a test is normed, this process of measuring a group has been completed to some extent.

**Normal language development.** The language acquisition of monolingual, bilingual, or bimodal children as measured by typical use, content, and form milestones.

**Object knowledge.** Receptive or expressive use of nouns, or transitive verbs, which is described typically as being affected by the action of the verb.

**Object relation.** The ways in which an object word relates to other words in an utterance.

**Objective.** A statement written in a specific form that describes how a particular student will meet an IEP goal.

**Objective-referenced tests.** See *Criterion-referenced tests*.

**Objective test.** The scoring of a test in which there is no possibility of difference of opinion among scorers as to whether responses are to be scored as right or wrong.

**Off-task.** A general term implying that the student is not doing what he or she is supposed to be doing. A student could be "off" one task by being "on" another.

**On-task behavior.** Student behavior that is appropriate to the task.

**One-to-one correspondence.** Matching items to pair them up such that one of one kind is matched with one of another kind; a cognitive skill.

**Open-ended questions.** Questions that require more than one word as an answer.

**Ordering.** Seriating according to some characteristic.

**Overlearning.** Practice, drill, and review beyond mastery to aid recall and memory.

**Paired reading.** Appropriate to beginning reading, in which a mature language user reads with an inexperienced reader and follows specific rules of assisting.

**Parallel talk.** Talking (signing or cueing) to describe what someone else (e.g. a child) is doing as he or she plays or solves a problem.

**Paraprofessional.** An individual without specialized training who provides assistance to the classroom teacher.

**Passive.** One of two ways (the other being the active voice) in which the relationship between a verb and the noun phrase can be expressed. "The fence was damaged by the wind" is an example of passive voice and is used when the writer or speaker does not know or does not wish to state the cause of the action.

**Phase/stage.** A period of development that is only roughly associated with age.

**Phonation.** To produce speech sounds.

**Phoneme.** The smallest unit of language sound.

**Phonetic.** Production of and differentiation between sounds that are not meaningful.

**Phonetics.** A study of all of the speech sounds in language and how these sounds are produced.

**Phonics.** The relationship between letters and sounds; for example, students are taught that *K* and *c* have the hard *C* sound, as in *kite* and *cat*.

**Phonologic.** Meaningful use of speech sounds.

**Phonology.** The establishment and description of the distinctive sounds of spoken language and the handshapes of signed language.

**Pitch.** The perception of a sound relative to its frequency.

**Place of articulation.** The position of the articulators in the oral cavity during the production of speech sounds; for example, labial, linguadental, velar; the location where a sign is made.

**Positive reinforcement.** The contingent presentation of a "desired" stimulus immediately after a response that increases the future rate or probability of occurrences of the response, or both.

**Pragmatics.** The study of the rules governing how language is used in social contexts.

**Preintentional.** Prior to the deliberate use of language.

**Prelocutionary.** Prior to language being used to convey a basic literal meaning (or propositional meaning).

**Precursor.** A behavior that precedes another behavior; for example, babbling is a typical precursor to one-word stage of language development.

**Prerequisite learning.** The information or skills that are necessary prior to working on sequentially more advanced topics or activities.

**Primary form target.** The skill in the area of language form that is in the most need of intervention.

**Primary reinforcers.** A stimulus (such as food) that may be said to have biological importance to an individual. Such stimuli are innately motivating (also called natural, unlearned, and unconditioned reinforcers).

**Probe.** A tentative exploratory form of investigation.

**Process feedback.** Providing individuals information about the *way* in which they do something. An example would be the steps that one use: to solve a problem rather than solely focusing on the solution.

**Pronoun.** A word that may replace a noun or a noun phrase. English is comprised of personal, possessive, demonstrative, interrogative, reflexive, and indefinite pronouns.

**Proportional data.** Provides an indication of the quality of a performance and an analysis of the number of correct or incorrect responses. Generally reported as a percentage or ratio.

**Prosody.** The overall rhythm, stress, and intonation of speech; also referred to as *suprasegmental features*.

**Psycholinguistics.** The field of study that blends aspects of two disciplines—psychology and linguistics—to examine the total picture of the language process.

**Public Law 94-142.** Federal legislation passed in 1975 and implemented in 1978. Called the Education for All Handicapped Children Act, PL 94-142 mandated that states and local school districts must provide a free, appropriate public education for all handicapped children.

**Punishment.** A consequent stimulus that decreases the future rate or the probability of occurrence of a behavior, or both.

**Queries.** Questions, asking for an expression of fact, opinion, belief, and so on.

**Random order.** Mixed in a chance manner that is unpredictable for the student.

**Rate.** The quantity, amount, or degree of something per unit of time. For example, a student may speak at the rate of 140 words per minute.

**Raw data.** The number of responses.

**Raw score.** The number of problems that are correct on a test.

**Recast.** When a mature language user reforms a child's utterance to add information of a specific type.

**Reciprocal teaching.** A particular approach to

teaching reading, in which the teacher and the student(s) eventually switch roles and independence is fostered.

**Recreational reading periods.** Periods of time in which people are left uninterrupted to read independently using a self-selected book or magazine.

**Reduplication.** Repetition of a syllable, a morpheme, a word, or a sign; for example, In Malay, *anak* means *child, anak anak* means *children.* In ASL, WORK can be reduplicated to mean WORK HARD, WORK + WORK, and so on.

**Referral.** Means a formal procedure, established by the local school district, by which a case study evaluation may be requested.

**Regular classrooms.** The classroom in which nonhandicapped children receive the majority of their educational program. Usually organized on a graded system.

**Regulatory function.** Controlling the behavior of others.

**Reinforcement.** Attention or reward for performance of behavior that is either positive or negative.

**Related services.** The developmental, corrective, and other supportive services that are required to assist a handicapped child to benefit from special education. Such services include: speech pathology and audiology, psychological services, physical and occupational abilities in children, counseling services, and medical services for diagnostic or evaluation purposes, transportation, school health services, social work services, and parent counseling and training.

**Reliability.** The extent to which scores on a test are consistent across items (internal consistency, split-half reliability), forms (alternate- or parallel-forms reliability), and time (test-retest reliability).

**Residential school.** School in which students live in addition to receiving academic and/or vocational training.

**Residual hearing.** The extent of hearing potential available to a hearing-impaired person.

**Resonation.** Process of modifying the laryngeal tone by altering the shape of the pharyngeal, oral, and nasal cavities.

**Resource room.** Educational setting in which identified exceptional students receive direct instruction in content areas needing remediation.

**Respiration.** Process of inhalation and exhalation, plus the resulting gas exchange.

**Response cost.** A procedure for the reduction of inappropriate behavior through withdrawal of specific amounts of a reinforcer, contingent upon the behavior's occurrence.

**Reverse analysis.** A task analysis procedure that focuses on a long-term goal and then, by working backwards, identifies the prerequisite steps needed to reach the goal.

**Rhythm.** Temporal patterns of stress, including syllable duration, total duration, and rate of speech. Natural linguistic boundaries (as in phrasing) contribute to overall rhythmic pattern.

**Role.** The part taken by a participant in any act of communication.

**Routine/conversational routine.** A predictable sequence of events learned together and used in a sequence.

**Saboteur.** Intentionally setting up language situations so that children or students are more likely to use the language that they have acquired or learned.

**Scaffolding.** Providing support for the development of skills, particularly language and literacy skills.

**Schedules of reinforcement.** The patterns of "timing" for delivery of reinforcers.

**Scope-and-sequence skills lists.** A list of behaviors that are arranged in hierarchical order. Each list focuses on a subject or an aspect of a subject. These lists provide educators with a developmental blueprint for assessing which skills students have or have not yet mastered.

**Screening.** Means the process of reviewing all children in a given group with a set of criteria for the purpose of identifying those children who may be in need of special education.

**Script.** Events and actions that are related to particular situations. A person's knowledge of a script can help in comprehending the language used with it.

**Seat work.** Independent activities for students that are designed to extend instruction.

**Segmental.** Pertaining to the phonemes with syllables and words.

**Self-contained class.** Students are placed in a

special education setting with one teacher for the entire day.

**Self-talk.**  Talking (signing or cueing) to describe what you are doing as you play or solve a problem.

**Semantic mapping.**  A categorical structuring of information in a graphic form. Networking is one example of semantic mapping. (See Chapter 5 for a diagrammed example.)

**Semantics.**  Study of language meaning and how it is acquired; the semantic component of language includes meanings and rules for linking meaning with words and with word sequences (phrases and sentences).

**Sense (of a language structure).**  Developing an understanding of the structure's meaning. Specific steps for analyzing a language structure for its meaning or sense appear in Chapter 7.

**Sensorimotor.**  A period of cognitive development when the child depends primarily on the motor reaction to sensory stimuli.

**Shaped-out signs.**  Signs formed by looking at sign-print and experimenting with handshape, movement, palm orientation, and placement based on pictures.

**Short-term objectives.**  Specific statements written in behavioral terms of what each student is to be taught; related to annual goals and incorporated into the IEP.

**Significant others.**  Parents, relatives, neighbors, older brothers and sisters, who are important to a student.

**Simultaneous.**  Occurring at the same time.

**Skill.**  The ability to use one's knowledge effectively and readily when performing some type of activity.

**Special education.**  Those instructional and resource programs and related services, unique materials, physical plant adjustments, and other special educational facilities, which, to meet the unique needs of exceptional children, modify, supplement, support or are in the place of the standard educational program of the public schools.

**Specialty teachers.**  Professionals who are responsible for providing educational services to hearing-impaired students in the ancillary areas of the curriculum. Examples include the speech and language pathologist, the art teacher, the gym teacher, the music teacher, and so on.

**Speech.**  Dynamic, neuromuscular process of producing speech sounds for communication. A verbal means of transmission.

**Speechreading.**  Lip reading. Student learns to distinguish sounds, words, and phrases as spoken by another.

**Spontaneous vocalizations.**  This refers to automatic vocalizations produced without specific modeling or request by another person. These vocalizations can consist of single sounds or combinations and need not be clearly articulated. They are often made for purposes of vocal play.

**Spontaneous connected language.**  Connected speech produced for the primary purpose of interpersonal communication. Such vocalizations should include language phonemes and should be clearly articulated.

**Standardized tests.**  See *Norm-referenced tests*.

**Stimulus/stimuli.**  Material(s) used to obtain a response.

**Strategy.**  The employment and management of a plan or a method of doing something.

**Stress.**  Variations in pitch, duration, and loudness of syllables in words, words in phrases, or phrases in sentences. Stressed syllables are referred to as "accent," and stressed words or phrases as "emphasis."

**Structural expansion.**  Making a sequence of linguistic units more complex.

**Structures.**  The arrangement of parts of an utterance.

**Subject-verb-compliance.**  Agreement; for example, "He run" is not in compliance; "She runs" is in compliance.

**Successive.**  Something occurring after another.

**Suprasegmental features.**  Qualities of sound that a student may be able to perceive or reproduce that can assist in expression and reception of speech, including pitch, duration, intensity, intonation patterns, and so on.

**Suprasegmental.**  Pertaining to the overall pattern of a phrase or a sentence, which reflects rhythm, stress, and intonation, that is, prosody.

**Suprasegmental devices.**  Paralinguistic mechanisms superimposed upon the verbal signal to change the form and meaning of the sentence by acting across the elements or segments of that sentence. Examples include intonation, stress, and inflection.

**Surface features.** Phonology and syntax of a language.

**Survey.** An alternative to formal and informal testing that provides a quick estimate of the best starting place for a student. Survey tests frequently accompany published materials.

**Syllable.** A unit of spoken language that consists of either a solitary vowel or diphthong, or that combines a vowel or diphthong with one or more consonants.

**Syntax.** The study of how words combine to form sentences and the grammatical rules that govern the formation of sentences.

**Systems.** Invented systems of communication for hearing-impaired students (e.g., SEE-1 and 2, Signed English, etc.).

**T-unit.** A group of words that can stand alone and make sense. T-units are used in analysis of sentence complexity. The number of units that can stand alone within a sentence is one indicator of sentence complexity.

**Targets (language targets).** Goals and/or objectives derived from the IEP process.

**Targets.** Skills that are the aim or goal of intervention.

**Task analysis.** The process of specifying the steps or components of a task for the purpose of delineating manageable instructional objectives.

**Taxonomy.** A classification of items into classes and subclasses. Taxonomic approaches have been used in phonology, syntax, semantics, and pragmatics. Examples appear in Chapters 5, 6, 7.

**Teacherese.** Based on the concept of motherese or parentese, in which adults talk in a simplified register to children or students, with the difference being that the teacher knows the use, content, and form abilities of the child and can aim input accordingly.

**Temporal concept.** The concept involving time.

**Time out.** A procedure of the reduction of inappropriate behavior whereby the student is denied access, for a fixed period of time, to the opportunity to receive reinforcement.

**Transition services.** Pertaining to the process and/or delivery involved as students pass from home to school, school to school, or from school years to adult life.

**Transitive action verbs.** An action verb that takes an object; for example; "They saw the accident." An intransitive verb does not take an object"; for example: "The children danced."

**Turn-taking.** The roles of speaker and listener change constantly.

**Types of language users.** Monolingual, bilingual, and bimodal users (either speakers or signers) of a language.

**Uncontractible copula.** Unreduced form of a *be* verb; for example, in response to the question "Who is hungry?" it is acceptable to say, "I am" but not to say, "I'm."

**Unit of instruction.** A sequential plan of instruction designed by instructional staff, which integrates the teaching of academic and social skills within the context of a theme, which builds on the previous experiences of the students.

**Use/pragmatics.** The study of the use of language in communications, particularly the relationship between sentences and the contexts and situations in which they are used.

**Utterance.** What is said by one person before or after another person speaks. An utterance can be one word, one phrase, or one sentence in length.

**Utterance-level skills.** Pragmatic or use skills at the utterance level, as contrasted with the conversational level. Describing, requesting, and responding are examples of utterance level skills.

**Validity.** The extent to which a test measures what it says it measures. Validity has different connotations for various kinds of tests and, therefore, different kinds of validity evidence.

**Verbal.** Spoken or signed and pertaining to a language or system.

**Visual clues.** Sign, speechreading, print, objects, or pictures, which represent the auditory message.

**Visualization.** Drawings that represent relationships and can serve as a link between written information and decontextualized conversations; these schema link old information with new information and help students organize their thoughts.

**Vocabulary expansion.** Creating a diversity to the meaning of known words or the learning of synonyms and antonyms for words.

**Voice quality.** Characteristics of voice, including nasality, stridency, harshness, pitch, and breathiness.

**Voicing.** The vibration of the vocal folds during the production of speech sounds.

**Wait time.** The amount of time that the teacher waits after asking a question before calling for the answer.

**Word processing.** A computer program that can be used to enter, store, revise, and print any form of written language.

**Writing process approach.** Teaching writing in a manner that emphasizes writing as a communication act. Emphasis is placed on planning, transcribing, reviewing, and revising.

**Writing process.** The act of writing while it is in progress, typically including recursive stages of planning, composing, revising, and editing.

**Writing mechanics.** Grammar, punctuation, capitalization, handwriting, and spelling.

**Written product.** The completed version of a writing task.

**Written expression.** Skills that are included in the ability to express oneself in writing.

**JUST FOR TODAY** . . . (roughly based on a column by Abigail Van Buren and the credo of the Alcoholics Anonymous):

Just for today, I will be a good teacher for this day only, and not wait until tomorrow to plan strategies to deal with all the things that hinder my work. I won't try to solve everything today. Yet, I will trust in the professional that I am and be an excellent teacher to all my students.

Just for today, I will be happy. I know that I am the person that can control my happiness and that my mood influences so greatly the spirit of my students. I will not dwell on thoughts that depress me. I will chase them out of my mind with happy, positive thoughts. And I will share these happy thoughts with the children in my care.

Just for today, I will accept the situation as it is. I will face reality. I will correct those things that I can correct and accept those things that I cannot correct.

Just for today, I will improve my mind or try something new. I will not be a mental loafer. I will force myself to read something that requires some effort, thought, and application. And I will evaluate whether this new challenge was a benefit to my students.

Just for today, I will do something to improve my health. I will take a walk with a friend and eat good meals. I will make a change that will improve the quality of my life.

Just for today, I will be totally honest. If someone asks me something I don't know, I'll simply say that I don't know.

Just for today, I'll do something that I've been putting off for a long time. I'll finally write that letter, order that material, talk to that parent, clean that closet, straighten out that drawer. . . .

Just for today, before I speak, I will ask myself, "Is that true? Is that kind?" And if the answer to either of these questions is negative, I won't say anything.

Just for today, I will make a conscious effort to be agreeable. I will look as good as I can, act courteously, not interrupt, really try to understand the sense of what someone is trying to communicate to me. I won't judge what others share. I will not try to improve anybody except myself.

Just for today, I will schedule some quiet time for myself. I might just sit alone in a quiet spot. I will reflect on my behavior and get a better perspective on my life.

Just for today, I will not be afraid. I will gather the courage to do what is right and take the responsibility for my own actions. I will expect nothing from my students, but I will realize that, as I give to my students, they will give to me.

Just for today, I will be happy, healthy, and at peace with myself as a teacher.

# Index

Barbara Luetke-Stahlman

John Luckner